# HUMAN MEMORY

# HUMAN MEMORY
## An Introduction to Research, Data, and Theory

Ian Neath

*Purdue University*

Brooks/Cole Publishing Company

I(T)P® An International Thomson Publishing Company

Pacific Grove • Albany • Belmont • Bonn • Cincinnati • Detroit • Johannesburg
London • Madrid • Melbourne • Mexico City • New York • Paris
Singapore • Tokyo • Toronto • Washington

Sponsoring Editor: *Marianne Taflinger*
Marketing Team: *Lauren Harp and Christine Davis*
Editorial Assistant: *Scott Brearton*
Production Editor: *Kirk Bomont*
Manuscript Editor: *Barbara Kimmel*
Permissions Editor: *Cat Morrison*

Interior and Cover Design: *Roy R. Neuhaus*
Cover Photo: *Scott Morgan*
Art Coordinator: *Jennifer Mackres*
Typesetting: *ColorType*
Cover Printing: *Phoenix Color Corporation*
Printing and Binding: *Maple-Vail Book Mfg. Group, Inc.*

*For more information, contact:*

BROOKS/COLE PUBLISHING COMPANY
511 Forest Lodge Road
Pacific Grove, CA 93950
USA

International Thomson Publishing Europe
Berkshire House 168-173
High Holborn
London WC1V 7AA
England

Thomas Nelson Australia
102 Dodds Street
South Melbourne, 3205
Victoria, Australia

Nelson Canada
1120 Birchmount Road
Scarborough, Ontario
Canada M1K 5G4

International Thomson Editores
Seneca 53
Col. Polanco
11560 México, D. F., México

International Thomson Publishing GmbH
Königswinterer Strasse 418
53227 Bonn
Germany

International Thomson Publishing Asia
221 Henderson Road
#05-10 Henderson Building
Singapore 0315

International Thomson Publishing Japan
Hirakawacho Kyowa Building, 3F
2-2-1 Hirakawacho
Chiyoda-ku, Tokyo 102
Japan

Printed in the United States of America

10 9 8 7 6 5 4 3 2 1

**Library of Congress Cataloging-in Publication Data**
Neath, Ian [date]
    Human memory : an introduction to research, data, and theory / Ian Neath.
        p.  cm.
    Includes bibliographical references and index.
    ISBN 0-534-34197-7
    1. Memory      I. Title
BF371.N43   1998
153.12—dc21                                     97-24356
                                                   CIP

*To A. M. S.*
*and*
*R. T. G. and H. T. G.*

**Ian Neath** is currently an associate professor in the Department of Psychological Sciences at Purdue University in West Lafayette, Indiana. He received a B.A. in history and psychology from Rice University in 1987 and a Ph.D. in cognitive psychology from Yale University in 1991. At Purdue, he regularly teaches both the undergraduate and graduate courses on human memory, as well as courses on introductory psychology, cognitive psychology, and simulation modeling. He has published many articles on memory in such professional journals as *Memory*, *Memory & Cognition*, *Learning & Memory*, and *The Journal of Memory and Language*. He has also authored or co-authored articles in *Animal Learning & Behavior*, *Psychonomic Bulletin & Review*, and *The Encyclopedia of Neuroscience*.

# Brief Contents

# Contents

# Contents

# Preface

This book is designed for use in both upper-division undergraduate and lower-division graduate courses on human memory. I wrote it because there were no books on memory that were really appropriate for the courses that I teach at Purdue. For the undergraduate memory course, I used to use Zechmeister and Nyberg's *Human Memory* (1982), but it is out of date, and the authors, unfortunately, have not offered a revised edition. For the graduate course, I have assigned sections of both Crowder's *Principles of Learning and Memory* (1976) and Murdock's *Human Memory* (1974). These texts provide sophisticated and insightful analyses of many problems in memory, and even though they are more than 20 years old, they remain useful reference books. Other books typically suffer from one of two problems: either their scope is too limited for a full semester course on human memory (e.g., Greene, 1992), or their scope is too inclusive (e.g., Anderson, 1995), including material that at Purdue is covered by a separate course on animal learning. Thus, this book covers what I cover in my two courses — although not all of the material is used in both courses — and additional readings from primary sources are assigned in the graduate course.

There are two unusual features of this book. First, there is an emphasis on theory and models with an extended discussion of some of the major quantitative models of memory. I was surprised when I could find introductory cognitive books (a lower-level course) that cover SAM, but no memory text that included the model. Because of SAM's enormous influence, knowledge of SAM, as well as of the other global memory models, is essential for understanding much of the most recent research on memory. Another special feature of this text, following the lead of Zechmeister and Nyberg, is an emphasis on research. Each chapter (with the exception of the first chapter, the global memory models chapter, and the developmental chapter) features a classic or important experiment that students can easily conduct, and the Appendix contains all the stimuli necessary to conduct the experiments. Indeed, the many similarities between this book and that of Zechmeister and Nyberg are entirely intentional.

One major problem in a text such as this concerns the relationship between the experimental data reported by a researcher and the theoretical explanation. Often in this book I report data but offer a theory very different from that proposed by the original author(s), primarily because there are too many different theories to mention every single one. Although this is not a new problem (Underwood, 1972), there does appear to be a proliferation of theories (Watkins, 1984). As an example, I discuss the results of Keppel and Underwood (1962), but I make no mention of their theoretical interpretation; similarly, I present Hyde and Jenkins (1973) as supporting levels of processing, whereas their interpretation was different. I never (to my knowledge) attribute a theoretical position to an author that is not clearly stated in the work, and I have tried to ensure that no unwarranted inferences will be drawn between a particular researcher and a particular theory. In addition, I often do not present the full experimental design when the complications in the original design might obscure the major point. For example, when discussing the Gerrig (1989) work that looks at the malleability of knowledge, I do not mention all of the conditions, such as the false versions and the control studies.

I have tried to achieve a balance between historically significant findings and current "state-of-the-art" research. One consequence of the former is that there are extensive references to memory research and theory during the early and middle parts of this century, including numerous references to people such as McGeoch, Postman, and Underwood. I was surprised to find that many memory textbooks include no citations to these (and many other) researchers whose ideas and work so profoundly affected the field. One consequence of including current work is that there are many equations in the book. Ideally, the equations will be a redundant restatement of the verbal description, but they have the advantage of being far more precise. None of the equations, however, require more mathematical ability than is needed for a basic statistics course.

Finally, there are many important topics that are not covered or that receive only minimal attention. The primary reason is that memory plays so central a role in cognitive functioning that almost all areas of experimental psychology could legitimately be included in a memory textbook. However, manuscripts are eventually due at the publishers, and I did not have time to include all of the topics that I would have liked. Hopefully, the book reflects a reasonably fair summary of the major areas of mainstream memory research.

# A Guide to the Book

Each chapter in this book is, to a large extent, self-contained and can be read in any order. Several features help this modular design, including defining the same concept in more than one chapter and providing numerous cross-references to other chapters. Nonetheless, certain groups of chapters will be easier to understand if read in sequence: Chapters 6, 7, and 8 should be read in order, and Chapter 10 should be read before Chapter 11. Chapter 17, on the other hand, can serve as either a review or as an introduction.

Chapter 2 situates current research within a larger historical perspective. Included is a brief overview of the contribution of philosophy to psychology's early history, as well as a discussion of the pioneering work of Hermann Ebbinghaus. The experiment replicates Ebbinghaus's famous forgetting function. The associationist tradition in memory that grew out of this early work is presented in some detail, with an emphasis on how it influenced research in the early and middle parts of the 20th century and served as the basis of connectionism.

Chapter 3 reviews work on sensory memory with an emphasis on whether there is evidence to support the idea that there exist separate memory systems for sensory information. Most of the chapter concerns visual and auditory modalities, but there is also a brief discussion of memory for odors, a sensory modality that has been rather understudied. The experiment focuses on the stimulus suffix effect.

Chapter 4 presents the common multistore, or modal, model of memory, with an in-depth examination of the evidence used to support a distinction between short-term store and long-term store. The chapter also discusses in some detail the classic work of Broadbent, Miller, Peterson and Peterson, Waugh and Norman, and Atkinson and Shiffrin, and includes a critical examination of the strengths and weakness of this approach. The experiment compares short-term recency effects with long-term recency effects.

Chapter 5 compares three current perspectives of immediate memory, Baddeley's (1986) Working Memory, Cowan's (1995) activation view, and Nairne's (1990) Feature Model. All of these views are presented in some detail to illustrate how theorists explain the huge amount of information we have about memory performance. The experiment demonstrates the word-length effect — better recall of short compared to long words.

Whereas Chapters 3 and 4 focus on structures, Chapter 6 focuses on processing, including both levels of processing and transfer appropriate processing. The relationship between the processing performed at study and the processing required at test is examined in detail, and the chapter concludes with presentation of Jacoby's (1991) processing dissociation framework, a technique designed to evaluate the contributions of different processes. The experiment in Chapter 6 illustrates the basic idea between levels of processing. These ideas lead into Chapter 7, which looks at three main views of forgetting, consolidation, decay, and interference. Here, the experiment examines the release from proactive interference effect seen in the Brown-Peterson paradigm.

Chapter 8 looks at implicit and explicit memory, particularly as they bear on the important issue of whether there are multiple memory systems. The experiment is a demonstration of repetition priming, the data most often used to support a distinction between implicit and explicit memory. The chapter compares the multiple systems view of Schacter and Tulving (1994), the transfer appropriate processing view of Roediger (1990), and the bias interpretation of Ratcliff and McKoon (1996).

Chapter 9 completes the discussion of multiple memory systems by presenting an overview of the biological bases of memory, including a discussion of simple neural circuits and a summary of methods of investigation. The experiment illustrates a simple behavioral measure for examining underlying neurological structure. Following this, there is a survey of research on amnesia.

Chapter 10 examines recognition memory, including a discussion of signal detection theory and how this can be used to assess discrimination and estimate response bias. The experiment details how to apply a signal detection analysis to recognition data, including a manipulation of response bias. Two early views, HAM and the class of generate-recognize models, are discussed, as well as more recent accounts. Also included are discussions of the remember-know paradigm, the mirror effect, and an overview of face recognition.

Chapter 11 presents three so-called global memory models. These models, SAM, MINERVA 2, and TODAM, are described in some detail and provide an illustration of how sophisticated current theories of memory can be. Each model can account for recognition and at least one other paradigm: for example, free recall for SAM, serial recall for TODAM, and schema abstraction for MINERVA 2. There is also an example of a connectionist model of memory, in this case a nonlinear back propagation model of recognition.

Chapters 12 and 13 examine the issue of representation. Chapter 12 focuses on knowledge and thus emphasizes a primarily propositional form of representation. The chapter includes both spreading activation accounts of semantic priming as well as the current compound cue theories, which extend the global memory models presented in the previous chapter. The experiment in this chapter examines typicality effects in categorization. Chapter 13 concentrates on visual imagery, arguing for the need for an analog form of representation. This chapter includes the early work of Paivio and Brooks, as well as the more recent work of Kosslyn and Shepard. Chapter 13 also discusses the issue of reality monitoring, including the Perky effect showing the difficulty in distinguishing between real and imaged stimuli. The experiment examines a prediction of Paivo's dual-coding theory, and the chapter concludes with a brief discussion of auditory and odor imagery.

Chapter 14 presents an overview of memory for "when," including a discussion of how people remember when particular events occurred, a section on autobiographical memory, and a comparison of various theories of dating events. Two models are compared in some detail, with an emphasis on how they account for both laboratory and real world data. The experiment assesses memory for when items were presented, which illustrates many of the same properties as memory for autobiographical events.

Chapter 15 concentrates on reconstructive processes in memory, including the role of schemas and general knowledge. The chapter includes a suggestion for making the concept of a schema less vague and capable of making predictions, and it presents a detailed presentation of memory illusions. Chapter 15 also explores the consequences of reconstructive memory for evaluating the memory of eyewitnesses, including the role of misinformation, hypnosis, and the cognitive interview and how factors such as emotion and arousal can affect accuracy. The experiment illustrates the phenomenon of memory for words not presented, and the chapter includes a discussion of implanting memories.

Chapter 16 looks at developmental issues, emphasizing qualitative differences in processing when infants, children and healthy older adults are compared to college students. Because of the difficulty of recruiting appropriate subjects, this chapter has no experiment.

Chapter 17 discusses ways to improve memory. Unlike books that focus only on the technical mnemonics, this chapter includes a much broader treatment and can serve as either a review or an introduction. The experiment duplicates a classic finding of better retention following interactive imagery as compared to no imagery. In addition, the chapter provides a critique of popular books, separating the useful and scientifically supported techniques from the useless and disproven.

# Instructor Support

To assist the teacher or student, I have created several demos that implement each of the major global memory models in Chapter 11 (SAM, MINERVA 2, and TODAM) for both IBM-compatible (DOS and Windows) and Macintosh computers. There are also versions of the Feature Model (Chapter 5) and Perturbation Theory (Chapter 14). You may download these programs, and a set of explanatory notes and suggested exercises, through the World Wide Web:

http://www.psych.purdue.edu/~neath/memory/memory.html

I'd be interested in your feedback and suggestions on how these programs, or any other part of the book, might be improved for future editions.

# Acknowledgments

Professionally, I am particularly indebted to three people: my undergraduate advisor, Michael J. Watkins of Rice University; my graduate advisor, Robert G. Crowder of Yale University; and my colleague James S. Nairne, at Purdue. Mike got me interested in human memory, and because of him I went on to graduate school in cognitive psychology rather than in history. Bob was the perfect advisor for me, treating me as a colleague from the first day and letting me pursue and develop my interests under his direction. At Purdue, Jim has fostered my interest in simulation modeling and constantly challenges me to be rigorous and thorough in my own thinking.

Several reviewers read the entire manuscript, and many more read portions; each made numerous insightful and critical comments that have greatly improved the manuscript. They are: Harriett Amster, University of Texas, Arlington; Barbara H. Basden, California State University, Fresno; Robert Campbell, Clemson University; James M. Clark, University of Winnipeg; Tim Curran, Case Western Reserve University; Ira Fischler, University of Florida; Peter Graf, University of British Columbia; Robert Greene, Case Western Reserve University; Denny C. LeCompte, University of Missouri–St. Louis; Wendy V. Parr, Victoria University of Wellington; Henry L. Roediger III, Washington University; J. Scott Saults, University of Missouri–Columbia; Jennifer R. Shelton-Young, Harvard University; Michael A. Stadler, University of Missouri–Columbia.

I also thank the staff at Brooks/Cole: Scott Brearton, Jennifer Mackres, Cat Morrison, and Roy R. Neuhaus. Both Marianne Taflinger and Kirk Bomont were a pleasure to work with, and Barbara Kimmel deserves much thanks for greatly improving the prose in the text. The folks at ColorType, especially Paul Bayfield, were invaluable in sorting out technical problems with the electronic submission of the figures.

I am especially fortunate that my colleagues at Purdue were willing to answer questions, provide references, and offer suggestions. In particular, Jacky Emmerton was kind enough to translate the original reports of the Japanese mnemonist Ishihara from German to English. Similarly, many virtual colleagues around the country and around the world promptly responded to my many electronic inquiries.

Aimée M. Surprenant read the entire book and has offered continuous support, advice, and encouragement from the beginning.

Finally, I am indebted to the many Purdue undergraduates who have taken Psyc 311, Human Memory, and have shown they can understand *all* the material included in the book if only I have high enough expectations.

*Sapiens nihil affirmat quod non probat*

*Ian Neath*

# References

Anderson, J. R. (1995). *Learning and Memory: An Integrated Approach*. New York: John Wiley and Sons.

Baddeley, A. D. (1986). *Working memory*. New York: Oxford University Press.

Cowan, N. (1995). *Attention and memory: An integrated framework*. New York: Oxford University Press.

Crowder, R. G. (1976). *Principles of Learning and Memory*. Hillsdale, NJ: Erlbaum.

Gerrig, R. J. (1989). Suspense in the absence of uncertainty. *Journal of Memory and Language, 28*, 633–648.

Greene, R. L. (1992). *Human Memory: Paradigms and Paradoxes*. Hillsdale, NJ: Erlbaum.

Hyde, T. S., & Jenkins, J. J. (1973). Recall of words as a function of semantic, graphic, and syntactic orienting tasks. *Journal of Verbal Learning and Verbal Behavior, 12*, 471–480.

Jacoby, L. L. (1991). A process dissociation framework: Separating automatic from intentional uses of memory. *Journal of Memory and Language, 30*, 513–541.

Keppel, G., & Underwood, B. J. (1962). Proactive inhibition in short-term retention of single items. *Journal of Verbal Learning and Verbal Behavior, 1*, 153–161.

Murdock, B. B. Jr. (1974). *Human Memory: Theory and Data*. Potomac, MD: Erlbaum.

Nairne, J. S. (1990). A feature model of immediate memory. *Memory & Cognition, 18*, 251–269.

Ratcliff, R., & McKoon, G. (1996). Bias effects in implicit memory tasks. *Journal of Experimental Psychology: General, 125*, 403–421.

Roediger, H. L., III. (1990). Implicit memory: Retention without remembering. *American Psychologist, 45*, 1043–1056.

Schacter, D. L., & Tulving, E. (1994). What are the memory systems of 1994? In D. L. Schacter & E. Tulving (Eds.), *Memory systems 1994*. Cambridge, MA: MIT Press.

Underwood, B. J. (1972). Are we overloading memory? In A. W. Melton and E. Martin (Eds.), *Coding Processes in Human Memory*. New York: Wiley.

Watkins, M. J. (1984). Models are toothbrushes. *Behavioral and Brain Sciences, 7*, 86.

Zechmeister, E. B., & Nyberg, S. E. (1982). *Human Memory: An Introduction to Research and Theory*. Monterey, CA: Brooks/Cole.

# CHAPTER ONE

# Introduction

*"There seems something more speakingly incomprehensible in the powers, the failures, the inequalities of memory, than in any other of our intelligences. The memory is sometimes so retentive, so serviceable, so obedient — at others, so bewildered and so weak — and at others again, so tyrannic, so beyond control! We are to be sure a miracle every way — but our powers of recollecting and of forgetting, do seem peculiarly past finding out."*

—Jane Austen

## Introduction to Human Memory

If we had no memory, in the broadest sense of the term, we would not be able to function. Memory is essential for all activities. When riding a bicycle, we rely on memory to provide the appropriate processes to keep our balance, keep the pedals turning, and navigate down the path. When reading, we rely on memory to provide knowledge about word definitions, facts, and concepts. We also need memory to keep track of the flow of ideas, why one sentence or paragraph of text follows another. When chatting with friends, we rely on memory to provide information about details of our own lives, what we did last week, or what happened at the ball game. When listening, we rely on memory to retain, however briefly, parts of the auditory signal so that it can be processed. When creating an image of what a room would look like with its furniture rearranged, we rely on memory to provide the structural descriptions that allow us to construct a mental picture. A person's identity and definition of self relies solely on memory, both for what the person has done, thought, and believed and for what others have said. Memory plays such an important and ever-present role that it is often overlooked. The only time most people pay attention to their memory is when it fails.

The study of memory seeks to understand these and many other aspects of memory. Like most people, researchers look for situations where memory fails. It is by comparing situations where memory is successful to ones where it fails that psychologists have discovered and documented the principles by which human memory operates. Although the research is not so far progressed that we can predict each individual's behavior in every

1

particular situation, the accumulated knowledge does allow us to predict general memory performance in a wide range of situations. The purpose of this book is to introduce you to this accumulated knowledge, to illustrate the process of designing and conducting diagnostic research, and to present a survey of the resultant theories that summarize and explain the data and make predictions about performance in novel situations. As you will see, our powers of remembering and forgetting can indeed be found out.

# Memory Metaphors

One of the central questions researchers must address when developing a theory or model is how best to think of memory. When most people think about memory — psychologists included — they typically conceive of a place where information is stored. As Roediger (1980) has noted, this spatial metaphor has dominated the study of memory: "We speak of *storing* memories, of *searching* for and *locating* them. We *organize* our thoughts; we *look* for memories that have been *lost,* and if we are fortunate, we *find* them" (p. 232).

In addition, many of the spatial metaphors contrived have typically been representative of the newest or most important technology available. For example, Aristotle, in his *De memoria et reminiscentia,* compared memory to a wax tablet, with forming a memory like making a seal on wax with a signet ring. The durability of the memory depended on the age and temperament of the person, just as the durability of an impression depends on the age and malleability of the wax.

> Some men in the presence of considerable stimulus have no memory. . . . With them the design makes no impression because they are worn down like old walls in buildings, or because of the hardness of that which is to receive the impression. For this reason the very young and the old have poor memories; they are in a state of flux, the young because of their growth, the old because of their decay. For a similar reason neither the very quick nor the very slow appear to have good memories; the former are moister than they should be, and the latter harder; with the former the picture has no permanence, with the latter it makes no impression. (Yates, 1966, p. 33)

Plato compared memory to an aviary, whereas Augustine compared memory to a cave — both spatial objects. Vives compared the faculty of memory to a body, claiming that both need regular exercise or they become lazy, sluggish, and inert. Francis Bacon compared the act of recollection to hunting a deer; if one cuts down the available space in which the deer can roam, the hunting is easier. Descartes, in *De homine,* used an analogy to the water-powered automata in the French royal gardens to describe simple reflexes and incorporated them into his conception of how the mind and body interacted (Herrnstein & Boring, 1965). John Locke thought of memory as an empty cabinet. By the early 20th century, memory was being compared to a gramophone, an updating of the wax tablet metaphor but with a more precise description of various problems (Pear, 1922).

By the mid-1950s, descriptions and theories of memory were borrowing much from the telephone system and from information theory (Broadbent, 1958), only to be eclipsed by the digital computer metaphor, with the interaction of hardware and software (Feigenbaum & Simon, 1962). This metaphor led directly to what is referred to as the dual-store or modal model of memory, with separate short- and long-term stores (see Chapter 4).

Perhaps the most unusual—but still spatial—metaphor compared memory to a cow's digestive system and the passage of information through the memory system to the passage of food through the various stomachs and orifices (Hintzman, 1974). Hintzman noted that the metaphor is invoked by phrases such as *food for thought, digesting information,* and *ruminating.* The process of forgetting was not explicitly described, but it was thought to be the reverse of "incremental learning: namely, excremental forgetting" (Hintzman, 1974, p. 85).

In all these views, memory is a place in which memories are stored, a position called the *structural view.* Consider the following alternative to the structural view:

> Memories, like perceptions and eventually sensations, have no separate existences. The memory of what you saw yesterday has no more existence until revived than the pain you felt in your arm before it was pinched. . . . In short, for the experiencing individual, memories do not exist before they are revived or recalled. Memories are not like filed letters stored in cabinets or unhung paintings in the basement of a museum. Rather, they are like melodies realized by striking the keys on a piano. Memories are no more stored in the brain than melodies in the keys of the piano. (Wechsler, 1963, pp. 150–151)

This second view, called the *proceduralist view,* emphasizes the processes that create and re-create the memory, rather than the structure or location in which a memory might be stored (Crowder, 1993). This idea was developed earlier by Bain (1855) and Hebb (1949).

Obviously, at some level, memories are stored somewhere; as we experience more and more, we remember more and more, and so structures must be important. Equally obvious, however, is that there is no one place that a memory is put. If, for example, one cell were responsible for the memory of my grandmother and that cell died (as cells do all the time), all memory for my grandmother would be permanently lost also. Although neither the structuralist nor proceduralist view can explain all memory phenomena, the field as a whole has come to emphasize process over structure. Even 20 years ago, Kintsch (1977) concluded that "many psychologists today are no longer satisfied with the box metaphor that underlies the earlier models. . . . Instead, a more dynamic conception of the memory system is evolving, with an emphasis on differential processes rather than on separate boxes" (p. 225). One important goal of this book is to introduce you to various theories of memory and to see how these theories are developed and evaluated.

# Memory Methodology

One problem with studying memory is that everyone has one and has experience with how it works. When a cognitive psychologist reports the results of a study, a common reaction is to exclaim, "My grandmother could've told me that!" However, the psychologist conducts experiments to determine, as objectively as possible, how memory works.

An experimental psychologist uses an established set of procedures that may or may not confirm your grandmother's own experience but that does (hopefully) produce reliable and replicable results. As a rule, experimental psychologists are particularly wary of any unsubstantiated claim, and this may be why it seems that a reference is cited for almost every statement made (Neath, 1998, Chap. 1).

The primary reason for this reliance on experimentation is that, although many conventional beliefs about memory are correct, many are not. For example, many people believe that photographic memory exists, and the majority of college students believe that hypnosis will recover repressed memories (Klatzky, 1984); neither appears to be the case (see Chapters 13 and 15, respectively). A properly conducted experiment — or more usually, a series of experiments — will provide evidence that either confirms or disconfirms such statements. Citing a research study ensures that theories are based on scientifically gathered data, rather than on general, untested speculations. Although many of the general findings may indeed be things that your grandmother knows, there is an important difference between basing conclusions on scientific research and hoping that untested folk wisdom is accurate.

A working definition of memory might be that it is the ability to use or revive information that was previously encoded or processed. Memory is never directly observed, and we need not even be aware of its influence; rather, its existence is inferred from some particular behavior or some change in level of performance. Therefore, the type of evidence needed to support the claim of memory versus no memory for a particular event requires special attention.

One goal of this text is to give you an appreciation for experimental design, and almost every chapter has a description of the procedures necessary to conduct a classic memory study. All the necessary stimuli are included in the Appendix, and no experiment requires any unusual or expensive equipment. Having conducted an experiment, you should be in a better position to appreciate the arguments that surround its theoretical interpretation.

When people first become acquainted with how experiments are designed and conducted, a common reaction is to wonder whether such artificial-looking procedures can say anything interesting about memory in ordinary, everyday situations. Many researchers have similar concerns, and in the past few years the debate over ecological validity has resurfaced. *Ecological validity* in this context refers to the extent to which an experiment in a controlled laboratory setting reflects what happens in ordinary, uncontrolled settings, usually dubbed "the real world." This recurring debate began again most recently when Ulric Neisser (1978) wrote, "If *X* is an interesting or socially significant aspect of memory, then psychologists have hardly ever studied *X*" (p. 4). He further claimed that most experimental findings were obvious or trivial and, most important, failed to generalize outside the laboratory. According to this view, research in the tradition of Bartlett (1932), whom we will discuss in Chapter 12, has fostered more important findings than has research in the tradition of Ebbinghaus (1885), whom we discuss in Chapter 2. For example, Bartlett in his research used sentences and prose passages rather than the nonsense syllables that Ebbinghaus used, and Bartlett examined memory in social settings, whereas Ebbinghaus tested only himself.

Two rebuttals to Neisser were quickly offered. First, Roediger (1990) pointed out that Neisser's claim is based on a rather limited review of the experimental literature. For example, many people Neisser cites as prime contributors to the "thundering silence" on practical issues actually spent a large portion of their careers studying these very topics. A good example is John McGeoch (see Crowder, 1992, for a brief biography). Although best known for his interference theory of forgetting (see Chapter 7), McGeoch also contributed substantially to what would now be called applied memory research. Another example, which will be discussed in more detail later on, is research demonstrating that distributed rather than massed practice produced better memory; if you allot 2 hours for practice, your memory will be better if you separate the practice into several smaller chunks (say, four half-hour blocks) than if you mass all the practice into one 2-hour block. Although these studies were usually conducted with artificial stimuli (nonsense syllables) in an artificial task (paired-associate learning) in an artificial environment (the laboratory), the results have consistently generalized to the "real world": information is retained longer if it is learned in several shorter sessions than in one longer session (for example, see Herrmann, Weingartner, Searleman, & McEvoy, 1992; Singh, Mishra, Bendapudi, & Linville, 1994). In fact, changing your study habits from massed study to distributed study is perhaps the easiest and most effective way to enhance your retention of information (see Chapter 17). It should not really be surprising that results do generalize from the laboratory to real life. As McGeoch and Irion (1952) put it, "life in the laboratory is just as 'real' as life may be anywhere else" (p. 8).

As an interesting side note, the work of Ebbinghaus, done in the "ecologically invalid" way, has consistently been replicated, whereas many of Bartlett's most well-known findings, done in a more "ecologically valid" way, have not. For example, the general shape of the forgetting function is the same as Ebbinghaus reported regardless of whether the stimuli are words or sentences (Slamecka & McElree, 1983) or television shows (Squire, 1989). Other examples are the difference between massed and distributed rehearsal cited above, and the effects of the time of day on memory (Petros, Beckwith, & Anderson, 1990). In contrast to this tradition of successful replication are some of Bartlett's most well-known findings. Bartlett had his subjects read a Native American folk tale called the "War of the Ghosts." Because his subjects were British, they had almost no knowledge of Native American customs, traditions, and symbolism, and so the story was particularly difficult to understand and recall. Bartlett reported that over successive recall attempts, more and more distortions were introduced. Although this result is presented in most texts, there are actually no successful replications of this result (see Gauld & Stephenson, 1967; Roediger, Wheeler, & Rajaram, 1993; Wheeler & Roediger, 1992). Of course, many of Bartlett's other studies on memory are easy to replicate, but these show similar patterns of results as those reported by Ebbinghaus.

A different rebuttal to Neisser's thesis was offered by Banaji and Crowder (1989). Their main point was that experiments (in any area) can be classified into one of four categories. The generalizability of the results of the experiment can be either high or low, and the ecological validity of the method can be either high or low. The four possibilities are shown in Table 1.1.

**Table 1.1**   A two-by-two array of approaches to science.

|  |  | Ecological validity of method | |
| --- | --- | --- | --- |
|  |  | Low | High |
| Generalizability of results | Low | Cell 1 | Cell 2 |
|  | High | Cell 3 | Cell 4 |

Source: Based on Banaji & Crowder (1989).

Banaji and Crowder noted that Cell 4, which represents high ecological validity and high generalizability of results, represents the ideal; Cell 1, which represents contrived, artificial methods with no generalizable findings, is the least desirable situation. Banaji and Crowder disagreed with Neisser in that they opted for Cell 3 as a better compromise than Cell 2. As support for their contention, they cited many studies with apparently low ecological validity of methods (such as displaying letters and words for 1/20th of a second) that have had an enormous impact on important everyday behaviors (such as reading).

Unfortunately, many experiments that fall within Cells 1 and 2 of the above array have been conducted and published. These studies contribute little to our knowledge of memory, and they can even hinder progress because methodological flaws have led to incorrect conclusions. Part of your job, as a student of memory, is to learn how to distinguish between those studies in Cells 1 and 2 and those in Cells 3 and 4.

## Memory Terminology

In 1972, Underwood posed this question to researchers studying human behavior: "Are we overloading memory?" Part of the problem, as he saw it, was the large number of different types of memory. If anything, the number of terms has proliferated since his article. Although Underwood was referring to overloading the subject's memory with all the different types of processing that could occur, he could also have been referring to the student of memory, who must try to retain the important distinctions among the many different proposed systems and subsystems. Table 1.2 lists some of the memory terms that will be encountered frequently.

In this text, when referring to a specific theory, I will use the terms listed in the far right column of Table 1.2. When referring to the same type of memory but without wishing to invoke a particular theory, I will use the terms listed in the middle column. The reason for this is that the theory-specific terms carry with them particular assumptions whereas the theory-neutral terms (as much as possible) do not. For example, the terms *episodic* and *semantic* usually imply separate memory systems along the lines proposed by Tulving (1972, 1983). In contrast, the terms *autobiographical memory* and *generic memory* refer to remembering the same kind of information as episodic and semantic memory, respectively, but are neutral on whether the systems are separate and are neutral on the

**Table 1.2** Theory-neutral and theory-specific terms for various kinds of memory.

| Type of Information | Theory-Neutral Term | Theory-Specific Term |
| --- | --- | --- |
| Sensations | Sensory Memory | Iconic Memory |
| | | Echoic Memory |
| | | PAS (Precategorical Acoustic Store) |
| Information to be retained only briefly | Immediate Memory | Short-Term Store |
| | | Short-Term Memory |
| | | Primary Memory |
| | | Working Memory |
| Information to be retained indefinitely | Generic Memory | Long-Term Store |
| | | Long-Term Memory |
| | | Secondary Memory |
| Personal history | Autobiographical Memory | Episodic Memory |
| Knowledge | Generic Memory | Semantic Memory |

Note: Terms in the far right column entail specific assumptions, especially about the division of memory, whereas terms in the middle column are intended to be neutral.

presumed underlying processes. Similarly, *working memory* is usually taken as implying Baddeley (1986) proposal, whereas immediate memory is the neutral equivalent, implying neither separate memory stores nor a monistic view. The terms *implicit* and *explicit memory* are not included in the table; the definitions for these are rather complex and will be provided in Chapter 8.

# References

Baddeley, A. D. (1986). *Working memory.* New York: Oxford University Press.

Bain, A. (1855). *The senses and the intellect.* London: John W. Parker and Son.

Banaji, M. R., & Crowder, R. G. (1989). The bankruptcy of everyday memory. *American Psychologist, 44,* 1185–1193.

Bartlett, F. C. (1932). *Remembering: A study in experimental and social psychology.* Cambridge: Cambridge University Press. (Reprinted 1977)

Broadbent, D. E. (1958). *Perception and communication.* New York: Pergamon.

Crowder, R. G. (1992). John A. McGeoch. In L. R. Squire (Ed.), *Encyclopedia of learning and memory.* New York: Macmillan.

Crowder, R. G. (1993). Systems and principles in memory theory: Another critique of pure memory. In A. F. Collins, S. E. Gathercole, M. A. Conway, & P. E. Morris (Eds.), *Theories of memory.* Hove, UK: Erlbaum.

Ebbinghaus, H. (1885). *Über das Gedächtnis: Untersuchungen zur experimentellen Psychologie.* Leipzig: Duncker and Humboldt. [Reprinted as H. E. Ebbinghaus (1964). Memory: A Contribution to Experimental Psychology (H. A. Ruger, Trans.). New York: Dover]

Feigenbaum, E. A., & Simon, H. (1962). A theory of the serial position effect. *British Journal of Psychology, 53,* 307–320.

Gauld, A., & Stephenson, G. M. (1967). Some experiments related to Bartlett's theory of remembering. *British Journal of Psychology, 58,* 39–49.

Hebb, D. O. (1949). *The organization of behavior: A neuropsychological theory.* New York: Wiley.

Herrmann, D. J., Weingartner, H., Searleman, A., & McEvoy, C. (Eds.). (1992). *Memory improvement: Implications for memory theory.* New York: Springer-Verlag.

Herrnstein, R. J., & Boring, E. G. (Eds.). (1965). *A source book in the history of psychology.* Cambridge, MA: Harvard University Press.

Hintzman, D. L. (1974). Psychology and the cow's belly. *The Worm Runner's Digest, 16,* 84–85.

Kintsch, W. (1977). *Memory and cognition.* New York: Wiley.

Klatzky, R. L. (1984). *Memory and awareness: An information-processing perspective.* New York: Freeman.

McGeoch, J. A., & Irion, A. L. (1952). *The psychology of human learning* (2nd ed.). New York: Longmans Green & Co.

Neisser, U. (1978). Memory: What are the important questions? In M. M. Gruneberg, P. Morris, & R. N. Sykes (Eds.), *Practical aspects of memory.* London: Academic Press.

Pear, T. H. (1922). *Remembering and forgetting.* London: Methuen.

Petros, T. V., Beckwith, B. E., & Anderson, M. (1990). Individual differences in the effects of time of day and passage difficulty on prose memory in adults. *British Journal of Psychology, 81,* 63–72.

Roediger, H. L., III. (1980). Memory metaphors in cognitive psychology. *Memory & Cognition, 8,* 231–246.

Roediger, H. L., III. (1990). Review of "Remembering Reconsidered: Ecological and Traditional Approaches to the Study of Memory." *American Journal of Psychology, 103,* 403–409.

Roediger, H. L., III, Wheeler, M. A., & Rajaram, S. (1993). Remembering, knowing, and reconstructing the past. In D. L. Medin (Ed.), *The psychology of learning and motivation: Advances in research and theory.* San Diego, CA: Academic Press.

Singh, S., Mishra, S., Bendapudi, N., & Linville, D. (1994). Enhancing memory of television commercials through message spacing. *Journal of Marketing Research, 31,* 384–329.

Slamecka, N. J., & McElree, B. (1983). Normal forgetting of verbal lists as a function of their degree of learning. *Journal of Experimental Psychology: Learning, Memory, and Cognition, 9,* 384–397.

Squire, L. R. (1989). On the course of forgetting in very long-term memory. *Journal of Experimental Psychology: Learning, Memory, and Cognition, 15,* 241–245.

Tulving, E. (1972). Episodic and semantic memory. In E. Tulving & W. Donaldson (Eds.), *Organization of memory.* New York: Academic Press.

Tulving, E. (1983). *Elements of episodic memory.* New York: Oxford University Press.

Underwood, B. J. (1972). Are we overloading memory? In A. W. Melton & E. Martin (Eds.), *Coding processes in human memory.* New York: Wiley.

Wechsler, D. B. (1963). Engrams, memory storage, and mnemonic coding. *American Psychologist, 18,* 149–153.

Wheeler, M. A., & Roediger, H. L., III (1992). Disparate effects of repeated testing: Reconciling Ballard's (1913) and Bartlett's (1932) results. *Psychological Science, 3,* 240–245.

Yates, F. A. (1966). *The art of memory.* Chicago: University of Chicago Press.

# CHAPTER TWO

# Historical Overview

*"Psychology has a long past, but only a short history."*
— *Hermann Ebbinghaus (Boring, 1950, p. ix)*

## A Short History

Although inquiries into the nature of memory began centuries ago and never really ceased, the early researchers' motivation and enthusiasm was partially offset by the lack of an appropriate set of rules, methods, and procedures for studying memory. In particular, the dominant method of inquiry was introspection. Many early researchers believed that, just as people can be trained to observe external events accurately (judges at gymnastics or diving competitions, for example), so could people be trained to observe their internal cognitive events. Introspectionists were trained to "observe" their own mental functioning and make repeated observations before coming to any conclusions. The main problem with this method, as Karl Marbe (1869–1953), a leading researcher at Würzburg, quickly found out, was that similar observers performing the same act often had different descriptions. In one of Marbe's experiments, subjects were asked to judge which of two objects was heavier; although his subjects were quite accurate at identifying the heavier object, they could not agree on the process whereby they made this decision. Marbe's disenchantment with introspection precipitated his change from experimental to applied psychology, where he developed aptitude tests for business and studied accident proneness with an eye to prevention (Zusne, 1975). As a method of inquiry, introspection has had a "dismal record of failure" in psychology (Bower & Clapper, 1989, p. 245). Although introspection has long been discredited as a method of scientific inquiry, the earliest philosophers and researchers gained many valuable insights using this method. It should be noted, however, that these same people made many errors through introspection as well.

## Antiquity and the Middle Ages

Many ancient cultures had gods or goddesses associated specifically with memory. In Egypt in 4000 B.C., Thoth was the god of learning, memory, and wisdom; in Greece in 1000 B.C., Mnemosyne (from whom we get terms such as mnemonic and mnemonist), mother of the muses, was the goddess of memory (Herrmann & Chaffin, 1988). Although there were undoubtedly many works on how to improve memory, the earliest surviving example dates from about 400 B.C. This fragment, known as the *Dialexeis* (Yates, 1966, pp. 29–30), suggests that the three most important aspects of remembering are to pay attention, to rehearse, and to use a formal mnemonic device known as the method of loci (see Chapter 17).

The first real memory theorists were Plato (427–347 B.C.) and Aristotle (384–322 B.C.). Plato believed that all essential truths are stored in memory and that learning is simply the process of recollecting these truths. He offered the following three metaphors for memory. The wax tablet model likens memory to impressions formed on a wax tablet; people might have a more or less retentive memory depending upon the age of the wax, the hardness of the wax, the depth of the impression, and so forth. He also compared knowledge to birds in an aviary, with each different species of bird being a different piece of knowledge. A particular bird might be in the bird house but off in a distant part and not immediately available. His third model, that of a scribe, views memory as a recording of experience, but it is a process that is subject to the whims of the scribe: "When the inscribing feeling writes truly, then true opinion and true propositions are formed within us in consequence of its work—but when the scribe within us writes falsely, the result is false" (Herrmann & Chaffin, 1988, p. 55).

Most of Aristotle's writing on memory is found in a brief essay called *De Memoria et Reminiscentia* ("On Memory and Reminiscences"). The title reflects a distinction that Plato draws in *Philebus*: memory is the power of retention, whereas recollection (or reminiscence) is the power of recall. Humans are said to have both, but other animals lack recollection. Recollection is based on associations, and an association is simply the connection of two mental events (ideas, thoughts, beliefs, memories). Philosophers and psychologists have identified three laws of association within the works of Aristotle: events tend to be associated when they occur close together in time or space (the law of contiguity), when they are similar (the law of similarity), and when they contrast with each other (the law of contrast).

In the Roman world, the emphasis was on practical aspects of memory rather than on theory. Both Cicero (106–43 B.C.) and Quintillian (40–96 A.D.) emphasized the role that memory played in oratory; Cicero emphasized the importance of order as an aid, and Quintillian emphasized exercise, both mental and physical (Burnham, 1888). An anonymous work written around 86 B.C. and known as *Ad Herennium* is the most famous pragmatic work on memory from that period (Yates, 1966) and was the basis for much of the work of subsequent scholars.

The third early memory theorist was Augustine (354–430 A.D.). He identified two kinds of memory, sense memory and intellectual memory (Burnham, 1888). Sense memory preserves and reproduces images of objects, including sounds, odors, and touch. Intellectual memory, on the other hand, is concerned with knowledge, including literature, science, philosophy, and so forth. He noted that having illusions of memory is possible, such as when "we fancy we remember as though we had done or seen it, what we never did or saw at all" (Burnham, 1888, p. 61). Augustine agreed with earlier scholars such as Plotinus (205–270 A.D.) that memory is not a simple, passive process but rather a complex series of actions that can affect the accuracy and the nature of the memory. This idea is reflected in one of Augustine's major concerns, retrieval. He compared memory to a cave in which were stored not the original events but images of the events. Whenever we attempt to recall something, we are limited by the associations of ideas. Augustine also mentioned one of the many paradoxes of memory: "we have not entirely forgotten anything if we can remember that we have forgotten it" (Herrmann & Chaffin, 1988, p. 119).

Relatively little survives from the dark ages, and much of the work on memory in the Renaissance concerns practical questions and much discussion of mnemonic techniques (see Carruthers, 1990; Yates, 1966). Thomas Aquinas (1224–1274) generally followed the views of Aristotle, and his main contribution was bringing the works of Aristotle to a wider audience, rather than adding anything new to views on memory. Until this point, there was relatively little emphasis placed on empirical testing of ideas. Most medieval scholars were more concerned with metaphysics and its relation to theology than with accumulating empirically based knowledge. A major change in attitudes is reflected in the works of Juan Luis Vives and Francis Bacon.

# The Beginning of Modern Psychology

Juan Luis Vives (1492–1540), a Spanish humanist who studied in Paris and taught for a while at Corpus Christi College, Oxford, is often regarded as one of the great empiricists of the Renaissance. His central focus was on practical uses of knowledge, and he is well known for his many works on education. In his main writing on psychology, *De anima et vita libri tres* ("Three Books on the Soul and Life") published in 1538, Vives calls for greater attention to observation and experiment and less reliance on ancient authorities. He discusses the association of ideas, following Aristotle's and Augustine's formulation, and discusses memory at length, including sections on a law of forgetfulness and on mnemonics. He identified three causes of forgetting: "either because the very picture in memory is erased or destroyed directly; or it is smeared and broken up; or because it escapes our searching" (Diamond, 1974, p. 256). Vives suggested writing down whatever one wanted to remember (Burnham, 1888), thus going against the strictures of Plato, who warned that writing down information "will create forgetfulness in the learner's souls, because they will not use their memories; they will trust to the external written characters and not remember of themselves" (Herrmann & Chaffin, 1988, p. 38). Vives also believed, however, that "if memory is not exercised, it grows dull, becoming slower each day, more sluggish and inert" (Diamond, 1974, p. 256).

Francis Bacon (1561–1626) also emphasized the practical value of empirical discoveries in contrast to the results of metaphysical speculation and introspection, and his approach and ideas influenced many other prominent British thinkers. He believed that the three great powers were memory, fancy, and reason. He offered many practical insights into improving memory that have since been demonstrated as effective, such as associating the event with something concrete, studying before sleeping to reduce interference, processing information in several different ways rather than simply repeating it in rote fashion, and reducing the size of the search set. This last suggestion was accomplished by means of a "prenotion":

> By Prenotion I mean a kind of cutting off of infinity of search. For when a man desires to recall anything into his memory, if he have no prenotion or perception of that he seeks, he seeks and strives and beats about hither and thither as if in infinite space. But if he have some prenotion, this infinity is at once cut off, and the memory ranges in a narrower compass; like the hunting of a deer within an enclosure. (Robertson, 1905, p. 168)

Bacon is also well known for his four Idols—preconceptions or biases that prevent or hinder the discovery of the real truth. The Idols of the Tribe are the generally agreed-upon ways of thinking; the Idols of the Den are biases created by a person's environment or education; the Idols of the Market Place are misconceptions based on loose use of vocabulary; and the Idols of the Theater are the blind acceptance of older ideas from tradition or authority. Despite his prominent role in establishing respect for the scientific method, Bacon did not think very highly of mathematics (Watson, 1968).

# British Empiricism and Continental Nativism

Thomas Hobbes (1588–1679) was the first unqualified reductionist of modern times and is generally considered the first in the line of British empiricists. Recognition of his influence was delayed, however, because he was suspected of being an atheist. He served as a secretary to Bacon for a short period and was undoubtedly influenced by Bacon's ideas. Hobbes thought that memory and imagination are decaying sensations and that all of cognition is based on sensation. He argued that qualities are not properties of the object but of the perceiver: a box is not red; rather, the perceiver has the sensation of the box's being red (Watson, 1968). Sensations lead to simple ideas, and various combinations of simple ideas lead to more complex ideas. The importance of this line of reasoning is that it implies that the mind can be analyzed mechanistically, that the study of the mind can be made scientific. This belief that ideas arise from sensations, and hence from experience, also makes Hobbes an empiricist and thus in opposition to René Descartes (1596–1650).

Descartes has been called the first great psychologist of the modern era, although not the first modern psychologist. The primary reason for the designation "great" is that he attempted, for the first time since Aristotle, to create an entirely new system of thought. The basis of his system was doubt, and the first principle of which he was sure was the famous *cogito, ergo sum:*

> I resolved that everything that ever entered into my mind was no more true than the illusions of my dreams. But immediately afterwards I noticed that whilst I thus wished to think all things false, it was absolutely essential that the "I" who thought this should be somewhat, and remarking that this truth "I think, therefore I am" was so certain and so assured that all the most extravagant suppositions brought forward by the sceptics were incapable of shaking it, I came to the conclusion that I could receive it without scruple as the first principle of the Philosophy for which I was seeking. (Watson, 1968, p. 150)

The essence of man, for Descartes, was a mind, a "thing which thinks." The mind is contrasted with the body, and this separating of mind and body into two different aspects came to be known as Cartesian Dualism. The mind and body can interact (Descartes localized the point of interaction as the pineal gland), but the mind can also act independently, as when it considers innate ideas. Whereas Hobbes concluded that the mind can be understood in mechanistic terms, Descartes argued that it cannot; only the body is amenable to such understanding. Whereas Hobbes believed in the accumulation of knowledge through sensations and experience, Descartes held that the most important ideas are innate. Innate ideas comprise the set of universal truths, and they are innate because they arise from consciousness alone and not from objects in the world. External objects may remind us of ideas, but ideas do not come to us from sensation (Watson, 1968).

Bacon's strong stance on using the experimental method for discovering knowledge was the basis for much of the work of John Locke (1632–1704). Locke is often mistakenly called the founder of associationism, but it was not until the fourth edition of his *Essay concerning humane understanding* (published in 1700) that he used the phrase "association of ideas" (Diamond, 1974; Watson, 1968). His entire philosophy, therefore, was formed without the need for the associationist ideas, and he mentions neither Hobbes nor Aristotle. Locke's importance comes more deservedly from his empirical approach and his conception of the mind as a tabula rasa (clean slate) or "the yet empty cabinet" (Watson, 1968, p. 184). This idea, present in Aristotle's work, claims that experience rather than innate or inborn factors is of most importance. Locke went even further, suggesting that when something is not currently being contemplated, it no longer exists:

> But our ideas being nothing but actual perceptions in the mind, which cease to be anything when there is no perception of them, this laying up of our ideas in the repository of the memory signifies no more but this, that the mind has a power in many cases to revive perceptions which it has once had. . . . And in this sense it is that our ideas are said to be in our memories, when indeed they are actually nowhere. (Burnham, 1888, pp. 70–71)

Locke did much to refine introspection and to set bounds on what could and could not be understood about human nature with his empirical method. Also, following Hobbes, he thought of ideas as comprising elements that could be studied and analyzed.

Gottfried Wilhelm Leibniz (1646–1716) not only rejected Locke's empiricism but also disagreed with the notion that ideas had no existence when not being contemplated. He argued that if nothing remained when one ceased to think about a certain idea, it would not be possible to recollect the idea at a later time. Instead, Leibniz argued that traces of ideas remain even when they are not being thought of, although they are unconscious.

The empiricism of Locke prevailed in Britain, however. David Hartley (1705–1757), who also believed that the mind is blank at birth and that sensations give rise to ideas, systematized the views of the British empiricists and associationists. For Hartley, memory is "that faculty by which traces of sensations and ideas recur or are recalled in the same order and proportion, accurately or nearly, as they were once actually presented" (Burnham, 1888, p. 83). He distinguished between "true" memories, recollections, and illusions of memory, or reveries: "All men are sometimes at a loss to know whether clusters of ideas that strike the fancy strongly, and succeed each other readily and immediately, be recollections or mere reveries. And the more they agitate the matter in the mind, the more does the reverie appear like a recollection" (Burnham, 1888, p. 84).

David Hume's (1711–1776) approach was to combine the experimental approach of Isaac Newton with Bacon and Locke's study of the human mind, the ultimate goal being an experimental science of the mind. Indeed, the subtitle of Hume's *Treatise of Human Nature* is *An attempt to introduce the experimental Method of Reasoning into Moral Subjects*. Hume noted that "the chief exercise of the memory is not to preserve the simple ideas, but their order and position" (Herrmann & Chaffin, 1988, p. 173). He also rediscovered two of Aristotle's principles of association — similarity and contiguity — but emphasized that his own third principle, cause and effect, was the most important. Hume recognized that associations are not automatic, and he used an analogy with gravitation to suggest the character of an association: "Here is a kind of Attraction, which in the mental world will be found to have as extraordinary effects as in the natural, and to shew itself in as many and as various forms" (Herrnstein & Boring, 1965, p. 348).

Immanuel Kant (1724–1804) distinguished three kinds of memorizing. The mechanical (*mechanisch*) method, which involves only frequent, literal repetition; the method of clever devices (*ingeniös*), which involves forming associations between items; and the method of reflection (*judiciös*), the best kind, which involves classification (Burnham, 1888). Kant has also been cited as a forerunner of connectionism (Van de Vijver, 1990). His *Kritik der reinen Vernunft* ("Critique of Pure Reason") attacked the empiricism of Hume, and Kant went so far as to say that "it was the warning voice of David Hume that first, years ago, roused me from dogmatic slumbers" (Herrnstein & Boring, 1965, p. 586). In trying to refute empiricism, Kant argued that humans are born with certain innate properties, and this nativistic approach contributed a highly influential philosophical background for psychological schools such as the Gestalt movement in perception. The conflicts between Locke and Descartes are echoed in the opposition between Hume and Kant, and, later, that between Helmholtz and Hering (Herrnstein & Boring, 1965).

James Mill (1773–1836), in his *Analysis of the Phenomena of the Human Mind* published in 1829, presents a thoroughly associationist view of memory but with several important insights. "In memory there is not only the idea of the thing remembered; there is also the idea of my having seen it. Now these two—1, the idea of the thing, 2, the idea of my having seen it—combined, make up, it will not be doubted, the whole of that state of consciousness which we call memory." The "idea of my having seen it" is also made up of two components, "the idea of my present self, the remembering self, and the idea of my past self, the remembered or witnessing self" (Burnham, 1888, p. 241).

Mill's son, John Stuart Mill (1806–1873), disagreed with his father's view of an infinite compounding of associations. Rather, he introduced the term *mental chemistry* to indicate that in combining simple elements, something new is created. Just as the properties of water are different from the properties of hydrogen and oxygen, the properties of a complex element may be different from those of the root elements. Mill thus anticipated Wundt and the Gestalt psychologists. Because of this view, Mill advocated studying complex ideas empirically rather than relying on observations of more simple elements.

Marie François Pierre Gonthier de Biran (1766–1824) was a French philosopher who took the name Maine de Biran from an estate named Le Maine that belonged to his father. A member of Louis XVI's royal guards, he was injured defending the king in 1789 at Versailles. On the subject of memory, his important work is *Influence de l'habitude sur la faculté de penser* ("Influence of habit on the faculty of thinking"), first published—without his name attached—in 1802 (Copleston, 1985). Although in his early works, Maine de Biran followed such thinkers as Condillac and Bonnet, he criticized and moved away from the empiricist school and became more of a Platonist (Copleston, 1985). He was careful to distinguish three types of memory systems: mechanical memory, which is concerned with motor tasks and operates largely at a nonconscious level; sensitive (or sensory) memory, which is concerned with feelings, affect, and fleeting sensations; and representative memory, which is concerned with conscious recollection of ideas and events (Schacter & Tulving, 1994).

Through Ravaisson, Maine de Biran's thought influenced the French philosopher Henri Bergson (1859–1941) (Copleston, 1985). Although best known for his work on topics other than memory—especially his *L'Évolution créatrice* ("Creative evolution") published in 1907—Bergson gave an extended treatment to the idea of fundamentally different kinds of memory in *Matière et mémoire* ("Matter and memory"), published in 1896. Like Maine de Biran, Bergson distinguished between two different memory systems. First, there is "a closed system of automatic movements which succeed one another in the same order and occupy the same time" (Copleston, 1985, p. 190). This form is similar to walking—a bodily habit—and is the type of memory that animals have, such as that possessed by a parrot taught to recite a passage of a poem. The second type is "pure memory," which represents and records "all the events of our daily life" (Copleston, 1985, p. 190). Because memory records everything, the function of the brain is to inhibit the majority of memories so that only those relevant or related to ongoing thought or action are recalled to consciousness. Bergson also argued that the brain is not a storehouse of memories but rather functions more as a telephone exchange. The neurological mechanisms permit various movements but do not themselves store memory (Copleston, 1985).

Alexander Bain (1818–1903) marks a transition. He belonged to the outgoing British associationist school early in his career and moved closer to the emerging German scientific psychology toward the end of the century (Zusne, 1975). He is noted for his attempts to connect psychology and physiology and, in particular, for his doctrine that "the renewed feeling occupies the very same parts and in the same manner as the original feeling" (Burnham, 1888, p. 243). For example, the recollection of language, according to this view, is suppressed articulation. Bain was also the founder of the British journal *Mind* in 1876.

Ernst Heinrich Weber (1795–1878) had a medical degree rather than a doctorate in philosophy, but his experiments to determine the smallest detectable difference between two weights set the groundwork for scientific psychology. Although he found that the absolute magnitude of the difference varied depending on the size of two weights compared, he noted that the difference had a constant relationship to the weight: for an increment in a stimulus to be just noticeably different, the size of the increment had to be a certain proportion of the stimulus. This formulation, known as Weber's Law, may have gone unnoticed had it not been for Fechner (Diamond, 1974).

# Scientific Psychology

Gustav Theodor Fechner (1801–1887) was the first scientific psychologist, and although he had a medical degree, his first interest was physics. He believed that the mind and body were aspects of the same unity (in contrast to Cartesian Dualism), and it was when he combined his interests in physics and philosophy that he initiated the field of psychophysics. According to Fechner, it was on the morning of October 22, 1850, while still in bed that he realized how to connect the body and the mind (Watson, 1968). The key, as he wrote ten years later in his *Elemente der Psychophysik* ("Elements of Psychophysics," published in Leipzig in 1860) was finding the quantitative relation between a mental sensation and the physical stimulus:

> Just as, in order to measure space, we need a physical yardstick which is contained in space, so, in order to measure the psychic, we will need something physical which underlies it. But insofar as we cannot directly observe the psychophysical activity which does directly underlie it, the stimulus which evokes that activity, and with which it waxes and wanes in regular fashion, will be able to serve in place of the yardstick. (Diamond, 1974, p. 685)

Fechner's Law — that sensation ($R$) is directly proportional to the logarithm of the stimulus ($S$) multiplied by a constant ($R = k \log S$) — was based on Weber's Law. This formulation of psychophysics directly inspired Hermann Ebbinghaus to apply similar methods to the study of a higher mental process, memory. It is interesting that Ebbinghaus worked outside of the influence of Wundt, the giant of 19th century psychology. Wilhelm Wundt (1832–1920) offered the first formal academic course in psychology in 1867 at the University of Heidelberg and founded the first psychology laboratory at the University of Leipzig in 1875 or 1879 (depending on the criteria). Watson (1968) suggests that the latter date is notable only for the appearance of the first student to do publishable research.

The scientific study of memory, then, did not begin until the latter part of the 19th century and had as its roots Aristotle's associationism, the philosophical orientation of the British empiricists, and the precision of Fechner's emerging psychophysics.

# Hermann Ebbinghaus

Hermann Ebbinghaus (1850–1909), generally identified as the first major scientific researcher of memory, received his doctoral degree in philosophy at Bonn in 1873 after serving in the army during the Franco-Prussian war. Although his dissertation concerned Hartmann's philosophy of the unconscious, Ebbinghaus also had an interest in history and philology (the study of literature and of relevant disciplines such as linguistics, language, and speech). After completing his dissertation, he spent seven years traveling around Europe and Britain. During this time, he came upon a copy of Fechner's *Elemente der Psychophysik* at a second-hand bookshop in Paris and became acquainted with and influenced by the empiricist tradition in Britain (Boring, 1950).

Ebbinghaus' contribution to the study of memory, published in 1885, was called *Über das Gedächtnis: Untersuchungen zur experimentellen Psychologie* ("Memory: A contribution to experimental psychology"). In it, he combined the techniques that Fechner had applied to the study of sensation with the topic of memory, long an important consideration of the British associationists. Although he is generally noted for being his only subject and for inventing nonsense syllables as his stimuli, these factors are neither problematic nor important. Ebbinghaus' far more significant and lasting contribution was that he was the first experimental psychologist, outside of psychophysicists, who understood and used the concepts of (1) measurement error, (2) distributions of observations around a mean, and (3) the importance of evaluating differences between two conditions in light of error associated with the respective means (Crowder, 1976). He is also well known for his forgetting function, which will be described below.

As befits the first scientific investigator of memory, Ebbinghaus reported what is perhaps the first true experiment on memory: he outlined two possible theories, derived a testable prediction that could distinguish between the two possibilities, and then conducted the experiment to evaluate the hypothesis. Indeed, the basic idea that came out of this research still has currency and serves as the basis for Johnson's (1991) distinctiveness model of serial learning.

Ebbinghaus (1885) conducted a series of experiments designed to demonstrate the existence of both forward and backward associations (see Figure 2.1). He learned lists of

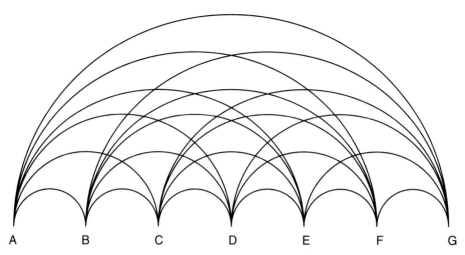

**Figure 2.1** An illustration of the possible associations among seven items in a list. According to Ebbinghaus, the first item, A, can be associated with item B through a direct association, and with items C, D, E, F, and G through remote associations. The less direct the association, the weaker the link.

16 syllables until he reached a certain criterion; in this case, he kept learning until he could repeat the list without error. After a delay, he measured his retention of the lists with the method of savings. In this method, a previously learned list is relearned and the difference between the time needed to learn the list to criterion the second time and the time it took to learn it originally represents the savings due to remembering. Ebbinghaus constructed "derived" lists where item 2 of the original list would be displaced 1, 2, 3, or 7 positions. For example, if the original list were I1, I2, I3, . . . , I16, then the derived list, skipping 1 syllable, would be I1, I3, I5, . . . , I2, I4, . . . , I16. If item I1 can serve as a cue, via a remote association, for item I3 in a derived list with 1 skipped syllable, and if it can serve as a cue, via a more remote association, for item I4 in a derived list with 2 skipped syllables, then learning one of these derived lists should take less time than learning a control list. If, on the other hand, there are only direct associations between adjacent items, there will be no advantage of a derived list over a control list because in both cases the direct association has been severed. Ebbinghaus found a mean savings of 33.3% in relearning the original list, a 10.8% saving when skipping 1 syllable, 7.0% when skipping 2 syllables, 5.8% when skipping 3 syllables, and 3.3% when skipping 7 syllables. In a control condition containing the same syllables but in random order, there was a savings of only 0.5%. According to Ebbinghaus, these findings support the idea of remote associations.

Ebbinghaus is probably most well known for the forgetting function, the first systematic investigation of forgetting. He first measured the amount of time required to learn (two errorless recitations) a list of 13 nonsense syllables. Then, he waited a specific period of time before relearning the same material and measured how long it took to relearn the

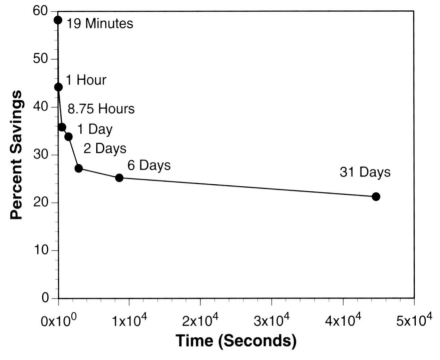

**Figure 2.2**   Retention of lists of nonsense syllables learned by Ebbinghaus as measured by the method of savings.   Source: Based on data from Ebbinghaus (1885).

lists. He reported the results in terms of percent savings. For example, in 12 tests, it took Ebbinghaus an average of 1081 seconds to learn a 13-item list of nonsense syllables. After a delay of 19 minutes, it took him an average of 498 seconds to relearn each list, a difference of 583. The formula (Ebbinghaus, 1885, p. 68) is

$$Q = \frac{100\Delta}{L - 85} \tag{2.1}$$

where $Q$ is the percent savings, $L$ is the time of first learning (including the two errorless recitations), $\Delta$ is the difference between $L$ and the second learning (both including the two recitations), and 85 is the time (in seconds) needed to say the two errorless recitations. The reason for subtracting this value is that Ebbinghaus was interested only in the savings of learning. In the example given above, he "saved" 58.2% of the time.

   Although the exact nature of the forgetting function can vary depending on the type of materials, the type of processing, the type of test, and so on, the basic shape appears relatively constant: the largest drop in performance occurs during the period immediately after the test (see Rubin & Wenzel, 1996). As shown in Figure 2.2, Ebbinghaus would

---

**Experiment    The Forgetting Function**

---

**Purpose:** To demonstrate the classic forgetting function using the method of savings.

**Subjects:** Thirty subjects are recommended. Ten should be assigned to the 1-Hour Group, ten to the 1-Day Group, ten to the 1-Week Group.

**Materials:** Table A in the Appendix lists 24 nonsense syllables with approximately equal association values. Create a list of 13 nonsense syllables by randomly selecting the syllables from the table. Write each syllable in large, clear form on a notecard. Each subject should get a different random ordering of items.

**Design:** Because each subject experiences only one condition, delay is a between-subjects factor.

**Procedure:** Inform the subjects that in this experiment they will be asked to learn a list of nonsense syllables. Show the subject the list of syllables at a rate of approximately 1 syllable every 2 seconds. Then, ask the subjects to repeat the list. Record the subject's responses. Then, show the subject the same list again, and ask the subject to repeat the list. Keep doing this until the subject can recall the list in order without making an error. Most subjects will require several trials before they recall the list. Keep track of how many trials are required to learn the list. Have the subjects in the 1-Hour group return after 1 hour, the subjects in the 1-Day group return after 1 day, and the subjects in the 1-Week group return after 1 week. Repeat the procedure, being careful to ensure that each subject receives the exact list in the same order during the second phase. Also, be careful not to tell the subject what will happen during phase 2.

**Instructions for Phase 1:** This experiment has two phases. In the first phase, you will be asked to learn a list of nonsense syllables. I will show the words, written on notecards, one at a time. After I have shown you all 13 items, I will ask you to recall the items in order. We will continue until you are able to recall all the items in order. Once you have recalled the items correctly, that will be the end of the first phase.

**Instructions for Phase 2:** For the second phase, I will ask you to relearn the list of items you originally learned 1 hour ago/1 day ago/1 week ago. We will follow the same procedure. I will show the words, written on notecards, one at a time. After I have shown you all 13 items, I will ask you to recall the items in order. We will continue until you are able to recall all of the items in order. Once you have recalled the items correctly, that will be the end of the experiment.

**Scoring and Analysis:** For each subject, count the number of trials required to learn the list the first time and the number of trials to relearn the list. To calculate percent savings, subtract the number of trials to relearn the list from the number of trials to originally learn the list. Then, divide this value by the number of trials to learn the list originally. For example, if it takes a subject 12 trials originally and 8 trials to relearn, the percent savings is $\frac{4}{12}$ or 33%. The x-axis should show the delay condition and the y-axis should show the number of lists. The graph should look similar to Figure 2.2, even though savings is plotted in terms of time rather than trials.

**Optional Enhancements:** Include more delay conditions, increase the number of subjects, and measure the time needed to learn and relearn the lists rather than just the number of trials.

Source: Based on an experiment by Ebbinghaus (1885).

have been at 100% at Time 0; waiting only 19 minutes resulted in a substantial drop in performance. By comparison, there is little overall loss from 2 days to 31 days.

Two points should be emphasized here. First, although Ebbinghaus is (rightly) viewed as the preeminent figure in the study of memory, some scientific research on memory occurred before his book (see, for example, Burnham, 1888; Murray, 1976; Schacter, Eich, & Tulving, 1978). Second, although the majority of his studies can be faulted for using only himself as a subject or for using nonsense syllables, all of his important findings replicate and have been at the center of much of the research and theory of the ensuing 100 years (Slamecka, 1985).

## Associationist Theories of Memory

Many theories in both animal learning and human memory that arose in the early part of the 20th century were based on associationist ideas like those discussed above. Although the word *associationist* is rarely seen in the current human memory literature, the influence of the associationist tradition is profound and widespread. In the last two sections of this chapter, we will briefly examine two ways in which associationist ideas were developed, were refined, and continue to affect current theory. The first topic concerns one of the most ubiquitous phenomena in memory research, which was first documented by Ebbinghaus (Crowder, 1976; Slamecka, 1985): the *serial position function*. The second reflects the desire to make the units of memory theory more like the units of the nervous system and is generally known as *connectionism*.

When people are asked to recall a series of items in order, they usually recall the first item very well (the primacy effect), the last item well (the recency effect), and the middle items quite poorly. In 1820, Thomas Brown accurately described the recency effect when he proposed the fourth of his secondary laws of association (Herrnstein & Boring, 1965). William James. (1890, p. 630) noted that "it is a matter of popular knowledge" that "other things equal, at all times of life recency promotes memory"; and Mary Calkins (1896) mentioned both primacy and recency in connection with her new method of paired associates. However, it was left to Ebbinghaus (1902) to document the relation between these components. By the time McGeoch (1942) wrote his classic text, he could devote some 50 pages to serial learning phenomena, could describe most of the curve's important characteristics, and could present several different theories explaining recency.

Foucault (1928) offered a theory based on a combination of two kinds of interference. When a series of items is being learned, each item can interfere with subsequent items (proactive interference) and each item can also interfere with memory for earlier items (retroactive interference). The first item is immune to proactive interference because no items come before it, and the final item is immune from retroactive interference because no items come after it. Items in the middle of the list, however, have interference of both kinds, and the middle item should have the most interference. The main problem with Foucault's view was in determining the contribution of each form of inhibition. A simple account would produce a symmetrical curve, but this did not describe the data well. Instead, the serial position curve for serial recall is asymmetrical, with worse performance closer to the end than the beginning of the list (Ward, 1937). Nonetheless, Foucault is remembered for attempting to explain effects of immediate memory with the same concepts used to explain memory performance after many trials or long delays. Melton. (1963) offered a related view but argued that just as interference can effect items in a list, so can similar effects of interference operate at the level of a single item. We shall see this idea applied to word-length effects in Chapter 5.

A similar theory, developed by Hull (1935) and his student Lepley (1934), was designed to build on the ideas of remote associations documented by Ebbinghaus. That is, in the series A, B, C, D, E, F, G, associations would develop between A and B, between A and C, and so on, and between B and C, between B and D, and so on (see Figure 2.1). To this idea, Hull and Lepley added an inhibitory mechanism, like Foucault's but based on a finding of Ivan Pavlov, known as trace conditioning. *Trace conditioning* involves a delay between presentation of a cue (called the *conditioned stimulus* or CS) and of the main stimulus (called the *unconditioned stimulus* or US). Pavlov (1927) noted that during the delay between the CS and US, animals would not respond, waiting until just before the US was presented before making their learned or conditioned response (CR). Pavlov concluded that the animals' response was being held in check by inhibition during the delay between the two events that had been associated.

Each item in a list is assumed to be connected via associations to every subsequent item in the list. In the 7-item list mentioned above, A can serve as a cue for recall of all subsequent items because it is associated with all subsequent items. In other words, A can be a CS for item G, the CR. During the wait, production of other responses will be inhibited. In this way, the central item has the most inhibition and the end items have the least; the serial position function is the result. Because there are more remote associations spanning middle items, recall should be worst in the middle of the list. That is, the C-D association falls in the middle of the A-E, A-F, A-G, B-E, B-F, and B-G associations. Items A and G are not spanned by any remote associations and so should be well recalled.

Two problems emerge from this view. First, while the point of maximum inhibition, according to the theory, should be the center of the list, experiments reveal that the curve is in fact slightly skewed toward the recency end of the list (see above). Second, there is no provision made for connections between trials; that is, the first item of list 2 is not subject to trace conditioning of the last item of list 1. Despite these shortcomings, the Hull-Lepley theory was still able to account for much of the serial position data, including the findings that (1) recency effects occur regardless of the list length (Robinson & Brown, 1926), (2) recency is independent of presentation rate (Hovland, 1938), (3) overall performance is better following distributed rather than massed learning (Ebbinghaus, 1885), and (4) both primacy and recency effects can be observed in animals other than humans (Warden, 1924). Although Hull later refined and extended the theory (Hull, Hovland, Ross, Hall, Perkins, & Fitch, 1940; Hull, 1943) to correct the two problems mentioned above, an additional problem remained unsolved: some of the mechanisms and processes invoked take many trials to develop, but the serial position curve can be observed in one trial.

A third type of theory involved the order of processing of the items. Ebbinghaus (1902) first proposed counting the number of promptings that were necessary before mastery for each serial position; he found that more were needed in the center of the list, and relatively fewer at the ends. In 1911, Ladd and Woodworth suggested that items might be associated with their serial position, a view often referred to as using *position-item associations*. Because the middle serial positions are less clearly defined than are positions at the end points, items in the middle of the list will have weaker associations with their respective positions than will primacy or recency items. (A revised version, Woodworth & Poffenberger, 1920, added *chaining* to middle items; we will discuss chaining a little later in this section.) One advantage of this system is that the positions are already known to the subject, and empirical support for the idea was reported in an experiment by Kreuger (1932).

Ebenholtz (1963) reported perhaps more convincing results in a study in which he had subjects learn a list for serial recall. The control condition presented entirely new items but two other conditions included some items from the original list. Of these, the coordinate condition kept the old items in the same position whereas the disparate condition had items in new positions. For example, if the original list were A B C D E F G H I, the coordinate condition might have the list Z B̲ Y D̲ X F̲ W H̲ V, whereas the disparate condition might have the list Z F̲ Y H̲ X B̲ W D̲ V. Performance on the control and disparate conditions was equivalent, showing basically no advantage of prior learning. Performance in the coordinate condition, however, was superior to performance in the other two conditions. Because the items remained in the same serial position, Ebenholtz interpreted this as evidence for position-item associations.

Ribback and Underwood (1950) noted the possibility of two distinct learning processes, both first documented by Ebbinghaus (1885). The first, type A, involves forward associations and the second, type B, involves backward associations. In addition to conducting experiments that demonstrated remote associations, Ebbinghaus (1885) had also documented the existence of backward associations. He used the same format of deriving lists from an original but, during testing, the derived lists had to be learned in inverted order. For example, if the original list was I1, I2, I3, . . . , I16, an inverted list would need to be learned as I16, I15, I14, . . . , I1. An inverted list with one skipped syllable would be I16, I14, . . . , I2, I15, I13, . . . I1. Ebbinghaus found a 12.4% savings for the original list when inverted, and a 5.0% savings for a list that was both inverted and that skipped one syllable. Because both savings were larger than the savings for a random list, Ebbinghaus concluded that backward associations must have been formed.

Ribback and Underwood assumed that because backward associations are more difficult to establish, type B learning takes longer, resulting in the skewed serial position curve. They tested this assumption using paired associates. First, subjects would learn syllables, such as QEL FIP. Then, subjects in the type A group would learn QEL FIP MYD, while those in the type B group would learn MYD QEL FIP. As predicted, type A learning was quicker, but type B learning also occurred. Although this theory received little additional attention, its main features were echoed in the later information processing models, such as Feigenbaum and Simon's (1962) EPAM (Elementary Perceiver and Memorizer), and a later extension by Hintzman (1968). This quantitative model of serial position effects stands midway between what came to be called *unitary* and *dual store* explanations of recency. While still rooted in multiple trial learning, the original model nonetheless posited "an immediate memory of limited size capable of storing information temporarily; and all access to an item by the learning processes must be through the immediate memory" (Feigenbaum & Simon, 1962, p. 310).

Three factors contributed to the decline of this type of research. First, some of the mechanisms and processes that are invoked in theories developed from multitrial learning take a long time to develop, but the serial position curve can be observed in a single trial. With increased emphasis on the results of a single learning trial, many different phenomena attracted attention, and this led to the formulation of the *modal model*. According to this view, memory first is temporarily stored in sensory memory systems (see Chapter 3) before being processed by two different structures, short-term store and long-term store (see Chapter 4).

A second factor was that the basic associationist model that became dominant was both incomplete and overly simplified, and the tests used to assess the predictive power of the model were at best inappropriate (see Slamecka, 1985, for a detailed discussion). Several researchers questioned the rationale behind the method of using derived lists (e.g., Hakes, James, & Young, 1964; Slamecka, 1964) and, once the question of remote associations was up in the air, the field focused most on a simple chaining view.

The *chaining hypothesis* refers to the idea that serial learning consists solely of forming associations between adjacent items. Just as a chain is made up of overlapping links, a list of items is made up of direct associations between adjacent items. For example, if a list of items A B C D E is learned, there should be a direct association between A and B, between B and C, and so on. One problem for the theory arises when a break in the chain occurs: As Lashley (1951) had pointed out, because there are only direct associations, any failure in a simple chaining model must result in failure to recall all subsequent items. The data, however, show that even when errors occur, later items can often be recalled successfully. (As we shall see in Chapter 11, the global memory model TODAM offers an elegant solution to this problem.)

A major problem arose from the types of tests used to evaluate the chaining view. Given that each link (except the first and last) serves as both a stimulus and a response, an obvious experimental technique was to reduce a list to its bare minimum, a form of paired-associates task. In a paired-associates task, subjects are asked to produce one item, B, when given another item, A, as a cue. If subjects are learning the list by using paired associations, then there should be savings, or *positive transfer,* when they are asked to learn certain pairs of items after learning a list. If subjects learn the list A B C D E, the idea went, they should learn the paired associates B-C, A-B, D-E, and so on faster than they learn a control list. The problem was that the results from a large series of experiments were mixed: although some researchers reported positive transfer — faster learning of the derived paired associates than of a control list — many more found no reliable transfer (for reviews, see Harcum, 1975; Young, 1968). The prediction was so clear-cut, simple, and elegant that a lack of positive results seems to have disheartened many researchers.

Slamecka (1985) has offered one explanation for these mixed results. In most of the research on derived lists in the 1960s, very little attention was paid to remote associations. Consider a list of items A to N and a series of derived paired associates such as E-F, B-C, and K-L. When learning the list, item L is cued not only by a direct association from K but also by remote associations from H, I, and J. When the paired-associates test is administered, these remote associations are not available because only K is presented. In other words, many of the cues the subject used during the first stage of learning — the remote associations — are removed at the time of the transfer test. Thus, if one accepts

Ebbinghaus' evidence for remote associations, the correct prediction is little or no positive transfer, which is exactly what the majority of studies found. This idea of memory being dependent on the relationship between the cues present at study and the cues present at test will play a large role in theories of forgetting and processing (see Chapters 6 and 7).

The third factor that contributed to the decline of associationist theories and research was the so-called cognitive revolution. Beginning in the 1920s, behaviorism came to dominate experimental psychology in the United States (Murray, 1995). According to this movement, unobservable constructs such as memory, imagery, and consciousness could not be studied rigorously and thus were deemed inappropriate topics for scientific study. Although behaviorists contributed much work on human memory, the major findings were less influenced by behaviorist theory and more concerned with empirical data. For example, McGeoch's (1942) highly influential text on human learning and memory was largely atheoretical, reflecting his belief that the study of memory was not yet ready for elaborate theories (Crowder, 1992). By the mid-1950s, two trends signaled the beginning of what came to be called *cognitive psychology*. First, there was a tremendous increase in applied psychology during and following World War II. Because of the central role that humans played in the research, people were viewed as a communications channel and as processors of information, similar to the equipment that was being designed. The second, related, trend was the development of computers and symbolic processing. Both of these trends led to the key concept that distinguished cognitive psychology from both the verbal learning approach and the behaviorist tradition: information. By 1967, the new field was well-enough established that the first influential text bearing the name *Cognitive Psychology* was published (Neisser, 1967). It should be noted that an earlier book of the same title was published nearly 30 years earlier (Moore, 1939) but had relatively little influence on the field (see Surprenant & Neath, 1997). Chapter 4 examines many of the influential memory models from this early period of cognitive psychology.

Thus, at the same time that a new, exciting conception of memory based on the computer metaphor of processing was on the rise, the associationist tradition was testing an incomplete, overly simplified model with inappropriate tests. The associationist view is by no means extinct—as illustrated by models such as Anderson and Bower's (1973) human associative memory, Raaijmakers and Shiffrin's (1981) search of associative memory, and Murdock's (1993) theory of distributed associative memory—but it does constitute a decided minority opinion in current memory research.

# Connectionist Networks

The associationist tradition has influenced most theories of learning and memory, including one of the most popular current approaches, *connectionism*. Connectionist networks, also known as neural networks or parallel distributed processing (PDP), can be seen as an attempt to model complex behavior with neuron-like components. Just as (to greatly simplify) the nervous system is composed of neurons and connections between them, con-

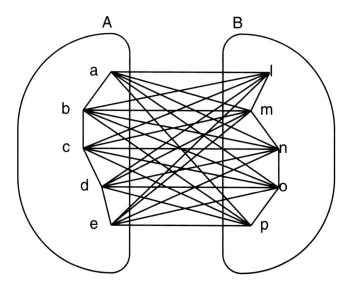

**Figure 2.3** William James' connectionist network designed to explain compound associations and "trains of thought." Source: Based on Figure 40 of James (1890).

nectionist models are composed of (1) simple processing units (or nodes) that can either fire or not, and (2) the connections between the nodes. The basic idea behind this approach goes back at least as far as Kant (Van de Vijver, 1990) and can be seen in the work of many associationist psychologists. For example, Thorndike's (1913) model of learning was, in fact, called *connectionism,* and Hull (1943; see also the collected papers of Hull in Amsel & Rashotte, 1984) offered the most complete early instantiation of such a system. As Hintzman (1993) put it, "The Hullians did not invent modern PDP systems, of course. But they might have, if they had owned Sun workstations or a Cray" (p. 375).

In his chapter on association, William James (1890, Chapter 14) includes an extended discussion of connectionist operating principles. Like many philosophers before him, James (1890) was intrigued by "the restless flight of one idea before the next" (p. 519), and he called the rules governing these associations the "principles of connection" (p. 520). The most basic of these is the law of neural habit:

> The amount of activity at any given point in the brain-cortex is the sum of the tendencies of all other points to discharge into it, such tendencies being proportionate (1) to the number of times the excitement of each other point may have accompanied that of the point in question; (2) to the intensity of such excitements; and (3) to the absence of any rival point functionally disconnected with the first point, into which the discharges might be diverted. (James, 1890, p. 534)

James (1890, p. 537) even provides a diagram of a connectionist network (see Figure 2.3). In his example, *a, b, c, d,* and *e* represent elementary nerves excited by the thought of a dinner party. Together, they constitute the dinner party, termed *A.* The event that follows is walking home through a frosty night, called B, represented by elementary nerves *l*, *m*, *n*, *o*, and *p*. According to this scheme, the thought of A will "awaken" the thought of B because "*a, b, c, d, e,* will each and all discharge into *l*" and "similarly they will discharge into *m, n, o,* and *p*; and these latter tracts will also each reinforce the other's action" (James, 1890, p. 536).

The reason that we are not continually stuck with just one train of thought is because of an element of randomness: "In no revival of a past experience are all the items of our thought equally operative in determining what the next thought shall be. Always some ingredient is prepotent over the rest" (James, 1890, p. 538).

Perhaps the first important advance that led to the modern era of connectionism was the publication of a paper by McCulloch and Pitts (1943). They conceived of the brain as a set of binary elements—processing units that could be either on or off. Because neuronal processing is characterized as either all or none, McCulloch and Pitts (1943) proposed that "neural events and the relations between them can be treated by means of propositional logic" (p. 115). During the 1960s, many proposed models were based on this idea (e.g., Grossberg, 1969; Konorski, 1967). For example, the basic element in the perceptron, a model developed by Rosenblatt (1958), was known as a threshold logic unit (TLU). Each TLU has several inputs, and the TLU will either fire (gives an output of 1) or not fire (gives an output of 0), depending on the amount of activation it receives from all of the input lines. The perceptron was able to discriminate between various patterns, responding with an output of 1 if the desired pattern was present and 0 if the pattern was not present. Furthermore, procedures were developed that enabled the perceptron to learn.

There were two major problems with the perceptron model. One was psychological. The procedure by which the model learned had the property that no learning took place when the model made a correct response; learning occurred only following an error. This seems implausible as a model of human behavior. The second problem was a limitation of the learning procedure: because there was only one set of connections between the input nodes and the output nodes, there was a limit on the type of problems that the model could address. The major difference between the perceptron and current models (e.g., Grossberg, 1988; Rumelhart & McClelland, 1986) is the addition of a layer of nodes between the input and output nodes and the development of learning algorithms that will work with these 3-layer architectures.

The operation of most current connectionist networks is simple at the root level; the most complex aspect is the learning algorithm, which we will consider in a later chapter. For now, we review the basic operation of a simple network (see Figure 2.4) from Rumelhart, Hinton, and Williams (1986).

A connectionist network has a few basic components. First, there are nodes or units that are neuronlike, in the sense that they either fire or do not fire. There are three types of nodes: input units receive activation from other networks, output units pass on activation to other networks, and hidden units receive no activation from outside of the local network. Each node has an activation threshold (the number in the middle of each node), which is the amount of energy required to make it fire. In Figure 2.4, the hidden node requires 3 or more units of activation before it will fire. Second, there are connections between the nodes (hence the term *connectionist*). In the typical model, each node has

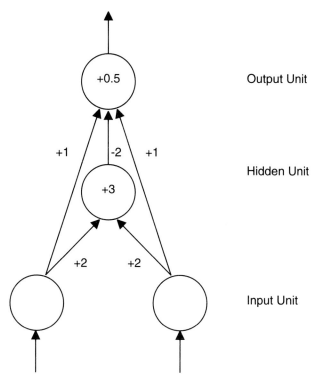

+0.5    Output Unit

+1    -2    +1    Hidden Unit

+3

+2    +2    Input Unit

**Figure 2.4**   A simple network, with one hidden unit, that can solve the XOR problem.
Source: Adapted from Rumelhart, Hinton & Williams, in Rumelhart & McClelland (1986).

multiple connections.  Third, these connections can be of two kinds, excitatory or inhibitory, depending on the weights. In Figure 2.4, the connections between the input
units and the hidden units are excitatory because the weights have a positive value (in this
case, +2). The connection between the hidden unit and the output unit is inhibitory because the weight is negative (−2). For simplicity, we assume that when a node fires, it
sends +1 units of activation along the connection. This value is modified by the weights
on the connection.

The model shown in Figure 2.4 was designed to solve the exclusive-or (XOR) problem. The XOR problem requires a specific solution: the output node should fire if and only
if there is exactly one active input node. If both input nodes are active or if neither input
node is active, then the output node should not fire. The actual operation is quite simple.
If neither input unit fires, there is no energy in the system and the output node will not
fire. If just the left input node is active, it will send +1 units of energy along each connection. The weight on the connection from the input unit to the hidden unit is +2, so the
total amount of energy arriving at the hidden unit is 2 × 1 or 2. This value is less than the
threshold of the hidden unit (3), so it does not fire. The weight on the connection from the
input unit to the output unit is +1, so the total amount of energy arriving at the hidden

unit is $1 \times 1$ or 1. This value is larger than the threshold, so the output unit fires. The same thing happens when just the right input unit fires. When both input units fire, we do not want the output node to fire. Both input nodes sent 2 units to the hidden unit. Thus, 4 units of energy arrive at the hidden unit, and this value is greater than the threshold. Because of this, the hidden unit will fire. It sends $+1 \times -2$ or $-2$ units of energy to the output node. To see whether the output node fires, we need to calculate the total amount of energy arriving there. Each input node sends $+1$ units, so the output node receives $+1$ units from the left input node, $+1$ units from the right input node, and $-2$ units from the hidden node. The sum is a net activation of 0, which is less than the threshold; therefore, the output unit does not fire when both inputs are active.

The learning algorithm is what sets the weights on the connections. Typically, before a connectionist network has "learned" anything, the weights are set to randomly determined values. Notice that this incorporates the idea of a clean slate (tabula rasa) of Locke and Aristotle. As each stimulus is presented, the model produces some output. If the output is correct, the weights are altered to make that response more likely; if the output is incorrect, the weights are altered to make that response less likely. A specific type of algorithm, known as *nonlinear back propagation,* is presented in detail in Chapter 11.

Of course, this model is very simple and solves only one problem, the XOR problem. But the principles behind it are the same as in the far more complex models we consider later, and this line of research is directly descended from the associationist tradition.

# Further Reading

This chapter has provided only the briefest of sketches, and the following sources are recommended for a more complete understanding of the history of experimental psychology in general and of memory research in particular. Every student of memory should read Ebbinghaus (1885), and Slamecka (1985) provides an excellent assessment of Ebbinghaus' contribution. Burnham (1888) provides an historical overview of early memory research, Murray (1976) discusses research on human memory in the 19th century, and Herrmann and Chaffin (1988) provide translations of much of the early work on memory. Yates (1966) offers an excellent history and analysis of mnemonic techniques, particularly in the middle ages, and Carruthers (1990) examines memory in the medieval period.

The classic history of experimental psychology is Boring (1950), and Watson (1968) also serves as an excellent starting point, offering biographical, philosophical, and psychological summaries of important figures in the history of psychology. Diamond (1974) and Herrnstein and Boring (1965) supply translations and short extracts of original sources. Both Warren (1921) and Robinson (1932) provide early histories of association psychology, and Anderson and Bower (1973) offer a brief but more modern overview. Although offering little by way of the role of associationist influences, Anderson and Hinton (1989) do provide an excellent brief history of neural networks in the modern era. Zusne (1975) offers a biological sourcebook of people who influenced psychology, and Watson (1915) provides some biographical information on Vives, a figure much overlooked by psychologists. Peters (1965) provides an edited and abridged version of Brett's classic *History of Psychology.*

# References

Amsel, A., & Rashotte, M. E. (1984). *Mechanisms of adaptive behavior: Clark Hull's theoretical papers, with commentary.* New York: Columbia University Press.

Anderson, J. A., & Hinton, G. E. (1989). Models of information processing in the brain. In G. E. Hinton & J. A. Anderson (Eds.), *Parallel models of associative memory (Updated ed.).* Hillsdale, NJ: Erlbaum.

Anderson, J. R., & Bower, G. H. (1973). *Human associative memory.* Washington, DC: Winston.

Boring, E. G. (1950). *A history of experimental psychology* (2nd ed.). New York: Appleton-Century-Crofts.

Bower, G. H., & Clapper, J. P. (1989). Experimental methods in cognitive science. In M. I. Posner (Ed.), *Foundations of cognitive science.* Cambridge, MA: MIT Press.

Burnham, W. H. (1888). Memory, historically and experimentally considered. *American Journal of Psychology, 2,* 39–90, 255–270, 431–464, 566–622.

Calkins, M. W. (1896). Association: An essay analytic and experimental. *Psychological Review Monograph Supplements* (No. 2).

Carruthers, M. (1990). *The book of memory: A study of memory in medieval culture.* New York: Cambridge University Press.

Copleston, F. (1985). *A history of philosophy: Vol. IX.* Garden City, New York: Image.

Crowder, R. G. (1976). *Principles of learning and memory.* Hillsdale, NJ: Erlbaum.

Diamond, S. (Ed.). (1974). *The roots of psychology: A sourcebook in the history of ideas.* New York: Basic Books.

Ebbinghaus, H. (1885). *Über das Gedächtnis: Untersuchungen zur experimentellen Psychologie.* Leipzig: Duncker and Humboldt. [Reprinted as H. E. Ebbinghaus (1964). *Memory: A contribution to experimental psychology.* H. A. Ruger, (Trans.). New York: Dover.]

Ebbinghaus, H. (1902). *Grundzüge der Psychologie.* Leipzig: von Veit.

Ebenholtz, S. M. (1963). Position mediated transfer between serial learning and a spatial discrimination task. *Journal of Experimental Psychology, 65,* 603–608.

Feigenbaum, E. A., & Simon, H. (1962). A theory of the serial position effect. *British Journal of Psychology, 53,* 307–320.

Foucault, M. (1928). Les inhibitions internes de fixation. *Année Psychologique, 29,* 92–112.

Grossberg, S. (1969). Some networks that can learn, remember, and reproduce any number of complicated space-time patterns: I. *Journal of Mathematics and Mechanics, 19,* 53–91.

Grossberg, S. (1988). *Neural networks and natural intelligence.* Cambridge, MA: MIT Press.

Hakes, D. T., James, C. T., & Young, R. K. (1964). A re-examination of the Ebbinghaus derived list paradigm. *Journal of Experimental Psychology, 68,* 508–514.

Harcum, E. R. (1975). *Serial learning and paralearning.* New York: Wiley.

Herrmann, D. J., & Chaffin, R. (Eds.). (1988). *Memory in historical perspective: The literature before Ebbinghaus.* New York: Springer-Verlag.

Herrnstein, R. J., & Boring, E. G. (Eds.). (1965). *A source book in the history of psychology.* Cambridge, MA: Harvard University Press.

Hintzman, D. L. (1968). Explorations with a discrimination net model for paired-associate learning. *Journal of Mathematical Psychology, 5,* 123–162.

Hintzman, D. L. (1993). Twenty-five years of learning and memory: Was the cognitive revolution a mistake? In D. E. Meyer & S. Kornblum (Eds.), *Attention and performance XIV:*

*Synergies in experimental psychology, artificial intelligences, and cognitive neuroscience*. Cambridge, MA: MIT Press.

Hovland, C. I. (1938). Experimental studies in rote-learning theory. II. Reminiscence with varying speeds of syllable presentation. *Journal of Experimental Psychology, 22,* 338–353.

Hull, C. L. (1935). The conflicting psychologies of learning—a way out. *Psychological Review, 42,* 491–516.

Hull, C. L. (1943). *Principles of behavior.* New York: Appleton-Century-Crofts.

Hull, C. L., Hovland, C. I., Ross, R. T., Hall, M., Perkins, D. T., & Fitch, F. B. (1940). *Mathematico-deductive theory of rote learning.* New Haven, CT: Yale University Press.

James, W. (1890). *The principles of psychology.* New York: Henry Holt and Company. [Reprinted as W. James (1983). *The principles of psychology.* Cambridge, MA: Harvard University Press]

Johnson, G. J. (1991). A distinctiveness model of serial learning. *Psychological Review, 98,* 204–217.

Konorski, J. (1967). *Integrative activity in the brain.* Chicago: University of Chicago Press.

Kreuger, W. C. F. (1932). Learning during directed attention. *Journal of Experimental Psychology, 15,* 517–527.

Ladd, G. L., & Woodworth, R. S. (1911). *Elements of physiological psychology.* New York: Scribners.

Lashley, K. S. (1951). The problem of serial order in behavior. In L. A. Jeffress (Ed.), *Cerebral mechanisms in behavior.* New York: Wiley.

Lepley, W. M. (1934). Serial reactions considered as conditioned reactions. *Psychological Monographs, 46* (No. 205).

McCulloch, W. S., & Pitts, W. H. (1943). A logical calculus of ideas immanent in nervous activity. *Bulletin of Mathematical Biophysics, 5,* 115–133.

McGeoch, J. A. (1942). *The psychology of human learning: An introduction.* New York: Longmans Green & Co.

Melton, A. W. (1963). Implications of short-term memory for a general theory of memory. *Journal of Verbal Learning and Verbal Behavior, 2,* 1–21.

Moore, T. V. (1939). *Cognitive psychology.* Philadelphia: Lippincott.

Murdock, B. B. (1993). TODAM2: A model for the storage and retrieval of item, associative, and serial-order information. *Psychological Review, 100,* 183–203.

Murray, D. J. (1976). Research on human memory in the nineteenth century. *Canadian Journal of Psychology, 30,* 201–220.

Murray, D. J. (1995). *Gestalt psychology and the cognitive revolution.* New York: Harvester Wheatsheaf.

Neisser, U. (1967). *Cognitive psychology.* New York: Appleton-Century-Crofts.

Pavlov, I. P. (1927). *Conditioned reflexes* (G. V. Anrep, Trans.). London: Oxford University Press.

Peters, R. S. (Ed.). (1965). *Brett's history of psychology.* Cambridge, MA: MIT Press.

Raaijmakers, J. G. W., & Shiffrin, R. M. (1981). Search of associative memory. *Psychological Review, 88,* 93–134.

Ribback, A., & Underwood, B. J. (1950). An empirical explanation of the skewness of the bowed serial position curve. *Journal of Experimental Psychology, 40,* 329–335.

Robertson, J. M. (Ed.). (1905). *The philosophic works of Francis Bacon* (R. C Ellis & J. Spedding, Trans.). London: Routledge & Kegan Paul.

Robinson, E. S. (1932). *Association theory today.* New York: The Century Co.

Robinson, E. S., & Brown, M. A. (1926). Effect of serial position upon memorization. *American Journal of Psychology, 37,* 538–552.

Rosenblatt, F. (1958). The perceptron: A probabilistic model for information storage and organization in the brain. *Psychological Review, 65,* 386–408.

Rubin, D. C., & Wenzel, A. E. (1996). One hundred years of forgetting: A quantitative description of retention. *Psychological Review, 103,* 734–760.

Rumelhart, D. E., Hinton, G. E., & Williams, J. R. (1986). Learning internal representations by error propagation. In D. E. Rumelhart & J. L. McClelland (Eds.), *Parallel distributed processing: Vol. 1.* Cambridge, MA: MIT Press.

Rumelhart, D. E., & McClelland, J. L. (1986). *Parallel distributed processing: Vol. 1.* Cambridge, MA: MIT Press.

Schacter, D. L., Eich, J. E., & Tulving, E. (1978). Richard Semon's theory of memory. *Journal of Verbal Learning and Verbal Behavior, 17,* 721–723.

Schacter, D. L., & Tulving, E. (1994). What are the memory systems of 1994? In D. L. Schacter & E. Tulving (Eds.), *Memory systems 1994.* Cambridge, MA: MIT Press.

Slamecka, N. J. (1985). Ebbinghaus: Some associations. *Journal of Experimental Psychology: Learning, Memory, and Cognition, 11,* 414–435.

Surprenant, A. M., & Neath, I. (in press). T. V. Moore's (1939) *Cognitive Psychology. Psychonomic Bulletin & Review.*

Thorndike, E. L. (1913). *The psychology of learning.* New York: Teachers College.

Van de Vijver, G. (1990). Schematism and schemata: Kant and the PDP. *Communication and Cognition, 23,* 223–233.

Ward, L. B. (1937). Reminiscence and rote learning. *Psychological Monographs, 49* (No. 220).

Warden, C. J. (1924). Primacy and recency as factors in cul-de-sac elimination in a stylus maze. *Journal of Experimental Psychology, 7,* 98–116.

Warren, H. C. (1921). *A history of the association psychology.* New York: Scribner.

Watson, F. (1915). The father of modern psychology. *Psychological Review, 22,* 333–353.

Watson, R. I. (1968). *The great psychologists: From Aristotle to Freud* (2nd ed.). Philadelphia: Lippincott.

Woodworth, R. S., & Poffenberger, A. T. (1920). *Textbook of experimental psychology.* (Mimeographed edition). New York: Columbia University Press.

Yates, F. A. (1966). *The art of memory.* Chicago: University of Chicago Press.

Young, R. K. (1968). Serial learning. In T. R. Dion & D. L. Horton (Eds.), *Verbal behavior and general behavior theory.* Englewood Cliffs, NJ: Prentice-Hall.

Zusne, L. (1975). *Names in the history of psychology: A biographical sourcebook.* New York: Halsted Press.

# Sensory Memory

*"Each sense organ of the body may be said to have its memory; and these memories are in a measure independent of each other."*

— *William H. Burnham (1888)*

## Sensory Memory

What is the purpose of memory? One purpose is to guarantee that even fleeting information will persist long enough so that it can be selected by the organism for further processing. For example, if you are driving on a freeway and a red or blue light flashes briefly behind you, it can disappear before you have time to think about it. However, if you had some system that could "play back" the event or could re-present the scene, you could then verify whether it was what you thought it was and decide whether or not to slow down. For visual information, this task is delegated to iconic memory, and for auditory information, to echoic memory.

## Iconic Memory

Jevons published a paper in 1871 describing "the power of numerical discrimination." He would toss a handful of beans in the air so that they would fall in a black tray, in the middle of which was a white box. Jevons' task was to estimate, without hesitating, the number of beans that fell in the white box, and he recorded both his estimates and the actual number for over 1000 trials. He found that for small numbers of beans, he was both accurate and fast in his estimates, but as the number increased, his accuracy decreased. Jevons' span of apprehension — the number of beans that he could attend to at one time — was approximately nine: when the number of beans falling into the white box was nine or higher, he was accurate only half of the time.

A more carefully controlled study was performed by Averbach (1963) using a tachistoscope, a device that presents visual information for very brief durations. Averbach varied the exposure duration, the time during which an array of black dots was visible. The number of dots that could be accurately reported depended on the exposure duration. There was a large benefit in increasing the exposure time from 40 ms to 150 ms,

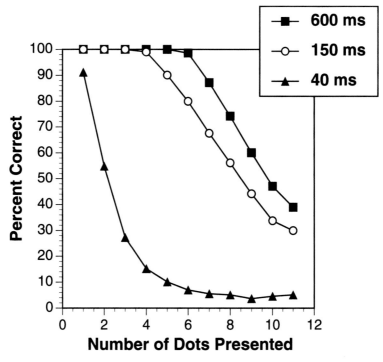

**Figure 3.1**   Averbach's span of apprehension. Percent correct estimates of the number of dots seen for three different exposure durations.   Source: Averbach (1963).

but very little benefit from increasing the duration from 150 ms to 600 ms. ("ms" stands for "milliseconds"; there are 1000 ms in 1 second.)  The results are shown in Figure 3.1. It is interesting to note that Averbach's estimate for the span of apprehension was similar to Jevons' estimate: when the number of stimuli is around eight or nine, estimates will be accurate only half the time.

These two studies used very simple stimuli (beans and dots) but found similar results. For a few stimuli, people can very accurately and very quickly report the correct number; with around four to eight items, performance is a little slower and a little less accurate; and for nine items or more, accuracy quickly falls off. But what about for more complicated items that have to be interpreted, such as letters?

George Sperling (1960) conducted a series of experiments to investigate this case. In a 3 × 4 matrix (see Figure 3.2), he presented some letters for 50 ms (or ¹⁄₂₀ sec) and asked his subjects to report all the letters they could see; his subjects could not report more than about four items on any one trial. The estimate of the span of apprehension for complex material, then, appeared much lower than for more simple material. However, Sperling's subjects claimed that they could "see" more than the four items reported; they just could not report all of them. This appeared consistent with the idea of iconic memory, a form of memory that maintains a large amount of visual information but for only brief periods. Although the subjects were introspecting, and, as we have already noted, introspection is not

| A | 2 | P | 9 |
| 3 | M | 7 | T |
| 5 | 7 | S | 4 |

**Figure 3.2**   An example of a 3 × 4 matrix that might be used in Sperling's (1960) experiment.

a reliable research method, it can generate hypotheses. Sperling devised a way of objectively testing this idea.

When you take any kind of test, you are not tested for everything that you know. For example, when you take the written portion of a driving test, you may get 20 questions about motor vehicle rules and regulations. If you get 15 out of 20 correct, the agency in charge infers that you know approximately 75% of the material. Rather than examining you on every possible motor vehicle question, the motor vehicle bureau tests only a portion of your knowledge and then estimates what you know about the untested information from the partial sample.

When this is done in psychology experiments, it is known as the partial report technique: you cue the subject which portion to recall, and then estimate the total number of items potentially available. What Sperling did was to cue his subjects to which row of the array to recall by playing one of three tones. If a high tone were played, the subject knew to recall just the top row (A2P9 in this example); a medium tone indicated that the middle row should be recalled; and a low tone meant that the bottom row should be recalled. A trial would go as follows. The display would be presented briefly, for perhaps 50 ms. Then, following a brief interval, a tone would be played, signaling which row to recall. Sperling systematically varied the duration of the interval between the offset of the display and the onset of the tone from 0 to 1 s. There was also a condition where the delay was −0.1 s, which means the tone was actually played 100 ms before the offset of the display. The results are shown in Figure 3.3.

Because there were three possible rows to recall and the subjects did not know until after they had heard the tone which row was the correct one, Sperling reasoned that the subjects had to attend to all of the items. Thus, he multiplied the number of items the subjects recalled by 3 to estimate the total amount of information available. For example, if a subject heard the high pitched tone and recalled three of the four items in the top row correctly, Sperling would estimate a total knowledge of nine items. What is most intriguing about Figure 3.3 is that if the tone is delayed by a second, then there is no partial report advantage; that is, the estimated number of letters available to the subject is equal to the actual number of letters recalled in the whole report procedure. Further work suggested that the partial report advantage disappears if the delay is as short as 500 ms.

Sperling (1960, 1967) concluded from these and other results that information is briefly registered in a sensory memory system and is almost totally available if accessed quickly enough. If the information is not soon attended to, however, it is rapidly lost. Although Sperling called this sensory store *visual information storage,* the name proposed by Ulric Neisser (1967) quickly became the dominant term: *iconic memory.*

The name *iconic memory* refers to the key property of the visual sensory store: iconic memory was thought to be precategorical, meaning that it preserves information in an unanalyzed form, rather like a picture or an icon of what was seen. The stimuli have not been

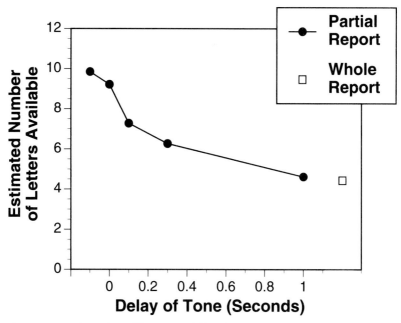

**Figure 3.3**   Estimated number of letters available when using the partial report technique (closed circles) as a function of the interval between the presentation of the letters and the presentation of the tone. The open square shows the results when using whole report.
Source: Sperling (1960).

categorized and there is not much processing of the image. To extract the information, the subject must scan the icon and then translate it into a more durable form. Sperling (1967) calculated that this scanning process took only about 10 ms per item. By comparison, it takes you about 250 to 300 ms to perform successive *saccades*—moving your eyes from one location to another and then focusing on the new location (Haber & Hershenson, 1973). Once the item is scanned, however, rehearsal is necessary or the information will be lost. Rehearsal is usually performed by recoding the information into its verbal name and repeating this name subvocally. Thus, when errors are made, they are likely to be based on acoustic similarity rather than on visual similarity: if the target letter is B, a person is more likely to say V than R.

One important question about iconic memory raises the possibility that it is not actually memory. For example, it is conceivable that iconic memory is just an afterimage, a perceptual phenomena based on the retina. If someone takes your photograph with a flash, you see an image of the flash persist, although the afterimage is of a black (or dark) blob rather than the intense white of the flash. This persistence has to do with chemical changes of photoreceptors in your eye's retina, rather than with memory. Similarly, if you stare at a bright red image for a minute or two and then look at a neutral wall, you will see an afterimage that has the same shape but is now green. Again, this image may persist for a minute or more. Afterimages are due to processes that occur within the eye, and some researchers have argued that iconic memory is also due to processes that occur in the eye. For example, Sakitt (1976; Sakitt & Long, 1979) has argued that the effects of iconic memory are due to activity of the rod cells in the retina.

The view that iconic memory is simply another form of afterimage makes certain predictions about how color information would be represented. Afterimages are complementary; that is, if you stare at a red stimulus, the afterimage is green; if you stare at a blue stimulus, the afterimage is yellow. If iconic memory is an afterimage, subjects should make systematic errors when asked to report items of a certain color, reporting the green items, for example, when asked to report the red ones. However, this does not occur; subjects *can* select items from iconic memory based on color (Banks & Barber 1977). This means that the original color rather than its complement is being retained, and at least some aspects of iconic memory are separate from the processes that give rise to afterimages.

More conclusive evidence comes from a study by Turvey (1973), who used brightness masking and pattern masking to distinguish between retinal-based properties and memory-based properties of iconic memory. In brightness masking, presentation of a target letter is followed by a brighter flash of light. This bright light masks, or hides, some of the information about the target and makes identification of the target letter more difficult. In pattern masking, a pattern rather than a light is presented after the target letter is shown; the patterns that Turvey used looked like Chinese characters. Brightness masking occurs when both the target letter and the brightness mask are presented to the same eye. If the target is presented to the left eye and the brightness mask is presented to the right eye, there is no masking. This suggests that brightness masking works by interfering with processes that occur within the eye, at the level of the retina. In contrast, pattern masking can occur when the target and the pattern masks are presented to different eyes. If the target is shown to the left eye and the pattern mask is shown to the right eye, masking can still occur. This suggests that pattern masking occurs at some point where information from both eyes has been combined. This aspect of pattern masking implies that some of iconic memory is controlled by more central processes, not totally controlled by more peripheral, or perceptual, processes.

Although it seems clear that some of iconic memory really is memory, there are three serious problems with Sperling's original interpretation (see Haber, 1983). Recall that iconic memory is supposed to be precategorical—that it preserves an unanalyzed representation of the original physical stimulus. If this is the case, then there should be no partial report advantage when the subjects are cued to recall the items by a category. In the original version of the experiment, subjects were cued by a tone that indicated physical location, which requires no categorization or deep analysis of the stimuli. Merikle (1980), on the other hand, cued subjects by categories. In his experiment, subjects were asked to recall just digits, just letters, or both. One can think of this as two different partial report tests with a whole-report control condition. Merikle not only found a partial report advantage when subjects were cued by category, he also found that the advantage was similar in magnitude to that of cueing by physical location. This implies that iconic memory is not precategorical, because people could select information to be recalled on the basis of a category label.

A second problem concerns the idea of output interference: the act of recalling one item can interfere with recall of the next item. Because of output interference, the more items you are required to remember, the less likely it is that you will recall the last one successfully. One important difference between partial report and whole report is that partial report reduces the amount of output interference. Sperling's original interpretation was that the icon decayed before all the information could be read off. A different interpretation might be that output interference is at least partially responsible for some of the difference. Some evidence consistent with this interpretation comes from an analysis that compared the number of times the first item in partial report was recalled correctly compared with the number of times the first item in whole report was recalled correctly. Dick (1971) found no difference between partial report and whole report for the first item, which suggests that output interference may play a large role in the advantage of partial report over whole report.

A final important concern involves the type of errors that the subjects make. It has already been noted that some of the errors are auditory confusion errors: reporting a letter that sounds like the actual target letter. Mewhort and Leppman (1985) conducted an experiment in which a row of letters was displayed for 50 ms and the subject's task was to decide if a target letter had appeared in the display. The experimenters varied the delay between the offset of the row of letters and the presentation of the probe. Subjects were equally as accurate when the delay was short as when it was long. Unlike Sperling's original study, there was no decrease in accuracy as the delay increased. Mewhort and Leppman ran a second version of the experiment in which the target was always in the display and the subject's task was to indicate the location of probe item. This time, accuracy did decrease as the delay increased, just as in Sperling's original study. Subjects appear to be forgetting location information—where an item was—rather than item information—what items were present (see also Mewhort, Campbell, Marchetti, & Campbell, 1981). A similar experiment was run using Sperling's original methodology with similar results: location errors increased as the delay increased, but item errors did not (Yeomans & Irwin, 1985).

At least some of the effects attributed to iconic memory, then, do appear to be due to real memory rather than to perception (controlled by central rather than by peripheral processes). On the other hand, there is evidence to suggest that subjects are not forgetting item information but rather are losing location information. Cowan (1995) suggests that the effects described above can be explained parsimoniously by dividing iconic memory into two phases (see also Coltheart, 1983). The briefer phase is a literal representation that lasts perhaps for only 150–250 ms and is a fundamentally different type of representation than one seen after longer intervals. For example, Di Lollo (1980) found that the persistence of a brief visual stimulus is inversely related to its physical duration: the longer a stimulus is shown, the shorter the reported persistence. Di Lollo proposed that a visual stimulus has a minimum duration of approximately 120 ms, starting at stimulus onset. As the physical duration increases, less of that 120 ms can be measured as "persistence." Subsequently, Di Lollo, Hogben, and Dixon (1994) suggested that the reason for this persistence is not the presence of the stimulus in a visual store but rather the emergence and continuation of a particular pattern of neural activity. Francis (1996) presents a detailed model of these and other visual sensory phenomena.

The second phase, which is probably not truly sensory, is characterized by the recoding of some features from the literal trace into other forms. One possibility for the increased location errors is that item information is recoded before location information is. This interpretation fits in well with studies demonstrating that people can identify items before they can locate them (Treisman & Gelade, 1980).

Current conceptions of iconic memory, then, have refined Sperling's original formulation. The duration of iconic memory proper is far shorter — around one fifth of the original estimate — and there is an immediate involvement of other processes to recode and categorize the information. It should not be surprising that the description of iconic memory has changed over time, nor does this reflect poorly on the original research. Rather, as we gain more information, theories need to be revised and made more precise, as is the case for iconic memory. As we shall see, the situation for echoic memory is quite similar.

# Echoic Memory

*Echoic memory,* also named by Neisser (1967), is the auditory analog of iconic memory. It gets its name from the idea that auditory information may persist in the form of an "echo" that can be attended to after the original stimulus is no longer present. Usually, this is most noticeable when someone says your name and you do not immediately hear it; after a brief interval, you realize that your name was said and you still seem to hear your name being spoken. Echoic memory has been studied in a variety of different ways, but one of the first studies used an analog of Sperling's (1960) technique.

Darwin, Turvey, and Crowder (1972) presented subjects with three lists of three digits. Each list took 1 s to present. One list was played over both the left and right channels of the speakers, so to the subject it sounded as if the digits were coming from directly in front. A second list was played simultaneously but only on the left channel. The third list was also played simultaneously but only on the right channel. In the partial report conditions, a visual signal would be projected after the lists had been presented to indicate which list should be recalled. For example, if the light appeared to the left, the subject should report the list that they heard coming from the left. The researchers varied the interval between the offset of the list and the onset of the signal from 0 to 4 s. In the whole report procedure, subjects were asked to recall all of the items. The results are reproduced in Figure 3.4.

There was a partial report advantage, indicating that subjects recalled more items on average when they had to recall only one list rather than all three. Although this advantage was not as large as with the visual modality, it lasted far longer. Darwin, Turvey, and Crowder also reported an in-depth analysis of the data from the partial report condition, in which subjects were asked to recall the three items in order. Subjects were much more accurate reporting the third item than either the first or second, and slightly more accurate reporting the first item than the second. The most obvious explanation for this result is that the third item partially masked the first two. Echoic memory, then, appeared similar to iconic memory with just two minor differences: echoic memory lasts longer, but it does not preserve as much information. There are several possible problems with this experiment (see Massaro & Loftus, 1996), and if this were the only sort of data available, the concept of echoic memory would be on very shaky ground. Probably because of these problems, many researchers began investigating echoic memory using different procedures.

We saw earlier that although a substantial portion of the effects originally attributed to iconic memory are due to a high-level, central process, some of the effects appear to be more peripherally located. A similar conclusion appears to apply to echoic memory. For example, Deatherage and Evans (1969) presented a target sound to a subject, and then

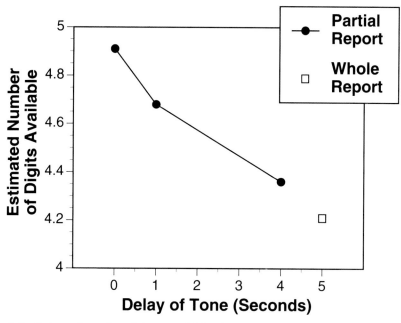

**Figure 3.4** Estimated number of digits available when using the partial report technique as a function of the interval between hearing the digits and the presentation of the visual signal. Source: Darwin, Turvey, & Crowder (1972).

also presented a masking sound. When both were presented to the same ear, identification of the target sound suffered, similar to brightness masking in the visual domain, where target and mask must be presented to the same eye. When the auditory mask and target were presented to different ears, there was no apparent masking.

Additional evidence for peripheral processes playing some role in echoic memory came from two papers published one after the other by Efron (1970a, 1970b). He presented subjects with a series of brief tones that lasted from 30 to 100 ms and asked the subjects to adjust a light such that it came on exactly when the tone ended. Efron found that regardless of the actual duration of the tone, its subjective duration was 130 ms. Cowan (1984) proposed that there are two echoic stores, one that retains information for up to approximately 300 ms, and one that retains information for longer periods, perhaps as long as 20 s. There appears good evidence that the shorter form is a distinct memory system and parallels the case for iconic memory (Cowan, 1995). Much of the evidence for the second, longer-lasting store comes from studies that examine the modality effect and the stimulus suffix (or simply suffix) effect (see Penney, 1989).

Both the modality and the suffix effects are observed when subjects are presented a series of items, typically a random ordering of the digits 1–9, and are asked to recall them in order. This recall procedure is known as *serial recall,* and the results are generally reported in terms of the proportion of items correctly recalled as a function of their input position. Auditory and visual presentation give rise to almost the same result with one important exception: there is a large advantage for the last one or two items in the list with

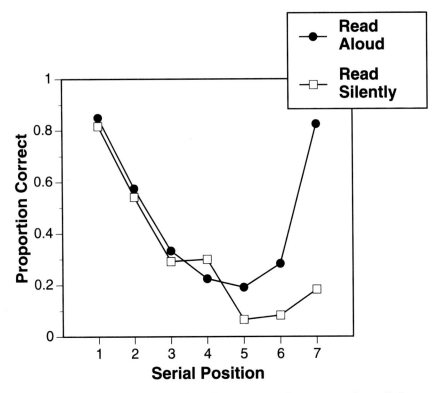

**Figure 3.5**   The modality effect in serial recall: proportion of items correctly recalled as a function of serial position when presentation modality is either reading silently (visual) or reading aloud (auditory).   Source: Conrad & Hull (1968).

auditory presentation compared to visual presentation (Corballis, 1966; Murray, 1966; Washburn, 1916, p. 74). Conrad and Hull (1968) presented all the items visually but required the subject to read the items aloud in one condition and silently in the other. The results are shown in Figure 3.5. There is usually little or no difference between reading items aloud and hearing them read (Crowder, 1970).

## Theories of Echoic Memory: PAS

The modality effect has most often been accounted for by *PAS* or *precategorical acoustic store* (Crowder & Morton, 1969), which is best seen as a specific theory of echoic memory. This view assumes that auditory to-be-remembered items are stored in a relatively uncategorized code for brief periods of time, around 2 s or so, in a modality-specific sensory memory system. The store is said to be *precategorical* because it contains unanalyzed information, and it is *acoustic* because it retains only acoustic information — or, more accurately, a representation of the acoustic information. Newly entering items interfere with already present items, but only if the new items are acoustically similar to the previous items. Forgetting in PAS is thus due to a specific form of retroactive interference: new items interfere with items that occurred earlier. Echoic memory, according to this view, provides a source of supplementary information that can be used to identify or recall an auditory item. The modality effect arises because auditory presentation of verbal material permits information about the one or two final items to remain in PAS, from which they can be recalled. Because visual presentation, by definition, contains no acoustic information, there will be no supplementary information available.

PAS makes several specific predictions about the modality effect. The *modality effect* refers to the enhanced recall of the final item when the presentation modality is auditory rather than visual. This enhanced recall is known as the *recency effect,* because the most recently presented items are remembered well. PAS predicts that when serial recall is the measure, there will be no recency effect observable with visual presentation. It is difficult to establish that something is not observable, because there could be many reasons for not finding a particular phenomenon. In this particular case, however, it is clear that this prediction has been confirmed and that there are no recency effects observable with visual presentation that are in any way comparable to those observed with auditory presentation (LeCompte, 1992).

A second prediction concerns the usefulness of the supplementary information in PAS. According to the theory, a recency effect will be observable to the extent that the acoustic information in PAS is useful for identifying the list items. There are several ways of varying the usefulness of the information. For example, if a list of homophones (such as *by, bye,* and *buy* or *pore, pour,* and *poor*) are presented, the acoustic information will be identical even though the items are different. In studies like these, it is important to make sure that all subjects pronounce the homophones in a similar way; in some dialects of English, for example, the word *poor* can have 1 syllable or 2 syllables. Crowder (1978a) verified that serial recall of homophones does not give rise to a recency effect. Another example of varying the usefulness of the acoustic information involves differences between vowels and consonants. Vowels are typically defined by relatively long sections of steady-state information. Consonants, on the other hand — particularly the stop consonants /b/, /d/, /g/, /k/, /p/, and /t/ — are distinguished primarily by very rapid bursts of dynamically changing information. Because PAS holds items with more steady-state information for longer periods than items with more transient information (Crowder, 1975), there will be more information concerning item identity in PAS when the stimuli are vowels than when they are consonants. Thus, according to this view, vowels should be recalled more accurately than consonants because the acoustic information describing a given vowel will last longer in PAS than will the corresponding information that describes a consonant. In addition, vowels that last longer should be recalled better and should produce larger recency effects than vowels that do not last as long. Again, these predictions have been confirmed (Crowder, 1973a, 1973b; Surprenant & Neath, 1996).

Not only did PAS offer a simple, elegant explanation of the modality effect, but it also accounted for the suffix effect within the same framework. The *suffix effect* is related to the modality effect, but it applies only when the presentation modality of the to-be-remembered items is auditory. In the suffix condition, an extra item follows the last to-be-remembered item. This item is typically the word *ready* or the digit 0, it is the same on every trial, and the subject is aware that this item need not be recalled. Even though the subject is told to ignore the suffix or to treat it merely as a sign to begin recall, the suffix

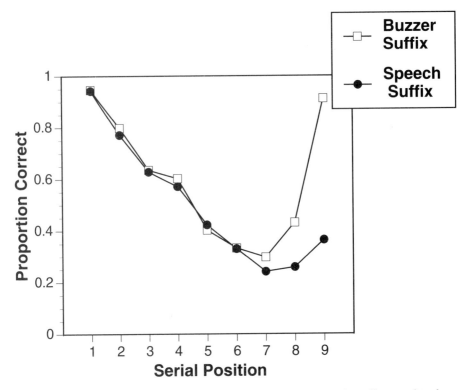

**Figure 3.6**  Serial recall of a nine-item list when an additional item, the suffix, is either the word *zero* or the sound made by a buzzer.   Source: Crowder (1972).

dramatically reduces recall of the final item (Crowder, 1967; Dallett, 1965). As Figure 3.6 shows, when the suffix is simply a tone or a buzzer, the data look similar to those for serial recall of standard auditory lists. When the suffix is speech, however, the shape of the serial position function resembles that for visually presented items: the recency effect is greatly attenuated (Crowder, 1972).

Repeated practice with the foreknowledge that the suffix will occur and will be the same item on each trial does not reduce the effect (Balota & Engle, 1981); and although continual presentation of the suffix token throughout the entire experimental session can weaken its potency (Watkins & Sechler, 1989), a reliable suffix effect still obtains. In general, a visual suffix will have little or no effect on an auditorily presented list of items (Morton & Holloway, 1970), and while the effect of the suffix diminishes over time such that a delay of 2 s is sufficient to remove most of the effect, this reduction cannot be attributed simply to delaying recall (Crowder, 1971) or to rhythmicity (Crowder, 1973c).

According to PAS, the suffix is interfering with information in echoic memory. The principles of interference during the early phases of PAS were very simple: a suffix would interfere to the extent that it was acoustically similar to the list items. Because of this, manipulations that alter acoustic factors will also affect the potency of the suffix, but manipulations that alter semantic or higher-level characteristics will not.

**Experiment**   The Stimulus Suffix Effect

**Purpose:**   To demonstrate the effect of a redundant item (the suffix) on immediate serial recall.

**Subjects:**   Twenty-four subjects are recommended. Twelve should be assigned to the suffix condition, and 12 to the control condition. Subject 1 should be in the suffix condition, Subject 2 in the control condition, Subject 3 in the suffix condition, and so on.

**Materials:**   Table B in the Appendix contains lists of the digits 1–9 in random order. For each subject, select 11 lists and write them down so that the experimenter can easily read them aloud and can easily keep track of the current list. For suffix subjects, add the digit 0 at the end of each of the lists. Also prepare answer sheets. The answer sheet should have 11 rows of boxes or blanks in which the subject will write down the responses.

**Design:**   Because the subjects experience only one condition, the effect of the suffix is a between-subjects manipulation.

**Procedure:**   The first list for each group is a practice list so that the subjects can familiarize themselves with the type of material, the speed of presentation, and the method of recall. The remaining 10 lists are the main trials from which data will be collected. Each list should be read aloud by the experimenter at a rate of 2 items per second. Try to place equal emphasis on each digit. Subjects should have approximately 20 seconds to write the digits down on their answer sheet before the next trial begins.

**Instructions for the Control Group:**   "This experiment tests your ability to recall a list of numbers in order. I will read a list of nine numbers, in random order, at a fairly quick pace. As soon as the list is over, I would like you to write down the digits in exactly the same order as you heard them. You should write down the first number in the first blank on your answer sheet, the second number in the second blank, and so on. Once you have written a number, you cannot alter it and you cannot go back and change earlier items. To be counted as correct, the digit must be in its original position. You may find that you cannot recall all of the items. If you are unsure, feel free to guess; it is better to guess than to omit an answer. The first list is a practice list." (If there are no questions following the practice list, proceed with the experimental lists. Make sure the subject is following the serial recall instructions.)

**Instructions for the Suffix Group:**   "This experiment tests your ability to recall a list of numbers in order. I will read a list of nine numbers, in random order, at a fairly quick pace. As soon as the list is over, I would like you to write down the digits in exactly the same order as you heard them. You will know when the list is over, because you will hear the number zero. You do not have to recall this item, and you should not write it down; the number zero will serve only as a cue to begin recalling the items. You should write down the first number in the first blank on your answer sheet, the second number in the second blank, and so on. Once you have written a number, you cannot alter it, and you cannot go back and change earlier items. To be counted as correct, the digit must be in its original position. You may find that you cannot recall all of the items. If you are unsure, feel free to guess; it is better to guess than to omit an answer. The first list is a practice list." (If there are no questions following the practice list, proceed with the experimental lists. Make sure the subject is following the serial recall instructions.)

**Scoring and Analysis:**   The practice list is not scored. For the remaining lists, count the number of times the first number was correctly written down in the first slot. This number will range from 0 to 10. Do the same for each serial position, counting the item

*(continued on next page)*

---

**Experiment**    The Stimulus Suffic Effect (*continued*)

---

correct only if it is the correct order. Construct two serial position functions, one for the suffix subjects and one for the control subjects. To do this, add up the individual subject data and divide by the number of subjects. To determine if the difference at the last serial position is statistically reliable, you can perform a *t* test for independent groups.

**Optional Enhancements:**    Present 21 lists to each group of subjects rather than 11. This will provide more observations and the data will show less random error. Record the stimuli onto cassette tape and add a tone (a computer beep, a note from a piano, etc.) at the end of the lists in the control condition. This will equate the time from the presentation of the ninth item until the beginning of recall in both conditions.

Source: Based on an experiment by Crowder (1972).

---

Morton, Crowder, and Prussin (1971) conducted the first extensive series of experiments on the suffix effect, and the main findings from their 17 experiments were consistent with the PAS interpretation. The magnitude of the suffix effect was not affected by (1) the meaning or predictability of the suffix; (2) whether the suffix was *uh* or *zero*; (3) the semantic relatedness of the suffix to list items; or (4) word frequency or emotionality of the suffix. The size of the suffix effect was reduced (1) when the acoustic properties of the suffix (such as its apparent spatial location, timbre, and pitch) were altered relative to the list items; (2) when the sex of the speaker changed from list items to suffix; and (3) when the speaker of the list items and suffix changed, even though they were of the same sex.

PAS offered a simple and elegant account for the effects described above, but evidence soon accumulated that this view had problems. In particular, three lines of evidence falsify the PAS account of suffix and modality effects. The first questions the precategorical nature of echoic memory by demonstrating that a stimulus' potency to function as a suffix depends on the context in which it is perceived (Ayres, Jonides, Reitman, Egan, & Howard, 1979; Neath, Surprenant, & Crowder, 1993). The second questions whether the store is sensitive only to acoustic information by demonstrating modality and suffix effects with clearly nonacoustic stimuli (e.g., Campbell & Dodd, 1980; Greene & Crowder, 1984; Nairne & Crowder, 1982; Nairne & Walters, 1983; Shand & Klima, 1981; Spoehr & Corin, 1978). The third involves demonstrations of modality and suffix effects when information in PAS should not be available (Conway & Gathercole, 1987; Gardiner & Gregg, 1979).

Ayres et al. (1979) challenged the precategorical interpretation of PAS by reporting an experiment in which the same, acoustically identical suffix reduced recall of the final item only when it was interpreted as human speech; when interpreted as a musical sound, this suffix did not affect recall. In a between-subjects design, three different groups received 30 seven-item lists of one-syllable words. The groups differed in which suffix was presented: either no suffix, a music suffix, or a speech suffix. The first group began serial recall of the words immediately after the seventh item, the music group heard what were labeled musical tones after the seventh item, and the speech group heard speech sounds as the suffix. The manipulation of interest was an ambiguous suffix *wa* that was presented to both suffix groups. Described as a "plunger-muted trumpet note sounding like a nasally spoken syllable" (p. 316), this suffix was referred to either as music or as speech, depending on the condition. Subjects in the speech condition were told that it was the syllable *wa,* and those in the music condition were told that it was a trumpet tone. The interesting result was that the effectiveness of the suffix was dependent on how the subjects were led to interpret it.

Whereas Ayres et al. (1979) made a nonspeech sound act as a speech sound, Neath, Surprenant, and Crowder (1993) did the opposite, making a speech sound act as a nonspeech sound. Two real animal noises, from a cow and a dog, were obtained from a sound effects collection. In addition, recordings of a male speaker saying "woof," "moo," and the digits 1 through 9 were digitized onto a computer. Finally, the same male speaker produced a sound, nominally "baa," that resembled the sound a sheep makes. Two groups of subjects were tested: the animal group was told that "after the ninth digit, an animal noise will indicate that the list is over and that you should get ready to recall the digits, in order," whereas the human group was told that "after the ninth digit, the same voice will pronounce a conventional animal sound to indicate that the list is over and that you should get ready to recall the digits, in order." Because the sheep suffix was the same physical item, according to PAS, it should have the same effect in the two groups. The results are displayed in Figure 3.7.

As in the Ayres et al. (1979) study, there was a robust context-dependent suffix effect. The sheep suffix reduced recall only when subjects interpreted it as human speech and not when they interpreted it as an animal sound. In Experiment 2, similar effects were demonstrated in a within-subjects design (Neath, Surprenant, & Crowder, 1993). Although PAS has seen several revisions (e.g., Crowder, 1978b; Greene & Crowder, 1984), no version can account for the context-dependent suffix effect, where the subject's interpretation of the suffix critically affects the potency of the suffix. PAS also faces problems from the many studies that demonstrate modality and suffix effects with clearly nonacoustic stimuli.

Spoehr and Corin (1978) reported a suffix experiment in which the experimenter read the to-be-remembered items aloud to the subject. On certain trials, however, the experimenter mouthed a suffix and the subject was able to lip-read (or *speech-read,* to use the correct term) the item. According to PAS, this lip-read suffix should have no effect on memory because interference in PAS occurs on the basis of acoustic similarity. Spoehr and Corin reported substantial suffix effects: A lip-read *zero* served as an effective suffix on a list of items presented aloud. Campbell and Dodd (1980) demonstrated that when subjects lip-read an entire list, a modality effect obtains; that is, lip-reading a list leads to the same excellent memory for the last item as does hearing a list. Using a single experimental setting, Nairne and Walters (1983) reported both modality and suffix effects with mouthed stimuli. In this procedure, subjects make all the gestures necessary for saying an item out loud but they make no sound. A silently mouthed suffix can also affect recall of items presented aloud (Nairne & Crowder, 1982).

Many variations on this basic paradigm have been reported. It is important to remember that a modality effect, in this larger sense, refers to a recall advantage for the final item presented in a particular modality compared to the last item presented visually. Lip-reading and silent mouthing both produce such modality effects. In addition, Nairne and McNabb (1985) demonstrated a tactile modality effect and Watkins and Watkins (1974) demonstrated a tactile suffix effect. The basic procedure was to use a paper clip to tap

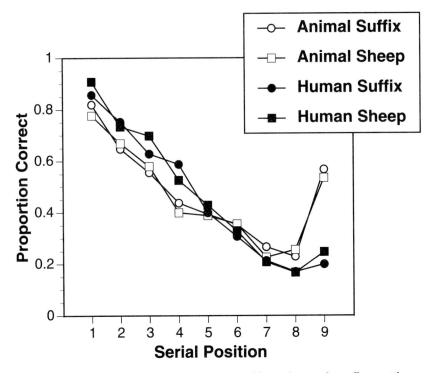

**Figure 3.7** Serial recall of a nine-item list when an additional item, the suffix, is either a real animal sound (animal suffix), a real English word (human suffix), or the same speech sound that is described as an animal sound (animal sheep) or as an English word (human sheep).
Source: Neath, Surprenant, & Crowder (1993).

subjects' fingers in a particular order. Subjects would be asked to recall the order in which different parts of their hand had been touched. To impose a suffix, the experimenter would tap the subjects' knuckles (lightly) with a pen. Other modalities show similar results. For example, for deaf subjects, there is evidence of modality and suffix effects when items are presented using American Sign Language (ASL) (Shand & Klima, 1981).

Finally, PAS faces problems from demonstrations of modality and suffix effects when there should be no information available in PAS. For example, Conway and Gathercole (1987) first presented subjects with a 30-item list of words, and then presented a list of 60 words in random order, 30 from the original list and 30 distractor items. The subjects' task was to say whether the item had been on the list. Words from the last part of the auditory list were better recognized than were words from the last part of the visual list. This is a problem for PAS because on average, the delay between the end of the list and the testing of the last few items would be far longer than the presumed duration of PAS. Similarly, Gardiner and Gregg (1979) found a modality effect for items that had been followed by auditory distractor activity. According to PAS, the auditory distractor items should have eliminated the information in PAS about the end-of-the-list items, and so there should not have been an auditory advantage. Similar problems arise with the PAS explanation of suffix effects. *Articulatory suppression* refers to a task where the subject is required to say an irrelevant item out loud and continuously during list presentation. According to PAS, this irrelevant auditory information should prevent a suffix effect because the articulatory suppression should remove any contribution from PAS. However, Surprenant, LeCompte, and Neath (1997) found reliable suffix effects even when subjects were engaged in articulatory suppression.

Although it might be tempting to posit tactile and sign-language sensory memory systems and different explanations when modality and suffix effects are observed after shorter versus longer intervals, it might be more profitable to search for a single explanation for all of these phenomena. Two accounts other than PAS have been offered as explanations for modality and suffix effects.

## Other Theories of Echoic Memory

*The Changing-State Hypothesis* One difference between a visual and an auditory item is that a visual item can be apprehended all at once whereas an auditory item requires some sequential processing. Campbell and Dodd (1980; see also Campbell & Dodd, 1987) suggest that this difference between relatively static and relatively dynamic stimuli could serve as the basis for modality and suffix effects. Both lip-read and silently mouthed stimuli change over time, just as auditory items do, and ASL is also a dynamic mode of presentation. There are at least two problems with this view, however. First, it cannot address the modality and suffix effects observed with tactile stimuli because tactile items more closely resemble simultaneous than sequential information. Second, tests of the changing-state hypothesis have generally not been supportive. For example, Crowder (1986) presented numbers on a computer screen in such a way that, for a given number, parts of the numeral would appear sequentially. It would take approximately the same time to draw the number 7 as to say the word *seven*. There was no advantage for these items relative to visual items presented in a more traditional way.

*The Primary Linguistic Code Hypothesis* Shand and Klima (1981) proposed an alternative account that disagreed about the key aspect of ASL. They claimed that speech is a primary linguistic code—that is, a preferred form of representing information in primary memory. When list items are presented in a secondary code, such as visual, the items have to be recoded to a format that is the basic code of the person. For native signers of ASL, the basic code will not be speech, but sign language. This is why ASL can give rise to modality and suffix effects. Lip-reading and silent mouthing are basically speech, but without the acoustic component.

There are problems associated with this view as well. Once again, it does not explain tactile modality and suffix effects. Second, it too has not fared well experimentally. For example, Manning, Koehler, and Hampton (1990) presented subjects with several different kinds of stimuli and forced the subjects to recode between formats. According to the primary linguistic hypothesis, recoding should interfere with modality and suffix effects, particularly when the items to be recoded are not the primary linguistic code to begin with. Modality and suffix effects obtained, however, even though they were not primary and even though recoding was occurring.

As with iconic memory, then, no view that posits a specialized sensory memory system appears capable of explaining all the relevant data. However, there does appear to be good evidence for a separate sensory memory system for very brief intervals for both modalities (Cowan, 1995; Massaro & Loftus, 1996). For the data from longer intervals — more than 250 ms or so — some theories can explain these data but they do not make recourse to sensory memory. The most successful of these theories, Nairne's (1988, 1990) feature model, attempts to explain not only modality and suffix effects but also the serial position function as a whole and many other effects associated with immediate memory. This view is presented in detail in Chapter 5.

One final aspect of the suffix effect is worth mentioning. Studies that explore suffix effects might seem an excellent example of research that lacks ecological validity. However, Schilling and Weaver (1983) simulated interaction between a directory assistance operator and a telephone customer to examine the effect of a telephone company policy that directed operators to say "Have a nice day" at the end of each transaction. As expected, when the telephone numbers were followed by the phrase "Have a nice day," there were reliable reductions in the subjects' ability to recall the telephone number accurately.

# Odor Memory

Studies of odor memory have lagged far behind studies of visual and auditory memory, and as a result the little that is known has not been integrated within a coherent framework. As Schab and Crowder (1995) emphasize, "too few data exist to permit broad conclusions about odor memory" (p. 10).

One aspect that parallels other forms of sensory memory is the question of whether odor memory is a separate sensory memory. Schab and Crowder (1995) take the view that recognition memory for odors follows the same principles as memory for visual or verbal stimuli. One type of study is to present a small number of odors, wait a short period, and then present a test odor; the subject's task is to say whether the target odor is one of the small set that was just presented. Although several studies have shown little forgetting of odors over 30 seconds (Engen, Kuisma, & Eimas, 1973), when the retention interval is extended to 2 minutes, there is a reliable decrease in performance (Gilmore, 1991, cited in Schab & Crowder, 1995). Another type of study uses more stimuli and far longer retention intervals. Here, too, performance decreases with increasing retention interval (Rabin & Cain, 1984). Elaborative rehearsal can help improve memory for odors (Lyman & McDaniel, 1990), just as it improves memory for verbal or visual information.

Herz and Eich (1995) take the opposite view. They point out that many studies show no forgetting of odors over either the short or the long term, although these studies are generally earlier than the ones cited by Schab and Crowder (1995). Odor memory also appears to be different in amnesic patients. For example, Mair, Harrison, and Flint (1995) reviewed evidence suggesting that in Korsakoff patients, odor memory is preserved whereas memory for words, colors, or faces is severely impaired. As another example, Herz and Eich (1995) emphasize that odor information has different properties with respect to interference with verbal information.

**Table 3.1**  The effects of proactive interference (learn A, learn B, tested on B) and retroactive interference (learn B, learn A, tested on B) for odors.

|              | Type of Interference | |
|--------------|:---:|:---:|
| Condition    | PI  | RI  |
| Control      | 72% | 68% |
| Experimental | 54% | 68% |

Source: Based on data from Lawless & Engen (1977).

For example, one prevalent finding with both visual and auditory information is that interference reduces performance (Underwood, 1957). In particular, memory for a particular item can be interfered with by information that you have already learned; this is called *proactive interference*. However, memory can also be interfered with by information that is presented after learning the key item but before the test is given; this is called *retroactive interference*. The suffix effect is a good example of retroactive interference. Lawless and Engen (1977) found evidence of proactive interference but no evidence of retroactive interference with odors. They asked subjects to associate a particular odor with a particular picture, and at the first test, were asked to indicate which odor went with which picture. To create interference, the experimenters had the subjects perform two learning trials, and on the second trial different pairings were used. For example, on the first trial, the raspberry odor might be paired with a picture of a Spanish beach, but on the second trial it might be paired with a picture of the Swiss Alps. At test, the subjects could be asked to recall the second pairing, in which case the first pairing might cause proactive interference; or subjects could be asked to recall the first pairing, in which case the second pairing might cause retroactive interference. The proportion correct for each of these groups is shown in Table 3.1, along with performance of a control condition. Performance was worse for the proactive interference condition, but there was no difference between the control group and the retroactive interference condition.

Both Schab and Crowder (1995) and Herz and Eich (1995) emphasize the paucity of evidence and the need for more data. At this point in time, the evidence is mixed with regard to whether odor memory is a separate memory system or more nearly follows the principles of memory proper. It is likely, however, that researchers will conclude, as with visual and auditory stimuli, that there is a very brief true sensory component.

# References

Averbach, E. (1963). The span of apprehension as a function of exposure duration. *Journal of Verbal Learning and Verbal Behavior, 2,* 60–64.

Ayres, T. J., Jonides, J., Reitman, J. S., Egan, J. C., & Howard, D. A. (1979). Differing suffix effects for the same physical suffix. *Journal of Experimental Psychology: Human Learning and Memory, 5,* 315–321.

Balota, D. A., & Engle, R. W. (1981). Structural and strategic factors in the stimulus suffix effect. *Journal of Verbal Learning and Verbal Behavior, 20,* 346–357.

Banks, W. P., & Barber, G. (1977). Color information in iconic memory. *Psychological Review, 84,* 536–546.

Burnham, W. H. (1888). Memory, historically and experimentally considered. *American Journal of Psychology, 2,* 39–90, 255–270, 431–464, 566–622.

Campbell, R., & Dodd, B. (1980). Hearing by eye. *Quarterly Journal of Experimental Psychology, 32,* 85–99.

Campbell, R., & Dodd, B. (Eds.). (1987). *Hearing by eye: The psychology of lip-reading.* London: Erlbaum.

Coltheart, M. (1983). Iconic memory. *Philosophical Transactions of the Royal Society of London B, 302,* 283–294.

Conrad, R., & Hull, A. J. (1968). Input modality and the serial position curve in short-term memory. *Psychonomic Science, 10,* 135–136.

Conway, M. A., & Gathercole, S. E. (1987). Modality and long-term memory. *Journal of Memory and Language, 26,* 341–346.

Corballis, M. C. (1966). Rehearsal and decay in immediate recall of visually and aurally presented items. *Canadian Journal of Psychology, 20,* 43–51.

Cowan, N. (1984). On short and long auditory stores. *Psychological Bulletin, 96,* 341–370.

Cowan, N. (1995). *Attention and memory: An integrated framework.* New York: Oxford.

Crowder, R. G. (1967). Prefix effects in immediate memory. *Canadian Journal of Psychology, 21,* 450–461.

Crowder, R. G. (1970). The role of one's own voice in immediate memory. *Cognitive Psychology, 1,* 157–178.

Crowder, R. G. (1971). Waiting for the stimulus suffix: Decay, delay, rhythm, and readout in immediate memory. *Quarterly Journal of Experimental Psychology, 23,* 324–340.

Crowder, R. G. (1972). Visual and auditory memory. In J. F. Kavanagh & I. G. Mattingly (Eds.), *Language by ear and by eye: The relation between speech and learning to read.* Cambridge, MA: MIT Press.

Crowder, R. G. (1973a). The representation of speech sounds in precategorical acoustic storage. *Journal of Experimental Psychology, 98,* 14–24.

Crowder, R. G. (1973b). Precategorical acoustic storage for vowels of short and long duration. *Perception & Psychophysics, 13,* 502–506.

Crowder, R. G. (1973c). The delayed stimulus suffix effect following arhythmic stimulus presentation. *Quarterly Journal of Experimental Psychology, 25,* 433–439.

Crowder, R. G. (1975). Inferential problems in echoic memory. In P. M. A. Rabbit & S. Dornic (Eds.), *Attention and performance V.* London and New York: Academic Press.

Crowder, R. G. (1978a). Memory for phonologically uniform lists. *Journal of Verbal Learning and Verbal Behavior, 17,* 73–89.

Crowder, R. G. (1978b). Mechanisms of auditory backward masking in the stimulus suffix effect. *Psychological Review, 85,* 502–524.

Crowder, R. G. (1986). Auditory and temporal factors in the modality effect. *Journal of Experimental Psychology: Learning, Memory, and Cognition, 12,* 268–275.

Crowder, R. G., & Morton, J. (1969). Precategorical acoustic storage (PAS). *Perception & Psychophysics, 5,* 365–373.

Dallett, K. (1965). "Primary memory": The effects of redundancy upon digit repetition. *Psychonomic Science, 3,* 237–238.

Darwin, C. J., Turvey, M. T., & Crowder, R. G. (1972). An auditory analogue of the Sperling partial-report procedure. *Cognitive Psychology, 3,* 255–267.

Deatherage, B. H., & Evans, T. R. (1969). Binaural masking: Backward, forward, and simultaneous effects. *Journal of the Acoustical Society of America, 46,* 362–371.

Dick, A. O. (1971). On the problem of selection in short-term visual (iconic) memory. *Canadian Journal of Psychology, 25,* 250–263.

Di Lollo, V. (1980). Temporal integration in visual memory. *Journal of Experimental Psychology: General, 109,* 75–97.

Di Lollo, V., Hogben, J. H., & Dixon, P. (1994). Temporal integration and segregation of brief visual stimuli: Patterns of correlation in time. *Perception & Psychophysics, 55,* 373–386.

Efron, R. (1970a). The relationship between the duration of a stimulus and the duration of a perception. *Neuropsychologia, 8,* 37–55.

Efron, R. (1970b). The minimum duration of a perception. *Neuropsychologia, 8,* 57–63.

Engen, T., Kuisma, J. E., & Eimas, P. D. (1973). Short-term memory of odors. *Journal of Experimental Psychology, 99,* 222–225.

Francis, G. (1996). Cortical dynamics of visual persistence and temporal integration. *Perception & Psychophysics, 58,* 1203–1212.

Gardiner, J. M., & Gregg, V. H. (1979). When auditory memory is not overwritten. *Journal of Verbal Learning and Verbal Behavior, 18,* 705–719.

Greene, R. L., & Crowder, R. G. (1984). Modality and suffix effects in the absence of auditory stimulation. *Journal of Verbal Learning and Verbal Behavior, 23,* 371–382.

Haber, R. N. (1983). The impending demise of the icon: A critique of the concept of iconic storage in visual information processing. *Behavioral and Brain Sciences, 6,* 1–54.

Haber, R. N., & Hershenson, M. (1973). *The psychology of visual perception.* New York: Holt, Rinehart & Winston.

Herz, R. S., & Eich, E. (1995). Commentary and envoi. In F. R. Schab & R. G. Crowder (Eds.), *Memory for odors.* Mahwah, NJ: Erlbaum.

Jevons, W. S. (1871). The power of numerical discrimination. *Nature, 3,* 281–282.

Lawless, H. T., & Engen, T. (1977). Associations to odors: Interference, mnemonics, and verbal labeling. *Journal of Experimental Psychology: Human Learning and Memory, 3,* 52–59.

LeCompte, D. C. (1992). In search of a strong visual recency effect. *Memory & Cognition, 20,* 563–572.

Lyman, B. J., & McDaniel, M. A. (1990). Memory for odors and odor names: Modalities of elaboration and imagery. *Journal of Experimental Psychology: Learning, Memory, and Cognition, 16,* 656–664.

Mair, R. G., Harrison, L. M., & Flint, D. L. (1995). The neuropsychology of odor memory. In F. R. Schab & R. G. Crowder (Eds.), *Memory for Odors.* Mahwah, NJ: Erlbaum.

Manning, S. K.,. Koehler, L, & Hampton, S. (1990). The effects of recoding and presentation format on recency and suffix effects. *Memory & Cognition, 18,* 164–173.

Massaro, D. W., & Loftus, G. R. (1996). Sensory and perceptual store. In E. L. Bjork & R. A. Bjork (Eds.), *Memory.* San Diego, CA: Academic Press.

Merikle, P. M. (1980). Selection from visual persistence by perceptual groups and category membership. *Journal of Experimental Psychology: General, 109,* 279–295.

Mewhort, D. J. K., Campbell, A. J., Marchetti, F. M., & Campbell, J. I. D. (1981). Identification, localization, and "iconic" memory: An evaluation of the bar-probe task. *Memory & Cognition, 9,* 50–67.

Mewhort, D. J. K., & Leppman, K. P. (1985). Information persistence: Testing spatial and identity information with a voice probe. *Psychological Research, 47,* 51–58.

Morton, J., Crowder, R. G., & Prussin, H. A. (1971). Experiments with the stimulus suffix effect. *Journal of Experimental Psychology Monograph, 91,* 169–190.

Morton, J., & Holloway, C. M. (1970). Absence of a cross-modal "suffix effect" in short-term memory. *Quarterly Journal of Experimental Psychology, 22,* 167–176.

Murray, D. J. (1966). Vocalization-at-presentation and immediate recall with varying recall methods. *Quarterly Journal of Experimental Psychology, 18,* 9–18.

Nairne, J. S. (1988). A framework for interpreting recency effects in immediate serial recall. *Memory & Cognition, 16,* 343–352.

Nairne, J. S. (1990). A feature model of immediate memory. *Memory & Cognition, 18,* 251–269.

Nairne, J. S., & Crowder, R. G. (1982). On the locus of the stimulus suffix effect. *Memory & Cognition, 10,* 350–357.

Nairne, J. S., & McNabb, W. K. (1985). More modality effects in the absence of sound. *Journal of Experimental Psychology: Learning, Memory and Cognition, 11,* 596–604.

Nairne, J. S., & Walters, V. L. (1983). Silent mouthing produces modality- and suffix-like effects. *Journal of Verbal Learning and Verbal Behavior, 22,* 475–483.

Neath, I., Surprenant, A. M., & Crowder, R. G. (1993). The context-dependent stimulus-suffix effect. *Journal of Experimental Psychology: Learning, Memory and Cognition, 19,* 698–703.

Neisser, U. (1967). *Cognitive Psychology.* New York: Appleton-Century-Crofts.

Penney, C. G. (1989). Modality effects and the structure of short-term verbal memory. *Memory & Cognition, 17,* 398–422.

Rabin, M. D., & Cain, W. S. (1984). Odor recognition: Familiarity, identifiability, and encoding consistency. *Journal of Experimental Psychology: Learning, Memory, and Cognition, 10,* 316–325.

Sakitt, B. (1976). Iconic memory. *Psychological Review, 83,* 257–276.

Sakitt, B., & Long, G. M. (1979). Spare the rod and spoil the icon. *Journal of Experimental Psychology: Human Perception and Performance, 5,* 19–30.

Schab, F. R., & Crowder, R. G. (1995). Odor recognition memory. In F. R. Schab & R. G. Crowder (Eds.), *Memory for odors.* Mahwah, NJ: Erlbaum.

Schilling, R. F., & Weaver, G. E. (1983). Effect of extraneous verbal information on memory for telephone numbers. *Journal of Applied Psychology, 68,* 559–564.

Shand, M. A., & Klima, E. S. (1981). Nonauditory suffix effects in congenitally deaf signers of American sign language. *Journal of Experimental Psychology: Human Learning and Memory, 7,* 464–474.

Sperling, G. (1960). The information available in brief visual presentations. *Psychological Monographs, 74* (Whole No. 11).

Sperling, G. (1967). Successive approximations to a model for short-term memory. *Acta Psychologica, 27,* 285–292.

Spoehr, K. T., & Corin, W. J. (1978). The stimulus suffix effect as a memory coding phenomenon. *Memory & Cognition, 6,* 583–589.

Surprenant, A. M., LeCompte, D. C., & Neath, I. (1997). Manipulations of irrelevant information: Suffix effects with articulatory suppression and irrelevant speech. Unpublished manuscript.

Surprenant, A. M., & Neath, I. (1996). The relation between discriminability and memory for vowels, consonants, and silent-center syllables. *Memory & Cognition, 24,* 356–366.

Treisman, A. M., & Gelade, G. (1980). A feature integration theory of attention. *Cognitive Psychology, 12,* 97–136.

Turvey, M. T. (1973). On peripheral and central processes in vision: Inferences from an information-processing analysis of masking with patterned stimuli. *Psychological Review, 22,* 142–147.

Underwood, B. J. (1957). Interference and forgetting. *Psychological Review, 64,* 49–60.

Washburn, M. F. (1916). *Movement and mental imagery.* Boston: Houghton Mifflin.

Watkins, M. J., & Sechler, E. S. (1989). Adapting to an irrelevant item in an immediate recall task. *Memory & Cognition, 17,* 682–692.

Watkins, M. J., & Watkins, O. C. (1974). A tactile suffix effect. *Memory & Cognition, 2,* 176–180.

Yeomans, J. M., & Irwin, D. E. (1985). Stimulus duration and partial report performance. *Perception & Psychophysics, 37,* 163–169.

# CHAPTER FOUR

# The Modal Model

*"There seems to be a presence-chamber in my mind where full consciousness holds court, and where two or three ideas are at the same time in audience, and an ante-chamber full of more or less allied ideas, which is situated just beyond the full ken of consciousness. Out of this ante-chamber the ideas most readily allied to those in the presence-chamber appear to be summoned in a mechanically logical way and to have their turn of audience."*

—*Sir Francis Galton (1883)*

## Primary Memory

The publication of Broadbent's *Perception and Communication* in 1958 and of the papers by Miller (1956), Brown (1958), and Peterson and Peterson (1959) mark the beginning of the modern history of viewing primary memory as a specialized store for briefly holding information. However, the idea of viewing memory as comprising multiple systems, one of which holds information for a brief period of time, goes back to the 19th century and even earlier (Burnham, 1888).

Memory had often been divided into multiple memory systems; for example, Burnham (1888, p. 575) documents forerunners of both iconic and echoic memory. Short-term store (STS) was based on what Exner called *primary memory* and Richet called *elementary memory* (Burnham, 1888). Although William James is usually given credit for coining the term *primary memory*, it was in fact Sigmund Exner (1846–1926), a physiological psychologist at Vienna, to whom James gives credit (James, 1890, p. 600). Exner's contribution was published in Ludimar Hermann's *Handbuch der Physiologie* in 1879 in Leipzig.

James (1890) distinguished *primary memory* from *memory proper,* tracing the concept back to Wilhelm Wundt's work on *Umfang.* This German term is difficult to translate precisely as there is no real English equivalent, but it implies a kind of immediate consciousness of that which is still present. James (1890) elaborates:

> The objects we feel in this directly intuited past differ from properly recollected objects. An object which is recollected, in the proper sense of the term, is one which has been absent from consciousness altogether, and now revives anew. . . . But an object of primary memory is not

thus brought back; it never was lost; its date was never cut off in consciousness from that of the immediately present moment. In fact, it comes to us as belonging to the rearward portion of the present space of time, and not to the genuine past. (pp. 608–609)

Short-term store (STS) of the late 1950s and early 1960s was a combination of the idea of primary memory with the computer metaphor of memory: it was of limited capacity, very short duration, primarily verbal in nature, and intended mainly as a buffer where information could be temporarily stored. And just as a computer memory "forgets" when the power is turned off, so too does STS "forget" when the maintenance process—rehearsal—is prevented. This view became so prevalent so quickly that, by 1963, Melton devoted a paper to discussing "whether single-repetition, short-term memory and multiple-repetition, long-term memory are a dichotomy or points on a continuum" (p. 3). Melton's cogent arguments against multiple stores notwithstanding, the ensuing two-store conception of memory reached its most explicit form with the papers by Waugh and Norman (1965), Atkinson and Shiffrin (1968), and Glanzer (1972) and the volume edited by Norman (1970). The resultant *modal model,* so termed by Murdock (1974), became the dominating, albeit not unanimous, view of memory. In this chapter, we will concentrate on the various forms this model took.

## Broadbent's Model

The most influential of the early approaches to primary memory was that of Donald Broadbent (1958). He characterized the human processor as a series of systems through which information flows, much as it does in electronic and communication systems. Information from the environment is received through the senses and is held temporarily in a preattentive sensory store (the S-system), the forerunner of iconic and echoic memory. From the S-system, information is filtered and arrives in a limited capacity store, the P-system. The P-system is the site of conscious awareness, and for Broadbent the combination of the S- and P-systems constituted immediate or primary memory. Note how these systems were foreshadowed by Galton (1883), as indicated by the opening quotation for this chapter. For information to remain in primary memory, it had to be rehearsed; without rehearsal, information was assumed to fade. Secondary or long-term memory was believed to be a third, more permanent memory system, and it was thought that information passes through primary memory on its way to more or less permanent storage. Three assumptions of Broadbent's view were retained by almost all subsequent models: (1) primary and secondary memory involve separate memory systems; (2) primary memory has a limited capacity; and (3) because information fades quickly in primary memory, information is retained only when it is actively rehearsed.

Recall that Sperling (1960) suggested that information in iconic memory needed to be recoded if it were to be maintained. Rather than store information in a form identical to its actual physical features, as sensory memory systems do, primary memory stores information in a speechlike code. Two early experiments by Conrad (1964) and Wickelgren (1965) quickly established that the main code in primary memory was an acoustic one. For example, Conrad (1964) presented subjects with lists of letters, some that looked the same but sounded quite different (such as V and X) and others that looked

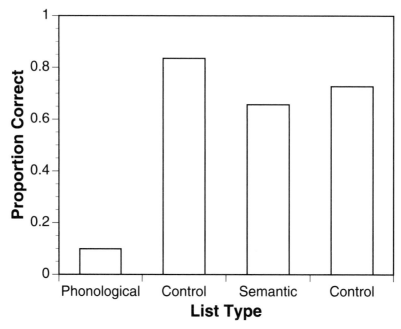

**Figure 4.1** Proportion of words correctly recalled as a function of list type. Source: Baddeley (1966).

quite different but sounded almost identical (such as V and C). Some subjects read the letters silently, and others heard the letters pronounced aloud. Surprisingly, Conrad found that regardless of whether the subjects had seen or heard the letters, any errors that were made tended to be based on acoustic similarity rather than on visual similarity. Both he and Wickelgren (1965) argued that the main code in primary memory is acoustic, suggesting that subjects are remembering the sound of the to-be-remembered items using some form of inner speech.

Baddeley (1966) found similar results. He presented subjects with four types of lists. In the phonologically similar list, the words sounded very similar, such as *man, mad, cap, can,* and *map.* The control1 list had words of similar frequency but different sounds: *pen, rig, day, bar,* and *sup.* In the semantically similar list, the words all meant the same thing: *big, huge, broad, long,* and *tall.* The control2 list was *old, late, thin, wet,* and *hot.* The results of the study are shown in Figure 4.1. Similarity of meaning had very little effect, but similarity of sound resulted in very poor performance. These results are entirely consistent with other studies that show that in primary memory the dominant code appears to be acoustic, a form of inner speech.

One way of testing the idea that information in primary memory utilizes inner speech is to prevent the subjects from subvocally rehearsing the items. If this is done successfully, the errors should no longer be based on acoustic similarity. Murray (1967) was the first to use a procedure known as *articulatory suppression* to prevent subvocal rehearsal. Throughout the presentation of the list items, the subject is required to say the word *the* over and over, out loud. Subjects were able to recall about two-thirds of the items that they had seen correctly, but the errors they made were now different. Without articulatory suppression, subjects were more likely to incorrectly recall an item that sounded like the target item than would be expected by chance alone. With articulatory suppression, this was no longer the case. Errors were not more likely to be acoustically similar items; they were also not more likely to be visually similar items. Although the mode of representing the information under conditions of articulatory suppression was not known, it was known that it was not visual.

Despite the observation that most people use a speech code to represent information in primary memory, this is neither a universal nor an obligatory code. Conrad (1972; see also Cowan, Cartwright, Winterowd, & Sherk, 1987; Locke & Fehr, 1970) demonstrated that young children do not show the same patterns of acoustic errors until they are around 5 or 6 years old. Even then, it takes several more years before their performance shows the same error pattern as that of adults.

The capacity of primary memory was a key question that many researchers attempted to address. The title of George Miller's (1956) paper began with the now famous phrase, "The magic number seven, plus or minus two," which reflects the most common estimates on the limitations of information processing. Miller (1956) arrived at this estimate after examining data from a variety of different paradigms, and he began the article with a parody of Senator Joseph McCarthy:

> My problem is that I have been persecuted by an integer. For seven years this number has followed me around, has intruded in my most private data, and has assaulted me from the pages of our most public journals. This number assumes a variety of disguises, being sometimes a little larger and sometimes a little smaller than usual, but never changing so much as to be unrecognizable. The persistence with which this number plagues me is far more than a random accident. There is, to quote a famous senator, a design behind it, some pattern governing its appearances. Either there really is something unusual about the number or else I am suffering from delusions of persecution. (p. 81)

Miller described the results from a number of different paradigms, all of which seemed to converge on the idea of a central limitation on people's ability to process information. His first topic concerns a finding that rarely fails to provoke disbelief: people are unable to learn to identify a set of items that vary along only one dimension if there are more than a few items. For example, in an absolute identification experiment, a subject might hear a set of nine tones that vary only in frequency. On each trial, one of these tones is played for the subject, who then tries to identify it. The subject is informed whether the response is correct and, if not, what the correct response should have been. The results of such an experiment are shown in Figure 4.2. The highest and lowest frequency tones are identified quite well (around 65% correct), but the closer to the middle of the set, the worse the performance. Generally speaking, once the number of items reaches about 8 or 9, subjects become unable to perform the task without errors; interestingly, errors persist regardless of the range and practice (Pollack, 1952, 1953; Shiffrin & Nosofsky, 1993).

When stimuli vary along more than one dimension, identification is much better. For example, most people can easily identify the 26 letters of the alphabet, even when they are handwritten. Because the letters vary along multiple dimensions, they are easier to discriminate from one another. When there is only one dimension involved — regardless of

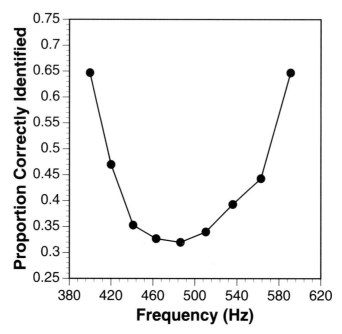

**Figure 4.2**   Proportion of times a particular tone was correctly identified using the method of absolute judgment.   Source: Neath & Knoedler (1997).

whether that dimension is frequency, length, height, or intensity—subjects will not be able to perform accurately once the number of items exceeds about 7.

A second topic that Miller discussed was the limitations of memory span. In 1887, Joseph Jacobs published a paper discussing his interest in measuring his students' mental capacity. His measure, known as the *memory span,* was defined as the number of items (usually digits) that can be repeated immediately in order 50% of the time. When this measure is used, the span is typically the same number that haunted Miller: 7, plus or minus 2. More specifically, 90% of the adult population is able to recall at least 5 items in order but not more than 8 (Matarazzo, 1972).

A third topic concerned the idea of a chunk. Miller (1956) reported the results from a series of experiments that studied recoding. Information can be recoded into higher-order units, called *chunks,* and this can lead to an increase in capacity. Simon (1974) expanded on Miller's ideas of a chunk, demonstrating that the number of chunks that can be recalled is variable. As shown in Table 4.1, when the stimuli comprised 1-syllable items, the number of syllables recalled was 7, the number of words recalled was also 7, and the number of chunks was also 7. However, when the stimuli comprised 3-syllable items, the number of syllables recalled increased to 18, the number of words recalled dipped slightly, and the number of chunks recalled also dropped slightly. The best performance (in terms of maximum number of syllables and words recalled) came with 8-word phrases; the worst performance (in terms of the number of chunks) was also with 8-word phrases.

Table 4.1 Memory span expressed in chunks for different kinds of material, either 1-, 2-, or 3-syllable words or 2-or 8-word phrases.

| | | Span | | |
|---|---|---|---|---|
| Stimuli | Syllables | Words | Imputed Chunks | Syllables per Chunks |
| 1-Syllable | 7 | 7 | 7 | 1.0 |
| 2-Syllable | 14 | 7 | 7 | 2.0 |
| 3-Syllable | 18 | 6 | 6 | 3.0 |
| 2-Word | 22 | 9 | 4 | 5.5 |
| 8-Word | 26 | 22 | 3 | 8.7 |

Source: Simon (1974).

Thus, with an increase in the amount of information in the chunk, there was a decrease in the number of chunks that could be remembered. Although the capacity of short-term store was an important issue at that time, the answer to the question depended on both the measure and the type of stimuli used. The limit on how much information could be retained in short-term store, then, was *not* constant.

# The Brown-Peterson Paradigm

Peterson and Peterson (1959) reported an experiment that used a procedure similar to one used by Brown (1958). Their purpose was to investigate the rate at which information is lost or decays in STS. The general procedure, now known as the *Brown-Peterson paradigm,* is for the experimenter to read a consonant trigram to a subject (three consonants in a row, such as DBX) and then read a 3-digit number out loud. The number of items is substantially less than almost everybody's memory span. The subject's task was first to count backward by 3 (or 4) from the 3-digit number for a certain amount of time. At the end of this period, the subject was asked to recall the three consonants in order. The purpose of the counting backward was to prevent rehearsal while minimizing overt interference: the digits were sufficiently different from the letters that they should not interfere. Peterson and Peterson varied how long the subjects counted backward, including conditions of 3, 6, 9, 12, 15, and 18 seconds (s). The results are shown in Figure 4.3. What is most noteworthy is that after as little as 18 s of counting backward, subjects could recall only about 10% of the items.

These results, along with those reported by Murdock (1961), Hellyer (1962), and Fuchs and Melton (1974), were generally interpreted as demonstrating the very rapid decay of information in short-term memory when rehearsal is prevented. In Chapter 7, we shall see that much of the data from the Brown-Peterson paradigm is inconsistent with a decay interpretation (Capaldi & Neath, 1995); rather, the reduced performance is due to

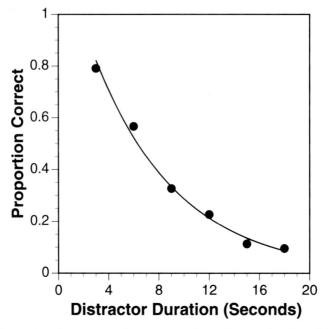

**Figure 4.3** Proportion of consonant trigrams correctly recalled as a function of the distractor task duration. Source: Peterson & Peterson (1959).

interference. Briefly, Keppel and Underwood (1962) demonstrated that if you examined performance on the very first trial of Brown-Peterson task, there was no difference in performance in the various delay conditions: it did not matter whether you had counted backward for 3 s or 18 s, performance was equal in the two conditions. At that time, however, less was known about the task, and so most researchers explained it in terms of decay from short-term store.

## Waugh and Norman's Model

To account for these and many other observations, many researchers divided memory into two structures. Of the many different versions, two particular models stand out as particularly influential. The first was the model developed by Waugh and Norman (1965), in which they specifically divided memory into *primary* and *secondary* memory, resurrecting the terms from James (1890). According to their model, perceived information first enters primary memory, a limited capacity structure. From primary memory, some information is lost by displacement, as newly arriving items "bump out" already existing items. Other information might be rehearsed and can thus remain in primary memory longer. Rehearsal also causes the information to be transferred to secondary memory, which has no capacity limitation. Recall can be based on information in either primary memory, secondary memory, or both.

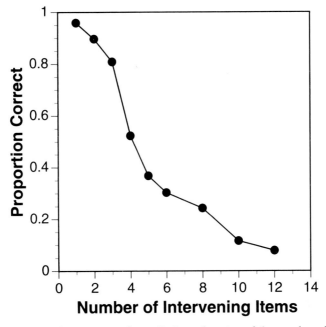

**Figure 4.4** Proportion of items correctly recalled as a function of the number of intervening items. The data plotted are averaged from the two presentation rates. Source: Waugh & Norman (1965).

According to the model, it should be possible to measure the capacity of primary memory. If items are continuously presented to a subject, there should be a point where primary memory is filled, and the new input displaces the old input. At this time, recall will be dependent solely on secondary memory for those items that have been displaced. If rehearsal is prevented, then at this point there should be no memory left for the items that were formerly in primary memory. Preventing rehearsal will ensure that the items are not refreshed in primary memory and are not transferred to secondary memory.

In one of their experiments, Waugh and Norman (1965) instructed subjects not to rehearse. To the extent that subjects followed these instructions, the items from primary memory should not be transferred to secondary memory. The researchers presented lists of 16 digits at a rate of either 1 digit per second or 4 digits per second. After all 16 items had been presented, a single item (a probe) was presented. The subject's task was to recall the digit that had followed the probe item in the original series. The results are replotted in Figure 4.4.

There was only a small and inconsistent effect of presentation rate; memory performance depended primarily on how many items had intervened between presentation and test. The farther back in the list the probe item was, the lower the probability of correctly recalling the next item. Waugh and Norman emphasized two key aspects of their data. First, there was a very sharp drop in performance after about 3 or 4 items. Second, the asymptote of the function approached 0. This means that after a large number of items intervened, the subjects could not recall the target item very accurately. This reinforced the idea that the instructions not to rehearse had been obeyed and that the digits had not been transferred to secondary memory. Waugh and Norman (1965) interpreted Peterson and Peterson's (1959) results as consistent with their view. The distracting activity would have displaced the information from primary memory, but what little rehearsal there was would have transferred some of the information to secondary memory. The approximately 10% recall after 18 seconds of distracting activity would reflect the secondary memory component in the Brown-Peterson task.

# Atkinson and Shiffrin's Dual-Store Model

The second model was developed in a series of papers by Richard Atkinson and Richard Shiffrin. Atkinson and Shiffrin (1968) distinguished between *structural* and *processing* components of memory. The structure is thought to be those parts of the memory system that do not change, whereas the control processes are thought to be flexible and under a person's control. Although often used as an example of a dual-store model, there are actually three structural components of memory. The first structures are the *sensory registers,* one for each modality. Visual information would enter a visual sensory register, auditory information would enter an auditory sensory register, and haptic (touch) information would enter a haptic sensory register. Atkinson and Shiffrin based their description of the visual sensory register on the work of Sperling, as described in Chapter 3. Relatively little was known then about the auditory sensory register, but as the model was developed, it took on the properties of echoic memory.

Short-term store (STS) closely resembles Broadbent's P-system. It is of limited capacity, very short duration, and intended mainly as a buffer where information could be temporarily stored. Long-term store (LTS), in contrast, is a permanent, unlimited capacity store. This is where all enduring memories are stored, including knowledge, personal history, and anything else that one remembers. All information eventually is completely lost from the sensory registers and the short-term store, whereas information in the long-term store is relatively permanent (although it may be modified or rendered temporarily irretrievable as the result of other incoming information).

All information entering LTS has to go through STS, and whenever an item is retrieved from LTS it again has to enter STS. It is important to note that information is not really transferred, for that implies that the original copy is lost. Rather, information is copied from one store to the other, leaving the original item in place. (Actually, the analogy of faxing is quite useful: usually a copy arrives at the destination, and most of the time it is legible. Some faxes do not "go through," however, and some of the information that arrives might not be readable.)

The emphasis of the Atkinson and Shiffrin (1968) model is on the control processes that manipulate the flow of information, and the flow of information is to a large extent under the subject's control. Control processes are "selected, constructed, and used at the option of the subject" and can be "readily modified or reprogrammed at the will of the subject" (Atkinson & Shiffrin, 1968, p. 90). Of the various control processes, the most important are rehearsal, coding, and retrieval. *Rehearsal* is necessary to preserve information in STS and copy it to LTS. The type of *coding*—what aspects of the information are registered—can determine what kinds of information will be remembered and what other information will be associated with it. *Retrieval* is most important for getting information from LTS, but the problem is more complicated than it might first appear. How does the retrieval process know what to look for, and how does it determine when to stop searching? Humans are particularly adept at knowing that they do not know something, and it is obvious that they are not performing an exhaustive search. (We will examine the retrieval process in Chapter 12.)

To make these issues a little more clear, let us follow a word through various stages of processing. A subject hears the word *cow* simultaneously spoken and presented visually on a computer screen. The physical properties of each stimulus will be represented in the respective sensory stores: the shape of the letters in iconic memory, and the sound of the word in echoic memory. Control processes in each sensory store determine which portions of the information get transferred to STS. It could be the fact that an uppercase *C* was presented, or the whole word *cow*, or the sound of the word, or the gender of the voice that presented it, or the color of the word, or the background noise that accompanied the word, or any other similar information. Let's assume that it was the sound of the word that was transferred, so that now STS contains acoustic information that defines the word *cow*.

Rehearsal could be simple rote—merely repeating the sound—or it could be elaborative, focusing on the meaning of the word, on the image of a cow, of things associated with cows, of a distant memory of cow tipping, and so on. Such associates (for example, the word *milk*, the sound of "moo," the image of a dairy cow) are copied from LTS to STS. STS, then, can store information in a variety of codes—visual, acoustic, verbal, and so on. Rehearsal is under the control of the subject, and, to a certain extent, so are the coding options. There is normally a preference for one kind of coding for a particular type of stimulus, but there is also great flexibility.

Atkinson and Shiffrin (1968) justified the division of memory into separate stores by citing several lines of converging evidence. First, they cited the papers by Miller, Broadbent, and Peterson and Peterson. They were aware of the Keppel and Underwood (1962) paper ascribing performance in the Brown-Peterson task to interference (discussed in Chapter 7), but Atkinson and Shiffrin suggested an alternative explanation. They noted that subjects in a Brown-Peterson experiment can devote attention to the to-be-remembered item for only a brief period of time before they have to begin counting backward. During this brief period, some of the information will get transferred to LTS. This explanation is supported by the observation that even after 18 s of counting backward, performance was not at 0; rather, subjects were recalling about 10% of the information. Interference occurs not in STS, according to this account, but in the search of LTS. Because of the interference in LTS, performance is determined almost entirely by STS.

Atkinson and Shiffrin (1968) assumed that the memory trace was composed of a multicomponent array consisting of a number of pieces of information, possibly redundant, correlated, or even in error. The traces do decay, but the decay rate can be affected by control processes. This would explain why sometimes presentation rate does not affect estimates of decay (e.g., Waugh & Norman, 1965) and sometimes it does (e.g., Conrad & Hille, 1958).

For simplicity, Atkinson and Shiffrin focused most on the auditory-verbal-linguistic, or a-v-l, aspect of both STS and LTS. They acknowledged that other forms of information can be represented in both STS and LTS, but most work at that time had explored memory for verbal stimuli. The reason for the three terms was that it became impossible to determine whether the format were acoustic, articulatory, or some other similar form (for example, Conrad, 1964; Hintzman, 1967).

Information can be transferred from STS to LTS via rehearsal. Again, the term *transfer* is actually a little misleading because it implies that the original information is actually moved. Rather, Atkinson, and Shiffrin meant that a copy was made in LTS. Although transfer was seen as an unvarying feature of the system, the amount and form of transfer could be affected by the particular control processes used. Most important, they assumed that transfer began and continued during the entire time an item was in STS.

The reason for assuming that transfer occurs throughout the time that an item resides in STS was the finding that learning takes place even when the subject is not trying to remember the material. For example, Hebb (1961) presented a series of 9-item lists to 40 subjects. The lists were made up of the digits 1–9, presented in random order, and the task was to recall the items in order. Most of the lists contained novel orderings, but one list was repeated every third trial. For example, a particular subject would see the exact same list on trials 3, 6, 9, 12, and so on until trial 24. The results, shown in Figure 4.5, have been replicated by Melton (1963) and more recently by McKelvie (1987). Even when those subjects who did notice the repetition were dropped from the analysis, the effect of repetition was still present. The key finding is that simple repetition of an item, even if the subjects are unaware of the repetition, leads to better performance.

Mechanic (1964) found similar results, but in a different paradigm. According to Atkinson and Shiffrin, performance on the repeated series improved because each time the items in the series were encountered, some of the information was transferred to LTS. The amount of transfer can vary with the task, and — at least in this paradigm — several repetitions were required before there was a meaningful difference between the repeated and novel series.

We will discuss LTS in more detail later (see Chapter 12); for now, we will just sketch out the basic features. There is no universal, unchanging process of transfer. Most likely, the transfer process results in multiple copies of the original item, each of which can be either partial or complete. The reason for this assumption were results like those of Brown and McNeill (1966) concerning the "tip of the tongue" phenomenon. This is the situation that occurs when you cannot recall a specific piece of information, but you can provide some correct information (such as the first letter or the number of syllables) and you can accurately predict whether or not you would recognize the correct answer. According to Atkinson and Shiffrin, the reason for this situation is that you have accessed a partial trace rather than a complete trace. Some of the information is correct, but there is not enough to allow successful recall. When presented with the correct answer, another retrieval attempt is made, this time with more information, and so a complete trace is likely to be found.

There are two main control processes in STS, retrieval and rehearsal. Although many theorists do not say much about retrieval from STS, Atkinson and Shiffrin emphasized the highly specialized nature of these processes. Because of decay, any retrieval process

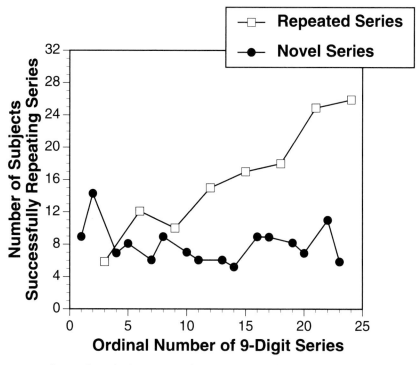

**Figure 4.5** The number of subjects, out of 40, who successfully recalled a 9-digit series as a function of the position of the 9-digit series within a set of 24 trials. The repeated series was the same 9-item list repeated every third trial. Source: Hebb (1961).

must be both very fast and highly efficient. The most likely candidate came from the work of Saul Sternberg, S. (1966). He presented subjects with a short list of items, such as 2, 5, 3, 8, which was followed by a test item, called the *probe*. A positive probe is an item that occurred in the list (such as 5 in the current example); a negative probe is an item that did not occur. Sternberg measured how long it took subjects to say that the probe item did or did not occur, and the results are shown in Figure 4.6.

Two features of the data are noteworthy. First, the addition of an extra item in the search set results in a consistent increase in reaction time of about 40 ms. Second, the data from the positive and negative probes are almost identical. The equation of the best-fitting straight line was $RT = 397 + 38\,n$, where $n$ is the number of items in the search set. This can be interpreted as saying that the basic task took approximately 400 ms to perform, with an additional 40 ms to compare each item. Similar results were found for nonverbal stimuli.

Sternberg interpreted these data as supporting an *exhaustive serial scanning model*. For a negative probe, this makes sense. The probe is compared with each item in the search set, one at a time (hence *serial*). Because the probe did not occur, the search must involve comparisons with every list item (hence *exhaustive*). But the same is true when the probe

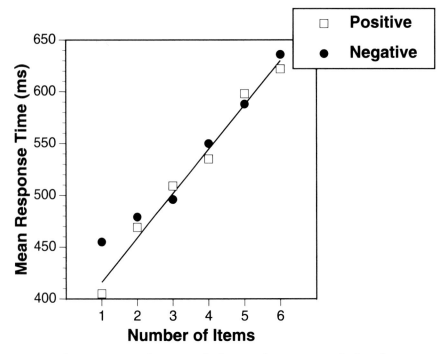

**Figure 4.6**   The mean time to determine whether a probe item was in the list of items (positive probe) or was not in the original list (negative probe) as a function of the number of items in the list.   Source: Sternberg (1966).

is positive. Although this may not sound very plausible, remember that we are dealing with STS, and any operation must be fast and efficient. Sternberg suggested that in order to keep the search fast, an *automatic process* is used. Once started, an automatic process must continue until completion; however, other processes can operate at the same time. Sternberg's idea is that the matching process is automatic, and, once a match is found, some note of this is made. At the end of the search, the subject examines the marker, and if it is positive, the subject presses the "yes" button; if negative, the subject presses the "no" button. Although consistent with the Atkinson and Shiffrin (1968) model, subsequent research has found the situation to be far more complex, and the simple serial exhaustive search interpretation is no longer tenable (see Van Zandt & Townsend, 1993).

The other major control process in STS is rehearsal. For the a-v-l part of STS, rehearsal was assumed to be like saying the items over and over. In certain situations, rehearsal can set up a buffer in which this rehearsal process is optimized. The buffer can be thought of as a bin that has a certain number of slots; each new item enters the rehearsal buffer and, if the buffer is already full, knocks out an item that is already there. Whether an item enters the rehearsal buffer is up to the subject, who directs the rehearsal process. There are two possibilities for determining which items get bumped. One is a method based on the duration of the item in STS, with the oldest item getting bumped first. The second is a random method, where an item in STS is randomly selected to be bumped. The rehearsal process will be discussed in more detail in later chapters.

Many theorists proposed models similar to those of Waugh and Norman (1965) and Atkinson and Shiffrin (1968), some offering only slight modifications and others adding extra systems; however, almost all shared the same basic structures and processes. This general view became the dominant framework and was termed the *modal model* after the statistical measure *mode* (Murdock, 1974). The mode is a measure of central tendency and is the value from a distribution of values that occurs most frequently. Many examples of similar models can be seen in the volume edited by Norman (1970), and the paper by Glanzer (1972) critically reviews much of the evidence that supports this general conception.

Even though the models have been presented as verbal theories, one version of the Atkinson and Shiffrin (1968) model was a formal, mathematical model that made specific predictions for many different paradigms. For example, assume that it takes 1.1 s for an item in STS to decay such that it can no longer be identified. Let's further assume that it takes 0.25 s to rehearse or refresh an item and that only one item can be rehearsed at a time. (These numbers, although somewhat arbitrary, are nonetheless plausible.) The result is that no more than five items could be consistently maintained in STS without information loss. Another set of assumptions concerned the probability that an item in STS will get successfully copied into LTS. This probability is determined by the duration and the quality of the rehearsal. The final assumptions concerned the probability that an item could be recalled. Among the parameters were ones for guessing, for the buffer size (how many items could be maintained in STS), the probability of entering the buffer, the transfer rate from STS to LTS, and the decay rate of information in STS. The result was an equation that, when the parameters were estimated, could be used to make precise predictions about how much information could be recalled in a variety of situations (see Atkinson & Shiffrin 1968, p. 129).

Note that whereas the Atkinson and Shiffrin (1968) version of the modal model was very precise, many other versions were far more vague and usually contained just the briefest description of how STS and LTS interacted. Indeed, many ignored some of the issues that Atkinson and Shiffrin considered and discussed at great length.

# The Serial Position Curve and the Modal Model

Many experiments that tested predictions of the modal model concerned the serial position function observable with free recall. When we examined the modality effect in Chapter 3, we saw that serial recall produced serial position curves. Free recall leads to similar looking curves, but there are two important differences. First, as can be seen in Figure 4.7, the recency effect seen in free recall is generally more pronounced relative to the primacy effect. Second, the recency effect in free recall can be observed with both auditory and visual presentation.

Kirkpatrick (1894) introduced the method of free recall, noting that few students "gave the words in order, and it was quite noticeable that the first and last words were less frequently omitted than any others" (p. 606). Because free recall is really unconstrained

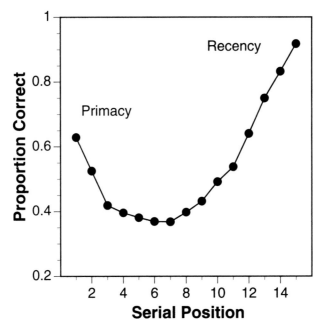

**Figure 4.7**   An idealized serial position curve showing the proportion of items correctly recalled in any order (free recall) as a function of input position.

recall, it is quite likely that different subjects are using different strategies; after all, the instructions just say, "Recall the items." Nonetheless, the various models that differentiated short-term from long-term store (e.g., Atkinson & Shiffrin, 1968; Glanzer, 1972; Waugh & Norman, 1965) not only explained the basic serial position effect but also made many predictions that were subsequently verified.

According to the modal model, primacy is due to the extra rehearsal the first few items get, which transfers them to LTS, and recency is due to the dumping of items from STS. For example, when the first item in a list is presented, subjects can devote 100% of their rehearsal to this item; when the second item is presented, subjects can devote only 50% of their rehearsal to this item. Because the first item is rehearsed more, it has a greater probability of being transferred to LTS. A strong prediction of the model, then, is that if the number of rehearsals per item can be measured, they will decline as more and more items are presented.

Rundus and Atkinson (1970) demonstrated this relationship by adopting a procedure that allowed them to measure the number of times an item was rehearsed. Subjects were told that they could rehearse whichever items they wanted to, but they must do it out loud. The subjects saw lists of 20 common nouns, and each word was presented for 5 seconds. The results, shown in Figure 4.8, show the predicted relationship between the number of rehearsals (shown on the right y-axis) and the proportion correctly recalled (shown on the

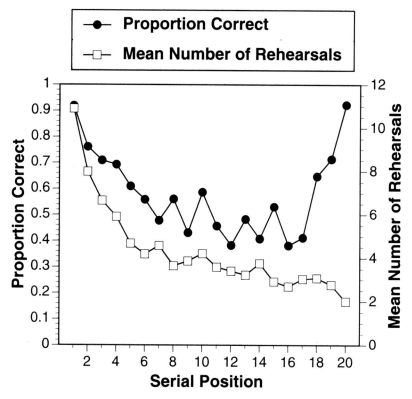

**Figure 4.8** The proportion of items correctly recalled as a function of its serial position and the mean number of rehearsals devoted to each item at each serial position. Source: Rundus & Atkinson (1970).

left y-axis). Early items received the most rehearsals and were recalled very well—the primacy effect. Items at the end of the list were also recalled well—the recency effect—but they had relatively few rehearsals. This finding is consistent with the modal model's claim that primacy is due to rehearsal and recency is due to dumping from short-term store. The middle items are not recalled well, but they also do not receive many rehearsals.

One might be concerned that the overt rehearsal procedure could introduce a confound: overt rehearsal might place extra demands on the cognitive system, altering the number of items that can be remembered. Although an appropriate concern, it does not seem warranted; Murdock and Metcalfe (1978) directly compared memory when rehearsal was covert or overt and found few differences.

According to the modal model, the primacy effect results from extra rehearsals, which increase the probability of transferring information to long-term store, and the recency effect results from dumping from short-term store. Analysis of output order confirms that

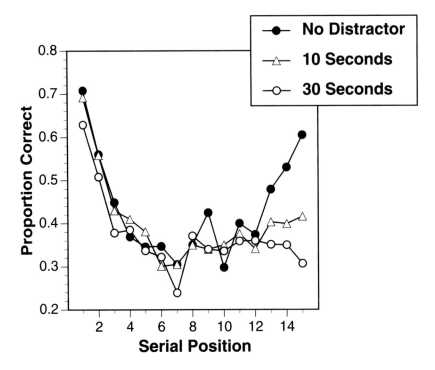

**Figure 4.9**   The proportion of items correctly recalled as a function of serial position in a free recall test when there is no distractor task, or when subjects are required to count backward for 10 or 30 seconds before recalling the items.   Source: Glanzer & Cunitz (1966).

the last few items are indeed recalled first (e.g., Welch & Burnett, 1924). A strong prediction of the model, then, is that if recall is delayed, the primacy effect should remain unaltered but the recency effect should disappear. Primacy will remain because once an item is in long-term store, it can be recalled after long delays. Recency will be eliminated because the items are not in long-term store, and items in short-term store cannot be retained for long.

To test this prediction, Glanzer and Cunitz (1966; see also Postman & Phillips, 1965) presented 15-item lists to subjects. In the control condition, subjects immediately recalled as many of the words as they could. In the other two conditions, subjects engaged in a distractor activity (counting backward) for either 10 or 30 seconds before recalling the items. The results are shown in Figure 4.9.

The control group showed the typical serial position function. Subjects in the two distractor groups recalled the same number of items as the control subjects but with one important exception: the longer they had to wait until recall, the fewer items from the end of the list were recalled. According to the modal model, this is because counting backward fills up short-term store with the numbers, and so the words are not available for output at the time of recall. The more numbers that are processed in short-term store, the less

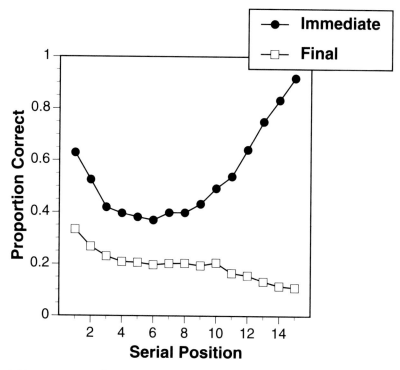

**Figure 4.10** Proportion of items correctly recalled on ten immediate tests (averaged together), and proportion of items correctly recalled from these lists on a surprise final free recall test as a function of serial position.   Source: Craik (1970).

chance there will be that a to-be-remembered item survives. Recall was not affected for earlier parts of the list because those items were recalled from long-term store.

Craik (1970) tested this idea in a different way. He presented subjects with 10 lists, each with 15 different words, and each list was followed by a free recall test. After recall of the 10th list, Craik surprised his subjects by asking them to recall all the words from all the lists. The idea is that after so much time has passed, this final free recall test would tap only long-term store. The results are shown in Figure 4.10.

As predicted by the modal model, recall of items that had occurred in the final positions of each of the ten lists were recalled worse than any other items, a so-called negative recency effect. Items that are recalled from long-term store are recalled better than those that were initially recalled from short-term store. (Craik had a different explanation, based on levels of processing, which we will consider in a later chapter.)

Another prediction is that a recency effect should be observed regardless of the length of the list. Murdock (1962) presented lists of either 20, 30, or 40 items for immediate free recall. The experimenter read each item aloud, and the items were presented at a rate of 1 item per s. Subjects had 90 s to write their responses, after which the next list began. For each list, there was a recency effect of approximately 7 items, with recall of the final item almost exactly the same in the three conditions. Between the primacy and recency portions of the curve, the recall was flat. Murdock (1962, p. 485) concluded that the recency effect "appears to be essentially independent of list length" (see also Postman & Phillips, 1965).

## Problems with the Modal Model

In the typical free recall experiment, subjects receive 12 or so list items and then recall those items immediately; a recency effect is typically observed. Glanzer and Cunitz (1966) added 30 seconds of distractor activity at the end of the list, and this eliminated the recency effect. Bjork and Whitten (1974) added distractor activity after *every* item in the list, including the final item. A word is shown, and then the subject performs a task that involves processing sufficient information to fill STS and that is sufficiently difficult that all of the subject's resources are diverted from rehearsal and to solving the task. Then the second word is shown, followed by another period of distracting activity. This is known as the *continual distractor task* because the subjects are continually distracted from rehearsing the to-be-remembered items. With this procedure, the recency effect reappeared. This finding has been replicated numerous times (e.g., Baddeley & Hitch, 1974, 1977; Glenberg, Bradley, Kraus, & Renzaglia, 1983; Tzeng, 1973).

An experiment reported by Watkins, Neath, and Sechler (1989) illustrates the essentials. They presented a 12-item list of words to subjects for free recall. After every word, the subjects heard the digits 1 through 9 presented one at a time in random order, and they had to recall the order of presentation of the digits. Thus, the subjects heard a word, then heard and recalled 9 digits in order, then heard the second item, then heard and recalled 9 digits in order, and so on throughout the list. The results are shown in Figure 4.11. The most important finding is that when distracting activity occurs after every item, including the final item, there is a substantial recency effect. Recall of the digits also showed a recency effect.

Recall that when Glanzer and Cunitz (1966) added distractor activity at the end of the list, the recency effect was eliminated. The explanation was that the distractor task removed the recency items from short-term store. When distractor activity occurs after every item, including the final item, the recency effect is again observed, even though the to-be-remembered list items should have been removed from short-term memory by the distractor task. These types of results led Bjork and Whitten (1974) to conclude that "the customary two-process theoretical account of immediate free recall is certainly incomplete, if not wrong" (p. 189).

Two recent studies have examined the effects of the distractor task in more detail. Koppenaal and Glanzer (1990) examined the effect of using more than one kind of distractor task. The arithmetic distractor task required that subjects read a 3-digit number from 100 to 999 out loud, add 1 to the number, and report the sum. The word distractor task required that subjects read six pairs of unrelated words out loud. One condition can be called *unchanging distractor* (subjects received either only the arithmetic task after every list item or only the word task after every list item), and the other condition can be called *changing distractor* (where the distractor task that followed the final list item was different from the distractor task that followed every other list item). Free recall in the unchanging distractor condition again yielded a recency effect, whereas recall in the changing distractor condition showed *no* recency effect.

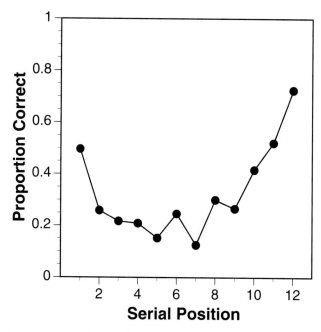

**Figure 4.11** The proportion of words freely recalled as a function of serial position in the continual distractor paradigm. Each word, including the final word, was followed by a distractor task in which the subject heard nine digits presented in random order and then recalled these items. Source: Watkins, Neath, & Sechler (1989).

---

**Experiment**    Recency Effects in Free Recall

**Purpose:**    To demonstrate the effect of distracting activity on the recency effect in free recall.

**Subjects:**    Thirty-six subjects are recommended; 12 should be assigned to the immediate condition, 12 to the delay condition, and 12 to the continual distractor condition. Subject 1 should be in the immediate condition, Subject 2 in the delay condition, Subject 3 in the continual distractor condition, Subject 4 in the immediate condition, and so on.

**Materials:**    Table C in the Appendix contains a list of 96 two-syllable words randomly drawn from the Toronto word pool. For each subject, construct 8 lists, each of which contains 12 words. Table B in the Appendix contains lists of the digits 1 through 9 in random order that will be used for the distractor task. Also prepare answer sheets with 8 rows of boxes or blanks in which the subject will write down the words. Subjects in the delay condition will need an answer sheet on which to write down the digits in order 8 times, and subjects in the continual distractor condition will need an answer sheet on which to write down the digits in order 96 times.

**Procedure:**    For the immediate group, read the list of 12 words to the subject at a rate of approximately 1 word every 2 s. At the end of the list, have the subject recall as many of the words as possible by writing them down, in any order, on the prepared answer

(continued on next page)

---

**Experiment**   Recency Effects in Free Recall (*continued*)

---

sheet. The only change for the delay group is to have the subjects engage in distractor activity after the final word and before recalling the words. Read a series of digits out loud at a rate of 1 digit per second and have the subjects recall the digits in order; then have the subjects recall the words. The only change for the continual distractor group is to have the subjects engage in distractor activity after every list item; thus, these subjects will hear and recall 12 lists of digits before recalling the words from that list.

**Instructions for the Immediate Group:**   "This experiment tests your ability to recall a list of words. I will read a list of 12 unrelated words, and as soon as the list is over, I would like you to write down as many words as you can remember. You can write down the words in any order, and it is better to guess than to leave a space blank. Any questions?"

**Instructions for the Delayed Group:**   "This experiment tests your ability to recall two different lists. I will read a list of 12 unrelated words, and then I'll read a list of the digits 1 through 9 in random order. I would like you to write down the digits in order on the first line on your answer sheet and then, when I indicate, write down the words. You can write down the words in any order, but you need to write down the digits in the original presentation order. It is better to guess than to leave a space blank. Any questions?"

**Instructions for the Continual Distractor Group:**   "This experiment tests your ability to recall two different lists. I will read a list of 12 unrelated words. After I read each word, I'll read a list of the digits 1 through 9 in random order. I would like you to write down the digits in order on the first line on your answer sheet. When you have finished, I will then read the second word on the list and then another list of digits. I will alternate reading a word and a list of digits until all 12 words have been read. At the end, I would like you to write down as many of the words as you can remember. You can write down the words in any order, but you need to write down the digits in the original presentation order. It is better to guess than to leave a space blank. Any questions?"

**Scoring and Analysis:**   For each list, count the number of times the first word was written down; it does not matter where the word was written down as long as it appeared on that list. This number will range from 0 to 8. Do the same for each of the other serial positions. Construct three serial position functions, one for each condition. To do this, add up the individual subject data, and divide by the number of subjects.

**Optional Enhancements:**   Score performance on the distractor task and plot recall as individual serial positions.

Source: Based on experiments by Glanzer & Cunitz (1966), Bjork & Whitten (1974), and Watkins, Neath, & Sechler (1989).

---

Koppenaal and Glanzer (1990) suggested that these results were consistent with the modal model. In a traditional continual distractor list, the subjects receive the same distractor task after every list item. Because of the extensive practice on the task, Koppenaal and Glanzer argued, subjects can learn to time-share, alternating their processing between rehearsing the list items to keep the last few in short-term memory and performing the distractor task. When the task changes, however, this disrupts the time-sharing mechanism, and the subjects can no longer perform both tasks adequately. Because an immediate response is demanded by the distractor task, the final words cannot be maintained in short-term memory and the recency effect is no longer observed.

This view makes at least three predictions. First, no changing distractor effect should be observable under incidental learning conditions. If subjects are unaware that there will be a recall test at the end of the list, there should be no reason for them to rehearse and keep the final items in short-term memory; nor should there be a need to develop the elaborate multitasking strategy. Without active rehearsal, the final list items should not be in short-term memory at the time of a surprise free recall test. Second, no changing distractor effect should be observable when the change in distractor activity occurs after the first list item. Koppenaal and Glanzer's (1990) account of the changing distractor effect hinges on the idea of rehearsal disruption: encountering a novel distractor task within a list disrupts a multitasking rehearsal strategy that permits the subject to both rehearse and perform the distractor task. When the first item is presented, the subject has no way of knowing whether the list is going to be in the changing or the unchanging condition; it is only when the second item and its distractor activity are presented that the subject knows whether the first item was followed by the different distractor task. However, even at this stage, it is not until the third item and its distractor task are presented that the subject knows which distractor task—the one after the first item or the one after the second item—is the unusual one. Performance should be identical in both the unchanging and changing conditions at position 1. Finally, if the distractor task changes after every list item, there should be no recency effect because there will have been no opportunity to develop the multitasking.

Neath (1993) tested these predictions. In Experiment 1, subjects were told that the experimenter was interested in what made people hesitate while reading aloud from a computer screen. Subjects were told that they would see three different kinds of stimuli that they should read as quickly and as clearly as they could. The stimuli were actually the same as those used by Koppenaal and Glanzer (1990), but subjects were unaware that a surprise recall test would occur. A surprise test was used so that it would be highly unlikely that the subjects would rehearse the list items. Each subject received only one list, and at the end of presentation subjects were asked to recall the words. Not only was there a recency effect in the unchanging distractor condition, there was a reliable changing distractor effect in the changing condition (see Figure 4.12). This result is problematic for Koppenaal and Glanzer's (1990) account because there should have been no information left in STS and thus no recency. And even if there were recency, there should be no effect of changing the distractor, because there was no rehearsal to disrupt.

A second experiment showed that recall is impaired for the first item if the first item is followed by the novel task. The effect is observable at any serial position.

In a final experiment, Neath (1993) again used an unchanging and a changing condition but also added a third condition in which a different distractor task occurred after every item—the continually changing condition. In this condition, each of the five list items was followed by a different distractor task. The rehearsal disruption account predicts a changing distractor effect at every serial position, and thus predicts no recency. However, there was a recency effect in the unchanging condition, no recency effect in the changing condition, and, contrary to the prediction of the rehearsal disruption account, there was also a recency effect in the continually changing condition. Thus, there is a recency

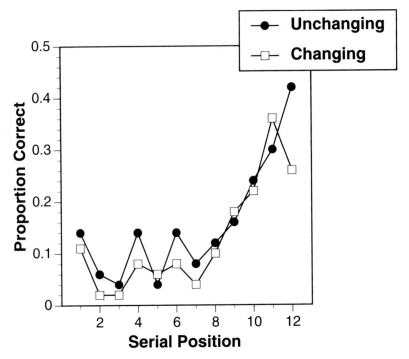

**Figure 4.12**   Mean number of words recalled in a surprise free recall test following incidental learning when the distractor task stays the same after every item (unchanging) and when there is a novel task after the final item (changing).   Source: Neath (1993).

effect for free recall of items when there is no distractor activity; the recency effect is eliminated when distractor activity follows just the final item; the recency effect returns when there is distractor activity after every item; the recency effect is again eliminated when the distractor task changes after the final item; and the recency effect again emerges when the distractor task changes after every item. These results are clearly problematic for any view that attributes recency to the dumping of items from short-term memory (see also Thapar & Greene, 1993).

## Additional Problems with the Modal Model

There are several other problems—some empirical and some logical—with most versions of the modal model. First, it is generally proposed within the modal model that whereas primary memory codes information on the basis of phonological or acoustic information, secondary memory codes items according to semantic information (Kintsch & Buschke, 1969). However, there is evidence of both acoustic interference in long-term memory (Dale & McGlaughlin, 1971) and semantic confusion errors in primary memory (Shulman, 1970, 1972).

Second, as Crowder (1976) pointed out, items in primary memory must be postcategorical because they already have their names. Because these names and other similar kinds of information presumably reside in secondary memory, there must have been some overlap. Although Atkinson and Shiffrin (1968) assume some contact of this sort, most versions do not. Unless information from sensory memory makes contact with long-term store prior to entry into short-term store, there will be no way of identifying or categorizing the information.

A third problem is related to the previous two. As Nairne (1996) points out, given the architecture of almost all versions of the modal model, there will always be contamination of one presumed store with the other. Information recalled from long-term memory has to pass through short-term memory on the way in and on the way out. Furthermore, information in primary memory has to be linked to information in secondary memory so that it can be identified and categorized in the first place. Any response from any task should reflect both stores, and, because of this inherent contamination, it would seem impossible to separate the types of codes.

The final problem concerns a variety of empirical results. Many studies demonstrate robust primacy effects when there is no rehearsal (Greene, 1986; Hockey & Hamilton, 1977; Neath & Crowder, 1996; Wixted & McDowell, 1989; Wright et al., 1990). Although rehearsal can affect the magnitude of the primacy effect (Rundus & Atkinson, 1970), rehearsal does not appear to be necessary. Just as there is growing evidence against the view that primacy is due to rehearsal, there is also substantial evidence that recency is not due to short-term memory. Numerous studies show parallel results between recency effects observed in so-called short-term settings and those observed over far longer-lasting time scales (Glenberg, Bradley, Kraus, & Renzaglia, 1983; Greene, 1986; Nairne, Neath, Serra, & Byun, in press; Neath, 1993; Neath & Crowder, 1990; Thapar & Greene, 1993). When the recency items take several weeks (or longer) to present and there is still a robust recency effect (Baddeley & Hitch, 1977; Pinto & Baddeley, 1991; Roediger & Crowder, 1976), attributing the recency effect to short-term memory is implausible.

This chapter has described the development of a structural view of short-term memory in some detail. The two reasons for this in-depth exploration are that (1) the modal model has exerted more influence on memory research for a longer time than any other view, and (2) the modal model is far more sophisticated than many descriptions suggest, with several formal mathematical versions. Nonetheless, the model has difficulty accounting for many results, and, consequently, most memory researchers came to emphasize the importance of processing rather than the importance of structures. The next chapter will examine current conceptions of immediate memory and will serve as an introduction to the now-dominant processing view of memory.

# References

Atkinson, R. C., & Shiffrin, R. M. (1968). Human memory: A proposed system and its control processes. In K. W. Spence & J. T. Spence (Eds.), *The psychology of learning and motivation, Vol. 2.* New York: Academic Press.

Baddeley, A. D. (1966). Short-term memory for word sequences as a function of acoustic, semantic, and formal similarity. *Quarterly Journal of Experimental Psychology, 18,* 362–365.

Baddeley, A. D., & Hitch, G. J. (1974). Working memory. In G. H. Bower (Ed.), *The psychology of learning and motivation, Vol. 8.* New York: Academic Press.

Baddeley, A. D., & Hitch, G. J. (1977). Recency reexamined. In S. Dornic (Ed.), *Attention and performance VI.* Hillsdale, NJ: Erlbaum.

Bjork, R. A., & Whitten, W. B. (1974). Recency-sensitive retrieval processes in long-term free recall. *Cognitive Psychology, 6,* 173–189.

Broadbent, D. E. (1958). *Perception and communication.* New York: Pergamon Press.

Brown, J. (1958). Some tests of the decay theory of immediate memory. *Quarterly Journal of Experimental Psychology, 10,* 12–21.

Brown, R., & McNeill, D. (1966). The "tip of the tongue" phenomenon. *Journal of Verbal Learning and Verbal Behavior, 5,* 325–337.

Burnham, W. H. (1888). Memory, historically and experimentally considered. *American Journal of Psychology, 2,* 39–90, 255–270, 431–464, 566–622.

Capaldi, E. J., & Neath, I. (1995). Remembering and forgetting as context discrimination. *Learning & Memory, 2,* 107–132.

Conrad, R. (1964). Acoustic confusions in immediate memory. *British Journal of Psychology, 55,* 75–84.

Conrad, R. (1972). Speech and reading. In J. F. Kavanagh & I. G. Mattingly (Eds.), *Language by ear and by eye: The relationships between speech and reading.* Cambridge, MA: MIT Press.

Conrad, R., & Hille, B. A. (1958). The decay theory of immediate memory and paced recall. *Canadian Journal of Psychology, 12,* 1–6.

Cowan, N., Cartwright, C., Winterowd, C., & Sherk, M. (1987). An adult model of preschool children's speech memory. *Memory & Cognition, 15,* 511–517.

Craik, F. I. M. (1970). Fate of primary memory items in free recall. *Journal of Verbal Learning and Verbal Behavior, 9,* 143–148.

Crowder, R. G. (1976). *Principles of learning and memory.* Hillsdale, NJ: Erlbaum.

Dale, H. C. A., & McGlaughlin, A. (1971). Evidence of acoustic coding in long-term memory. *Quarterly Journal of Experimental Psychology, 23,* 1–7.

Fuchs, A. H., & Melton, A. W. (1974). Effects of frequency of presentation and stimulus length on retention in the Brown-Peterson paradigm. *Journal of Experimental Psychology, 103,* 629–637.

Galton, F. (1883). *Inquiries into human faculty and its development.* London: Dent.

Glanzer, M. (1972). Storage mechanisms in recall. In G. H. Bower & J. T. Spence (Eds.), *The psychology of learning and motivation, Vol. 5.* New York: Academic Press.

Glanzer, M., & Cunitz, A. R. (1966). Two storage mechanisms in free recall. *Journal of Verbal Learning and Verbal Behavior, 5,* 351–360.

Glenberg, A. M., Bradley, M. M., Kraus, T. A., & Renzaglia, G. J. (1983). Studies of the long-term recency effect: Support for the contextually guided retrieval hypothesis. *Journal of Experimental Psychology: Learning, Memory and Cognition, 9,* 231–255.

Greene, R. L. (1986). A common basis for recency effects in immediate and delayed recall. *Journal of Experimental Psychology: Learning, Memory and Cognition, 12,* 413–418.

Hebb, D. O. (1961). Distinctive features of learning in the higher animal. In J. F. Delafresnaye (Ed.), *Brain mechanisms and learning: A symposium.* Oxford: Blackwell Scientific Publications.

Hellyer, S. (1962). Frequency of stimulus presentation and short-term decrement in recall. *Journal of Experimental Psychology, 64,* 650.

Hintzman, D. L. (1967). Articulatory coding in short-term memory. *Journal of Verbal Learning and Verbal Behavior, 6,* 312–316.

Hockey, R., & Hamilton, P. (1977). The basis of the primacy effect: Some experiments with running memory. *Quarterly Journal of Experimental Psychology, 29,* 49–63.

Jacobs, J. (1887). Experiments on "prehension." *Mind, 12,* 75–79.

James, W. (1890). *The principles of psychology.* New York: Henry Holt and Company. [Reprinted as W. James (1983). *The principles of psychology.* Cambridge, MA: Harvard University Press.]

Keppel, G., & Underwood, B. J. (1962). Proactive inhibition in short-term retention of single items. *Journal of Verbal Learning and Verbal Behavior, 1,* 153–161.

Kintsch, W., & Buschke, H. (1969). Homophones and synonyms in short-term memory. *Journal of Experimental Psychology, 80,* 403–407.

Kirkpatrick, E. A. (1894). An experimental study of memory. *Psychological Review, 1,* 602–609.

Koppenaal, L., & Glanzer, M. (1990). An examination of the continuous distractor task and the long-term recency effect. *Memory & Cognition, 18,* 183–195.

Locke, J. L., & Fehr, F. S. (1970). Young children's use of the speech code in a recall task. *Journal of Experimental Child Psychology, 10,* 367–373.

Matarazzo, J. D. (1972). *Wechsler's measurement and appraisal of adult intelligence (5th ed.).* Baltimore: Williams & Wilkins.

McKelvie, S. J. (1987). Learning and awareness in the Hebb digits task. *The Journal of General Psychology, 114,* 75–88.

Mechanic, A. (1964). The responses involved in the rote learning of verbal materials. *Journal of Verbal Learning and Verbal Behavior, 3,* 30–36.

Melton, A. W. (1963). Implications of short-term memory for a general theory of memory. *Journal of Verbal Learning and Verbal Behavior, 2,* 1–21.

Miller, G. A. (1956). The magical number seven plus or minus two: Some limits on our capacity for processing information. *Psychological Review, 63,* 81–97.

Murdock, B. B. (1961). The retention of individual items. *Journal of Experimental Psychology, 62,* 618–625.

Murdock, B. B. (1962). The serial position effect of free recall. *Journal of Experimental Psychology, 64,* 482–488.

Murdock, B. B. (1974). *Human memory: Theory and data.* Hillsdale, NJ: Erlbaum.

Murdock, B. B., & Metcalfe, J. (1978). Controlled rehearsal in single-trial free recall. *Journal of Verbal Learning and Verbal Behavior, 17,* 309–324.

Murray, D. J. (1967). The role of speech responses in short-term memory. *Canadian Journal of Psychology, 21,* 263–276.

Nairne, J. S. (1996). Short-term/working memory. In E. L. Bjork & R. A. Bjork (Eds.), *Memory.* New York: Academic Press.

Nairne, J. S., Neath, I., Serra, M., & Byun, E. (in press). Positional distinctiveness and the ratio rule in free recall. *Journal of Memory and Language.*

Neath, I. (1993). Contextual and distinctive processes and the serial position function. *Journal of Memory and Language, 32,* 820–840.

Neath, I., & Crowder, R. G. (1990). Schedules of presentation and temporal distinctiveness in human memory. *Journal of Experimental Psychology: Learning, Memory and Cognition, 16,* 316–327.

Neath, I., & Crowder, R. G. (1996). Distinctiveness and very short-term serial position effects. *Memory, 4,* 225–242.

Neath, I., & Knoedler, A. J. (1997). Dimensional distinctiveness and increasing primacy effects in perception, recognition and sentence processing. Unpublished manuscript.

Norman, D. A. (Ed.) (1970). *Models of human memory.* New York: Academic Press.

Peterson, L. R., & Peterson, M. J. (1959). Short-term retention of individual items. *Journal of Experimental Psychology, 61,* 12–21.

Pinto, A. C., & Baddeley, A. D. (1991). Where did you park your car? Analysis of a naturalistic long-term recency effect. *European Journal of Cognitive Psychology, 3,* 297–313.

Pollack, I. (1952). The information of elementary auditory displays. *Journal of the Acoustical Society of America, 24,* 745–749.

Pollack, I. (1953). The information of elementary auditory displays. II. *Journal of the Acoustical Society of America, 25,* 765–769.

Postman, L., & Phillips, L. W. (1965). Short-term temporal changes in free recall. *Quarterly Journal of Experimental Psychology, 17,* 132–138.

Roediger, H. L. I., & Crowder, R. G. (1976). A serial position effect in recall of United States presidents. *Bulletin of the Psychonomic Society, 8,* 275–278.

Rundus, D., & Atkinson, R. C. (1970). Rehearsal processes in free recall: A procedure for direct observation. *Journal of Verbal Learning and Verbal Behavior, 9,* 99–105.

Shiffrin, R. M., & Nosofsky, R. M. (1993). Seven plus or minus two: A commentary on capacity limitations. *Psychological Review, 101,* 357–361.

Shulman, H. G. (1970). Encoding and retention of semantic and phonemic information in short-term memory. *Journal of Verbal Learning and Verbal Behavior, 9,* 499–508.

Shulman, H. G. (1972). Semantic confusion errors in short-term memory. *Journal of Verbal Learning and Verbal Behavior, 11,* 221–227.

Simon, H. A. (1974). How big is a chunk? *Science, 183,* 482–488.

Sperling, G. (1960). The information available in brief visual presentations. *Psychological Monographs, 74,* (Whole No. 11).

Sternberg, S. (1966). High speed scanning in human memory. *Science, 153,* 652–654.

Thapar, A., & Greene, R. L. (1993). Evidence against a short-term-store account of long-term recency effects. *Memory & Cognition, 21,* 329–337.

Tzeng, O. J. L. (1973). Positive recency effect in a delayed free recall. *Journal of Verbal Learning and Verbal Behavior, 12,* 436–439.

Van Zandt, T., & Townsend, J. T. (1993). Self-terminating versus exhaustive processes in rapid visual and memory search: An evaluative review. *Perception & Psychophysics, 53,* 563–580.

Watkins, M. J., Neath, I., & Sechler, E. S. (1989). Recency effect in recall of a word list when an immediate memory task is performed after each word presentation. *American Journal of Psychology, 102,* 265–270.

Waugh, N. C., & Norman, D. A. (1965). Primary memory. *Psychological Review, 72,* 89–104.

Welch, G. B., & Burnett, C. T. (1924). Is primacy a factor in association formation? *American Journal of Psychology, 35,* 396–401.

Wickelgren, W. A. (1965). Short-term memory for phonemically similar lists. *American Journal of Psychology, 78,* 567–74.

Wixted, J. T., & McDowell, J. J. (1989). Contributions to the functional analysis of single-trial free recall. *Journal of Experimental Psychology: Learning, Memory and Cognition, 15,* 685–697.

Wright, A. A., Cook, R. G., Rivera, J. J., Shyan, M. R., Neiworth, J. J., & Jitsumori, M. (1990). Naming rehearsal, and interstimulus interval effects in memory processing. *Journal of Experimental Psychology: Learning, Memory and Cognition, 16,* 1043–1059.

# CHAPTER FIVE

# Current Perspectives on Immediate Memory

*"While simple qualitative conceptual models have proved very useful, one eventually reaches a point at which some form of detailed and preferably quantitative model is necessary if the concepts are to develop."*

—Alan Baddeley (1994, p. 363

The previous chapter chronicled the development of the idea of separate memory stores, one devoted to memory for the short term and one for memory for the long term. In this chapter, we examine three current views of immediate memory in some detail. Given our extensive knowledge of human performance in this area, it is a challenge to develop a theory that can satisfactorily explain all the relevant data and make novel predictions. Each of the views has its strengths and weaknesses.

Alan Baddeley's (1986) Working Memory is perhaps the single most influential current model of immediate memory. Although initially a theory of memory for the short term, it has been extended to other areas such as reading and language comprehension (see Gathercole & Baddeley, 1993). The second approach characterizes immediate memory as the subset of information that currently has a heightened state of activation (e.g., Cowan, 1988, 1993, 1995; Schneider & Detweiler, 1987; Shiffrin & Schneider, 1977). Although this view is quite similar to Working Memory, there are several major differences. The third model is the Feature Model (Nairne, 1988, 1990; Neath & Nairne, 1995), which not only explains the same basic phenomena as Working Memory but can also explain memory effects previously attributed to echoic memory (see Chapter 3).

## Working Memory

Alan Baddeley and his colleagues (see Baddeley, 1986; Baddeley & Hitch, 1974) have developed what is currently the most influential view of immediate memory. Part of their goal was to examine more closely the idea of immediate memory as a place where many basic cognitive operations are carried out, hence the name of the system. The modal model (discussed in the previous chapter) was seen as too limited and restrictive. In contrast, Working Memory is seen as the combination of a central executive—a controlling attentional mechanism—and a number of subsidiary slave systems (see Figure 5.1). The

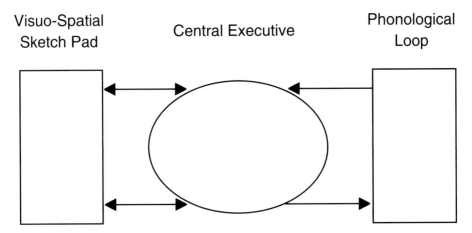

Figure 5.1    A simplified representation of Baddeley's Working Memory system.
Source: Based on Baddeley (1990).

central executive coordinates activities within the slave systems, two of which have been studied extensively. (We will postpone discussion of the visuo-spatial sketch pad, which sets up and manipulates visual images, until the chapter on imagery.) The slave system known as the phonological loop will be of primary concern, as this is the system that handles the phenomena previously attributed to short-term store.

## The Phonological Loop

The phonological loop has two main components: the phonological store and the articulatory control process. The phonological store is a memory store that can retain speech-based information for a short period of time. The traces within the store are assumed to fade and decay within about 1 to 2 seconds, after which they are no longer usable. The second component is the articulatory control process, which is responsible for two different functions: it can translate visual information into a speech-based code and deposit it in the phonological store; and it can refresh a trace in the phonological store, offsetting the decay process. One of the fundamental assumptions of Working Memory is that the articulatory control process controls subvocal rehearsal and that this is analogous to overt rehearsal, where subjects would be saying the item out loud. The amount of verbal information that can be retained is therefore a trade-off between the decay rate (which is assumed to be fixed for a given type of item) and the covert rehearsal rate (which can vary). If rehearsal of a particular item does not occur within a certain amount of time, the memory trace for that item will have decayed too far to be usable. The phonological loop was designed to explain four basic findings: the phonological similarity effect, effects of articulatory suppression, the irrelevant speech effect, and the word-length effect (Baddeley, 1986, 1992, 1994).

*Phonological similarity*    The phonological similarity effect refers to the finding that memory is worse for items that sound alike than for items that differ (Baddeley, 1966; Conrad,

**Table 5.1**  The proportion of items correctly recalled as a function of presentation modality, phonological similarity, and articulatory suppression. With no articulatory suppression, dissimilar lists are recalled better than similar lists. With articulatory suppression, there is no phonological similarity effect for visual items, but the effect remains for auditory items. Note that articulatory suppression also greatly reduces overall performance.

|          | Silent | | Articulatory Suppression | |
|----------|------------|---------|------------|---------|
|          | Dissimilar | Similar | Dissimilar | Similar |
| Visual   | 0.93       | 0.73    | 0.57       | 0.58    |
| Auditory | 0.82       | 0.32    | 0.45       | 0.19    |

Source: Data from Peterson & Johnson (1971).

1964; see Figure 4.1). The sequence PGTCD is harder to recall from memory than the sequence RHXKW because the items in the first sequence share similar sounds. The phonological similarity effect occurs for both visual and auditory presentation because, according to the Working Memory view, items are retained in a speech-based code in the phonological store. If the items are presented aloud, then they have immediate access to the store because they are already in the appropriate, speech-based code. If the items are presented visually, however, they need to be translated into a phonological code by the articulatory control process. A strong prediction is that if we somehow prevent the visual items from being translated by the articulatory control process, then the phonological similarity effect should disappear for visually presented items because they cannot be translated into the appropriate code for deposit into the phonological store. Thus, one way of preventing translation is to have the subject engage in articulatory suppression, the second phenomenon that Working Memory was designed to account for.

*Articulatory suppression*  When subjects engage in articulatory suppression (Murray, 1968), they repeatedly say a word, such as *the,* over and over out loud. According to the Working Memory view, this occupies the articulatory control process, which is needed for both overt and covert articulation. Therefore, there should be no covert rehearsal using the articulatory control process during articulatory suppression. Without covert rehearsal, visual information cannot be translated into a phonological code and so cannot be placed into the phonological store; therefore, there should be no phonological similarity effect. Auditory items, on the other hand, have direct access to the phonological store because they do not need to be translated. Because auditory information can enter the phonological store without the articulatory control process, there should still be a phonological similarity effect for auditory items. As shown in Table 5.1, this is indeed what happens: articulatory suppression removes the phonological similarity effect for visually presented items, but the effect remains for auditory items (Baddeley, Lewis, & Vallar, 1984; Estes, 1973; Levy, 1971; Longoni, Richardson, & Aiello, 1993; Murray, 1968; Peterson & Johnson, 1971).

*The irrelevant speech effect*   The third phenomenon that Working Memory was designed to account for is the irrelevant speech effect. Colle and Welsh (1976) had two groups of subjects recall visually presented consonants, but one group saw the consonants while some irrelevant speech was played in the background. Relative to the subjects in the quiet condition, subjects who heard irrelevant speech were not as successful in recalling the information. According to Working Memory, the phonemes from the irrelevant speech enter into the phonological store and interfere with the information about the visually presented items. Given this explanation, we can make three predictions. First, articulatory suppression should remove the irrelevant speech effect because the articulation will prevent the visually presented items from entering the phonological store. Although the irrelevant speech can still enter the store, the to-be-remembered items will not. Second, because the basis is interference at the level of the phoneme, it should not matter whether the irrelevant speech is a single phoneme or a multisyllable word: what is important is the similarity of the phonemes in the irrelevant speech to the phonemes in the to-be-remembered items. Third, nonspeech items, like tones, should not produce an irrelevant speech effect. Salamé and Baddeley (1982) confirmed these predictions.

*The word-length effect*   The fourth phenomenon that Working Memory was designed to account for is the word-length effect: the finding that short words (man, dog) are recalled better than are long words (gentleman, canine). Mackworth (1963) first reported the high correlation between reading rate and memory span, but because she was interested primarily in identifying limits in iconic memory (or the *visual image,* as she termed it), she did not measure word length precisely. Nonetheless, over five experiments with a variety of stimuli including pictures, letters, digits, and colors, she found that "the amount reported was proportional to the speed of reporting the individual items" (Mackworth, 1963, p. 81). Watkins (1972) and Watkins and Watkins (1973) reported effects of word-length as a function of modality and serial position in both free and serial recall. In all cases, words of one syllable were recalled better than were words of four syllables.

Baddeley, Thomson, and Buchanan (1975) systematically explored the effect of word length in terms of pronunciation time. They demonstrated that even when items are equated for meaning and word frequency, if one set of words takes less time to pronounce than another set, memory will be better for the shorter items. Their stimuli from Experiment 6 are reproduced in Table 5.2. The stimuli were selected so that the only important

**Table 5.2**   Examples of the stimuli used in Experiment 6. Note that the word *aluminium* is spelled and pronounced differently in Britain and the United States.

| One Syllable | Two Syllables | Three Syllables | Four Syllables | Five Syllables |
|---|---|---|---|---|
| Stoat | Puma | Gorilla | Rhinoceros | Hippopotamus |
| Mumps | Measles | Leprosy | Diphtheria | Tuberculosis |
| Greece | Peru | Mexico | Australia | Yugoslavia |
| Maine | Utah | Wyoming | Alabama | Louisiana |
| Zinc | Carbon | Calcium | Uranium | Aluminium |

Source: Baddeley, Thomson, & Buchanan (1975).

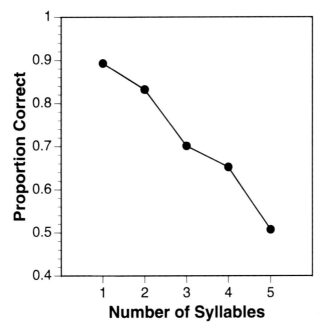

**Figure 5.2**  Proportion of words correctly recalled as a function of the number of syllables.
Source: Baddeley, Thomson, & Buchanan (1975).

difference was the number of syllables. Each list contained the name of an animal, a disease, a place for education, a country, a city, and so forth. Figure 5.2 shows the results of the study: As the number of syllables in the words increased, the proportion of words that could be recalled decreased.

Baddeley, Thomson, and Buchanan (1975) also plotted their data in a different form, measuring the reading rate of their subjects (in words per second). When this measure is used, rather than just syllables, the relationship between the time to say a word and the ability to recall a series of items becomes even more striking. These results are shown in Figure 5.3, indicating a linear relationship between how long it takes to pronounce a word and the level of recall.

This basic finding, the word-length effect, is captured in a very simple equation. One critical assumption is that overt pronunciation rate is correlated with the inner subvocal rehearsal rate. Given this assumption, the relationship between memory span, $s$, for verbal items of type $i$ can be described as a linear function of pronunciation rate, $r$, and the duration of the verbal trace, $\tau$ (Schweickert, Guentert, & Hersberger, 1990):

$$s_i = r_i \tau \tag{5.1}$$

Perhaps the most compelling evidence supporting this view is the relative consistency of the presumed rate of decay, $\tau$. As Schweickert and Boruff (1986) put it, "The mean of these trace duration estimates is 1.6 s. Considering the variety of methods for presenting the stimuli and measuring the spans and pronunciation rates, one is struck more by the

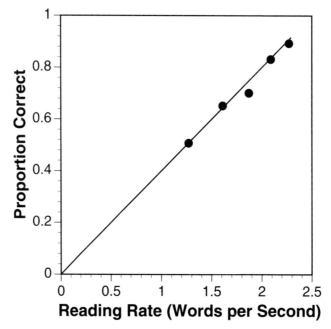

**Figure 5.3**    Proportion of words correctly recalled as a function of time required to read the words in words per second.    Source: Baddeley, Thomson, & Buchanan (1975).

agreement than by the differences" (p. 420). The consistency of this finding has led the word-length effect to be seen as "the best remaining solid evidence in favor of temporary memory storage" (Cowan, 1995, p. 42).

This relationship, regardless of the underlying theoretical explanation, has important implications. For example, one component of many intelligence tests is a memory span task. Subjects are tested to see how many items—often digits—they can recall in order. Ellis and Hennelly (1980) showed that apparent differences in IQ and memory span between Welsh- and English-speaking subjects may be ascribed to the relatively longer time needed to say the Welsh digits compared to the English digits. Because digits 1–9 take longer to pronounce in Welsh than in English, this reduces the number of items that can be correctly recalled. Bilingual Welsh-English speakers have higher memory spans and higher measures of intelligence when tested in English than when tested in Welsh. It appears that the language most optimized for digit span is Cantonese (cited in Naveh-Benjamin & Ayres, 1986), where the average digit span approaches nine or even more items, rather than seven for English.

Further evidence supporting the idea that the critical factor is the time needed to say the word was reported by Cowan, Day, Saults, Keller, Johnson, and Flores (1992). They constructed a list of long and short words that varied only in the time needed to pronounce the items: both groups of words had the same number of syllables, the same number of letters, and a similar set of phonemes. The long words were *coerce, humane, morphine, voodoo,* and *zygote,* and the five short words were *decor, ember, hackle, pewter,* and *wiggle.* Even with these stimuli, there was a robust word-length effect.

The explanation of the word-length effect, according to Working Memory, is that the number of items that can be immediately recalled depends on how often each item can be subvocally rehearsed by the articulatory control process. This process is used to refresh the decaying traces in the phonological store, and the shorter the items (in terms of pronunciation time), the more items can be rehearsed before a particular trace decays. One prediction of this view is that the word-length effect should be removed for both auditory and visual items under conditions of articulatory suppression, because articulatory suppression prevents the items from being rehearsed with the subvocal articulatory control process.

Baddeley, Thomson, and Buchanan (1975, Experiment 8) presented subjects with five-word lists for immediate serial recall. There were two word lengths (1 and 5 syllables), two presentation modalities (auditory and visual), and two articulatory conditions (suppression and no suppression). According to the Working Memory view, articulatory suppression prevents subjects from registering visually presented items in the phonological

---

**Experiment**   The Word-Length Effect

**Purpose:**   To demonstrate the effect of word length on immediate serial recall.

**Subjects:**   Twenty subjects are recommended.

**Materials:**   Table D in the Appendix contains eight short words and eight long words. Construct ten lists of five words each using these words in a different random order for each subject. Each subject will need an answer sheet on which they will write their responses. It is useful to have five spaces marked for the subjects to write down each response.

**Design:**   This is a completely within-subjects design because each subject receives each level of the experimental condition, word length.

**Procedure:**   Inform the subjects that this is an experiment on memory. Tell them that they will hear a list of five words and that they will be asked to recall the words in order. Read each list aloud at the rate of 1 word per second. As soon as the last word is read, the subjects should begin writing down their responses. For this experiment, serial recall is required. With serial recall, the subject must write down the first word first, the second word second, and so forth. If they cannot remember a word, have them write in an X and then proceed to the next word. They are not allowed to go back and change their responses. Allow about 20 seconds for recall, then read the next list.

**Instructions:**   "This is an experiment on memory. I will read five words out loud, and then I would like you to recall them in order. Simply write the first word you heard in the first blank on your answer sheet, then write the second, and so on. It is important that you write the words in order. If you cannot remember a particular word, write an X in that blank and proceed to the next word. You are not allowed to go back and fill in a blank or change a response once you have written it down. Any questions?"

**Scoring and Analysis:**   For each subject, count the number of words recalled in order for each word length and compute the average. A one-way analysis of variance with length as a repeated measure can be used to analyze the results.

Source: Adapted from an experiment by Baddeley, Thomson, & Buchanan (1975).

store because the articulatory control process is not available. Although auditory items have automatic access to the phonological store, articulatory suppression prevents rehearsal of these items because the articulatory control process is not available. Baddeley, Thomson, and Buchanan observed appropriate effects of word length for the no suppression groups, but articulatory suppression eliminated the word-length effect *only* for the visual group: the effect of word length remained in the auditory modality with articulatory suppression group. Because articulatory suppression should remove the word-length effect regardless of presentation modality, the finding that the word-length effect remained for auditory items is problematic for the Working Memory view.

Baddeley (1986) argued that subjects may be rehearsing during recall, refreshing the decaying trace in the phonological store while simultaneously recalling items. This is more likely for auditory items because they are automatically registered in the phonological store and do not require conversion using the articulatory control process during presentation. If this is the case, then requiring articulatory suppression not only during presentation but also throughout recall should eliminate the word-length effect for auditory items. Baddeley, Lewis, and Vallar (1984, Experiment 4) conducted an experiment almost identical to Experiment 8 of Baddeley, Thomson, and Buchanan (1975). Five-item lists of auditory items were presented for immediate serial recall; the short words had one syllable and the long words had five syllables. The main difference was that whereas Baddeley et al. (1975) had subjects engage in articulatory suppression only during presentation, Baddeley et al. (1984) had subjects engage in articulatory suppression during both presentation and throughout the entire recall period. The data are summarized in Table 5.3. The word-length effect was present when suppression occurred only during presentation but was eliminated when suppression continued throughout the recall period. To the extent that subvocal rehearsal is prevented during both presentation and recall, there will be no word-length effect, just as Working Memory predicts (Baddeley, 1992).

Another prediction concerns the interaction between word length, articulatory suppression, and phonological similarity. Articulatory suppression should remove the word-length effect for both visual and auditory items, but it should remove the phonological similarity effect only for visual items, not for auditory items. We have discussed both of these findings separately. However, the Working Memory view predicts that, at the same

**Table 5.3**  Percentage of short and long words correctly recalled as a function of two types of articulatory suppression. Articulatory suppression eliminates the word-length effect for auditory items only when it occurs during both presentation and recall.

|        | Quiet | Suppression Presentation Only | Quiet | Suppression Presentation and Recall |
|--------|-------|-------------------------------|-------|-------------------------------------|
| Short  | 83.7  | 71.0                          | 78.0  | 46.9                                |
| Long   | 62.0  | 53.7                          | 61.0  | 41.7                                |

Source: Data in the first two columns come from Experiment 8 of Baddeley, Thomson & Buchanan (1975), and data in the second two columns came from Baddeley, Lewis, & Vallor (1984).

Table 5.4   The percentage of auditory items correctly recalled as a function of word length, phonological similarity, and articulatory suppression. With no articulatory suppression, dissimilar lists are recalled better than similar lists, and short lists are recalled better than long lists. With articulatory suppression, there is still a phonological similarity effect, but the word-length effect (52.0 versus 49.4 and 25.0 versus 17.5) is eliminated.

|       | Silent | | Articulatory Suppression | |
|-------|------------|---------|------------|---------|
|       | Dissimilar | Similar | Dissimilar | Similar |
| Short | 86.2       | 63.2    | 52.0       | 25.0    |
| Long  | 73.7       | 31.2    | 49.4       | 17.5    |

Source:  Data from Longoni, Richardson, & Aiello (1993).

time that articulatory suppression is removing the word-length effect, the phonological similarity effect should be removed for visual but remain for auditory. This is exactly what happens (Longoni, Richardson, & Aiello, 1993; see Table 5.4).

## Critique of Working Memory

There are several problems with the Working Memory view as outlined above, over and beyond the difficulty in thinking about how three different manipulations, such as word length, phonological similarity, and articulatory suppression, interact. With regard to the irrelevant speech effect, there are several studies that cannot replicate the key finding that the magnitude of the irrelevant speech effect is related to the phonological similarity between the relevant and irrelevant items (Jones & Macken, 1995; LeCompte & Shaibe, 1997). Second, it has been shown that pure tones disrupt serial recall (Jones & Macken, 1993; LeCompte, Neely, & Wilson, 1997), and thus the irrelevant speech effect may not require speech. Both of these findings contradict predictions of Working Memory (see also Martin, 1993).

A second problem concerns several findings about the word-length effect. For example, the word-length effect is larger for visually presented items than for auditory items (Baddeley, Thomson & Buchanan, 1975, Experiment 8; Watkins & Watkins, 1973), but Working Memory says nothing about why this occurs. Similarly, the word-length effect changes as a function of serial position (Cowan et al., 1992), but Working Memory says nothing about serial position effects.

Perhaps even more problematic, Caplan, Rochon, and Waters (1992) have reported negative word-length effects, where shorter words are recalled worse than longer words. In their experiment, the short words took, on average, 546 ms to say and the long words took 720 ms. However, only 65.6% of the short words were recalled, compared to 76.4% of the long words. Working Memory says that if an item takes longer to say, it will be recalled less well, but these data show the opposite finding. Caplan, Rochon, and Waters (1992) suggest that the important factor in determining the word-length effect is a difference in the number of phonemes, but it is unclear why their stimuli resulted in a negative

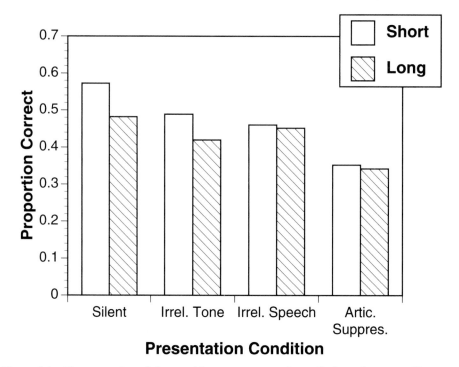

**Figure 5.4**   The proportion of short and long items correctly recalled as a function of four presentation conditions. In both the silent and irrelevant tone conditions, there is a word-length effect; but in the irrelevant speech and articulatory suppression conditions, the word-length effect is eliminated.   Source: Neath, Surprenant, & LeCompte (1996).

word-length effect when the stimuli of Cowan et al. (1992) produced a positive word-length effect. Although this result has yet to be explained completely, it directly contradicts a fundamental prediction of Working Memory.

A third problem concerns interactions among the four basic phenomena. According to Baddeley's (1986) Working Memory, articulatory suppression affects the articulatory control process whereas irrelevant speech "impairs performance by corrupting the phonological store" (p. 90). Although irrelevant speech may lower overall performance, because of some corruption of traces within the phonological store, it should have no effect on the articulatory control process and thus no differential effect on long and short words. However, as Figure 5.4 shows, irrelevant speech eliminates the word-length effect, just as articulatory suppression does (Neath, Surprenant, & LeCompte, in press). Articulatory suppression eliminates the word-length effect because it prevents rehearsal, but it is difficult to see why irrelevant speech would prevent rehearsal. A related finding is that irrelevant speech also eliminates the phonological similarity effect for visual items but not for auditory items (LeCompte, Surprenant, & Neath, 1997). Thus, irrelevant speech and articulatory suppression have similar effects on both the word-length effect and the phonological similarity effect, but Working Memory does not explain why.

There are also problems concerning the fundamental assumption that the inner voice and covert articulatory control process are intimately related to overt speed of speaking. For example, Baddeley and Wilson (1988) tested a patient with anarthria—an inability to speak despite retaining the ability to comprehend language and communicate by other means. This patient had a normal digit span and showed typical phonological similarity and word-length effects. Thus, although overt speaking was disrupted, none of the effects attributed to covert rehearsal were disrupted. Because of this finding, Baddeley and Wilson refined Working Memory to suggest that the articulatory control process is tied not to overt speech but to some more central aspect of speech planning.

Even with this refinement, there are problems with the model. Martin, Blossom-Stach, Yaffee, and Wetzel (1995) presented a case study of a patient, MP, whose speech production was severely impaired. The cause of the impairment was determined to be a central disruption of motor programming, rather than problems with the peripheral muscles necessary for articulation. Despite his articulatory problems, MP demonstrated normal memory span for auditory presentation as well as a robust word-length effect. Thus, even when central motor processes are disrupted, word-length effects can still be observed.

A second example comes from the study of two patients who, although they showed similar deficits, nonetheless showed different patterns of performance. Vallar and Baddeley (1984, 1987) described a patient known as PV, who had a severely reduced memory span and thus, according to Working Memory, a defective articulatory control process. If one assumes that PV's articulatory control process was already disrupted, then requiring articulatory suppression—to disrupt the articulatory control process—should have had no effect. PV's performance was not made worse by requiring articulatory suppression, thus apparently confirming the Working Memory interpretation. The problem arises from a study reported by Butterworth, Campbell, and Howard (1986; see also Howard & Butterworth, 1989) describing a patient known as RE who also had a reduced memory span. Given the similarities to PV, Working Memory would predict similar impairments on other tasks. However, PV exhibited a comprehension deficit, due—according to Working Memory—to a deficit in the articulatory control process, whereas RE did not. Martin (1995) summarized other evidence against a Working Memory interpretation of sentence comprehension deficits in aphasics.

Perhaps the most important problem with the Working Memory explanation of basic memory effects is that it is a purely verbal model and is quite imprecise and incomplete in its descriptions. For example, it says that phonologically similar items will not be well remembered, but it does not specify how they interfere with each other. As another example, given visual items presented under articulatory suppression, the Working Memory view says the information is not in the phonological store but does not specify how or where the information is being retained. As a third example, Working Memory does not relate these findings to other phenomena observed in immediate-memory experiments.

Working Memory should be seen as an ongoing process in which the ideas are being refined and more precisely specified. Given the complexity of topic, it should not be surprising that a simple model does not fare well. It remains to be seen whether modifications can be made that will correct or resolve the problems mentioned above or whether quantitative versions, as Baddeley (1994) advocates, can be made that give the model more precision in its operation and predictions (for example, Burgess & Hitch, 1992).

Nonetheless, Working Memory remains a useful heuristic for the general effects, even if it cannot gracefully handle the more intricate interactions.

# Immediate Memory as Activation

The second current view of immediate memory is that it is a subset of information that currently has a heightened state of activation (for example, Cowan, 1988, 1993; Shiffrin, 1993). This view is similar to Baddeley's (1986, 1994) Working Memory and is sometimes (confusingly) also called working memory (but with lowercase letters). The main similarities between the two are the use of decay as the fundamental cause of forgetting over the short term and the role of immediate memory as the "place" where cognitive "work" is performed. The activation view differs from Baddeley's Working Memory in that it does not divide immediate memory into separate subsystems, such as the visuo-spatial sketchpad or the phonological loop, and it emphasizes the role of attention.

There are at least two different approaches within the activation view. One (for example, Schneider & Detweiler, 1987) has as its goal a simulation model and specifies in great detail how the proposed system operates. The second approach (e.g., Cowan, 1995) has as its goal "to pare down the features of their model until they reach the core assumptions in which they believe solidly on the basis of already-existing data" (p. 18). Thus, they favor simplicity over testability: "It appears most efficient for the time being to try to stay near the most basic level of the hypothesis space until the fundamental issues are resolved, even though this results in a model too general to make specific predictions in many situations" (Cowan, 1995, p. 24). We shall examine the latter view, because the more complex versions (e.g., Anderson, 1983; Schneider & Detweiler, 1987) can be seen as variants of the former. With the exception of providing many elaborations and subdivisions, the major difference between Anderson (1983) and Cowan (1988) is that the former does not include sensory stores and omits mention of selective attention. The major difference between Schneider and Detweiler (1987) and Cowan (1988) is similarly the division into 8 separate modules (visual, auditory, speech, lexical, semantic, motor, mood, and context), each of which is embedded in a connectionist network. Cowan's view, then, is a framework that has many possible instantiations.

Cowan's (1988, 1995) view has four basic assumptions. First, it assumes that the number of items that can be retained over a short duration is greater than the number of items that can be held in the focus of attention. Therefore, there is a distinction (similar to Galton, 1883; see the quotation at the beginning of Chapter 4) between representations that are currently the focus of attention and other activated items that are just beyond the focus. Immediate memory is defined as that portion of permanent knowledge that is in a heightened state of activation, but only a very small fraction of information in memory can be active at one time. When some information becomes activated, there must be some mechanism or process that can deactivate it. The second main assumption is that the central mechanism by which information is deactivated is decay. Decay occurs over time unless some other process, such as rehearsal or attention, reactivates the information. The third assumption is that there exists a separate sensory store, which can retain sensory information for brief periods (on the order of several hundred ms; see Chapter 3). The fourth assumption is that there is a central executive that directs attention and controls

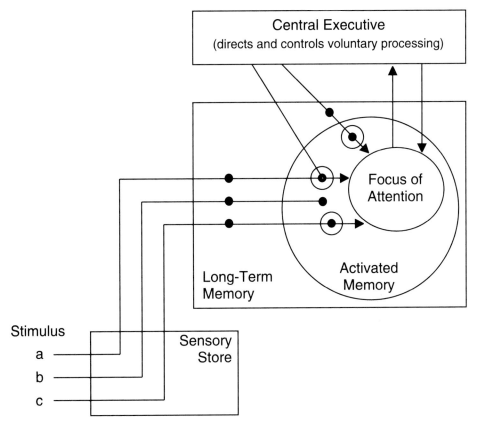

**Figure 5.5** A schematic representation of the activation view of immediate memory.
Source: Adapted from Cowan (1988).

voluntary processing. It can select information (whether from sensory store or from long-term memory or activated memory) to be in the focus of attention, and it controls the voluntary processing that is then performed on the information.

Figure 5.5 illustrates the basic operation with three types of stimuli (*a*, *b*, and *c*). The arrows show the basic time course, although the underlying processes are thought to be continuous. Stimuli *a* and *b* are unchanged items (they have been experienced before) and ordinarily would not attract attention. Stimulus *a* is selected for more elaborate processing, but this requires some attention and the involvement of the central executive. Stimulus *b* is not selected, and although some features will be encoded, the resultant information will be less rich than for stimulus *a*. Stimulus *c* is a novel item, one that has not been seen before or recently, and so it attracts attention.

There are three main problems with this approach. First, as proponents readily acknowledge (see Cowan, 1995), it is very difficult to derive a prediction—as opposed to a post-hoc explanation—from this type of model. For example, how would this model predict the finding that articulatory suppression eliminates the word-length effect for both visual and auditory items but that articulatory suppression eliminates the phonological similarity effect for visual but not for auditory items? Could this view predict what will happen to the word-length effect when subjects hear irrelevant speech?

Second, the term *activation* is often not defined very precisely. Typically, researchers use operational definitions to specify what is meant by activation. For example, activation is usually defined by reference to a particular behavioral task; thus, Cowan (1993) offers one definition as "the temporary state of memory representations that would allow these representations to have a priming effect on subsequent stimuli" (p. 162). Although the concept has widespread acceptance, particularly for priming data, there are other explanations of priming (see Chapter 12). Some researchers suggest that activation corresponds to a pattern of activity across a subset of individual neurons. This suggestion runs into problems, however, for there are many instances when the nervous system uses a change in the rate of firing to code information, rather than activity versus no activity.

The third problem concerns the assumption of deactivation. Although the concept of decay has been used without controversy within connectionist networks (e.g., Rumelhart & McClelland, 1986), the concept has been vigorously and repeatedly rejected in the memory literature (McGeoch, 1932; Osgood, 1953; see Chapter 7). The main objection has been that time is not a causal agent: iron rusts over time, but time does not cause rust, oxidation does. In memory, information appears lost over time, but time should not be given the causal role; some other activity (usually defined as interference) that unfolds over time should be the causal agent. The underspecification of how activated information becomes deactivated, and whether it can become inhibited, is a major omission in this view.

In defense of the activation view, its proponents (see Cowan, 1993, 1995) recognize these weaknesses and note that more development is necessary. It is conceivable that these problems may be solved or greatly mitigated with further theoretical work and more precise descriptions.

# The Feature Model

The Feature Model (Nairne, 1988, 1990) was designed to account for the major effects observed when memory is tested using immediate serial recall, including many of the phenomena described in Chapters 3 and 4 such as the recency effect, the modality effect, and the suffix effect. The model gets its name from the fact that items are assumed to be represented as a set of features, a common modeling assumption (see Chapter 11). In its most simple form, this assumption states that any item can be represented by a string of +1s, −1s, and 0s. As an analogy, think of a small black-and-white television set. If you look at the screen up close, you will find that each pixel can take on three values: black, white, or broken. The screen uses the same pixels to represent an ice hockey game, a debate, or an advertising disclaimer. If you were to freeze the screen at any instant and write down the values of each pixel, you would be representing the information as a series of (mostly) +1s and −1s. The value of pixel number 824 is meaningless by itself; it does not tell you whether you are watching a sporting event or a disclaimer that not all plates go up in value. Rather, it is the ordered set of values that represents the particular display. In the Feature Model, then, no one feature in a vector is meaningful.

The Feature Model assumes that there are only two types of features. Modality-dependent features represent the conditions of presentation, including presentation modality, whereas modality-independent features represent the nature of the item itself and are generated through internal processes, such as categorization and identification. Regardless of whether you read the word *dog* silently to yourself or hear someone else say "dog," the modality-independent information will be the same. On the other hand, if you hear the word *dog,* the modality-dependent features might represent information such as the person's accent, whether the speaker was male or female, and so on. If you saw the word *dog,* the modality-dependent feature might represent information such as whether the word was in upper or lower case, what color it was, and so on. Internally generated traces can contain only modality-independent features because there was no modality. The modality-dependent features will be used to account for the effects previously attributed to echoic memory. Unlike other accounts that place the locus of echoic memory in a separate structure (Crowder & Morton, 1969), the Feature Model follows Watkins and Watkins (1980) in that modality dependent-information is viewed as just part of a common memory trace.

The Feature Model also distinguishes between primary and secondary memory. Primary memory has no capacity limits, and items in primary memory do not decay. Rather, the major function of primary memory is to construct and maintain cues that may indicate which items were recently presented (see also Raaijmakers & Shiffrin, 1981). The Feature Model assumes that all memory is cue driven (see Watkins, 1979). The only loss of information from primary memory occurs from interference: newly entering items can interfere with items that are already in primary memory. A simplifying assumption is that an item can interfere only with the immediately preceding item (see Figure 5.6). At the end of the presentation of a typical list, primary memory will consist of partially degraded traces. In the memory test, subjects must match the degraded primary memory traces with the appropriate intact trace in secondary memory.

For each partially degraded trace in primary memory, the subject tries to select an appropriate recall candidate by comparing the degraded trace with intact traces in the secondary memory search set. Typically, the secondary memory search set will consist of items presented on the most recent list, but this is not necessarily always the case. For example, when the same to-be-remembered items are repeated on each list or if the items constitute a well-established group (such as the digits 1–9), the subject will use the appropriate secondary memory search group. However, when the to-be-remembered items come from a larger group (such as unique items on each trial), the search group is likely to be larger.

Even though a subject may have correctly matched a degraded primary memory trace with its intact secondary memory counterpart, the item still may not be produced by the subject. In general, subjects tend not to recall an item more than once, even if that item actually appeared more than once on the original list (see Hinrichs, Mewaldt, & Redding, 1973). The Feature Model includes this type of output interference. Suppose the subject is trying to find a match for primary memory trace number 2, but mistakenly selects from secondary memory the item that matches the fifth primary trace; the fifth item will be recalled (and scored as incorrect because it is in the wrong order). When it comes time to match primary memory trace number 5, the subject might select the appropriate secondary memory item. However, the subject has already produced this as a response and so is less willing to write this item down again.

|   | Item Presented | Primary Memory |
|---|---|---|
| 1 | [+1 −1 +1 +1, +1 −1 +1 −1] | [+1 −1 +1 +1, +1 −1 +1 −1] |
| 2 | [−1 −1 +1 −1, −1 −1 −1 −1] | [+1  0  0 +1, +1  0 +1  0]<br>[−1 −1 +1 −1, −1 −1 −1 −1] |
| 3 | [+1 −1 −1 −1, +1 +1 −1 +1] | [+1  0  0 +1, +1  0 +1  0]<br>[−1  0 +1  0, −1 −1  0 −1]<br>[+1 −1 −1 −1, +1 +1 −1 +1] |
| 4 | [−1 +1 −1 −1, −1 +1 +1 +1] | [+1  0  0 +1, +1  0 +1  0]<br>[−1  0 +1  0, −1 −1  0 −1]<br>[+1 −1  0  0, +1  0 −1  0]<br>[−1 +1 −1 −1, −1 +1 +1 +1] |

**Figure 5.6**  An example of what might happen when four items are presented, assuming perfect encoding and an overwriting probability of 1.0. The first four features represent modality-independent information, and the second four represent modality-dependent information. Item 1 is represented accurately in primary memory, but when item 2 is presented, any features in item 1 that overlap with features in item 2 are overwritten (set to 0). The same thing happens when item 3 is presented. Only the last item is completely intact. However, rehearsal can take place: this consists of generating an item, and a generated item can contain only modality-independent features. The rehearsed item(s) can overwrite the modality independent features of the final item, but the modality-dependent features will be intact.

The final assumptions needed to get the model up and running concern the number of features. Going back to the television analogy, you can see an elephant on a 13-inch screen almost as easily as on a 35-inch screen. There will be some differences in resolution, but the smaller screen will be satisfactory and can convey all the necessary information. As the left panel of Figure 5.7 shows, there is almost no advantage of using a large number of features compared to a small number of features (see also Neath & Nairne, 1995). The reason that the absolute number of features is unimportant is because the rule that decides whether a primary and secondary memory trace match relies on the relative number or proportion of matching features. Thus, items were assumed to have 20 modality-independent features (this number was picked to minimize the time required to run the simulation and has no other significance).

It is assumed that auditory presentation gives rise to more modality-dependent features than visual presentation does. Nairne (1988, 1990) discussed the reasons for this in detail, but the basic idea is the acknowledgment that primary memory traces do not exist in a vacuum; rather, they exist as part of a stream of ongoing mental activity (see Johnson & Raye, 1981; Nairne & McNabb, 1985). When interpreting a primary memory trace, the subject needs to discriminate the trace not only from other traces but also from traces that are generated internally. By definition, traces that are generated by purely internal activity contain only modality-independent features and lack some of the information that accompanies perception of an external item (Suengas & Johnson, 1988; Surprenant, 1992; see also the section on Real versus Imagined Events in Chapter 13).

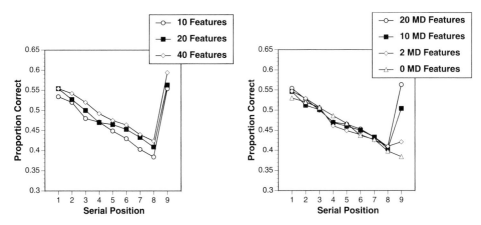

**Figure 5.7**    The left panel shows the proportion of items correctly recalled as a function of the number of features. The three lines show predicted performance (1) when there are 10 modality-independent and 10 modality-dependent features, (2) when there are 20 of each kind, and (3) when there are 40 of each kind. As the figure shows, there is almost no effect of increasing the absolute number of features. The right panel shows the effect of changing the number of modality-dependent features when the number of modality-independent features is held constant at 20. Parameter values not specified were the same as those in Table 5.5.

An extensive literature shows that both visual presentation and subvocal rehearsal produce similar effects (for reviews, see Baddeley, 1986; Crowder, 1976). Thus, a visually presented item will be quite similar to an internally generated item. Because there is also evidence of differences between visually and auditorily presented items, we end up with a scheme in which auditory items have more modality-dependent features than do visual items, which in turn have more modality-dependent features than do internally generated items (Nairne, 1988, 1990; for further converging evidence, see Surprenant & Neath, 1996). The right panel of Figure 5.7 shows the effect of decreasing the number of modality-dependent features when the number of modality-independent features is held constant.

What makes the Feature Model seem complex is that it can simulate many different processes simultaneously. Fortunately, each individual process is simple and straightforward, and the key processes are precisely described using four simple equations. What follows is a description of a typical trial in which a subject hears a list of nine digits in random order and then recalls them in order (immediate serial recall).

Each to-be-remembered item is made up of features. Because it is auditory presentation, we assume there are 20 modality-independent features and 20 modality-dependent features, each of which is randomly set to values of +1 or −1. These 40 features represent the first item presented. The second item presented also contains 40 features. Retroactive interference occurs, with features from item 2 overwriting features of item 1; specifically, if modality-independent feature number 5 of item 2 has the same value as modality-independent feature number 5 of item 1, then item 1's feature 5 is overwritten by replacing the original value with a value of 0. The parameter $F$ in the model determines how

**Table 5.5**  Parameters and typical parameter values for the Feature Model.

| Description | Symbol | Typical Value |
|---|---|---|
| Attention constant | $b$ | 1.0 |
| Recovery scaling constant | $c$ | 2.0 |
| Number of recovery attempts | $r$ | 2 |
| Probability of overwriting | $F$ | 1.0 |
| Distance scaling constant | $a$ | 9 |
| Number of modality-independent features | | 20 |
| Number of modality-dependent features: | | |
|    Auditory | | 20 |
|    Visual | | 2 |
| Number of segments: | | |
|    Short | | 1 |
|    Long | | 10 |
| Probability of segment error | | 0.10 |

likely overwriting is (see Table 5.5); in most situations, $F$ is set to 1.0, which ensures that overwriting will occur if the features are the same.

Then the third item is presented, then the fourth, and so on. The final item is followed not by any external information but by rehearsal. Because subvocal rehearsal has, by definition, no modality-dependent information (there is no modality!), only the modality-independent features of the final item are subject to overwriting. At the end of list presentation, primary memory contains a trace of each of the items presented. In the typical case, these traces will be degraded because certain features will have been overwritten. The final item, however, will have its modality-dependent features intact.

The subject now tries to match each primary memory item with an intact secondary memory trace. Because we are considering the case in which nine digits are presented in random order, the subject will limit the search to the representations of the nine digits in secondary memory. Beginning with the first item, each primary memory item is compared with all secondary memory items in the comparison set. In general, the secondary memory item with the fewest mismatching features will be selected as the candidate for recall. Thus, the secondary memory trace chosen as the response for a particular degraded primary memory trace will typically be that trace with the largest proportion of matching features, relative to the other choices currently available in the secondary memory search set. The absolute number of features is not as important as the proportion of matching features. This can be expressed mathematically as:

$$P_i(SM_j/PM_i) = \frac{s(i,j)}{\displaystyle\sum_{k=1}^{n} s(i,k)} \tag{5.2}$$

This equation describes the probability of sampling a particular secondary memory trace, $SM_j$, as a potential recall response for a primary memory trace, $PM_i$. If $i$ and $j$ have the same value, then this is a correct match; if $i$ and $j$ have different values, then it is a mismatch. The numerator is simply the similarity between primary memory trace $i$ and secondary memory trace $j$. As the similarity increases, the probability of sampling the secondary memory trace *increases*. The denominator is the sum of the similarity between primary trace $i$ and all secondary memory items in the search set. As this value increases, the probability of sampling the particular secondary memory trace *decreases*. The size of the search set is $n$, which in the case of recalling nine digits would be 9. The probability of sampling, then, is a ratio; the larger the denominator, the lower the sampling probability. This equation is a version of Luce's (1963) choice rule.

The similarity between two items $i$ and $j$ is related to a measure of distance ($d$). By using the distance as a negative exponent for the mathematical constant $e$, we ensure that the similarity value is less than 1.

$$s(i,j) = e^{-d_{ij}} \qquad (5.3)$$

The distance between two memory traces $i$ and $j$ ($d_{ij}$) is calculated by adding the number of mismatched features, $M$, and dividing by the number of compared features, $N$ (see Equation 5.4). $M_k$ is simply the number of times a particular feature position, $x_{ik}$, does not equal feature position $x_{jk}$. If the primary memory trace $i$ has a 0 for feature 3, and the secondary memory trace has a $+1$, then this is counted as a mismatch. The parameter $a$ is a scaling parameter; we adjust this value to raise or lower overall performance levels. The final parameter, $b_k$, is an attentional parameter that could be used to weight particular feature comparisons. For example, more attention might be given to certain modality-dependent features in a data driven task than in a conceptually driven task (e.g., Roediger, Weldon, & Challis, 1989). In all simulations reported, $b_k$ was set to 1.0 and so it does not affect any of the results. Similarity is thus related to the proportion of mismatched features, and the more mismatches there are, the larger $d_{ij}$ will be. The larger $d_{ij}$ is, the smaller $s$ is.

$$d_{ij} = \frac{a \sum_{k=1}^{N} b_k M_k}{N} \qquad (5.4)$$

If a subject selects as a response to a degraded primary memory trace an incorrect secondary memory trace, the subject will typically not choose that particular secondary memory trace again. This is the output interference described above and more precisely defined in Equation 5.5.

$$P_r = e^{-cr} \qquad (5.5)$$

This equation says that the probability of actually producing a sampled item as a response ($P_r$) is related to the number of times the item has already been recalled on the current trial ($r$). The parameter $c$ is a scale constant, uniformly set to 2.0 (see Table 5.5). Again, we use the product of the scale constant and the number of times an item has been recalled as a negative exponent. This says that the probability of recovering an item decreases the more times it has previously been recalled.

What follows is a partial listing of the memory phenomena that the Feature Model can successfully simulate. Unless otherwise noted, the parameters needed to produce each simulation are those listed in Table 5.5.

## Simulations Using the Feature Model

*The serial position function*    Recall generally declines over serial positions because of output interference. Items presented later in the list have a greater chance of being mistakenly recalled early on and so are less likely to be produced even if sampled. The pronounced recency effect seen in serial recall of auditory items arises because the modality-dependent features of the last list item are not subject to overwriting. Consequently, there will be extra information available to make a better match between a degraded primary memory item and the appropriate secondary memory item. To the extent that a presentation modality provides useful modality-dependent features (for example, tactile, lip-read, mouthed), there will be a modality effect (see the right panel of Figure 5.7). To the extent that a presentation modality does not provide useful modality-dependent features, there will not be a modality effect. Visual presentation leads to very little useful extra information, and so recency effects are not seen with visual presentation and serial recall (LeCompte, 1992). Another way of reducing the usefulness of the modality dependent information is to use homophones (such as *pear, pare, pair* or *pour, poor, pore*). When a list of auditory homophones is presented, there is no recency effect (Crowder, 1978). According to the Feature Model, this is because the undegraded modality-dependent features of the final item will contribute almost no useful information for matching the degraded trace to the original item; the right panel of Figure 5.7 shows these effects. Standard auditory presentation uses 20 modality-independent and 20 modality-dependent features. Standard visual presentation uses 20 modality-independent and 2 modality-dependent features. If the 20 modality-dependent features are all set to be the same (as in the case with homophones), there will be no recency effect.

*The suffix effect*    The suffix effect occurs whenever the modality-dependent features of the final item are overwritten. Thus, a speech suffix will overwrite some of the modality-dependent features of a list of speech items because these features are likely to be similar. Thus, visual suffixes should have little or no effect on auditory list items, and physically similar suffixes should have far larger effects than semantically similar suffixes do (because the locus of recency lies in residual modality-dependent features). The less similar the suffix, the smaller the suffix effect (Morton, Crowder, & Prussin, 1971). If the suffix is grouped in with the list items, then there will also be a suffix effect on more than just the final items because of the increased search set (see Nairne, 1990). This approach has been used to explain the context-dependent suffix effect (see Neath, Surprenant, & Crowder, 1993), as well as modality and suffix effects that are observed in modalities with no apparent acoustic component, such as tactile (Nairne & McNabb, 1985; Watkins & Watkins, 1974), or mouthed or lip-read (Nairne & Crowder, 1982; Spoehr & Corin, 1978) stimuli. To simulate the suffix effect, an additional auditory item is presented but not recalled. Its modality-dependent features will overwrite some of the modality-dependent features of the last to-be-remembered item and will make performance roughly equivalent to a visual condition.

*Grouping effects* The Feature Model can predict the appropriate modality-based grouping effects. When a temporal gap is inserted in a list, performance is enhanced for auditory items, but there is little or no effect on visual items (Frankish, 1985; Ryan, 1969). A temporal gap preserves the modality-dependent features of the item immediately prior to the gap in the auditory case, and so the auditory condition can be conceived of as 2 (or more) smaller lists. The reduction in the search set size provides an overall increase in performance relative to the ungrouped condition, and the removal of overwriting of the modality-dependent features of each end-boundary item produces mini serial position functions (see Figures 11 and 12 of Nairne, 1990). There is almost no advantage for visual items in a grouped list because there are far fewer modality-dependent features to be preserved.

*Phonological similarity* The Feature Model also accounts for the observation that phonological similarity impairs serial recall performance (Crowder, 1978). Because sampling probability is conceived as the ratio of similarities, any increase in similarity increases the value of the denominator relative to the numerator, resulting in overall worse performance. Phonological similarity is simulated in the Feature Model by manipulating the number of overlapping features; on average, there will always be some similarity between adjacent items. Phonological similarity is modeled by setting a minimum number of similar features. For example, in a control or phonologically dissimilar condition, each of the 20 modality-independent features is randomly set to be $\pm 1$. Under these conditions, there will be some featural overlap, but it will be essentially random. In a phonologically similar condition, however, a certain number of features (for example, 13 out of the 20) are set to the same value, +1 for example, and the remaining features (in this case, 7) are randomly set to $\pm 1$. There will be at least 13 overlapping features, but some of the other 7 may also overlap.

*Articulatory suppression* When subjects engage in articulatory suppression, they repeatedly say a constant item out loud, and this constant piece of information is assumed to be incorporated into the memory trace of each individual item. Because articulatory suppression reduces performance for both auditory and visual items, articulatory suppression is implemented by setting half of the modality-independent features of each item to a constant value. This has the net result of increasing the similarity of the items, producing decrements in the ability to match a degraded trace correctly with the appropriate undegraded trace. As Nairne (1990) demonstrated, the Feature Model produces the appropriate interaction between phonological similarity effects in the two modalities when tested with and without articulatory suppression. Articulatory suppression eliminates the phonological similarity effect for visual items because the modality-independent features become more similar. Visual items have so few modality-dependent features that they add essentially no information that would be useful for matching the phonologically dissimilar traces relative to the phonologically similar traces. Auditory items, however, have many more modality-dependent features, and even though the modality-independent features have become more similar for both groups, enough modality-dependent features are different in the phonologically dissimilar condition to give an advantage over the phonologically similar items.

*Word-length effects*   The word-length effect is implemented based on an idea originally suggested by Melton (1963). The basic idea is that the more parts there are, the more opportunities there are to make a mistake. To take an extreme example, if you have a jigsaw puzzle with only 2 pieces, it is very difficult to put the pieces together incorrectly. On the other hand, a 100-piece puzzle allows you to make far more mistakes in assembly. Just as a list can be divided into items, an item can be divided into segments. The Feature Model assumes that long words have more segments than short words, and further assumes that the segments have to be assembled at some stage during the recall process. For example, Caplan, Rochon, and Waters (1992) suggested that the segments could correspond to the phonological structure of the items and that the word-length effect arises when this information is being used in preparation for recall. The Feature Model has a parameter that corresponds to the number of segments (see Table 5.5). For simplicity, it is assumed that there is a fixed probability of assembling each segment incorrectly; as a result, long words have a greater probability of being assembled incorrectly because they possess more segments. If a segment error occurs at any point in the assembly process, half of the modality-independent features of the trace are set to 0, and the remaining half are left unchanged. The modality-independent features are affected because word-length effects obtain with both visual and auditory presentation.

Although some segments may undoubtedly be more critical than others to the identification of a particular item (e.g., Brown & Hulme, 1995), Neath and Nairne (1995) chose the simplifying assumption that any segmental error will result in an equal loss of information. Regardless of the number of segmental assembly errors, it seems likely that some information will remain, even if that information is only disassembled segments; thus, we again chose a simplifying assumption that no more than half of the modality-independent features could be affected. As a result, when modeling word-length effects, the probability of an individual segment error was the same for auditory and for visual items, as well as for long and for short words. Long words simply had more segments than short words did (see Neath & Nairne, 1995, for more details).

Watkins and Watkins (1973) found that the recall difference between short and long visual items was greater than the difference between short and long auditory items. The Feature Model correctly predicts this finding of a larger word-length effect for visual items than for auditory items (see Table 5.6). The reason is straightforward: the word-length effect is implemented in the feature model as affecting only modality-independent features. Because auditory presentation results in more modality-dependent features than does visual presentation, the effects of a word-length manipulation will affect a smaller proportion of elements in a vector that represents an auditory item, other things being equal.

*Interactions*   The strongest test of the Feature Model so far has been to see if it predicts the correct interactions between the effects modeled above. For the most part, each main effect (word length, phonological similarity) was modeled independently, and it could eas-

**Table 5.6** The predicted interaction between presentation modality and word length. The word-length effect is larger (i.e., there is a larger difference between recall of short and long words) for visually presented items than for auditory items. The parameters were as listed in Table 5.5.

|            | Visual | Auditory |
|------------|--------|----------|
| Short      | 0.433  | 0.478    |
| Long       | 0.322  | 0.414    |
| Difference | 0.111  | 0.064    |

**Table 5.7** The predicted interaction between phonological similarity, word length, and articulatory suppression. Similar items had a minimum of 10 identical features, long items had 10 segments, and short items had 1 segment. Compare with Table 5.4.

|       | Silent | | Articulatory Suppression | |
|-------|------------|---------|------------|---------|
|       | Dissimilar | Similar | Dissimilar | Similar |
| Short | 0.608      | 0.412   | 0.496      | 0.321   |
| Long  | 0.558      | 0.349   | 0.507      | 0.320   |

ily be the case that when several effects are performed simultaneously within the model, it will produce inappropriate results. However, the model does predict the correct interactions. Table 5.7 shows the results of one such simulation where the effects of word length, articulatory suppression, and phonological similarity are combined. The silent-dissimilar condition is really the control condition, and the word-length manipulation has its effect by increasing the number of mismatches between corresponding primary and secondary memory traces. Because a long word is less likely to be assembled correctly, it is less likely to be matched correctly with the secondary memory trace. Comparing the silent-dissimilar with the silent-similar condition, the phonological similarity manipulation reduces performance by increasing the number of mismatching features between a primary memory trace and the correct secondary memory trace. The reason for this increase is that more overwriting will occur if all the items in the list are phonologically similar: Overwriting changes an element's value to 0, and the secondary memory traces do not contain any zeros. This is independent of the word-length manipulation, and so word-length effects should be seen for both similar and dissimilar items.

Articulatory suppression is modeled by adding a constant value of 1 to a random half of the modality-independent features, making the degraded primary memory traces more similar to each other. This will make the correct discrimination more difficult because there is less of a difference in the number of mismatching features between a primary memory trace and correct and incorrect secondary memory traces. This effect masks the

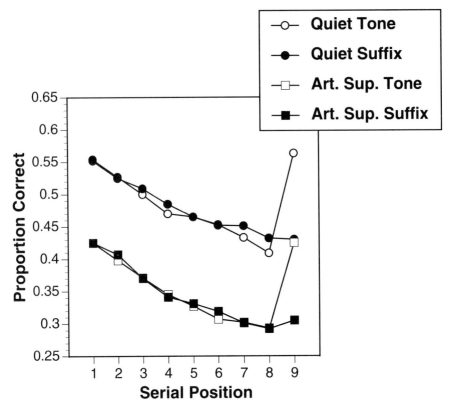

**Figure 5.8**   An example of a novel prediction of the Feature Model. Using the same parameter settings as for the previous simulations, the model predicts that a suffix effect will still be seen when subjects engage in articulatory suppression. The simulation models immediate serial recall of a list of nine digits presented auditorily and followed by either a tone or a suffix.

word-length effect because so many features have already been changed that assembly errors are not detectable with standard stimuli.

As one final example of the predictions the model makes, a simulation was run that included the suffix effect and articulatory suppression. Both of these effects were implemented separately, but the Feature Model allows the combination. The model predicts that suffix effects will still be observed under articulatory suppression, and this prediction has been confirmed empirically (Surprenant, LeCompte, & Neath, 1997). The term *predict* in conjunction with the Feature Model means that the results will be seen regardless of the parameter settings. Overall performance can be made better or worse, and slight variations can be made to appear, but the pattern shown in Figure 5.8 will always be observed. In fact, the model *cannot* be made to produce results where, under articulatory suppression, there is no suffix effect. Notice also that for all the simulation results presented and for all the findings discussed, the basic parameter values are as listed in Table 5.5.

## Critique of the Feature Model

Although the Feature Model has had remarkable success in accounting for many of the basic phenomena observed when memory is assessed immediately, there are several weaknesses. First, the Feature Model does not produce the appropriate error patterns. For example, in a test of immediate serial recall, when subjects fail to recall the third item of a list in the third position, they are most likely to recall it either second or fourth. The Feature Model does not. Nairne (1990) has suggested this could be addressed by incorporating perturbation theory (see Chapter 14), but it remains to be seen whether this will work.

A second major problem is that the Feature Model does not include any process for incorporating time. Many demonstrations have shown that increasing the time between the presentation of an item and recall can actually *increase* the likelihood of recall (e.g., Glenberg, Bradley, Kraus, & Renzaglia, 1983; Neath & Crowder, 1990, 1996). Of course, there are also many demonstrations that increasing the time between presentation and test decreases the likelihood of recall. Because there is no role for time in the Feature Model, it cannot address these data.

Obviously, there are many results that have not yet been addressed by the Feature Model. For example, when simulating a six-item mixed list (three short items and three long items) with forward serial recall, the feature model predicts no reliable differences for the first four positions but does predict an advantage for the last item in the long-short condition, relative to the last item in the short-long condition. Cowan and associates (1992; see also Cowan, Wood, & Borne, 1994) observed differences in both list halves, and at the final position the ordering of conditions was the reverse. It is possible that the addition of overwriting during recall could remedy this incorrect prediction, although this possibility has not been explored in detail.

The Feature Model does have some distinct advantages over Working Memory, whether Baddeley's (1986, 1994) version or the less-well specified activation view of Cowan (1988, 1995). First, the Feature Model can address effects at different serial positions, including modality and suffix effects observable with auditory as well as tactile stimuli, whereas the Working Memory and activation views cannot. Second, it can readily explain negative word-length effects, as described above, whereas Working Memory cannot. Perhaps the most important advantage, however, is that the Feature Model is a precise statement of what happens during the entire study and retrieval process. The predictions are unambiguous because the model provides numbers that are easily compared. As such, it also provides a check on human reasoning, which can be quite fallible, and it can be used to generate novel predictions (e.g., Surprenant & Neath, 1996).

# Summary of Current Immediate Memory Theories

The majority of theories currently used to explain immediate memory phenomena are based on Baddeley's (1986) Working Memory. Although we have examined only two — Baddeley's Working Memory and the "working memory as activated memory" view — there are many other versions (Martin, Shelton, & Yaffee, 1994; Richardson, 1996). All of these views maintain that some form of decay is required and that this imposes a fundamental limit on the amount of information that can be retained. The other major theory is Nairne's (1990) Feature Model. This differs from Working Memory approaches in that it does not use the concept of decay; rather, memory performance is made worse by interference.

# References

Anderson, J. R. (1983). *The architecture of cognition*. Cambridge, MA: Harvard University Press.

Baddeley, A. D. (1966). Short-term memory for word sequences as a function of acoustic, semantic, and formal similarity. *Quarterly Journal of Experimental Psychology, 18,* 362–365.

Baddeley, A. D. (1986). *Working memory*. New York: Oxford University Press.

Baddeley, A. D. (1992). Working memory. *Science, 255,* 556–559.

Baddeley, A. D. (1994). Working memory: The interface between memory and cognition. In D. L. Schacter & E. Tulving (Eds.), *Memory systems 1994*. Cambridge, MA: MIT Press.

Baddeley, A. D., & Hitch, G. J. (1974). Working memory. In G. H. Bower (Ed.), *The psychology of learning and motivation, Vol. 8*. New York: Academic Press.

Baddeley, A. D., & Lewis, V. J. (1984). When does rapid presentation enhance digit span? *Bulletin of the Psychonomic Society, 22,* 403–405.

Baddeley, A. D., Lewis, V. J., & Vallar, G. (1984). Exploring the articulatory loop. *Quarterly Journal of Experimental Psychology, 36,* 233–252.

Baddeley, A. D., Thomson, N., & Buchanan, M. (1975). Word length and the structure of short-term memory. *Journal of Verbal Learning and Verbal Behavior, 14,* 575–589.

Baddeley, A. D., & Wilson, B. (1988). Comprehension and working memory: A single case neuropsychological study. *Journal of Memory and Language, 27,* 479–498.

Brown, G. D. A., & Hulme, C. (1995). Modeling item length effects in memory span: No rehearsal needed? *Journal of Memory and Language, 34,* 594–621.

Burgess, N., & Hitch, G. J. (1992). Toward a network model of the articulatory loop. *Journal of Memory and Language, 31,* 429–460.

Butterworth, B., Campbell, R., & Howard, D. (1986). The uses of short-term memory: A case study. *Quarterly Journal of Experimental Psychology, 38A,* 705–738.

Caplan, D., Rochon, E., & Waters, G. S. (1992). Articulatory and phonological determinants of word-length effects in span tasks. *Quarterly Journal of Experimental Psychology, 45A,* 177–192.

Colle, H. A., & Welsh, A. (1976). Acoustic masking in primary memory. *Journal of Verbal Learning and Verbal Behavior, 15,* 17–32.

Conrad, R. (1964). Acoustic confusions in immediate memory. *British Journal of Psychology, 55,* 75–84.

Cowan, N. (1988). Evolving conceptions of memory storage, selective attention, and their mutual constraints within the human information processing system. *Psychological Bulletin, 104,* 163–191.

Cowan, N. (1993). Activation, attention, and short-term memory. *Memory & Cognition, 21,* 162–168.

Cowan, N. (1995). *Attention and memory: An integrated framework*. New York: Oxford University Press.

Cowan, N., Day, L., Saults, J. S., Keller, T. A., Johnson, T., & Flores, L. (1992). The role of verbal output time in the effects of word length on immediate memory. *Journal of Memory and Language, 31,* 1–17.

Cowan, N., Wood, N. L., & Borne, D. N. (1994). Reconfirmation of the short-term storage concept. *Psychological Science, 5,* 103–106.

Crowder, R. G. (1976). *Principles of learning and memory.* Hillsdale, NJ: Erlbaum.

Crowder, R. G. (1978). Memory for phonologically uniform lists. *Journal of Verbal Learning and Verbal Behavior, 17,* 73–89.

Crowder, R. G. (1982). The demise of short-term memory. *Acta Psychologica, 5,* 291–323.

Crowder, R. G. (1993). Short-term memory: Where do we stand? *Memory & Cognition, 21,* 142–145.

Crowder, R. G., & Morton, J. (1969). Precategorical acoustic storage (PAS). *Perception & Psychophysics, 5,* 365–373.

Ellis, N. C., & Hennelly, R. A. (1980). A bilingual word-length effect: Implications for intelligence testing and the relative ease of mental calculations in Welsh and English. *British Journal of Psychology, 71,* 43–52.

Estes, W. K. (1973). Phonemic coding and rehearsal in short-term memory for letter strings. *Journal of Verbal Learning and Verbal Behavior, 12,* 360–372.

Frankish, C. (1985). Modality-specific grouping effects in short-term memory. *Journal of Memory and Language, 24,* 200–209.

Gathercole, S. E., & Baddeley, A. D. (1993). *Working memory and language.* Hove, UK: Erlbaum.

Glenberg, A. M., Bradley, M. M., Kraus, T. A., & Renzaglia, G. J. (1983). Studies of the long-term recency effect: Support for a contextually guided retrieval theory. *Journal of Experimental Psychology: Learning, Memory and Cognition, 9,* 231–255.

Hinrichs, J. V., Mewaldt, S. P., & Redding, J. (1973). The Ranschberg effect: Repetition and guessing factors in short-term memory. *Journal of Verbal Learning and Verbal Behavior, 12,* 64–75.

Howard, D., & Butterworth, B. (1989). Developmental disorders of verbal short-term memory and their relation to sentence comprehension: A reply to Vallar and Baddeley. *Cognitive Neuropsychology, 6,* 455–463.

Johnson, M. K., & Raye, C. L. (1981). Reality monitoring. *Psychological Review, 88,* 67–85.

Jones, D. M., & Macken, W. J. (1993). Irrelevant tones produce an irrelevant speech effect: Implications for phonological coding in working memory. *Journal of Experimental Psychology: Learning, Memory, and Cognition, 19,* 369–381.

Jones, D. M., & Macken, W. J. (1995). Phonological similarity in the irrelevant speech effect: Within- or between-stream similarity? *Journal of Experimental Psychology: Learning, Memory, and Cognition, 21,* 103–115.

LeCompte, D. C. (1992). In search of a strong visual recency effect. *Memory & Cognition, 20,* 563–572.

LeCompte, D. C., Neely, C. B., & Wilson, J. R. (1997). Irrelevant speech and irrelevant tones: The relative importance of speech to the irrelevant speech effect. *Journal of Experimental Psychology: Learning, Memory, and Cognition, 23,* 472–483.

LeCompte, D. C., & Shaibe, D. M. (1997). On the irrelevance of phonology to the irrelevant speech effect. *Quarterly Journal of Experimental Psychology, 50A,* 100–118.

LeCompte, D. C., Surprenant, A. M., & Neath, I. (1997). Irrelevant speech eliminates the phonological similarity effect for visual but not auditory items. Unpublished manuscript.

Levy, B. A. (1971). Role of articulation in auditory and visual short-term memory. *Journal of Verbal Learning and Verbal Behavior, 10,* 123–132.

Longoni, A. M., Richardson, J. T. E., & Aiello, A. (1993). Articulatory rehearsal and phonological storage in working memory. *Memory & Cognition, 21,* 11–22.

Luce, R. D. (1963). Detection and recognition. In R. D. Luce, R. R. Bush, & E. Galanter (Eds.), *Handbook of mathematical psychology.* New York: Wiley.

Mackworth, J. F. (1963). The duration of the visual image. *Canadian Journal of Psychology, 17,* 62–81.

Martin, R. C. (1993). Short-term memory and sentence processing: Evidence from neuropsychology. *Memory & Cognition, 21,* 176–183.

Martin, R. C. (1995). Working memory doesn't work: A critique of Miyake et al.'s capacity theory of aphasic comprehension deficits. *Cognitive Neuropsychology, 12,* 623–636.

Martin, R. C., Blossom-Stach, C., Yaffee, L. S., & Wetzel, W. F. (1995). Consequences of a motor programming deficit for rehearsal and written sentence comprehension. *Quarterly Journal of Experimental Psychology, 48A,* 536–572.

Martin, R. C., Shelton, J. R., & Yaffee, L. S. (1994). Language processing and working memory: Neuropsychological evidence for separate phonological and semantic capacities. *Journal of Memory and Language, 33,* 83–111.

McGeoch, J. A. (1932). Forgetting and the law of disuse. *Psychological Review, 39,* 352–370.

Melton, A. W. (1963). Implications of short-term memory for a general theory of memory. *Journal of Verbal Learning and Verbal Behavior, 2,* 1–21.

Morton, J., Crowder, R. G., & Prussin, H. A. (1971). Experiments with the stimulus suffix effect. *Journal of Experimental Psychology Monograph, 91,* 169–190.

Murray, D. J. (1968). Articulation and acoustic confusability in short-term memory. *Journal of Experimental Psychology, 78,* 679–684.

Nairne, J. S. (1988). A framework for interpreting recency effects in immediate serial recall. *Memory & Cognition, 16,* 343–352.

Nairne, J. S. (1990). A feature model of immediate memory. *Memory & Cognition, 18,* 251–269.

Nairne, J. S., & Crowder, R. G. (1982). On the locus of the stimulus suffix effect. *Memory & Cognition, 10,* 350–357.

Nairne, J. S., & McNabb, W. K. (1985). More modality effects in the absence of sound. *Journal of Experimental Psychology: Learning, Memory and Cognition, 11,* 596–604.

Naveh-Benjamin, M., & Ayres, T. J. (1986). Digit span, reading rate, and linguistic relativity. *Quarterly Journal of Experimental Psychology, 38A,* 739–751.

Neath, I., & Crowder, R. G. (1990). Schedules of presentation and temporal distinctiveness in human memory. *Journal of Experimental Psychology: Learning, Memory and Cognition, 16,* 316–327.

Neath, I., & Crowder, R. G. (1996). Distinctiveness and very short-term serial position effects. *Memory, 4,* 225–242.

Neath, I., & Nairne, J. S. (1995). Word-length effects in immediate memory: Overwriting trace-decay theory. *Psychonomic Bulletin & Review, 2,* 429–441.

Neath, I., Surprenant, A. M., & Crowder, R. G. (1993). The context-dependent stimulus-suffix effect. *Journal of Experimental Psychology: Learning, Memory and Cognition, 19,* 698–703.

Neath, I., Surprenant, A. M., & LeCompte, D. C. (in press). Irrelevant speech eliminates the word-length effect. *Memory & Cognition.*

Nosofsky, R. M. (1986). Attention, similarity, and the identification-categorization relationship. *Journal of Experimental Psychology: General, 115,* 39–57.

Osgood, C. E. (1953). *Method and theory in experimental psychology.* New York: Oxford University Press.

Peterson, L. R., & Johnson, S. T. (1971). Some effects of minimizing articulation on short-term retention. *Journal of Verbal Learning and Verbal Behavior, 10,* 346–354.

Raaijmakers, J. G. W., & Shiffrin, R. M. (1981). Search of associative memory. *Psychological Review, 88,* 93–134.

Richardson, J. T. E. (Ed.). (1996). *Working memory and human cognition.* New York: Oxford University Press.

Roediger, H. L., III, Weldon, M. S., & Challis, B. H. (1989). Explaining dissociations between implicit and explicit measures of retention: A processing account. In H. L. Roediger III & F. I. M. Craik (Eds.), *Varieties of memory and consciousness: Essays in honour of Endel Tulving.* Hillsdale, NJ: Erlbaum.

Rumelhart, D. E., & McClelland, J. L. (Eds.). (1986). *Parallel distributed processing, Vol. 1.* Cambridge, MA: MIT Press.

Ryan, J. (1969). Grouping and short-term memory: Different means and patterns of groups. *Quarterly Journal of Experimental Psychology, 21,* 137–147.

Salamé, P., & Baddeley, A. D. (1982). Disruption of short-term memory by unattended speech: Implications for the structure of working memory. *Journal of Verbal Learning and Verbal Behavior, 21,* 150–164.

Schneider, W., & Detweiler, M. (1987). A connectionist/control architecture for working memory. In G. H. Bower (Ed.), *The psychology of learning and motivation, Vol. 21.* New York: Academic Press.

Schweickert, R., & Boruff, B. (1986). Short-term memory capacity: Magic number or magic spell? *Journal of Experimental Psychology: Learning, Memory and Cognition, 12,* 419–425.

Schweickert, R., Guentert, L., & Hersberger, L. (1990). Phonological similarity, pronunciation rate, and memory span. *Psychological Science, 1,* 74–77.

Shiffrin, R. M. (1993). Short-term memory: A brief commentary. *Memory & Cognition, 21,* 193–197.

Shiffrin, R. M., & Schneider, W. (1977). Controlled and automatic human information processing: II. Perceptual learning, automatic attending, and a general theory. *Psychological Review, 84,* 127–190.

Spoehr, K. T., & Corin, W. J. (1978). The stimulus-suffix effect as a memory coding phenomenon. *Memory & Cognition, 6,* 583–589.

Suengas, A. G., & Johnson, M. K. (1988). Qualitative effects of rehearsal on memories for perceived and imagined complex events. *Journal of Experimental Psychology: General, 117,* 377–389.

Surprenant, A. M. (1992). *The mind's ear: Imagery for vowels and consonants.* Unpublished doctoral dissertation, Yale University.

Surprenant, A. M., LeCompte, D. C., & Neath, I. (1997). *Manipulations of irrelevant information: Suffix effects with articulatory suppression and irrelevant speech.* Unpublished manuscript.

Surprenant, A. M., & Neath, I. (1996). The relation between discriminability and memory for vowels, consonants, and silent center vowels. *Memory & Cognition, 24,* 356–366.

Vallar, G., & Baddeley, A. D. (1984). Phonological short-term store, phonological processing and sentence comprehension: a neuropsychological case study. *Cognitive Neuropsychology, 1,* 121–141.

Vallar, G., & Baddeley, A. D. (1987). Phonological short-term store and sentence processing. *Cognitive Neuropsychology, 4,* 417–438.

Watkins, M. J. (1972). Locus of the modality effect in free recall. *Journal of Verbal Learning and Verbal Behavior, 11,* 644–648.

Watkins, M. J. (1979). Engrams as cuegrams and forgetting as cue overload: A cueing approach to the structure of memory. In C. R. Puff (Ed.), *Memory organization and structure.* New York: Academic Press.

Watkins, M. J., & Watkins, O. C. (1973). The postcategorical status of the modality effect in serial recall. *Journal of Experimental Psychology, 99,* 226–230.

Watkins, M. J., & Watkins, O. C. (1974). A tactile suffix effect. *Memory & Cognition, 2,* 176–180.

Watkins, O. C., & Watkins, M. J. (1980). The modality effect and echoic persistence. *Journal of Experimental Psychology: General, 109,* 251–278.

# CHAPTER SIX

# Perspectives on Processing

*"We soon forget what we have not deeply thought about."*

—*Marcel Proust*

The three previous chapters have emphasized memory as a structure. For example, in the modal model, one of the most important aspects that determines whether an item will be recalled is the memory store that holds the item: an item stored in short-term memory will be remembered differently than will an item in long-term memory or sensory memory. During the 1970s, a different view became increasingly popular—one that shifted the emphasis from the underlying store as the most important factor to the type of processing that was performed.

## Levels of Processing

Craik and Lockhart (1972) offered the first detailed view suggesting that processing was more important than the underlying theoretical structure. They made four key assumptions. First, they conceptualized memory as the result of a successive series of analyses, each at a deeper level than the previous one, that are performed on the to-be-processed information. An example of a shallow level is processing an item on the basis of how it sounds; an example of a deep level is processing an item on the basis of its meaning. It is important to note that there really are no discrete levels; rather, there is a continuum from shallow to deep. Second, Craik and Lockhart assumed that the deeper the level, the more durable the resulting memory. If you need to remember an item for a long time, it is better to use a deep level of processing, such as focusing on its meaning, than to use a more shallow level, such as how the item sounds. Third, the levels of processing view assumes that rehearsal can be relatively unimportant. Memory improvements are due to deeper levels of analysis, not to repeating an item over and over. Rehearsal will be beneficial only to the extent that it induces a deeper level of processing. This type of rehearsal, known as Type II or *elaborative rehearsal,* will improve memory; simple rote repetition, known as Type I or *maintenance rehearsal,* will not improve memory.

The final assumption has to do with how memory should be studied rather than with specifics of the theory. Because the emphasis is on processing rather than on structure,

Craik and Lockhart (1972) argued that the most informative research will occur when the experimenter has control over the processing. When subjects are intentionally trying to learn, they might use the processing they think most appropriate, and this may not be the processing the experimenter wanted. Therefore, researchers should use an incidental learning procedure. In this procedure, the subject is unaware that the material being processed will be tested later on; rather, the subject simply processes the material in the way suggested by the experimenter.

> The interesting thing to do is to systematically study retention following different orienting tasks within the incidental condition, rather than to compare incidental with intentional learning. Under incidental conditions, the experimenter has a control over the processing the subject applies to the material that he does not have when the subject is merely instructed to learn and uses an unknown coding strategy. (Craik & Lockhart, 1972, p. 677)

One implication is that intent to learn is not necessarily an important variable in memory research. Indeed, Postman (1964, p. 190) had earlier concluded the same thing, that "intent per se is not a significant variable in learning."

One early experiment that seemed to support many of the assumptions of the levels of processing view, including the relative unimportance of intentionality, was reported by Hyde and Jenkins (1973). They actually used 22 different conditions, but we shall examine only a few in detail. The to-be-remembered items were 24 common words presented auditorily. Following presentation, the subjects were asked to recall as many of these items as they could in any order they liked (free recall). The groups of subjects differed primarily in the orienting instructions given to them and in whether they were told in advance of the free recall test.

One group of subjects was given a shallow task, such as checking the words for the presence of the letters E or G. A second group was given the slightly deeper task of identifying the part of speech, such as noun or verb. A third group was asked to rate the frequency, or how common the word is. A fourth group was asked to rate each word on how pleasant or unpleasant it was. Half the subjects in each of these groups were told that they would also need to remember the items for a later test (the intentional group); the other half were told nothing about the memory test (the incidental group). Finally, a control group was told simply to remember the words for a later free recall test. The results are shown in Figure 6.1.

There are three particularly important findings. First, looking only at the incidental groups, the deeper the level of processing, the more words were recalled. For example, those subjects performing pleasantness ratings recalled more items than did those doing E-G checking. Second, subjects in the incidental pleasantness condition recalled as many, if not more, words than did subjects in the intentional control condition. This finding supports Postman's assertion, quoted above, that other factors may be more important than intent to remember. Finally, there was very little difference in performance between the incidental and intentional groups that were given the same orienting instructions. For example, those subjects performing the part of speech judgment recalled the same number of words regardless of whether they knew about the recall test.

The results from Hyde and Jenkins' (1973) study support many of the assumptions of Craik and Lockhart (1972) levels of processing framework. A different set of experiments supported the idea that maintenance rehearsal has little or no effect on memory.

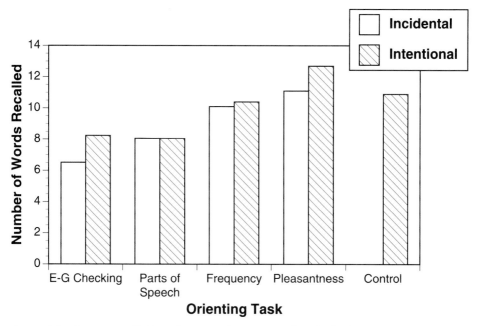

**Figure 6.1**   Amount recalled as a function of orienting task and whether subjects were told a memory test would be given.   Source: Hyde & Jenkins (1973).

Craik and Watkins (1973) tested the idea that maintenance rehearsal does not lead to improved memory. They induced subjects to use maintenance rehearsal by giving them special instructions. Subjects were asked to listen to a list of items and report the last word that began with a particular letter. If the critical letter were G, the subject could ignore all words until one was encountered that began with G. For example, in the list DAUGHTER, OIL, RIFLE, GARDEN, GRAIN, TABLE, FOOTBALL, ANCHOR, GIRAFFE, the first word the subject would rehearse would be GARDEN. The subject would rehearse this item for only a moment before GRAIN replaced it. GRAIN would be rehearsed for longer, because GIRAFFE does not appear for a while. The operational definition of how long an item was rehearsed was termed $i$, the number of intervening words. GRAIN had an $i$ value of 3, GARDEN had an $i$ value of 0, and some items had $i$ values as large as 12. At the end of each trial, the subject would report the one item required and the next trial would begin. The final manipulation of interest involved a surprise final recall test. Ten minutes after the final trial, Craik and Watkins asked the subjects to report as many of the critical items as they could, both the final ones, which they had already reported, as well as those that were not the final items. Craik and Watkins found that final recall was unrelated to the $i$ value: recall of an item was uncorrelated with how long it had been rehearsed using maintenance rehearsal.

This result poses a problem for the modal model because it suggests that time spent in short-term store can be unrelated to subsequent recall. Further research has generally replicated the finding of little or no effect of maintenance rehearsal. For example, Nairne

(1983) replicated these results for free recall but also tested recognition. In a recognition test, subjects can indicate whether they do or do not recognize an item as being from a particular list. Nairne found increased "yes" responding with increased rehearsal, but this does not necessarily mean that overall memory was more accurate. Subjects were

---

**Experiment   Levels of Processing**

**Purpose:** To demonstrate the basic levels of processing phenomena.

**Subjects:** Forty subjects are recommended. Ten should be assigned to the intentional *E-G* group, 10 to the incidental *E-G* group, 10 to the intentional pleasantness group, and 10 to the incidental pleasantness group.

**Materials:** Table E in the Appendix lists 25 common, 2-syllable nouns. For each subject, present these in a different, random order. The orienting responses require answer sheets with numbers from 1 to 25. Additional sheets will be required for the free recall test.

**Design:** Because each subject experiences only one condition, both intentionality and level of processing are between-subjects factors. The basic design is a 2 × 2 factorial.

**Procedure:** Inform the subjects that this is an experiment on information processing. Describe the orienting task that each group will get, and explain how they will respond on the answer sheets. Do not give out the response sheets for the free recall task; it is very important that the subjects in the incidental conditions do not expect a memory test. For those subjects in the intentional conditions, inform them that they will be tested for their memory for the words later on. Read each word aloud, allowing 3 seconds for the subject's response. After reading the words, remove the first answer sheet before giving them the second. This way, they won't be able to use their previous responses as cues. Allow as much time as needed for the free recall test.

**Instructions for E-G:** "This is an experiment on information processing. I will read a list of 25 words, and I would like you to indicate whether there is an *E* or a *G* in the word. If the word has either an *E*, a *G*, or both, please write Y next to the number on the response sheet. If the word has no *E*s or *G*s, please write N. Please be as accurate as you can, but you will have only 3 seconds per word to make your response." To the intentional group, add: "At the end, you will be tested for your memory for the words."

**Instructions for Pleasantness:** "This is an experiment on information processing. I will read a list of 25 words, and I would like you to indicate whether you think the word represents something pleasant or unpleasant. If you think the word is pleasant, please write P next to the number on the response sheet. If the word is unpleasant, please write U. Please be as accurate as you can, but you will have only 3 seconds per word to make your response." To the intentional group, add: "At the end, you will be tested for your memory for the words."

**Instructions for Test:** "Please write down as many of the 25 words as you can remember. Feel free to write them down in any order."

**Scoring and Analysis:** For each subject, count the number of words recalled and compute an average for each group. The results should be similar to those plotted in Figure 6.1. A 2 × 2 between-subjects analysis of variance can be performed on the individual subject data.

**Optional Enhancements:** Include a control group that receives intentional instructions but no orienting instructions.

Source: Based on an experiment by Hyde and Jenkins (1973).

**Table 6.1** Two ways of accounting for basic memory phenomena. Reading the table down shows the structural view: if an item is in STS, then its format will be phonological, the capacity small, etc. Omitting the top row shows the processing view: If an item is encoded phonologically, then the capacity is small and the duration is around 30 s. The first line becomes irrelevant.

| Store | Sensory | STS | LTS |
|---|---|---|---|
| Format | literal copy | phonological | semantic |
| Rehearsal | not possible | maintenance | elaborative |
| Capacity | medium | small | infinite |
| Duration | 500–2000 ms | up to 30 s | minutes to years |

more likely to say "yes" both (1) to items that were from the list (a correct response, known as a "hit") and (2) to items that were not from the list (an incorrect response known as a "false alarm"). When this tendency is taken into account using signal detection theory and measuring accuracy with $d'$ (see Chapter 9), there was no relation between rehearsal and performance.

Table 6.1 illustrates how the same results can be interpreted by two very different views. According to the modal model, it is the memory structure that determines the properties. If short-term store is used, the code will be phonological, the capacity will be relatively small, maintenance rehearsal will keep the item in the store, and without rehearsal, the maximum duration is about 30 s. What levels of processing did was basically eliminate the top row. According to levels of processing, if a subject processes an item at the phonological level, then the subject will not be able to remember very many items for very long.

Although levels of processing as a theoretical description can account for many experimental findings — including some findings that the modal model cannot — it has two major problems. The first major problem with levels of processing is that one of its key assumptions is circular. It is assumed that deeper levels of processing lead to better memory, and when there is better memory, we attribute it to a deeper level of processing. Although most researchers will concede that E-G checking is intuitively more shallow than pleasantness ratings, there is no independent method for determining, before a memory experiment, whether process A is deeper or more shallow than level B. Craik and Tulving (1975) reported 10 experiments that attempted to define levels objectively. For example, one idea was that deeper levels of processing require more time to perform than shallower levels do. Unfortunately, they observed that it is possible to construct a situation such that a deep task requires 0.83 s to complete and leads to 82% correct, and a shallow task takes 1.70 s to complete but leads to only 57% correct.

The lack of an objective definition of a level might have been overcome had there not been a second major problem, this one concerning an omission. Levels of processing focused almost exclusively on encoding and said relatively little about retrieval. The second major processing view developing in the 1970s, transfer appropriate processing, began as a way of rectifying this omission. Despite its major problems, however, levels of processing had an enormous impact on the field and influenced many current theories of memory.

## Transfer Appropriate Processing

The primary difference between levels of processing and transfer appropriate processing is that the latter includes retrieval. According to this view, a process leads to better performance not because it is deeper but because it is appropriate given the kind of test that will be conducted. In general, deep tasks do lead to better performance than do shallow tasks on free recall tests, but free recall is not the only way of testing memory. Morris, Bransford, and Franks (1977) demonstrated that a shallow level of processing can lead to better performance than a deep level when tested in a particular way. This demonstration clearly disconfirms an assumption of levels of processing.

Morris, Bransford, and Franks (1977) presented 32 sentences auditorily to the subjects, and in each sentence, a word was missing. In one condition, subjects judged whether a target word filled in the blank. For example, the sentence might be "The (blank) had a silver engine" and the target word might be *train*. In a different condition, subjects judged whether the target word rhymed with another. In this case, the sentence might be "(Blank) rhymes with legal" and the target word might be *eagle*. Subjects indicated "yes" or "no" to each kind of question and were unaware that a later memory test would be given. So far, this is just like a standard levels of processing experiment, with subjects performing incidental learning under two different sets of orienting instructions. But the researchers changed the paradigm by including two types of tests. One test was a standard recognition test, where a target word was presented and subjects were asked whether it had been seen previously. The second test was a rhyming recognition test, where subjects were asked whether a word rhymed with one of the target words. In the example given above, the standard recognition test might have as a test item the word *train* or the word *eagle*. The rhyming recognition test might have as test items the word *plane* (which rhymes with *train*) and *regal* (which rhymes with *eagle*). The results are shown in Figure 6.2.

With a standard recognition test, the deeper orienting task (whether the word fit in the sentence) led to better performance than did the more shallow task (whether the word rhymed). However, with the rhyme recognition test, the shallow task led to better performance than did the deep task. Levels of processing assumed that deeper processing leads to better performance, but the data in Figure 6.2 show that this is true only for some kinds of tests; on other tests, shallow processing can be better than deep. Morris, Bransford, and Franks (1977) interpreted their results as supporting a theory called *transfer appropriate processing*. A type of processing will lead to better memory performance if it is appropriate for the particular test; no one type of processing is good for all tests.

One qualification should be added. Fisher and Craik (1977) replicated the results of Morris, Bransford, and Franks (1977), ruling out several uninteresting interpretations of the data. They emphasized, however, that although rhyme encoding followed by a rhyme cue led to better performance than did semantic encoding followed by a rhyme cue, semantic encoding followed by a semantic cue led to the best performance. This can be seen in the data of shown in Figure 6.2. According to Fisher and Craik (1977), the reason is that semantic encoding leads to a more specific cue, which in turn leads to enhanced discriminability from competing cues. For example, there are only limited number of possible phonemic cues, compared to an almost infinite number of semantic cues. This is related to Watkins' (1979) cue overload principle, which states that there are only so many items that can be associated with a cue before the cue begins to lose its effectiveness.

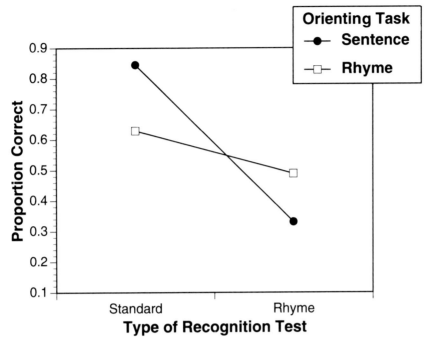

**Figure 6.2**  Overall proportion correct on a standard or rhyme recognition memory test following either a sentence (semantic) or rhyme (nonsemantic) orienting task.  Source: Morris, Bransford, & Franks (1977).

The more items that are associated with a cue, the less effective the cue will be in eliciting the desired item.

## Organization and Distinctiveness

The levels of processing framework includes the idea that a deeper level of processing produces a more distinctive cue than does a shallow level of processing. The more distinctive an item, the more different it is from competing items (see also the discussion of distinctiveness in Chapter 7). At the same time, however, there is a large body of literature that demonstrates that organization helps memory. When incorporating information into an organization, what matters most are the similarities. As Hunt and McDaniel (1993, p. 421), wondered, "How can both similarity and difference be beneficial to memory?"

As used in the memory field, *organization* refers to relationships among the information that is to be remembered, and it formed a cornerstone of gestalt theory (Katona, 1940; Koffka, 1935). Subjects recall more words from a categorized list than from an uncategorized list. For example, Deese (1959) found that subjects recalled about 49% of the words from a list that contained high associates (such as flower, insect, bees), compared to only 37% of the words from a random list. The effects of organization can be quite powerful. Mandler (1967) had four groups of subjects examine 52 words. Of most interest here is that subjects who were asked to sort the cards into categories of their own choosing recalled as many of the words on a surprise test as did subjects who were specifically asked to memorize the words.

A related phenomenon is called *clustering*. Bousfield (1953) presented subjects with a 60-word list made up of 15 instances of four categories (animals, names, professions, and vegetables). The words were presented in random order. Bousfield observed that subjects were likely to cluster their responses; that is, they were likely to recall two or more items from the same category sequentially even though the items were separated in the list. The lists do not need to be categorized in such a blatant fashion in order to see clustering (for example, Tulving, 1962).

One resolution has been to say the paradox that both similarity and difference helps is more apparent than real. In other words, both are important because both reflect particular types of processing. Hunt and his colleagues (Hunt & Einstein, 1981; Hunt & McDaniel, 1993) emphasize the importance of relational and item-specific processing, arguing that organization emphasizes relational processing (how the items fit together), whereas item-specific processing emphasizes the particular to-be-remembered item. Memory performance is best when both processes occur. A specific example is provided in Chapter 14, at the end of the section "Item and Order Information."

For now, the important point is that both relational and item-specific processing are important. Without knowledge of the to-be-remembered item itself, memory will be quite poor. Even if the item is known, however, relational processing can help provide cues that quickly produce the desired target information. This interaction between the processes performed at encoding and those performed at retrieval is highlighted in our next topic, the encoding specificity principle.

# The Encoding Specificity Principle

Tulving (1972, 1983) described a principle that is consistent with the results from the transfer appropriate processing paradigm that he proposed and empirically evaluated over the last 20 years called the *encoding specificity principle*. According to this principle, the recollection of an event or a certain aspect of it depends on the interaction between the properties of the encoded event and the properties of the retrieval information. Tulving calls this particular process *ecphory*, from a Greek word meaning "to be made known." An ecphoric process, then, is a process by which "retrieval information is brought into interaction with stored information" (p. 178). Because it is the interaction that is important, both the study and test conditions must be specified before any meaningful statements can be made about memory processes. Tulving (1983, p. 239) lists three specific kinds of meaningless statements: (1) absolute statements about the memorability of items; (2) absolute statements concerning the effectiveness of different kinds of encoding operations; and (3) absolute statements about effectiveness of different types of cues. The only way such statements can be meaningful is if both the study and the test conditions are well specified.

We have already examined one good example: the statement "deep processing at study is better than shallow processing" is inaccurate unless the statement is amended to include a description of the test. Another example concerns the difference between a

**Table 6.2**  The probability of recall when study cues and retrieval cues are varied.

| | Retrieval Cue | | |
|---|---|---|---|
| Study Cue | None | Weak | Strong |
| None | 0.49 | 0.43 | 0.68 |
| Weak | 0.30 | 0.82 | 0.23 |

Source:  Data from Thomson & Tulving (1970).

strong cue and a weak cue. A *strong cue* is a word that elicits a desired target word most of the time. When people hear the word *bloom,* most will respond with *flower* as the first word they think of. A *weak cue* is a word that elicits the target word only rarely. When people hear *fruit,* they respond with *flower* only about 1% of the time. You might be tempted to conclude that strong cues are better than weak cues, but this is the sort of absolute statement that Tulving (1983) argues is meaningless. The reason is that weak cues can be made more effective than strong cues depending on what happens at study and at test. In one experiment, Thomson and Tulving (1970) presented some target words alone at study, and some with a weak cue. At test, there were three cue conditions: no cue, a weak cue, or a strong cue. The results, expressed as probability of recall, are shown in Table 6.2.

First, note that *bloom* (a strong cue) can be an effective cue, as in the case where no study cues were provided and subjects were expecting a free recall test. However, note also that when a weak cue was presented at encoding, the weak cue at test was better than both no cue (0.82 versus 0.30) and the strong cue (0.82 versus 0.23).

Perhaps the most surprising implication of this view is that an item is not necessarily the best cue for itself. In a typical recognition experiment, the subject first sees a series of items, and then these items, along with new ones, are presented for a judgment. For each item, the subject is instructed to say either "old" or "new" to indicate whether it was on the list of original items. As we shall see in Chapter 11, it is possible to arrange a situation in which an item cannot be correctly recognized when the item itself is used as a cue, but the subject is able to recall the item. This finding, known as *recognition failure of recallable words,* can be explained only by theories that take into account processing at both encoding and retrieval. We now examine this idea in more depth by focusing on one paradigm.

# Context and Memory

Many early experimental psychologists studied context effects or, more accurately, the change in performance when information is studied in one context and remembered in a different context (e.g., Carr, 1925; McGeoch, 1932). For example, Abernathy (1940) demonstrated that students who were tested in the same classroom in which they were taught did better on tests than did students who were tested in a different classroom. Such effects are predicted by the encoding specificity principle and, more generally, by any view of memory that emphasizes processing.

You should not be unduly worried about this result; changing classrooms from study to test often produces no decrement (e.g., Saufley, Otaka, & Bavaresco, 1985) because of at least three factors. First, most classrooms are quite similar, so a change from one to another will not be a very dramatic change; second, only a limited amount of studying occurs in the first classroom, with much taking place in libraries, dorm rooms, and other places; and third, students are taking the tests for a grade in a course, and so it should not be surprising that they do everything they can to do well. Even if worried, there are ways to overcome potential context effects. Smith (1979) had subjects learn 80 words in a distinctive basement room. They were then given a recognition test on some of the words so that they would think that this phase of the experiment was over and would not rehearse the words during the next 24 hours. The next day, all subjects were given a surprise free recall test. One group was tested in the same basement room (same context), one was tested in a soundproof booth located in a computer room on the fifth floor (different context), and the third group was also tested in the booth but was given additional instructions. This third group of subjects was told to try to reinstate their memory for the basement room before trying to recall any items; they were asked to list attributes of the original room, and then try to recall the words. The same-context group recalled 18 words, on average. The different-context group recalled significantly fewer items, only 12. The third group, the different-context plus image group, recalled 17.2 items, almost the same amount as the first group. It appears that environmental contextual information can be reinstated and can be used to compensate for a change in location.

There are many different ways that context has been defined, although all share a similar distinction. For example, Wickens (1987) distinguished between Context Alpha and Context Beta; Context Alpha refers to "the environmental surrounds in which some event exists or occurs. . . . [There is] no implication that the context or the environment influences the event or is related to it in any significant way." This may be contrasted with Context Beta, which is the "situation in which one stimulus event combines with another stimulus event to define the correct response or meaning of the event" (pp. 135–146).

Perhaps the most famous experiment that manipulated Context Alpha was reported by Godden and Baddeley (1975). Their subjects were members of a university diving club who were asked to learn a list of words either on land or 20 feet underwater. They were then tested either on land or underwater with four conditions: two match conditions, where the environment (either on land or underwater) was the same at both learning and testing, and two mismatch conditions, where the environment was different at learning and testing. Regardless of where they were learning or recalling, the subjects wore their diving apparatus. There was a 4-minute interval between study and test, to allow enough time for the subjects to change environment. The results are reproduced in Figure 6.3. Subjects clearly recalled more words when the study and test environments matched than when they mismatched, regardless of whether subjects were underwater or on land. When there was a mismatch, recall suffered. One practical implication for divers is that if they memorize dive tables on land, they may not remember them very well when needed (e.g., Martin & Aggelton, 1993). A better instructional technique is to have the divers learn the material underwater as well as on dry land.

One potential confound might be that the actual movement necessary to change environments was causing the memory deficit, rather than the changed environment itself. To rule out this possibility, Godden and Baddeley conducted a second experiment. Half of

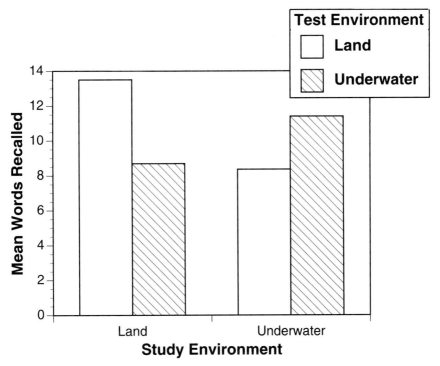

**Figure 6.3** Mean number of words recalled as a function of study and test environments.
Source: Godden & Baddeley (1975).

the subjects again learned a list of words and were then tested for recall on land. The other half also learned the list and were tested on land, but they were also required to enter the pool, swim a short distance, dive to a depth of 20 feet, and then return to land prior to recall. If the movement itself was the cause of the interference, then there should be a difference in performance between the two groups. If the change in environment itself was the cause of the deficit, then there should be no difference. There was no difference; the disruption between study and test did not cause the decreased recall.

An example of Context Beta comes from a study by Light and Carter-Sobell (1970). They presented sentences to subjects that contained a two-word phrase that was capitalized and underlined, such as "The STRAWBERRY JAM tasted great." Subjects were told to expect a memory test for the underlined-capitalized phrases. After presenting all the sentences, a recognition test was given. Half of the phrases were old, meaning they were ones the subjects had seen, and half were new, meaning they had not been seen by the subjects. Some of the old phrases contained the same noun as the original sentence but now the noun was paired with a new adjective, such as TRAFFIC JAM. The subjects were supposed to respond on the basis of the noun, so that if they saw JAM, they should indicate that it was one of the studied items regardless of whether the adjective was the same or different. When JAM was presented in the same context, subjects correctly recognized it about 65% of the time, but when it was in a new context, they recognized it only about 25% of the

time. This is an example of Context Beta because the adjective was essential for determining the meaning of the word.

A *context-dependent memory effect,* then, refers to the observation that memory can be
worse when tested in a new or different context relative to performance in a condition in
which the context remains the same. Context can be manipulated in a variety of ways.
For example, Schab (1990) filled a small room with the odor of chocolate either at study,
at test or at both. Even after a 24-hour delay, subjects' performance on a surprise test
was better when the odors matched. This experiment also provides empirical validation
for the famous anecdote reported by Marcel Proust in the first novel of *Remembrance of
Things Past.*

*State-dependent memory* refers to a similar finding as with context-dependent memory,
and indeed many theorists view them as essentially the same (e.g., Capaldi & Neath,
1995). A person's state can be changed by altering the affective or the pharmacological
state from study to test. The first person to describe the concept that what has been
learned in a certain state of mind is best remembered in that state was a French aristocrat,
Marquis de Puységur, in 1809 (Eich, 1989). More recently, Morton Prince (1910) conjec-
tured that people have difficulty remembering their dreams not because they do not want
to but because they cannot, because of the dissimilarity of the two states. In 1934,
Susukita demonstrated that something learned while calm cannot be recalled when in a
state of shock but can be recalled at a later time when calm is restored. In this particular
instance, a state of shock was induced when an earthquake hit. Although the typical finding is similar, some researchers vary the environment, some the pharmacological state, and
some the affective state or mood of the person.

Bartlett and Santrock (1979) altered the affective state of their subjects so that they
were either in a happy or a neutral mood at study, and a happy or a neutral mood at test.
Performance was better when the moods matched than when they mismatched. Similar
results have been reported by Bower (1981). Although there are several well-documented
failures to find mood-dependent memory effects, a review by Eich (1995) goes a long way
towards delineating when such effects will or will not be seen. First among these conditions is producing a strong, sincere mood.

Goodwin, Powell, Bremer, Hoine, and Stern (1969) demonstrated state-dependent
memory using alcohol. Some subjects received 10 oz of 80-proof vodka either at study, at
test, or at both; other subjects remained sober. Not surprisingly, performance was best
when subjects were sober at both study and test. Perhaps more surprising is the finding
that the worst performance was when subjects were intoxicated at study and sober during the test. In fact, subjects were worse in this condition than when the mismatch was
the other way around—sober at study and intoxicated at test (see Table 6.3). Similar
state-dependent memory effects have been shown using marijuana (Eich, Weingartner,
Stillman, & Gillin, 1975) and nicotine (Peters & McGee, 1982).

Weingartner and Faillace (1971) conducted a state-dependent memory experiment
with two different groups of subjects. One group was made up of chronic alcoholics with
documented histories of long-term alcohol abuse; the other group was made up of an
equal number of nonalcoholics who were closely matched to the alcoholic subjects with
respect to age, education, and other demographic variables. The test session was held
two days after initial learning, during which subjects tried to recall as many of the target

**Table 6.3**  Mean number of errors of recall as a function of encoding and testing state.

| Encoding | Retrieval | |
|---|---|---|
| | Sober | Intoxicated |
| Sober | 1.25 | 2.25 |
| Intoxicated | 4.58 | 2.50 |

Source:  Goodwin, Powell, Bremer, Hoine, & Stern (1969).

words as they could. The subjects from both groups were either intoxicated or sober at study, and intoxicated or sober at test. In this experiment, intoxication was defined as having 1.6 ml of alcohol per kg of body weight. Both groups of subjects showed state-dependent memory effects.

There is an interesting asymmetry seen with state-dependent memory in which a shift from intoxication to sobriety impairs memory more than a shift from sobriety to intoxication (Eich, 1989; Overton, 1984). For example, as Table 6.3 shows, there is a larger difference between recalling items encoded during intoxication while in an intoxicated state than while in a sober state (mean errors of 2.50 versus 4.58), and a smaller effect of recalling items encoded during sobriety while in a sober state than while in an intoxicated state (mean errors of 1.25 versus 2.25). As Eich (1989) points out, this asymmetry can be seen in the studies of Eich et al. (1975) with marijuana, Peters and McGee (1982) with nicotine, and Bartlett and Santrock (1979) with mood. Furthermore, it is seen in the Weingartner and Faillace (1971) study in both the alcoholic and the nonalcoholic control groups. If we label the sober state as normal for the nonalcoholics and the intoxicated state as normal for the alcoholics, then the pattern is identical: performance is worse when switching from the unusual to normal condition than when switching from the normal to unusual condition, regardless of which condition is normal, sober or intoxicated.

The interpretation advanced by several theorists to explain such asymmetry is actually quite simple (e.g., Barry, 1978; Capaldi & Neath, 1995; Eich, 1980). The context in which a person — or other animal, because all these context-(alpha and beta) and state-dependent memory effects can be observed in dogs, rats, and pigeons (e.g., Asratian, 1965; Bouton, 1993; Rescorla, Durlach, & Grau, 1985) — learns some information provides cues that the subject can use to remember the information (see Chapter 7 for more detail). There will always be some N (or normal) cues encoded because there will always be some aspect that is unchanged. It can be assumed that drugs add U (or unusual) cues to the representation, with N or normal state cues being little affected. For chronic alcoholics, being sober is unusual, and so the absence of the effects of alcohol provides the U cues. The N-to-N or U-to-U groups show generally good retention because the cues encoded at study (either N or U) are the cues that are useful at test. The N-to-U group shows the intermediate level of performance because there were N cues present both during test and study. The U-to-N group shows the worst performance because the U cues present at study are absent at test.

One advantage of this view is that it makes a specific prediction: in an experiment in which context is changed, the change in context can be overcome if the experimenter provides useful cues to the subject. We have already seen one example of this, where the experimenter told the subject to reinstate the missing context mentally (Smith, 1979). This can be thought of as providing some of the missing U cues. Another example comes from a study reported by Eich and Birnbaum (1982), in which subjects were asked to learn a list of words in either a sober or an intoxicated state. When tested after a change in drug state, retrieval was poor, as is usually the case. However, some of the subjects in the changed-state condition were given additional cues (such as, "think of all the flowers that you can"). Providing a category name gave the subject additional useful cues, and recall was much improved (Eich & Birnbaum, 1982).

Note that in almost all of these cases, a recall test rather than a recognition test was used. There are many reports of failures to obtain a context-dependent memory effect when recognition is used (e.g., Godden & Baddeley, 1980; Smith, Glenberg, & Bjork, 1978), and there are also reports of failures to obtain mood-dependent memory effects with recognition (Eich & Metcalfe, 1989). Context-, mood-, or state-dependent memory effects are larger (1) with tests like free recall that require internally generated cues, rather than tests like cued-recall or recognition that also have externally provided cues; and (2) when the tests emphasize conceptually driven tasks (those that focus on word meanings and relationships between words) rather than data driven tasks (those that stress perceptual processing). This latter aspect is nicely illustrated in a series of experiments reported by Eich and Metcalfe (1989). Before describing the experiment, however, it is necessary to describe some methods and define some terms.

Johnson and Raye (1981) defined *cotemporal thought* as "the sort of elaborative and associative processes that augment, bridge, or embellish ongoing perceptual experience but that are not necessarily part of the veridical representation of perceptual experience" (p. 443). Eich and Metcalfe suggested that, if a person is in a happy mood, then the cotemporal thought that occurs should lead to large mood-dependent memory effects if the cotemporal thought is allowed to be important. To test this hypothesis, they used a procedure, first described by Heller (1956) and more recently by Slamecka and Graf (1978), that gives rise to the generation effect (see Chapter 14 for more discussion).

In the typical generation-effect experiment, subjects are asked to read an item on half of the lists, and they are asked to generate an item on the remaining trials. For example, subjects may see a category cue followed by two words, one in upper case. Subjects are instructed that they will need to remember the uppercase word for a later memory test. In the generate condition, subjects see exactly the same display except that only the initial letter is given for the uppercase words: the subjects have to generate the word themselves. The typical finding is that generated words are remembered much better than are the read words.

Milkshake flavors: chocolate : VANILLA         Read condition
Milkshake flavors: chocolate : V_____         Generate condition

Eich and Metcalfe (1989) combined a generation-effect procedure with a mood-manipulation procedure. Half of the subjects were induced to be happy at study, and half were induced to be sad. Of the happy subjects, half were induced to be happy again 24 hours later at the surprise recall test, and half were induced to be sad. Within the four

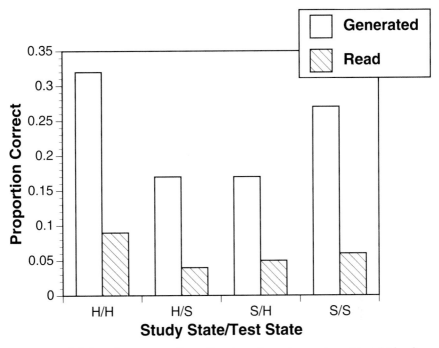

**Figure 6.4** Probability of correct recall as a function of mood at study and test (either happy or sad) and whether the item was generated or read. Source: Eich & Metcalfe (1989).

groups delineated by mood, half of the subjects read the target item, and half generated the target item. Mood changes were induced by playing either happy (Mozart's *Eine Kleine Nachtmusik*) or sad (Albinoni's *Adagio in G minor*) music and to think either happy or sad thoughts. The results are displayed in Figure 6.4.

Subjects recalled more words when their moods matched than when the moods were mismatched, regardless of whether they read or generated the items. However, when the words were generated, not only was recall superior, but the size of mood congruency effect was larger. These data, and others reported in the same article, support the idea that, to the extent thoughts are important in the processing of information, there will be large effects of environment, state, and mood congruency. Context- and state-dependent memory can be seen as examples of transfer appropriate processing. When the processing done at study (such as relying on U cues) is not appropriate for the processing required at test (generating a response based on primarily N cues), memory will be impaired. The addition of the missing cues, however, can dramatically increase the amount of information remembered. This type of finding—increased recall under one set of testing conditions relative to another set of testing conditions—has important implications for forgetting, a subject we turn to in the next chapter.

There is an important distinction between mood-dependent memory, which is shown in Figure 6.4, and mood-congruent effects. *Mood congruency* refers to the finding that a given mood tends to cue memories that are consistent with that mood, rather than memories that are inconsistent (Blaney, 1986; Hertel, 1992). For example, Teasdale and Russell (1983) had subjects learn a list of negative, neutral, or positive words. At test, subjects were induced to be either happy or sad and then were asked to recall as many words as they could. The sad subjects recalled more negative words than the happy subjects did, but the happy subjects recalled more positive words than the sad subjects did. The reason for mood-congruency effects is that the mood serves as a cue, and positive events are associated with positive moods and negative events with negative moods. A particular type of mood can cue memories that are associated with that mood.

# The Process Dissociation Framework

The levels of processing and transfer appropriate processing views stimulated a lot of research on the effects of different kinds of processing. One potential problem concerns how to attribute specific effects to specific processes; several processes are used at the same time, and until quite recently it appeared quite difficult to separate the effects of different operations. Jacoby (1991) recently developed a technique for separating different processes that may be operating. Thus far, it has been applied to only a few types of processes, but it should be relatively straightforward to apply the logic to other settings.

Jacoby and his colleagues (1991; Jacoby, Toth, & Yonelinas, 1993) were interested in separating intentional retrieval processes from incidental processes. (This topic is of critical importance in the implicit memory literature and will be discussed further in Chapter 8.) On many tasks, performance improves simply because an item has been perceived a little earlier. Even though the subject may be completely unaware of this influence, performance can be enhanced. For example, if you happened to read the word *toboggan,* and a little later were doing a crossword puzzle where *toboggan* was the answer, you would be more likely to get the answer than someone who had not recently read the word. This sort of process is sometimes termed an *automatic* or *incidental process.* By contrast, an *intentional process* would be one where the subject intentionally tried to recall an item. Because both of these processes usually contribute to performance on various tests (Richardson-Klavehn & Bjork, 1988), it has been difficult to determine the properties and effects of each. One way to separate them, Jacoby (1991) suggests, is to have two groups of subjects study a set of words. One group will receive an inclusion test, in which both processes are allowed to contribute; the other group receives an exclusion test, in which only automatic or incidental processes can contribute. The retrieval cues available to the subject are kept constant; the sole difference between an inclusion test and an exclusion test is the instructions given to the subject. By comparing performance on both tests, it becomes possible to separate the effects of each process.

To see how this logic works, it is easiest to follow a specific example. In Phase 1, all subjects heard a list of items. In Phase 2, more items were presented, but this time in one of two conditions. In the full-attention condition, the subjects simply read the words. In the divided-attention condition, the subjects also had to listen to a tape-recorded series of numbers and indicate when they heard three odd digits in a row. The divided-attention manipulation was designed to reduce the influence of the recollective process while leaving the automatic process unaffected. At test, the subjects received a stem completion task,

**Table 6.4** The probability of completing the stem with a studied item on both inclusion and exclusion tests for experiments. "Read" and "Heard" correspond to whether the item came from Phase 1 or Phase 2 of presentation.

| Attention | Performance Component | | | |
|---|---|---|---|---|
| | Read | | Heard | |
| | Inclusion | Exclusion | Inclusion | Exclusion |
| Full | 0.61 | 0.36 | 0.47 | 0.34 |
| Divided | 0.46 | 0.46 | 0.42 | 0.37 |

Source: Jacoby, Toth, & Yonelinas (1993).

where they were asked to complete the stem to make a valid English word. The stems could be presented in one of two colors, green or red. If the subjects saw a green stem, they were asked to use it as a cue to remember a word from either Phase 1 or Phase 2; if they could not remember a word, they were asked to complete it with the first word that came to mind. A green stem, then, signaled an inclusion test. If the subjects saw a red stem, they were again asked to use it as a cue to remember a word from either Phase 1 or Phase 2 and to make sure that they did *not* write any of these words as responses. A red stem signaled an exclusion test. Table 6.4 shows the probability of responding with an old word, from two versions of this experiment. Note that in the exclusion condition, subjects were instructed not to write down any old items. In general, performance is worse under divided than under full attention, particularly for the inclusion task. Performance was equivalent for the "heard" words because attention was not manipulated there. This is an important condition because it provides a check on the attention manipulation: if performance were not different between read and heard words, we would not have confidence in the division of attention manipulation.

How can we separate the recollective process from the automatic process using these data?

On an *inclusion* test, the probability of responding with a studied item (either read or heard) is the probability of conscious recollection ($R$) plus the probability that a word came to mind automatically ($A$) when there is a failure of conscious recollection ($1 - R$). Because the second part is a conditional probability, we need to multiply both components together to reflect the fact that both need to occur.

$$Inclusion = R + A(1 - R) \tag{6.1}$$

For an *exclusion* test, the word will be produced only when conscious recollection fails ($1 - R$) and when the word automatically came to mind ($A$).

$$Exclusion = A(1 - R) \tag{6.2}$$

Because Equations 6.1 and 6.2 share similar terms, Equation 6.2 can be rewritten as

$$Inclusion = R + Exclusion \tag{6.3}$$

**Table 6.5**   Estimates of the contribution of recollective and
automatic processes for the words that were read calculated from
the data presented in Table 6.4.

| Attention | Estimate | |
|---|---|---|
| | Recollection | Automatic |
| Full | 0.25 | 0.47 |
| Divided | 0.00 | 0.46 |

Source: Jacoby, Toth, & Yonelinas (1993).

or

$$R = Inclusion - Exclusion \qquad (6.4)$$

If we divided Equation 6.2 by $(1 - R)$, we can solve for $A$:

$$A = \frac{Exclusion}{1 - R} \qquad (6.5)$$

Using the values in Table 6.4, we can now calculate estimates of R and A for the words that were read. We focus on this condition because it was only here that the divided-attention manipulation was performed. The estimate of R for the full-attention condition in Experiment 1b is calculated using Equation 6.4: $R = 0.61 - 0.36$, which is 0.25. The estimate of $A$ for the same condition is calculated using Equation 6.5: $A = 0.36/(1 - 0.25)$, which is 0.47. For the divided-attention condition, $R = 0.46 - 0.46$, which is 0, and $A = 0.46/(1 - 0)$, which is 0.46. The values are summarized in Table 6.5.

The estimates of R and A suggest that the processing dissociation framework can separate the influences of two different processes. Divided attention was designed to minimize the effect of conscious recollective processes, because the subject was required to attend to the irrelevant vigilance task. As Table 6.5 shows, the contribution of R was reduced to 0. However, attention should not affect the automatic component, and indeed the estimates of A are identical in both the divided- and full-attention conditions. Jacoby, Toth, and Yonelinas (1993) performed several more replications to ensure that the results obtained here were not a fluke. In particular, in a second experiment, they again obtained an estimate of R in a divided-attention condition of 0.0.

There have been some criticisms of this approach, centering around the issue of independence of the intentional and automatic processes. For example, Richardson-Klavehn, Lee, and Joubran (1994) suggest that both processes may operate in a symbiotic fashion: an item suggested by the automatic process may then be considered by the intentional process. The question of independence of these processes is explored in detail in an exchange between Jacoby and his colleagues (Jacoby, Begg, & Toth, 1997; Jacoby & Shrout, 1997) and Curran and Hintzman (1997; Hintzman & Curran, 1997). It is unclear at the moment whether this criticism is important or trivial, and future empirical work is needed. Nonetheless, this is an exciting approach to investigating and separating processes.

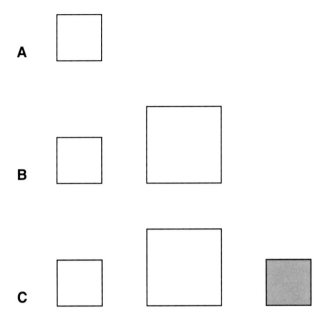

**Figure 6.5**   An illustration of how different dimensions become relevant. When asked to name the figure in A, the answer is a square, in B, the answer is a small square, but in C, the answer is a small white square.

# What Is Encoded?

The studies on state-, mood-, and context-dependent memory suggest that even when presented with a single word, people also encode lots of other factors related to their mood and their environment. Furthermore, as we shall see in the next chapter, people also seem to encode all kinds of information about the word itself, including whether it is a noun or adjective, whether it has one or two syllables, whether it was presented in red or green, whether it was presented in upper- or lowercase, and so on. Is this much information really being encoded? One way to view this question is that an awful lot of processing — mostly encoding information on a large number of dimensions — occurs even in the 500 ms that a word is available for study.

There is a different way of viewing this, however. Many of the dimensions that subjects appear to encode may be apparent at test only when particular comparisons are made. For example, describe the object in Figure 6.5A. Most people will say "a square." However, when asked to describe the same object when placed next to another item, as in Figure 6.5B, they now describe it as a small square. With two other items, as in Figure 6.5C, they describe it as a small white square.

Thus, there is a difference between a nominal stimulus and a functional stimulus. The *nominal stimulus* is what the experimenter thinks the subject is encoding, and the *functional stimulus* is what the subject actually encoded. In general, the functional stimulus is likely to include many elements of the context and many idiosyncratic associations. Taking heed

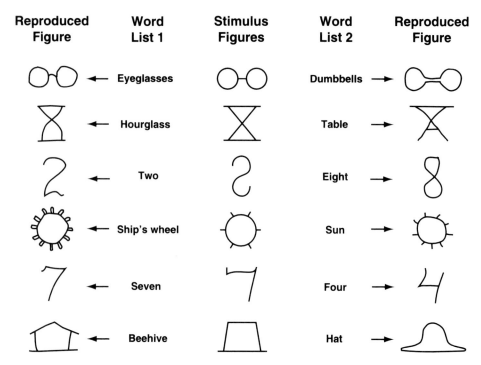

| Reproduced Figure | Word List 1 | Stimulus Figures | Word List 2 | Reproduced Figure |
|---|---|---|---|---|
| | ← Eyeglasses | | Dumbbells → | |
| | ← Hourglass | | Table → | |
| | ← Two | | Eight → | |
| | ← Ship's wheel | | Sun → | |
| | ← Seven | | Four → | |
| | ← Beehive | | Hat → | |

**Figure 6.6** Several examples of the types of items presented by Carmichael, Hogan, and Walter. Source: Carmichael, Hogan, & Walter (1932).

of an assumption from levels of processing, memory is a byproduct of processing information, and the processing can add to or subtract from the nominal stimulus.

One famous example of this process is the study reported by Carmichael, Hogan, and Walter (1932; see also Moore, 1910). The subjects were told that they would see a picture and that they would be asked to reproduce the figure as accurately as possible. As each figure was shown, the experimenter would say, "The next figure resembles . . ." and would say a name. For example, one group of subjects was told that an ambiguous figure (such as those shown in the center column of Figure 6.6) resembles "eyeglasses," and a second group was told that it resembles "dumbbells." Although the task was to reproduce the figure "as accurately as possible," most subjects changed the figure so that it more closely resembled the verbal label. Examples of some reproductions are also shown in Figure 6.6.

The point is, of course, that the nominal stimulus is the figure itself, but the functional stimulus—how the subject encoded the item—was slightly different. The subject paid attention to the verbal label, and this affected how the figure was encoded. Similar effects are observable when the labels are provided only at test (Hanawalt & Demarest, 1939). The way the information is processed at study or is processed at test can distort the original information. (We shall examine reconstructive processes in more detail in Chapter 15.)

Both of these illustrations fit in nicely with the type of processing views discussed above. People may not be aware of every dimension they encode, because many of these dimensions are not relevant for the task and are apparent only when compared with other stimuli. In addition, the processes used at both study and test can distort the original item by either adding features, removing features, or both. One advantage of viewing memory from a processing perspective, then, is that these systematic changes are predicted because memory is seen as the byproduct of the processing performed. Memory is not like a library, in which a verbatim copy is stored on a shelf and remains unchanged until retrieved. Rather, the item can be changed during encoding and can be changed during retrieval. Although these changes can lead to a reduction in performance, this should not necessarily be seen as forgetting, as we shall see in the next chapter.

# References

Abernathy, E. M. (1940). The effect of changed environmental conditions upon the results of college examinations. *Journal of Psychology, 10*, 293–301.

Asratian, E. A. (1965). *Compensatory adaptations, reflex activity and the brain.* New York: Pergamon Press.

Barry, H. (1978). Stimulus attributes of drugs. In H. Anisman & G. Bignami (Eds.), *Psychopharmacology of aversively motivated behavior.* New York: Plenum.

Bartlett, J. C., & Santrock, J. W. (1979). Affect-dependent episodic memory in young children. *Child Development, 50*, 513–518.

Blaney, P. H. (1986). Affect and memory: A review. *Psychological Bulletin, 99*, 229–246.

Bousfield, W. A. (1953). The occurrence of clustering in the recall of randomly arranged associates. *Journal of General Psychology, 49*, 229–240.

Bouton, M. E. (1993). Context, time, and memory retrieval in the interference paradigms of Pavlovian learning. *Psychological Bulletin, 114*, 80–99.

Bower, G. H. (1981). Mood and memory. *American Psychologist, 36*, 129–148.

Capaldi, E. J., & Neath, I. (1995). Remembering and forgetting as context discrimination. *Learning & Memory, 2*, 107–132.

Carmichael, L., Hogan, H. P., & Walter, A. A. (1932). An experimental study of the effect of language on the reproductions of visually perceived forms. *Journal of Experimental Psychology, 15*, 73–86.

Carr, H. A. (1925). *Psychology: A study of mental activity.* New York: Longmans, Green.

Craik, F. I. M., & Lockhart, R. S. (1972). Levels of processing: A framework for memory research. *Journal of Verbal Learning and Verbal Behavior, 11*, 671–684.

Craik, F. I. M., & Tulving, E. (1975). Depth of processing and the retention of words in episodic memory. *Journal of Experimental Psychology: General, 104*, 268–294.

Craik, F. I. M., & Watkins, M. J. (1973). The role of rehearsal in short-term memory. *Journal of Verbal Learning and Verbal Behavior, 12*, 599–607.

Curran, T., & Hintzman, D. L. (1997). Consequences and causes of correlations in process dissociation. *Journal of Experimental Psychology: Learning Memory, and Cognition, 23*, 496–504.

Deese, J. (1959). Influence of inter-item associative strength upon immediate free recall. *Psychological Reports, 5*, 305–312.

Eich, E. (1989). Theoretical issues in state dependent memory. In H. L. Roediger III & F. I. M. Craik (Eds.), *Varieties of memory and consciousness: Essays in honour of Endel Tulving.* Hillsdale, NJ: Erlbaum.

Eich, E. (1995). Searching for mood dependent memory. *Psychological Science, 6,* 67–75.

Eich, E., & Birnbaum, I. M. (1982). Repetition, cueing, and state dependent memory. *Memory & Cognition, 10,* 103–114.

Eich, E., & Metcalfe, J. (1989). Mood-dependent memory for internal versus external events. *Journal of Experimental Psychology: Learning, Memory, and Cognition, 15,* 443–455.

Eich, J. E. (1980). The cue-dependent nature of state-dependent retrieval. *Memory & Cognition, 8,* 157–173.

Eich, J. E., Weingartner, H., Stillman, R. C., & Gillin, J. C. (1975). State-dependent accessibility of retrieval cues in the retention of a categorized list. *Journal of Verbal Learning and Verbal Behavior, 14,* 408–417.

Fisher, R. P., & Craik, F. I. M. (1977). Interaction between encoding and retrieval operations in cued recall. *Journal of Experimental Psychology: Human Learning and Memory, 3,* 701–711.

Godden, D. R., & Baddeley, A. D. (1975). Context-dependent memory in two natural environments: On land and underwater. *British Journal of Psychology, 66,* 325–331.

Godden, D. R., & Baddeley, A. D. (1980). When does context influence recognition memory? *British Journal of Psychology, 71,* 99–104.

Goodwin, D. W., Powell, B., Bremer, D., Hoine, H., & Stern, J. (1969). Alcohol and recall: State dependent effects in man. *Science, 163,* 1358.

Hanawalt, N. G., & Demarest, I. H. (1939). The effect of verbal suggestion in the recall period upon the reproduction of visually perceived forms. *Journal of Experimental Psychology, 25,* 159–174.

Heller, N. (1956). An application of psychological learning theory. *Journal of Marketing, 20,* 248–254.

Hertel, P. (1992). Emotion, mood, and memory. In L. R. Squire (Ed.), *Encyclopedia of learning and memory.* New York: Macmillan.

Hintzman, D. L., & Curran, T. (1997). More than one way to violate independence: Reply to Jacoby and Shrout (1997). *Journal of Experimental Psychology: Learning, Memory, and Cognition, 23,* 511–513.

Hunt, R. R., & Einstein, G. O. (1981). Relational and item-specific information in memory. *Journal of Verbal Learning and Verbal Behavior, 20,* 497–514.

Hunt, R. R., & McDaniel, M. A. (1993). The enigma of organization and distinctiveness. *Journal of Memory and Language, 32,* 421–445.

Hyde, T. S., & Jenkins, J. J. (1973). Recall of words as a function of semantic, graphic, and syntactic orienting tasks. *Journal of Verbal Learning and Verbal Behavior, 12,* 471–480.

Jacoby, L. L. (1991). A process dissociation framework: Separating automatic from intentional uses of memory. *Journal of Memory and Language, 30,* 513–541.

Jacoby, L. L., Begg, I. M., & Toth, J. P. (1997). In defense of functional independence: Violations of assumptions underlying the process-dissociation procedure? *Journal of Experimental Psychology: Learning, Memory, and Cognition, 23,* 484–495.

Jacoby, L. L., & Shrout, P. E. (1997). Toward a psychometric analysis of violations of the independence assumption in process dissociation. *Journal of Experimental Psychology: Learning, Memory, and Cognition, 23,* 505–510.

Jacoby, L. L., Toth, J. P., & Yonelinas, A. P. (1993). Separating conscious and unconscious influences of memory: Measuring recollection. *Journal of Experimental Psychology: General, 122,* 139–154.

Johnson, M. K., & Raye, C. L. (1981). Reality monitoring. *Psychological Review, 88,* 67–85.

Katona, G. (1940). *Organizing and memorizing: Studies in the psychology of learning and teaching.* New York: Columbia University Press.

Koffka, K. (1935). *Principles of gestalt psychology.* London: Routledge & Kegan Paul.

Light, L. L., & Carter-Sobell, L. (1970). Effects of changed semantic context on recognition memory. *Journal of Verbal Learning and Verbal Behavior, 9,* 1–11.

Mandler, G. (1967). Organization and memory. In K. W. Spence & J. T. Spence (Eds.), *The psychology of learning and motivation, Vol. 1.* New York: Academic Press.

Martin, K. M., & Aggelton, J. P. (1993). Contextual effects on the ability of divers to use decompression tables. *Applied Cognitive Psychology, 7,* 311–316.

McGeoch, J. A. (1932). Forgetting and the law of disuse. *Psychological Review, 39,* 352–370.

McGeoch, J. A. (1942). *The psychology of human learning: An introduction.* New York: Longmans Green & Co.

Moore, T. V. (1910). The process of abstraction: An experimental study. *California University Publications in Psychology, 1,* 73–197.

Morris, C. D., Bransford, J. D., & Franks, J. J. (1977). Levels of processing versus transfer appropriate processing. *Journal of Verbal Learning and Verbal Behavior, 16,* 519–533.

Nairne, J. S. (1983). Associative processing during rote rehearsal. *Journal of Experimental Psychology: Learning, Memory, and Cognition, 9,* 3–20.

Overton, D. A. (1984). State dependent learning and drug discriminations. In L. L. Iverson, S. D. Iverson, & S. H. Snyder (Eds.), *Handbook of psychopharmacology, Vol. 18.* New York: Plenum.

Peters, R., & McGee, R. (1982). Cigarette smoking and state-dependent memory. *Psychopharmacology, 76,* 232–235.

Postman, L. (1964). Short-term memory and incidental learning. In A. W. Melton (Ed.), *Categories of human learning.* New York: Academic Press.

Prince, M. (1910). The mechanism and interpretation of dreams. *Journal of Abnormal Psychology, 5,* 139–195.

Rescorla, R. A., Durlach, P. J., & Grau, J. W. (1985). Contextual learning in Pavlovian conditioning. In P. D. Balsam & A. Tomie (Eds.), *Context and learning.* Hillsdale, NJ: Erlbaum.

Richardson-Klavehn, A., & Bjork, R. A. (1988). Measures of memory. *Annual Review of Psychology, 39,* 475–543.

Richardson-Klavehn, A., Lee, M. G., & Joubran, R. (1994). Intention and awareness in perceptual identification priming. *Memory & Cognition, 22,* 293–312.

Saufley, W. H., Jr., Otaka, S. R., & Bavaresco, J. L. (1985). Context effects: Classroom tests and context independence. *Memory & Cognition, 13,* 522–528.

Schab, F. R. (1990). Odors and the remembrance of things past. *Journal of Experimental Psychology: Learning, Memory and Cognition, 16,* 648–655.

Slamecka, N. J., & Graf, P. (1978). The generation effect: Delineation of a phenomenon. *Journal of Experimental Psychology: Human Learning and Memory, 4,* 592–604.

Smith, S. M. (1979). Remembering in and out of context. *Journal of Experimental Psychology: Human Learning and Memory, 5,* 460–471.

Smith, S. M., Glenberg, A. M., & Bjork, R. A. (1978). Environmental context and human memory. *Memory & Cognition, 6,* 342–353.

Susukita, T. (1934). Untersuchung eines auß erordentlichen Gedächtnisses in Japan (II). *Tohoku Psychologica Folia, 2,* 15–42.

Teasdale, J. D., & Russell, M. L. (1983). Differential effects of induced mood on the recall of positive, negative, and neutral words. *British Journal of Clinical Psychology, 22,* 163–171.

Thomson, D. M., & Tulving, E. (1970). Associative encoding and retrieval: Weak and strong cues. *Journal of Experimental Psychology, 86,* 255–262.

Tulving, E. (1962). Subjective organization in free recall of "unrelated" words. *Psychological Review, 69,* 344–354.

Tulving, E. (1972). Episodic and semantic memory. In E. Tulving & W. Donaldson (Eds.), *Organization of memory.* New York: Academic Press.

Tulving, E. (1983). *Elements of episodic memory.* New York: Oxford University Press.

Watkins, M. J. (1979). Engrams as cuegrams and forgetting as cue overload: A cueing approach to the structure of memory. In C. R. Puff (Ed.), *Memory organization and structure.* New York: Academic Press.

Weingartner, H., & Faillace, L. A. (1971). Alcohol state-dependent learning in man. *Journal of Nervous and Mental Disease, 153,* 395–406.

Wickens, D. D. (1987). The dual meanings of context: Implications for research, theory, and applications. In D. S. Gorfein & R. R. Hoffman (Eds.), *Memory and learning: The Ebbinghaus Centennial Conference.* Hillsdale, NJ: Erlbaum.

# CHAPTER SEVEN

# Principles of Forgetting

*"We are told that the famous Athenian Themistocles was endowed with wisdoms and genius on a scale quite surpassing belief; and it is said that a certain learned and highly accomplished person went to him and offered to impart to him the science of mnemonics, which was then being introduced for the first time; and that when Themistocles asked what precise result that science was capable of achieving, the professor asserted that it would enable him to remember everything; and Themistocles replied that he would be doing him a greater kindness if he taught him to forget what he wanted than if he taught him to remember."*

*— Marcus Tullius Cicero*

Historically, there have been three main views of forgetting: (1) forgetting occurs due primarily to storage problems, (2) forgetting is due primarily to decay of information, and (3) forgetting is due primarily to retrieval failures. In this chapter, we examine consolidation theory, interference theory, and a theory based on discrimination.

## Consolidation Theory

Consolidation theory is not really a theory of forgetting but rather a theory of why information is not stored in the first place. Müller and Pilzecker (1900) argued that learning is not complete at the time that practice or rehearsal ends. Rather, a process known as *perseveration* occurs for a while afterward, and the longer this perseveratory period, the stronger or more consolidated the memory trace. If anything occurs to interrupt this perseveration, then the trace may not have the chance to become consolidated and recall will not be possible. This idea has substantial biological plausibility. Hebb (1949) proposed that memory is a persistent change in both (1) the relationship between neurons (or groups of neurons, which he called cell assemblies), either through structural modification or biochemical events; and (2) the changes within a particular neuron that affect communication with its neighbors (see Chapter 9). An obvious suggestion was that perseveration is short-term memory and that the consolidated trace is long-term memory.

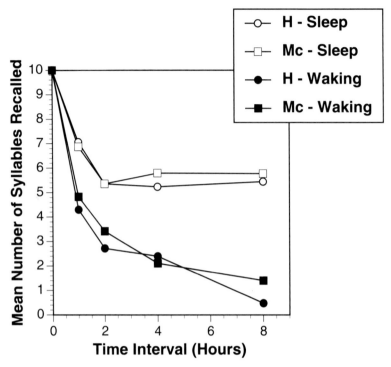

**Figure 7.1**    Mean number of syllables correctly recalled by two subjects who either slept or remained awake for varying time intervals after learning.    Source: Jenkins & Dallenbach (1924).

Three key predictions are made by any version of consolidation theory. First, a period of mental inactivity (or neuronal inactivity) is more conducive to perseveration—and hence to more consolidation—than is a period of activity. Memory should be better, then, following a rest period (such as a nap) than following a period of activity (such as engaging in some distractor task). Second, if the perseveration period is interrupted, then the trace cannot be consolidated and the item will not be stored. Memory should be worse, then, following some event that prevents consolidation. Third, if consolidation is prevented, the item should *never* be recalled because the essential storage phase was not completed.

There is ample evidence for the first of these predictions. Ebbinghaus (1885) noted that forgetting is retarded by sleep or, more precisely, that the rate of forgetting is slowed when a period of sleep occurs between study and test. Jenkins and Dallenbach (1924) performed a more systematic investigation in which they had two subjects live in the lab for a period of time. The subjects learned lists of items and then were asked to recall them after 1, 2, 4, or 8 hours of sleep or wakefulness. As Figure 7.1 shows, subjects were able to recall more of the items following a period of sleep than following a period of wakefulness.

According to consolidation theory, the interpretation is simple: when the perseveration process is interrupted by other mental or neuronal activity, the trace cannot be consolidated. The longer the perseveratory process, the better the information will be consolidated and the more likely it will be remembered. This interpretation is consistent with another experiment by Dallenbach, but this time the subjects were cockroaches. Minami and Dallenbach (1946) investigated the effects of inactivity when sleep was not involved. They first conditioned roaches to elicit an avoidance response. Some roaches were then allowed to engage in normal activity, whereas others were wrapped in cotton wool and placed in matchboxes. The idea was to prevent the roaches from moving and to minimize stimulation. These restricted roaches showed greater retention of the avoidance response than did the roaches that were allowed to engage in normal activity.

One example often cited as supporting the second prediction of consolidation theory—that if perseveration is interrupted, then the trace cannot be consolidated and the item will not be stored—is retrograde amnesia. With retrograde amnesia, people cannot recall the events that occurred before the trauma. According to consolidation theory, the perseveratory activity was interrupted by the trauma and thus the consolidation process could not be completed. Therefore, the events that occurred right before the trauma were not stored and could not be remembered.

Most experimental studies that tested consolidation theory used rats as subjects and induced amnesia by subjecting the rats to electroconvulsive shock (ECS). One side effect of ECS, in both humans and other animals, is retrograde amnesia. A typical study, and one that is widely cited, was performed by Duncan (1949). He first trained rats using an avoidance procedure. A rat was placed in a two-chambered box and received a mild foot shock if it had not moved to the other side of the chamber within 10 seconds. Rats can learn this task rather quickly. Duncan varied the interval between completion of the avoidance response and the administration of ECS, using intervals from 20 s to 4 hr; a control group received no ECS. Consistent with consolidation theory, the longer the delay between the response and the administration of ECS—or in terms of the theory, the longer perseveration was allowed to continue—the better the memory for the learning episode (see Figure 7.2). The estimate of time needed for consolidation was approximately 1 hour.

One problem with this experiment is that it requires an active response on the part of the rat to demonstrate learning, but there are two reasons the rat might not move after receiving ECS. First, the animal may have forgotten the avoidance response that it had learned and so does not remember to move to the other side of the chamber to avoid a foot shock. A second view suggests that rats may have inadvertently been subjected to a conditioned fear experiment and may be opting for the lesser of two evils: a move to the other side of the chamber could serve as a cue for ECS, and the animal may prefer the mild foot shock to the severe ECS. Thus, the rat may remain stationary because of amnesia or because of fear.

An experiment by Chorover and Schiller (1965) tested this idea. Rather than require an active response to signify remembering, their experiment required the animal to remain stationary. The experiment involved placing a rat on a raised platform. Because the rat's natural inclination is to avoid exposed, high places, the animal would quickly step off the platform. When this happened, the rat received a mild foot shock; if the rat stayed on the platform, nothing would happen. Chorover and Schiller again varied the interval between the learning episode (stepping down) and the administration of ECS. Note that this time, however, the rat should remain on the platform if it has learned fear of the ECS. If, on the other hand, it does not remember the foot shock, then it should step down. Whereas

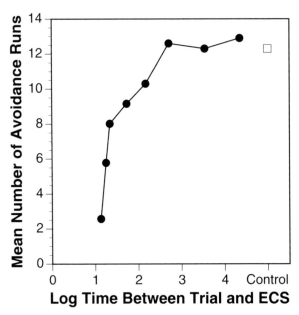

**Figure 7.2**   Mean number of avoidance runs made by different groups of rats that differed only in the duration of the interval between the learning trial and the ECS. The x-axis is in log units. The corresponding values are 20 s, 40 s, 60 s, 4 min, 15 min, 1 hr, 4 hr, and 14 hr.
Source: Duncan (1949).

Duncan estimated that consolidation takes 1 hr, Chorover and Schiller estimated that consolidation is complete within 10 s. If ECS is administered within 10 s of the learning, then there is retrograde amnesia. If ECS is delayed for more than 10 s, then memory for the learning episode will remain. This estimate of 10 s, although obtained on rats, coincided nicely with conceptions of the duration of information in short-term memory. But two experiments challenged the interpretation of these findings.

The third prediction of consolidation theory is that, if consolidation is prevented, the item should *never* be recalled. Quartermain, McEwan, and Azmitia (1972) tested this prediction using a similar procedure to that used by Chorover and Schiller. The main difference was that whereas Chorover and Schiller tested *all* animals 24 hr after the administration of ECS, Quartermain et al. tested some animals 48 and 72 hr after ECS. There was evidence of amnesia in those animals tested 24 or 48 hr after ECS, but no evidence of amnesia after the 72-hr test. The suggestion is that in the 24- and 48-hr groups, the memory was actually stored but was rendered temporarily unavailable by the ECS; after 72 hr, the memory again became available. This directly contradicts the third prediction of consolidation theory: interrupting the perseveration phase should prevent the storage of information. But Quartermain et al. demonstrated that the information is stored, it is just not retrieved.

A final study reinforces this interpretation. Miller and Springer (1972) argued that if the memory is stored but is just temporarily unavailable, providing a reminder to the animals should remove all traces of amnesia. They followed a similar procedure as the researchers in the previous studies, but they gave some rats a second foot shock after ECS had been administered. The reminder foot shock was given outside the experimental chamber, so it did not constitute another learning trial. The control group, which did not receive a reminder, showed amnesia, whereas the experimental group did not.

Although there is much evidence against a strong form of consolidation theory (Crowder, 1982; Keppel, 1984; Spear & Riccio, 1994), a weaker form undoubtedly is correct: some biological changes may indeed affect an organism's ability to store information. This weaker form, though, has yet to provide a link between the physiological processes and the cognitive consequences. As knowledge of psychobiological processes continues, it may be possible to again entertain a serious version of consolidation theory. Until that time, there are several other major theories of forgetting that make more accurate predictions and offer more insights into why forgetting occurs.

# Interference Theory

A competing view of forgetting was also being developed during the same time as consolidation theory, but rather than suggesting that the information never entered the memory system, it proposed that other information somehow caused interference. John McGeoch played a central role in the first stages of the development of interference theory. In 1932, he argued that time-based decay theories are not valid scientific explanations of behavior. Specifically, he argued that just as iron rusts over time, memories are forgotten over time, but in neither case is time the causal agent. For iron, it is the process of oxidation that causes rust, and this process must, of necessity, unfold over time. The same is true for forgetting: it must, of necessity, unfold over time, but something else, analogous to oxidation, occurs as time passes. McGeoch suggested that other material, which is processed as time passes, causes interference. Notice that the experiments by Dallenbach reported above can be interpreted as supporting an interference explanation.

Interference can be either retroactive or proactive, which is best illustrated by considering a hypothetical experiment. In a paired-associate experiment, subjects are asked to learn arbitrary pairings of two items, such as DOG and ROOF, CAR and DESK, and so forth. At test, they will be prompted with DOG and asked to respond with the correct answer, ROOF. These items are often represented by the term A-B. If subjects learn a second list that contains entirely new items, C-D (such as PHONE-COFFEE), there will be relatively little interference. In other words, memory for the A-B relationship will not be affected very much by learning the C-D relationship. If, however, the subjects learn a list that reuses the A items but pairs them with new, D items, there will be interference. If DOG-ROOF is the A-B pairing, DOG-COFFEE might be the A-D pairing. When tested later for the A-B items, the A-D associations will produce what is called retroactive interference (RI) because A-D interferes with something learned earlier. This is illustrated in the top part of Table 7.1.

The bottom part of Table 7.1 illustrates the procedure for inducing proactive interference (PI). Note that we are again testing memory of the A-B items, but subjects in the experimental group learn the A-D associations first. This will cause proactive interference because already-learned information will interfere with newer information. Although the stimuli and methods described may often seem artificial, the principles apply equally as

Table 7.1   A schematic illustration of two experimental designs in which subjects are tested for the memory of A-B relationships. The top design produces retroactive interference and the bottom design produces proactive interference.

|              | Learn First | Learn Second | Tested on | Interference |
|--------------|-------------|--------------|-----------|--------------|
| Experimental | A-B         | A-D          | A-B       | RI           |
| Control      | A-B         | C-D          | A-B       |              |
| Experimental | A-D         | A-B          | A-B       | PI           |
| Control      | C-D         | A-B          | A-B       |              |

well in real-world settings (see, for example, Bower, 1978). Indeed, as we shall see in Chapter 15, the typical experiment on the effects of misleading information on eyewitnesses is nothing more than a fancy A-B–A-D paradigm (Crowder, 1976): the original material is B, and the misleading information is D.

Underwood (1957) dramatically documented the effects of proactive interference. He combined the results of 14 studies and simply plotted them all on the same graph, shown in Figure 7.3. What he found was that the more previous trials a subject had with a particular task, the lower the performance. That is, if a person has had three previous trials and everything else is held constant, performance on the fourth trial will be worse because there is interference from the first three trials. Although there were some suggestions of how to incorporate PI into interference theory, relatively little was proposed in terms of a specific mechanism. This lack of a specific mechanism for PI was one major reason for the diminishing popularity of interference theory in general (Zechmeister & Nyberg, 1982). Despite this omission, interference theory greatly influenced all subsequent theories of forgetting.

Consolidation theory may be seen as one form of interference theory, but one in which interference occurs during storage. In McGeoch's (1932, 1942) three-factor theory of forgetting, the initial main formulation of interference theory, the locus of the interference was placed at retrieval. McGeoch assumed that retrieval failures occur because unwanted memories are retrieved instead of the desired memory. The A-D learning does not erase or remove the memories of the A-B learning, and the memories of the A-B pairing do not decay or fade over time; rather, both B and D coexist as memories for the correct response to A. In McGeoch's theory there is no forgetting in the sense of loss of information; forgetting is a temporary performance problem. Rather than a loss of information, there is a lapse in retrieving it. McGeoch identified three mechanisms that can cause interference: response competition, altered stimulus conditions, and set.

Response competition occurs when two or more items are potential responses to a memory query. For example, when cued with A-?, both B and D compete as potential responses, and this competition reduces the probability that either one will be offered as a response. Much research on this aspect of interference theory was conducted and Crowder (1976) provides an excellent discussion and review. The main question concerned how best to test for the relative strength of the B and D responses so that different explanations of response competition could be further explicated. For example, Melton and

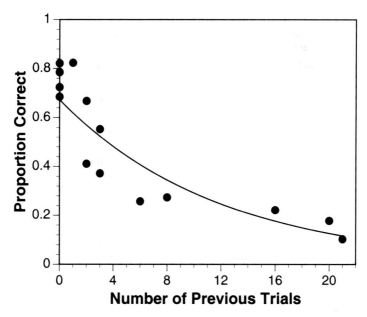

**Figure 7.3**   Proportion correct plotted as a function of the number of previous trials. Data were collected from 14 different studies.   Source: Underwood (1957).

Irwin (1940) used an A-B–A-D paired associate task, much like the one illustrated in Table 7.1. Subjects in the control condition learned to associate a series of items with cues, the A-B learning, and then "rested" for 30 min. Other groups had either 5, 10, 20, or 40 trials learning A-D paired associates, and then all groups were tested for the original A-B material. If response competition were causing all of the forgetting, then all of the errors in the groups with interpolated learning should be D responses, rather than the desired B responses. Melton and Irwin demonstrated that this was not the case — that the difference in recall between the control and the experimental groups could not be attributed solely to intrusion or competition from D items. They suggested that subjects actually unlearned the original A-B material during the interpolated learning. However, the unlearning hypothesis quickly ran into the same problem that consolidation theory did: it is easy to find situations in which information that is supposed to be completely lost from the memory system reappears (Capaldi & Neath, 1995). For example, Postman and his colleagues (Postman, 1961; Postman, Stark, & Fraser, 1968) demonstrated that specific A-B–A-D associations are not actually lost, as the unlearning hypothesis predicted, but are available when different forms of testing are used.

The second of McGeoch's original three factors was *altered context* or *altered stimulus conditions*. Animal learning theorists distinguish between the nominal stimulus and the functional stimulus; for example, if a tone consistently precedes a mild foot shock, then rats will learn to avoid the shock by moving. From the experimenter's perspective, the tone is the important stimulus and nothing else. From the animal's perspective, however, the tone is only a *nominal* stimulus: additional sources of information also serve as cues. The total of all the cues that the animal attends to is the *functional* stimulus. For example, if the conditioning takes place in a white box, then the functional stimulus may be both a tone and a white environment. When placed in a black box and the tone is played, the animal may not respond, but this does not mean that the animal has forgotten; rather, it could mean that the functional stimulus (white + tone) is no longer present to elicit the response.

Similar effects had long been known with humans as well (Carr, 1925; McGeoch, 1932). As discussed in the previous chapter, Abernathy (1940) demonstrated that students who were tested in the same classroom they were taught in did better than students who were tested in a different classroom. Subsequent research has consistently supported the idea that altered stimulus conditions, or more generally, contextual factors, play a major role in most kinds of forgetting.

The third factor in McGeoch's three-factor theory was set. *Set* can be thought of as a special version of context effects, such as when the subject is using an inappropriate mind set. The typical example is failing to recognize a friend from college when you happen to run into the person during a visit home. The idea is that, when at home, you are most likely to search through your list of "home friends" to identify the familiar face, but because this person is not a "home friend," you find no match. If you used the correct mind set —"friends from college"—then you would have recognized this person.

A related phenomenon is known as *part-set cuing*. When people are asked to recall items from a list they have just studied or to produce examples from a well-known category, having a subset — part of a set — of those items available at recall usually does not help and can even impair performance. For example, Slamecka (1968) had subjects hear a list of words twice. The control subjects were given a blank sheet of paper and were asked to write down as many of the words as they could. The experimental subjects were given a sheet of paper on which were 5 (or 15, or 25) of the words and were asked to supply the remaining 25 (or 15 or 5) items. The data of interest are the proportion of words recalled that were not cues. Slamecka found that the groups that had received part of the set as a cue recalled fewer items than did the control group. That is, the experimental group that received 15 words as cues could produce (on average) only 38% of the remaining words, compared to 50% for the control group. Although there is still no complete account for all of the part-set cuing data (see Nickerson, 1984), one interpretation is that the cues disrupt the normal strategy.

McGeoch's influence was so profound that there are no theories of forgetting from long-term memory that propose decay as the main explanation. Within the realm of immediate memory, however, the most common view of forgetting has long been decay.

# Decay versus Interference

The Brown-Peterson paradigm is one area in which both a decay explanation and one based on interference were offered. Recall that in the Brown-Peterson paradigm, subjects are given three letters and are then asked to count backward (or perform some other distracting activity) for a specified amount of time. The typical finding is that after about 20 seconds of counting backward, very few people can recall the letters. Indeed, many textbooks still cite the results of Peterson and Peterson (1959) as supporting the rapid decay of information in short-term memory. We have already described the basic results

**Table 7.2**   Proportion of items correctly recalled, displayed as blocks of 12 trials for 2 different sets of delay.

|            | Block 1 | Block 2 | Block 3 | Block 4 |
|------------|---------|---------|---------|---------|
| 3 and 6 s  | 0.57    | 0.66    | 0.70    | 0.74    |
| 15 and 18 s| 0.08    | 0.15    | 0.09    | 0.12    |

Source: Data from Peterson & Peterson (1959).

from the Brown-Peterson paradigm in Chapter 4 and saw how they were used as evidence for a separate short-term store and for advocating a major role for decay to explain the loss of information. An enormous amount of research has been conducted in this paradigm precisely because of its importance for theories of memory. This research has generally not favored the decay explanation.

The first major challenge to the decay explanation was reported by Keppel and Underwood (1962). Remember that Underwood (1957) found that, over a large number of studies, subjects' performance decreased as they received more and more trials. PI could operate in the Brown-Peterson paradigm because all of the consonant trigrams on all of the trials were very similar: the more previous trials that the subjects had seen, the worse their performance may have been. In fact, Peterson and Peterson were aware of this, and analyzed their data to see whether PI was operating. They divided the 48 trials into blocks of 12 and combined performance in the two shortest and the two longest conditions. The proportion of items correctly recalled is displayed in Table 7.2. Peterson and Peterson (1959) concluded that there was no PI because performance actually got better in the 3 and 6 s conditions over blocks. If there were PI, performance would be expected to get worse.

The only difference between Peterson and Peterson's (1959) analysis and that of Keppel and Underwood (1962) was that the latter researchers examined the first four trials individually, rather than averaging over the first 12 trials. When they did so, Keppel and Underwood found substantial evidence for proactive interference. On Trial 1, there was no forgetting regardless of how long the subjects counted backward (see Figure 7.4). Forgetting was observed only on subsequent trials, and by as few as 3 trials, performance was quite poor.

The important point is that recall does not differ on the very first trial when tested after 3 s or after 18 s. Equivalent performance has been repeatedly demonstrated when the first trial is analyzed (Baddeley & Scott, 1971; Cofer & Davidson, 1968; Fuchs & Melton, 1974; Gorfein, 1987; Turvey, Brick, & Osborn, 1970; Wright, 1967). A decay explanation, such as the one usually invoked to explain the Peterson and Peterson (1959) results, says that the more time elapses, the more decay will occur. Showing equivalent performance for the 3 and 18 s groups is inconsistent with this prediction. The reason that Peterson and Peterson (1959) did not observe PI was that it had already occurred within the 12 trials that composed Block 1.

The decay view and the interference view make different predictions. Wickens, Born, and Allen (1963; see also Wickens, 1970, 1972) tested a strong prediction of the PI interpretation of the Brown-Peterson results. Proactive interference will build up when the list items are all highly similar. If the stimulus type is changed, however, there should be

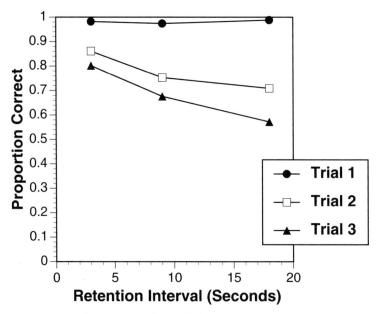

**Figure 7.4**   Proportion of items correctly recalled in a Brown-Peterson procedure at three different retention intervals on the first, second, and third trials.   Source: Keppel & Underwood (1962).

---

**Experiment   Buildup and Release of PI**

**Purpose:** To demonstrate the buildup and release of proactive interference in the Brown-Peterson paradigm.

**Subjects:** Forty subjects are recommended; ten should be assigned to each group. Two groups receive the same type of items on all four trials, and two groups change to a different type of item on Trial 4.

**Materials:** Table F in the Appendix lists 32 consonant trigrams. Number trigrams can be obtained from Table B by taking the first 3 digits, then the second 3 digits, and so forth. Table G lists several names of categories. For each subject, present novel items. There should also be two answer sheets: one for the category items and one for the trigrams. You will also need a stopwatch.

**Design:** One group of subjects will receive only letters, and one will receive only numbers. For the remaining subjects, one group will receive letters for the first three trials and numbers on the fourth, and the other group will receive numbers for the first three trials and letters on the fourth. Because each subject experiences only one condition, this is a between-subjects design.

**Procedure:** Inform the subjects that this is an experiment on information processing. Describe the two tasks and explain how subjects should respond on the answer sheets. Read

(continued)

less PI. Thus, on the first three trials, the researchers had subjects hear three consonants, then perform some distracting activity, and then recall the consonants. On the fourth trial, half of the subjects were switched from consonants to numbers. Performance in the switched group was much better than in the control group, regardless of the direction of the change (digits to letters or letters to digits). The PI account, then, predicts the increase in performance when the type of stimuli is changed. The decay view, on the other hand, cannot predict an increase in performance.

The amount of reduction, or release from PI, can be calculated easily (see Figure 7.5). If $x$ is the difference in performance between the experimental and control groups on trial 4, and $y$ is the difference between the control group on Trial 4 and the control group on Trial 1, then the percent release from PI is equal to $(x/y) \times 100$. If the release is 100%, then performance on the fourth trial is the same as performance on the first trial. If it is close to 0, there is no release.

Most release from PI phenomena are symmetric; that is, you get the same amount of release when switching from consonants to numbers as when switching from numbers to consonants. This symmetry indicates that it is the change in materials that is crucial, rather than the fact that one type of material is easier to recall than another. Switching from words to numbers gives an 85% release; switching from auditory to visual also gives about an 85% release. Changing taxonomic category (such as from types of cars to Russian novelists) gives a 65% release. Changing the number of syllables gives only a 15% release. Changing from one part of speech to another (verbs to nouns) gives less than a 5% release. One particularly interesting release concerns what is known as the *semantic differential*. If all the words on the first three trials have similar meanings, such as something pleasant

---

**Experiment    Buildup and Release of PI** (*continued*)

each trigram aloud, immediately name a category, and ask the subject to name as many examples of that category as they can. Record the examples of the category that the subject produces. After 10 s, ask the subject to report the trigram; then, begin the next trial. On the fourth trial, change the type of material for half of the subjects.

**Instructions:** "This is an experiment on information processing. I will read three items out loud, which I will ask you to recall in order. Before you recall them, I will name a category (such as DOG), and I would like you to name as many examples as you can as quickly as you can. For example, you would say "Poodle, corgi, greyhound, pekinese, Great Dane, English setter" as quickly as you can. When I signal, you will stop and report the three items in order. Then, I'll give you the next three items and a new category. Any questions?"

**Scoring and Analysis:** For each subject, count the number of trigrams recalled in order and compute an average for each group. The results from the two groups that receive the same items can be averaged together, and the results from the two groups that have a change can be averaged together. The results should be similar to those plotted in Figure 7.5.

**Optional Enhancements:** Include more subjects in each group.

Source: Based on an experiment by Wickens (1972).

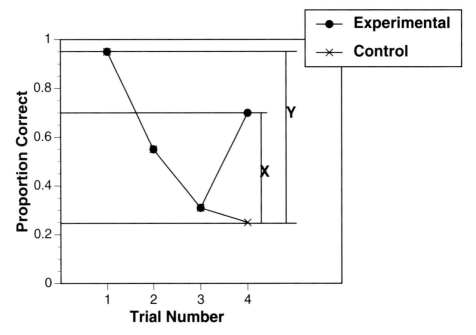

**Figure 7.5**  Idealized data showing release from proactive interference in the Brown-Peterson paradigm. *X* is the difference in performance between the experimental group (who have a different type of stimulus material on Trial 4 than on the previous trials) and the control group (who have the same type of stimulus material). *Y* is the difference in performance between the control group on Trial 1 and Trial 4.

(sunny, enjoy, happy), but the words on the last trial mean something different (kill, death, illness), then there is about a 55% release from PI. Wickens (1972) reports many such measures.

Release from PI is not limited to the typical laboratory paradigm. Gunter, Berry, and Clifford (1981) demonstrated release from PI when testing subjects' memory for news items taped off the evening news. The news stories were classified as being either domestic or international, and subjects saw several stories from one category, and then either another from the same category or one from the other category. Subjects showed a 70% release. Blumenthal and Robbins (1977) have shown buildup and release of PI when answering questions about prose passages, suggesting that this might affect performance on standardized tests. Dempster (1985) tested this directly, demonstrating the buildup of PI on comprehension questions like those used on the ACT and SAT.

Turvey and Egan (1970) changed two dimensions at the same time and found that performance on Trial 4 was equal to performance on Trial 1 regardless of whether the retention interval was 5 or 15 s. Other results consistent with the proactive interference explanation were reported by Loess and Waugh (1967). If recall is being reduced by PI, then one way to decrease the amount of PI is to separate the trials. Loess and Waugh found that with very long intervals between trials (such as 300 s), there was no difference in performance as a function of trial number even when the subjects were counting backward for

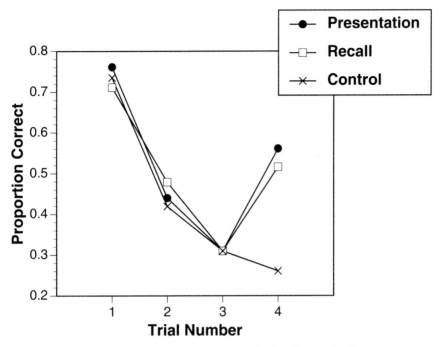

**Figure 7.6**   Proportion of items correctly recalled on the first four trials of a Brown-Peterson procedure as a function of type of cue.   Source: Gardiner, Craik, & Birtwistle (1972).

18 seconds. Subjects were about 60% accurate on Trial 1 and were still around 60% correct on Trial 4. Both results are inconsistent with an explanation that attributes forgetting to the rapid loss of information from short-term memory.

Several studies have tried to pin down the locus of the release from PI effect. An early suggestion was that when a change in stimulus properties occurs, subjects devote extra attention to the novel item. There are two problems with this account. One is that subjects are often unaware of the changes, particularly with the semantic differential, and yet they still show release from PI. A second problem is that other manipulations designed to affect the amount of attention do not yield any release (MacLeod, 1975).

A more promising idea is that it is a retrieval effect. Gardiner, Craik, and Birtwistle (1972) examined this hypothesis using two categories of items, each of which could be divided into subgroups. Some subjects received types of games, others types of flowers. Unnoticed by the subjects, the first three trials would all be indoor games (or wildflowers), and the fourth trial would be outdoor games (or garden flowers). All subjects received this subtle change in categories, but only two of the groups were informed of the change. One group was informed *prior* to presentation of the fourth trial, and the other group was informed *after* presentation of the fourth trial but prior to recall. Nothing extra was said to the control subjects. The results are shown in Figure 7.6.

The control subjects were affected by the buildup of PI, and this continued through Trial 4. If the change is unnoticed, then there will be no release from PI; but both the presentation and recall groups showed an equivalent release from PI. Gardiner and associates argued that this release must be a retrieval effect because that is the only place both groups had the category change information at the same time: the recall group could still take advantage of the change, even though they were unaware of this subtle change in category at encoding.

# Relative Distinctiveness

A similar kind of retrieval hypothesis also suggests an explanation for the data reported by Turvey, Brick, and Osborn (1970). Although they had five conditions, we will restrict our attention to only three, which conditions differed only in the duration of the retention interval (how long the subjects performed the distracting activity). One group counted backward for 10 s, one for 15 s, and one for 20 s. The proportion of items correctly recalled was equivalent on the first trial (0.85, 0.93, and 0.93, respectively). The proportion of items correctly recalled was also equivalent on the fourth trial (0.33, 0.30, and 0.30, respectively). Note that these results are already inconsistent with a decay explanation, because more decay should have occurred with the longer intervals.

On the fifth trial, Turvey and associates had every group perform the distracting activity for 15 s; thus, one group's retention interval increased, one group's remained the same, and the third group's retention interval decreased. On this fifth trial, performance was not equivalent: the 10 s group got worse (down to 0.20), the 15 s group remained constant (0.28), and the 20 s group got better (up to 0.38). A change in the duration of the distracting activity is not sufficient to obtain a release from PI, because one group actually performed worse after the change. However, Baddeley (1976) offered an explanation that attributes it to the relative duration of the distractor activity rather than the absolute duration.

Imagine three groups of subjects who receive two trials in a Brown-Peterson procedure. The first item is presented at Time 0, and the second item is presented after 20 s. Up until recall of the second item, everything is the same in the three groups. The second item is recalled either 10, 20, or 30 s after it was presented, as illustrated in Table 7.3.

Baddeley (1976) calculated a ratio of the times involved. The duration between the presentation of the first item (P1) and the test for the second item (R2) is 30 s for Group A, 40 s for Group B, and 50 s for Group C. The duration between the presentation of the second item (P2) and the test for the second item (R2) is 10 s for Group A, 20 s for Group

**Table 7.3**  Three groups that receive presentation of the first item at the same time and presentation of the second item at the same time; but recall of the second item occurs after varying delays.

| Group | *Time (seconds)* | | | | | | P1-R2 | P2-R2 | Ratio |
| | 0 | 10 | 20 | 30 | 40 | 50 | | | |
|---|---|---|---|---|---|---|---|---|---|
| A | P1 | | P2 | R2 | | | 30 s | 10 s | 3:1 |
| B | P1 | | P2 | | R2 | | 40 s | 20 s | 2:1 |
| C | P1 | | P2 | | | R2 | 50 s | 30 s | 1.67:1 |

**Table 7.4**    Three conditions from Turvey, Brick, & Osborn (1970) represented in the same way as in Table 7.3.

| Group | Time (seconds) | | | | | | | | | P4-R5 | P5-R5 | Ratio |
|---|---|---|---|---|---|---|---|---|---|---|---|---|
| | 0 | 5 | 10 | 15 | 20 | 25 | 30 | 35 | 40 | | | |
| 10 | P4 | | P5 | | | R5 | | | | 10 | 15 | 0.67 |
| 15 | P4 | | | P5 | | | R5 | | | 15 | 15 | 1.00 |
| 20 | P4 | | | | P5 | | | | R5 | 20 | 15 | 1.33 |

B, and 30 s for Group C. These figures and the resultant ratios are also shown in Table 7.3. The prediction is that the group with the largest ratio will show the best performance because Baddeley suggested, at the time of the recall attempt for item 2, what will primarily determine recall is the subject's ability to correctly distinguish the second item from the first item. The closer in time the recall test is to the presentation of the second item and the farther away the recall test is from the presentation of the second item, then the better the recall of the second item. It is this idea that the ratio is capturing.

The same reasoning can be applied to the Turvey, Brick, and Osborn (1970) data, shown in Table 7.4. The fourth item is presented at Time 0 (an arbitrary starting point). The fifth item is presented either 10, 15, or 20 s later, according to the group. The recall test for the fifth item occurs 15 s later. The same ratios as before are calculated, and again the larger the ratio, the better the recall of the fifth item.

This example contains a few simplifications. For example, the first three items are not factored in, and the time intervals are not exactly those that appeared in the experiment (for example, we have omitted the time needed to recall). However, this analysis applies even if we factor all these things in; it is just more complex. Similar analyses based on temporal discrimination have been used to explain serial position effects observed in recognition (Neath, 1993) and in memory for items within a sentence (Neath & Knoedler, 1994).

One particularly interesting phenomenon that this type of view emphasizes is that memory performance can get *better* as time passes. In one experiment, Neath and Knoedler (1994) presented subjects with a series of digitized photographs of snowflakes. These stimuli were chosen because people are unable to assign verbal labels to them, and thus the stimuli cannot be rehearsed verbally (Goldstein & Chance, 1970). These flakes were presented for 1 s on a computer screen with a 1 s gap—or interstimulus interval (ISI)—between each flake. The recognition test occurred after a retention interval (RI) of either 0, 2, or 5 s. For the test, the snowflake shown was either one from the immediately preceding list or one the subjects had not seen before. Only one recognition judgment was performed after each list. The results are shown in Figure 7.7. With a short retention interval, memory for the first item is at chance levels whereas the last item is almost perfectly recognized. As the retention interval increases in duration, performance on the last item decreases and performance on the first item increases.

The most intriguing finding is that memory for the first item improves as time elapses, a finding that has been replicated elsewhere (Neath, 1993; Wright, Santiago, Sands, Kendrick, & Cook, 1985). This result is predicted by the dimensional distinctiveness model (DDM). Based on a model suggested by Murdock (1960) and derived from the

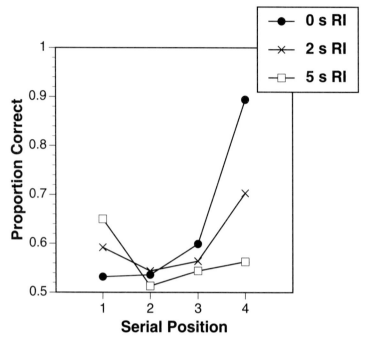

**Figure 7.7**   The proportion of items correctly recognized as a function of serial position and retention interval. Contrary to predictions based on decay or consolidation theories, there is an absolute increase in performance at the first serial position as the interval between presentation and test increases.   Source: Neath & Knoedler (1994).

ideas of the gestalt psychologist Koffka (1935), DDM also reflects the analysis offered by Baddeley (1976) and described above. DDM defines distinctiveness as the extent to which a stimulus stands out from other stimuli and emphasizes the relation between a given stimulus and the other members of the ensemble. The concept of distinctiveness is thus not applicable to an item in isolation, and the distinctiveness of a particular item can change depending on the other items in the list. For example, if the item at position 6 of a 12-item list is red and all the other items are black, item 6—the red item—will be very distinctive and very well recalled. If, on the other hand, all the items are red, then item 6 will not be very distinctive, even though it is the same item in both cases (von Restorff, 1933; Wallace, 1965).

Distinctiveness can, in principle, be calculated for any set of stimuli that vary along any dimension, whether temporal, physical, or some other dimension, although most of the work heretofore has focused on temporal distinctiveness. The reason is that in the typical memory experiment, the stimuli are equated for concreteness, length, frequency, and so forth, and so the stimuli vary systematically only along a temporal dimension. The position of the item along the relevant dimension—here temporal—is determined by calculating the sum of each ISI (in seconds) following the item in question and the RI following the final item. The temporal position of an item is calculated by giving each item an initial value of 1. The final item in the list is multiplied by the duration of the RI, while all other items are multiplied by the duration of the ISI and then added to the sum of the value of the following item. For example, if the RI is 1 s and each ISI is 1 s, the serial/temporal values ($s$) of a four-item list, beginning with the first item, would be 4, 3, 2, and 1. The final item in the list is a distance of 1 from the recaller whereas the first item is a distance of 4 from the recaller.

These temporal values then undergo a log transformation, a process based on Weber's Law (see Chapter 2; see also Helson, 1964), yielding the preliminary discriminability of that item ($d$). For the example given above, these log values would be 1.39, 1.10, 0.69, and 0.00, respectively. A distinctiveness value of each item ($\delta$) is calculated according to Equation 7.1, where $n$ is the number of items in the list and $k$ is the serial position of the current item.

$$\delta_k = \sum_{j=1}^{n} |d_k - d_j| \qquad (7.1)$$

All Equation 7.1 really does is calculate a measure of how different each item is from all of the other items. We take the absolute value of the difference because we do not care which number is larger, just what the size of the difference is. Thus, $\delta_1$ is equal to $(1.39 - 1.39) + (1.39 - 1.09) + (1.39 - 0.70) + (1.39 - 0.00)$, or 2.37. We then do this for the other items and get values of 1.79, 1.79, and 3.18. [Actually, Neath (1993) used a slightly different equation for the middle items, but it is omitted here for the sake of simplicity.] Finally, these values are normalized. This means that they are converted to a scale that reflects the relative size of these numbers. To do this, we add up all the values, which is 9.13, and then divide each $\delta$ value by 9.13 to get the distinctiveness of each item relative to the other items on the list; we get 0.26, 0.20, 0.20, and 0.35.

What happens to the $\delta$ values when the RI is increased? Using the same example, but changing the RI to 5, we get the following serial/temporal values: 8, 7, 6, and 5. The logs of these values are 2.08, 1.95, 1.79, and 1.61. $\delta_1$ is equal to $(2.08 - 2.08) + (2.08 - 1.95) + (2.08 - 1.79) + (2.08 - 1.61)$, or 0.89. We then do this for the other items and get values of 0.62, 0.62, and 0.99. The sum of these $\delta$ values is 3.13 and the normalized values are 0.29, 0.2, 0.2, and 0.32. Notice that with an increase in the duration of the retention interval, the DDM predicts that primacy will increase (0.26 becomes 0.29) and recency will decrease (0.35 becomes 0.32).

Wright and his colleagues have shown similar increases in performance over time as Neath and Knoedler (1994) showed, but Wright showed that this finding holds for pigeons and monkeys as well (Wright et al., 1985). Wheeler (1995) has demonstrated, in a different paradigm, increased performance over time when there is no opportunity for further rehearsal or learning. Any theory of forgetting must explain not only why memory is often worse as time passes, but also why memory is sometimes better.

## Forgetting as Discrimination

One theory of forgetting that can explain better performance as time elapses views memory and forgetting as a discrimination problem. According to Capaldi and Neath (1995), during learning, the organism not only processes the material to be learned but also associates that material with a variety of internal and external contextual cues. What ends up being processed is a multi-dimensional complex of stimuli. Forgetting will occur if the stimulating conditions at test do not sufficiently discriminate between the desired memory and some other competing memories, or if the stimuli at test elicit no memories at all. To the extent that the test cues do discriminate, then the organism will remember. Thus, forgetting is simply a performance deficit resulting from inadequate stimulus conditions. This approach suggests that forgetting, in the sense of permanent loss, does not occur: there is only a failure to perform due to a difference between the stimulus conditions prevailing at encoding and at test.

The question of permanent loss versus temporary lapse is an important one, but it is difficult if not impossible to answer. If an organism learns something at Time 1, demonstrates memory for it at Time 2, but demonstrates no memory for it at Time 3, has the information been permanently lost or is this simply a temporary retrieval deficit? In 1929, H. C. Blodgett reported an experiment demonstrating that a lack of performance was at least sometimes not a lack of learning or memory. He placed hungry rats in a complex maze and gave them food when they found their way through. These rats quickly learned the shortest route. He placed a second group of hungry rats in the maze but did not reward them. Not surprisingly, the performance of these animals did not improve over trials. With the introduction of food rewards, however, the error scores of the second group of animals plummeted to that of the first group that had been rewarded with food from the outset. This seminal study illustrates the important proposition that a lack of performance does not necessarily indicate a lack of learning — or, in memory terms, a lack of performance does not necessarily indicate a loss of previously learned information. Whenever an item is not recalled, it is possible that it is only temporarily inaccessible and that with a change in conditions or testing methods, the subject will be able to produce it (Tulving & Pearlstone, 1966).

Loftus and Loftus (1980) took the position that there is permanent loss of information. Their evidence was mostly negative in nature, demonstrating that neither hypnosis (see Chapter 15) nor neurological studies by Wilder Penfield (see Chapter 17) support the idea of permanent storage. The one line of evidence used to support their position came from the misleading eyewitness information paradigm, which we will discuss in Chapter 15. Capaldi and Neath (1995) took the opposite position. Although agreeing with Loftus and Loftus in their analysis of the hypnosis and Penfield studies, Capaldi and Neath suggested that the temporary lapse view made more predictions supported by empirical evidence than the permanent loss view did. In particular, they cited (literally) dozens of studies that demonstrated memory for information previously thought to be permanently lost (see also Miller & Grahame, 1991). To be clear, the temporary lapse view says that if a person (or animal) demonstrates memory for something at Time N, then that partiular memory will be potentially available at all subsequent times as long as the retrieval cue is appropriate. The lapse view does not say that people remember everything they see or hear.

Two examples will serve here: one where memory performance became better with the addition of a useful retrieval cue, and one where memory for various items seems to have lasted at least 50 years. Eich and Birnbaum (1982) asked subjects to learn a list of words in either a sober or intoxicated state. When tested after a change in drug state, retrieval was poor, as is usually the case (see Chapter 6). However, some of the subjects in the changed state condition were given an additional retrieval cue (e.g., think of all the flowers that you can). These subjects were then able to recall many of the items that they

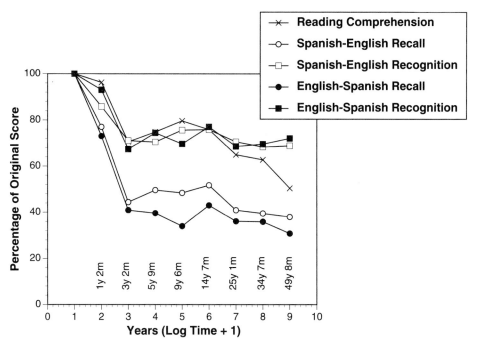

**Figure 7.8**   Amount of Spanish remembered over intervals from 1 year 2 months (1y 2m) to 49 years 8 months (49y 8m) expressed as a percent of original learning. Any value over 0 indicates that some material was remembered.   Source: Adapted from Bahrick (1984).

previously could not. The temporary lapse view predicts that when the appropriate retrieval cue is presented, evidence of memory — as opposed to memory loss — will be observed, as in the case of Eich and Birnbaum (1982). The trick, of course, is finding the right retrieval cue.

The temporary lapse view also predicts that, under appropriate testing conditions, there should be evidence of retention regardless of the delay between study and test. Perhaps the most impressive data on permanent retention come from the studies reported by Harry Bahrick and his colleagues. Bahrick, Bahrick, and Wittlinger (1975) demonstrated that although memory for people who attended the same high school over 50 years ago may be very poor when tested with recall, when tested with a cued-recognition test, performance was surprisingly accurate. For recognition of pictures of high school classmates, accuracy remained as high as 80 to 90% for more than 35 years. Similar feats of retention (in what has been dubbed "the permastore") have been demonstrated in mathematics (Bahrick & Hall, 1991), for city streets and locations (Bahrick, 1983) and for the Spanish language (Bahrick, 1984). In this latter study, Bahrick tested 773 people who had taken Spanish in high school and collected objective evidence of their original proficiency, including measures of grades, amount of practice, and years of study. He also administered a test to measure current understanding; the results are shown in Figure 7.8 as a percent of original performance. Although there was a substantial drop during the first three years, there was basically no further loss over the next 50 years. Ebbinghaus (1885) reported similar results: when relearning certain stanzas from Byron's *Don Juan* after a 30-year interval, he still showed savings.

Each view, permanent loss and temporary lapse, has its proponents and detractors. For the time being, it is worthwhile to remember the basic predictions each view makes. The permanent loss view suggests the information is gone forever, whereas the temporary lapse view suggests that under different conditions with different ways of testing, the information might still be revealed. The studies cited above (see also Capaldi & Neath, 1995; Miller & Grahame, 1991) are predicted by the temporary lapse view but not by the permanent loss view.

Although covered in more detail in the next chapter, results from experiments studying implicit memory also seem to support the temporary lapse view. For example, there is a paradigm known as *repetition priming*. In these experiments, subjects are typically presented with a word fragment that can be completed with only one valid word. For example, toboggan might be the target word and _o_ogg_n might be the word fragment; some subjects have recently seen the word *toboggan* on a prior list and others have not. Repetition priming refers to the finding that those subjects who have seen *toboggan* recently are more likely to complete the word fragment correctly than are those subjects who did not, even if the former subjects are unaware of their prior exposure to the word. Effects of repetition priming can be detected after a delay as long as 16 months in college students (Sloman, Hayman, Ohta, Law, & Tulving, 1988) and after a delay as long as 12 months in amnesics (Tulving, Hayman, & MacDonald, 1991). Such feats of retention after a single exposure are better explained by the temporary lapse than by the permanent loss view.

# References

Abernathy, E. M. (1940). The effect of changed environmental conditions upon the results of college examinations. *Journal of Psychology, 10,* 293–301.

Baddeley, A. D. (1976). *The psychology of memory.* New York: Basic Books.

Baddeley, A. D., & Scott, D. (1971). Short-term forgetting in the absence of proactive interference. *Quarterly Journal of Experimental Psychology, 23,* 275–283.

Bahrick, H. P. (1983). The cognitive map of a city — 50 years of learning and memory. In G. H. Bower (Ed.), *The psychology of learning and motivation, Vol. 17.* New York: Academic Press.

Bahrick, H. P. (1984). Semantic memory content in permastore: Fifty years of memory for Spanish learned in school. *Journal of Experimental Psychology: General, 113,* 1–29.

Bahrick, H. P., Bahrick, P. C., & Wittlinger, R. P. (1975). Fifty years of memories for names and faces. *Journal of Experimental Psychology: General, 104,* 54–75.

Bahrick, H. P., & Hall, L. K. (1991). Lifetime maintenance of high school mathematics content. *Journal of Experimental Psychology: General, 120,* 20–33.

Blodgett, H. C. (1929). The effect of the introduction of reward upon the maze performance of rats. *University of California Publications in Psychology, 4,* 113–134.

Blumenthal, G. B., & Robbins, D. (1977). Delayed release from proactive interference with meaningful material: How much do we remember after reading brief prose passages? *Journal of Experimental Psychology: Human Learning and Memory, 3,* 754–761.

Bower, G. H. (1978). Interference paradigms for meaningful propositional memory. *American Journal of Psychology, 91*, 575–585.

Capaldi, E. J., & Neath, I. (1995). Remembering and forgetting as context discrimination. *Learning & Memory, 2*, 107–132.

Carr, H. A. (1925). *Psychology: A study of mental activity.* New York: Longmans, Green.

Chorover, S. L., & Schiller, P. H. (1965). Short-term retrograde amnesia in rats. *Journal of Comparative and Physiological Psychology, 59*, 73–78.

Cofer, C. N., & Davidson, E. H. (1968). Proactive interference in STM for consonant units of two sizes. *Journal of Verbal Learning and Verbal Behavior, 7*, 268–270.

Crowder, R. G. (1976). *Principles of learning and memory.* Hillsdale, NJ: Erlbaum.

Crowder, R. G. (1982). General forgetting theory and the locus of amnesia. In L. S. Cermak (Ed.), *Human memory and amnesia.* Hillsdale, NJ: Erlbaum.

Dempster, F. N. (1985). Proactive interference in sentence recall: Topic-similarity effects and individual differences. *Memory & Cognition, 13*, 81–89.

Duncan, C. P. (1949). The retroactive effect of electroshock on learning. *Journal of Comparative and Physiological Psychology, 42*, 32–44.

Ebbinghaus, H. (1885). *Über das Gedächtnis: Untersuchungen zur experimentellen Psychologie.* Leipzig: Duncker and Humboldt. [Reprinted as H. E. Ebbinghaus (1964). Memory: A Contribution to Experimental Psychology (H. A. Ruger, Trans.). New York: Dover.]

Eich, E., & Birnbaum, I. M. (1982). Repetition, cuing, and state dependent memory. *Memory & Cognition, 10*, 103–114.

Fuchs, A. H., & Melton, A. W. (1974). Effects of frequency of presentation and stimulus length on retention in the Brown-Peterson paradigm. *Journal of Experimental Psychology, 103*, 629–637.

Gardiner, J. M., Craik, F. I. M., & Birtwistle, J. (1972). Retrieval cues and release from proactive inhibition. *Journal of Verbal Learning and Verbal Behavior, 11*, 778–783.

Goldstein, A. G., & Chance, J. E. (1970). Visual recognition memory for complex configurations. *Perception & Psychophysics, 9*, 237–241.

Gorfein, D. S. (1987). Explaining context effects on short-term memory. In D. S. Gorfein & R. R. Hoffman (Eds.), *Memory and learning: The Ebbinghaus Centennial Conference.* Hillsdale, NJ: Erlbaum.

Gunter, B., Berry, C., & Clifford, B. R. (1981). Proactive interference effects with television news items: Further evidence. *Journal of Experimental Psychology: Learning, Memory, and Cognition, 7*, 480–487.

Hebb, D. O. (1949). *The organization of behavior: A neuropsychological theory.* New York: Wiley.

Helson, H. (1964). *Adaptation-level theory.* New York: Harper & Row.

Jenkins, J. G., & Dallenbach, K. M. (1924). Obliviscence during sleep and waking. *American Journal of Psychology, 35*, 605–612.

Keppel, G. (1984). Consolidation and forgetting theory. In H. Weingartner & E. S. Parker (Eds.), *Memory consolidation: Psychobiology of cognition.* Hillsdale, NJ: Erlbaum.

Keppel, G., & Underwood, B. J. (1962). Proactive inhibition in short-term retention of single items. *Journal of Verbal Learning and Verbal Behavior, 1*, 153–161.

Koffka, K. (1935). *Principles of gestalt psychology.* London: Routledge & Kegan Paul.

Loess, H., & Waugh, N. C. (1967). Short-term memory and inter-trial interval. *Journal of Verbal Learning and Verbal Behavior, 6*, 455–460.

Loftus, E. F., & Loftus, G. R. (1980). On the permanence of stored information in the human brain. *American Psychologist, 35,* 409–420.

MacLeod, C. M. (1975). Release from proactive interference: Insufficiency of an attentional account. *American Journal of Psychology, 88,* 459–465.

McGeoch, J. A. (1932). Forgetting and the law of disuse. *Psychological Review, 39,* 352–370.

McGeoch, J. A. (1942). *The psychology of human learning: An introduction.* New York: Longmans Green.

Melton, A. W., & Irwin, J. M. (1940). The influence of degree of interpolated learning on retroactive inhibition and the overt transfer of specific responses. *American Journal of Psychology, 53,* 173–203.

Miller, R. R., & Grahame, N. J. (1991). Expression of learning. In L. Dachowski & C. F. Flaherty (Eds.), *Current Topics in Animal Learning: Brain, Emotion, and Cognition.* Hillsdale, NJ: Erlbaum.

Miller, R. R., & Springer, A. D. (1972). Recovery from amnesia following transorneal electroconvulsive shock. *Psychonomic Science, 28,* 7–8.

Minami, H., & Dallenbach, K. M. (1946). The effect of activity upon learning and retention in the cockroach. *American Journal of Psychology, 59,* 1–58.

Müller, G. E., & Pilzecker, A. (1900). Experimentalle Beitrage zur Lehre vom Gedachtnis. *Zeitschrift fur Psychologie, 1,* 1–300.

Murdock, B. B., Jr. (1960). The distinctiveness of stimuli. *Psychological Review, 67,* 16–31.

Neath, I. (1993). Distinctiveness and serial position effects in recognition. *Memory & Cognition, 21,* 689–698.

Neath, I., & Knoedler, A. J. (1994). Distinctiveness and serial position effects in recognition and sentence processing. *Journal of Memory and Language, 33,* 776–795.

Nickerson, R. S. (1984). Retrieval inhibition from part-set cuing: A persisting enigma in memory research. *Memory & Cognition, 12,* 531–552.

Peterson, L. R., & Peterson, M. J. (1959). Short-term retention of individual items. *Journal of Experimental Psychology, 61,* 12–21.

Postman, L. (1961). The present status of interference theory. In C. N. Cofer (Ed.), *Verbal learning and verbal behavior.* New York: McGraw-Hill.

Postman, L., Stark, K., & Fraser, J. (1968). Temporal changes in interference. *Journal of Verbal Learning and Verbal Behavior, 7,* 672–694.

Quartermain, D., McEwen, B. S., & Azmitia, E. C., Jr. (1972). Recovery of memory following amnesia in the rat and mouse. *Journal of Comparative and Physiological Psychology, 76,* 521–529.

Slamecka, N. J. (1968). An examination of trace storage in free recall. *Journal of Experimental Psychology, 76,* 504–513.

Sloman, S. A., Hayman, C. A. G., Ohta, N., Law, J., & Tulving, E. (1988). Forgetting in primed fragment completion. *Journal of Experimental Psychology: Learning, Memory, and Cognition, 14,* 223–239.

Spear, N. E., & Riccio, D. C. (1994). *Memory: Phenomena and principles.* Boston: Allyn & Bacon.

Tulving, E., Hayman, C. A. G., & MacDonald, C. A. (1991). Long-lasting perceptual priming and semantic learning in amnesia: A case experiment. *Journal of Experimental Psychology: Learning, Memory, and Cognition, 17,* 595–617.

Tulving, E., & Pearlstone, Z. (1966). Availability versus accessibility of information in memory for words. *Journal of Verbal Learning and Verbal Behavior, 5,* 381–391.

Turvey, M. T., Brick, P., & Osborn, J. (1970). Proactive interference in short-term memory as a function of prior-item retention interval. *Quarterly Journal of Experimental Psychology, 22,* 142–147.

Turvey, M. T., & Egan, J. F. (1970). Release from proactive interference in short-term memory as a function of change in visual and phonemic structure and retention interval. *Perception & Psychophysics, 7,* 169–172.

Underwood, B. J. (1957). Interference and forgetting. *Psychological Review, 64,* 49–60.

von Restorff, H. (1933). Analyse von Vorgangen in Spurenfeld. I. Über die Wirkung von Bereichsbildung im Spurenfeld. *Psychologische Forschung, 18,* 299–342.

Wallace, W. P. (1965). Review of the historical, empirical, and theoretical status of the von Restorff phenomenon. *Psychological Bulletin, 63,* 410–424.

Wheeler, M. A. (1995). Improvement in recall over time without repeated testing: spontaneous recovery revisited. *Journal of Experimental Psychology: Learning, Memory, and Cognition, 21,* 173–184.

Wickens, D. D. (1970). Encoding categories of words: An empirical approach to meaning. *Psychological Review, 77,* 1–15.

Wickens, D. D. (1972). Characteristics of word encoding. In A. W. Melton & E. Martin (Eds.), *Coding Processes in Human Memory.* Washington, DC: Winston.

Wickens, D. D., Born, D. G., & Allen, C. K. (1963). Proactive inhibition and item similarity in short-term memory. *Journal of Verbal Learning and Verbal Behavior, 2,* 440–445.

Wright, A. A., Santiago, H. C., Sands, S. F., Kendrick, D. F., & Cook, R. G. (1985). Memory processing of serial lists by pigeons, monkeys, and people. *Science, 229,* 287–289.

Wright, J. H. (1967). Effects of formal interitem similarity and length of retention interval on proactive inhibition in short-term memory. *Journal of Experimental Psychology, 75,* 366–395.

Zechmeister, E. B., & Nyberg, S. E. (1982). *Human memory: An introduction to research and theory.* Pacific Grove, CA: Brooks/Cole.

# CHAPTER EIGHT

# Implicit Memory and Multiple Memory Systems

*"As has often been shown by recent writers . . . we have not memory, but memories."*
— *William H. Burnham (1888)*

In Chapter 7, the idea was presented that memory might fundamentally be a discrimination problem. If this is the case, it was suggested, it should be possible to take a situation where an organism shows no evidence of memory, change the test conditions slightly to make the discrimination task easier, and then demonstrate that the information was retained. One area of research that has attracted much attention over the last few years concerns just such a situation. In this chapter, we examine implicit memory and contrast it with explicit memory. We then use this analysis to shed some light on other proposed distinctions (especially the episodic-semantic distinction) and compare the multiple systems view to the unitary view.

## Implicit Memory

An initial problem in this area is to define the appropriate terms. Roediger (Roediger, Weldon, Stadler, & Riegler, 1992) uses the terms *incidental* and *intentional* to refer to the learning task, and *implicit* and *explicit* to refer to the test; Jacoby (1984) uses *incidental* and *intentional* to refer to the test; Schacter and Tulving (1994) use *implicit* and *explicit* to refer to both the task and to the form of memory; and Johnson and Hasher (1987; see also Richardson-Klavehn & Bjork, 1988) use *indirect* and *direct* to refer to the test, and *implicit* and *explicit* to refer to the form of memory. Furthermore, there is a separate but related area of research that examines implicit learning (for example, Reber, 1993). All of this can be quite confusing. In this text, we use *incidental* and *intentional* to refer to the learning instructions, *indirect* and *direct* to refer to the test, and *implicit* and *explicit* to refer to the type of memory used by the subject. To keep from being completely unambiguous, however, we shall retain *implicit learning* as the term referring to the nonconscious acquisition of structured information.

The majority of situations considered in this book so far have been examples of direct tests of memory following intentional learning instructions; the subject is aware that the situation will require a memory test and tries to memorize the information (intentional learning). At test, the subject is aware of the particular learning episode that should be recalled, and the test instructions make direct reference to the learning episode (direct test). The type of memory used in this situation has been called *explicit memory*.

We examined incidental learning instructions in Chapter 6 in conjunction with the orienting instructions typically given in a levels of processing experiment. Learning is incidental because the instructions require that subjects focus on some information processing goal (such as pleasantness ratings) other than on remembering the information. An indirect memory test, in contrast to a direct test, occurs when "the instructions refer only to the task at hand, and do not make reference to prior events" (Richardson-Klavehn & Bjork, 1988, p. 478). The type of memory used in this situation has been called implicit memory.

## Indirect Tests of Implicit Memory

It is important to clarify three points with respect to implicit and explicit memory. First, as Table 8.1 illustrates, there are four different combinations of learning—incidental and intentional—and testing—indirect and direct. Many studies in this area fit in Cell 1 of the table, because the subject did not intentionally learn the items and was not aware of the relationship between the test and the study phase. Most of the studies presented earlier in the text (Chapters 4 and 5) fall in Cell 4, because the subject is asked to study a list of words and at test is asked to recall the list of words just studied. Many experiments have been conducted (many levels of processing studies) that would fit in Cell 2—implicit learning but explicit testing (for example, Postman & Phillips, 1954). For example, subjects are not told of the memory test prior to study, but at test they are asked to refer back to the study episode. Roediger, Weldon, Stadler, and Riegler (1992) reported an experiment that included all four cells. Although the majority of studies that we will focus on in this chapter fit in Cell 1, it is important to note that there are other ways of assessing memory.

Second, implicit memory and implicit learning are not at all equivalent to subliminal perception. *Subliminal perception* refers to when a stimulus is presented so quickly or so quietly that it is not consciously perceived. The most famous example occurred in New Jersey in 1957, when James Vicary reported that after he flashed the message "Buy Popcorn" on the screen during a movie, popcorn sales increased by over 50%. This is subliminal perception because the theater patrons were unaware that the message had been presented. (It turns out that this episode never happened; Vicary admitted that he faked the report to try to revive his failing marketing business: see Pratkanis, 1992; Rogers,

**Table 8.1**   Four possible ways of combining implicit and explicit study and test instructions: Learning can be incidental or intentional, and the test can be an indirect or a direct measure.

|  |  | Test Instructions | |
| --- | --- | --- | --- |
|  |  | *Indirect* | *Direct* |
| *Study Instructions* | *Incidental* | Cell 1 | Cell 2 |
|  | *Intentional* | Cell 3 | Cell 4 |

1993.) In an implicit memory study, the subjects are aware of the stimuli as they are presented; they are simply unaware that the memory test that follows is directed toward these items.

Third, although implicit memory has received most attention during the last few years, it is not a new discovery. For example, Schacter (1989) mentions two 19th-century investigators—Dunn (1845) and Korsakoff (1889)—who accurately described implicit memory. Even Ebbinghaus (1885, p. 2; cited by Richardson-Klavehn & Bjork, 1988) claimed that prior experiences can be retained without awareness. And Claparède described an anecdote from 1911 that conforms to an indirect test of implicit memory (Claparède, 1951; see Schacter, 1987, for an historical review).

# Implicit Learning

The term *implicit learning* usually refers to "the process by which knowledge about the rule-governed complexities of the stimulus environment is acquired independently of conscious attempts to do so" (Reber, 1989, p. 219). There has been a long history of research on this topic; McGeoch and Irion (1952, p. 210 ff) review the early research and Reber (1993) reviews more recent work.

One common method of studying implicit learning is to examine how people learn artificial grammars. These types of studies typically have two phases. First, there is an acquisition phase, where subjects are exposed to strings of letters that are consistent with the grammar; second, there is a testing stage, where the subject's knowledge of the grammar is assessed.

A Markovian artificial grammar is simply a way of specifying which letters may precede and follow other letters. Figure 8.1 illustrates a simple such system. In this system, the string PTTVPS is grammatical (it can be generated by the system), whereas the string PTTXS is not grammatical (it cannot be generated by the system). These systems are nice for studying implicit learning because they are complex enough that conscious strategies will be of little use; yet novel so the experimenter is assured the subject enters the situation with no preexisting knowledge; and the stimuli are synthetic and arbitrary. This last point is important because if implicit learning can be observed with such impoverished, artificial stimuli, it demonstrates the power and flexibility of this mode of learning (see Reber, 1993).

In one study (Reber, 1967), subjects were asked to learn strings with three to eight letters in each string. Although this is intentional learning (study these lists for an upcoming test) with a direct test (recall the strings you just studied), Reber was most interested in the implicit learning that occurred. One group of subjects learned strings that were grammatical according to a Markovian artificial grammar such as the one in Figure 8.1. Another group learned random strings that conformed to no grammar. On the first trial, both groups averaged about 18 errors when recalling the strings; this demonstrates the difficulty of the task. Both groups did improve, but the group that received the grammatical strings made fewer errors than did the group with random strings. By the end of seven trials, the grammatical group was averaging fewer than three errors compared to about eight for the random group. Furthermore, subjects in the grammatical group could then use information acquired implicitly to judge quite accurately whether or not novel

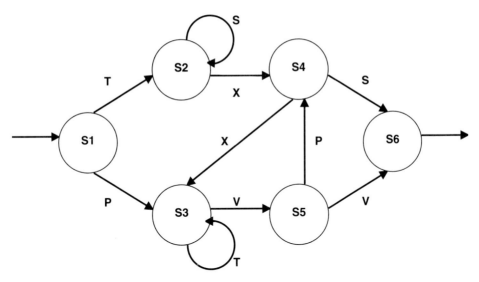

**Figure 8.1**  An example of an artificial grammar. Each state (e.g., S1) represents a random choice: a certain proportion of the time, the result is one direction (chose "T") and the rest of the time, the result is the other direction (chose "P"). To generate a string, one simply keeps moving through the grammar system until exiting at S6. The two shortest strings are TXS and PVV. Other grammatical strings include: TSXXVPS, PVPS, PTVPXTVPS, and TSXS.
Source: Reber (1993).

strings were grammatical. However, the subjects were not able to describe the rules they used to decide, and those subjects who did venture detailed accounts invariably provided rules that would not work. Implicitly learned information appears difficult to vocalize.

One key aspect that affects whether structure can be implicitly learned is the degree of organization present in the string (cf. Garner, 1974). The stimuli do not have to be perfectly predictable; for example, Cleeremans and McClelland (1991) demonstrated that even a noisy grammar — one where approximately 15% of the stimuli are random — can be implicitly learned. However, changes in the organization of the sequences can affect learning.

A study reported by Stadler (1995) illustrates the complexity of the issue. Stadler's task was implicit serial pattern learning, in which subjects were asked to press one of four keys as quickly as they could. When an asterisk appeared in any of four locations (labeled A, B, C, and D), the subject was prompted to press a corresponding key as quickly as possible to indicate the asterisk's location. There were several different sequences of locations — such as BCADBCA, DACBDAC, CDBACDB, and ABDCABD — and these locations would be repeated during the course of the experiment. Because accuracy becomes quite high, the dependent variable was response time. In all conditions, subjects' response times systematically decreased, illustrating learning. As the subjects learned the sequence, they became able to anticipate the next location and so they could respond more quickly. Specifically, their average response time on the learned sequences was approximately 220 ms faster than on unlearned sequences.

The important data come from comparing the performance in the control condition to that in three other conditions. Stadler (1995) used three conditions, because when disrupting the organization of a structure, it is also possible to change other factors. By examining several different variables, he could determine the relative importance of each factor. One condition clearly affected the organization, one clearly affected the processing demands placed on the subject, and the third did both. The first condition was the *pauses* condition. In this condition, the subject did not have to do anything other than respond as the control subjects did; thus, there should be little or no resources diverted from learning. However, because the time between the subject's response and the next item could vary, this should disrupt the organization of the sequence. The second condition was the *memory load* condition, in which the subject was asked to retain a list of seven letters over several trials. This should require some additional processing resources compared to the control groups. However, because the letters were presented prior to a block of trials and the responses were collected after the block, the task should not interrupt processes responsible for organizing the stimuli during the block. In the final condition, the *tone counting* condition, subjects were asked to count the number of times they heard a particular tone. The tone could occur after the subject made a particular response, thereby disrupting a sequence; but the subject also had to report the number of tones heard at the end of a block, thereby requiring additional processing resources compared to the control group.

The memory load task reduced performance; the difference in response times from learned to unlearned sequences dropped from 200 ms to 159 ms. However, both the tone counting and pauses conditions disrupted performance even more, down to 82 ms and 93 ms, respectively. What this means, according to Stadler, is that implicit learning is affected far more by changes in the structure or organization of information to be learned, and is far less affected by tasks that require more processing.

Reber (1993) argued that such implicit learning accounts for most of the learning about the structure of the environment. The arguments supporting this position are too complex to be summarized here, and the reader is referred to Reber's book. Nonetheless, it is clear that highly complex structures and patterns of information can be learned largely without the subject's awareness. Although the information is learned without awareness, it is sometimes possible for subjects to become aware and use this knowledge (Mathews, 1990; Mathews, Buss, Stanley, Blanchard-Fields, Cho, & Druhan, 1989). A recent issue of the journal *Psychonomic Bulletin & Review* contains a symposium that critically considers the relationship between implicit learning and other forms of learning and memory (Roediger, 1997). Given all these findings, it should not be surprising that information learned incidentally can greatly affect memory performance.

# Experimental Dissociations

To illustrate how implicit memory is assessed by an indirect test, consider the following typical experiment. There are two phases and two groups of subjects. In Phase I, the subjects are shown a long list of words (maybe 100 or so) and are asked to perform some task, such as making pleasantness ratings. The rating task ensures that the subjects process the information. In the list of words seen by the experimental group, a small proportion will be words of interest. Thus, the experimental group may see 10 key words that the control group does not see. In Phase II, some time later, the subject is asked to complete another task, unrelated to the first. The subject is given a long list of word fragments—such as _o_ogg_n—and is asked to fill in the blanks to make a complete word. There is no mention of the previous list of words, and there is often a delay between the two phases. In this example, the control subjects did not see the only valid English word that completes this fragment (toboggan), but the experimental subjects did see this word on the list. Implicit memory is demonstrated when more experimental subjects complete the word fragment correctly than control subjects do. The task is incidental because the subject was not intentionally trying to study the words during Phase I, and it is indirect because the subject was not trying to recall the list of words during Phase II.

A measure commonly used is *repetition priming:* the processing of something a second time is benefited from having processed it previously. (A second type of priming is *association priming,* which refers to the observation that response times are often faster if a second item is semantically related to or associated with the first item. This type of priming will be discussed in Chapter 12.) Priming is typically the difference between the mean proportion of fragments completed by the experimental group and the mean proportion completed by the control group. A priming score of 0 indicates no difference, and any positive value (such as 0.10) indicates better performance for the experimental group. A direct test of memory, on the other hand, would have required the subjects to recall as many of the words from the study session as they could, or to decide whether a target item shown during the test period was one of the words studied. It turns out that one of the critical issues in current memory research—the nature and number of different memory systems—has been addressed using dissociations between indirect and direct tests of memory.

A *dissociation* occurs when one variable, such as presentation modality or word frequency, is shown to affect one test differently than another. For example, when Test A is given, subjects do better with visual than with auditory presentation; when Test B is given, the opposite pattern is observed—performance is better with auditory than with visual presentation. The discovery of such a dissociation can support the idea that the two tests tap into different memory systems. Beginning in the early 1980s, several dissociations were demonstrated between indirect and direct tests, which led researchers to think that implicit and explicit memory were two different systems. Here, we consider only two dissociations.

Tulving, Schacter, and Stark (1982) conducted an experiment with three phases. In Phase I, subjects were asked to learn a list of 96 words. In Phase II, which occurred 1 hour later, subjects received a word-fragment completion test or a recognition test on 48 of the studied words. Phase III took place 7 days later, when the tests were given for the other 48 studied words. Of most interest is the change in memory performance over time for both the direct (recognition) and indirect (fragment completion) tests; the results are shown in Figure 8.2. For the recognition test, performance declined over the retention interval: the subjects correctly recognized fewer words after 7 days than after 1 hour. For the word-fragment completion test, the measure of interest is the amount of priming— the proportion of times the fragment was accurately completed when it was a studied item compared to the number of times it was accurately completed when it was a nonstudied

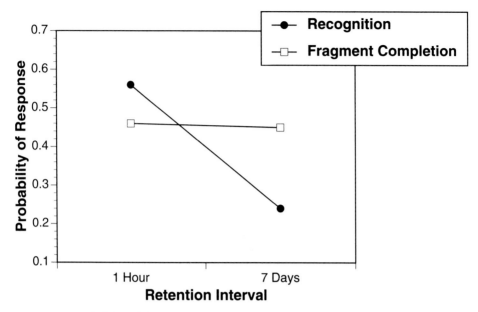

**Figure 8.2**    Probability of observing priming in a word-fragment completion task and probability of correctly recognizing words after a 1-hour or 1-week retention interval. Source: Tulving, Schacter, & Stark (1982).

item. This value remained the same after a 1-week delay as after a 1-hour delay. This represents a dissociation, because the independent variable — duration of the retention interval — affected the direct and indirect measures differently. The longer the retention interval, the worse the performance on the direct test; but retention interval had no measurable effect on the indirect test.

A second type of dissociation was demonstrated by Graf and Schacter (1987). Chapter 7 included a discussion of interference theory, emphasizing the prevalence of both retroactive interference (RI) and proactive interference (PI) as causes of memory failure. Graf and Schacter reported an experiment in which RI and PI affected direct tests of memory but did not affect indirect tests.

In Phase I, subjects studied word pairs, such as SHIRT-WINDOW. These first pairs will be called A-B pairs. Subjects were asked to generate and read aloud a sentence that related the words in a meaningful manner, such as "The boy threw the shirt out of the window." This is incidental learning because the subjects were not asked to learn the word pairs. In Phase II, the subjects did the same processing to a second list of word pairs. In the control condition, this list contained all new words and so was called the C-D list. In the experimental condition, this list was designed to produce interference by reusing the first words from Phase I. These interference lists, then, are called A-D lists. Both groups of subjects would be tested on the original A-B pairs, so this design would lead to retroactive interference: processing the A-D list can interfere with information already processed, the A-B list. Another set of subjects also received two learning sessions, but these were arranged so as to cause proactive interference. These subjects processed the A-D or C-D pairs in Phase I, and the A-B pairs in Phase II. They were then tested on the A-B pairs. This is proactive interference because information already processed (the A-D pairs) can interfere with new information (the A-B pairs). The design is sketched out in Table 8.2.

The direct test was cued recall; the subject was provided with the A word and the first few letters of a B word and was asked to complete the stem with the originally studied word. This is a direct test because the subject is asked to refer back to a specific learning

---

**Experiment    Priming Word-Fragment Completion**

**Purpose:** To demonstrate repetition priming effects in a word fragment completion task.

**Subjects:** Twenty subjects are recommended. Ten should be assigned to the experimental group, and ten to the control group.

**Materials:** Table H in the Appendix lists 60 word fragments. For each subject, present 20 of these words (with no letters missing). A convenient way is to create a booklet with 1 word per page. You will also need an answer sheet containing all 60 word fragments (with the letters missing) in random order. Make sure that none of the first 10 word fragments were on the study list.

**Design:** One group of the subjects will participate in both the study and test phases, whereas the control group will participate in only the test phase. Because each subject experiences only one condition, this is a between-subjects design.

**Procedure (Phase I):** Inform the subjects in the experimental group that this is an experiment on information processing that has several parts. Tell them to read each word silently to themselves. They should look at each word for 5 seconds before turning the page and going on to the next word.

**Instructions (Phase I):** "This is an experiment on information processing. On each page of your booklet, you will see a word. I would like you to read it silently to yourself. After you have seen all the words, I will give you further instructions. Please turn the page when I say the word *turn*. Any questions?"

**Procedure (Phase II):** Collect all of the booklets and wait 10 minutes after subjects have processed the words before giving the test sheet. During the interval, you can have the subjects perform any other task that does not involve words (such as recall of lists of 9 items, circling all the occurrences of the digit 6 on a sheet of paper). Then tell them the next phase consists of completing word fragments.

**Instructions (Phase II):** "In this phase of the experiment, you will see a list of word fragments. For each fragment, I would like you to try to fill in the missing letters to make a valid English word. Any questions?"

**Scoring and Analysis:** For each subject in the control group, count the number of word fragments accurately completed. Do the same for the experimental group. Of most interest are the fragments that the experimental group studied. The experimental group should have completed more words than the experimental group. The difference between the proportion correct for each group (experimental minus control) is the amount of priming.

**Optional Enhancements:** Include more subjects in each group, and include another group that has a longer delay (such as 24 hours) between study and test.

Source: Adapted from Tulving, Schacter, & Stark (1982).

**Table 8.2**   Schematic representation of the conditions tested by Graf and Schacter (1987).

|              | Phase I | Phase II | Tested on | Interference |
|--------------|---------|----------|-----------|--------------|
| Experimental | A-B     | A-D      | A-B       | RI           |
| Control      | A-B     | C-D      | A-B       |              |
| Experimental | A-D     | A-B      | A-B       | PI           |
| Control      | C-D     | A-B      | A-B       |              |

episode. The indirect test was word-fragment completion; the subject was provided with the A word and stem of a B word and was asked to complete the stem with the first word that came to mind. This is an indirect test because the task can be completed without reference to the learning episode. To minimize the chance that subjects became aware of the relationship between the word-fragment completion test and the study episode, only 12 A-B pairs were tested out of 44 other items. A third, separate group of subjects received only Phase III; this group provides a baseline of how many fragments would be completed when there was no opportunity to learn. The subjects in the control and experimental conditions performed more accurately than the baseline subjects did, confirming that memory was indeed playing a role. The rest of the results are shown in Table 8.3.

First consider the retroactive interference manipulation. On the direct test, the control subjects performed more accurately than the experimental subjects did (.55 versus .40), demonstrating the presence of RI. On the indirect test, however, the control and experimental subjects performed at about the same levels, indicating no interference. The pattern is the same for the proactive interference condition: on the direct test, the control subjects outperformed the experimental subjects (.67 versus .45), whereas performance was equivalent on the indirect test. This represents a dissociation, because the manipulation of both RI and PI affected performance on one kind of test (direct) but had no effect on another test (indirect).

Although there are numerous dissociations between implicit and explicit memory, there are also numerous situations where parallel effects occur (Richardson-Klavehn & Bjork, 1988, p. 525). For example, performance on both direct and indirect tests benefits

**Table 8.3**   The proportion of stems correctly completed in a cued recall test (direct) or word-fragment completion test (indirect) in either a retroactive or proactive interference design.

|           | Retroactive Interference | | Proactive Interference | |
|-----------|---------|--------------|---------|--------------|
| Test Type | Control | Experimental | Control | Experimental |
| Direct    | .55     | .40          | .67     | .45          |
| Indirect  | .34     | .32          | .32     | .35          |

Source: Based on data from Graf & Schacter (1987).

from repetition of the to-be-tested material (Graf & Mandler, 1984) and suffers when attention is divided during study (Eich, 1984). One reason for this might be that no test (direct or indirect) relies solely on one type of memory, explicit or implicit. Explicit memory can be used on an indirect test, as when a subject notices that several of the word fragments can be completed with words from the pleasantness ratings task (Richardson-Klavehn & Bjork, 1988). Similarly, implicit memory can be used on a direct test, as when implicit memory facilitates encoding of recognition probes (Jacoby & Dallas, 1981). It was for this reason that Jacoby and his colleagues (Jacoby, Toth, & Yonelinas, 1993) developed the process dissociation framework presented in Chapter 6.

# Theoretical Accounts of Implicit Memory

There are four main accounts of the implicit memory data (for extensive reviews of data and theories, see Richardson-Klavehn & Bjork, 1988; Roediger & McDermott, 1993): the activation view (Graf & Mandler, 1984), the multiple memory systems approach (Tulving & Schacter, 1990), the transfer appropriate processing view (Roediger, Weldon, & Challis, 1987), and the bias view (Ratcliff & McKoon, 1996).

## The Activation View

This account, perhaps currently the least popular of the four, holds that the priming seen on indirect tests is attributable to the temporary activation of preexisting representations. This activation occurs automatically, without the need for extensive or intentional processing on the part of the subject. Because the activation is automatic and occurs without elaborative processing, there is no contextual information available that would make the item appear as part of an episode. This view readily explains certain aspects of performance on indirect tests. For example, this view predicts that there should be priming in the absence of elaborative processing (see Jacoby & Dallas, 1981) because priming is the result of automatic processes. Furthermore, in amnesics, there should be normal priming of information that is already known, but no such priming of novel word pairs (see Cermak, Talbot, Chandler, & Wolbarst, 1985). As we will see in Chapter 9, amnesics often show impairment on tasks that require processing contextual information; however, because the activation view says that context is not important, amnesics should still show priming for information they already know.

Several types of findings pose serious problems for the activation view, however. First is the finding that some indirect tests show priming after a delay as long as 16 months in college students (Sloman, Hayman, Ohta, Law, & Tulving, 1988) and after a delay as long as 12 months in amnesics (Tulving, Hayman, & MacDonald, 1991). If priming is automatic, temporary activation, the time frame involved should be seconds or minutes, not months or years. Second, under certain circumstances, amnesics demonstrate priming of newly acquired information (see Graf & Schacter, 1985). This finding poses a problem because the activation view assumes that temporary activation of preexisting representations is the primary cause of priming. However, if newly acquired information can be primed, it calls into question the assumption concerning preexisting representations. The activation explanation has not fared well of late, and it has been eclipsed by the other proposals.

# Multiple Memory Systems

The multiple memory systems view is put forward most strongly by Tulving and Schacter (1990; Schacter & Tulving, 1994). In its simplest form, it holds that many dissociations between direct and indirect tests of memory arise because the tests tap different underlying memory systems. In particular, Schacter (1994) identifies the perceptual representation system (PRS) as a separate memory system responsible for many of the effects seen on indirect tests. The PRS is responsible for "the facilitated identification of perceptual objects from reduced cues as a consequence of a specific prior exposure to an object" (Schacter, 1994, p. 234). Before describing this proposed system more completely, it is first necessary to define what is meant by a memory system. By necessity, the discussion begins with the assumption that there are multiple memory systems, although not all researchers agree on this point. For example, the following discussion uses the proposed distinction between episodic and semantic memory to illustrate the requirements for proposing different systems, but many researchers question whether there is sufficient evidence to differentiate these systems (see below).

What is a system? Schacter and Tulving (1994) define a memory system by describing what a memory system is not. First, a memory system is not a memory process: "A memory process refers to a specific operation carried out in the service of memory performance" (Schacter & Tulving, 1994, p. 12). This definition includes encoding, rehearsal, retrieval, and so forth. Second, a memory system is not a memory task. A recognition task does not imply a recognition memory system distinct from other memory systems. There is often an implicit isomorphism between certain tasks, such that most free recall tasks tap episodic memory, but this need not be the case. Except for highly unusual circumstances, a given memory task is not a pure measure of a particular memory process, let alone a particular memory system (Jacoby, 1991). A final confusion is that implicit memory and explicit memory are not memory systems (Schacter & Tulving, 1994). Rather, these terms refer to situations where memory is expressed without awareness (implicit) or with awareness (explicit) of the original learning episode.

Different researchers have offered different definitions of a memory system, and at least some of the confusion about what is and what is not a system is due to inconsistent or contradictory definitions. Part of the problem is that experimental research into different memory systems is relatively recent. Another part is that, as experimental evidence accumulates, the definitions are continually being refined and made more precise. Currently, the most well-thought-out definition of a memory system is offered by Schacter and Tulving (1994, pp. 14–20), who describe three main criteria.

*Class-inclusion operations.*   A memory system enables the organism to perform a very large number of tasks of a particular class or category, regardless of the specific details about the tasks. For example, one proposed memory system is episodic memory, which is the conscious recollection of personally experienced episodes. It does not matter what the personally experienced episode is; it could be a birthday party, the time your dog was nearly hit by a car, the first day at college, or any other event. All operations dealing with these types of memories occur within the episodic memory system. If there is damage to the system, then all kinds of personally experienced memories will be affected, but other cognitive operations should remain intact. Thus, certain forms of amnesia can interfere with episodic memory but not with recollection of historical facts, which are assumed to be in a different system, namely semantic memory.

*Properties and relations.* The second criteria proposed by Schacter and Tulving (1994) is that a memory system must be described in terms of a property list: an enumeration of its features and aspects by which its identity can be determined and its relation to other systems can be specified. These properties include the rules of operation, the kind of information that is processed, the neural substrate, and a statement about the system's evolutionary purpose. In addition to these properties, the proposed system must have a definite relationship to other systems. For example, episodic memory relies on parts of semantic memory, but semantic memory does not depend on episodic memory in any way.

*Convergent dissociations.* As we have already noted, *single dissociations* occur when a particular independent variable, such as word frequency, has two different effects depending on the test — recall versus recognition. Weaker forms of dissociation occur when the independent variable has a larger effect on one test than on another, or has an effect on only one test and not on the other. Single dissociations provide no evidence for postulating a new memory system, according to Schacter and Tulving (1994). However, *convergent dissociations* are multiple single, or double, dissociations that use a variety of tasks, a variety of materials, a variety of populations, and a variety of techniques. If a proposed memory system is indeed a memory system, then these multiple dissociations will all converge on the same conclusion.

On the basis of the criteria outlined above, Schacter and Tulving (1994) offer five memory systems and nearly a dozen subsystems (see Table 8.4). The two main divisions are between procedural and declarative memory. *Procedural memory* is involved with learning behavioral and cognitive skills and algorithms. A rule of thumb is that if you can say you know how to do something, it is a good candidate for a form of procedural memory. Sample tasks include riding a bicycle, typing (if you are a touch typist), and even performing complex skills like solving puzzles. In contrast, *declarative memory* is involved with knowing "that" rather than knowing "how." For example, if you know that 2 plus 2 equals 4, the information is said to be declarative.

The subsystems of procedural memory include those responsible for learning motor skills, simple conditioning, and simple associative learning (Schacter & Tulving, 1994). Procedural memory is also thought to be responsible for learning about patterns and regularities in the environment that unfold over time, even quite complex ones (Reber, 1993). For example, many attributions of cause and effect have their basis, according to Reber, in implicit learning.

The perceptual representation system (PRS) mentioned before is another form of nondeclarative memory, and Schacter (1994) views it as a separate memory system. This system is important in identifying words and objects but is nondeclarative in the sense that it is typically involved in nonconscious operations. Within the PRS, there are three subsystems: one handles visual input, one handles auditory input, and the final one handles descriptions of objects.

**Table 8.4**    Major memory systems and their subsystems.

| System | Other Name(s) | Subsystems |
|---|---|---|
| Procedural | Nondeclarative | Motor skills |
|  |  | Cognitive skills |
|  |  | Simple conditioning |
|  |  | Simple associative learning |
| Perceptual Representation |  | Visual word form |
|  |  | Auditory word form |
|  |  | Structural description |
| Primary Memory | Working Memory | Visual |
|  |  | Auditory |
| Semantic | Generic | Spatial |
|  | Factual | Relational |
|  | Knowledge |  |
| Episodic | Personal |  |
|  | Autobiographical |  |
|  | Event memory |  |

Source: Based on Schacter & Tulving (1994).

The three remaining systems belong on the declarative side, and all three involve cognition. Primary memory, as we saw in Chapters 4 and 5, has had a long history, at times being called short-term store, at times short-term memory, and at times working memory. The system listed in Table 8.4 follows Baddeley's (1986) general description of two subsystems—one for visual-spatial information and another for auditory-verbal information.

The final two systems—episodic and semantic memory—take their names and general characteristics from Tulving (1972, 1983). The *semantic memory* system (also known as knowledge or generic memory) processes factual information. If you can recollect that George Washington was the first President of the United States, that information comes from your semantic memory system. *Episodic memory* (also known as autobiographical memory) differs from semantic memory in that it includes recollection of personal involvement. An example will help illustrate the essential difference. Suppose that you know nothing about the vice presidents of the United States. One day, while waiting for an appointment, you read in an old magazine about Maine's commemoration of the 100th anniversary of the death of Hannibal Hamlin (1809–1891), Abraham Lincoln's first vice president. You immediately think of elephants crossing the Alps to fight Romans, confusing the more famous Carthaginian with the less famous granite-state native son. A few days later, you happen to watch a television quiz show and Hamlin's name occurs again. Although the bare fact that he was Lincoln's first vice president may be in semantic memory, all of the details that you recollect about the learning episode—such as the fact that you were reading an old magazine, that you thought of the more famous Hannibal, that you were so bored you were reading a magazine that was several years old, that the room was stuffy and hot—are due to episodic information. Finally, suppose that several years later, you again recollect Hamlin's name, but this time you are unaware of the source. In one sense, Hamlin has become Washington's equal: you cannot recall anything about the learning episode.

If there is some uncertainty about what constitutes a system, there is even less agreement about what distinguishes a subsystem from system. According to Schacter and Tulving (1994), the important difference is that

> whereas systems are characterized by different rules of operation, as embodied in property lists and relations, subsystems, we suggest, are distinguished primarily by different kinds of information (subsystems share the principal rules of operations of their superordinate system, but they differ from one another with respect to the kinds of information each one processes) and different brain loci (although subsystems are all instantiated in the neural circuitry that defines their superordinate system, they can occupy distinct loci within the broader network). . . . Whereas postulating of full-blown systems requires satisfaction of all three of our major criteria, postulating of subsystems requires satisfaction of the first (class inclusion operations) and third (converging dissociations) but not the second (property lists and relations, with the corresponding emphasis on different rules of operation). (p. 19)

Despite these attempts at clarification, a major weakness is the lack of consensus on what the systems are and even on what the criteria should be, even among proponents of the multiple systems view. For example, some researchers think of episodic and semantic memory as subsystems rather than as two distinct systems (Johnson & Chalfonte, 1994; Squire, 1994). Others propose systems not included in the Schacter and Tulving hierarchy, such as the sensory memory systems proposed by Cowan (1995). Indeed, according to some criteria, there could be as many as 25 different memory systems (Roediger, 1990b).

## Transfer Appropriate Processing

The explanation of dissociations between direct and indirect tests of memory according to transfer appropriate processing (TAP) (see Chapter 6) has been most completely articulated by Roediger and his colleagues (see Blaxton, 1989; Roediger, Weldon, & Challis, 1987) and proceeds from four assumptions. First, a given type of processing will lead to better memory performance if it is appropriate for the particular test (see Morris, Bransford, & Franks, 1977; Tulving & Thomson, 1973). The important point here is that different types of processing lead to good performance on different types of tests; there is no one type of processing that will lead to optimal performance on all tests. Second, direct and indirect tests of memory typically require different retrieval operations. In particular, the typical tasks chosen for direct and indirect tests differ not only in the presumed underlying memory being tapped (explicit versus implicit) but also in the type of information required. Third, most indirect tests used have relied primarily on perceptual processing. For example, a fragment completion task requires processing the individual letters rather than focusing on an item's meaning. Roediger calls this kind of processing *data driven,* a term introduced by Jacoby (1983). Finally, most direct tests used have relied primarily on the encoded meaning of concepts. For example, most subjects will focus on word meanings and relationships between the words on recall and recognition tasks. Roediger calls this kind of processing *conceptually driven* (Jacoby, 1983).

To be clear, not all indirect tests are data driven and not all direct tests are conceptually driven. Indeed, the key experiments that support the transfer appropriate processing view compare data driven indirect tests to conceptually driven indirect tests. Another point of clarification concerns the terms *data driven* and *conceptually driven,* which represent not a dichotomy, but rather two end points on a continuum. In practice, most tasks will have both data driven and conceptually driven processes operating; what concerns Roediger and his colleagues is which type of processing predominates.

A study by Blaxton (1989) examined two types of indirect tests and two types of direct tests. One indirect and one direct test were predominantly data driven, and one indirect and one direct test were predominantly conceptually driven. Blaxton chose presentation modality as the key independent variable. According to dissociation logic, if indirect tests are tapping a separate system, then presentation modality should affect both indirect tests in the same way. On the other hand, if the transfer appropriate processing view is correct, then it should not matter whether the test is direct or indirect. According to this view, data driven tasks should show one pattern of results, and conceptually driven tasks should show a different pattern.

First, all subjects saw (visual condition) or heard (auditory) a list of words; then several different kinds of tests were administered. To illustrate the different test types, consider the target word *bashful.* The direct, data driven test was graphemic cued recall; a grapheme, for this test, was a word that had similar letters in similar locations, such as *bushel,* and subjects were instructed to recall a word from the list that had similar letters. This test is thus direct (subjects are instructed to recall words from the list) and data driven (processing needs to focus on the physical features rather than on meaning). The indirect, data driven test was word-fragment completion; the word fragment was b_sh_u_, and subjects were asked to complete the fragment with the first word that came to mind. This is an indirect test because no mention was made of the study items. The direct, conceptually driven test was free recall; subjects were asked simply to recall as many of the words as they could. The indirect, conceptually driven test was a test of general knowledge. The question was, "Which of the seven dwarves comes first alphabetically?" It is indirect because subjects need not refer back to the learning episode, but it is conceptually driven because the test requires processing of meaning rather than merely of physical features.

The results are shown in Figure 8.3: consistent with the transfer appropriate processing view and contrary to the multiple systems view, performance was better on data driven tasks (the upper- and lower-left graphs) with visual presentation, and performance was equivalent or slightly better on conceptually driven tasks (upper- and lower-right graphs) with auditory presentation. The multiple systems view predicted that both direct tasks would be similar, whereas the results showed that both data driven tasks were similar. According to Blaxton's (1989) interpretation, the type of test (direct or indirect) did not matter as much as the type of processing that predominates (data driven or conceptually driven).

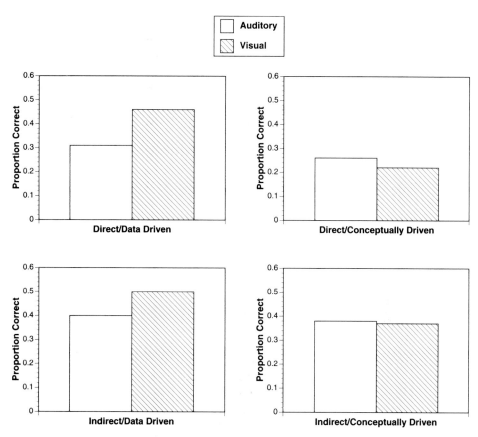

**Figure 8.3** Proportion correct as a function of test type (direct or indirect) and task type (data driven or conceptually driven) and presentation modality. Source: Blaxton (1989).

## The Bias View

The bias view (Ratcliff & McKoon, 1996) begins with the observation that none of the preceding views actually explains the phenomenon. In a repetition priming task, there is an increase in the probability of responding (or a decrease in the time needed to respond) when an item has been seen recently. The multiple systems view (Schacter & Tulving, 1994) explains these results by postulating three separate memory systems: there is one system for auditory words, one for visual words, and one for structural descriptions. However, saying that these effects occur because of the memory system responsible does not really explain them. The transfer appropriate processing view (Roediger, 1990a) also has difficulty explaining these results because of the possibility of circularity. Repetition priming will be observed when there is appropriate transfer of the study and test processing, but evidence for appropriate transfer of processing comes from observing priming. It is possible that converging operations, such as the process dissociation framework (Jacoby, 1991) can eliminate the circular reasoning, but currently this is more a promise than a fact.

A central component of the bias view is that bias entails both costs and benefits. Many studies of repetition priming have been set up to see only benefits (such as better performance or reduced response times). Ratcliff and McKoon (1996) surveyed several studies and report new data that illustrate both costs and benefits in 3 different repetition priming paradigms, each of which has previously been attributed to separate memory systems.

*Bias with auditory words.* Ratcliff, Allbritton, and McKoon (1997) had subjects listen to two lists of words, the second of which was presented in noise to make the task difficult. Each word on the second list fell in one of three conditions: (1) it was a new word (novel), (2) it was a word that was also in the first list (repeated), or (3) it was a word that was similar to a word on the first list (similar). The measure of interest was the probability of identifying items in the second list. Novel words (the control condition) were correctly identified about 60% of the time. A repetition priming effect was seen for the repeated items, with more items correctly identified — 65% — than in the control condition. Most important, there was a cost for similar items, with only 55% correctly identified.

*Bias with visual words.* Ratcliff and McKoon (1996) reported an experiment that examined bias effects with a stem completion task. In the first phase, 32 words were presented on a computer screen, and subjects were asked to make a rating of how pleasant these words were. In the second phase, four letters appeared in the center of the screen, and subjects were asked to say, as quickly as they could, a word that began with those letters. As before, there were novel, repeated, and similar conditions. The mean response time to say a word to a novel 4-letter stem was 1363 ms. Repetition priming was observed in the repeated condition, with response time decreasing to 1156 ms. In the similar condition, performance was slowest, with a mean response time of 1561 ms.

*Bias with objects.* In a typical object decision experiment, subjects see a series of line drawings of possible and impossible objects (see Figure 8.4). There are two lists, and for each object, subjects are asked to decide as quickly as they can whether the object is possible. The typical finding is that only possible objects show repetition priming; there appears to be no advantage of being exposed to an impossible object during an earlier phase of the experiment (Schacter, Cooper, & Delaney, 1990; Schacter, Cooper, Delaney, Peterson, & Tharan, 1991). This finding of repetition priming for possible objects and no repetition priming for impossible objects is consistent with the idea of separate memory systems, one of which is devoted to processing objects.

Ratcliff and McKoon (1995) also presented subjects with line drawings of possible or impossible objects. In their standard condition, they replicated the finding of enhanced performance for possible objects on list 2 if they had been seen previously on list 1, and no enhancement for impossible objects. According to the bias view, however, one reason for this finding may be the contribution of episodic recollection. For example, recalling that you have seen an object before biases you to say that the object is possible. This recollective process could hide the effects of repetition priming on impossible objects by biasing subjects to respond with "possible." This idea was tested by using two different ways of minimizing conscious recollection. In one version, the subjects were given a memory load; that is, they were asked to keep seven digits in memory while making their deci-

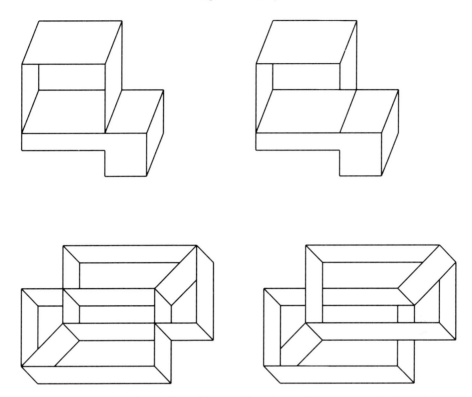

**Figure 8.4**   An example of possible and impossible objects, of the sort used in object decision experiments.   Source: Adapted from Ratcliff & McKoon (1995).

sions. The second version implemented a deadline procedure, in which subjects were required to respond more quickly than usual. The idea here is that the object decision response must be made before the episodic information becomes available. The results are shown in Table 8.5.

When recollective processes were allowed (the column labeled "replication"), the results duplicated the finding of repetition priming only for possible objects (0.67 versus 0.58) and not for impossible objects (0.42 versus 0.41). However, when the influence of the recollective processes was minimized by a deadline procedure, the results were different: repetition priming was seen for both possible (0.64 versus 0.54) and impossible (0.48 versus 0.33) objects. The results from the memory load condition, which should also minimize the contributions of recollection, were the same as those of the deadline experiment. In other words, impossible objects also have an advantage when seen a second time. Ratcliff and McKoon (1996) extend this result to show both benefits (i.e., repetition priming) and costs (i.e., worse performance) for object identification.

The bias view, then, not only is able to account for all these results, but, more important, it actually predicted them. That is, the bias view predicts that in all instances of repetition priming (which it views as a benefit of repetition), it should be possible to show

**Table 8.5**  The proportion of possible and impossible objects labeled "possible" in three different experiments (replication, deadline, and memory load) as a function of prior exposure.

|  |  | Proportion Labeled "Possible" | | |
| --- | --- | --- | --- | --- |
| Study Form | Test Form | Replication | Deadline | Memory Load |
| Possible | Possible | 0.67 | 0.64 | 0.66 |
| Not Presented | Possible | 0.58 | 0.54 | 0.61 |
| Impossible | Impossible | 0.42 | 0.48 | 0.42 |
| Not Presented | Impossible | 0.41 | 0.33 | 0.34 |

Source: Ratcliff & McKoon (1995).

a decrement in performance (which it views as a cost of repetition). A model that allows for both qualitative and quantitative predictions within the perceptual identification paradigm has been developed (see Ratcliff & McKoon, 1997), and it seems likely that similar approaches can be made for the other paradigms.

# Comparing Bias, TAP, and the Multiple Systems Views

Both the bias and transfer appropriate processing (TAP) views hold that postulating multiple memory systems is not needed to explain the currently available data. Moreover, models developed from the bias view (Ratcliff & McKoon, 1997) specify at least some of the processes that are responsible for repetition priming, and so can be seen as complementing, rather than competing with, TAP.

The major strength of the transfer appropriate processing view is the emphasis on processing information and of viewing memory as a process (see Craik & Lockhart, 1972; Kolers & Roediger, 1984), especially as a discrimination process (see Capaldi & Neath, 1995). Because of this emphasis, TAP predicts dissociations based on processing rather than on the underlying memory system. For example, Blaxton (1989) predicted that her data driven tests would benefit from visual presentation regardless of whether the test was thought to tap implicit memory (the indirect test) or explicit memory (the direct test). Similarly, Balota and his colleagues demonstrated dissociations between two tasks thought to tap semantic memory (Balota & Neely, 1980) and between two tasks thought to tap episodic memory (Balota & Chumbley, 1984). The more similarities that are found between tasks that are thought to tap different systems, the more problematic the multiple systems view becomes. Another strength of TAP is its ability to account for age-related declines in memory (see Chapter 16).

One weakness of the TAP view is that it says relatively little about the phenomenon of conscious awareness in differing types of tasks. A second problem is that, although it distinguishes between perceptual and conceptual processing, the TAP approach does not yet include more fine-grained distinctions (Roediger & McDermott, 1993). Thus, the TAP view cannot currently explain certain dissociations between two conceptually driven tasks (McDermott & Roediger, 1996; Tenpenny & Shoben, 1992).

Much of the evidence for multiple memory systems comes from people with various forms of brain damage. According to proponents of the multiple systems view (Tulving, 1986), it is by studying the pattern of deficits in these patients that memory researchers will be able to specify the number and type of memory systems. In the next chapter, we examine the biological basis of memory and the various forms of memory deficits that commonly occur. As we shall see, however, without further work, this area may pose a serious problem. For example, according to the multiple systems view, implicit memory system is spared in amnesia, and so tests that tap implicit memory will show unimpaired performance. The question arises, How do we know if a test taps implicit memory? The answer is usually because performance is unimpaired. Currently, there is no way out of this circular reasoning (see Ratcliff & McKoon, 1996).

A second problem concerns a priori predictions about dissociations between memory systems, which applies even for the most widely accepted of the different systems, the episodic-semantic distinction (Hintzman, 1984; McKoon, Ratcliff, & Dell, 1986; Neely, 1989). The most severe criticism has been that there is often no prediction ahead of time which variables will result in a dissociation between episodic and semantic memory and which variables will not. Furthermore, there is no way of predicting the way the variables will affect performance in each system. Consider one example that involves the fan effect. After learning a set of sentences that contain a fact about a person and a location, subjects are given a recognition test. The *fan effect* is the finding that response times to say that a particular sentence has been seen previously increase when the number of facts related to the person in the sentence or the location also increases (Anderson, 1974). The important point as far as the distinction between episodic and semantic memory is concerned, as McKoon, Ratcliff, and Dell (1986) point out, is that this fan effect is observed in episodic tasks but not in semantic tasks. There is nothing in the distinction between episodic memory and semantic memory that would lead anyone to predict this result. Although it is a dissociation, it is not predicted; if the result had been the reverse, the distinction would still be supported! As Hintzman (1984, p. 241) put it, "If one wants to claim that a dissociation outcome supports the episodic-semantic distinction, one must show that the dissociation is predicted by theory that embodies the distinction."

Tulving and Schacter (1990) agree that there are many similarities between tasks thought to tap one memory system and tasks thought to tap a separate system. They state that these " 'parallel effects' are theoretically uninteresting, since some similarities would be expected of all forms of memory—otherwise it would be difficult to justify their general label" (p. 305). The goal facing multiple systems theorists is to develop a theoretical account that predicts which variables will show dissociations between different systems and which variables will behave in a parallel fashion.

A third area of weakness concerns findings of dissociations within a particular memory system. As mentioned above, Balota and his colleagues demonstrated dissociations between two tasks thought to tap semantic memory (Balota & Neely, 1980) and between two tasks thought to tap episodic memory (Balota & Chumbley, 1984). Others have shown independence between two tasks thought to tap implicit memory (Witherspoon & Moscovitch, 1989).

However, as the number of proposed memory systems increases, the systems view becomes more like a processing view. If a memory system is defined as broadly as the neural structures that underlie performance on a particular task (Crowder, 1993; Roediger & Srinivas, 1993), then there is no difference between processing and systems views. Indeed, Crowder (1993) has suggested that "the number of different memory systems is a count of the number of different information processing ensembles that can be recruited to do the cognitive work required for a task" (p. 145).

The area of implicit memory research has been characterized as "by far the most heavily studied area in cognitive psychology at present" (Greene, 1992, p. 172). Given the rate at which new information is accumulating, it should be clear relatively soon whether the processes and systems views are indeed converging. Even though we have examined this debate so far only in terms of implicit memory, the debate plays an important role in understanding impaired memory performance in the elderly (see Chapter 16) and in various clinical populations. We will examine amnesia in the next chapter, after reviewing the basic anatomy and biology of the brain and nervous system.

# References

Anderson, J. R. (1974). Retrieval of propositional information from long-term memory. *Cognitive Psychology, 6,* 451–474.

Baddeley, A. D. (1986). *Working memory.* New York: Oxford University Press.

Balota, D. A., & Chumbley, J. I. (1984). Are lexical decisions a good measure of lexical access: The role of word frequency in the neglected decision stage. *Journal of Experimental Psychology: Human Perception and Performance, 10,* 340–357.

Balota, D. A., & Neely, J. H. (1980). Test-expectancy and word-frequency effects in recall and recognition. *Journal of Experimental Psychology: Human Learning and Memory, 6,* 576–587.

Blaxton, T. A. (1989). Investigating dissociations among memory measures: Support for a transfer-appropriate processing framework. *Journal of Experimental Psychology: Learning, Memory, and Cognition, 15,* 657–668.

Capaldi, E. J., & Neath, I. (1995). Remembering and forgetting as context discrimination. *Learning & Memory, 2,* 107–132.

Cermak, L. S., Talbot, N., Chandler, K., & Wolbarst, L. R. (1985). The perceptual priming phenomenon in amnesia. *Neuropsychologia, 23,* 615–622.

Claparède, E. (1951). Reconnaissance et moiité. In D. Rapaport (Ed.), *Organization and pathology of thought.* New York: Columbia University Press.

Cleeremans, A., & McClelland, J. L. (1991). Learning the structure of event sequences. *Journal of Experimental Psychology: General, 120,* 235–253.

Cowan, N. (1995). *Attention and memory: An integrated framework.* New York: Oxford.

Craik, F. I. M., & Lockhart, R. S. (1972). Levels of processing: A framework for memory research. *Journal of Verbal Learning and Verbal Behavior, 11,* 671–684.

Crowder, R. G. (1993). Systems and principles in memory theory: Another critique of pure memory. In A. F. Collins, S. E. Gathercole, M. A. Conway, & P. E. Morris (Eds.), *Theories of memory.* Hove, UK: Erlbaum.

Dunn, R. (1845). Case of suspension of the mental faculties. *Lancet, 2,* 588–590.

Ebbinghaus, H. (1885). *Über das Gedächtnis: Untersuchungen zur experimentellen Psychologie.* Leipzig: Duncker and Humboldt. [Reprinted as H. E. Ebbinghaus (1964). Memory: A Contribution to Experimental Psychology (H. A. Ruger, Trans.). New York: Dover.]

Eich, E. (1984). Memory for unattended events: Remembering with and without awareness. *Memory & Cognition, 12,* 105–111.

Garner, W. R. (1974). *The processing of information and structure.* Hillsdale, NJ: Erlbaum.

Graf, P., & Mandler, G. (1984). Activation makes words more accessible, but not necessarily more retrievable. *Journal of Verbal Learning and Verbal Behavior, 23,* 553–568.

Graf, P., & Schacter, D. L. (1985). Implicit and explicit memory for new associations in normal and amnesic subjects. *Journal of Experimental Psychology: Learning, Memory, and Cognition, 11,* 501–518.

Graf, P., & Schacter, D. L. (1987). Selective effects of interference on implicit and explicit memory for new associations. *Journal of Experimental Psychology: Learning, Memory, and Cognition, 13,* 45–53.

Greene, R. L. (1992). *Human memory: Paradigms and paradoxes.* Hillsdale, NJ: Erlbaum.

Hintzman, D. L. (1984). Episodic versus semantic memory: A distinction whose time has come—and gone? *Behavioral and Brain Sciences, 7,* 240–241.

Jacoby, L. L. (1983). Remembering the data: Analyzing interactive processes in reading. *Journal of Verbal Learning and Verbal Behavior, 22,* 485–508.

Jacoby, L. L. (1984). Incidental versus intentional retrieval: Remembering and awareness as separate issues. In L. R. Squire & N. Butters (Eds.), *The neuropsychology of memory.* New York: Guilford.

Jacoby, L. L. (1991). A process dissociation framework: Separating automatic from intentional uses of memory. *Journal of Memory and Language, 30,* 513–541.

Jacoby, L. L., & Dallas, M. (1981). On the relationship between autobiographical memory and perceptual learning. *Journal of Experimental Psychology: General, 110,* 306–340.

Jacoby, L. L., Toth, J. P., & Yonelinas, A. P. (1993). Separating conscious and unconscious influences of memory: Measuring recollection. *Journal of Experimental Psychology: General, 122,* 139–154.

Johnson, M. K., & Chalfonte, B. L. (1994). Binding complex memories: The role of reactivation and the hippocampus. In D. L. Schacter & E. Tulving (Eds.), *Memory Systems 1994.* Cambridge, MA: MIT Press.

Johnson, M. K., & Hasher, L. (1987). Human learning and memory. *Annual Review of Psychology, 38,* 631–668.

Kolers, P. A. (1973). Remembering operations. *Memory & Cognition, 1,* 347–355.

Kolers, P. A., & Roediger, H. L., III. (1984). Procedures of mind. *Journal of Verbal Learning and Verbal Behavior, 23,* 425–449.

Korsakoff, S. S. (1889). Etude médico-psychologique sur une forme des maladies de la mémoire. *Revue Philosophique, 28,* 501–530.

Mathews, R. C. (1990). Abstractness of implicit grammar knowledge: Comments on Perruchet and Pacteau's analysis of synthetic grammar learning. *Journal of Experimental Psychology: General, 119,* 412–416.

Mathews, R. C., Buss, R. R., Stanley, W. B., Blanchard-Fields, F., Cho, J. R., & Druhan, B. (1989). Role of implicit and explicit processes in learning from examples: A synergistic effect. *Journal of Experimental Psychology: Learning, Memory, and Cognition, 15,* 1083–1100.

McDermott, K. B., & Roediger, H. L., III. (1996). Exact and conceptual repetition dissociate conceptual memory tests: Problems for Transfer Appropriate Processing theory. *Canadian Journal of Psychology, 50,* 57–71.

McGeoch, J. A., & Irion, A. L. (1952). *The psychology of human learning (2nd ed.).* New York: Longmans Green.

McKoon, G., Ratcliff, R., & Dell, G. S. (1986). A critical evaluation of the semantic/episodic distinction. *Journal of Experimental Psychology: Learning, Memory, and Cognition, 12,* 295–306.

Morris, C. D., Bransford, J. D., & Franks, J. J. (1977). Levels of processing versus transfer appropriate processing. *Journal of Verbal Learning and Verbal Behavior, 16,* 519–533.

Neely, J. H. (1989). Experimental dissociations and the episodic/semantic memory distinction. In H. L. Roediger III & F. I. M. Craik (Eds.), *Varieties of memory and consciousness: Essays in honour of Endel Tulving.* Hillsdale, NJ: Erlbaum.

Postman, L., & Phillips, L. W. (1954). Studies in incidental learning: I. The effects of crowding and isolation. *Journal of Experimental Psychology, 48,* 48–56.

Pratkanis, A. R. (1992). The cargo-cult science of subliminal persuasion. *Skeptical Inquirer, 16,* 260–272.

Ratcliff, R., & McKoon, G. (1995). Bias in the priming of object decisions. *Journal of Experimental Psychology: Learning, Memory, and Cognition, 21,* 754–767.

Ratcliff, R., & McKoon, G. (1996). Bias effects in implicit memory tasks. *Journal of Experimental Psychology: General, 125,* 403–421.

Ratcliff, R., & McKoon, G. (1997). A counter model for implicit priming in perceptual word identification. *Psychological Review.*

Ratcliff, R., Allbritton, D. W., & McKoon, G. (1997). Bias in auditory priming. *Journal of Experimental Psychology: Learning, Memory, and Cognition, 23,* 143–152.

Reber, A. S. (1967). Implicit learning of artificial grammars. *Journal of Verbal Learning and Verbal Behavior, 6,* 317–325.

Reber, A. S. (1989). Implicit learning and tacit knowledge. *Journal of Experimental Psychology: General, 118,* 219–235.

Reber, A. S. (1993). *Implicit learning and tacit knowledge: An essay on the cognitive unconscious.* New York: Oxford University Press.

Richardson-Klavehn, A. & Bjork, R. A. (1988). Measures of memory. *Annual Review of Psychology, 39,* 475–543.

Roediger, H. L., III. (1990a). Implicit memory: Retention without remembering. *American Psychologist, 45,* 1043–1056.

Roediger, H. L., III. (1990b). Implicit memory: A commentary. *Bulletin of the Psychonomic Society, 28,* 373–380.

Roediger, H. L., III. (1997). Implicit learning: A symposium. *Psychonomic Bulletin & Review, 4,* 1.

Roediger, H. L., III, & McDermott, K. B. (1993). Implicit memory in normal human subjects. In H. Spinnler & F. Boller (Eds.), *Handbook of neuropsychology.* Amsterdam: Elsevier.

Roediger, H. L., III., & Srinivas, K. (1993). Specificity of operations in perceptual priming. In P. Graf & M. E. J. Masson (Eds.), *Implicit memory: New directions in cognition, development and neuropsychology.* Hillsdale, NJ: Erlbaum.

Roediger, H. L., III, Weldon, M. S., & Challis, B. H. (1987). Explaining dissociations between implicit and explicit measures of retention: A processing account. In H. L. Roediger, III & F.

I. M. Craik (Eds.), *Varieties of memory and consciousness: Essays in honour of Endel Tulving.* Hillsdale, NJ: Erlbaum.

Roediger, H. L., III, Weldon, M. S., Stadler, M. L., & Riegler, G. L. (1992). Direct comparison of two implicit memory tests: Word fragment and word stem completion. *Journal of Experimental Psychology: Learning, Memory, and Cognition, 18,* 1251–1269.

Rogers, S. (1993). How a publicity blitz created the myth of subliminal advertising. *Public Relations Quarterly, 37,* 12–17.

Schacter, D. L. (1987). Implicit memory: History and current status. *Journal of Experimental Psychology: Learning, Memory, and Cognition, 13,* 501–518.

Schacter, D. L. (1989). On the relation between memory and consciousness: Dissociable interactions and conscious experience. In H. L. Roediger, III & F. I. M. Craik (Eds.), *Varieties of memory and consciousness: Essays in honour of Endel Tulving.* Hillsdale, NJ: Erlbaum.

Schacter, D. L. (1994). Priming and multiple memory systems: Perceptual mechanisms of implicit memory. In D. L. Schacter & E. Tulving (Eds.), *Memory systems 1994.* Cambridge, MA: MIT Press.

Schacter, D. L., Cooper, L. A., & Delaney, S. M. (1990). Implicit memory for unfamiliar objects depends on access to structural descriptions. *Journal of Experimental Psychology: General, 119,* 5–24.

Schacter, D. L., Cooper, L. A., Delaney, S. M., Peterson, M. A., & Tharan, M. (1991). Implicit memory for possible and impossible objects: Constraints on the construction of structural descriptions. *Journal of Experimental Psychology: Learning, Memory, and Cognition, 17,* 3–19.

Schacter, D. L., & Tulving, E. (1994). What are the memory systems of 1994? In D. L. Schacter & E. Tulving (Eds.), *Memory systems 1994.* Cambridge, MA: MIT Press.

Sloman, S. A., Hayman, C. A. G., Ohta, N., Law, J., & Tulving, E. (1988). Forgetting in primed fragment completion. *Journal of Experimental Psychology: Learning, Memory, and Cognition, 14,* 223–239.

Squire, L. R. (1994). Declarative and nondeclarative memory: Multiple brain systems supporting learning and memory. In D. L. Schacter & E. Tulving (Eds.), *Memory systems 1994.* Cambridge, MA: MIT Press.

Stadler, M. A. (1995). Role of attention in implicit learning. *Journal of Experimental Psychology: Learning, Memory, and Cognition, 21,* 674–685.

Tenpenny, P., & Shoben, E. J. (1992). Component processes and the utility of the conceptually-driven/data-driven distinction. *Journal of Experimental Psychology: Learning, Memory, and Cognition, 18,* 25–42.

Tulving, E. (1972). Episodic and semantic memory. In E. Tulving & W. Donaldson (Eds.), *Organization of memory.* New York: Academic Press.

Tulving, E. (1983). *Elements of episodic memory.* New York: Oxford University Press.

Tulving, E. (1986). What kind of a hypothesis is the distinction between episodic and semantic memory? *Journal of Experimental Psychology: Learning, Memory, and Cognition, 12,* 307–311.

Tulving, E., Hayman, C. A. G., & MacDonald, C. A. (1991). Long-lasting perceptual priming and semantic learning in amnesia: A case experiment. *Journal of Experimental Psychology: Learning, Memory, and Cognition, 17,* 595–617.

Tulving, E., & Schacter, D. L. (1990). Priming and human memory systems. *Science, 247,* 301–306.

Tulving, E., Schacter, D. L., & Stark, H. (1982). Priming effects in word-fragment completion are independent of recognition memory. *Journal of Experimental Psychology: Human Learning and Memory, 8,* 336–342.

Tulving, E., & Thomson, D. M. (1973). Encoding specificity and retrieval processes in episodic memory. *Psychological Review, 80,* 352–373.

Witherspoon, D., & Moscovitch, M. (1989). Stochastic independence between two implicit memory tasks. *Journal of Experimental Psychology: Learning, Memory, and Cognition, 15,* 22–30.

# CHAPTER NINE

# Memory, the Brain, and Amnesia

*"Memory is no abstract property of the mind, but a universal property of nerves."*
— *William H. Burnham (1888, p. 264)*

In 1904, Richard Semon introduced the term *engram* — the set of changes in the nervous system that represents stored memory (Schacter, 1982). The next logical question is, Where is the engram? Although it seems obvious that memories must be stored in the brain, and although our knowledge of biological and physiological processes is advancing at an ever-accelerating rate, we still know relatively little about the biological basis of memory. The goal of this chapter, therefore, is to provide a general overview of the underlying biological processes and brain structures that support memory and an appreciation for the difficulties in conducting this kind of research. We begin with a brief overview of how neurons work, and follow with a description of the basic architecture of the brain. Then we can examine ideas concerned with the biological basis of memory and amnesia.

## The Neuron

The current view is that memory involves "a persistent change in the relationship between neurons, either through structural modification or through biochemical events within neurons that change the way in which neighboring neurons communicate" (Squire, 1987, p. 7). This concept was first introduced by Ramon y Cajal (1894) and has been restated in various forms by people like Konorski (1948), Hebb (1949), and Kandel (1977). Memory can thus be seen as a specific form of a more general biological process known as neural plasticity. *Plasticity* refers to the idea that a neuron can change either structurally or functionally in a way that is long lasting. One form of plasticity that has been of particular interest is *synaptic plasticity,* the changes that occur at and around the synapse.

There are two main types of cells in the nervous system, glial cells and neurons. Glia provide the basic support system for neurons and perform a variety of maintenance functions, including holding the structure together, supplying nutrients, and maintaining the chemical environment. Neurons are the cells that process information, receiving, integrating, and transmitting messages. Sensory neurons gather information that originates

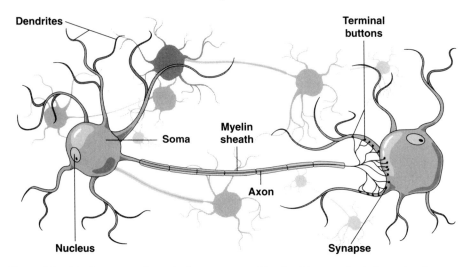

**Figure 9.1**    The key parts of a typical interneuron. The dendrites receive information from other neurons, the soma or cell body contains the nucleus of the cell, and the axon transmits the information to other neurons. The axon is often covered by the myelin sheath, which serves as insulation and increases the speed at which the message is sent. The point at which the ends of the axon connect with the dendrites of the next neuron are the synapses.

outside of the system (such as sights and sounds), and motor neurons provide instructions to muscles that inform them when and how to move. The majority of neurons, however, are interneurons—neurons that communicate only with other neurons and not with muscles or the outside world.

Figure 9.1 shows a simplified drawing of the major parts of the prototypical interneuron. A neuron normally consists of dendrites, which receive information, the soma (or cell body), and an axon, which transmits information to another neuron or group of neurons.

Neurons can vary in size, shape, and many other properties, but their basic operation is quite clear. The neural impulse is a complex electrochemical reaction. There is a difference in electrical charge between the inside and the outside of the cell body caused by the presence, in differing amounts, of (1) sodium, potassium, or calcium for a positive charge, and (2) chloride for a negative charge. The cell membrane is semipermeable; that is, at different times it will allow different types of ions to permeate, or pass through. At rest, there are more negative ions inside the cell, and more positive ions outside the cell. Thus, relative to the outside, the cell is negatively charged.

When a neuron is stimulated, either by other neurons or by a sensory event, the neuronal membrane becomes more permeable to positive ions. These positive ions rush into the cell, attracted by the large number of negative ions inside. Relative to the outside, the cell becomes less negative, creating an action potential. This is the name given to a brief change in the cell's electrical charge, and this voltage change is the message sent down the axon. A neural impulse is simply an electric current that flows along an axon as a result of an action potential. Before a neuron can fire again, the positive ions have to be pumped out of the cell, restoring the resting voltage. If the axon is insulated with a myelin sheath, the signal can travel faster. Some diseases, such as multiple sclerosis, destroy the myelin sheath, which results in loss of coordination, movement, and eventually cognitive processes.

Neural firing works on the all-or-none principle, like pulling a trigger on a gun. Once the trigger is pulled a certain amount, a bullet is fired. The bullet travels at the same velocity no matter how weakly or strongly the trigger is pulled. Neurons typically convey strength information not by increasing the voltage change sent down the axon but by changing the frequency of firing. For example, a stronger stimulus might cause a neuron to fire more rapidly, but each individual neural impulse will be of the same magnitude as when a weaker stimulus elicits firing.

The gap between the end of the axon of one neuron and the dendrites of another is called the synapse. It has been estimated that there are $6 \times 10^{13}$ synapses in the human cortex (Shepard & Koch, 1990). The chemicals that transmit the neural impulse over this gap are called neurotransmitters, and they are stored in small sacks called synaptic vesicles. An arriving neural impulse induces a chemical reaction that releases a particular kind or set of neurotransmitters into the synapse. These molecules diffuse across the synapse (from the presynaptic membrane to the postsynaptic membrane) and reach the dendrites of the receiving neuron, attaching themselves to receptor sites on the dendrites. This generates a postsynaptic potential (or PSP), which can be one of two kinds. An excitatory PSP increases the likelihood that the receiving neuron will open the ion channels and begin the process for an action potential; an inhibitory PSP causes the voltage to remain or become even more negative, thus decreasing the likelihood of an action potential. The neurotransmitters are then either neutralized or broken down by enzymes, freeing up the receptor sites, or are taken up by the synaptic vesicles. Each neuron can have as many as 15,000 synapses receiving information from thousands of other neurons and can send signals to many thousands more; thus neurons are more than just simple relay stations.

## Neural Circuits

To give a better idea of how neurons communicate, Figure 9.2 shows a simplified version of a circuit suggested by Hawkins (1989) as the basis of several forms of memory in the mollusk *Aplysia*. (For more precise details, see Hawkins, 1989). In *Aplysia*, the respiratory chamber — or mantle cavity — that houses the gill is covered by a protective sheet known as the mantle shelf. This shelf ends in the siphon, a fleshy spout. When the siphon or the mantle shelf is touched, the siphon, mantle shelf, and gill contract and withdraw into the mantle cavity. This reflex can be modified by experience, and so demonstrates habituation, sensitization, and classical conditioning.

In *habituation,* the animal learns to ignore a relatively weak stimulus that repeatedly touches its mantle shelf or siphon without causing harm or damage. The magnitude of the gill and siphon reflex will be greatly reduced for minutes to hours, depending upon the situation. Habituation is seen only when the organism remembers the stimulus. For the shorter form of habituation, the cellular cause is a decrease in the amount of neurotransmitter released at the synapses that the sensory neurons make on the motor neurons

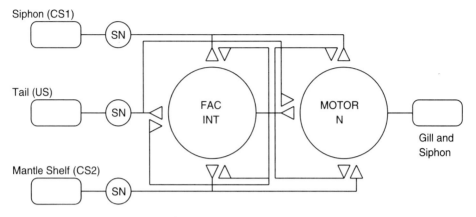

**Figure 9.2**   Partial neural circuit for the Aplysia gill and siphon withdrawal reflex and its modification by tail stimulation. Mechanosensory neurons (SN) from the siphon, mantle, and tail excite gill and siphon motor neurons. The sensory neurons also excite facilitator interneurons, which produce presynaptic facilitation at all of the terminals of the sensory neurons.   Source: Hawkins (1989).

and interneurons. The reason for the depression of neurotransmitters is thought to be a decrease in the amount of calcium ($Ca^{2+}$) that flows into the axon terminals of the sensory neurons with each action potential. The depletion may also involve a reduction in the amount of transmitter available.

*Sensitization* is another form of learning that can be thought of as the opposite of habituation. In habituation, the animal learns to ignore weak stimuli because they have little or no noxious effects. In sensitization, the animal learns to respond to weak stimuli because other stimuli have recently had noxious or harmful effects. As with habituation, the effects can last from minutes to weeks.

Sensitization uses the same cellular locus as habituation and also uses a change in the amount of neurotransmitter released (in this case, an increase), but it is far more complex than habituation. Hawkins (1989, p. 77) described the following five steps (see Figure 9.2).

1. Stimulating the tail activates a group of facilitator neurons which synapse on or near the terminals of the sensory neurons and act there to enhance transmitter release. This process is called presynaptic facilitation.
2. The transmitters released by the facilitator neurons, which include serotonin and a small peptide (SCP), activate an adenylate cylcase, which increases the level of free cyclic AMP in the terminals of the sensory neurons.
3. Elevation of free cyclic AMP, in turn, activates a second enzyme, a cAMP-dependent protein kinase.
4. The kinase acts by means of protein phosphorylation to close a particular type of $K^+$ channel and thereby decreases the total number of $K^+$ channels that are open during the action potential.

5. A decrease in K$^+$ current leads to broadening of subsequent action potentials, which allows a greater amount of Ca$^{2+}$ to flow into the terminal and thus enhances transmitter release.

In addition, Hawkins (1989) adds, "recent evidence suggests that sensitization may also involve mobilization of transmitter to release sites, perhaps through Ca$^{2+}$/calmodulin- or Ca$^{2+}$/phospholipid-dependent protein phosphorylation" (p. 77). Needless to say, the description of this simple form of learning and memory in a simple organism that uses only a few neurons is very complex.

*Classical conditioning* is a form of associative learning and memory; the animal has to remember a particular association. In classical conditioning, an organism learns to associate a particular signal, the CS or conditioned stimulus, as indicating that a particular event, the US or unconditioned stimulus, will shortly occur. In the case of the *Aplysia*, the US is a shock applied to the tail, which gives rise to a robust UR (unconditioned response), a variety of defensive reactions. Prior to training, the CS, a weak signal presented to the siphon, results in almost no responding. With repeated pairings of the CS and US, the CS begins to elicit a CR (conditioned response)—the siphon withdrawal reflex—which gains in magnitude. At test, the CS is presented alone and a robust siphon withdrawal reflex occurs. This preparation also shows the other properties of classical conditioning, including extinction and spontaneous recovery (Carew, Walters, & Kandel, 1981).

The cellular mechanism responsible for supporting classical conditioning is an elaboration of the one that supports sensitization. Some aspects occur in the sensory neuron itself, with a presynaptic facilitation caused by an increase in the action potential duration and a Ca$^{2+}$ influx. However, it is still unclear which aspects interact with the presynaptic facilitation to amplify it, and which step in the biochemical reactions is sensitive to the changed action potential (Hawkins, 1989).

Even though this is a greatly simplified description of the circuit, it is still complex and there are still aspects that are not known or well understood. The *Aplysia* is a relatively simple organism with only some 20,000 neurons, some of which are so large they can be seen with the naked eye. By contrast, it has been estimated that the average college student loses 10 times as many neurons in one day (Dowling, 1992). The point, of course, is to illustrate the complexity of identifying particular neural circuits that underlie complex memory functions in humans. At this point, there is some degree of certainty over general locations within the brain, and there is the promise of a much more precise and complete knowledge within the near future.

# The Brain

The brain is an approximately 3-pound, walnut-like object that contains billions of interacting neurons. There are three major regions: the hindbrain, the midbrain, and the forebrain (see Figure 9.3).

The hindbrain is at the lower end and controls regulation of basic body functions. Connecting the brain and the spinal cord is the medulla, which is responsible for breathing and circulation. The pons, above the medulla, is a bulbous structure that regulates the sleep-wake cycle and includes a bridge of fibers that connects the brain stem with the rest

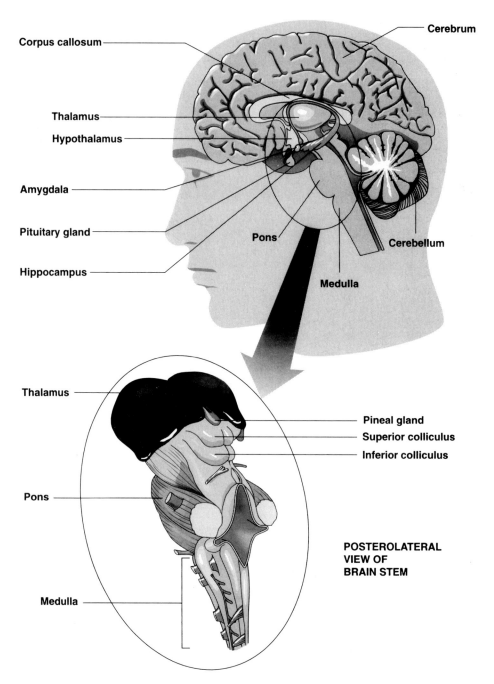

**Figure 9.3** Some major areas and important structures of the brain.

of the brain. The cerebellum is a large structure that is critically involved with the coordination of movement.

The midbrain lies between the hindbrain and the forebrain. Included within this region is the tectum, which is involved with reflexive responses such as ducking, and part of the reticular formation, which begins in the hindbrain. This area is associated with vigilance and arousal, and damage to this area often results in a coma. There is also an important set of dopamine-releasing neurons in the substantia nigra. Dopamine is a neurotransmitter often used by neurons that control smooth motor movement. Damage to these dopamine-producing neurons is related to Parkinson's Disease, often characterized by tremors, reduced control over voluntary movement, and muscular rigidity.

The forebrain is associated with complex thought and cognition. The thalamus, the hypothalamus, and the limbic system form the core of the forebrain and are located at the top of the brain stem. Over them is the cerebrum, which may contain as much as two-thirds of all the neurons within the central nervous system. The cerebrum is covered by a wrinkled surface called the cerebral cortex; the reason for the wrinkles is so that more surface area (up to 1.5 square feet or 2500 square centimeters) can fit within the skull. The elevations are called gyri, the small valleys are called sulci, and the large valleys are called fissures.

The thalamus can be thought of as a sensory relay station, integrating almost all sensations (the exception being odor) before passing them on to the appropriate areas of cortex for further processing. The hypothalamus is below the thalamus and is involved with regulating the autonomic nervous system, emotion, and what has sometimes been dubbed the four Fs: feeding, fighting, fleeing, and reproduction. In addition, it regulates hormone production within the endocrine system. The limbic system, which includes parts of the hypothalamus, is not a very well-defined system. It is a group of structures that surrounds the thalamus, and includes the amygdala, the septum, and the hippocampus. The amygdala is an evaluation system and contributes to feelings of fear, anger, and so forth. Damage to the amygdala results in an inability to evaluate environmental stimuli appropriately, for example, by trying to evaluate a visual stimulus by taste. The role of the hippocampus will be discussed in more detail later in this chapter.

A distinction is often made between *cortical* and *subcortical* regions. These terms refer to areas either within the cortex or below the cortex. The cortex, or cerebrum, is divided into two halves, referred to as hemispheres, that are separated by a central fissure. At the bottom of the fissure lies the corpus callosum, a bundle of fibers that connects the two hemispheres and allows them to communicate with each other. Each cerebral hemisphere is divided into four lobes (see Figure 9.4).

The frontal lobe is responsible for motor control and contains an area called the primary motor cortex. Different parts of the motor cortex control different parts of the body, and the more precision needed for motor control (e.g., fingers, tongue), the larger the area of motor cortex associated with it. The motor cortex occupies only a small region of the frontal lobes, and the functions of the remaining areas are more speculative.

Behind the frontal lobe is the parietal lobe, which includes the somatosensory cortex. This region processes sensory information, including touch, temperature, and pain. As with the primary motor cortex, larger regions of the somatosensory cortex are associated with more precise sensory receivers. Below the parietal lobe is the temporal lobe (near the

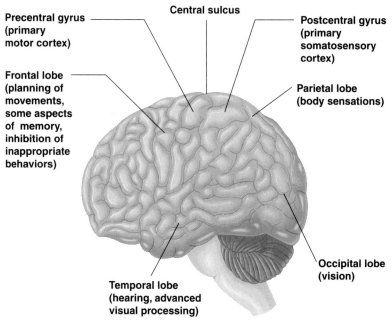

**Central sulcus**

**Precentral gyrus
(primary
motor cortex)**

**Postcentral gyrus
(primary
somatosensory
cortex)**

**Frontal lobe
(planning of
movements,
some aspects
of memory,
inhibition of
inappropriate
behaviors)**

**Parietal lobe
(body sensations)**

**Temporal lobe
(hearing, advanced
visual processing)**

**Occipital lobe
(vision)**

**Figure 9.4**    Areas of the cortex: the lobes.

temples), which contains the primary auditory cortex and controls hearing. Finally, be-hind the parietal and temporal lobes is the occipital lobe, which contains the primary visual cortex, where most visual signals are sent and where most visual processing occurs.

## Methods of Investigation

Lesion studies have provided much of the basic data about brain function, and both clin-ical patients and laboratory animals have been used. For example, when a stroke occurs in one hemisphere, it can lesion or destroy certain areas. By determining which areas are affected and by noting behavioral changes, a tentative assignment can be made between area and function. In laboratory animals, more precise lesions are possible and appropri-ate control groups can be used. In many cases, however, the animal's brain function and organization can be quite different, so great care must be taken in choosing the appropri-ate model. The most common criticism of this method is typically, "How can the function of a complex, highly interrelated system be understood by placing a hole in the middle of it?" (Squire, 1987, p. 175). When a structure such as the hippocampus is lesioned and retention of some learned information is impaired, how do we know that it is the hip-pocampus per se rather than some fibers that pass through that caused the loss? The an-swer is that gross lesioning techniques cannot provide much in the way of precise answers, and most researchers do not do this. Rather, researchers look for converging evidence, combining data from lesion procedures with results from other paradigms to see if they all point to—or converge on—one answer. By precision lesioning, psychologists have begun to map out the circuitry of some elementary forms of learning and memory (Byrne & Berry, 1989; Donegan, Gluck, & Thompson, 1989; McGaugh, Weinberger, & Lynch, 1990).

The intracarotid amobarbital perfusion test—better known as the Wada test after Juhn Wada, who devised it (Calvin & Ojemann, 1994)—provides evidence about the division of functioning between the two hemispheres. A short-acting anesthetic (amobarbital) is injected into the left carotid artery, and the front two-thirds of the left hemisphere stop working for approximately 2 minutes. By noting which behavioral and cognitive operations are no longer functional, the researcher can assign those operations to the temporarily deactivated hemisphere. This test is usually done prior to brain surgery to ensure that certain areas (such as the left temporal lobe) are undamaged before removing parts of a different area (the right temporal lobe). More detailed information can be obtained by direct stimulation of various areas of the brain. Both of these techniques are limited to clinical patients, often those with severe epilepsy or other dysfunctions.

A more common technique is imaging (see Kolb & Whishaw, 1990). Researchers use CT (computerized tomography), MRI (magnetic resonance imaging), and PET (positron emission tomography) scans. Generally, these techniques show either activity levels at various brain sites or detailed structural information.

CT scans (also known as computerized axial tomography or CAT scans) are useful for examining brain structure. The patient's head is surrounded by a set of X-ray transmitters and receptors so that X-rays are directed through the brain along different orientations. A computer analyzes how much radiation arrives at each destination and converts this information into a photograph of the brain's structure. This technique is often used to detect damage caused by trauma or disease, such as degeneration caused by Alzheimer's disease.

MRI is based on the effects that strong magnetic fields have on the alignment of hydrogen atoms. Again, a computer analyzes the changes in alignment when the magnetic field is repeatedly disrupted by radio waves. Brain structure is revealed because hydrogen concentrations vary in different areas. MRIs are thought to be safe but are quite costly.

A PET scan, by contrast, provides information about ongoing activity rather than about structure (see Posner & Raichle, 1994). Neurons use glucose, a form of sugar, as a source of energy and so the more active neurons in the brain take up larger amounts of glucose. For a PET scan, the patient is injected with radioactive glucose, and the amount of radiation emitted by various parts of the brain is then measured and analyzed. The results are usually shown as a color map, with red representing those areas that have the most emissions—indicating that they were very active and had absorbed a relatively large amount of radioactive glucose—and colors farther along the color spectrum show lower levels of emissions. One important detail to remember about PET scans is that the images typically displayed are computed. In a "raw" image of a PET scan, many different areas of the brain would be involved. The subtraction technique involves taking multiple scans, and subtracting one image scanned when the subject is doing one task from another image of the same subject doing a related task. In theory, the resulting image shows those areas that were more active on the second task than on the first.

For example, Tulving (1989) asked a subject to think about an autobiographical memory, an event that the person had personally experienced, or to think about something general, such as the history of astronomy that the person had not directly experienced. The particular procedure used here was to inject a small amount of radioactive gold into the bloodstream and to use gamma-ray detectors that encircled the subject's head. Tulving (1989) found evidence of greater blood flow in the frontal portions of cortex when the subject was thinking about autobiographical information, and greater blood flow in the posterior portions of cortex when thinking about generic information.

Two other common techniques involve EEGs and ERPs. Electroencephalograms (EEGs) measure the pattern of electrical activity through electrodes attached to the scalp. The resulting information measures brain activity at a relatively gross level. More recently, measuring event-related potentials (ERPs) has become a common technique. These are momentary changes in electrical activity in the brain associated with the presentation of a particular stimulus or with a particular type of processing (Näätänen, 1992). ERPs are analyzed in terms of positive or negative changes, relative to a baseline, within a particular time span. For example, a negative change that occurs between 300 and 500 ms after the stimulus is known as an N400 ERP.

Paller, Kutas, and McIsaac (1995) had subjects complete a recognition judgment (a direct test) and perform a lexical decision task (an indirect test). In this latter task, subjects were asked to respond as quickly as they could as to whether a target item was a valid word or a nonword. Prior to these tasks, the subjects were asked to perform an imagery judgment (is the object referred to by the word larger or smaller than the computer monitor) or a syllable judgment (does the word have one syllable or more than one syllable). The researchers found that subjects recognized imaged words better than words that were in the syllable judgment, but found that these tasks did not affect the lexical decision task. So far, this dissociation fits in with the type of studies reported in the last chapter, where some measures affect direct tests of memory but do not affect indirect tests. Paller, Kutas, and McIsaac (1995) also recorded ERPs. They found that when conscious recollection was occurring, as indexed behaviorally by the improved recognition performance for the imagery words, there was a more positive ERP observable between 500 and 900 ms after stimulus presentation than when the syllable words were presented. They suggested that this ERP correlates with degree of recollective processing and may be another useful way of separating automatic from recollective processes (see also Chapter 6).

There are also behavioral tests that can be used, which rely on getting a particular hemisphere to control or have priority in performing some task. For example, stimuli can be presented to subjects so that they are initially processed by just the left hemisphere or just the right hemisphere. Although the information will quickly be transmitted to the other hemisphere, differences in processing time can allow the researcher to infer differences in capabilities. Klatzky and Atkinson (1971) presented either pictures or letters and had subjects then make a decision about whether the stimulus had appeared in an immediately preceding list. By having the subjects fixate to the left of the display area, the stimulus would be presented in the right visual field and thence projected to the left hemisphere. Fixating to the right of the display area would mean the stimulus was presented in the left visual field and would be projected to the right hemisphere. Klatzky and Atkinson found that when the stimuli required a verbal code, right-handed subjects were faster when the stimuli was presented to the left hemisphere (856 ms) than to the right hemisphere (902 ms). When the stimuli required a spatial code, subjects were faster when the stimuli were presented to the right hemisphere (809 ms) than to the left hemisphere

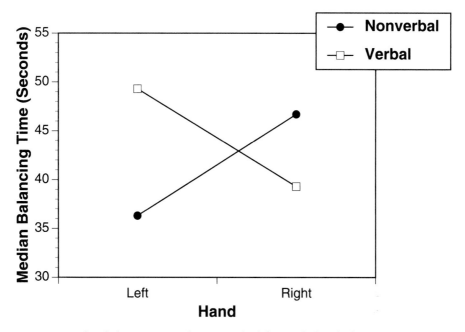

**Figure 9.5**   Median balancing time when using the left or right hand when concurrent vocalization was required (verbal) or not required (nonverbal).   Source: Based on data from Kinsbourne & Cook (1971).

(828 ms). These results were obtained regardless of which hand was used for responding. Koenig, Wetzel and Caramazza (1992) reported similar findings.

Similar techniques have been used with other tasks. For example, Urcuioli, Klein, and Day (1981) found differences in a categorization task: whereas category matching relied more on the left hemisphere, category membership tasks were less localized. Another behavioral test is to use classical conditioning and present the CS to one visual field or another. Using this technique, Hellige (1975) used a conditioned blink procedure and found systematic differences in speed and type of responding depending upon the hemisphere that received the CS.

Kinsbourne and Cook (1971) reported a study that compared performance on a balancing task when the subject was asked either to vocalize or to remain silent. The subjects, all of whom were right-handed, first practiced balancing a wooden dowel on the left and right index fingers. They balanced the dowel for 1 minute on the left index finger and then, after a 1 minute rest, balanced the dowel for 1 minute on the right index finger. The criterion was to be able to have a mean balancing time in excess of 5 minutes for the 20 experimental trials. The subjects then attempted to balance the dowel for as long as they could while vocalizing or while remaining silent. The results are shown in Figure 9.5.

Kinsbourne and Cook (1971) found the predicted benefit of longer balancing times on the right hand in the nonverbal condition and shorter balancing times on the right hand in the verbal condition. The reason, they suggest, is because the left hemisphere, which controls the right hand, is also the seat of language. The surprising result was that the opposite pattern was observed for the left hand: longer balancing times in the verbal condition than in the silent. Their interpretation is that the task to verbalize helped performance on the left hand by distracting the subjects just enough that they did not focus too much attention on balancing. Regardless of the correct interpretation, the results show laterality effects on a behavioral measure.

A final technique used to ascribe function to brain areas, and also to distinguish between different memory systems, is logical rather than methodological. A *dissociation* is said to have been shown when an independent variable differentially affects performance on two different tests. For example, word frequency refers to how often a word is used in written and spoken language. When the test is free recall, high-frequency words are recalled better than low-frequency words; when the test is recognition, low-frequency words are recognized better than high-frequency words (Gregg, 1976). This is an example of a single dissociation. Another example occurs when damage occurs to a specific brain

---

**Experiment   Laterality of Language**

**Purpose:** To demonstrate the laterality of language by inducing interference on a balancing task.

**Subjects:** Twenty right-handed subjects are recommended. Subjects should indicate that they write and throw with their right hand and that they use their right hand to brush their teeth. The reason for using right-handed subjects is that the left side of the brain is the seat of language in almost all right-handed people but for only approximately 70% of left-handed people (Corballis, 1980).

**Materials:** You will need a wooden rod, approximately 46 cm long, 1.3 cm in diameter, and weighing approximately 105 g. You will also need a set of sentences for the subject to verbalize (you can make these up yourself) and a stopwatch.

**Procedure:** Each subject should practice balancing the dowel for 1 minute on the right index finger. Allow 15 minutes for practice. Then, 10 subjects should be tested on the conditions in the order RN (right-nonverbal) followed by RV (right-verbal) and ten subjects should be tested on the conditions in the order RV followed by RN.

**Instructions:** "We are interested in how long you can balance this rod on your index finger while standing. Try to keep the rod balanced for as long as possible, moving your whole body if necessary."

**Additional Instructions for the Verbal Trials:** "While you balance the rod, I would like you to repeat the following sentences out loud." (Read the sentences.)

**Scoring and Analysis:** For each subject, calculate the median balancing time (in seconds) for both conditions. The median is the value that is in the middle; there are an equal number of values above and below the median. Then, average the median balancing times. A paired-group *t* test can be used to test for significance. The results should replicate the data for the right hand shown in Figure 9.5.

**Optional Enhancements:** Include the left hand. In this case, present the conditions in the order RN, LN, RV, LV and LV, RV, LN, RN.

Source: Based on an experiment by Kinsbourne & Cook (1971).

area. Patients with damage to Broca's area have trouble producing fluent speech — called Broca's aphasia — whereas similar subjects without this damage do not have this difficulty. A double dissociation is said to have been shown when two different independent variables have opposite effects on two different tests. In neuropsychology, a double dissociation is often expressed as finding two patients of whom Patient A is impaired on Task 1 but not on Task 2, whereas Patient B is impaired on Task 2 but not on Task 1.

In practice, the logic of dissociations and double dissociations is not as simple as described above. For example, Shallice (1988) devotes three chapters to discussing what inferences may be drawn on the basis of various kinds of dissociations. Neely (1989) points out many other potential problems that may prevent the logic from being valid. In fact, he includes a set of "prescriptions" that a researcher should follow when designing an experiment in order to avoid common interpretive difficulties. Even though both authors emphasize that dissociations can serve as a valuable tool for distinguishing different underlying systems, both also emphasize that it is very difficult to construct the appropriate series of experiments. Certainly, dissociations from a single experiment or from a single study should be looked on with skepticism. As in other areas of scientific inquiry, replication under appropriately stringent conditions is needed in order to draw firm conclusions.

# Localized versus Distributed Storage

There are two basic historical conceptions of where memory might be stored. A *localized view* comes from early research that showed specialized memory structures in the brain, such as Broca's area for speech production (Broca, 1861). The *distributed view* arose from the idea that mental activity was due to integrated activity of many different components of the brain. In particular, Lashley (1929) found that although the extent of the lesions in rats was positively correlated with memory impairment, there was no relationship between the location of the lesions and memory impairment. Lashley (1950) concluded that memories were not stored "anywhere" but rather were stored everywhere.

The resolution between these two views lies in the size of the area under consideration. As Squire's (1987) review shows, memory is widely distributed, but different loci store different aspects of the whole.

> Memory is distributed in that no single memory center exists, and many parts of the nervous system participate in the representation of a single event. Memory is localized in that the representation of a single event involves a limited number of brain systems and pathways, and each part of the brain contributes differently to the representation. . . . The most likely site of storage is the set of particular cortical processing systems that are engaged during the perception, processing, and analysis of the material being learned. (p. 123)

For memories such as your last Christmas Day meal, the components of the memory are distributed over a variety of areas and within a particular area; certain cell assemblies contribute different parts of the whole picture. To further complicate matters, some of the information that you recall is clearly not from the original event but from other sources. Did you have mashed potatoes? Probably, but perhaps you are guessing about this because many people have mashed potatoes. Thus, you do not have a single place where memories are stored.

If much of memory is localized in the assemblies that processed the original event, and if memory is a persistent change in the way neurons communicate, an intriguing question is, Why doesn't perception also change? The answer to this question has two parts. First, perception does in fact change; but, second, it changes slowly because only a portion of cortical cells within a particular assembly are plastic (for example, Fuster & Jervey, 1981). This slow change is not noticed and decreases as the organism ages. For example, monkeys' capabilities to perceive touch and other sensations using their hands depends on the amount of somatosensory cortex assigned to that body part. Studies with monkeys have shown that the amount of somatosensory cortex devoted to the hand and fingers can expand and contract, depending on the experimental manipulation (Kaas, 1995). Similar changes in perception with experience and (presumably) changed neuronal communication can also be seen in humans' "higher-level" cognitive processes: upside-down and even mirrored text can be more quickly interpreted after practice (Kolers, 1979); and chess experts perceive chess layouts differently than do novices (Chase & Simon, 1973). Indeed, the cortex seems remarkably plastic (Fuster, 1995).

# Amnesia

There are two main classes of amnesia. With *retrograde amnesia* a person is unable to remember details that were learned prior to the event that caused the amnesia. A concussion can often lead to retrograde amnesia: the person cannot remember what happened during the few minutes or hours prior to the blow to the head. Retrograde is the type of amnesia discussed in Chapter 7 in conjunction with consolidation theory. The other main form is *anterograde amnesia;* a person is unable to learn new information following some brain trauma. It is possible, of course, for a person to experience both kinds simultaneously.

Within these types of amnesia, there are three main ways of classifying people: by cause, by damage, or by functional deficit. Classification by cause is most useful when investigating prognosis. For example, patients with amnesia due to chronic alcoholism are likely to have a different prognosis than are those with amnesia due to viral encephalitis. This criteria is less useful for psychological purposes, though, because within a category, patients can have more or less severe cases. The degree of severity will affect the type and extent of deficits, and so the memory data can be ambiguous.

Some studies classify patients on the basis of the location of the brain damage. In many cases, if similar brain structures are damaged, the behavior impairment is similar regardless of the cause. The major problem with this approach is the current crudity of brain localization techniques. For example, when the hippocampus, a structure often implicated with memory impairment, is damaged, not only is the structure itself affected but also many fibers that pass through the hippocampus. For most lesions in humans, the damage is rarely localized and instead affects many different areas.

A third way of classifying amnesics is by their functional deficit. That is, there exists a group of patients who, regardless of the etiology and localization of their deficits, have similar patterns of memory behavior. For example, one common type of deficit is known as the *amnesic syndrome.* Although pure cases are rare and there is a wide range of vari-

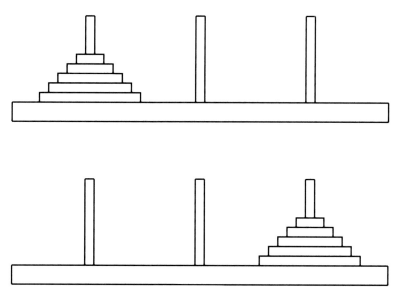

**Figure 9.6** The Tower of Hanoi problem. The goal is to move five disks from the leftmost peg (top panel) to the rightmost peg (bottom panel). Only one disk may be moved at a time, and a larger disk cannot be placed on top of a smaller disk. The optimal solution requires 31 moves.

ability, the basic characteristics are quite robust. The amnesic syndrome can arise from Korsakoff's syndrome, where prolonged alcohol abuse leads to a thiamine deficiency and subsequent brain damage. It can also occur from viral encephalitis, from lesions due to trauma or surgery, and from lack of oxygen.

Wilson and Baddeley (1988) described one such case, a 59-year-old patient known as K. J. whose amnesia resulted from meningitis. On intelligence tests, K. J. performed well above average and displayed no evidence of perceptual deficits. He showed no noticeable impairment on immediate memory tasks, including the Brown-Peterson task, and his basic knowledge was unaffected. For example, he could verify sentences such as "Canaries are yellow" (true) or "Bats are birds" (false) as quickly and as accurately as appropriate control subjects. His memory for the details of his own life were well preserved, at least up until the time near his illness. His performance on implicit learning tasks was near normal. For example, he could learn to solve the Tower of Hanoi puzzle (see Figure 9.6), as well as other procedural tasks such as reading reversed text. The main locus of his deficit was in retrieving episodic information. He had problems learning the names of new therapists and could not navigate in new environments or recall what he had seen on television or read in the newspaper. If tested immediately, he could recall even fairly complex paragraphs; after a short delay, however, he could recall almost nothing.

The major problem in the amnesia literature is that neither amnesia itself nor its behavioral tasks or consequents are as yet precisely described. Even within a type of amnesia (such as Korsakoff patients), there is often uncertainty about how one patient's symptoms compare with another. For example, Weiskrantz (1985) reported on the use of the difference between the IQ score and the memory quotient (MQ) of the Weschsler Memory Scale. This difference is known as IQ-WMQ. The larger this difference, the more impaired the subject. By comparing the IQ-WMQ scores of different types of patients, Weiskrantz found that amnesics with the same numerical score are sometimes classified as "severe" amnesics by one researcher and as "moderate" by another. Many studies include no objective numerical assessment of the severity of the amnesia.

As one example of another problem, many reports describe only one level of task; thus, some studies report that patients can solve visual maze learning tasks, whereas other studies with apparently similar subjects report that their patients cannot. A better method is to include at least two levels of difficulty. This was done with H. M., a patient with profound amnesia (see the next section), and it was found that he could learn the simple version of the maze but not the complex version (Milner, Corkin, & Teuber, 1968). Perhaps these and other problems prompted Cermak (1982) to state, "Finding an amnesic to support one's thesis is neither difficult nor sufficient" (p. 44). Nonetheless, there has been an enormous amount of progress in understanding at least the character of human amnesic syndrome and related memory deficits (Parkin, 1997). Although the issues are too complex and the literature too large to be reviewed completely in one chapter, it is nonetheless possible to offer an overview.

## H. M.: A Case Study

The most often cited case study of amnesia is that of H. M. (see Scovile & Milner, 1957). In 1953, when he was 27, H. M. underwent an experimental surgical procedure that bilaterally severed his hippocampus to try to alleviate chronic epileptic seizures. As a result of the surgery, the previously intractable seizures became controllable by medication, and thus the surgery was a partial success. However, the surgery also produced a severe disruption of memory performance. After the operation, H. M. lived with his parents, and since 1980 has lived in a nursing home. The severity of the memory impairment and the complete disruption of his life cannot be overemphasized. For example, although his father died in 1967 and his mother in 1977, in 1986 H. M. thought he was still living with his mother and was unsure of whether his father was alive (Parkin, 1993). In general, H. M. is able to perform within the normal range on tasks that have an immediate test, and he shows almost no memory for information when the test is delayed.

The case of H. M. has been used to support (1) the role of the hippocampus in memory, (2) the distinction between long- and short-term memory, (3) the distinction between procedural and declarative memory, and (4) the distinction between implicit and explicit memory. There are problems with each of these interpretations.

H. M. is often cited as evidence supporting the hypothesis that the hippocampus is critically involved in mediating memory (Milner, Corkin, & Teuber, 1968). The problem is that the surgeon lesioned not only the hippocampus proper but also caused damage to the amygdala, the larger hippocampal formation, the surrounding cortex, the subiculum and surrounding tissue, the fornix-fimbria, and probably the thalamus (Horel, 1994; Weiskrantz, 1985). Thus, attributing the memory deficit in H. M. solely to the hippocampus is highly questionable.

Because H. M. has a memory span well within the normal range (Wickelgren, 1968), his case has also been used as evidence for the distinction between short- and long-term memory. The problems with this argument are similar to those presented in Chapter 4 as problems with the modal model's account of memory in normal subjects. In addition, there is a further logical problem. Having normal memory for the short term and impaired memory for the long term does not necessarily imply that a normal short-term memory exists separately from an impaired long-term memory. As Crowder (1989) put it, "evidence for (a distinct subsystem of) short-term storage is not at all the same as evidence that people . . . store things over the short term" (p. 280).

A more recent claim has been that case studies like that of H. M. support a distinction between procedural and declarative memory (Cohen & Eichenbaum, 1993; Squire, 1987). A rule of thumb is that if you say you know how to do something, then it is a good candidate for a form of procedural memory but if you say you know that something is so, it is a good candidate for declarative memory. H. M., as well as many other amnesics, show evidence of procedural learning. For example, Cohen, Eichenbaum, Deacedo, and Corkin (1985) found that amnesics performed equivalently on the Tower of Hanoi problem (see Figure 9.6) as did matched control subjects. On the first day, the control subjects required an average of 48.6 moves compared to 46.7 for the amnesics. By the fourth day of training (with four trials per day), both groups exhibited learning: the control subjects required only 34.1 moves compared to 33.5 for the amnesics. Optimal performance is 31 moves. Note that the amnesics did not remember the previous trials and did not remember the rules. On each trial, the goal and rules had to be explained again.

Results from the Tower of Hanoi study, as well as many others, support the claim that procedural memory is unimpaired and declarative memory is impaired. However, this distinction is too simplistic and overlooks many problems (McCarthy & Warrington, 1990). For example, it depends on the particular definition of what constitutes procedural and what constitutes declarative memory, and many researchers disagree on which tasks tap which purported system. As another example, there are several documented cases of amnesics like H. M. who can learn new declarative information (see Glisky & Schacter, 1987; Schacter, 1985) and who are impaired on procedural tasks (see Warrington & Weiskrantz, 1974; Winocur & Weiskrantz, 1976).

The most recent application of cases like that of H. M. have been to support the difference between implicit and explicit memory (see Chapter 8). This will be discussed below after first considering some other theoretical accounts.

## Theoretical Accounts of Amnesia

There have been several different general explanations of amnesia. One possibility is that amnesics do not encode information as well as control subjects do. This seems unlikely, however, given that Korsakoff patients show similar patterns of enhancement when coding instructions are manipulated (see Cermak & Reale, 1978; Meudell, Mayes, & Neary, 1980). Similar conclusions come from a more recent study that varied both encoding and retrieval conditions (Dalla-Barba & Wong, 1995). Another possibility is that amnesics simply forget faster than control subjects do. Huppert and Piercy (1978a) tested Korsakoff patients and control subjects after equating for initial level of learning; that is, photographs were presented at a much slower presentation rate to the amnesic subjects so that their recognition score equaled that of the control subjects. The subjects were tested

**Table 9.1**   Proportion correct on three different tests for both control and amnesic subjects.

| Test | Control Subjects | Amnesic Subjects |
|------|:---:|:---|
| Recall | 48% | 14% |
| Recognition | 94% | 59% (Chance = 50%) |
| Fragmented Words | 96% | 94% |

Source: Warrington & Weiskrantz (1970).

after one day and one week, and there was no evidence of faster forgetting. Similar results have been reported by others (for example, Carlesimo, Sabbadini, & Fadda, 1995; Kopelman, 1985).

Two more enduring theories have focused on retrieval problems. Warrington and Weiskrantz (1968, 1970) suggested that one important factor was interference. They used a procedure in which a list of items (words or pictures) was displayed and, after an interval, a fragment of each item or the first letter or two was presented as a cue. With these partial cues, the ability of the amnesic subjects to recall the information was greatly enhanced (see Table 9.1). Performance on both free recall and recognition tests was substantially lower for the amnesic subjects; when a fragment served as a partial cue, however, performance improved dramatically. Warrington and Weiskrantz (1974) also showed equivalent performance for amnesic and control subjects on a cued-recall test.

The idea is that the cue or partial fragment can help reduce interference, and overcoming this deficit restores performance to normal or near normal levels. Why, then, does recognition show a large disadvantage? On a yes-no recognition test, there is no cue to the subject that the item being presented was a studied item, whereas on a cued-recall test, the cue is part of a studied item. Consistent with this interpretation, Weiskrantz (1982) found that although amnesics are good at learning new associations where links already exist (such as soldier-army), they become progressively worse as the relatedness of the items decreases. To the extent that indirect tests of implicit memory are relatively immune from interference (Graf & Schacter, 1987; see Chapter 8), this would explain why amnesics show relatively unimpaired performance on these tasks.

The second enduring theory has to do with the role of context. One of the few studies to show a qualitative rather than just a quantitative difference between amnesics and control subjects was reported by Huppert and Piercy (1978b). On Day 1, Korsakoff patients and alcoholic control subjects were shown 80 color photographs of various complex scenes. Half of these photographs were shown once, and half were shown three times. On Day 2, the subjects saw a different list of 80 photographs; again, half of the photographs were shown once, and half were shown three times. The test began 10 minutes after the end of presentation of the photographs on Day 2. The subjects were told that they would see a long series of test photographs. They were also told that they had seen all of the test photographs before, either today (Day 2) or yesterday (Day 1), and that half of the photographs had been shown once, and half shown three times. The subject's task was to indicate when the photograph was shown, and how many times it had been shown; the results are shown in Figure 9.7.

The control subjects were quite accurate, replicating other judgments of frequency (see Hasher & Chromiak, 1977). In the right half of Figure 9.7, the D2F1 (day 2, fre-

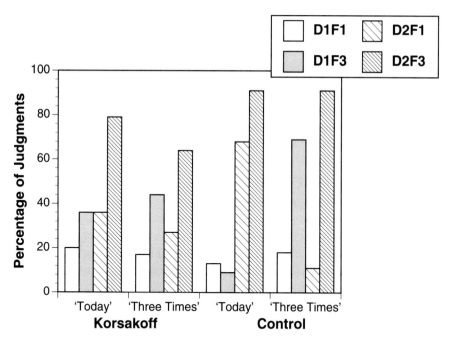

**Figure 9.7**    Percentage of "Today" and "Three Times" judgments for Korsakoff patients and alcoholic control subjects. D1 and D2 refer to Day 1 and Day 2 and F1 and F3 refer to presented once and presented three times respectively.    Source: Huppert & Piercy (1978b).

quency 1) and D2F3 (day 2, frequency 3) items were accurately judged as being seen today (day 2) and the D1F3 (day 1, frequency 3) and D2F3 were accurately judged as being shown three times. The Korsakoff patients, however, showed a different pattern. They were as likely to respond with "today" for D1F3 and D2F1 pictures; furthermore, they were more likely to respond "three times" for D2F1 than D1F1. The results are consistent with the idea that the amnesic subjects were relying on familiarity, and an item could be familiar either because it occurred on the same day as the test or because it occurred three times on the previous day. Similar results have been reported by Meudell, Mayes, Ostergaard, and Pickering (1985).

One interpretation of these results is that the Korsakoff patients were relying on the strength of the memory trace to make their judgments, whereas the control subjects were relying on both strength and contextual recollection. This interpretation gains further support from the results of a study reported by Parkin, Montaldi, Leng, and Hunkin (1990). They found that Korsakoff patients could quite accurately distinguish old from new items after a brief delay as long as the distractor (new) items had not been seen previously. When the distractors had been seen previously, the Korsakoff patients could no longer do the task. Because they had been seen previously, the distractor items appeared to be as familiar as the test items. Amnesic syndrome, then, apparently leaves an automatic familiarity process intact but interferes with the recollective process. This interpretation also dovetails nicely with the results of Jacoby's (1991) process dissociation framework, discussed in Chapter 6.

# Amnesia and Implicit Memory

In the previous chapter, we contrasted the multiple memory systems view of implicit memory with the transfer appropriate processing view. Both views have problems with some recent data. As noted in Chapter 8, Blaxton (1989) reported data consistent with the idea that a distinction between data driven and conceptually driven processing is more important than is a distinction based on indirect versus direct tests. However, the transfer appropriate processing has problems with a recent study that used amnesics. Cermak, Verfaellie, and Chase (1995) showed that amnesic patients were impaired on a direct test of cued recall but were unimpaired on indirect tests, regardless of whether the indirect test was data driven or conceptually driven. The distinction between direct and indirect was more important than was the distinction between data driven and conceptually driven.

Cermak and his colleagues (Cermak, Verfaellie, & Chase, 1995; Cermak & Verfaellie, 1992) have attempted to reconcile these problems by emphasizing the role of fluency (or familiarity) and context. The idea is that the typical indirect test is not only data driven but also emphasizes the role of familiarity. The typical direct test, by contrast, is usually conceptually driven but also emphasizes the role of context.

Cermak, Verfaellie, Butler, and Jacoby (1993) used a version of Jacoby's false fame procedure (Jacoby, Woloshyn, & Kelley, 1989) to test this idea. A group of amnesics (seven Korsakoff patients, and six with amnesia from other causes) and a control group of chronic alcoholics saw a list of 40 names drawn from the Boston telephone book. In Experiment 1, the subjects were told that the names were from the phone book and were nonfamous; in Experiment 2, the subjects were told the names came from *Who's Who* and were of famous people. The subjects were told to remember this information because it would help them in the next phase. The subjects then saw a list of 120 names and were asked to judge whether the person was famous. Of these names, 60 were famous, 30 were from the list of nonfamous names that had been studied, and 30 were nonfamous names that had not been seen before. The results of the fame judgment task are shown in Table 9.2, along with what perfect performance should look like.

When the subjects were told that the studied names were all of nonfamous people, the amnesic subjects showed a robust false fame effect: they judged 29.2% of the old nonfamous people as actually being famous. According to Cermak and associates (1993), they were very likely to judge an old nonfamous name as famous because of its familiarity. In contrast, the alcoholic control subjects showed no false fame effect: they judged only 9.4% of old nonfamous names as famous. The control subjects were able to use contextual information to determine that if they recollected that an item had been on the first list, it must be nonfamous despite its familiarity. When the subjects were told that the studied names were all of famous people, the control subjects now judged more old nonfamous names as famous than the amnesics did (70.3% compared to 43.1%). The control group was again able to use information to attribute the familiarity of a name to its occurrence on the first list: the group thus judged very few of these names as famous in Experiment 1 but judged the majority famous in Experiment 2. Whereas the control group went from 9.4% to 70.3% judged famous, the amnesics went from 29.2% to only 43.1% judged famous, a difference that was not statistically reliable. This latter result is consistent with the idea that the amnesics could not attribute the familiarity of the names to the appropriate source (Schacter, Harbluk, & McLachlan, 1984). The difference between the alcoholics

**Table 9.2** Percentage of names identified as famous when subjects were told that the old nonfamous names were nonfamous or were famous.

|  | Percentage of Names Identified as Famous | | |
|---|---|---|---|
|  | *Famous* | *Old Nonfamous* | *New Nonfamous* |
| *Told That Studied Items Were Nonfamous* | | | |
| Alcoholic | 53.2 | 9.4 | 8.8 |
| Amnesic | 36.7 | 29.2 | 16.9 |
| Perfect | 100 | 0 | 0 |
| *Told That Studied Items Were Famous* | | | |
| Alcoholic | 77.2 | 70.3 | 10.3 |
| Amnesic | 53.3 | 43.1 | 23.6 |
| Perfect | 100 | 100 | 0 |

Source: Based on data from Cermak et al. (1993).

and amnesics is also consistent with current views that recognition consists of two components, a recollective process and a familiarity assessment (see Chapter 10).

Thus, amnesics will generally show normal performance whenever the task relies primarily on familiarity or on fluency; these tasks are generally indirect tasks. Amnesics will generally show impaired performance whenever the task relies primarily on contextual discrimination; these tasks are generally direct tasks. However, both types of processing can be recruited for each type of task, hence some of the dissociations between indirect and direct and between conceptually driven and data driven. According to this view, one reason for the lack of immediate memory deficits is that the subject does not need to determine which context is the appropriate cue. On tasks where there is a delay, there is a deficit because, on explicit tasks at least, there is no indication of which context should be used. Indirect tests usually do not require a reinstatement of context, and thus performance is preserved here also. From this perspective, it is not necessary to postulate multiple memory systems to explain differences between amnesic and control performance or to explain differences between direct and indirect tests. This position still cannot explain all of the data; but it appears more capable than others (Cermak, Verfaellie, & Chase, 1995).

# Where Is Memory?

One of the most widespread views of the cause of amnesia is that it is damage to the hippocampus or hippocampal formation (Squire, 1987). If this view is accurate, it supports the idea that the hippocampus and surrounding structures are critical for successful memory. Indeed, one of the most cited lines of evidence supporting the role of the hippocampus comes from studies of H. M. More and more researchers, however, are suggesting that the role of the hippocampus has been overstated. There are many reasons for this change, including the fact that H. M. suffered damage not only to the hippocampus but also to a large portion of surrounding cortex (Horel, 1994; Weiskrantz, 1985), and also the finding that many lesions outside the hippocampus produce symptoms like classical human amnesia syndrome (Baddeley & Wilson, 1988; Corkin, Cohen, Sullivan, Clegg, Rosen, & Ackerman, 1985; De Renzi, 1982).

Another reason is that on evolutionary grounds, it would not be adaptive to have memory functioning that relied so heavily on just one structure, such as the hippocampus. Reliance on a central memory organ would be too dangerous because damage to this one organ would eliminate all memories. Reliance on a central memory organ would also be problematical on anatomical grounds because it would require all processing to be routed through that organ. If the hippocampus were the most important center for memory, it follows that all of the information processed must go from the perceptual processing center to the hippocampus and back again. This leads researchers who emphasize the role of the hippocampus in memory to posit what Horel (1994) calls "anatomical extension cords." For example, if damage to one area, such as the frontal lobes, produces amnesia, researchers who support the central role of the hippocampus have to argue that there must also be some damage to a connection to the hippocampus for the memory deficit to occur. Typically, however, only the damage to the one area (in this example, the frontal lobes) is clearly seen, and there is little evidence for damage to the hippocampus.

So where is memory in the brain? As Horel (1994) noted, "[T]erms like 'memory' and 'perception' have truly global referents, and were invented without reference to the brain, and the brain, though exquisitely divisible, is not necessarily going to be divided according to terms that are used to divide components of intact human behavior" (p. 277).

Although the hippocampus may be involved with some types of memory, it is not necessarily the case that the hippocampus is centrally important to all memory. Rather, it is more likely that memory is not the function of any single structure but is a part of local operations carried out in all cortical areas where the information to be remembered is processed and perceived. This view is echoed by many others (Crowder, 1993; Roediger & Srinivas, 1993) and makes a strong prediction: a local lesion will cause not only a loss of local function, but also the memory for that function. The "anatomical extension cord" from the area of lesion to the hippocampus may not be needed.

# References

Baddeley, A. D. (1986). *Working memory.* New York: Oxford University Press.

Baddeley, A. D., & Wilson, B. A. (1988). Frontal amnesia and the dysexecutive syndrome. *Brain and Cognition, 7,* 212–230.

Blaxton, T. A. (1989). Investigating dissociations among memory measures: Support for a transfer-appropriate processing framework. *Journal of Experimental Psychology: Learning, Memory, and Cognition, 15,* 657–668.

Broca, P. (1861). Remarques sur le siège de la faculté du langage articulé, suives d'une observation d'aphemie. *Bulletin et Mémoires de la Société anatomique de Paris, 2,* 330–357.

Byrne, J. H., & Berry, W. O. (1989). (Eds.). *Neural models of plasticity: experimental and theoretical approaches.* San Diego: Academic Press.

Calvin, W. H., & Ojemann, G. A. (1994). *Conversations with Neil's brain: The neural nature of thought and language.* Reading, Mass: Addison-Wesley.

Capaldi, E. J., & Neath, I. (1995). Remembering and forgetting as context discrimination. *Learning & Memory, 2,* 107–132.

Carew, T. J., Walters, E. T., & Kandel, E. R. (1981). Classical conditioning in a simple withdrawal reflex in Aplysia californica. *Journal of Neuroscience, 1,* 1426–1437.

Carlesimo, G. A., Sabbadini, M., & Fadda, L. (1995). Forgetting from long-term memory in dementia and pure amnesia: Role of task, delay of assessment and aetiology of cerebral damage. *Cortex, 31,* 285–300.

Cermak, L. S. (1982). The long and short of it in amnesia. In L. S. Cermak (Ed.), *Human memory and amnesia.* Hillsdale, NJ: Erlbaum.

Cermak, L. S., & Reale, L. (1978). Depth of processing and retention of words by alcoholic Korsakoff patients. *Journal of Experimental Psychology: Human Learning and Memory, 4,* 165–174.

Cermak, L. S., & Verfaellie, M. (1992). The role of fluency in the implicit and explicit task performance of amnesic patients. In L. R. Squire & N. Butters (Eds.), *The neuropsychology of memory* (2nd ed.). New York: Guilford.

Cermak, L. S., Verfaellie, M., Butler, T., & Jacoby, L. L. (1993). Attributions of familiarity in amnesia: Evidence from a fame judgment task. *Neuropsychology, 4,* 510–518.

Cermak, L. S., Verfaellie, M., & Chase, K. A. (1995). Implicit and explicit memory in amnesia: An analysis of data-driven and conceptually driven processes. *Neuropsychology, 9,* 281–290.

Chase, W. G., & Simon, H. A. (1973). The mind's eye in chess. In W. G. Chase (Ed.), *Visual information processing.* New York: Academic Press.

Cohen, N. J., & Eichenbaum, H. (1993). *Memory, amnesia, and the hippocampal system.* Cambridge, MA: MIT Press.

Cohen, N. J., Eichenbaum, H., Deacedo, B. S., & Corkin, S. (1985). Different memory systems underlying acquisition of procedural and declarative knowledge. In D. S. Olton, E. Gamzu, & S. Corkin (Eds.), *Memory dysfunctions: An integration of animal and human research from preclinical and clinical perspectives.* New York: New York Academy of Sciences.

Corballis, M. C. (1980). Laterality and myth. *American Psychologist, 35,* 284–295.

Corkin, S., Cohen, N. J., Sullivan, E. V., Clegg, R. A., Rosen, R. J., & Ackerman, R. H. (1985). Analysis of global memory impairments of different etiologies. *Annals of the New York Academy of Sciences, 444,* 10–40.

Crowder, R. G. (1989). Modularity and dissociations of memory systems. In H. L. Roediger, III & F. I. M. Craik (Eds.), *Varieties of memory and consciousness: Essays in honour of Endel Tulving.* Hillsdale, NJ: Erlbaum.

Crowder, R. G. (1993). Systems and principles in memory theory: Another critique of pure memory. In A. F. Collins, S. E. Gathercole, M. A. Conway, & P. E. Morris (Eds.), *Theories of memory.* Hove, UK: Erlbaum.

Dalla-Barba, G., & Wong, C. (1995). Encoding specificity and intrusion in Alzheimer's disease and amnesia. *Brain and Cognition, 27,* 1–16.

De Renzi, E. (1982). Memory disorders following focal neocortical damage. *Philosophical Transactions of the Royal Society of London B, 298,* 73–83.

Donegan, N. H., Gluck, M. A., & Thompson, R. F. (1989). Integrating behavioral and biological models of classical conditioning. In R. D. Hawkins & G. H. Bower (Eds.), *Computational models of learning in simple neural systems.* San Diego, CA: Academic Press.

Dowling, J. E. (1992). *Neurons and networks: An introduction to neuroscience.* Cambridge, MA: Harvard University Press.

Fuster, J. M. (1995). Gradients of cortical plasticity. In J. L. McGaugh, N. M. Weinberger, & G. Lynch (Eds.), *Brain and memory: Modulation and mediation of neuroplasticity.* New York: Oxford University Press.

Fuster, J. M., & Jervey, J. P. (1981). Inferotemporal neurons distinguish and retain behaviorally relevant features of visual stimuli. *Science, 212,* 952–955.

Glisky, G. L., & Schacter, D. L. (1987). Acquisition of domain-specific knowledge in organic amnesia: Training for computer-related work. *Neuropsychologia, 25,* 893–906.

Graf, P., & Schacter, D. L. (1987). Selective effects of interference on implicit and explicit memory for new associations. *Journal of Experimental Psychology: Learning, Memory, and Cognition, 13,* 45–53.

Gregg, V. H. (1976). Word frequency, recognition and recall. In J. Brown (Ed.), *Recall and recognition.* London: Wiley.

Hasher, L., & Chromiak, W. (1977). The processing of frequency information: An automatic mechanism? *Journal of Verbal Learning and Verbal Behavior, 16,* 173–184.

Hawkins, R. D. (1989). A simple circuit model for higher-order features of classical conditioning. In J. H. Byrne & W. O. Berry (Eds.), *Neural models of plasticity: Experimental and theoretical approaches.* San Diego: Academic Press.

Hebb, D. O. (1949). *The organization of behavior: A neuropsychological theory.* New York: Wiley.

Hellige, J. B. (1975). Hemispheric processing differences revealed by differential conditioning and reaction time performance. *Journal of Experimental Psychology: General, 104,* 309–326.

Horel, J. A. (1994). Some comments on the special cognitive functions claimed for the hippocampus. *Cortex, 30,* 269–280.

Huppert, F. A., & Piercy, M. (1978a). Dissociation between learning and remembering in organic amnesia. *Nature, 275,* 317–318.

Huppert, F. A., & Piercy, M. (1978b). The role of trace strength in recency and frequency judgments by amnesic and control subjects. *Quarterly Journal of Experimental Psychology, 30,* 347–354.

Jacoby, L. L. (1991). A process dissociation framework: Separating automatic from intentional uses of memory. *Journal of Memory and Language, 30,* 513–541.

Jacoby, L. L., Woloshyn, V., & Kelley, C. M. (1989). Becoming famous without being recognized: Unconscious influences of memory produced by dividing attention. *Journal of Experimental Psychology: General, 118,* 126–135.

Kaas, J. H. (1995). The plasticity of sensory representations in adult primates. In J. L. McGaugh, N. M. Weinberger, & G. Lynch (Eds.), *Brain and memory: Modulation and mediation of neuroplasticity.* New York: Oxford University Press.

Kandel, E. R. (1977). Neuronal plasticity and the modification of behavior. In J. M. Brookhart & V. B. Mountcastle (Eds.), *Handbook of physiology: The nervous system, Vol. 1.* Bethesda, MD: American Physiological Society.

Kinsbourne, M., & Cook, J. (1971). Generalized and lateralized effects of concurrent verbalization on a unimanual skill. *Quarterly Journal of Experimental Psychology, 23,* 341–345.

Klatzky, R. L., & Atkinson, R. C. (1971). Specialization of the cerebral hemispheres in scanning for information in short-term memory. *Perception & Psychophysics, 10,* 335–338.

Koenig, O., Wetzel, C., & Caramazza, A. (1992). Evidence for different types of lexical representations in the cerebral hemispheres. *Cognitive Neuropsychology, 9,* 33–45.

Kolb, B., & Whishaw, I. Q. (1990). *Fundamentals of human neuropsychology* (3rd ed.). New York: Freeman.

Kolers, P. A. (1979). A pattern-analyzing basis of recognition. In L. S. Cermak & F. I. M. Craik (Eds.), *Levels of processing in human memory.* Hillsdale, NJ: Erlbaum.

Konorski, J. (1948). *Conditioned reflexes and neuron organization.* Cambridge, England: Cambridge University Press.

Kopelman, M. D. (1985). Rates of forgetting in Alzheimer-type dementia and Korsakoff's Syndrome. *Neuropsychologia, 15,* 527–541.

Lashley, K. S. (1929). *Brain mechanisms and intelligence: A quantitative study of injuries to the brain.* Chicago: University of Chicago Press.

Lashley, K. S. (1950). In search of the engram. In *Symposium of the society for experimental biology, Vol. 4.* New York: Cambridge University Press.

McCarthy, R. A., & Warrington, E. K. (1990). *Cognitive neuropsychology: A clinical introduction.* San Diego, CA: Academic Press.

McGaugh, J. L., Weinberger, N. M., & Lynch, G. (Eds.). (1990). *Brain organization and memory: Cells, systems, and circuits.* New York: Oxford.

Meudell, P. R., Mayes, A. R., & Neary, D. (1980). Orienting task effects of the recognition of humorous material in amnesia and normal subjects. *Journal of Clinical Neuropsychology, 2,* 1–14.

Meudell, P. R., Mayes, A. R., Ostergaard, A., & Pickering, A. (1985). Recency and frequency judgments in alcoholic amnesics and normal people with poor memory. *Cortex, 21,* 487–511.

Milner, B., Corkin, S., & Teuber, H. L. (1968). Further analysis of the hippocampal amnesic syndrome: 14-year follow-up study of H. M. *Neuropsychologia, 6,* 215–234.

Näätänen, R. (1992). *Attention and brain function.* Hillsdale, NJ: Erlbaum.

Neely, J. H. (1989). Experimental dissociations and the episodic/semantic memory distinction. In H. L. Roediger III & F. I. M. Craik (Eds.), *Varieties of memory and consciousness: Essays in honour of Endel Tulving.* Hillsdale, NJ: Erlbaum.

Paller, K. A., Kutas, M., & McIsaac, H. K. (1995). Monitoring conscious recollection via the electrical activity of the brain. *Psychological Science, 6,* 107–111.

Parkin, A. J. (1987). *Memory and amnesia.* Oxford: Basil Blackwell.

Parkin, A. J. (1993). *Human memory.* Oxford: Basil Blackwell.

Parkin, A. J. (1997). *Memory and amnesia* (2nd ed.). Oxford: Basil Blackwell.

Parkin, A. J., Montaldi, D., Leng, N. R. C., & Hunkin, N. (1990). Contextual cueing effects in the remote memory of alcoholic Korsakoff patients. *Quarterly Journal of Experimental Psychology, 42A,* 585–596.

Posner, M. I., & Raichle, M. E. (1994). *Images of mind.* New York: Scientific American Library.

Ramon y Cajal, S. (1894). La fine structure des centres nerveux. *Proceedings of the Royal Society of London, 55,* 444–468.

Roediger, H. L., III, & Srinivas, K. (1993). Specificity of operations in perceptual priming. In P. Graf & M. E. J. Masson (Eds.), *Implicit memory: New directions in cognition, development and neuropsychology.* Hillsdale, NJ: Erlbaum.

Schacter, D. L. (1982). *Stranger behind the engram.* Hillsdale, NJ: Erlbaum.

Schacter, D. L. (1985). Multiple forms of memory in humans and animal. In N. M. Weinberger, J. L. McGaugh, & G. Lynch (Eds.), *Memory systems of the brain.* New York: Guilford.

Schacter, D. L. (1994). Priming and multiple memory systems: Perceptual mechanisms of implicit memory. In D. L. Schacter & E. Tulving (Eds.), *Memory systems 1994.* Cambridge, MA: MIT Press.

Schacter, D. L., Harbluk, J. L., & McLachlan, D. R. (1984). Retrieval without recollection: An experimental analysis of source amnesia. *Journal of Verbal Learning and Verbal Behavior, 23,* 593–611.

Schacter, D. L., & Tulving, E. (1994). What are the memory systems of 1994? In D. L. Schacter & E. Tulving (Eds.), *Memory systems 1994.* Cambridge, MA: MIT Press.

Scovile, W. B., & Milner, B. (1957). Loss of recent memory after bilateral hippocampal lesions. *Journal of Neurological and Neurosurgical Psychiatry, 20,* 11–12.

Semon, R. (1904). *Die Mneme als erhaltendes Prinzip im Wechsel des organischen Geshehens.* Leipzig: Engelmann.

Shallice, T. (1988). *From Neuropsychology to Mental Structure.* Cambridge, UK: Cambridge University Press.

Shepard, G., & Koch, C. (1990). Introduction to synaptic circuits. In G. Shepard (Ed.), *The synaptic organization of the brain.* New York: Oxford.

Squire, L. R. (1987). *Memory and brain.* New York: Oxford.

Tulving, E. (1989). Remembering and knowing the past. *American Scientist, 77,* 361–367.

Urcuioli, P. J., Klein, R. M., & Day, J. (1981). Hemispheric differences in semantic processing: Category matching is not the same as category membership. *Perception & Psychophysics, 29,* 343–351.

Warrington, E. K., & Weiskrantz, L. (1968). New method of testing long-term retention with special reference to amnesia patients. *Nature, 217,* 972–974.

Warrington, E. K., & Weiskrantz, L. (1970). Amnesic syndrome: Consolidation or retrieval? *Nature, 228,* 628–630.

Warrington, E. K., & Weiskrantz, L. (1974). The effect of prior learning on subsequent retention in amnesia patients. *Neuropsychologia, 16,* 169–176.

Weiskrantz, L. (1982). Comparative aspects of studies of amnesia. *Philosophical Transactions of the Royal Society of London B, 298,* 97–109.

Weiskrantz, L. (1985). On issues and theories of the human amnesic syndrome. In N. M. Weinberger, J. L. McGaugh, & G. Lynch (Eds.), *Memory systems of the brain.* New York: Guilford.

Wickelgren, W. A. (1968). Sparing of short-term memory in an amnesic patient: Implications for a strength theory of memory. *Neuropsychologia, 6,* 235–244.

Wilson, B. A., & Baddeley, A. D. (1988). Semantic, episodic, and autobiographical memory in a postmeningitic amnesic patient. *Brain and cognition, 8,* 31–46.

Winocur, G., & Weiskrantz, L. (1976). An investigation of paired-associate learning in amnesic patients. *Neuropsychologia, 14,* 97–110.

# C H A P T E R   T E N

# Recognition

*"A similar result comes about when a definite setting is only nascently aroused. We then feel that we have seen the object already, but when or where we cannot say, though we may seem to ourselves to be on the brink of saying it. . . . It tingles, it trembles on the verge, but does not come. Just such a tingling and trembling of unrecovered associates is the penumbra of recognition that may surround any experience and make it seem familiar, though we know not why."*

— *William James (1890)*

People often say that although they cannot quite think of the answer, they would know it if they saw it. In other words, people believe that a recognition test is "easier" than a recall test, although as will be seen below, this statement is often wrong. The essential difference between recall and recognition tests was described by Hollingworth (1913): in a recall test, the experimenter provides the context and the subject has to retrieve the target, whereas in a recognition test, the experimenter provides the target and the subject has to retrieve the context.

One classic experiment illustrates why many people think recognition is "easy." Shepard (1967) presented subjects with lengthy series of stimuli, and then at test presented two stimuli. One stimulus was from the list that the subjects had just studied, and one was a similar item that had not been seen. Some subjects saw 540 words, some saw 612 sentences, some saw 1224 sentences, and some saw 612 photographs. Subjects correctly recognized 88% of the words, 89% of the 612 sentences and 88% of the 1224 sentences, and almost 100% of the pictures. Some subjects who had seen the pictures were tested one week later, and even after that length of time, they still correctly recognized 87% of the pictures.

Shepard's test is known as a *two alternative forced choice,* or 2AFC test. In many college courses, your knowledge is assessed using a 4AFC test, where four alternatives are provided. The advantage of this technique is that the experimenter can manipulate the type and number of distractor words. This method is very useful because it can give detailed information about the type of errors people make. For example, when adults make an error, they typically select an item that is related to the correct item by meaning (Underwood & Freund, 1968), whereas third-graders typically select an item that sounds like or is acoustically related to an old item (Bach & Underwood, 1970).

**Table 10.1**   Possible outcomes in a yes-no recognition test. The probability of a hit is 1 minus the probability of a miss, and the probability of a false alarm is 1 minus the probability of a correct rejection. Thus, the probability of a hit plus the probability of a miss equals 1.0. The probability of a false alarm plus the probability of a correct rejection equals 1.0. Usually, researchers report only hits and false alarms.

|            |       | Subject's Response | |
|------------|-------|------|------|
|            |       | *Old* | *New* |
| *Test Item* | *Old* | Hit | Miss |
|            | *New* | False Alarm | Correct Rejection |

A second type of recognition test is often referred to as a yes-no recognition test. Subjects see a series of items, and then at test are presented with a single item, which they indicate is either from the studied list or is not from the studied list. Items that were originally presented are known as old items, and items that were not shown in the study list are known as new items. The main difference between the two types of tests is what is presented at test. With the yes-no method, only one item at a time is presented at test, and subjects have to indicate whether this item is old or new (see Table 10.1). In the forced choice procedure, two (or more) items are presented, and the subject has to indicate which one item was an old item. The new items in either test are referred to as distractors or lures.

Although the yes-no method might appear simple, it raises a very complicated issue. Subjects respond by indicating whether the item is old or new, and the test item can be old or new. This means that they can make two types of correct responses and two types of incorrect responses.

Imagine a situation in which you are given a yes-no recognition test. The experimenter tells you that you will receive $1 for every hit (responding "old" when the item is old) and will be penalized only 1 cent for every false alarm (responding "old" when the item is new). You are likely to respond old on almost every trial simply to maximize the amount of money. Imagine the reverse situation, where you are penalized $1 for every false alarm and rewarded with 1 cent for every hit. Now, you are likely to respond "new" on almost every trial to minimize your financial loss. Although extreme, these cases illustrate the large role that response bias can play in altering subjects' behavior, which is independent of their actual ability to tell whether an item is old or new (discrimination). There have been many different ways of trying to correct for guessing in the yes-no procedure, but the most common is to apply ideas from signal detection theory (Green & Swets, 1966).

# Signal Detection Theory

*Signal detection theory* was initially developed to examine performance in perception experiments where the subject's task was to detect the presence of a signal (a tone, for example) when presented against a background of noise. The two possible situations are noise only

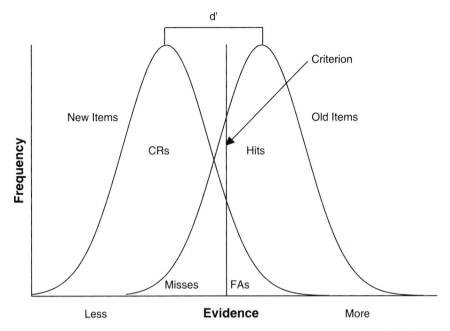

**Figure 10.1** Signal detection theory as applied to yes-no recognition memory. The subject evaluates the evidence supporting the idea that the item is old or new. Old items are assumed to appear more familiar, on average, than new items, although there will often be some overlap. The distance between the means of these distributions is $d'$, a measure of discriminability. The subject adopts a criterion, and items with more familiarity will be judged "old" (a "yes" response), whereas items with less familiarity will be judged "new" (a "no" response). Items that fall to the right of the criterion but are from the New Item distribution are false alarms. Items that fall to the left of the criterion but are from the Old Item distribution are misses.

or signal and noise. According to signal detection theory, the subject's response will be based partly on true ability to discriminate signal plus noise from noise only, and partly on response bias. This is also the situation confronting smoke detectors. There will always be some smoke particles in the air (perhaps from slightly burned toast or accumulated dust on a powerful lamp), but the important decision concerns whether this smoke is of sufficient concentration to indicate an important fire. The detector must be sensitive enough to detect smoke (detect that there are smoke particles), but it must also decide whether the smoke particles detected constitute an actual fire.

When applied to recognition, signal detection theory assumes that old and new items differ in how familiar they appear to the subject. The average new item will appear less familiar than the average old item because the old items have been processed more recently. If we could somehow assess the familiarity of all the old items for a particular subject and plot the number of items at each level of familiarity, we would end up with a distribution like the one shown in Figure 10.1 labeled "Old Items." If we did the same thing for all of the distractor or lure items, we would get the distribution labeled "New Items" in Figure 10.1. The difference between the averages of these two distributions is called $d'$ (pronounced "dee prime") and is the measure of bias-free discriminability. If old and new items

**Table 10.2**   Sample $d'$ values for different hit and false alarm rates. $p(\mathrm{H})$ is the probability of a hit, $p(\mathrm{FA})$ is the probability of a false alarm, $Zsn$ is the $z$-score corresponding to 1 minus the hit rate (or signal + noise), $Zn$ is the $z$-score corresponding to 1 minus the false alarm rate (or noise). $d'$ is $Zn - Zsn$ and $C$ is $0.5 \times (Zn + Zsn)$.

| $p(\mathrm{H})$ | $p(\mathrm{FA})$ | $Zsn$ | $Zn$ | $d'$ | $C$ |
|---|---|---|---|---|---|
| 0.90 | 0.90 | −1.282 | −1.282 | 0.00 | −1.282 |
| 0.90 | 0.70 | −1.282 | −0.524 | 0.76 | −0.904 |
| 0.90 | 0.02 | −1.282 | 2.054 | 3.34 | 0.384 |
| 0.50 | 0.02 | 0.000 | 2.054 | 2.05 | 1.029 |

appear equally familiar, then the difference between the means of the distributions will be 0. A $d'$ of 0, then, represents the case where the distributions overlap and the subject cannot tell the difference. The more familiar the old items are relative to the new items, the greater the difference between the distributions and the larger $d'$. Typically, values of between 1 and 2 usually represent good yes-no recognition performance.

If an experimenter uses a yes-no recognition test and reports only the proportion of items correctly recognized as old (hits), there is no way to assess the performance of the subjects. Table 10.2 illustrates why this is the case. The first three rows all have hit rates of 90%, but $d'$ ranges from 0 to 0.76 to 3.34. A $d'$ of 0 means the subjects could not discriminate between old and new items, even though the hit rate is near perfect. Why is this the case? Because the false alarm rate is varying also. The last row shows how a hit rate of 50% can mean better discriminability than a hit rate of 90% when different false alarm rates are taken into account. The measure of response bias when applying signal detection theory to recognition memory is $C$ (see Snodgrass & Corwin, 1988, for why $C$ is preferred to $\beta$). A value greater than 0 indicates a conservative response bias, a tendency to respond "new" more often than "old." A value less than 0 indicates a liberal bias — a tendency to respond "old" more often than "new." A well-analyzed study of yes-no recognition memory will present both the hit and the false alarm rates, a measure of discriminability ($d'$), and a measure of response bias ($C$). If there are hit or false alarm rates of 1 or 0, there is a standard correction so that $d'$ and $C$ may still be calculated (see Snodgrass & Corwin, 1988).

Signal detection theory is not the only way of analyzing data from yes-no recognition tasks. $A'$ is a nonparametric analog of $d'$ (Pollack & Norman, 1964) and has been shown to be highly correlated with $d'$ (Snodgrass, Volvovitz, & Walfish, 1972). It ranges from 0 to 1, with 0.5 reflecting chance performance. Because of the way it is calculated, it allows analysis of data from subjects who have hit or false alarm rates of 0, and it also does not require homogenous variance. Snodgrass, Levy-Berger, and Haydon (1985) show how to calculate $A'$. The appropriate measure of bias for $A'$ is $B''_D$. This measure ranges from −1 to +1 with 0 indicating no bias; a positive number indicates a conservative bias (see Donaldson, 1992).

A third method is generally referred to as the two-high-threshold model (see Feenan & Snodgrass, 1990). The name comes from the idea that there is a threshold for old items and a threshold for new items (hence "two thresholds"), and only items that

**Experiment**    Recognition and Signal Detection Theory

**Purpose:** To demonstrate the use of signal detection theory in analyzing yes-no recognition tests.

**Subjects:** Thirty subjects are recommended; 10 should be assigned to the neutral condition, 10 to the conservative condition, and 10 to the liberal condition. Subject 1 should be in the neutral condition, Subject 2 in the conservative condition, Subject 3 in the liberal condition, Subject 4 in the neutral condition, and so on.

**Materials:** Table C in the Appendix contains a list of 96 two-syllable words randomly drawn from the Toronto word pool. For each subject, construct a list of 48 words in random order. The answer sheet should have all 96 words (in random order) followed by OLD and NEW.

**Procedure:** For each group, read the first set of instructions, followed by the list of 48 words to the subject at a rate of approximately 1 word every 2 seconds. At the end of the list, read the instructions appropriate for each group. Give subjects the prepared answer sheet and have them circle either OLD or NEW for each item.

**Instructions for All Groups:** "I will read you a long list of words. After I have finished reading the words, I will give you a memory test. I will tell you more about the test after I have read the words."

**Instructions for the Neutral Group:** "On the answer sheet, you will see a list of 96 words. Half of these words came from the list I just read, and half are new words. I would like you to circle OLD or NEW beside each word to indicate if it was on the list. Because half of the words are new, if you are unsure of your response, it is no better to guess OLD than to guess NEW because each response is equally likely to be correct. Any questions?"

**Instructions for the Conservative Group:** "On the answer sheet, you will see a list of 96 words; 25% of these words came from the list I just read, and 75% are new words. I would like you to circle OLD or NEW beside each word to indicate if it was on the list. Because 75% of the words are NEW, if you are unsure of your response, it is better to guess NEW than to guess OLD because you will be more likely to be correct. Any questions?"

**Instructions for the Liberal Group:** "On the answer sheet, you will see a list of 96 words; 75% of these words came from the list I just read, and 25% are new words. I would like you to circle OLD or NEW beside each word to indicate if it was on the list. Because 75% of the words are OLD, if you are unsure of your response, it is better to guess OLD than to guess NEW because you will be more likely to be correct. Any questions?"

**Scoring and Analysis:** For each list, count the number of times an old pair was judged to be old (hits) and the number of times a new pair was judged to be old (false alarms). $d'$ is easy to calculate, particularly if you have access to a spreadsheet program such as Micro-Soft® Excel™. $d' = Zn - Zsn$, where $Zn$ is the $z$-score of $1$ − the probability of a false alarm, and $Zsn$ is the $z$-score for $1$ − the probability of a hit. In Excel, if the proportion of hits is in cell A1, the formula for $Zsn$ is NORMINV(1-A1,0,1). If the proportion of false alarms is in cell B1, the formula for $Zn$ is NORMINV(1-B1,0,1). $C = 0.5$ $(Zn + Zsn)$. If Excel or other equivalent software is not available, many books (e.g., Snodgrass, Levy-Berger, & Haydon, 1985) contain tables of $z$ scores from which both $d'$ and $C$ can easily be calculated.

**Optional Enhancements:** Include more subjects in each condition and collect a measure of confidence. For each item, after the old/new judgment, have the subject write down a number from 1 to 6 to indicate confidence. A 1 means very low confidence, a 6 means very high confidence.

Source: Based on an experiment by Knoedler (1996).

exceed the threshold will be recognized (hence "high"). The discrimination measure is $Pr$, also known as the corrected recognition score. It is simply the difference between the hit and false alarm rates. $Br$ is the bias measure, and is the false alarm rate divided by 1 minus $Pr$. A value of $Br$ greater than 0.5 indicates a liberal response bias, and a value less than 0.5 indicates a conservative response bias.

Feenan and Snodgrass (1990) recommend reporting not only hit and false alarm rates and $d'$ and $C$, but also $Pr$ and $Br$. They demonstrate that some effects are observable in only a subset of these measures (see also Knoedler, 1996). For example, in their Experiment 1, subjects saw line drawings and were then given a recognition test in either the same context or a different context. The hit rate was larger when the pictures were tested in the same context compared to when they were tested in a different context, but there was no difference in the false alarm rates. Similarly, there was a difference in the $Pr$ measure of discrimination but not in $d'$. Both measures of bias, however, revealed a large and statistically significant effect of changing the context: with a different context, subjects responded more conservatively than when the test context was the same as the study context. Although it is better to report a complete analysis, for many of the studies reported in this section, we will focus on only one measure to make the presentation more concise.

# Single Process Models of Recognition

Early theories of recognition were of a class known as *single process models*. For example, Yntema and Trask (1963) proposed a tagging model of recall and recognition in which each item is tagged when it occurs. To determine whether a word had been presented on a list, the subject would examine the word in generic memory and look to see whether there is a tag. The tag encodes not only the mere fact of presentation but also the relative time of occurrence. This view explains why people are very accurate at judging which of two words occurred first (Yntema & Trask, 1963), because all that needs to be done is to examine the tags. It also explains why distractor words that are similar to target words are often incorrectly labeled "old" (Anisfeld & Knapp, 1968). For example, seeing the word *beach* might make the subject think of *ocean,* and *ocean* gets tagged along with *beach*.

A second type of single process model was strength theory (Bahrick, 1970; Wickelgren & Norman, 1966). The basic idea was that the more recently a particular item was experienced, the stronger or more familiar it seemed. Strength could be used as the dimension along a signal-detection type analysis.

The key limitation in both of these models is that they contain only a single process. With only a single mechanism, the same manipulation has to have the same effect; there is no provision for different processes. Evidence inconsistent with both of these views comes from studies that report different effects of one manipulation depending on whether the test is recall or recognition.

Eagle and Leiter (1964) presented subjects with a list of 36 words and told them they would have to remember the words. This was the intentional learning condition. Subjects recalled 15.2 words and recognized 23.7 words. In the incidental learning condition, a different group of subjects was given the same 36 words and told to classify the words based on part of speech. When a surprise memory test was given, the subjects recalled only 11.4 words and recognized 27.0 words. The key result, shown in Figure 10.2, is that recall is higher when intentional instructions are given than when incidental instructions

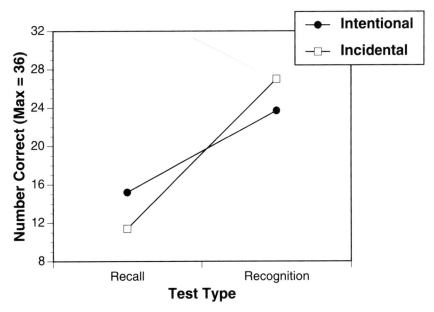

**Figure 10.2**   The interaction between learning instructions (intentional versus incidental) and test type (free recall or recognition).   Source: Eagle & Leiter (1964).

are given (15.2 versus 11.4), but the opposite is true for recognition: performance is better when incidental instructions are given than when intentional instructions are given (23.7 versus 27.0). Estes and Da Polito (1967) have found similar results. One reason may be that when intentional instructions are given, subjects can engage in appropriate strategies to organize the material, and organization has larger benefits for recall than recognition does (Kintsch, 1970; Mandler, 1967; see also Hunt & Einstein, 1981).

A second result of interest is the differential effect of word frequency. High-frequency words are recalled better than low-frequency words are, but low-frequency words are recognized more accurately than are high-frequency words (Deese, 1961; Gregg, 1976; Hall, 1954). Word frequency is normally expressed as the number of times the word is likely to be encountered per million words. This is computed by counting the number of occurrences in several different kinds of written documents (such as newspapers, novels, and magazines). Kinsbourne and George (1974) presented subjects with a 16-item list of words that were either of high frequency (words that occurred no fewer than 200 times per million) or of low frequency (words that occurred no more than 15 times per million). Half of the subjects received a free recall test, and half received a recognition test; the results are shown in Figure 10.3. More high-frequency words were recalled than low-frequency words were, but more low-frequency words were recognized than high-frequency words were.

Neither single process model can account for these results. Because there is only a single process, a manipulation such as word frequency or intentionality must have the same effect on both recall and recognition. To overcome the limitations of single-process models, researchers quickly developed a class of two-stage models known as generate-recognize models.

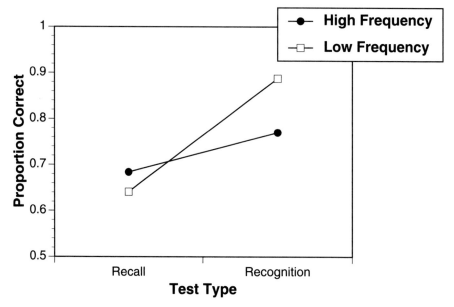

**Figure 10.3**   The word-frequency effect in recall and recognition.   Source: Based on data from Kinsbourne & George (1974).

# Generate-Recognize Models

Single process models were quickly replaced by a class of two-stage models collectively known as *generate-recognize models* (Anderson & Bower, 1972; Bahrick, 1970; Kintsch, 1970). According to these models, recall is made up of two processes whereas recognition is made up of only one. In a free recall test, subjects must first generate a set of plausible candidates for recall. Once the set is generated, the subject then has to confirm whether each word is worthy of being recalled. (It is unfortunate that the second stage is called "recognition," which leads to confusion with a recognition test.) In a recognition test, the subject does not need the generation stage; the experimenter has provided the candidate. All that is left is the confirmation or recognition stage.

How would such a model explain the two findings mentioned above? Anderson and Bower's (1973) version, called HAM (human associative memory), begins with the assumption that words are stored in an associative network of nodes (see Chapter 12). Each node represents both a word and the concept represented by the word, and the nodes are connected by pathways to related nodes. As each word is presented, the node gets tagged with a contextual marker. Contextual markers contain information about salient stimuli that occurred; for example, a clock could be ticking, a door could slam, a siren could be heard, and so forth. If one word is associated with another word, the pathway can also be tagged. This is a little like Hansel and Gretel: as they went through the forest, they left bread crumbs to mark their passage, with the hopes of retracing their steps. At recall, the subject follows the contextual markers to generate a set of plausible candidates.

The second stage, recognition, examines the number of associations between the target word and the context associated with the particular list. If there is sufficient contextual evidence, the subject is willing to say "old." If there is not sufficient evidence, the subject will say "new." Thus, the signal-detection analysis shown in Figure 10.1 is again applicable; recall will be enhanced to the extent that there is a rich network and that lots of pathways have been tagged, and recognition will be enhanced to the extent that individual words are associated with particular contextual elements.

The intentional/incidental learning dissociation is easily explained. When learning is incidental, the subject does not associate words in the list with each other because there is no reason to do so; this will hurt recall during the generation stage. However, because the subject focuses entirely on one word at a time, there will be a strong association between the word and the contextual elements; this will help recognition. When learning is intentional, most subjects will adopt a strategy of associating each word in the list with other words. According to HAM, this will set up a richly marked network with lots of pathways tagged and will facilitate generation. This helps recall. Because the subject focuses on associating words with each other, this will result in only weak associations between a given word and context; this will hurt recognition.

A similar analysis explains the word-frequency effect. High-frequency words tend to have more associates and thus more pathways. Subjects should be able to find a shorter, more direct path between the nodes for a given list of short items. Low-frequency words, on the other hand, have fewer associates and can take longer to read. This makes it less likely that a short path can be obtained and so hurts recall. However, because many low-frequency words are unusual looking, they can take longer to process and thus lead to more item-context associations; this helps recognition. Indeed, the more unusual looking the word, the better the recognition of the item (Zechmeister, 1972).

There is one major problem with most versions of generate-recognize models: they require that if a word can be recalled, it must also be recognized (Watkins & Gardiner, 1979). Because the second stage is the stage that both recall and recognition have in common, a successful outcome at this stage in one test means a successful outcome at this stage for the other test. The reason a word can often be recognized when it is not recalled is due to the extra preliminary stage on a test of recall: even though it was not generated, it was capable of being recognized. For example, you may not be able to recall the name of the actor who starred in one of your favorite films, but as soon as someone suggests the name, you can accurately recognize it. Thus, recall failure of recognizable words is quite common. Tulving and his colleagues (Tulving & Thomson, 1973; Watkins & Tulving, 1975) have demonstrated a phenomenon known as *recognition failure of recallable words*. That is, contrary to the prediction of generate-recognize models, a word can be recalled even though it cannot be recognized.

The procedure used by Watkins and Tulving (1975) is shown in Table 10.3 (but simplified a little). The first two steps consist of a traditional paired-associate task, where the task is to recall the second word given the first word as a cue. In Step 3, the critical list is presented, but note that it is not immediately tested. The important aspect of Step 3 is that the cue word is a weak associate of the target words (see Chapter 6). In Step 4, the subject is given a free association test, where the subjects generate as many associates as they can think of to a target word. This target word (TABLE) is a strong associate of the target word in the previous step (CHAIR), and so the subject usually provides the response term

**Table 10.3**   One procedure used to demonstrate recognition failure (step 5b) of recallable (step 6) words.

| Step | Procedure | Example |
|------|-----------|---------|
| 1a | List 1 presented | *badge*-BUTTON |
| 1b | Cued recall of List 1 | *badge*-<u>button</u> |
| 2a | List 2 presented | *preach*-RANT |
| 2b | Cued recall of List 2 | *preach*-<u>rant</u> |
| 3 | List 3 presented | *glue*-CHAIR |
| 4a | Free association stimuli presented | table |
| 4b | Free association responses made | table <u>chair</u> <u>cloth</u> <u>desk</u> <u>dinner</u> |
| 5a | Recognition test sheets presented | DESK   TOP   CHAIR |
| 5b | Recognized items circled | (DESK)   TOP   CHAIR |
| 6 | Cued recall of List 3 | *glue*-<u>CHAIR</u> |

Source: Based on Watkins & Tulving (1975).

from Step 3. In Step 5, the subject is given a forced-choice recognition test; this is where recognition failure can occur. The final step is the cued-recall test for the list presented in Step 3. This is where the subject produces the word that could not be recognized in the previous step. Watkins and Tulving (1975) found that 49% of the recalled items were not recognized. In Experiments 2 through 6, this value varied from a low of 16% to a high of 62%. They also determined, by using various techniques, that "the hocus pocus procedures of the early experiments turned out not to have been necessary to produce the phenomenon of recognition failure of recallable words" (p. 26).

There are many variations on this procedure, and more will be said about its interpretation in Chapter 11. However, based on the encoding specificity idea presented in Chapter 6, the explanation is quite straightforward. Contrary to the fundamental assumption of generate-recognize theory, recognition and recall *both* depend on the cues available at test. In the situation concocted by Watkins and Tulving, the cues available at test were better in the recall test than in the recognition test. Recognition is not easier than recall, and recall is not easier than recognition; performance on each test depends upon the cues available.

## Beyond Simple Generate-Recognize

One change that can be made to a simple generate-recognize model to allow it to account for recognition failure of recallable words is to have a search process occur during the recognition phase. For example, it is possible to have the same search and confirmation process operate in both recognition and recall (Jacoby & Hollingshead, 1990). The main problem with this approach is that subjects can very quickly and with a great deal of confidence correctly say that an item was not presented (Atkinson & Juola, 1974). Given the speed and confidence with which subjects reject an item, it seems unlikely that an extensive search of memory occurs every time.

Several researchers have suggested a process whereby recognition can utilize a search but can also rely on a simple familiarity process (Atkinson & Juola, 1973; Mandler, 1980). The idea is that a measure of familiarity is instantly computed. If this value is very large, then the subject gives a very rapid "old" response. If this value is very low, then the subject gives a very rapid "new" response. It is only for the intermediate familiarity values that a search takes place. A fundamental assumption is that the process to assess familiarity is faster than the search process.

Mandler (1980) is careful to distinguish two types of recognition judgments: simple recognition, in which a judgment of prior occurrence is made, and identification. The former process may be accomplished solely by an evaluation of the familiarity of the item, but the latter requires both familiarity and retrieval. Familiarity is related to the ease of processing the item: the more recently the item has been perceived, the easier it is to perceive the item at test. Both processes, familiarity and retrieval, are assumed to be initiated simultaneously. Although not directly applied to the recognition-failure-of-recallable-words paradigm, Mandler's (1980) model has mechanisms that should allow it to produce the appropriate pattern. In the procedure detailed in Table 10.4, there is a relatively long delay between learning and the recognition test. This delay could lower the feelings of familiarity until they fall into the intermediate range, and performance must then rely more on the retrieval component. Because the target word in the recognition test is presented in a different context than the study context, the retrieval phase is presented with inappropriate cues. The recall test (Step 6) provides appropriate cues, and so the retrieval process will succeed. Note that this idea is similar to the encoding specificity idea presented in Chapter 6.

Mandler (1980) did report a simulation of a study of recognition that supports the above analysis. Subjects studied word pairs and then received a variety of tests. For example, a subject would study the pair A-B, and then recognition would be assessed when just A was presented, when just B was presented, and when both A and B were presented. According to the analysis outlined above, performance will be better for the A-B items than for either A or B individually. This is exactly what Table 10.4 shows. In particular, notice that whereas both the hit rate and false alarm rate improve when both A and B are presented for test, there is a larger difference in the false alarm rate. The results are nicely

**Table 10.4**  Observed and predicted hit rate and false alarm rate for word pairs.

| Items | Hits | | False Alarms | |
|-------|----------|-----------|----------|-----------|
|       | Observed | Predicted | Observed | Predicted |
| A  | 0.76 | 0.79 | 0.18 | 0.23 |
| B  | 0.77 | 0.79 | 0.23 | 0.22 |
| AB | 0.86 | 0.81 | 0.06 | 0.04 |

Source: Mandler (1980).

predicted by the model. The single A and B items are being tested in a new context, and so performance is worse than when tested in the old context (both items together).

Given the success on the recognition component, Mandler (1980) looked at recognition performance of B when B has been either recalled or not recalled (using data from Rabinowitz, Mandler, & Barsalou, 1977). According to the analysis presented above, the familiarity values for recognizing B should be relatively constant and in the intermediate range. This will cause more reliance on the retrieval component. When B was recalled, it was correctly recognized with a probability of 0.69; when B was not recalled, it was recognized with a probability of 0.41. Despite this large difference, the estimates of the familiarity component were identical and were in the intermediate range: 0.40 and 0.39, respectively. A combination of familiarity and retrieval, then, can produce the recognition-failure-of-recallable-words result.

Gillund and Shiffrin (1984) conducted three experiments to test the assumption that both familiarity and a search process are important. The basic idea was to force subjects to respond very quickly or to make them wait a while. Thus, the average response time in the fast response condition was approximately 500 ms, compared to 2.5 to 3 s in the slow condition. In the fast condition, subjects should be relying more on the familiarity process, whereas in the slow condition, they should be relying more on the search process. Gillund and Shiffrin reported two main results. First, and not surprisingly, subjects were more accurate in the slow condition than in the fast condition. Second, and more important, there were no other differences between slow and fast responses. To the extent that the two processes are different, Gillund and Shiffrin argued, there should have been some interactions. Because they did not observe any interactions, they argued that a search process for recognition was not required and that recognition could be based solely on familiarity.

Current models of recognition are part of the so-called global memory models, such as SAM (Gillund & Shiffrin, 1984), MINERVA 2 (Hintzman, 1988), and TODAM (Murdock, 1982). These models, along with a connectionist model of recognition, are presented in the next chapter. Interestingly, however, the type of view suggested by Mandler (1980) may make a comeback of sorts: the two mechanisms he suggested accord nicely with results from a relatively new paradigm.

## Remember versus Know

One relatively recent change in recognition methodology concerns the *remember-know procedure* (Gardiner, 1988; Tulving, 1985), although the ideas behind it were well articulated by Mandler (1980). In this procedure, subjects are given a recognition test and are asked to indicate whether they actually remember the information (have a conscious recollection of the information's occurrence on the study list) or just somehow know the answer (know that the item was on the list but have no conscious recollection of its actual occurrence). In Tulving's (1985) study, the first using remember-know methodology, subjects studied pairs of words where the second word was a member of the category indicated by the first word, such as *musical instrument–viola.* The subjects then received a standard free recall test, and then a cued-recall test with the category name as a cue, and finally a cued-recall test with the category name as a cue plus the first letter of the target item. The proportion of "remember" judgments decreased over the three kinds of tests and also decreased with increasing retention interval, relative to overall recognition performance.

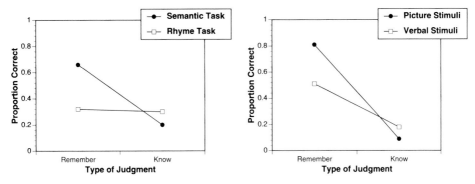

**Figure 10.4**  Two differences between remember and know judgments. The left panel shows the basic level of processing effect, and the right panel shows the picture superiority effect but only for remember judgments.   Source: Based on data from Rajaram (1993).

Several other variables have been found that have different effects on remember compared to know responses, most of which have been reported by Gardiner and his colleagues. Gardiner (1988) found a levels of processing (Chapter 6) effect on remember judgments but not on know judgments, and also found a generation effect (Chapter 7) for remember judgments but not for know judgments. Gardiner and Java (1990) found the standard better recognition of low-frequency than high-frequency words for remember judgments but not for know judgments. Gardiner and Parkin (1990) had subjects engage in a secondary task during study and found that this divided attention manipulation disrupted remember judgments but not know judgments. And Gardiner and Java (1991) have also shown that performance as assessed by remember judgments decreases more quickly over a 6-month period than does performance on know judgments.

As an explanation, Gardiner (Gardiner & Parkin, 1990; Gardiner & Java, 1993) has suggested that remember judgments are influenced by conceptual and attentional factors, whereas know judgments are not; rather, they are possibly based on a procedural memory system, much like Schacter's (1994) PRS. This distinction sounds much like that between factors that affect explicit memory and those that affect implicit memory (see Chapter 8).

Rajaram (1993) reported a series of experiments that examined remember-know judgments in more detail. Her first experiment replicated Gardiner's (1988) findings in that there was a large level of processing effect on remember judgments but no effect (if anything, a slight reversal) on know judgments (see the left panel of Figure 10.4). Her second experiment involved showing either pictures or words at study and just words at test. The task was to say whether either the word or the picture named were seen previously. The standard picture superiority effect (Madigan, 1983) was observed for remember judgments: performance was better for pictures than for words. However, there was again a reversal for know judgments: words were better than pictures (see right panel of Figure 10.4). Although this is consistent with the idea that remember judgments are based on the explicit system and know judgments are based on implicit memory, it is also consistent with the idea that remember judgments may depend more on recollective processes whereas know judgments are based more on familiarity.

Rajaram's (1993) final experiments compared know judgments to judgments of confidence. In addition to remember and know judgments, Rajaram had subjects categorize the items they had responded to with "old" in terms of whether they were sure or not sure. She again found a difference between remember and know judgments, but, importantly, there was no difference in terms of confidence ratings. This suggests that know judgments are not based solely on the perceived confidence of the subject.

There are three current accounts of the remember-know data. The first emphasizes the similarity between remember judgments and episodic memory and between know judgments and procedural or implicit memory (Gardiner & Parkin, 1990). A second emphasizes Mandler's (1980) distinction between two different aspects of recognition but refines the idea to encompass areas other than just recognition (see Rajaram, 1993). A third view emphasizes the process dissociation framework of Jacoby (Yonelinas & Jacoby, 1995; see Chapter 6). These views may not be mutually exclusive, and further work is needed to refine the ideas involved. However, this line of research promises to be an interesting exploration of how consciousness and awareness interact with memory.

## The Mirror Effect

One aspect of recognition that has received much attention in recent years is the mirror effect (Brown, Lewis, & Monk, 1977; Glanzer & Adams, 1985). In its most simple form, the mirror effect describes a regularity when examining performance on a variety of different kinds of recognition tests (such as yes-no, forced choice, multiple choice, rating scale). A mirror effect is observed when "The type of stimulus that is accurately recognized as old when old is also accurately recognized as new when new. The type that is poorly recognized as old when old is also poorly recognized as new when new" (Glanzer & Adams, 1985, p. 8).

One example of a mirror effect concerns the effect of word frequency on recognition memory. Generally, low-frequency words are recognized more accurately than high-frequency words are (see above). However, word frequency also shows a mirror effect. Both of these effects can be seen in the data shown in Table 10.5. Rao and Proctor (1984) had subjects see a list of 120 words and then presented a recognition test of 240 words. The

**Table 10.5**   The mirror effect (higher hit rates and lower false alarm rates in low-frequency than high-frequency words) and the word-frequency effect in recognition.

|  | Word Frequency | |
| --- | --- | --- |
|  | High | Low |
| Hits | 27.84 | 31.00 |
| False Alarms | 10.20 | 7.63 |
| $d'$ | 1.36 | 1.88 |

Source: Based on data from Rao & Proctor (1984).

**Table 10.6**   The number of reports (separate studies or, in the case of the pictures versus words, separate experiments) found that meet the criteria and the number that show a mirror effect.

| Variable | Number of Reports | Number Showing a Mirror Effect |
|---|---|---|
| Word Frequency | 24 | 23 |
| Concreteness | 9 | 8 |
| Meaningfulness | 13 | 9 |
| Pictures vs. Words | 8 | 6 |
| Miscellaneous | 26 | 17 |
| Total | 80 | 63 |

Source:  Glanzer & Adams (1985).

mirror effect can be seen clearly in their data: the number of hits was *higher* for the low-frequency words than for the high-frequency words, and at the same time the number of false alarms was *lower* for the low-frequency compared to the high-frequency words. The standard word-frequency effect can be seen in the larger $d'$ value for the low- compared to the high-frequency words.

One reason this finding has attracted a great deal of attention is that the mirror effect seems pervasive. In their initial review, Glanzer and Adams (1985) reviewed all the published recognition studies they could find in which (1) a within-subjects design was used in which two (or more) levels of the variable were assessed and (2) the authors reported sufficient data (hit rates and false alarm rates for each stimulus class) to make the study useful. The results are shown in Table 10.6.

The one notable departure from the mirror effect comes from studies in the miscellaneous category that looked at recognition for normal as opposed to transformed text. With the transformed text studies removed, the number of mirror effects observed becomes 17 out of 22. Another possible exception is rare words (Wixted, 1992). Since the initial report, many studies have demonstrated mirror effects with other types of stimuli, including frequency discrimination (Greene & Thapar, 1994), associative information (Hockley, 1994), presentation rate (Ratcliff, Sheu, & Gronlund, 1992), age of the subject (Bäckman, 1991), and recency (Glanzer, Adams, & Iverson, 1991). It can also be seen with incidental learning (Glanzer & Adams, 1990) and when latency rather than accuracy is used as the response (Hockley, 1994). Even though they were excluded from the survey, experiments that use between-subject designs also show the mirror effect (Glanzer & Adams, 1985).

Having established the generality of the mirror effect, the next question is whether this effect is important or trivial. It could be the case that the mirror effect is an artifact of the way recognition data is analyzed. For example, there is a "mirror effect" that occurs between false alarm rates and the correct rejection rates. As false alarm rates increase, correct rejection rates decrease. This is an uninteresting mirror effect, however, because the false alarm rate and the correct rejection rate *must* add to 1.0 (see Table 10.1). Is this the case for the mirror effect between hit rates and false alarm rates?

The consensus is that the mirror effect is not an artifact (Glanzer & Adams, 1985; Hintzman, Caulton, & Curran, 1994). One reason for this conclusion is that hit rates and

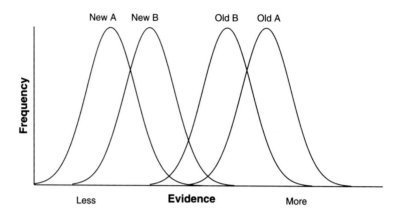

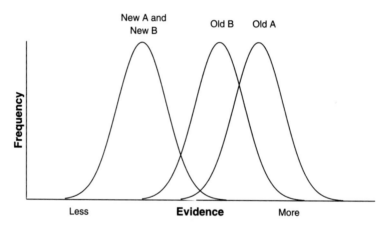

**Figure 10.5** The top panel shows the required ordering of the four distributions of A and B stimuli according to signal detection theory if the mirror effect is to be seen. The bottom panel shows the most likely ordering of the distributions, where unstudied (new) items are unlikely to differ. Source: Adapted from Glanzer & Adams (1985).

false alarm rates can, in theory, vary independently; for any given hit rate, the false alarm rate can still be anywhere between 0.0 and 1.0. In the example in the preceding paragraph, false alarm and correct rejection rates cannot vary independently; if the false alarm rate is 0.2, then the correct rejection rate will be 0.8. A second reason is that the actual pattern is not what is most likely. Let A represent a stimulus class in which old items are called "old" more often than B items, and also in which new items are called "new" more often than B items. To see a mirror effect, the distributions of these items needs to be ordered such that New A < New B < Old B < Old A. This is shown graphically in the top panel of Figure 10.5. Note that this is not the only possible ordering: it is possible that all old items would share a distribution, or that all new items would share a distribution. In fact, given that none of the new items have been studied, the most reasonable pattern is that the New A and New B distributions overlap, as shown in the bottom panel of Figure 10.5. However, the mirror effect is clearly the rule and not the exception.

Given that the mirror effect is both general and important, another important issue concerns its relationship to theories of recognition. The mirror effect clearly eliminates from contention all theories of recognition based on a unidimensional conception of strength or familiarity (Brown, Lewis, & Monk, 1977; Glanzer & Adams, 1985, 1990; Hintzman, Caulton, & Curran, 1994). In other words, the models of recognition described in the next chapter (SAM, MINERVA 2, and TODAM), which all rely on a unidimensional conception of familiarity, cannot explain all instances of the mirror effect. Currently, it is unclear whether these models can be modified to account for the mirror effect, whether a two-dimensional construct of familiarity is required, or whether a new type of theory is required (Glanzer, Adams, Iverson, & Kim, 1993; Hintzman, Caulton, & Curran, 1994). Whatever the outcome, the mirror effect will play a large role in theory development in the future.

# Face Recognition

Face recognition needs to be distinguished from face identification, a more difficult task. *Face identification* is being able to supply the name (and perhaps other details) that goes with a particular face, a form of paired-associate learning. *Face recognition,* on the other hand, is deciding whether a particular face has been seen before. Bahrick (1984) reported a study in which college teachers were asked to both identify and recognize faces of former students. One variable of particular interest was the retention interval—the time since the semester ended in which the student was in class. Bahrick's results are shown in Table 10.7. Face identification was consistently less accurate than face recognition.

It turns out that people make an extraordinary number of face identification and face recognition errors. Young, Hay, and Ellis (1985) had 22 subjects keep track of all of the errors they made recognizing and identifying people over an 8-week period. They reported 1008 errors, nearly 6 errors per day per subject. Of these, 114 were failures to recognize a person. Subjects rely heavily on physical features to recognize people—especially hair, forehead, eyes, and nose (Ellis, 1975)—and when these features change, recognition can fail. A second common error was mistakenly identifying one person as another; there were 314 such incidents, the most common being thinking an unfamiliar person is a familiar one. A third common error (233 reports) involved recognizing a person

**Table 10.7** Percent correct recognition and identification of students' faces by their college teachers.

|                | 11 Days | 1 Year | 4 Years | 8 Years |
|----------------|---------|--------|---------|---------|
| Recognition    | 69.0    | 47.5   | 31.0    | 26.0    |
| Identification | 35.5    | 6.0    | 2.5     | 0.0     |

Source: Based on data from Bahrick (1984).

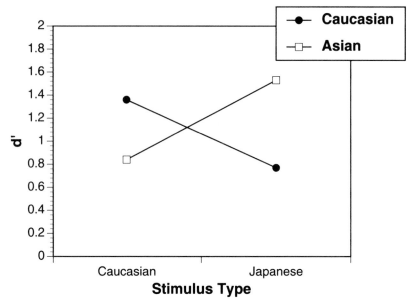

**Figure 10.6**   Accuracy (measured by $d'$) in recognizing Caucasian or Japanese faces as a function of the subject's race.   Source:   O'Toole, Deffenbacher, Valentin, & Abdi (1994).

but failing to identify the person (as opposed to incorrectly identifying the person). These errors typically involved a slight acquaintance in a novel context, such as meeting your dentist in the grocery store. The fourth common error (190 incidents) was failing to recall the name of a person. In most cases, other information such as occupation was nearly always recalled. This finding, the so-called name effect, has been replicated: McWeeny, Young, Hay, and Ellis (1987) found that it took subjects longer to provide a name than an occupation. One nice control in this study was that the names and occupations were the same; for example, one face would be described as Mr. Baker, whereas a different face would be described as that of a baker. It was easier to say the occupation "baker" than the name "Baker."

Faces of people of the same race as the subject tend to be recognized slightly more accurately than are faces of people from different races. For example, O'Toole, Deffenbacher, Valentin, and Abdi (1994) had a group of Caucasian subjects and a group of Asian subjects study Caucasian and Japanese faces. They performed a signal detection analysis on the recognition data, which is shown in Figure 10.6. Caucasian subjects recognized Caucasian faces more accurately than they did Japanese faces, whereas Asian subjects recognized Japanese faces more accurately than they did Caucasian faces. Similar conclusions have been reached by Valentine and Endo (1992) and Vokey and Read (1992).

Similar to the other-race effect just described is the *face-inversion effect*. If even a very familiar face is shown upside down, the probability of correctly identifying or recognizing the face drops precipitously (Yin, 1969; Valentine, 1988). This face-inversion effect has played a large role in the question of whether face recognition is a special process (see below). A face does not have to be shown rotated a full 180° to see a decrease in performance. A change in orientation of 45° (such as full face to three-quarter view) reliably impairs performance, and a change of 90° (full face to profile) results in even worse performance (Baddeley & Woodhead, 1983).

As with words and other stimuli, a form of priming can be observed with faces. If two well-known faces that are associated with each other are presented one after the other, the second face is identified more quickly than if it were an unfamiliar face (Bruce & Valentine, 1986). Thus, presenting a picture of Abbott will make recognition of Costello faster than if Abbott were not presented. Interestingly, if subjects believe that a face they are looking at belongs to a criminal, then it is remembered more accurately (Honeck, 1986). The severity of the crime did not correlate with accuracy.

Two issues concerning face recognition and identification are how to explain the various phenomena and whether they involve a special process. Ellis and Young (1989) concluded that face recognition is special but not unique: faces are not the only stimuli to take advantage of it. The reasons Ellis and Young offer to support their view that face recognition is special are (1) that neonates show a preference for faces over nonfaces; (2) that face recognition has a different developmental history than other phenomena; (3) that faces are very difficult to identify upside down, the face-inversion effect; and (4) that there appears to be a special neural substrate that supports face recognition. Each of these factors will be discussed briefly.

The first line of evidence offered by Ellis and Young (1989) to support the conclusion that face recognition is special concerns the finding that newborn infants appear to display a preference for faces relative to nonfaces. However, the pattern of data is quite complicated. First, several studies show that face preference can disappear in infants at around 2 months of age, only to return a little later (see Maurer, 1985). Furthermore, other types of pictures show a similar privileged status; for example, infants may show a preference for pictures of normal over scrambled cars (Levine, 1989). Rather than arguing for specialness, this result could be seen as a general preference for coherence, or even for closed forms. A similar criticism has been offered against the second line of evidence: the special development history of face recognition. It turns out that this is not unique: both voice recognition and tonal memory have similar patterns of development (Carey & Diamond, 1980).

The third line of evidence concerned the face-inversion effect. Diamond and Carey (1986) suggested that expertise — or, more accurately, a lack of expertise — may explain the face-inversion effect. Subjects have a great deal of experience recognizing upright faces but almost no experience recognizing upside-down faces. Diamond and Carey used photographs of dogs as control stimuli for faces, and recruited experts in judging dogs. The dog experts showed a difference in recognizing upside-down from upright dogs, just as people show a difference in recognizing inverted from upright faces. The novices, people with little familiarity with particular dog breeds, did not show a difference. Similar explanations have been offered to explain the other race effect. Valentine (1988) also views face recognition as more a matter of expertise than as a special process. His conclusion comes from examining studies of inverted faces; rather than saying an upside-down face disrupts the special face recognition process, he argues that people have almost no experience with the task.

Ellis and Young's (1989) final point is that there appears to be some evidence of special neural substrates supporting face recognition. For example, the right hemisphere appears to be more involved in face recognition than the left, and several researchers have found cells in monkeys that respond only when the animal looks at faces. Furthermore, there is the phenomenon termed prosopagnosia, which refers to the inability to recognize familiar faces after certain brain injuries. As with the other points, this line of evidence is open to alternative explanations. For example, Levine, Banich, and Koch-Weser (1988) suggest that face recognition is not special but is similar to other tasks that tap particular processes situated in the right hemisphere. In one study, they found a similar pattern of localized neural responding when the stimuli were houses. As another example, Dalesbred sheep have cells that respond to faces of sheep, dogs, and humans (Kendrick & Baldwin, 1987); however, at least one set of cells responded to familiar Dalesbred sheep rather than to unfamiliar Dalesbred sheep. A familiarity or expertise argument could again account for these findings. (Oddly, human and dog faces were responded to by the same cells, although the interpretation of this is not clear.)

Although there is still debate over whether face recognition is special, there is little evidence to support the argument that face recognition is unique. Even such proponents as Ellis and Young think of it as only one of several special processes that have a similar set of properties. As more neurological evidence becomes available, there may be more consensus on the issue of how special face recognition is. In addition to advances in neurological study, analyses by several formal models of face recognition may also help. For example, a recent connectionist model has simulated the other-race effect based solely on the degree of experience with various kinds of faces (O'Toole et al., 1994). Similar existence proofs may be forthcoming from Bruce and Young's (1986) influential functional model, which has recently been implemented in a connectionist network (Burton, Bruce, & Johnston, 1990).

# References

Anderson, J. R., & Bower, G. H. (1972). Recognition and retrieval processes in free recall. *Psychological Review, 79,* 97–123.

Anderson, J. R., & Bower, G. H. (1973). *Human associative memory.* Washington, DC: Winston.

Anisfeld, M., & Knapp, M. (1968). Association, synonymity, and directionality in false recognition. *Journal of Experimental Psychology, 77,* 171–179.

Atkinson, R. C., & Juola, J. F. (1973). Factors influencing speed and accuracy of word recognition. In S. Kornblum (Ed.), *Attention and performance IV.* New York: Academic Press.

Atkinson, R. C., & Juola, J. F. (1974). Search and decision processes in recognition memory. In D. H. Krantz, R. C. Atkinson, R. D. Luce, & P. Suppes (Eds.), *Contemporary developments in mathematical psychology, Vol. 1.* San Francisco: Freeman.

Bach, M. J., & Underwood, B. J. (1970). Developmental changes in memory attributes. *Journal of Educational Psychology, 61,* 292–296.

Bäckman, L. (1991). Recognition memory across the adult life span: The role of prior knowledge. *Memory & Cognition, 19,* 63–71.

Baddeley, A. D., & Woodhead, M. (1983). Improving face recognition ability. In S. M. A. Lloyd-Bostock & B. R. Clifford (Eds.), *Evaluating witness evidence.* Chichester, UK: Wiley.

Bahrick, H. A. (1967). Decision processes in memory. *Psychological Review, 74,* 462–480.

Bahrick, H. A. (1970). Two-phase model for prompted recall. *Psychological Review, 77,* 215–222.

Bahrick, H. A. (1984). Memory for people. In J. E. Harris & P. E. Morris (Eds.), *Everyday memory, actions and absentmindedness.* London: Academic Press.

Brown, J., Lewis, V. J., & Monk, A. F. (1977). Memorability, word frequency and negative recognition. *Quarterly Journal of Experimental Psychology, 29,* 461–473.

Bruce, V., & Valentine, T. (1986). Semantic priming of familiar faces. *Quarterly Journal of Experimental Psychology, 38A,* 125–150.

Bruce, V., & Young, A. (1986). Understanding face recognition. *British Journal of Psychology, 77,* 305–327.

Burton, A. M., Bruce, V., & Johnston, R. A. (1990). Understanding face recognition with an interactive activation model. *British Journal of Psychology, 81,* 361–380.

Carey, S., & Diamond, R. (1980). Maturational determination of the developmental course of face encoding. In D. Caplan (Ed.), *Biological studies of mental processes.* Cambridge, MA: MIT Press.

Clark, S. E., & Gronlund, S. D. (1996). Global matching models of recognition memory: How the models match the data. *Psychonomic Bulletin & Review, 3,* 37–60.

Deese, J. (1961). From the isolated verbal unit to connected discourse. In C. N. Cofer (Ed.), *Verbal learning and verbal behavior.* New York: McGraw-Hill.

Diamond, R., & Carey, S. (1986). Why faces are and are not special: An effect of expertise. *Journal of Experimental Psychology: General, 251,* 111–126.

Donaldson, W. (1992). Measuring recognition memory. *Journal of Experimental Psychology: General, 121,* 275–278.

Eagle, M., & Leiter, E. (1964). Recall and recognition in intentional and incidental learning. *Journal of Experimental Psychology, 68,* 58–63.

Ellis, H. D. (1975). Recognising faces. *British Journal of Psychology, 66,* 29–37.

Ellis, H. D., & Young, A. W. (1989). Are faces special? In A. W. Young & H. D. Ellis (Eds.), *Handbook of research on face processing.* Amsterdam: North-Holland.

Estes, W. K., & Da Polito, F. (1967). Independent variation of information storage and retrieval processes in paired-associate learning. *Journal of Experimental Psychology, 75,* 18–26.

Feenan, K., & Snodgrass, J. G. (1990). The effect of context on discrimination and bias in recognition memory for pictures and words. *Memory & Cognition, 18,* 517–527.

Gardiner, J. M. (1988). Functional aspects of recollective experience. *Memory & Cognition, 16,* 309–313.

Gardiner, J. M., & Java, R. I. (1990). Recollective experience in word and nonword recognition. *Memory & Cognition, 18,* 23–30.

Gardiner, J. M., & Java, R. I. (1991). Forgetting in recognition memory with and without recollective experience. *Memory & Cognition, 19,* 617–623.

Gardiner, J. M., & Java, R. I. (1993). Recognition memory and awareness: An experiential approach. *European Journal of Cognitive Psychology, 5,* 337–346.

Gardiner, J. M., & Parkin, A. J. (1990). Attention and recollective experience in recognition memory. *Memory & Cognition, 18,* 579–583.

Gillund, G., & Shiffrin, R. M. (1984). A retrieval model for both recognition and recall. *Psychological Review, 91,* 1–67.

Glanzer, M., & Adams, J. K. (1985). The mirror effect in recognition memory. *Memory & Cognition, 13,* 8–20.

Glanzer, M., & Adams, J. K. (1990). The mirror effect in recognition memory: Data and theory. *Journal of Experimental Psychology: Learning, Memory, and Cognition, 16,* 5–16.

Glanzer, M., Adams, J. K., & Iverson, G. J. (1991). Forgetting and the mirror effect in recognition memory: Concentering of underlying distributions. *Journal of Experimental Psychology: Learning, Memory, and Cognition, 17,* 81–93.

Glanzer, M., Adams, J. K., Iverson, G. J., & Kim, K. (1993). The regularities of recognition memory. *Psychological Review, 100,* 546–567.

Green, D. M., & Swets, J. A. (1966). *Signal detection theory and psychophysics.* New York: Wiley.

Greene, R. L., & Thapar, A. (1994). Mirror effect in frequency discrimination. *Journal of Experimental Psychology: Learning, Memory, and Cognition, 20,* 946–952.

Gregg, V. H. (1976). Word frequency, recognition, and recall. In J. Brown (Ed.), *Recall and recognition.* New York: Wiley.

Hall, J. F. (1954). Learning as a function of word frequency. *American Journal of Psychology, 67,* 138–140.

Hintzman, D. L. (1988). Judgments of frequency and recognition memory in a multiple-trace memory model. *Psychological Review, 95,* 528–551.

Hintzman, D. L., Caulton, D. A., & Curran, T. (1994). Retrieval constraints and the mirror effect. *Journal of Experimental Psychology: Learning, Memory, and Cognition, 20,* 275–289.

Hockley, W. E. (1994). Reflections of the mirror effect for item and associative recognition. *Memory & Cognition, 22,* 713–722.

Hollingworth, H. C. (1913). Characteristic differences between recall and recognition. *American Journal of Psychology, 24,* 532–544.

Honeck, R. P. (1986). A serendipitous finding in face recognition. *Bulletin of the Psychonomic Society, 24,* 369–371.

Hunt, R. R., & Einstein, G. O. (1981). Relational and item-specific information in memory. *Journal of Verbal Learning and Verbal Behavior, 20,* 497–514.

Jacoby, L. L., & Hollingshead, A. (1990). Toward a generate/recognize model of performance on direct and indirect tests of memory. *Journal of Memory and Language, 29,* 433–454.

Kendrick, K. M., & Baldwin, B. A. (1987). Cells in temporal cortex of conscious sheep can respond preferentially to the sight of faces. *Science, 236,* 448–450.

Kinsbourne, M., & George, J. (1974). The mechanism of the word-frequency effect on recognition memory. *Journal of Verbal Learning & Verbal Behavior, 13,* 63–69.

Kintsch, W. (1970). Models for free recall and recognition. In D. A. Norman (Ed.), *Models of human memory.* New York: Academic Press.

Knoedler, A. J. (1996). Discrimination, response bias, and context: An explanation for elusive environmental context effects in recognition memory. Doctoral dissertation, Purdue University.

Levine, S. C. (1989). The question of faces: Special is in the brain of the beholder. In A. W. Young & H. D. Ellis (Eds.), *Handbook of research on face processing.* Amsterdam: North-Holland.

Levine, S. C., Banich, M. T., & Koch-Weser, M. P. (1988). Face recognition: A general or specific right hemisphere capacity? *Brain and Cognition, 8,* 303–325.

Madigan, S. (1983). Picture memory. In J. C. Yuille (Ed.), *Imagery, memory, and cognition: Essays in honour of Allan Paivio.* Hillsdale, NJ: Erlbaum.

Mandler, G. (1967). Organization and memory. In K. W. Spence & J. T. Spence (Eds.), *The psychology of learning and motivation, Vol. 1.* New York: Academic Press.

Mandler, G. (1980). Recognizing: The judgment of previous occurrence. *Psychological Review, 87,* 252–271.

Maurer, D. (1985). Infants' perception of facedness. In T. N. Field & N. Fox (Eds.), *Social perception in infants*. Norwood, NJ: Ablex.

McWeeny, K. H., Young, A. W., Hay, D. C., & Ellis, A. W. (1987). Putting names to faces. *British Journal of Psychology, 78*, 148–150.

Murdock, B. B. (1982). A theory for the storage and retrieval of item and associative information. *Psychological Review, 89*, 609–626.

O'Toole, A. J., Deffenbacher, K. A., Valentin, D., & Abdi, H. (1994). Structural aspects of face recognition and the other-race effect. *Memory & Cognition, 22*, 208–224.

Pollack, I., & Norman, D. A. (1964). A nonparametric analysis of recognition experiments. *Psychonomic Science, 1*, 125–126.

Rabinowitz, J. C., Mandler, G., & Barsalou, L. W. (1977). Recognition failure: Another case of retrieval failure. *Journal of Verbal Learning and Verbal Behavior, 16*, 639–663.

Rajaram, S. (1993). Remembering and knowing: Two means of access to the personal past. *Memory & Cognition, 21*, 89–102.

Rao, K. V., & Proctor, R. W. (1984). Study-phase processing and the word frequency effect in recognition memory. *Journal of Experimental Psychology: Learning, Memory, and Cognition, 10*, 386–394.

Ratcliff, R., Sheu, C.-F., & Gronlund, S. D. (1992). Testing global memory models using ROC curves. *Psychological Review, 99*, 518–535.

Schacter, D. L. (1994). Priming and multiple memory systems: Perceptual mechanisms of implicit memory. In D. L. Schacter & E. Tulving (Eds.), *Memory systems 1994*. Cambridge, MA: MIT Press.

Shepard, R. N. (1967). Recognition memory for words, sentences, and pictures. *Journal of Verbal Learning and Verbal Behavior, 6*, 156-163.

Snodgrass, J. G., & Corwin, J. (1988). Pragmatics of measuring recognition memory: Applications to dementia and amnesia. *Journal of Experimental Psychology: General, 117*, 34–50.

Snodgrass, J. G., Levy-Berger, G., & Haydon, M. (1985). *Human experimental psychology*. New York: Oxford University Press.

Snodgrass, J. G., Volvovitz, R., & Walfish, E. R. (1972). Recognition memory for words, pictures, and words + pictures. *Psychonomic Science, 27*, 345–347.

Tulving, E. (1985). Memory and consciousness. *Canadian Psychology, 26*, 1–12.

Tulving, E., & Thomson, D. M. (1973). Encoding specificity and retrieval processes in episodic memory. *Psychological Review, 80*, 352–373.

Underwood, B. J., & Freund, J. S. (1968). Errors in recognition learning and retention. *Journal of Experimental Psychology, 78*, 55–63.

Valentine, T. (1988). Upside-down faces: A review of the effect of inversion upon face recognition. *British Journal of Psychology, 79(4)*, 471–491.

Valentine, T., & Endo, M. (1992). Towards an exemplar model of face processing: The effects of race and distinctiveness. *Quarterly Journal of Experimental Psychology, 44A*, 671–204.

Vokey, J. R., & Read, J. D. (1992). Familiarity, memorability, and the effect of typicality on the recognition of faces. *Memory & Cognition, 20*, 291–302.

Watkins, M. J., & Gardiner, J. M. (1979). An appreciation of generate-recognize theory of recall. *Journal of Verbal Learning and Verbal Behavior, 18*, 687–704.

Watkins, M. J., & Tulving, E. (1975). Episodic memory: When recognition fails. *Journal of Experimental Psychology: General, 104*, 5–29.

Wickelgren, W. A., & Norman, D. A. (1966). Strength models and serial position in short-term recognition memory. *Journal of Mathematical Psychology, 3,* 316–347.

Wixted, J. T. (1992). Subjective memorability and the mirror effect. *Journal of Experimental Psychology: Learning, Memory, and Cognition, 18,* 681–690.

Yin, R. K. (1969). Looking at upside-down faces. *Journal of Experimental Psychology, 81,* 141–145.

Yntema, D. B., & Trask, F. P. (1963). Recall as a search process. *Journal of Verbal Learning & Verbal Behavior, 2,* 65–74.

Yonelinas, A. P., & Jacoby, L. L. (1995). The relation between remembering and knowing as bases for recognition: Effects of size congruency. *Journal of Memory and Language, 34,* 622–643.

Young, A. W., Hay, D. C., & Ellis, A. W. (1985). The faces that launched a thousand slips: Everyday difficulties and errors in recognising people. *British Journal of Psychology, 76,* 495–523.

Zechmeister, E. B. (1972). Orthographic distinctiveness as a variable in word recognition. *American Journal of Psychology, 85,* 425–430.

# CHAPTER ELEVEN

# Global Memory Models

*"As far as the laws of mathematics refer to reality, they are not certain; and as far as they are certain, they do not refer to reality."*

—*Albert Einstein*

Formal models are increasing in both popularity and sophistication in the study of human memory and in experimental psychology as a whole. Although there are many potential problems with using mathematical descriptions, there are also many advantages (Lewandowsky, 1994). Perhaps the most compelling advantage is that they provide an excellent check on human reasoning, particularly for situations in which there are complex interactions between several different variables. Hintzman (1991) offers the following example of when a formal model might have prevented an embarrassing claim:

> A recent textbook on learning has a chapter on sociobiology, which contains the following claim regarding sexual promiscuity: "While adultery rates for men and women may be equalizing, men still have more partners than women do, and they are more likely to have one-night stands." ... It is clear from the context that this does not hinge on the slight plurality of women to men (which would make it trivial), and that homosexual partners do not count. I challenge anyone to set up a formal model consistent with the claim—that is, there must be equal numbers of men and women, but men must have more heterosexual partners than women do. (While you are at it, derive the prediction about one-night stands.) An effort to set up such a model could have helped the authors avoid making a mathematically impossible claim. (p. 41)

Of course, there are other errors that formal models can make that people do not, such as programming errors, but to the extent that human reasoning and mathematical reasoning converge on the same answer, we can be more certain that we have not made an error of the type that Hintzman describes.

There are several models of memory that are usually referred to as umbrella models: they attempt to model, in a formal, quantitative fashion, human memory in a variety of different tasks, including both recall and recognition. When models are applied to many different experimental paradigms, they cannot be tailored to fit a particular finding. The same process that simulates recall of abstract words is also used to simulate recognition with differing proportions of distractor items. One advantage is that models will often uncover relationships between different paradigms or will suggest different explanations that may have been overlooked.

In this chapter, four prominent global memory models are presented: SAM, which stands for search of associative memory (Raaijmakers & Shiffrin, 1981; Gillund & Shiffrin, 1984; Mensink & Raaijmakers, 1988); MINERVA 2, which is the second version of a model named after the Greek goddess of wisdom (Hintzman, 1984, 1986, 1987, 1988); and TODAM, which stands for theory of distributed associative memory (Murdock, 1983, 1984; Lewandowsky & Murdock, 1989). The fourth model is actually a class of models: nonlinear back propagation connectionist models. Each model will be used to illustrate different advantages and disadvantages of using simulation models as a tool for analyzing human memory. For a review of other influential simulation models, see Raaijmakers and Shiffrin (1992).

# SAM

Because Richard Shiffrin was a principal architect of SAM (Raaijmakers & Shiffrin, 1981; Gillund & Shiffrin, 1984), it should come as no surprise that SAM retains many properties of the highly successful dual-store model (Atkinson & Shiffrin, 1968). Short-term memory is viewed as a limited-capacity buffer that serves two roles: it affects which items will get stored in long-term memory, and it is used to assemble retrieval cues that access information in long-term memory. Long-term memory is assumed to be an (almost) unlimited set of interconnected (or associated) concepts. Information in long-term memory is assumed to be permanent; there is no erasing or decaying or forgetting of information in long-term memory. All instances of apparent forgetting are retrieval failures; successful retrieval depends on the cue that is used, with context playing a particularly important role.

A key concept in the SAM model is the image. An *image* is an interconnected feature set that contains information about the context in which the item was learned, the item itself (its meaning, its name, and so on), and its relation with other images. When trying to recall something, a person assembles a set of cues in short-term memory and then uses these to activate various images in long-term memory. *Sampling* refers to the selection of an image and *recovery* refers to the process of getting information out of the image. Just because an item is sampled does not necessarily mean that the information within that image is recovered. Although this might sound odd, consider what can happen when you search for a book in the library. You might be interested in how people recognize faces, and so you assemble a cue, the index number for the human memory section of the Purdue psychology library (153.1). You next go to that section of the library and sample from the set of books whose call numbers begin with 153.1. Simply sampling these books does not, however, mean that you will find something about face recognition. Many of the memory books will discuss this process, and to the extent that they do, you will recover some information about basic face recognition. However, more information can be found with a slightly different cue (152.1), where you will find entire books that discuss research on face perception.

The associative retrieval structure is created by processes that occur in the storage buffer. The buffer has a fixed size, $r$, and once this capacity is exceeded, a replacement rule determines which items are lost. The first version of SAM (Raaijmakers & Shiffrin, 1981) assumed that each item in the buffer had an equal probability of being replaced (e.g., 1/r). Later versions (Gillund & Shiffrin, 1984) used a different rule where the oldest item in the buffer was replaced. Rehearsal, the basis for incrementing the strength of three types of associations, is shared over all items currently in the buffer. Thus, if only a few items are in the buffer, associative strengths will increase more than if the buffer is full.

The time spent in the buffer determines context strength, or the degree of association between the item and context. Interitem strengths—associations between two items—are determined by the amount of time the two items spend in the buffer together. The strength of the association between an item and itself is also determined by the time spent in the buffer. Although this might sound like an odd sort of association, this will become important during the sampling phase, where this strength will determine whether a cue will sample the appropriate image. Four parameters are involved here: $a$ is used with context associations, $b$ with interitem strengths, and $c$ with associations between the word and itself. The last association is between two items from the same list that did not share time in the buffer; this residual associative strength is represented by a parameter called $d$. This last parameter is not directly calculated, but any two items in the retrieval structure that were not rehearsed together can have some associative strength. Thus, $d$ is similar to $b$ but is typically much smaller.

The strength of the association between the context, $C$, and a particular item, $W_i$, is given by Equation 11.01. The parameter $n$ refers to the number of items that are simultaneously maintained in the buffer, $t_i$ is the time that item $W_i$ spends in the buffer, and $a$ is simply the context association parameter described above. The strength of the association between a particular item, $W_i$, and another item, $W_j$, is given by Equation 11.02. It is almost identical to 11.01 except that $t_{ij}$ is the amount of time word$_i$ and word$_j$ spend in the buffer together, and $b$ is the interitem associative strength parameter. Finally, the strength of the association between an item, $W_i$, and itself is given by Equation 11.03. This equation is exactly the same as equation 11.01, except that $a$ is replaced by the self-association parameter $c$.

$$S(C, W_i) = \frac{at_i}{n} \qquad (11.01)$$

$$S(W_j, W_i) = \frac{bt_{ij}}{n} \qquad (11.02)$$

$$S(W_i, W_i) = \frac{ct_i}{n} \qquad (11.03)$$

There is one more storage assumption that adds variability to the strengths discussed above. This variability is needed primarily for recognition. Basically, there is a $\frac{1}{3}$ probability that a starting strength $x$ will remain unchanged, a $\frac{1}{3}$ probability that the strength will be increased, and a $\frac{1}{3}$ probability that the strength will be decreased. The parameter that controls this is called $v$, and the resulting stored strength is called $y$. Equation 11.04 describes this process.

$$y = \begin{cases} (1-v)x; \\ x; \\ (1+v)x; \end{cases} \qquad (11.04)$$

Once an item, or more accurately, an image, is stored, the free recall retrieval cycle can begin. The first step is assembling a retrieval cue in the short-term buffer. For most applications, sampling begins with just a context cue, followed by the context cue plus whatever item was just recalled. This cue is used to probe for images in long-term memory, and the images sampled and recovered can then be used as cues for the remaining items. This process continues until some ending criterion is reached.

The general course of the free recall retrieval process can be thought of as a flowchart, as shown in Figure 11.1. This particular chart illustrates the retrieval cycle described in more detail by Gillund and Shiffrin (1984). In the flowchart, the retrieval cycle begins by using context as the cue. The process continues until there have been $kmax$ total failures; these failures are counted using the variable $k$. A failure occurs if the sampled item is not recovered, or if the chosen item has been sampled on an earlier cycle (even if, on the earlier cycle, the item was not recovered). The other failure criterion, $lmax$, determines how long the model will use the just-recalled item, $w_j$, as a probe. Failures of this type are counted with the variable $l$. After $lmax$ successive failures with a particular cue, the model shifts to the default cue, using just the context alone.

Formally, the probability of sampling ($P_s$) a particular item in the recall set ($W_i$) when the context ($C$) is used as a cue depends upon the strength of the association between the item and the context, divided by the sum of the strengths of the association between the context and the other items in the recall set. Mathematically, this can be expressed as

$$P_s(W_i \mid C) = \frac{S(C, W_i)}{\sum_{k=1}^{n} S(C, W_k)} \qquad (11.05)$$

where $n$ is the number of items in the recall set and is usually the number of items in the list. The associative strength between the context and the word depends on how long the item was in the temporary buffer and how many other items were simultaneously present. The strength can also be modified by altering the value of the parameter $a$. When an item, $W_j$, has been recalled, the model shifts to using context plus the item as a cue. Basically, two more terms are added to Equation 11.05, and these terms reflect (1) the associative strength between the item desired and the item used as a cue, and (2) the associative strength between the item used as a cue and all the other items in the recall set. Mathematically, Equation 11.05 becomes:

$$P_s(W_i \mid C, W_j) = \frac{S(C, W_i)S(W_j, W_i)}{\sum_{k=1}^{n} S(C, W_k)S(W_j, W_k)} \qquad (11.06)$$

Once an item has been sampled, it still needs to be recovered. Recovery can be thought of as the process by which information is extracted from the image, and this process may or may not be successful. Just as there are two sampling equations (11.05 and 11.06), there are also two recovery equations (11.07 and 11.08), which vary depending on whether the cue was just the context or the context plus an item.

$$P_R(W_i, \mid C) = 1 - \exp[-S(C, W_i)] \qquad (11.07)$$

$$P_R(W_i, \mid C, W_j) = 1 - \exp[-S(C, W_i) - S(W_j, W_i)] \qquad (11.08)$$

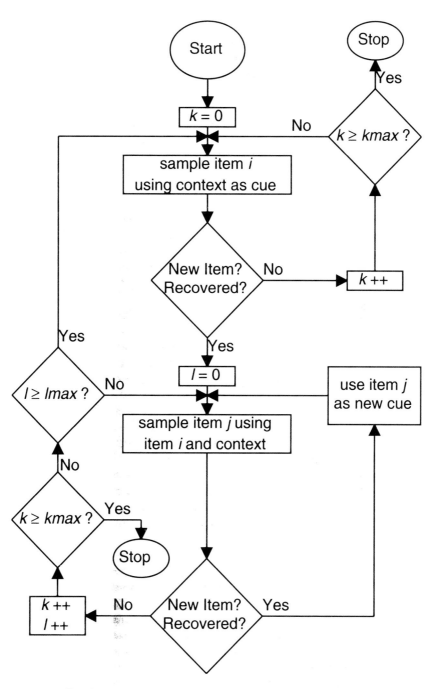

**Figure 11.1**  A flowchart representing the Gillund and Shiffrin (1984) SAM retrieval cycle for free recall.  Source: Gillund & Shiffrin (1984).

For a yes-no recognition test, it is assumed that recognition is determined by a direct-access familiarity process; there is no search. The subject probes memory with two cues, the context and the tested item. The total activation of long-term store in response to the probe is a measure of the familiarity not only of that particular item, but also of all other images in memory. For this reason, Gillund and Shiffrin (1984) termed this a measure of *global familiarity*. The subject makes a yes or no decision based on the global familiarity; if the value reaches some criterion, the subject responds "yes." In the typical case, the main recognition equation is very similar to the main sampling equation above. The familiarity of an item, when probing using context and the item itself, is given by the sum, over all the items in the recall set, of the product of the associative strength of the context with each item and the associative strength between the target and each item.

$$F(C,W_j) = \sum_{k=1}^{n} S(C,W_k) S(W_j,W_k) \qquad (11.09)$$

Once the familiarity is determined, a criterion must be set; this value, indicated by $Cr$, is a free parameter of the model. Typically, it is set so that it is close to the crossing points for the familiarity values of the target and distractor distributions. The idea is based on signal detection theory, described in the previous chapter. (In fact, for the sake of convenience, the performance of the model on recognition tasks is often described in terms of $d'$). For the simulations reported in Gillund and Shiffrin (1984), the appropriate formula was specified in terms of the mean value of the distractor distribution and the mean value of the target distribution.

$$Cr = 0.455(M_d + M_t) \qquad (11.10)$$

It should be quite clear that SAM is complex and that it will be most useful if incorporated into a computer simulation. This is exactly how most of the simulation modeling has been conducted. However, given the verbal description and the equations presented above, several properties of SAM should be evident. For example, SAM accounts for the serial position curve in free recall in much the same way as the dual-store model does. The recency effect is attributed to output from the buffer at the time of recall. The primacy effect is attributed to the more beneficial rehearsal the first few items get, because they do not share processing with other items, yielding stronger associations. The probability of recalling or recognizing a particular item decreases as the length of the list of to-be-remembered items increases (Murdock, 1962; Strong, 1912). According to SAM, list length affects memory performance in the two tests differently. In free recall, increasing the list length reduces the probability of sampling a particular item. In recognition, the variance of both the target and distractor distributions increases, and so there is more overlap between the two; as a result, $d'$ decreases.

Table 11.1 lists the main parameters in SAM, but most of SAM's properties depend on the setting of just four parameters: $a$, $b$, $c$, and $d$. The effect of each of these parameters on recall and recognition performance is shown in Figure 11.2.

The context parameter $a$ acts only as a scale factor for recognition and so does not affect performance. In free recall tasks, an increase in $a$ will increase the probability of recovering an item (but has no effect on sampling probability), and so free recall performance will improve.

**Table 11.1** The main parameters and their default values in SAM.

| Parameter | Value | Function |
|---|---|---|
| $a$ | 0.250 | context associations |
| $b$ | 0.200 | inter-item associations |
| $c$ | 0.150 | self associations |
| $d$ | 0.075 | residual associations |
| $v$ | 0.500 | variability in association |
| $t$ | 2.000 | presentation rate (seconds per item) |
| $r$ | 4 | capacity of buffer |
| $Cr$ | 1.000 | criterion |
| $ll$ | 20 | list length |
| $kmax$ | 30 | number of attempts using just context as a cue |
| $lmax$ | 8 | number of attempts using context plus a previously recalled item as a cue |

Increases in the interitem associative parameter $b$ will improve performance on recognition tasks by raising the familiarity of the target distribution (but not of the distractor distribution). This parameter has a similar beneficial effect on free recall, improving recovery and also, in a less apparent way, decreasing self-sampling. *Self-sampling* is the tendency for an item, when used as a cue, to sample itself rather than other items.

Parameter $c$ is the self-coding parameter, and by increasing associations between the item and itself, recognition performance improves because the familiarity of the target distribution is increased with no change in the distractor distribution. In free recall, on the other hand, an increase in $c$ reduces performance because self-sampling is increased. (Recall that self-sampling decreases performance because, when an item is used as a cue, it samples itself rather than another item in the list.)

Increases in the residual parameter $d$ decrease recognition performance by increasing the familiarity of the distractors more than the familiarity of the targets and by increasing the overall variance of both distributions. Increases in $d$ benefit free recall by increasing recovery probabilities and also by decreasing self-sampling.

Using only these four parameters, SAM is able to simulate many of the empirical results seen with both recall and recognition. In particular, it offers an explanation for the differential effects of intentionality and word frequency on recall and recognition, and can also address the recognition-failure-of-recallable-words phenomenon.

*Intentionality.* Subjects tend to recall more items under intentional learning instructions than under incidental instructions, but subjects can often recognize more items under incidental instructions (Eagle & Leiter, 1964; Estes & Da Polito, 1967). According to SAM, increased intentionality leads to increased interitem coding because, if subjects know a test is forthcoming, their usual strategy is to relate the words to each other. Increased interitem coding is modeled by increasing parameter $b$, which, as can be seen in Figure 11.2, leads to an increase in performance in both recall and recognition. However, increased in-

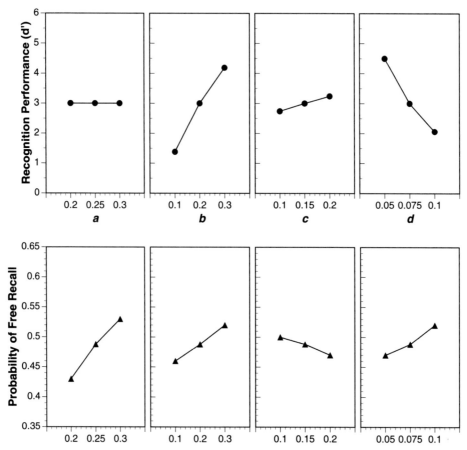

**Figure 11.2**   The effects of varying just *a, b, c,* and *d,* when all other parameters are held constant, on recognition and recall.   Source: Gillund & Shiffrin (1984).

teritem coding is usually associated with decreased self-coding. This is modeled by decreasing parameter *c,* which, as can be seen in Figure 11.2, helps recall but hurts recognition. Simulation results are shown in Table 11.2: As *b* increases and *c* decreases, recognition decreases and free recall increases.

*Word-frequency effect.*   The typical finding is that high-frequency words are recalled better than low-frequency words, but low-frequency words are recognized better than high-frequency words in lists of pure high- or low-frequency; in mixed lists, recall of high- and low-frequency words is often equal (Gregg, 1976). The residual association between any two items not rehearsed together, or between any distractor and any list item, is assumed to be frequency-dependent. The parameter *d* is assumed to be larger for high-frequency words than for low-frequency words. For words that are rehearsed together, it is assumed that high-frequency cues are stronger than low-frequency cues—that *b* for high-frequency words is larger than *b* for low-frequency words. The parameters *a* and *c*

**Table 11.2**  Simulation results using the Gillund and Shiffrin (1984) version of SAM for recognition and recall of a 20-item list presented at a rate of 1 item every 2 seconds. For recognition, the hit rate, false alarm rate, and $d'$ are shown; for recall, the proportion correct is shown. The criterion, $Cr$, was calculated according to Equation 11.10 and was approximately 1.0 for the first three simulations and approximately 0.5 for the last simulation. Parameters not shown were identical in all simulations and were those listed in Table 11.1.

| Condition | Hit Rate | False Alarm | $d'$ | Recall | $b$ | $c$ | $d$ |
|-----------|----------|-------------|------|--------|-----|-----|-----|
| Intentional | 0.935 | 0.056 | 3.097 | 0.503 | .22 | .10 | 0.075 |
| Incidental | 0.940 | 0.042 | 3.287 | 0.451 | .18 | .25 | 0.075 |
| High Freq | 0.921 | 0.044 | 3.118 | 0.479 | .20 | .15 | 0.075 |
| Low Freq | 0.954 | 0.012 | 3.931 | 0.424 | .10 | .15 | 0.035 |

are not frequency-dependent. Finally, the criterion will be different in the recognition phase for high- and low-frequency words. Although three parameters are changed ($b$, $d$, and $Cr$), this results in the appropriate pattern for pure and mixed lists (see Table 11.2).

There is a pure-list advantage for high-frequency words in recall for a combination of two reasons. Any item sampled by a high-frequency word has a greater probability of being recovered because of the higher strength values. In pure high-frequency lists, only high-frequency cues are used, and in pure low-frequency lists, only low-frequency cues are used. In a mixed list, a high-frequency word is just as likely to sample a low-frequency word as a high-frequency word, and then both types are equally likely to be recovered. There is a consistent recognition advantage for low-frequency words regardless of the list composition. The residual parameter $d$ has a smaller value for low-frequency words, and lower values increase recognition performance.

*Recognition failure of recallable words.*  SAM can also explain the other major problem facing a model of both recall and recognition: recognition failure of recallable words. Although the storage assumptions are the same for both recall and recognition, the retrieval assumptions are quite different. In SAM, recall requires a search, and a successful search means that an item was both sampled and recovered. Recognition, on the other hand, is based on a measure of global familiarity. Under certain circumstances, some searches will succeed in sampling and recovering an item even though the item may not reach the recognition familiarity criterion. One reason that an item may not reach the recognition familiarity criterion is because of change in context, and SAM can easily model context effects: when the context changes, both $a$ and $c$ will change, and when the meaning of an item changes, changes in $b$ will occur (see Gillund & Shiffrin, 1984, for details).

*Summary of SAM.*  SAM has been an enormously successful and influential model of recall and recognition. With only a few parameters, all of which are related to psychologically plausible concepts, SAM is able to explain memory performance in a wide variety of situations and different paradigms. It is also currently being used in conjunction with compound-cue theory (see Chapter 12) to explain associative priming effects in generic memory. It is not without problems, however. First, because of the way the associative structure is set up, SAM suffers many of the same problems as the dual-store model does (see Chapter 4). Second, although Table 11.2 shows that SAM can simulate the mirror effect seen with word frequency, SAM cannot account for all aspects of the mirror effect (see Chapter 10).

# MINERVA 2

One of the main goals in developing MINERVA 2 was to explain memory for individual experiences (episodic memory) and memory for abstract concepts (generic or semantic memory) within a single system (Hintzman, 1984). Primary memory plays a very minor role, either sending a retrieval cue or probe to secondary memory or receiving the reply, termed the *echo*.

The model assumes "(1) that only episodic traces are stored in memory, (2) that repetition produces multiple traces of an item, (3) that a retrieval cue contacts all memory traces simultaneously, (4) that each trace is activated according to its similarity to the retrieval cue, and (5) that all traces respond in parallel, the retrieved information reflecting their summed output" (Hintzman, 1984, p. 96). It is clear how this might capture episodic memory phenomena. Generic memory follows from the assumption that although a separate trace of each episode is stored, the traces are activated in parallel by a retrieval cue, and abstractions can be constructed through the summed responses of those traces that are most strongly activated by the cue.

The repetition of an item improves memory performance not by strengthening a particular trace but rather by redundancy, by creating multiple copies. When a probe is presented to secondary memory, it is simultaneously matched with every memory trace. Each trace is activated according to its similarity to the probe, and the echo that is returned to primary memory represents the summed reactions of all traces to the probe. Because a trace contributes to the echo only to the extent that it is activated, only similar traces will make substantive contributions. There is no process by which a particular memory trace can be isolated and further examined.

Information about an event or experience is represented as a vector, an ordered list of feature values. Each feature can take a value of +1, −1, or 0. Each feature of an event or experience in primary memory is encoded in secondary memory with a probability $L$, a learning parameter. In a secondary memory trace description, a 0 means either that the feature is irrelevant or that it was never stored.

Let $P_j$ be the value of feature $j$ in the probe, $T_{i,j}$ be the value of feature $j$ in trace $i$, and $N_r$ be the number of relevant features — the number of features that are not 0 in either the probe or the trace. The similarity of a particular trace, $i$, to the probe is

$$S_i = \sum_{j=1}^{N} P_j T_{i,j} \frac{1}{N_r} \tag{11.11}$$

In this equation, $S_i$ acts as a correlation coefficient; when the probe and trace are identical, it takes a value of +1, and when the probe and trace are orthogonal, it takes a value of 0. Although values close to −1 are mathematically possible, they rarely occur in simulations. Imagine a probe item with a vector of feature values [1, −1, −1, 1, −1]. The similarity between this probe item and a trace vector [1, −1, 1, 1, −1] would be [(1 × 1) + (−1 × −1) + (−1 × 1) + (1 × 1) + (−1 × −1)]/5 = (1 + 1 − 1 + 1 + 1)/5 = 0.80.

A trace will be activated to the extent that it is similar to the probe. The activation level, $A_i$, is the cube of the similarity value:

$$A_i = S_j^3 \tag{11.12}$$

Because a cube is taken, the activation will preserve the sign of similarity measure. In addition, if there is little similarity between the trace and the probe, the activation will be close to zero. For the example given above, the activation would be 0.8 × 0.8 × 0.8 = .512. An item that is less similar (such as $S_i = 0.4$) would have much less activation (0.064).

The echo that is returned has two properties, intensity and content. The intensity, $I$, of an echo is found by summing the activation levels of all the traces, M. It can be thought of as a measure of familiarity, and it is used when modeling recognition and frequency judgments.

$$I = \sum_{i=1}^{M} A_i \tag{11.13}$$

The content of the echo, $C_j$, is the activation pattern across features. The activation of a particular feature, $j$, in the echo is given by:

$$C_j = \sum_{i=1}^{M} A_i T_{i,j} \tag{11.14}$$

Traces activated by the probe can contain information that was not originally in the probe. For example, an experience might be learning to associate a name with a particular face. Features 1 to 10 might represent information about the face, whereas features 11 to 20 might represent information about the name. Recalling a name upon presentation of the face could involve assembling a probe with features 1–10 containing information about the face and features 11–20 set to 0, and focusing on the content of features 11–20 in the returning echo (for example, examining $C_{11}$ through $C_{20}$).

The resemblance between the original and the retrieved information is usually not perfect. One attractive feature of MINERVA 2 is that it offers an elegant way of sharpening or deblurring the returned echo. The echo can be used as a second probe, and the second echo can be used as a third probe, and so forth. After a few iterations, the resultant echo is more like an acceptable response than the first echo, and it is often an almost perfect copy of the original (see Hintzman, 1986). Recognition (hit rate) depends on the intensity of the echo and thus depends, in part, on the degree to which the target probe matches the subset of target features probed for. In addition, the learning rate will affect performance: the more features there are, the higher the intensity of the echo.

We will focus on just two aspects of MINERVA 2. First, it demonstrates that both episodic and semantic memory processes can be accounted for within a single memory system: second, it sheds more light on the recognition-failure-of-recallable-words phenomenon. In both cases, MINERVA 2 has served as an analysis tool to demonstrate that

**Figure 11.3** Examples of a prototype, a low-level distortion exemplar, and a high-level distortion exemplar.   Source: After stimuli used by Posner, Goldsmith, & Welton (1967).

alternate conceptions to the standard view can predict and account for the same pattern of results.

Although there is wide acceptance of the distinction between episodic and semantic memory systems (Tulving, 1983), many researchers have documented both empirical and logical problems with the distinction (McKoon, Ratcliff, & Dell, 1986; Neely, 1989; see also Chapter 8). One purpose of MINERVA 2 was to see if it could produce the appropriate pattern of results in both an episodic task and a semantic task. If it could, MINERVA 2 would stand as an existence proof: it is possible to produce the correct results without postulating separate systems.

Hintzman (1986) applied MINERVA 2 to the question of how abstract knowledge is related to specific experience. According to multiple systems theorists, repeated exposure to individual examples produces traces in episodic memory and also an abstract representation of the category in semantic memory (Tulving, 1983). In contrast, Hintzman took the view that only traces of individual episodes are stored and that abstract representations are simply a product of the way these individual traces are activated at retrieval. In this conception, there is no need for a semantic memory system. To see if this view was plausible, Hintzman simulated many findings from a research paradigm known as a *schema abstraction task* (Posner & Keele, 1968).

In the typical experiment, subjects may be trained to classify random dot patterns into three categories (Homa, Cross, Cornell, Goldman, & Schwartz, 1973). Each category has a different number of members which are called exemplars, in this case 3, 6, and 9. All exemplars are distortions of the prototype, but the subjects never see the actual prototype and are not told that such a prototype exists. During learning, a particular pattern is shown, and the subject classifies it as belonging to category A, B, or C. Subsequent feedback informs the subject what the correct response should have been. After learning to classify these 18 patterns, the subjects are then tested on their ability to classify five other patterns: (1) the training exemplars, which are now called "old" exemplars; (2) the three prototypes, none of which have been seen previously; (3) new exemplars that are relatively low-level distortions of the prototypes; (4) new exemplars that are relatively high-level distortions of the prototypes; and (5) random arrangements of dots. Figure 11.3 illustrates the relationship between a low-level and a high-level distortion and the category prototype.

Among the results of interest are the following: (1) Subjects tend to classify the old exemplars more accurately than prototypes on an immediate test, but classification is

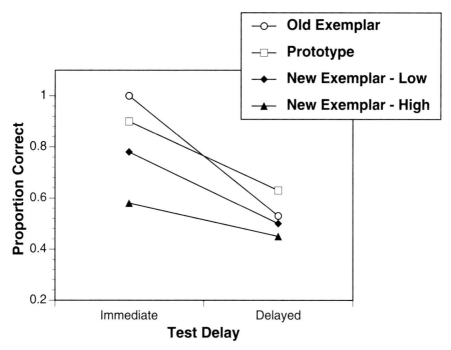

**Figure 11.4**   Correct classification for the 6-item category as a function of probe type (old exemplar, prototype, low-distortion new exemplar, and high-distortion new exemplar) and test delay (immediate and delayed).   Source: Adapted from Hintzman (1986).

either equal or slightly worse for old exemplars than for prototypes on a delayed test. (2) Old exemplars are classified more accurately than new exemplars on both immediate and delayed tests. (3) New exemplars that are low-level distortions of the prototypes are classified more accurately than new high-level distortions on both immediate and delayed tests. (4) Classification of new patterns is better for large categories (categories with more instances) than small categories. (5) Random patterns are more likely to be assigned to a large category than to a small category.

MINERVA 2 can simulate all five key results (Hintzman, 1986). For this simulation, each memory trace has 23 features ($n = 23$), with the first 10 coding the category name and the last 13 coding the stimulus pattern. The model is told of the appropriate category, just as the subjects were. Three prototypes were generated randomly, and exemplars were generated by multiplying a random 2 (low level) or 4 (high level) features from the last 13 by −1. Storage occurred as described above, and testing consisted of presenting the stimulus pattern as a cue (feature values 1 through 10 were set to 0 on the probe) and examining the category name portion of the echo content. To simulate a delayed test, each stored feature was set to 0 with a probability of 0.75 and then was retested. Figure 11.4 shows some of the results from one simulation for the category with six items.

First, MINERVA 2 correctly simulates differential forgetting rates for the prototype and old exemplars, with best performance on the immediate test for old exemplars but best performance on the delayed test for prototypes. Second, old exemplars are consistently categorized better than are new exemplars. Third, new exemplars of low distortion are categorized better than are new exemplars of high distortion. Not shown is the fourth finding: performance for the 9-item category was better than for the 6-item category, which in turn was better than performance in the 3-item category. The fifth result described above — that random patterns are more likely to be assigned to a large category than to a small category — was also simulated by MINERVA 2. Of the random patterns tested, 22% were assigned to the 3-item category, 31% to the 6-item category, and 34% to the 9-item category. The remaining items were assigned to a "junk" category, meaning that no clear response was given. These simulation results are not dependent on particular parameter settings; Hintzman (1986) replicated these results with different settings, in addition to reporting several other simulations.

The important point for our purposes is that MINERVA 2, which simply stores every item experienced, can reproduce the key findings from the schema abstraction paradigm. Although it is possible to account for the results by postulating a separate semantic memory system, MINERVA 2 illustrates that it is possible to account for the data without such a separate system.

The second topic of interest for MINERVA 2 is the recognition-failure-of-recallable-words paradigm. As described in more detail in Chapter 10, it is possible to set up a situation where an item can be recalled but cannot be recognized (Watkins & Tulving, 1975). Because this result seems counterintuitive, numerous studies have explored many different factors. When the proportion of words recognized is plotted against the proportion of words recognized that were also recalled, a regular pattern emerges; this pattern is known as the Tulving-Wiseman law (Tulving & Wiseman, 1975; Flexser & Tulving, 1978), and it looks like Figure 11.5. The diagonal (dashed) line represents what should happen if there is no correlation between recall and recognition. The actual data, replotted from dozens of studies, falls on the curved (solid) line but always above the dotted line. This indicates that there is a positive correlation between the two scores.

There is an ongoing controversy about how to interpret this result (for example, compare Hintzman, 1992, with Tulving & Flexser, 1992). The key for our purposes is that the diagonal is supposed to mean that recognition and recall are independent processes. In MINERVA 2, recall and recognition use the same memory trace, and so performance on the two tests should be correlated. In other words, if MINERVA 2 were used to simulate recognition failure of recallable words, the simulation results should show a positive correlation and fall in the area where data from human subjects fall. Curiously enough, this is *not* what happens when the simulations are actually run.

Hintzman (1987) ran simulations of recognition failure of recallable words in which the model learned a list of cue-target pairs. Each pair had 20 elements; the cue was represented by the first 10 features, and the target by the second 10 features. For the cued-recall test, only the cue was used as a probe, and the model's answer was the last 10 features of the echo. For the recognition test, just the target was used as a probe. If the target had been previously recalled, the resulting echo was added to the distribution of recalled echoes. If the target had not been recalled, the echo was added to the distribution

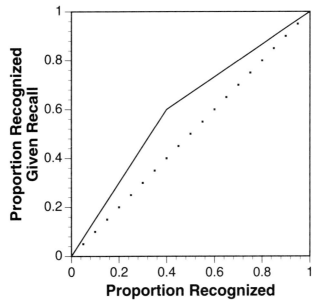

**Figure 11.5**   A representation of the Tulving-Wiseman law. If recall and recognition are uncorrelated, performance should fall on the diagonal (dotted) line. Data plotted from many studies falls above the diagonal, in the region shown by the curved (solid) line.

of nonrecalled echoes. The new distributions were obtained by probing with new, random vectors. Remember that in a recognition test MINERVA 2 uses the echo intensity; it is these intensities that are collected together to generate the distributions. With the distributions assembled, a signal detection analysis can be performed (see Chapter 10).

With standard parameters (e.g., $L = 0.45$ and list lengths of between 8 and 32), the data from MINERVA 2 fell *exactly* on the diagonal. Mathematically, this can be interpreted as stochastic independence: recall and recognition are independent. However, because we know that recall and recognition in MINERVA 2 are not independent, something else must be going on.

According to this analysis, there are two ways of obtaining independence. First, recall and recognition might be truly independent. Second, there could be one or more variables which are positively correlated with both measures and one or more variables that are negatively correlated with both measures. For example, both recall and recognition benefit when more target features are stored (through the parameter $L$). The second variable could be variation in intralist similarity. High similarity is known to decrease the probability of correctly recalling an item on a cued-recall list (due to interference) but increase the probability of responding "old." The complicated aspect of this is that it is not similarity per se but rather variation in similarity that could produce the negative correlation. Simulations reported by Hintzman (1987) confirmed this analysis. By varying the number of features encoded and the variation in similarity, he was able to move the data points either above the diagonal or below the diagonal.

What does this imply about recognition failure of recallable words? Because MIN-ERVA 2 usually produces results that indicate independence and it is known that MIN-ERVA 2's processes are not independent, it suggests that the Tulving-Wiseman law may be an artifact of as yet unexplored factors. One possibility is that variation in intralist similarity and degree of encoding might be affecting the results. Notice that the simulations from MINERVA 2 do not prove this interpretation; rather, they again serve as an existence proof. Hintzman's argument is presented in more detail in Hintzman (1992); Tulving (Tulving & Flexser, 1992) provides an alternate explanation.

*Summary of MINERVA 2.*    MINERVA 2 was designed to account for recognition and cued recall. It has successfully shown that a model that does not distinguish between episodic and semantic memory can nonetheless produce the appropriate pattern of results, as seen in the schema abstraction results shown in Figure 11.4. Furthermore, it can explain not only recognition data but also frequency data; that is, it can simulate the results of tests that ask people to judge how many times they have seen a particular item. Perhaps its most important feature is the ability to deblur an ambiguous echo without recourse to an external memory source. (We shall discuss this issue in more detail in conjunction with TODAM.) As was the case with SAM, MINERVA 2 is not perfect. It cannot explain the mirror effect (see Chapter 10), and because there are so few parameters, it cannot address other aspects of memory. Nonetheless, MINERVA 2 is perhaps the most impressive model, if only because it can do so much with so few assumptions and parameters.

# TODAM

Murdock's (1982, 1983, 1993, 1995; Lewandowsky & Murdock, 1989) Theory of Distributed Associative Memory (TODAM) is a very different kind of model than the two previously considered. It was designed to explain memory for serial order and recognition. Individual memories are stored in a distributed fashion; in other words, there is one memory storage system that is involved with every memory. In the simulation version, there is a common memory vector, $\mathbf{M}$. Just as in connectionist models, each element in this vector is involved with storing every memory. TODAM can also be seen as an existence proof: in this case, that it is possible to store and retrieve information from a common memory vector.

In TODAM, vectors are centered at 0, which means that the middle location is location 0 and so there are an equal number of features to the left and to the right of this middle position. Each vector has $N$ features, where $N$ is theoretically a large number but in practice is on the order of 200 or so. The features in the vector are randomly drawn from a normal distribution with a mean of 0 and a standard deviation ($\sigma$) of $\sqrt{1/N}$. Basically, what this means is that the vectors will have certain properties; for example, if a vector is multiplied by itself, the product is 1.

Two mathematical procedures make TODAM tick. The first is called *convolution* and is represented by the symbol $*$, and the second is *correlation,* which is represented by the symbol #. (This type of correlation is unrelated to Pearson's correlation, with the symbol $r$.) TODAM assumes that there is a main memory vector that stores two kinds of information: item information, which lets the system recall which information was presented, and associations between items, which lets the system recall in the appropriate order. Information is entered into the main memory vector by convolution and is retrieved via correlation.

At the time when item $j$ is encoded, the state of memory vector $\mathbf{M}$ can be represented as

$$\mathbf{M}_j = \alpha \mathbf{M}_{j-1} + \gamma f_j + w_j f_j * f_{j-1} \tag{11.15}$$

$\mathbf{M}_{j-1}$ is the state of the memory vector prior to learning the current item, item $j$. $\alpha$ is a noise or forgetting parameter that can vary between 0 and 1. The vector that represents item $j$ is represented by $f_j$. The parameter $\gamma$ is a weighting factor that increases or decreases the relative importance of item information. The parameter $w_j$ is a weighting factor that increases or decreases the relative importance of associative information. Finally, $f_j * f_{j-1}$ is a representation of associative information — in particular, the convolution of the current item with the previous item. Thus, the state of the memory vector after learning item $j$ is the prior state altered by a little noise plus item $j$ plus an association between item $j$ and the item that preceded item $j$.

Convolution is a relatively straightforward procedure; the only trick is in keeping track of which particular elements are involved in each step. Eich (1982) gives a good description of convolution in a memory model and illustrates the procedure step by step. If $L$ is $(N-1)/2$, and $x$ ranges from $-L$ to $L$, then to convolve two vectors, $\mathbf{A}$ and $\mathbf{B}$:

$$(\mathbf{A} * \mathbf{B})_x = \sum_{i=-L}^{L} (\mathbf{A}_i \cdot \mathbf{B}_{x-i}) \tag{11.16}$$

Serial recall is cue driven, and the first cue used is a context cue. The idea is that the subject is told to recall the list of items that was just presented, and this is the cue to initiate retrieval. Retrieval is done through the process of correlation, an approximate inverse of convolution. If two vectors, $\mathbf{A}$ and $\mathbf{B}$, are correlated, then

$$(\mathbf{A} \# \mathbf{B})_x = \sum_{i=-L}^{L} (\mathbf{A}_i \cdot \mathbf{B}_{x+i}) \tag{11.17}$$

Because of the way that associative information is encoded, the cue for item $j$ is item $j - 1$. The result will be a noisy, blurry, but potentially interpretable vector known as $f'$. Thus,

$$f_{j-1} \# \mathbf{M} = f'_j \tag{11.18}$$

Context, then, is the cue for $f_1$, $f_1$ is the cue for $f_2$, $f_2$ is the cue for $f_3$, and so on. This procedure is known as *chaining*, and it works well until one of the items is not recalled. The result of correlation is a blurry but potentially interpretable vector, and the model interprets this vector by computing the dot product between the recovered vector and the possible candidates. If this value is within acceptable limits, then the item is interpreted and produced. (The dot product of two vectors, $a$ and $b$, is also a vector, the first element is the product of the first elements of $a$ and $b$, the second element is the product of the second elements of $a$ and $b$, and so on.) If an item is not recalled, the link in the chain is missing; in the typical chain model of memory (see Chapter 2), recall must necessarily stop at this point. This problem has limited the development of models of serial order for

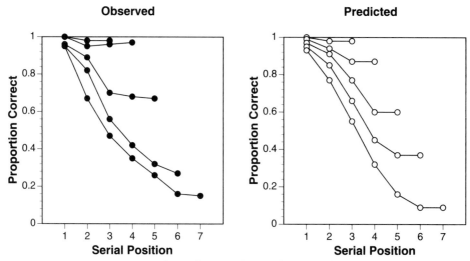

**Figure 11.6**   Proportion correctly recalled in order as a function of various list lengths. As soon as one item was incorrectly recalled, no further items in the list were scored as correct. Source: Adapted from Lewandowsky & Murdock (1989).

years (see Young, 1968), and one of the contributions of TODAM is a way around this problem. Regardless of its interpretation, $f'_j$ will be used as the cue for the next item. Because the memory vector **M** contains both item and associative information, it turns out that $f'_j$ can be a useful cue even if it is uninterpretable itself.

One intriguing aspect of TODAM's behavior is that several items can be stored in the common memory vector and then retrieved, and the simulation results closely resemble what subjects do. For example, Drewnowsk and Murdock (1980) presented subjects with lists of 3, 4, 5, 6, and 7 items for immediate serial recall. The left panel of Figure 11.6 shows some of their data. A response was scored as correct only if it was reported in the correct order; thus, as soon as one error was made, no other responses were counted as correct. The predictions of TODAM are shown in the right panel, which is clearly capturing the important aspects of the data.

TODAM has also been applied to recognition (Murdock, 1982), and, as with SAM and MINERVA 2, recognition is based on a measure of familiarity. In TODAM's case, familiarity is defined as the dot product of the probe, $f$, and the main memory vector, **M**:

$$f \cdot M = \sum_{i=-L}^{L} (f_i \cdot M_i) \qquad (11.19)$$

If this value is greater than some criterion, then the response is "old"; if it is less than the criterion, then the response is "new." Hockley and Murdock (1987) have developed a sophisticated decision mechanism for interpreting the familiarity value that can predict both accuracy and latency, which is outlined in Figure 11.7.

The memory comparison stage reflects the result of Equation 11.19, a measure of familiarity. One of the key assumptions is that there is always some noise present in the

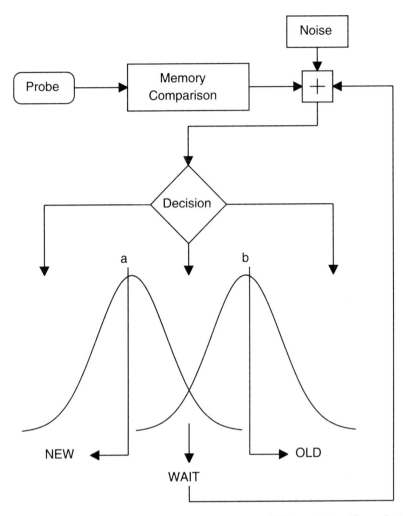

**Figure 11.7**   A schematic representation of the decision model for TODAM. The probe is the item presented for a recognition judgment, and the memory comparison stage is based on assessing familiarity via Equation 11.19. Noise (in the form of random variability) is added, and this is the input to the decision system. If this input is less than *a* or greater than *b*, a decision of "new" or "old" (respectively) is made. If the input falls in between, then the system enters a wait interval, during which a new value of random noise is added to the familiarity value and *a* and *b* are moved slightly closer together. This cycle continues until a decision is made.   Source: Adapted from Hockley & Murdock (1987).

memory system. Each time through the decision cycle, random noise is added to the original output of the memory system. The combined value is then compared to two criteria, *a* and *b*. If the value is less than *a*, a "new" decision is made; if it is greater than *b*, an "old" decision is made. If the value falls in between, then a wait interval occurs. A different random noise value is added to the output of the model, and *a* and *b* are moved closer together. The more wait intervals, the longer the response until (usually) the value falls either below $a$ or above $b$. Formally, the time to make a decision, $T$, is given by

$$T_{(k)} = (k^2 + k + 2)BCT \qquad\qquad (11.20)$$

where $k$ is the number of previous cycles and $BCT$ is the base cycle time, the time to complete one cycle. Typically, a value of 17.5 ms is used for $BCT$. This means that the fastest possible decision time is 35 ms, which would occur when an immediate "old" or "new" response is given. With an immediate response, $k$ would be 0, and so $T_0 = 2 \times BCT$.

Figure 11.8 shows an application of this decision model. The data come from an experiment reported by Hockley (1982) in which 80 words were presented once and 80 words were presented three times. Each time a word was presented, the subject was asked to decide whether the word had already appeared in the list. The lag between the first and second presentation of an item and the second and third presentation of an item could vary between 0 (the items appeared successively) and 40 (40 items intervened). The mean correct response times (in milliseconds) are shown for the second (2P) and third (3P) presentations, as well as the proportion correct. The best fit of the decision model is shown with the solid lines, with the original data shown as data points. The model produces an impressive fit (see Hockley & Murdock, 1987, for more details).

Although TODAM has successfully predicted many serial order phenomena, it has at least one important problem that is of central importance not only in TODAM itself but also in any simulation model that produces a result that needs to be interpreted. This process is often referred to as *deblurring*. TODAM utilizes the concept of a competitor set, a set of items that the subject thinks is likely to have occurred on the trial, to aid in this process. For example, many experiments use numbers, letters, or some other relatively small set. In TODAM, $f'_j$ is compared to the items in the competitor set, and whichever item is most similar is the interpretation of $f'_j$. If this is a correct match, then the model is judged to have recalled the appropriate item and the item is removed from the competitor set. The reason for this removal is that subjects rarely repeat an item. The recalled item is then convolved back into the main memory vector to implement the idea that the subjects remember which items they have recalled.

The problem arises when $f'_j$ is matched with an incorrect item. In this case, there are two options. One is to remove the best matching item from the competitor, but this will prevent the model from producing recency effects. The reason is straightforward (Nairne & Neath, 1994). If there is a pool of 8 items in the competitor set, the 8th item has the most chances of being mistakenly recalled. If it is matched inappropriately to $f'_j$ and removed, then the model cannot recall the 8th item when the appropriate time comes. Another way is to remove the correct item anyway (Lewandowsky & Murdock, 1989). If this method is adopted, then TODAM can produce recency effects (see Figure 11.9). By the time the last item is ready to be recalled, it is also the only item left in the competitor set; so as long as things have not gone disastrously awry, $f'_j$ will always be matched with the last item because there is no other possibility.

Removing the correct item solves the problem of a lack of recency, but it introduces another: If the system does not know that $f'_j$ is really item 2, how does it know to remove item 2 from the competitor set? The solution to the problem is neither trivial nor obvious (Lewandowsky & Li, 1994), and it remains unclear whether the solution solves all of the related problems.

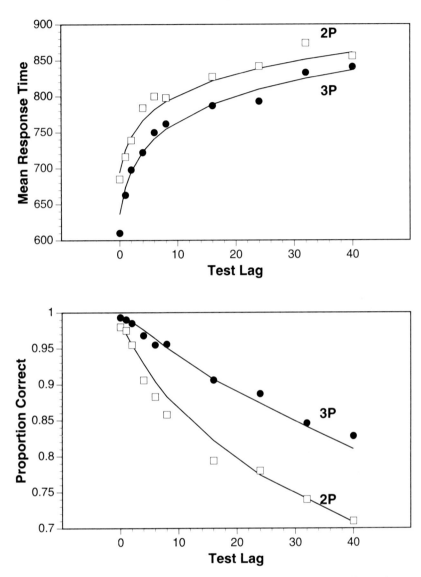

**Figure 11.8** The data points show observed data and the solid lines show the predictions for response times (top panel) and accuracy (bottom panel) as a function of test lag.
Source: Adapted from Hockley & Murdock (1987).

*Summary of TODAM.*  TODAM was designed to account for serial order and recognition. Its most impressive accomplishment is to demonstrate that a model that consists of a single main memory vector can store items and successfully recall or recognize them. As such, it illustrates that, in principle, distributed memory models can work. TODAM also has successfully fit a variety of serial order and recognition data. One problem is the

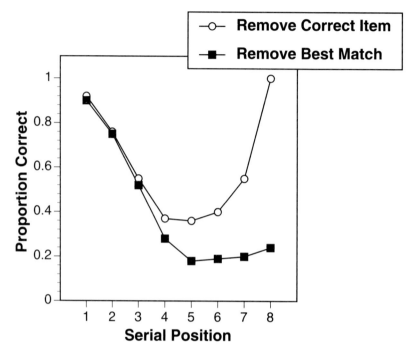

**Figure 11.9**  Two ways of removing items from the pool of competitors. If the correct item is removed from the competitor set, then the model produces recency. If the item that was actually matched to $f'_j$ is removed, then there is no recency.  Source: Nairne & Neath (1994).

manner in which an item is deblurred; the original system does not work, and it remains to be seen if this problem can be fixed. A major challenge facing theorists is to develop a psychologically plausible method of deblurring that simulates human data. Like the other models discussed above, TODAM also cannot account for the mirror effect (see Chapter 10).

## Connectionist Models

The implementation of neurallike circuitry in computer simulation models is known variously as *connectionism*, *neural networks*, or *parallel distributed processing*. These types of models have enjoyed tremendous popularity in many areas of cognitive psychology (see Chapter 2 for a brief history). As far as memory is concerned, their success has been less pronounced. As Ratcliff (1992) summarized it, "Few of the [neural network] models, however, have been seriously applied to the same range of experimental data in memory as the global memory models. It has been shown (McCloskey & Cohen, 1989; Ratcliff, 1990) that it is far from trivial to get models of this class to account for more than a few of the major trends in experimental data" (p. 431). The reason turns out to be rather straight-

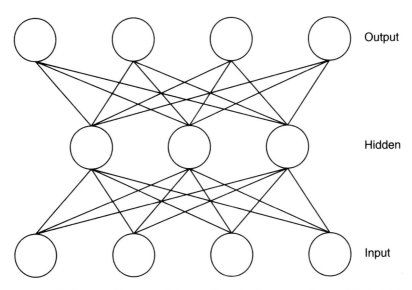

**Figure 11.10**   The basic architecture of the nonlinear back propagation models tested in recognition judgments.   Source: Ratcliff (1990).

forward: the very mechanism that allows these models to learn is also what causes them to forget.

One problem with studying connectionist models is that there are such a large number of possible variants. Most models can be instantiated in a three-layer architecture, and thus most models differ from others primarily in terms of the learning algorithm used. Ratcliff (1990) focused his attention on a class of connectionist models known as *nonlinear back propagation models,* a name that describes the learning mechanism. Most of Ratcliff's tests were with a model that looked like the one shown in Figure 11.10. There are four input nodes, each of which is connected to three hidden units; the hidden units in turn are each connected to four output units. The basic paradigm was simulating studying a list of words, and then being tested for recognition. Each "word" in the simulation was represented by a four-element vector of 0s and 1s (such as [1 0 0 1]), and the model was judged to have correctly recognized an old item if it reproduced a vector very similar to the input vector. For example, [0.94  0.04  0.04  0.96] would be judged as correct.

During study, a vector would be presented to the input nodes. The activation that arrives at a particular hidden node $i$ is simply the sum of all the activation that arrives over the four connections. For each connection, the value of the $j$th item in the vector ($O_j$) is multiplied by the weight on the connection between input node $j$ and hidden node $i$ ($w_{ij}$). The sum of all of these connections is the net activation ($net_i$):

$$net_i = \sum_j w_{ij}O_j \qquad (11.21)$$

The hidden nodes are connected to the output nodes. The function that describes these connections is called a *logistic sigmoid function,* which basically, converts numbers to a range from 0 to 1. It is useful to keep the activations in the range from 0 to 1 for easy interpretation and, more important, so that the values being used in the model do not become too large to work with. The particular logistic sigmoid function used to calculate the activation that arrives at output node i ($O_i$) is:

$$O_i = \frac{1}{1 + \exp^{-net_i}} \tag{11.22}$$

Prior to training, the weights are set to random values to reflect the fact that the network does not yet know anything. The first time through, the output that the model gives will be quite different from the desired output. The difference between the actual output ($O_i$) and the desired output ($t_i$) is represented by $\delta_i$ and is calculated by

$$\delta_i = (t_i - O_i)O_i(1 - O_i) \tag{11.23}$$

The error value, $\delta_i$, is then used to change the weights on the connections so that the actual output on the next learning trial will be closer to the desired output. The change in weights between the output and hidden nodes ($\Delta w_{ij}$) is calculated by multiplying the error value by a learning rate parameter ($\eta$) and by the jth value of the original vector ($O_j$):

$$\Delta w_{ij} = \eta \delta_i O_j \tag{11.24}$$

The weights between the hidden nodes and the input nodes use a slightly different error value which is calculated by

$$\delta_j = O_i(1 - O_i)\sum_k w_{ik}\delta_k \tag{11.25}$$

Then, the same equation as before (11.24) is used to calculate the actual change, but the new error value ($\delta_j$) is used instead of the old ($\delta_i$).

Ratcliff (1990) used two learning conditions. In the first, the model learned four words through what is known as *simultaneous presentation:* the four words are studied according to the following scheme: 1 2 3 4, 1 2 3 4, 1 2 3 4, 1 2 3 4, and so on.   The results are shown in Table 11.3.

So far, so good. The problem is that humans do not learn this way. They usually experience *sequential* presentation; that is, they study word 1 for a period of time, then word 2, and so on through the list, but once each item is finished with, it is not restudied be-

**Table 11.3**   Results of recognition simulations with a three-layer nonlinear back propagation network when the four to-be-remembered stimuli are trained using simultaneous presentation.

| Study | | | | Test | | | | Response | | | |
|---|---|---|---|---|---|---|---|---|---|---|---|
| 1 | 0 | 0 | 0 | 1 | 0 | 0 | 0 | 0.94 | 0.04 | 0.05 | 0.02 |
| 0 | 1 | 0 | 0 | 0 | 1 | 0 | 0 | 0.05 | 0.94 | 0.04 | 0.02 |
| 0 | 0 | 1 | 0 | 0 | 0 | 1 | 0 | 0.04 | 0.05 | 0.94 | 0.02 |
| 0 | 0 | 0 | 1 | 0 | 0 | 0 | 1 | 0.03 | 0.04 | 0.04 | 0.95 |

Source: Data from Ratcliff (1990).

**Table 11.4**   Results of recognition simulations with a three-layer nonlinear back propagation network when the four to-be-remembered stimuli are trained using simultaneous presentation for the first three items but sequential presentation for item 4.

| Study | | | | Test | | | | Response | | | |
|---|---|---|---|---|---|---|---|---|---|---|---|
| 1 | 0 | 0 | 0 | 1 | 0 | 0 | 0 | 0.77 | 0.01 | 0.01 | 0.90 |
| 0 | 1 | 0 | 0 | 0 | 1 | 0 | 0 | 0.01 | 0.75 | 0.01 | 0.92 |
| 0 | 0 | 1 | 0 | 0 | 0 | 1 | 0 | 0.01 | 0.01 | 0.73 | 0.95 |
| 0 | 0 | 0 | 1 | 0 | 0 | 0 | 1 | 0.03 | 0.04 | 0.04 | 0.95 |

Source: Ratcliff (1990).

fore test. Ratcliff tried a version of sequential learning: the network had the same number of learning trials, but the order of study was 1 2 3, 1 2 3, 1 2 3, . . . , 4 4 4, . . . . The results are shown in Table 11.4.

Although the most recent item is well remembered, recognition performance of the first three items drops dramatically. As can be seen in Table 11.4, the problem is that the last element of the vectors representing the first three items is contaminated by the last element in the vector representing the final item. Furthermore, the value of the other elements is greatly reduced. It turns out that this is a general problem: In several other simulations, Ratcliff tried various ways of minimizing this rapid forgetting including (1) modifying only some of the weights, (2) adding more hidden units, (3) longer vectors, (4) bigger networks, and various combinations of these. None of these greatly changed performance of the model.

The discussion of connectionist networks in Chapter 2 emphasized that memory is distributed over every node and every connection; there is no one place where the information resides. Each weight is involved in memory for each item. When the items are learned using simultaneous presentation, the model is basically finding one solution for all four problems. When the items are learned using sequential presentation, the model does not have to care about any item other than the one it is currently processing. Once the weights are established for this one item, the next item is presented. The model does not give a hoot about what it just learned; it adjusts the weights to learn the next problem. Therefore, the model is subject to catastrophic interference. Notice that it is the learning algorithm (changing the weights so that the actual output is more similar to the desired output) that also governs forgetting: changing the weights will change the output of what was previously learned.

*Summary of Connectionist Models.*   We have examined only one class of connectionist models but found an important limitation: whenever a realistic training sequence is used, the models suffer from catastrophic interference. It remains to be seen whether this problem is inherent in models that use other learning algorithms. Although there are successful connectionist models of other cognitive phenomena, there is currently no connectionist model comparable to SAM, MINERVA 2, or TODAM in terms of scope and accuracy of predictions.

# Summary of Global Memory Models

SAM, MINERVA 2, and TODAM have been applied to an impressive range of memory phenomena with notable success. It is because of their wide applicability that they are often referred to as *global memory models*. Although fitting a model to data does not mean that the model is arriving at the same result the same way that people do, such fitting does serve as an existence proof. Furthermore, simulation models provide an excellent check on human reasoning, particularly for situations in which there are complex interactions between several different variables. It should be emphasized that simulation models are not always better than purely verbal theories. Just as there are vague and inaccurate verbal theories of memory, there can also be vague and inaccurate simulation models. As far as the three global memory models that have been discussed in this chapter go, however, there are no verbal theories of comparable precision and breadth.

# References

Atkinson, R. C., & Shiffrin, R. M. (1968). Human memory: A proposed system and its control processes. In K. W. Spence & J. T. Spence (Eds.), *The psychology of learning and motivation, Vol. 2*. New York: Academic Press.

Drewnowski, A., & Murdock, B. B., Jr. (1980). The role of auditory features in memory span for words. *Journal of Experimental Psychology: Human Learning and Memory, 6*, 319–332.

Eagle, M., & Leiter, E. (1964). Recall and recognition in intentional and incidental learning. *Journal of Experimental Psychology, 68*, 58–63.

Eich, J. M. (1982). A composite holographic associative recall model. *Psychological Review, 89*, 627–661.

Estes, W. K., & Da Polito, F. (1967). Independent variation of information storage and retrieval processes in paired-associate learning. *Journal of Experimental Psychology, 75*, 18–26.

Flexser, A. J., & Tulving, E. (1978). Retrieval independence in recognition and recall. *Psychological Review, 85*, 153–171.

Gillund, G., & Shiffrin, R. M. (1984). A retrieval model for both recognition and recall. *Psychological Review, 91*, 1–65.

Gregg, V. H. (1976). Word frequency, recognition and recall. In J. Brown (Ed.), *Recall and recognition*. London: Wiley.

Hintzman, D. L. (1984). MINERVA 2: A simulation model of human memory. *Behavior Research Methods, Instruments, & Computers, 16*, 96–101.

Hintzman, D. L. (1986). "Schema abstraction" in a multiple-trace memory model. *Psychological Review, 93*, 411–428.

Hintzman, D. L. (1987). Recognition and recall in MINERVA 2: Analysis of the "recognition-failure" paradigm. In P. E. Morris (Ed.), *Modeling cognition*. Chichester, UK: Wiley.

Hintzman, D. L. (1988). Judgments of frequency and recognition memory in a multiple-trace memory model. *Psychological Review, 95*, 528–551.

Hintzman, D. L. (1991). Why are formal models useful in psychology? In W. E. Hockley & S. Lewandowsky (Eds.), *Relating theory and data: Essays in honor of Bennet B. Murdock*. Hillsdale, NJ: Erlbaum.

Hintzman, D. L. (1992). Mathematical constraints on the Tulving-Wiseman law. *Psychological Review, 99*, 536–542.

Hockley, W. E. (1982). Retrieval processes in continuous recognition. *Journal of Experimental Psychology: Learning, Memory, and Cognition, 8*, 497–512.

Hockley, W. E., & Murdock, B. B., Jr. (1987). A decision model for accuracy and response latency in recognition memory. *Psychological Review, 94*, 341–358.

Homa, D., Cross, J., Cornell, D., Goldman, D., & Schwartz, S. (1973). Prototype abstraction and classification of new instances as a function of number of instances defining the prototype. *Journal of Experimental Psychology, 101*, 116–122.

Lewandowsky, S. (1994). The rewards and hazards of computer simulations. *Psychological Science, 4*, 236–243.

Lewandowsky, S., & Li, S. C. (1994). Memory for serial order revisited. *Psychological Review, 101*, 539–543.

Lewandowsky, S., & Murdock, B. B., Jr. (1989). Memory for serial order. *Psychological Review, 96*, 25–57.

McCloskey, M., & Cohen, N. J. (1989). Catastrophic interference in connectionist networks: The sequential learning problem. In G. H. Bower (Ed.), *The psychology of learning and motivation, Vol. 23*. New York: Academic Press.

McKoon, G., Ratcliff, R., & Dell, G. S. (1986). A critical evaluation of the semantic/episodic distinction. *Journal of Experimental Psychology: Learning, Memory, and Cognition, 12*, 295–306.

Mensink, G.-J., & Raaijmakers, J. G. W. (1988). A model for interference and forgetting. *Psychological Review, 95*, 434–455.

Murdock, B. B., Jr. (1962). The serial position effect of free recall. *Journal of Experimental Psychology, 64*, 482–488.

Murdock, B. B., Jr. (1982). A theory for the storage and retrieval of item and associative information. *Psychological Review, 89*, 609–626.

Murdock, B. B., Jr. (1983). A distributed memory model for serial-order information. *Psychological Review, 90*, 316–338.

Murdock, B. B., Jr. (1993). TODAM2: a model for the storage and retrieval of item, associative, and serial-order information. *Psychological Review, 100*, 183–203.

Murdock, B. B., Jr. (1995). Developing TODAM: three models for serial-order information. *Memory & Cognition, 23*, 631–645.

Nairne, J. S., & Neath, I. (1994). A critique of the retrieval/deblurring assumptions of TODAM. *Psychological Review, 101*, 528–533.

Neely, J. H. (1989). Experimental dissociations and the episodic/semantic memory distinction. In H. L. Roediger III & F. I. M. Craik (Eds.), *Varieties of memory and consciousness: Essays in honour of Endel Tulving*. Hillsdale, NJ: Erlbaum.

Posner, M. I., Goldsmith, R., & Welton, K. E., Jr. (1967). Perceived distance and the classification of distorted patterns. *Journal of Experimental Psychology, 73*, 28–38.

Posner, M. I., & Keele, S. W. (1968). On the genesis of abstract ideas. *Journal of Experimental Psychology, 77*, 353–363.

Raaijmakers, J. G. W., & Shiffrin, R. M. (1981). Search of associative memory. *Psychological Review, 88*, 93–134.

Raaijmakers, J. G. W., & Shiffrin, R. M. (1992). Models for recall and recognition. *Annual Review of Psychology, 43*, 205–234.

Ratcliff, R. (1990). Connectionist models of recognition memory: Constraints imposed by learning and forgetting functions. *Psychological Review, 97,* 285–308.

Ratcliff, R. (1992). Models of memory. In L. R. Squire (Ed.), *Encyclopedia of learning and memory.* New York: Macmillan.

Strong, E. K. (1912). The effect of length of series upon recognition memory. *Psychological Review, 19,* 447–462.

Tulving, E. (1983). *Elements of episodic memory.* New York: Oxford University Press.

Tulving, E., & Flexser, A. J. (1992). On the nature of the Tulving-Wiseman function. *Psychological Review, 99,* 543–546.

Tulving, E., & Wiseman, S. (1975). Relation between recognition and recognition failure of recallable words. *Bulletin of the Psychonomic Society, 6,* 79–82.

Watkins, M. J., & Tulving, E. (1975). Episodic memory: When recognition fails. *Journal of Experimental Psychology: General, 104,* 5–29.

Young, R. K. (1968). Serial learning. In T. R. Dixon & D. L. Horton (Eds.), *Verbal behavior and general behavior theory.* Englewood Cliffs, NJ: Prentice-Hall.

# CHAPTER TWELVE

# Knowledge

*"I consider that a man's brain originally is like a little empty attic, and you have to stock it with such furniture as you choose. . . . It is a mistake to think that the little room has elastic walls and can distend to any extent. Depend upon it there comes a time when for every addition of knowledge you forget something that you knew before."*

—*Sherlock Holmes*

*"The more you put in a brain, the more it will hold."*

—*Nero Wolfe*

Knowledge refers to what you know. You probably know the capital of Canada, the number of states in the United States, your telephone number, the number of legs on an ostrich, several types of dinosaurs, the color of carrots, the texture of sandpaper, the taste of sea water, and perhaps even the air-speed velocity of an unladen European swallow. Perhaps more surprising than the amount of things you know is the amount of things you know that you do not know. For example, you probably know that you do not know the name of the 44th element in the periodic table (molybdenum), the name of William McKinley's first vice president (Garret A. Hobart), or the name of the 1959 Nobel Prize winner for literature (Salvatore Quasimodo). In this chapter, we look at various explanations for how people organize and retrieve information from semantic or generic memory. Although *semantic* memory is the most common term, a better term is Hintzman's (1978) *generic* memory, for three reasons: first, the topic is about everyday, ordinary knowledge (hence, generic); second, it includes information other than purely semantic information (having to do with words and meanings); and finally, the term *semantic memory* is usually taken as implying that semantic and episodic memory are separate systems (Tulving, 1972, 1983), which should be a separate issue from the study of knowledge.

## Propositions and Concepts

Before examining the most common views of generic memory, we need to define and explain some terms. The most common class of models that attempt to explain generic memory rely on concepts and propositions. A *proposition* is simply a relationship between two concepts that has a truth value. For example, a proposition might be that "A canary can sing." Singing is a concept and canary is a concept; this statement becomes a proposition because the concepts are arranged such that the truth of the statement can be verified. Even though most of the propositions we consider will be in the form of English sentences, this need not be the case. English is simply a convenient way of expressing the information, and people who speak different languages are assumed to have similar propositional representations.

A *concept,* then, is simply a mental representation of something. More technically, a concept is "an idea that includes all that is characteristically associated with it" (Medin, 1989, p. 1469). It could be a type of animal such as aardvark, a part of speech such as adjective, or an idea such as justice. Although words are frequently used to name concepts, a concept is more than a word and does not have to be a verbal entity. An analogy might be that a concept is like the entry in a dictionary that follows the word rather than the word itself.

One final point we need to consider is how best to test the models that will be described. The main problem is that everybody knows that birds fly, canaries sing, and animals eat. If we used an *accuracy* measure like proportion correct, everyone would score near 100% correct and there would be no observable differences. Instead of accuracy, researchers have used *latency* as their behavioral measure. Measurements of how quickly a person can respond are usually called *response times* and are conveniently abbreviated as RT. The key data, therefore, will come from seeing how quickly people process various types of information. One common test is to measure how long it takes people to verify that a proposition is true or false, and another is to measure how long it takes people to verify that a target item is a valid word. This latter test is known as a *lexical decision test.*

# Collins and Quillian's Hierarchical Model

Collins and Quillian (1969) converted a model for storing generic information in a computer (Quillian, 1967, 1969) into a testable model of human knowledge. Figure 12.1 shows the organization and illustrates the key features. Each black dot represents a category name (or concept), arranged in a hierarchical fashion so that the most general concepts are at the top and more specific instances are further down. Thus, canaries are a type of bird, and birds are a type of animal. The properties that most animals have in common are represented at the level of the animal concept; those that birds share but that other animals do not are at the level of bird; and those that distinguish canaries from other birds are down at the level of canary. This general principle is known as *cognitive economy,* because each property is listed as few times as possible. If asked whether canaries fly, the subject responds by retrieving the knowledge that canaries are birds and that birds can fly; it can then be inferred that canaries can fly. Ostriches cannot fly, and this information is stored at the level of ostrich to prevent an incorrect inference.

How does this model make testable predictions to see whether this organization is a plausible model for how people organize knowledge? The Collins and Quillian model makes predictions about how long it will take a person to verify a sentence. Suppose a person is asked to verify two sentences: "A canary can sing" and "A canary can fly." The model

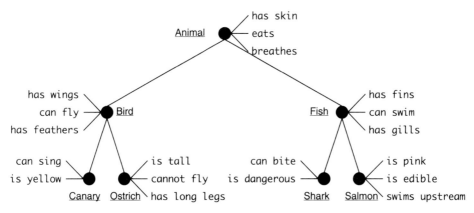

**Figure 12.1**  Hypothetical generic memory structure for a three-level hierarchy. The properties are not meant to be exhaustive, but rather illustrative.   Source: Collins & Quillian (1969).

shown in Figure 12.1 predicts slower responding to the second sentence than to the first. To verify the second sentence, the subject starts at the canary node but then has to move up the hierarchy one level to confirm that the desired property is there. No such travel is necessary for the first sentence; the property is stored at the same level as the category.

To state the predictions as precisely as possible, Collins and Quillian (1969) made three assumptions. First, they assumed that both retrieving a property and traversing the hierarchy take time. Second, they assumed that the times are additive whenever one step is dependent on the completion of another. For example, to verify the sentence "A canary can fly," retrieving the property "can fly" is dependent on first moving up the hierarchy. The additive assumption simply means that the time to complete both steps is the sum of completing each step individually. Third, Collins and Quillian assumed that the time to retrieve a property is independent of the level of the hierarchy.

Collins and Quillian (1969) presented subjects with two kinds of sentences to verify. Sentences that involved properties were called P sentences, and those that involved superset relations were called S sentences. In addition, there were three possible levels of the hierarchy. A 0-level sentence involves properties or supersets at the same level. For example, a P0 sentence might be "A canary can sing." An S0 sentence might be "A canary is a canary." Any sentence that involved moving one level up the hierarchy was called either an S1 or P1 sentence; a sentence that involved moving two levels was called an S2 or P2 sentence. In three experiments, Collins and Quillian (1969) presented true and false sentences from knowledge bases similar to that shown in Figure 12.1. For example, a true P1 sentence from a Games knowledge base might be "Badminton has rules." A false sentence might be "Hockey is a race."  Other knowledge domains tested included trees and beverages.

The model predicts two parallel lines, with the property line higher than that for superset questions. As Figure 12.2 shows, this is exactly what happens. The difference between P0 and P1, and P1 and P2 is about 75 ms, as is the difference between S1 and S2. The difference between P1 and S1 and P2 and S2 is about 225 ms. These measures can be interpreted as suggesting that it takes about 75 ms to retrieve a property, regardless of the

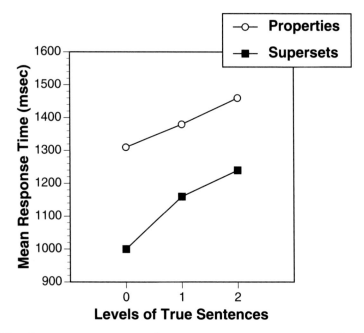

**Figure 12.2**   Mean response time to verify property or superset sentences as a function of how many levels need to be traveled.   Source: Collins & Quillian (1969).

level in the hierarchy, and that it takes about 225 ms to travel up a level. Given the simplicity of the model, it is remarkably accurate in its predictions.

There were two main problems with this version of the model. First, and most important, there is no clear way of explaining performance on the false sentences. Collins and Quillian considered three different hypotheses: (1) the contradiction hypothesis, where search stops when a contradiction is reached; (2) the unsuccessful search hypothesis, where search stops after a certain criterion is reached; and (3) the search and destroy hypothesis, where search continues until all possible connections are evaluated. None gave a good account of performance. The second main problem was that the Collins and Quillian (1969) model was proposed as a specific test of the most simple version of the model, and it made assumptions that were more strict than necessary (see Collins & Loftus, 1975). For example, although the description appears to suggest that each item is stored only once, Collins and Quillian (1969, p. 242) acknowledge there are often multiple representations and that structures may not be perfectly hierarchical.

## The Feature Overlap Model

The next major model was developed by Smith and his colleagues (Smith, Shoben, & Rips, 1974), who assumed that the meaning of a concept is not a single unit but a set of features or attributes. There are two types of features, defining and characteristic. *Defining features* are essential, whereas *characteristic features* are typical. This relationship is not

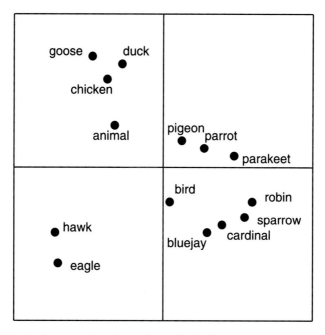

**Figure 12.3**  A multidimensional scaling solution for birds.  Source: Rips, Shoben, & Smith (1973).

an either-or situation, however; a particular feature can be more defining or more characteristic. For example, some features of robins are that (1) they are bipeds, (2) they have wings, (3) they have red breasts, (4) they perch in trees, and (5) they are not domesticated. Feature (3) is probably the most defining, and features 1 and 5 are the least defining.

One way of obtaining evidence consistent with this idea is to have subjects rate how typical various instances of various categories are. Rips, Shoben, and Smith (1973) found that robins and sparrows were thought to be more typical birds than are chicken and geese. These judgments are consistent with the idea that subjects are using characteristic features. A more sophisticated way of representing these data is to use *multidimensional scaling*. This procedure basically converts similarity ratings to distance: the more similar two items are judged to be, the closer the items are when plotted. One such solution is shown in Figure 12.3. Note that goose, duck, and chicken are close together (they are similar) but are far away from robin and sparrow. Notice also that these three birds are closer (more similar) to the concept of an animal than to the concept of a bird. One implication of this view is that category membership is not all or none; rather, membership within a category is a matter of degree.

Further evidence consistent with the idea that the meaning of a concept is a set of features or attributes was reported by Rips (1975). He had subjects read a report about a fictitious island that contained several kinds of animals: geese, ducks, eagles, hawks, robins, sparrows, ostriches, and bats. As can be seen in Figure 12.3, the first three pairs are widely spaced, but each item in the pair is close to the other item. Subjects were told that one species had been diagnosed with a contagious disease, and they were asked to estimate the percentages of other animals that also had the disease. The results are shown in

**Table 12.1**  Estimated rates of infection for five species when told that a sixth species was infected. The boldface figures are for birds that are most similar to the infected species.

| Infected Species | Estimated Percent Infection Rate | | | | | |
|---|---|---|---|---|---|---|
| | Goose | Duck | Robin | Sparrow | Hawk | Eagle |
| Goose | – | **74** | 17 | 18 | 16 | 13 |
| Duck | **81** | – | 18 | 18 | 43 | 35 |
| Robin | 26 | 30 | – | **79** | 35 | 41 |
| Sparrow | 32 | 27 | **66** | – | 49 | 43 |
| Hawk | 40 | 27 | 27 | 29 | – | **63** |
| Eagle | 17 | 16 | 26 | 29 | **72** | – |

Source: Based on Rips (1975).

Table 12.1. The species closest to the infected bird in Figure 12.3 was the species with the highest estimated infection rate. As the species became more distant, the predicted infection rate decreased.

Rips' (1975) study is important because it provides converging evidence. Although he used different subjects and a very different task, the results are consistent with those from

---

**Experiment    Typicality Effects and Inferences**

**Purpose:** To demonstrate how typicality can affect inferences.

**Subjects:** Thirty-six subjects are recommended.

**Materials:** Table 12.1 above lists six of the eight animals needed; ostrich and bat should also be included. You will also need an answer sheet on which subjects can write their responses. This answer sheet should have all eight animal names in a different random order for each subject.

**Procedure:** Inform the subjects that in this experiment they will be asked to make estimates of how many animals from various species are infected by a particular disease. One-sixth of the subjects should be given sparrow as the infected species, one-sixth should be given robin, and so forth. No subjects are told that bat or ostrich are infected.

**Instructions:** "Imagine an island has been discovered that contains eight different species of animals. These are listed on your answer sheet. Scientists have found that the [name of infected bird]s are infected with a contagious disease. We would like you to estimate how many of the other animals are likely to be infected. On your answer sheet, please write down a number from 0% to 100% to indicate how many of each species is likely to be infected. Any questions?"

**Scoring and Analysis:** For each infected species, calculate the average percent infection rate for the other five species of birds. The data should look like Table 12.1.

**Optional Enhancements:** Increase the number of subjects, making sure to keep an even multiple of 6. Use other types of animals or adapt the experiment to other types of materials.

Source: Based on an experiment by Rips (1975).

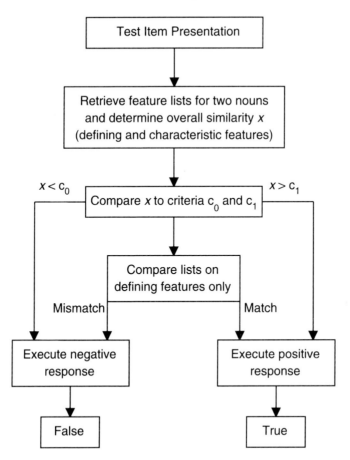

**Figure 12.4**  The two-stage decision process for feature comparison.  Source: Smith, Shoben, & Rips (1974).

the multidimensional scaling procedure. This is called *converging evidence* because both sets of results converge or point to the same answer (Garner, Hake, & Ericksen, 1956). Furthermore, it shows how information in generic memory can affect performance on other tasks.

According to the *feature overlap model,* how does a person decide whether a robin is a bird? The basic processes involved are outlined in Figure 12.4. After the proposition is presented, the first process is to retrieve the list of features for both concepts. These feature lists contain both characteristic and defining features. It is assumed that the lists are organized with the most defining features listed first, with subsequent features being less defining and more characteristic. The feature lists of the two concepts in the proposition are then compared and an overall measure of similarity or overlap, $x$, is computed. What happens next depends on the value of $x$. There are two critera, an upper value $c_1$ and a lower value $c_0$. If $x$ is greater than $c_1$, there is a high degree of overlap (which indicates a match) and so a positive response is made. If $x$ is lower than $c_0$, there is very little overlap (which indicates a mismatch) and so a negative response is made. When $x$ has extreme values, only one decision stage is necessary. If $x$ is greater than the lower criterion but less than the upper criterion, there is some overlap; so an immediate "false" response cannot be given, but there is not enough overlap to give an immediate "true" response. This is where the second decision stage occurs; this second stage separates the more defining features from the characteristic features. For example, although bats have several characteristic features of birds (for example, they both fly), bats have different defining features (they are mammals whereas birds are not). Comparing all features would produce an intermediate value for $x$, and then the defining features would be examined. This second comparison is more analytic than the first, which can be thought of as more holistic.

This model can account for all the data that the Collins and Quillian (1969) hierarchical model can, as well as for several results that the former model could not. For example, subjects more quickly verify that "A robin is a bird" than that "A robin is an animal." The hierarchical model says this is because there are two levels of hierarchy to travel for the second sentence, compared to only one in the first. The Smith et al. (1974) model says this is because robins share more features with the concept bird than with the concept animal. In Figure 12.3, robin is closer to bird than to animal, which indicates that there is more feature overlap between robins and birds than between robins and animals.

The second finding from Collins and Quillian (1969) was that people are faster to verify sentences like "A canary can sing" than "A canary can fly." In the hierarchical model, this was because the properties were stored at different levels of the hierarchy. In the feature overlap model, this is explained by the ordering of features within the feature list. The most defining feature is listed first, which in the case of canaries would be things like is yellow, can sing, and so forth. Farther down the list are features that are less defining, such as can fly, has wings. The farther down the list of features the particular property, the longer it will take to verify the sentence.

The feature overlap model has two major advantages. It can handle false responses, which occur when the featural overlap between two concepts is very small. But even more important, it can handle different kinds of false responses. For example, subjects more quickly indicate that the proposition "Magnesium is an animal" is false than the proposition "A tree is an animal" (Collins & Quillian, 1970). This is because animals and trees are both living things and will have some features in common, whereas magnesium is inanimate.

The model is not without problems, the most important of which concerns the distinction between defining and characteristic features. For categories such as triangle, there are defining features: a 3-sided, closed figure whose interior angles add to 180°. If a shape has these features, it is a triangle; if it does not, then it is not a triangle. For nontechnical categories though, such as ones people use everyday (furniture, cars, tools), there is no such thing as a defining feature. This problem, well known in philosophy (Wittgenstein, 1953), is illustrated by asking subjects to answer a simple question: Can you name one feature that all games have in common? For every suggestion, one can easily find a game for which the feature is not true or can find something that is not a game but has that feature. The feature overlap model requires this distinction in order to have two stages, but the distinction is probably not valid for the majority of categories.

A second problem is that the feature overlap model restricts the kind of information that can be brought to bear on a task. Because the key decision processes are based only on feature comparison, other sources of knowledge are excluded from the categorization process. For example, another common task to uncover the properties of generic memory is called *production frequency*. Here, subjects are given either a category name and are asked to name an example, or are given an example and are asked to name the category. Depending on which item is given first, different results occur. Loftus (1973) found, for example, that although insect is often mentioned as the category for butterfly, butterfly is rarely mentioned as an example of an insect. The problem for the feature overlap model is how to explain these differences when the same set of features is recruited for each comparison.

## Collins and Loftus' Spreading Activation Model

Collins and Loftus (1975) proposed a revision of the basic hierarchical model to take into account the problematic findings for both models described above. The key idea, expanded and clarified from earlier versions, is that activation spreads from one or two concepts to all related concepts. The main differences between this model and the earlier versions are that implied or suggested constraints are explicitly disavowed. For example, the spreading activation model (1) is not strictly hierarchical or, to phrase the same idea slightly differently, relaxes the notion of cognitive economy so that some concepts can be represented multiple times; (2) has links between concepts that have differential travel time; and (3) explicitly allows activation to spread from both category and exemplar nodes. Collins and Loftus list 13 assumptions about the spreading activation model's operation; we list only a subset.

*Assumption 1:* When a concept is processed, activation spreads out along all paths; the strength of the activation decreases as the number of paths increase.

*Assumption 2:* Only one concept can be processed at a time, but once processed activation can spread in parallel.

*Assumption 3:* Activation decreases over time and/or activity.

*Assumption 5:* The more properties two concepts have in common, the more links there are between the concepts. For example, most vehicles are very similar, so they will have many interconnecting links, but most red things share only one feature (color) and so will have very few links (see Figure 12.5).

*Assumption 8:* The decision process requires enough evidence to exceed a positive or negative criterion. Evidence comes from examining intersections, points where activation from different sources meet.

Related are assumptions 9 through 13, which detail the types of positive and negative evidence available. Finding an intersection involving a superordinate category, or properties that match, or exclusive subordinates (such as male and female), or counterexamples, are all types of evidence that can be used to render a decision, either positive or negative.

Chang (1986) compared the hierarchical model and the spreading activation model in the following way: "As easy as it was to falsify the hierarchical-network model, it is just as difficult to disprove the present spreading-activation theory; but, at the same time, as easy as it was to [generate] empirical implications of the earlier model, it is just as difficult at present to derive unequivocal predictions [of the revised model]" (p. 217). Because of these problems, the Collins and Loftus (1975) version is probably best viewed as a framework rather than as a precise, testable model, and for that reason we do not provide

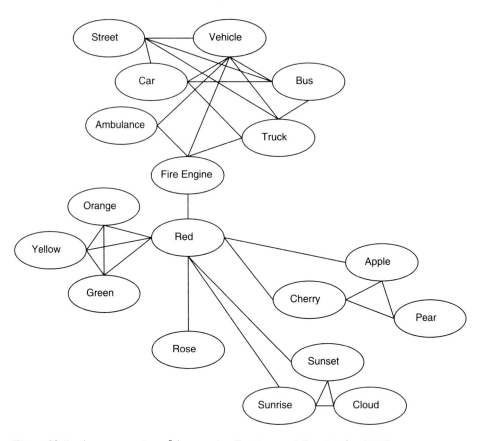

**Figure 12.5** A representation of Assumption 5.   Source: Collins & Loftus (1975).

a detailed analysis of its predictions about verifying propositions. We will examine it in more detail in the section comparing its account of association priming with the account offered by compound cue theories.

Spreading activation quickly became the dominant explanation for theories of generic memory (Anderson, 1983a), as well as word production (Dell, 1986) and word perception (McClelland & Rumelhart, 1981; Rumelhart & McClelland, 1982). Indeed, connectionist models, which have been applied to numerous areas in psychology, can be thought of as spreading activation models. Although each of these versions is more specific and detailed than the original proposal, each is based on the same idea.

## Knowing That You Don't Know

Before continuing with a discussion of the core feature of spreading activation, it is worthwhile to pause and consider how people decide that they do not know something. There has been relatively little work on this area compared to research on what people do know.

For example, all of the models discussed above emphasized how people respond "true" or "false," but they gave no option for a "don't know" response.

One notable exception is a series of experiments reported by Glucksberg and Mc-Closkey (1981). In their first experiment, they had subjects memorize a set of sentences, such as: John has a pencil; John doesn't have a shovel; Bill has a bowl; Bill doesn't have a magazine. After learning these sentences, subjects were given a variety of questions that could be answered true, false, or don't know. The true sentences were the same as the studied sentences, whereas the false sentences contradicted some aspect of a studied sentence (such as John doesn't have a pencil; Bill has a magazine). The don't know sentences contained names and objects that had been studied but in new combinations (Bill has a pencil; John doesn't have a magazine). Subjects were asked to decide true, false, or don't know as fast as they could.

Subjects took 1596 ms to correctly respond "true" to true test items and 1688 ms to correctly respond "false" to false items. They required only 1337 ms to correctly respond "don't know." An analysis of errors illustrated the same pattern: subjects made about 12% errors on true items, 12% errors on false items, but only 2% errors on don't know items. People can thus be both faster and more accurate to say they don't know than to respond with what they do know.

Glucksberg and McCloskey's (1981) second experiment tested an interesting idea. They hypothesized that people will take more time to respond "don't know" if they have explicitly stored the fact that they don't know something compared to when they have not explicitly stored that fact. The design was similar to the previous experiment, except that some sentences contained information about what was not known (such as, It is unknown whether John has a chair). An explicit don't know test item might be "John has a chair" or "John doesn't have a chair," whereas an implicit don't know test item would be the same as in the previous experiment. The results are shown in Table 12.2. When the subjects had explicit knowledge that the information was not known, it took them longer to respond and they were less accurate than when they did not have explicit knowledge about their lack of information.

Glucksberg and McCloskey (1981) suggested that don't know decisions are made by a two-stage process. First, the subject examines whether there are any relevant facts about the question. If there are none, then a quick "don't know" response is made. If there is some information available, the second stage begins in which there is a more detailed examination of the facts. If the information is still not sufficient to answer the question, then a slow "don't know" response is made.

**Table 12.2** Mean response time and mean error rate for true, false, explicitly stored uncertain, and not stored uncertain test items.

|  | True | False | Explicit Don't Know | Implicit Don't Know |
|---|---|---|---|---|
| Response Time (ms) | 1888 | 2093 | 1892 | 1594 |
| Error Rate (%) | 4.8 | 7.3 | 4.0 | 1.4 |

Source: Data from Glucksberg & McCloskey (1981).

**Table 12.3**  Mean response times.

| Top String | Bottom String | Example | Mean RT | % Errors |
|---|---|---|---|---|
| Word | Associated word | nurse-doctor | 855 | 6.3 |
| Word | Unassociated word | nurse-butter | 940 | 8.7 |
| Word | Nonword | bread-marb | 1087 | 27.6 |
| Nonword | Word | besk-doctor | 904 | 7.8 |
| Nonword | Nonword | besk-marb | 884 | 2.6 |

Source: Data from Meyer & Schvaneveldt (1971).

# Priming

Spreading activation can essentially be reduced to one main finding: priming. Unfortunately, the term *priming* can refer to at least two different effects. In Chapter 8, we examined *repetition priming* in conjunction with implicit memory: the processing of something a second time benefits from having processed it previously. A second type of priming is *association priming,* which refers to the observation that response times are often faster if a second item is related to or associated with the first item. Thus, in repetition priming the target item is processed twice, whereas in association priming the target item is processed only once.

To give a specific example of association priming, in one experiment two strings of letters were shown, one above the other. If both were valid words, the subject was asked to respond "yes." If one or both strings were not words, the subject was asked to respond "no." The results are shown in Table 12.3.

Subjects responded faster when both strings were related words (nurse-doctor, bread-butter) than when they were unrelated (doctor-butter, bread-nurse) by approximately 85 ms (Meyer & Schvaneveldt, 1971). When the first string was a nonword, response times were also fast but as a result of the task: there is no need to process the second string if the first one gives sufficient information to answer the question. Subjects were slowest when the first word was a word and the second was a nonword. Spreading activation models provide a simple explanation: as the first word is read, the relevant concept is activated. Activation spreads to related concepts so that by the time the second word is read, its relevant concept is already partially active. This saves time in processing the second item and produces a decrease in response time.

Priming can be seen when the stimuli are more complex than single words. For example, Ashcraft (1976) demonstrated priming with topics. Sentences that involved high-frequency properties, such as "A sparrow has feathers" were verified in approximately 1330 ms. If a second sentence, such as "A robin can fly" followed, there was priming: response times decreased to approximately 1200 ms.

Neely (1977) demonstrated that expectations can affect priming using a lexical decision task. Subjects were asked to judge as quickly and as accurately as they could whether a target was a word or a nonword. (We will ignore the responses to nonwords; they are there primarily to keep the subjects honest.) In one condition, subjects were told that if

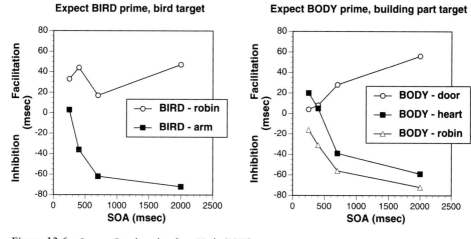

**Figure 12.6**   Source: Based on data from Neely (1977).

the first word (the prime) was BIRD, then the second word (target) would be a type of bird. These subjects might see BIRD followed by ROBIN. In a second condition, subjects were told that if the prime was BODY, then the target would be a building part. These subjects might see BODY followed by DOOR. Neely also manipulated two other variables. One is called stimulus onset asynchrony, or SOA. This is simply the amount of time between the presentation of the first item and the presentation of the second: an SOA of 0 ms means the two items are presented simultaneously; an SOA of 2000 ms means presentation of the second item began 2 seconds after the presentation of the first item began. The final variable was whether the prime-target relationship was as advertised: occasionally, subjects who were expecting BIRD-ROBIN might see BIRD-ARM. Subjects who were expecting a category shift (BODY-DOOR) occasionally might see BODY-ARM.

The results are shown in Figure 12.6 as a function of the amount of facilitation or inhibition with respect to baseline performance. Baseline performance is simply the time taken to respond when the prime was XXX rather than a word. The left panel of Figure 12.6 shows the results for the subjects who were not expecting a category shift: the open circles are for trials where no shift occurred, and the closed squares are for trials where a shift did occur. The right panel shows the results for subjects who were expecting a category shift. At the shortest SOA, there was priming for semantically related items (BIRD-ROBIN and BODY-HEART). However, as the SOA increased, the expectations of the subject come into play: BIRD-ROBIN priming continues (left panel) whereas BODY-HEART priming disappears (right panel). Neither BIRD-ARM nor BODY-ROBIN showed priming; indeed, as the SOA increases, inhibition increases. Neither group expected this pairing, and both pairs contain unrelated words. The final data come from the BODY-DOOR group in the right panel. These subjects were expecting this relationship, but there was no priming with short SOAs. Because priming here is dependent on expectations, it takes some time to be observable; by 2000 ms SOA, however, BODY primed DOOR (when expected) as well as BIRD primed ROBIN.

These results are consistent with the idea that there are at least two components involved with priming. First, there is an automatic component that is independent of the subject's intentions or expectations. This is seen in Neely's (1977) data when related items, such as BODY-HEART, show priming at short SOAs even though the subject was not expecting this relationship. The second component is more strategic and reflects the subject's expectations. Thus, BODY can prime DOOR but only after a relatively long SOA; there is no priming seen at short SOAs. Most models focus on the automatic aspect because it is more likely to yield information about the basic structure of generic memory than the intentional component is, which reflects strategies the subject is currently using. It should be noted that further research (Neely, Keefe, & Ross, 1989) has revealed that the process is more complex than described above.

Spreading activation models are such dominant models that many people use the terms *priming* and *activation* as synonyms (Ratcliff & McKoon, 1988). Indeed, the concept of activation is so well accepted that it is widely used in other areas of research. For example, one current view of immediate memory uses activation and decay of activation as the key theoretical idea (see Chapter 5). Immediate memory, according to this view, is that portion of permanent knowledge that is in a heightened state of activation. Because only a very small fraction of information in memory can be active at one time, these views also need to posit some mechanism or process, usually decay, that can deactivate it.

The most fundamental findings that support a spreading activation approach are the association priming data discussed above. These results are widely considered to be the most direct evidence possible: all the subject is required to do is process one word after processing a related item. According to spreading activation, as the first word is read, the relevant concept is activated. Activation spreads to related concepts so that by the time the second word is read, its relevant concept is already partially active.

If the spreading activation account of association priming is called into question, then spreading activation as a general concept, in theories of both immediate and generic memory, can also be called into question. Compound cue theory, a more recent explanation of association priming, does indeed call into question the fundamental assumption of spreading activation theory.

# Alternatives to Spreading Activation

One relatively recent competitor to spreading activation is a class of models known as *compound cue models* (Dosher & Rosedale, 1989; Ratcliff & McKoon, 1988). The basic idea is that instead of selecting items that have been activated by spreading activation, generic memory functions more the way other forms of memory function. Ratcliff and McKoon's (1988; McKoon & Ratcliff, 1992) model, for example, is based on a process similar to that used by SAM (Gillund & Shiffrin, 1984; see Chapter 11), a model designed to explain both free recall and recognition data. However, Ratcliff and McKoon point out that two other models (also discussed in Chapter 11)—MINERVA 2 (Hintzman, 1986) and TODAM (Murdock, 1982)—both can implement the main idea.

In SAM (Gillund & Shiffrin, 1984), items in memory are represented as images. An *image* is an interconnected feature set that contains information about (1) the context in which the item was learned, (2) the item itself (its meaning, its name, etc.), and (3) its relation with other images. In a memory test, the subject assembles a set of cues in short-term memory and then uses these to probe various images in long-term memory. In a recognition test, the result of this probe, called *familiarity*, is used to decide whether to respond "old" or "new." The familiarity of an item depends on the strength of the associations between the cues used and the target item, as well as between the target item and other items in memory. The familiarity of an item, when probing using context and the item itself, is given by the following equation (described in more detail in Chapter 11):

$$F(C,W_j) = \sum_{k=1}^{n} S(C,W_k) S(W_j,W_k) \tag{12.1}$$

This formula calculates the familiarity ($F$) when both the context ($C$) and the item itself ($W_j$) are used as cues. The strength of the association between the context and a given item in memory ($W_k$) and the strength of the association between the item itself and a given item in memory are multiplied. This is done for all $n$ items in memory, and the results are added together. (This process was discussed at length in Chapter 11.)

The first change is the assumption that items presented to the system can join together to form a compound cue; thus, another item is added to the equation above. The familiarity when the two items plus the context are used as cues will be the sum of the products of the strengths of the associations. If $X$ represents the preceding item in the compound (the prime), then $S(X,W_k)$ would appear at the end of the equation, like this:

$$F(C,W_j,X) = \sum_{k=1}^{n} S(C,W_k) S(W_j,W_k) S(X,W_k) \tag{12.2}$$

The familiarity value will be a combination of familiarity to both items that form the compound. For example, if NURSE is seen right after DOCTOR, then the compound of DOCTOR and NURSE as a cue will result in more familiarity than if just NURSE is the cue. Familiarity will be greater when the two items forming the compound cue have a large number of common associates because the strengths to each individual cue are multiplied. For example, imagine two items, A and B, that share many associates, I, J, K, and L. The strength of the association between A and I is large, and the association between B and I is large; when these strengths are multiplied, the result is even larger. Now imagine a third item, C, that is not associated with I, J, K, or L; in other words, item C has few associates in common with item A. The strength of the association between A and I is still large, but the strength of the association between C and I is small; a large number is now multiplied by a small number. The actual equation used is a little more complicated because the current item (NURSE) is given more importance than the preceding item (DOCTOR):

$$F(C,W_j,X) = \sum_{k=1}^{n} S(C,W_k) S(W_j,W_k)^{(1-P)} S(X,W_k)^{P} \tag{12.3}$$

$P$ is a value that ranges from 0 to 1. If $P$ is set to 0, then $S(X,W_k)^P$ becomes 1 and the prime is ignored. As $P$ increases, more weight is given to the prime.

There is one other change to SAM; some way needs to be devised to relate familiarity to response time. Ratcliff and McKoon (1988) used a previously well-studied diffusion model (Ratcliff, 1978), which basically converts high values of familiarity to fast and accurate positive ("Yes") response times, low values of familiarity to fast and accurate negative ("No") response times, and intermediate values to slower and less accurate positive and negative response times.

# Comparing Spreading Activation and Compound Cue Models

Although relatively few studies directly compare predictions of spreading activation models and compound cue models, some differences have been noted. The compound cue model referred to below is described more completely by Ratcliff and McKoon (1988, 1995), and a spreading activation account is described by McNamara (1992a, 1992b).

*Priming.*   *Spreading activation* models account for association priming by assuming that activation spreads from one concept to related concepts; the more directly related the concept, the more priming will occur. *Compound cue theory* accounts for association priming by assuming that both the prime and the target form a cue; because they have associates in common, there is more familiarity. There is no such thing as activation within compound cue theory.

*Priming onset.*    Priming onset refers to how quickly priming is evident. Early versions of spreading activation theories (Collins & Quillian, 1969; Collins & Loftus, 1975) assumed that the onset of priming was a function of the number of intervening concepts, or links. These models predict that priming should take longer to see for CANARY-ANIMAL than CANARY-BIRD. (Do not confuse priming with sentence verification; in priming, subjects respond whether the target is a word or not. Responses to the target are facilitated when then prime is associated with it relative to when the prime is unrelated.)  The compound cue model predicts no difference in priming onset because the same computations are performed regardless of how related the items may be. Ratcliff and McKoon (1981) varied the duration of the SOA to determine when priming was first evident and found that, when words rather than sentences were used, there was no difference in response times for primes that are closer together (CANARY-BIRD) than for primes that are farther apart (CANARY-ANIMAL). Spreading activation models have since been revised to account for this finding by allowing the spread of activation from concept to concept to be much faster (on the order of 5 ms per link).

*Decay of priming.*    As more items intervene between the prime and target, the amount of facilitation decreases. Compound cue models account for this by having the prime replaced by the intervening item within the compound cue (Ratcliff & McKoon, 1988). Although the compound cue could include any number of items, if more than one or two nonassociated items are included, the effects of priming will be minimal. This places a limit on the model's prediction of how long the target can be delayed and still have priming. If priming is seen after ten intervening items, for example, compound cue theory is disproven. Spreading activation models, on the other hand, typically have activation decrease as a function of time (Anderson, 1983b, McClelland & Rumelhart, 1981). There is nothing within the structure of these models that places a limit on how many intervening items can occur.

*Multiple meanings.*    There is evidence that when an ambiguous word is presented, both meanings are primed immediately but only the appropriate meaning remains primed (Swinney, 1979). For example, the word *bank* can refer to a place where money is kept or to the side of a river; the word *bug* can refer to an insect or to a covert listening device. Spreading activation explains this priming effect by assuming that decay of activation occurs to both meanings; the "correct" meaning is kept active, however, by activation from other words compatible with the context of the sentence. The compound cue model states that no decay occurs because no activation occurs; rather, a compound cue that contains an ambiguous word will give a high value of familiarity. When the ambiguous word is replaced in the cue by a later word, then only the appropriate meaning will have a high familiarity value.

*Mediated priming.*    Mediated priming refers to priming seen when two items that are unrelated (LION and STRIPES) can become related by a third, mediating item (here, TIGER). According to spreading activation models, activation spreads from LION to STRIPES via the mediating link of TIGER. LION and TIGER are related, and TIGER and STRIPES are related. Compound cue theories posit that no mediation is necessary. If the two components in the compound are sufficiently familiar, then there will be priming. One measure related to familiarity should be co-occurrence: how often two words are experienced together. McKoon and Ratcliff (1992) showed that mediated priming (LION-STRIPES, mediated presumably by TIGER) resulted in as much facilitation as nonmediated priming of words that co-occur frequently (DEER-GRAIN, where no obvious item associated with deer also is related to grain). There is currently much ongoing work examining mediated priming, but both views can predict the basic effect.

Given that both views are consistent with the main data, which is the better explanation? Spreading activation is still currently the most widely accepted view of how information in generic memory is retrieved. One reason is because it is intuitively appealing: the basic idea of spreading activation captures the introspection of how one item word or idea can lead to another.

The main weakness of the spreading activation view is the lack of specificity. Most versions (one exception is Anderson, 1983a) are so vague that it is difficult to derive a strong, a priori prediction (see Chang, 1986). Related to this is a logical problem (see Ratcliff & McKoon, 1994). Suppose each word has 20 other words associated with it; this assumption is reasonable, given data on word association norms (Postman & Keppel, 1970). Presenting one prime would activate 20 words, and each of those would activate another 20. If activation is allowed to spread, as is required to explain mediated priming (McNamara & Altarriba, 1988), then each of these 400 active words would activate another 20. From one prime, 8000 words are now active, roughly an eighth of the words that the typical adult English speaker knows. McNamara (1992b) has demonstrated mediated priming with four items (e.g., MANE-STRIPES, presumably mediated by LION and TIGER). According to the account of mediated priming offered by spreading activation theories, 32,000 words are now active, approximately half of the typical English speaker's vocabulary.

Compound cue theory has two major advantages. First, it is more well specified, via the equations that describe the processes, than spreading activation models are. It is easy for different researchers to agree on the predictions that it makes, and the predictions can be made before the experiment. Second, it uses the mechanisms and processes of the global memory models (see Chapter 11) and so relates memory performance from generic memory to performance on recall and recognition tasks. There are also two main problems with compound cue theory. First, the rules for determining which items will form a compound cue are not yet well specified. Second, there is some question about the accuracy of one of its predictions. The words *spider* and *ant* are related but they are not associated. In other words, when people are asked to say the first thing that comes into their head when they hear the word *spider,* they do not say *ant.* Compound cue theory predicts that priming should occur because of the semantic relatedness, but some researchers (Shelton & Martin, 1992) found no priming, whereas others (McKoon & Ratcliff, 1992) have found priming. It remains unclear how to interpret these mixed results.

# How Is Generic Memory Organized?

Despite its apparent simplicity, the answer to the question of how generic memory is organized is likely to be complex, elusive, and a long way off. Categories can be organized at different levels of abstraction, some being very broad (furniture), some being less broad (chair), and some being quite specific (rocking chair). These have been termed (respectively) *superordinate, basic,* and *subordinate level categories* (Rosch & Mervis, 1975). What is particularly intriguing is that basic level categories (chair, dog, car) seem to be learned first, are the level at which objects are named, and show remarkable cross-cultural consistency (Rosch, Mervis, Gray, Johnson, & Bayes-Braem, 1976). Basic level categories are neither the most inclusive nor the most specific, but they do seem to have a special status relative to other levels of categorization.

The idea that concepts are organized by similarity has intuitive appeal. For example, people seem to group many things together on the basis of shared perceptual qualities. However, as Medin (1989) has argued, rather than being organized by similarity, concepts are organized around theories. According to this view (Murphy & Medin, 1985), the relationship between a concept and an example of that concept is similar to the relationship between theory and data. An example must have the right explanatory relationship to the theory that organizes the concept, rather than merely being similar. We will examine this idea further by focusing on one particular area of research.

One currently popular approach is to examine people who have deficits in particular aspects of generic memory operation: they can identify certain types of items but have difficulty identifying other items. One early suggestion was that generic memory might be organized by different categories, such as animate versus inanimate things.

Warrington and Shallice (1984) described four people who had recovered from herpes encephalitis but who had sustained both left and right temporal lobe damage. In one task, two subjects were asked to identify pictures of living things and nonliving things; in another task, they heard a word and were asked to provide a definition. The results are shown in Table 12.4. For example, when asked to define *ostrich,* JBR responded with

**Table 12.4**  Performance by two subjects with damage to both left and right temporal lobes on two generic memory tasks. Although subjects' ability to identify and define living things is grossly impaired, their ability to identify and define nonliving things is relatively intact.

| Subject | Living Things | Nonliving Things |
|---------|---------------|------------------|
| *Picture Identification* | | |
| JBR | 6% | 90% |
| SBY | 0% | 75% |
| | | |
| *Spoken Word Definition* | | |
| JBR | 8% | 79% |
| SBY | 0% | 52% |

Source: Based on data from Warrington & Shallice (1984).

"unusual." When asked to define *wasp,* SBY responded with "bird that flies." Even though these subjects were not perfect in identifying or defining all nonliving things, their performance was much better than for living things. Similar results have been reported by other investigators (De Renzi & Lucchelli, 1994; Farah, McMullen, & Meyer, 1991; Pietrini, Nertimpi, Vaglia, Revello, Pinna, & Ferro-Milone, 1988; Sartori, Miozzo, & Job, 1993).

One tempting conclusion is that generic memory organizes information about living things and nonliving things differently, such that it is possible to sustain damage to one area but have the other area relatively intact. Such a simple principle quickly became more complicated because there were subtypes that did not fit in with the category. For example, De Renzi and Lucchelli (1994) reported that their subject, Felicia, had only mild impairment for naming body parts, which technically are living, but she had severe impairment for professions, which are clearly not animate. Similarly, performance showed impairment for food items, of which some are living (e.g., potatoes, beans) and some are nonliving items (e.g., Coca Cola, spaghetti, and ice cream). Thus, Warrington and Shallice (1984; Warrington & McCarthy, 1983) suggested that the relevant difference was actually based on different properties. In general, visual features are of more importance in discriminating living things, whereas function is more important for discriminating nonliving things.

Farah and McClelland (1991) explored this idea by constructing a simulation model and then lesioning the part of the model responsible for visual features in generic memory. The basic architecture of the model is shown in Figure 12.7. Generic memory consists of two different types of knowledge: visual and functional. Input to the system can be either verbal (e.g., hearing a word) or visual (e.g., seeing a picture).

What is most intriguing are the results from simulations where Farah and McClelland damaged part of the model. They removed the visual component of generic memory by altering the weights on the connections or, in some cases, by disconnecting the units entirely. As the left panel of Figure 12.8 shows, when visual generic memory is damaged,

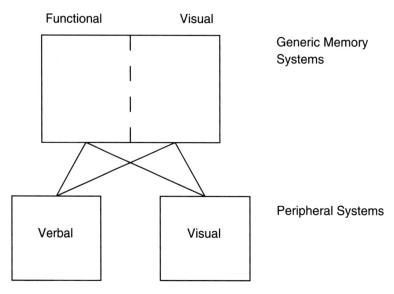

**Figure 12.7**   A schematic representation of the Farah and McClelland parallel distributed processing model of generic memory.   Source: Farah & McClelland (1991).

performance for nonliving things declines only slightly, whereas performance for living things declines to almost 0. This pattern is similar to that seen in Table 12.4. When visual generic memory is left intact and functional generic memory is damaged, there is no deficit apparent for living things and only a slight loss for nonliving things. This is also what subjects show (De Renzi & Lucchelli, 1994).

The results of the simulation are consistent with the organizational scheme proposed by Warrington and Shallice (1984). They do not, of course, prove that the scheme is correct, or that it is the only way of organizing information. Rather, they serve as an existence proof. Can a generic memory system that distinguishes between visual or perceptual information and functional information give rise to the sorts of deficits seen in subjects with bilateral temporal lobe damage? The answer is yes, but with qualifications.

The sensory/functional view can capture the broad pattern, but it fails to produce some deficits that are very fine grained. For example, Hillis and Caramazza (1991) described two patients, PS and JJ, who had contrasting deficits: PS showed a pervasive deficit in processing animal terms, whereas JJ showed a pervasive deficit in processing all categories tested except for animals. In both cases, processing for only animals rather than all living things was the exception. As another example, Hart, Berndt, and Caramazza (1985) described a patient, MD, whose deficit was limited to naming fruits and vegetables. This distinction cannot be captured by the sensory/functional view.

Although deficits in processing certain types of information from generic memory may suggest how it is organized, there is still no definitive view, and it is likely that this controversy will persist. Nonetheless, it is suggestive that many of the deficits described in a recent review by Caramazza, Hillis, Leek, and Miozzo (1994) correspond to basic level categories (see above).

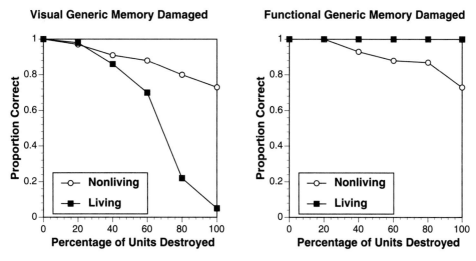

**Figure 12.8**   Simulation results from the Farah and McClelland model showing the effects of damaging increasing proportions of visual generic memory (left panel) or functional generic memory (right panel).    Source: Farah & McClelland (1991).

# Capacity and Acquisition

We began the chapter with two opposing viewpoints by two famous geniuses. It turns out that Nero Wolfe is better informed than Sherlock Holmes. Two series of experiments by Voss and his colleagues (Chiesi, Spilich, & Voss, 1979; Spilich, Vesonder, Chiesi, & Voss, 1979) illustrate the point. Using the criterion of baseball knowledge, subjects were divided into two groups; those with a lot of knowledge about baseball and those with very little. All subjects heard a fictional account of half an inning of a baseball game. Subjects with more knowledge of baseball remembered more of the specific details, provided a more organized response, and included more details relevant to the outcome of the game than did those subjects with less knowledge. Finally, high-knowledge subjects were able to predict the outcome better than low-knowledge subjects were. Existing knowledge, then, allows people to interpret new information, provides structures that add meaning to events, and allows people to make predictions. The more you know about something, the easier it is to acquire new related information; in that sense, the more you know, the more you can know.

There are at least two different ideas about how generic memory develops. One simple notion might be that as new information is received, it is categorized, labeled, and assigned to the relevant location within generic memory (placed at the appropriate level of the hierarchy in Collins and Quillian's structural model, or entered with appropriate connections in spreading activation models). This structure and set of connections can be quite different from that which supports episodic memory. This view predicts that there should be differences between episodic and generic memory, and such dissociations have been found. However, as discussed in Chapter 9, this view is as yet unable to predict the precise nature of the dissociations and has a difficult time accounting for dissociations within one system.

A quite different explanation is offered by MINERVA 2 (Hintzman, 1986; see Chapter 11). In this model, only episodic traces are stored, with each new episode producing a new trace. Generic memory results from parallel activation of all episodic traces, with the generic information being abstracted from the summed responses of those traces that are most strongly activated by the cue. If a compound cue mechanism is added (see Ratcliff & McKoon, 1988), then MINERVA 2 can account easily and parsimoniously for both episodic (recall and recognition) and generic (priming, schemas, and abstractions) memory within a single system. All dissociations, according to this view, arise from different processing requirements, since the same memory system is supporting both types of memory performance.

As this chapter has shown, people's knowledge is complex, richly organized, and wonderfully fast. It is the ability to draw on this resource that distinguishes human cognitive capabilities from other animals and from machines. We will examine the functions of knowledge in other memory situations in more detail in Chapter 15, especially where they lead to systematic biases in what people perceive, encode, and recall.

# References

Anderson, J. R. (1983a). A spreading activation theory of memory. *Journal of Verbal Learning and Verbal Behavior, 22,* 261–295.

Anderson, J. R. (1983b). *The architecture of cognition.* Cambridge, MA: Harvard University Press.

Ashcraft, M. H. (1976). Priming and property dominance effects in semantic memory. *Memory & Cognition, 4,* 490–500.

Caramazza, A., Hillis, A., Leek, E. C., & Miozzo, M. (1994). The organization of lexical knowledge in the brain: Evidence from category- and modality-specific deficits. In L. A. Hirschfeld & S. A. Gelman (Eds.), *Mapping the mind: Domain specificity in cognition and culture.* New York: Cambridge University Press.

Chang, T. M. (1986). Semantic memory: Facts and models. *Psychological Bulletin, 99,* 199–220.

Chiesi, H. L., Spilich, G. J., & Voss, J. F. (1979). Acquisition of domain-related information in relation to high- and low-domain knowledge. *Journal of Verbal Learning and Verbal Behavior, 18,* 257–273.

Collins, A. M., & Loftus, E. F. (1975). A spreading-activation theory of semantic processing. *Psychological Review, 82,* 407–428.

Collins, A. M., & Quillian, M. R. (1969). Retrieval time from semantic memory. *Journal of Verbal Learning and Verbal Behavior, 8,* 240–247.

Collins, A. M., & Quillian, M. R. (1970). Does category size affect categorization time? *Journal of Verbal Learning and Verbal Behavior, 9,* 432–438.

De Renzi, E., & Lucchelli, F. (1994). Are semantic systems separately represented in the brain? The case of living category impairment. *Cortex, 30,* 3–25.

Dell, G. S. (1986). A spreading-activation theory of retrieval in sentence production. *Psychological Review, 93,* 283–321.

Dosher, B. A., & Rosedale, G. (1989). Integrated retrieval cues as a mechanism for priming in retrieval from memory. *Journal of Experimental Psychology: General, 118,* 191–211.

Farah, M. J., & McClelland, J. L. (1991). A computational model of semantic memory impairment: Modality specificity and emergent category specificity. *Journal of Experimental Psychology: General, 120,* 339–357.

Farah, M. J., McMullen, P. A., & Meyer, M. M. (1991). Can recognition of living things be selectively impaired? *Neuropsychologia, 29,* 185–193.

Garner, W. R., Hake, H. W., & Ericksen, C. W. (1956). Operationism and the concept of perception. *Psychological Review, 63,* 149–159.

Gillund, G., & Shiffrin, R. M. (1984). A retrieval model for both recognition and recall. *Psychological Review, 91,* 1–65.

Glucksberg, S., & McCloskey, M. (1981). Decisions about ignorance: Knowing that you don't know. *Journal of Experimental Psychology: Human Learning and Memory, 7,* 311–325.

Hart, J., Berndt, R. S., & Caramazza, A. (1985). Category-specific naming deficit following cerebral infarction. *Nature, 316,* 439–440.

Hillis, A. E., & Caramazza, A. (1991). Category-specific naming and comprehension impairment: A double dissociation. *Brain, 114,* 2081–2094.

Hintzman, D. L. (1978). *The psychology of learning and memory.* San Francisco: Freeman.

Hintzman, D. L. (1986). "Schema abstraction" in a multiple-trace memory model. *Psychological Review, 93,* 411–428.

Loftus, E. F. (1973). Category dominance, instance dominance, and categorization time. *Journal of Experimental Psychology, 97,* 70–74.

McClelland, J. L., & Rumelhart, D. E. (1981). An interactive activation model of context effects in letter perception: Part 1. An account of basic findings. *Psychological Review, 88,* 375–407.

McKoon, G., & Ratcliff, R. (1992). Spreading activation versus compound cue accounts of priming: Mediated priming revisited. *Journal of Experimental Psychology: Learning, Memory, and Cognition, 18,* 1155–1172.

McNamara, T. P. (1992a). Priming and constraints it places on theories of memory and retrieval. *Psychological Review, 99,* 650–662.

McNamara, T. P. (1992b). Theories of priming: I. Associative distance and lag. *Journal of Experimental Psychology: Learning, Memory, and Cognition, 18,* 1173–1190.

McNamara, T. P., & Altarriba, J. (1988). Depth of spreading activation revisited: Semantic mediated priming occurs in lexical decisions. *Journal of Memory and Language, 27,* 545–559.

Medin, D. L. (1989). Concepts and conceptual structure. *American Psychologist, 44,* 1469–1481.

Meyer, D. E., & Schvaneveldt, R. W. (1971). Facilitation in recognizing pairs of words: Evidence of a dependence between retrieval operations. *Journal of Experimental Psychology, 90,* 227–234.

Murdock, B. B., Jr. (1982). A theory for the storage and retrieval of item and associative information. *Psychological Review, 89,* 609–626.

Murphy, G. L., & Medin, D. L. (1985). The role of theories in conceptual coherence. *Psychological Review, 92,* 289–316.

Neely, J. H. (1977). Semantic priming and retrieval from lexical memory: Roles of inhibitionless spreading activation and limited-capacity attention. *Journal of Experimental Psychology: General, 106,* 226–254.

Neely, J. H., Keefe, D. E., & Ross, K. L. (1989). Semantic priming in the lexical decision task: Roles of prospective prime-generated expectancies and retrospective semantic matching. *Journal of Experimental Psychology: Learning, Memory, and Cognition, 15,* 1003–1019.

Pietrini, V., Nertimpi, T., Vaglia, A., Revello, M. G., Pinna, V., & Ferro-Milone, F. (1988). Recovery from herpes simplex encephalitis: Selective impairment of specific semantic categories with neuroradiological correlation. *Journal of Neurology, Neurosurgery, and Psychiatry, 51,* 1284–1293.

Postman, L., & Keppel, G. (1970). *Norms of word association.* San Diego, CA: Academic Press.

Quillian, M. R. (1967). Word concepts: A theory and simulation of some basic semantic capabilities. *Behavioral Science, 12,* 410–430.

Quillian, M. R. (1969). The teachable language comprehender: A simulation program and theory of language. *Communications of the ACM, 12,* 459–476.

Ratcliff, R. (1978). A theory of memory retrieval. *Psychological Review, 85,* 59–108.

Ratcliff, R., & McKoon, G. (1981). Does activation really spread? *Psychological Review, 88,* 454–462.

Ratcliff, R., & McKoon, G. (1988). A retrieval theory of priming in memory. *Psychological Review, 95,* 385–408.

Ratcliff, R., & McKoon, G. (1994). Retrieving information from memory: Spreading-activation theories versus compound-cue theories. *Psychological Review, 101,* 177–184.

Ratcliff, R., & McKoon, G. (1995). Sequential effects in lexical decision: Tests of compound-cue retrieval theory. *Journal of Experimental Psychology: Learning, Memory, and Cognition, 21,* 1380–1388.

Rips, L. J. (1975). Inductive judgments about natural categories. *Journal of Verbal Learning and Verbal Behavior, 14,* 665–681.

Rips, L. J., Shoben, E. J., & Smith, E. E. (1973). Semantic distance and the verification of semantic relations. *Journal of Verbal Learning and Verbal Behavior, 12,* 1–20.

Rosch, E., & Mervis, C. B. (1975). Family resemblances: Studies in the internal structure of categories. *Cognitive Psychology, 7,* 573–605.

Rosch, E., Mervis, C. B., Gray, W. D., Johnson, D. M., & Bayes-Braem, P. (1976). Basic objects in natural categories. *Cognitive Psychology, 8,* 382–439.

Rumelhart, D. E., & McClelland, J. L. (1982). An interactive activation model of context effects in letter perception: Part 2. The contextual enhancement effect and some tests and extensions of the model. *Psychological Review, 89,* 60–94.

Sartori, G., Miozzo, M., & Job, R. (1993). Category-specific naming impairment? Yes. *Quarterly Journal of Experimental Psychology, 46A,* 489–504.

Shelton, J. R., & Martin, R. C. (1992). How semantic is automatic semantic priming? *Journal of Experimental Psychology: Learning, Memory, and Cognition, 18,* 1191–1210.

Smith, E. E., Shoben, E. J., & Rips, L. J. (1974). Structure and process in semantic memory: A featural model for semantic decisions. *Psychological Review, 81,* 214–241.

Spilich, G. J., Vesonder, G. T., Chiesi, H. L., & Voss, J. F. (1979). Text processing of domain-related information for individuals with high- and low-domain knowledge. *Journal of Verbal Learning and Verbal Behavior, 18,* 275–290.

Swinney, D. (1979). Lexical access during sentence comprehension: (Re)consideration of context effects. *Journal of Verbal Learning and Verbal Behavior, 18,* 645–659.

Tulving, E. (1972). Episodic and semantic memory. In E. Tulving & W. Donaldson (Eds.), *Organization of memory.* New York: Academic Press.

Tulving, E. (1983). *Elements of episodic memory.* New York: Oxford University Press.

Warrington, E. K., & McCarthy, R. (1983). Category specific access dysphasia. *Brain, 106,* 859–878.

Warrington, E. K., & Shallice, T. (1984). Category specific semantic impairments. *Brain, 107,* 829–854.

Wittgenstein, L. (1953). *Philosophical investigations* (G. E. M. Anscombe, Trans.). Oxford: Blackwell.

# CHAPTER THIRTEEN

# Imagery

*"Any single Circumstance of what we have formerly seen often raises up a whole Scene of Imagery."*

—*Joseph Addison*

Scientific research on imagery is a relatively recent occurrence, primarily because of the emphasis that behaviorists placed on overt behavior. Imagery, by its very nature, is internal, and asking subjects about their images seemed exactly like introspection. Because introspection as a method of inquiry was quickly shown to have a "dismal record of failure" in psychology (Bower & Clapper, 1989, p. 245), research on imagery was out of the provenance of respectable psychologists. In the late 1960s, this attitude began to change as several researchers demonstrated that imagery could be objectively studied without recourse to introspection.

## Analog versus Propositional Representations

One common definition of a *proposition* is that it is the smallest unit of knowledge that has a truth value. Propositions are usually represented as English sentences (at least in English-speaking countries), but they are not necessarily tied to language. Rather, a proposition is a basic unit of meaning that is either true or false and cannot be made any smaller without losing the truth value. For example, a proposition might be "Lafayette is north of Indianapolis" or "A robin has wings." No part of these propositions can be removed and still leave the proposition with a truth value.

An *analog form* of representation, by contrast, is one that preserves the structure of the original information in a more or less direct manner. A map is a good example of an analog form of representation; a map preserves the spatial structure of the actual physical environment but changes many other aspects of the information. It is often convenient to use a picture as an illustration of an analog form of representation. Just as propositions are not English sentences, analog representations are not pictures. What is important is that some aspect of the physical structure is represented in an accurate way in a more or less direct manner.

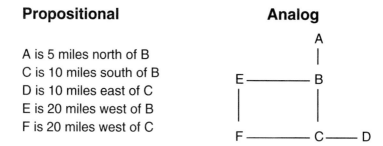

**Figure 13.1**   A comparison of a propositional and an analog way of representing the same information about distances between six cities.

A good way to see the difference between an analog and a propositional form of representation is to compare the way the same information might look in each format. In Figure 13.1, both forms contain information about the relationships between six cities. However, most people would prefer the analog form to the propositional form because it is more readily useful for the purpose of navigating. For some forms of information, a propositional code might be more useful, whereas for other forms of information, an analog form might be more useful.

The general idea at issue for the visual imagery literature is whether results from visual imagery experiments require two forms of representation or whether a propositional form can account for all the results. Almost all theorists agree that propositional forms are needed for representing knowledge; the question is whether analog forms are needed for imagery. At a general level, it is convenient to think of verbal codes (particularly knowledge and sentences) as being represented by propositions. In this chapter, we will see that it is equally convenient to think of visual codes (particularly visual images) as analog representations.

# The Dual-Task Method

In 1968, Lee Brooks reported a series of experiments in which he had subjects perform two tasks simultaneously. The logic behind the dual-task method is that people can perform multiple tasks simultaneously as long as the resources required do not overlap. For example, many people can walk and chew gum at the same time; however, probably nobody can chew gum and whistle at the same time. The obvious reason is that the same resources are required in the latter task (moving the mouth, tongue, and lips), whereas different resources are required in the former case (legs versus mouth). Therefore, Brooks had one task that was designed to require verbal processing and a second task that was designed to require spatial processing. He also devised two ways of responding, one of which required verbal answers and one of which required the subject to point to the correct answer.

Brooks (1968) used a verbal task and a verbal response, and a spatial task and a spatial response. In the verbal task, subjects were given sentences such as, "A bird in the hand is not in the bush." The task was to identify each word as being a noun (respond "yes") or

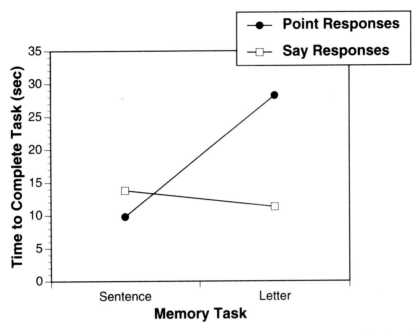

**Figure 13.2**   Time required to answer "yes" or "no" by speaking or pointing when the task involves processing either a sentence or an image.   Source: Brooks (1968).

not a noun (respond "no"). Responses could be either verbal (saying the answer) or spatial (pointing to the answer). When pointing their answer, subjects had to point to a Y or N printed in irregularly staggered columns on a sheet of paper. In the imagery task, the subject was asked to imagine the outline of a letter, such as the letter F, and then to imagine a marker beginning at the lower left and moving around the outside. At each corner, the subjects were asked to indicate if it were an extreme top or bottom corner. For the letter F, correct responding would be "Yes," "Yes," "No," "No," and so on.

The results are shown in Figure 13.2. Note that the subject had to keep either the sentence or the image of the letter in memory while performing the response. When both the task and the response mode tapped the same mode of representation (letter form and pointing, sentence and speaking) responses were slower than when the task and response mode tapped different modes of representation (letter form and speaking, sentence and pointing). These results are consistent with the idea that there are two forms of representation: one corresponding roughly to a propositional or verbal format, and the other to an analog or spatial format. In the original report, Brooks (1968) included several other experiments to eliminate other possible explanations of his data.

Den Heyer and Barrett (1971) replicated these results but used a paradigm in which both verbal and spatial aspects came from the same stimulus. Subjects briefly saw a grid in which several letters were placed; then, one of three events occurred. One was to do nothing for 10 seconds; this was the control group. A second was to add several two-digit numbers, and the third was to compare three small grids and decide which was the odd one

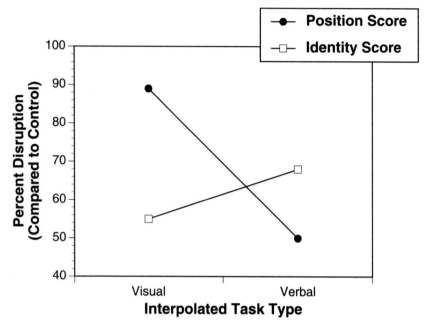

**Figure 13.3**   Percent disruption caused by an interpolated task compared to no interpolated task. Position scoring indicates that the correct cells were marked as having letters, regardless of whether the letter was correct. Identity scoring indicates that the correct letters were recalled regardless of which cell they were placed in. A disruption score of 0 would mean performance was the same as in the control group; larger scores mean more disruption.   Source: den Heyer & Barrett (1971).

out. Then the memory test was given, in which the original grid was displayed again, and the subject's task was to enter the appropriate letters into the appropriate cells. Two different scores were calculated. The position score indicated how many cells were correctly marked as containing a letter, regardless of whether the letter entered was the correct one. The identity score indicated how many letters were correctly recalled, regardless of whether they were placed in the correct location.

The results are shown in Figure 13.3. The scores are shown in a measure called percent disruption. Essentially, this score shows how much worse performance was in the two conditions with interpolated activity than in the control condition, in which there was no activity. A score of 0% would indicate equivalent performance, and the larger the score, the more the interpolated activity disrupted performance. The pattern of results is the same as in Brooks' (1968) study: a visual interpolated task affected memory for location (measured by the position score) far more than it affected memory for specific letters (measured by identity score). Conversely, a verbal interpolated task affected memory for specific letters far more than it affected memory for location.

Segal and Fusella (1970) found analogous results using auditory and visual stimuli: if subjects were asked to image a visual stimulus, they were worse at detecting a visual stimulus than an auditory one. Conversely, if they were asked to image an auditory stimulus, they were worse at detecting an auditory stimulus than a visual one. This is a modern demonstration of the Perky effect, named after Perky (1910). These findings are consistent with the idea of two forms of representation, propositional and analog. Much of the early theoretical work was done by Allan Paivio.

# Paivio's Dual-Coding Theory

According to Paivio's (1971, 1986) dual-coding theory, words representing concrete objects can be encoded in two different ways, whereas words representing abstract objects can be encoded in only one way. For example, *dog* can be encoded using both a verbal code (the word itself) and a visual code (an image of a dog). The word *idea,* on the other hand, probably has no visual code: what would an image of an idea look like? It may be possible to generate an image that is associated with *idea,* such as a lightbulb going on over a person's head, but that is not nearly as direct a coding as an image of a dog.

Because concrete words have two potential codes compared to only one for abstract words, the dual-coding view predicts that concrete words should be remembered better; this is exactly what happens (Paivio, 1969). Furthermore, other things being equal, pictures are remembered better than words representing those pictures, the so-called picture

---

**Experiment   Dual-Coding Theory**

**Purpose:** To demonstrate the advantage for concrete words over abstract words.

**Subjects:** Twenty subjects are recommended.

**Materials:** Table 1 in the Appendix lists 80 abstract words and 80 concrete words of approximately equal word frequency and length. For each subject, create 10 lists of concrete words and 10 lists of abstract words; each list should have 8 different words. The first 10 lists should have 5 abstract and 5 concrete lists. You will also need an answer sheet on which subjects can write their responses.

**Design:** Because each subject experiences both conditions, concreteness is a within-subjects factor.

**Procedure:** Inform the subjects that in this experiment they will be asked to learn lists of words. Read each list at a rate of 1 word every 2 seconds. Then allow 30 seconds for free recall. Give a short break after 10 lists.

**Instructions:** "In this experiment, I will read you a list of words, and then I would like you to write down as many as you can remember on the answer sheet. Feel free to write the words in any order you like, and feel free to guess. After you have recalled each list, the next one will begin. Any questions?"

**Scoring and Analysis:** For each subject, count the number of concrete words recalled and the number of abstract words recalled. A paired *t* test can be used to verify that the means are different.

**Optional Enhancements:** Plot the data as a function of serial position.

Source: Based on an experiment by Paivio (1969).

superiority effect (Madigan, 1983; Paivio, 1971). The reason for the better performance is that there are two types of attributes processed for concrete items; even if one of them fails to be useful, a second code is potentially retrievable. The benefit of concrete over abstract can be magnified if subjects are told to image the two objects interacting in some fashion. For example, Schnorr and Atkinson (1969) found that subjects could recall more than 80% of items when given imagery instructions, compared to about 40% when rote rehearsal instructions were used. However, imagery instructions do not have to be given for the advantage to be seen, and, perhaps even more surprising, the advantage is seen in a free reconstruction of order test. In this test, a subject sees a list of words presented and is then given the list items in a new order. The task is to reconstruct the original presentation order. Even though all the words are given back to the subject, the concrete words are still remembered more accurately than the abstract words are (Neath, 1997).

There is a fair degree of similarity between Paivio's (1971, 1986) dual-code theory and the idea of the phonological loop and visuo-spatial sketch pad in Baddeley's (1986; Baddeley & Hitch, 1974) Working Memory, as well as other proposals (Potter, 1979). The major difference between the two views is that whereas dual-coding assumes multiple memory codes that are modality specific, the other views include some more generic code common to both abstract and concrete information (Marschark, 1992).

Even with the success of dual-coding theory in accounting for these and other findings, there remained much experimental work to be done to confirm the analog nature of visual imagery and to investigate further the properties of this system when engaged in more active processing of the image. Thus, studies turned away from examining the structure and emphasized more the function or dynamic properties of the analog form of representation.

# Mental Rotation

If visual imagery is represented within an analog system that preserves the structure of the physical environment, then certain physical laws should be observed in imagery tasks. For example, if you hold a cube in your hand and rotate it 180°, the cube must first be rotated 1°, and then another degree, and so forth. In other words, the cube has to pass through all intermediate orientations before completing the full 180°. This is a physical law in the real world. If the system representing visual information is preserving the spatial structure of the real world, as the studies by Brooks (1968) and den Heyer and Barrett (1971) suggest, then the same law should hold true when subjects image a cube rotating 180°.

Note that this need not be the case. In fact, in a truly efficient system, it is far quicker to simply flip the image 180° than to calculate each intervening orientation. When you ask a computer graphics program to rotate an object 180°, this is exactly what the computer does: a simple flip. To demonstrate that the imagery representation system is analog, one needs to show that an image of a rotated cube passes through all intermediate orientations.

This is exactly what Roger Shepard and his colleagues demonstrated (Cooper & Shepard, 1973; Shepard & Metzler, 1971; much of the work is reprinted in Shepard & Cooper, 1983). Shepard used objects that were made out of cubes (see Figure 13.4). Two

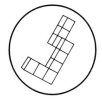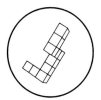

**Figure 13.4** Two pairs of objects used in mental rotation studies. The subjects were shown the forms on the left and asked to decide if the form on the right was the same object, only rotated. Source: Shepard & Metzler (1971).

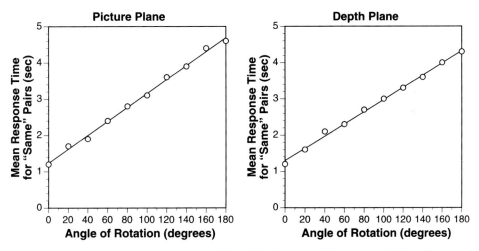

**Figure 13.5** Mean response time to correctly say that the pair of objects matched as a function of the angle of rotation in degrees. The left panel shows objects that were rotated in the picture plane and the right panel shows objects that were rotated in depth. Source: Shepard & Metzler (1971).

such objects were shown, one on the left (the standard) and one on the right (the target). The subject was asked to decide if the target was the same as the standard, only rotated. Although the target was often not the same as the standard, the data of interest come when the target and standard were the same. In particular, Shepard was interested in how long it would take subjects to indicate that the objects were the same as a function of the degree of rotation. The results are shown in Figure 13.5.

The relationship between the distance to rotate an object and the response time to decide that the two matched was linear. This illustrates the same property as in the real world, that the further you rotate a cube in your hand, the longer it will take you, assuming the speed of rotation is constant. Notice also that it did not seem to matter which direction the rotation occurred, in either the picture plane (seeing an object rotate like the hands on a clock) or in the depth plane (seeing the top of the clock move towards you, and then continue down as the bottom of the clock swings away from you and then up). Further work suggested that for particular individuals, the speed of rotation was constant (Finke, 1989).

Of particular interest are the reaction times for both 0° and 180°. The time taken to compare the two objects when both are in the same orientation can be taken as a baseline of how long the task and response take. Any extra time can be attributed to the time to rotate. If subjects were simply flipping the object 180°, then the response time at this angle of rotation should be quite fast; the data clearly show that it was the slowest. This is consistent with the idea that the subjects were rotating through all intermediate positions.

# Distinguishing Propositional from Analog Representation

Kosslyn (1976) reported an experiment consistent with the idea that both propositional and analog forms of representation are available. He selected features that were either highly associated or only marginally associated with a particular object. For example, claws are highly associated with the concept of a cat, whereas heads are not highly associated, even though cats have them. In addition, one of the features was small in relation to the main object, and the other large. Kosslyn's task was to have subjects verify statements, such as "Cats have claws" and "Cats have heads." He predicted that if subjects were instructed to form an image, they should respond fastest to the larger feature. In an image of a cat, the head is easier to "see" than the claws. However, if subjects were not instructed to use imagery, then the subjects should respond fastest to the most highly associated item. As Figure 13.6 shows, this is exactly what happened.

Any theory of knowledge based on propositions would predict that subjects can retrieve information more quickly when the two concepts are highly associated than when they are less associated (Anderson, 1976). When no specific instructions are given, subjects will use a propositional form to get the answer because it is faster. Thus, subjects verified the statement "Cats have claws" faster than the statement "Cats have heads." However, when imagery instructions are given, subjects will generate an image and then answer the question based on the image. They will be able to retrieve information about a large part more quickly than a small part. Thus, subjects verified the statement "Cats have heads" faster than the statement "Cats have claws" because in the image the head is larger than the claws.

Recall that Shepard and Metzler (1971) discovered a linear relationship between response time and degree of rotation. Kosslyn, Ball, and Reiser (1978) discovered that the same linear relationship holds for distance. They reported a study in which subjects first memorized a map of an island, on which were seven objects such as a hut, a swamp, a beach, and a well. These objects created 21 distances ranging from 2 cm to 19 cm. After subjects demonstrated that they had learned the map locations, the "mental scanning" phase of the experiment began. The subjects were asked to examine their image of the map and to focus on the named object, imagining a small speck hovering over the location. A second location was named, and the subject was asked to move the speck in a direct straight-line path and to press a button when the speck arrived at the destination. Kosslyn and his colleagues observed a linear relationship between distance scanned and response time; indeed, the correlation was 0.97.

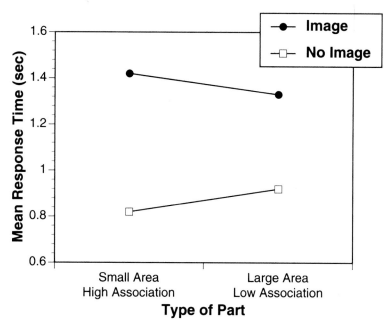

**Figure 13.6**   The time needed to verify a statement in which the part was either small but highly associated or large but had only a low association as a function of instructions. Propositional theory predicts the results when no imagery instructions are given, but an analog theory better accounts for the results when imagery instructions are given.   Source: Kosslyn (1976).

# Arguments Against Imagery

One of the most influential critics of the analog view of imagery is Zenon Pylyshyn (1973, 1979, 1981). Regardless of the outcome of the imagery debate, Pylyshyn's critiques forced the research to become more rigorous, objective, and careful. Although the three objections are listed separately, they are not mutually exclusive and they can operate simultaneously. Furthermore, other arguments were offered against the need for a separate form of representation (Anderson, 1978).

One of Pylyshyn's objections is the possibility that *experimenter bias* was determining the outcome of the experiment. It is well known that the expectations of the experimenter can influence how a subject responds in a particular situation (Rosenthal, 1966). For example, Intons-Peterson (1983) has shown that subtle cues provided by the experimenter can change the way the subject responds within an imagery experiment.

A second argument made by Pylyshyn is that subjects are using their tacit knowledge to guide their responses. *Tacit knowledge* is information people possess that reflects their beliefs about how things should work but that may not be verbalizable. (Tacit knowledge is often thought to be similar to implicit learning; see Chapter 8.) For example, because of interactions with the environment, people tacitly know that it takes more time to travel a long distance than a short distance at a given speed. They may not be able to formulate

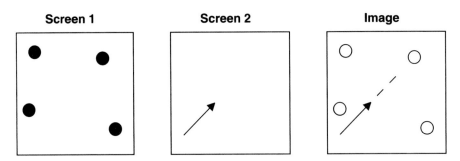

**Figure 13.7**   The subject saw the left panel for 5 seconds, and then it disappeared. One second later, the middle panel was presented. The arrow could appear anywhere and could be in any orientation. Subjects reported deciding whether the arrow pointed to a dot by imagining they were scanning from the tip of the arrow along the direction specified until they hit a dot or a boundary. This strategy is represented in the right panel.   Source: Finke & Pinker (1982).

the equation rate × time = distance, but they are tacitly aware of this relationship. When asked to scan a visual image, subjects may assume that it should work just as physical motion does and so produce a linear relationship. The tacit knowledge point, then, says that the linear relationship between distance scanned and time to respond is due to the fact that subjects expect it to work this way.

A final argument suggests that task demands may be affecting the results. *Task demands* are similar to experimenter bias, except that it is the task itself, rather than any cues provided by the experimenter, that causes the subject to behave in one way rather than another. For example, when told that they are in an imagery experiment, the task is quite different than when no mention is made of the task.

To address Pylyshyn's first objection, Jolicoeur and Kosslyn (1985) conducted a replication of the Kosslyn et al. (1978) map study to see whether the experimenter's expectations affected the results. They told some of the experimenters to expect a U-shaped function between response time and distance scanned. Despite the expectations of the experimenters, the usual linear function was found and the Kosslyn et al. (1978) results were replicated. Although some results may be influenced by experimenter bias, the linear relationship between distance scanned and time to scan does not appear to be one of them.

An experiment by Finke and Pinker (1982) answered the last two criticisms. In this experiment, subjects saw a display that contained a random pattern of dots (see Figure 13.7). After 5 seconds, this display disappeared, followed 1 second later by a display that contained only an arrow. The task was to indicate whether the arrow pointed to any of the previously seen dots and to press a button to indicate yes or no.

Notice that in this experiment there is no mention of scanning, of forming an image, or even of the key variable — the distance between the tip of the arrow and the location of the dot. Nonetheless, the results were similar to those observed in other mental scanning studies: the farther the distance from the tip of the arrow to the dot, the longer the response time. Kosslyn (1980) provides a model that addresses in detail how visual images might be constructed and manipulated.

# Imagery and Perception

Despite the evidence supporting the analog view, there are still plausible theories of imagery that rely on propositional representations. For example, Humphreys and Bruce (1989) detail how both images and percepts may be built up from a common underlying propositional system. Regardless of which view ultimately explains the most data, both suggest great commonalities between the visual perception system and the visual imagery system.

Some of the most striking evidence comes from studies that tested patients with various visual deficits (reviewed by Farah, 1988). For example, Riddoch and Humphreys (1987) reported a case in which acquired cerebral color blindness (in which a patient loses the ability to perceive certain colors) was accompanied by a similar deficit in imagery for color. Levine, Warach, and Farah (1985) tested two patients, one with visual localization impairment and one with visual object identification impairment. The patient with object identification difficulties also had difficulties with tasks that required the formation of a visual image of an object. The patient with localization problems was unable to describe the relative locations of items in an image.

A final example concerns patients with unilateral visual neglect. Patients with damage to the right parietal lobe often fail to detect stimuli presented in the left visual field, even though their basic perceptual processes apparently are normal (Posner, Walker, Friedrich, & Rafal, 1984). (Information from the left visual field goes to the right hemisphere, and information from the right visual field goes to the left hemisphere.) This deficit is known as *unilateral visual neglect,* and patients with this disorder show a similar disorder in visual imagery tasks: Bisiach and his colleagues (Bisiach & Luzzatti, 1978; Bisiach, Luzzatti, & Perani, 1979) have demonstrated that when their patients were asked to imagine a famous square in Milan (with which the subjects were familiar), they failed to report landmarks that were in the left side of the scene. When the task was repeated, but the patients were asked to describe the square from a different side, the previously neglected information was now reported, because it was on the right side. On the basis of these and other studies, Farah (1988) concluded that "for all of the types of selective visual deficits due to cortical lesions in which imagery has been examined, parallel imagery deficits have been observed" (p. 312). One interpretation of how perception and imagery interact is offered by Farah (1989).

Another area of research relevant to the relationship between imagery and perception is called *memory psychophysics.* In perceptual psychophysics, a standard technique is *magnitude estimation;* subjects rate a set of stimuli along some particular dimension, such as size. The main restriction on the estimates is that they must preserve ratio properties. For example, if a subject sees a particular stimulus and rates it as a 10 and then sees a stimulus that is perceived to be twice as long, the subject should give a 20, an estimate twice as large as the first. Typically, the estimated value ($e$) is related to the actual value ($a$) by a power function:

$$e = a^x \qquad\qquad (13.1)$$

Kerst and Howard (1978) obtained magnitude estimations for distance (using centers of major U.S. cities) and area (of various states), and the exponents were calculated to be

1.04 and 0.79. Thus, subjects typically overestimated distance and underestimated area. Kerst and Howard also ran an imagery condition in which subjects first studied a map of the United States and then made judgments about distance and area from memory. The exponents in the imagery condition were calculated to be 1.10 and 0.60 for distance and area judgments, respectively. The important point is that the imagery exponents were the square of the perceptual exponents; that is, $1.04 \times 1.04 = 1.08$, and $0.79 \times 0.79 = 0.62$. What this means, according to Kerst and Howard, is that in the imagery condition, the subjects were reperceiving the stimuli. There was a transformation during the encoding, when the actual distances were transformed with an exponent of 1.04. During the imagery phase of the experiment, the stimuli in memory, now an image, were reperceived and underwent another transformation with an exponent of 1.04. These results have been replicated (Moyer, Bradley, Sorensen, Whiting, & Mansfield, 1978).

Algom and his colleagues (Algom, Wolf, & Bergman, 1985) conducted an extensive series of experiments on both perceptual and memory psychophysics that generally support the reperceptual hypothesis, at least for area judgments. The general methodology was to have subjects estimate the area of a rectangle given information about its height and width. This information could be provided entirely perceptually, entirely through memory, or in a mixture. Although the memory exponent was often close to the square of the perceptual exponent, there were several conditions under which this relationship did not hold. In all conditions, however, the memory exponent was smaller than the appropriate perceptual exponent. The researchers also found that whenever both perceptual and remembered information needed to be combined, the memory transformation dominates. Algom, Wolf, and Bergman (1985) concluded that their results support the analog view of imagery because of the "definitive evidence of second-order isomorphism between internal and external physical relations" (p. 469).

One final type of result consistent with the idea of some overlap between the visual imagery and visual perception systems comes from studies of visual imagery in congenitally blind subjects. These subjects, who have never seen anything, still show concreteness effects and effects attributable to visual imagery (DeBeni & Cornoldi, 1988). Indeed, Kerr (1983) replicated the results of Kosslyn's map study (Kosslyn, Ball, & Reiser, 1978; Jolicoeur & Kosslyn, 1985) using blind subjects and a 3-dimensional rendering of the map. These results are consistent with the idea that visual imagery is an analog form of representation that preserves spatial relationships. To the extent that the congenitally blind subjects had no deficit neurologically, then the standard visual imagery patterns should be observed.

# Real versus Imagined Events

Given the similarities between visual imagery and visual perception, it might seem likely that the two events can sometimes be confused. The area of research that investigates how accurate people are at distinguishing real from imagined events is called *reality monitoring.*

Johnson and Raye (1981) described the most influential account of reality monitoring. According to their view, there are two ways to distinguish real (external) events from imagined (internal) events. The first is by an evaluation of the qualitative attributes. Externally produced memories are likely to contain a rich representation of sensory attributes, including color, texture, intensity, and so forth. To the extent that a memory contains a rich encoding of sensory attributes and is highly detailed, it is likely to be an externally produced event. In contrast, internally generated events will lack some of the sensory information and will be less detailed and less integrated with contextual information. They will often contain evidence of related cognitive processing, such as reasoning or decision making, that was necessary to generate the memory in the first place. For many memories, an evaluation of these details will quite often determine the origin of the event, external or internal.

Many events — perhaps even a majority — will fall in a middle range. Although there are some features indicative of an external origin, there are also a number of features that indicate an internal origin. For these, Johnson and Raye (1981) propose a second kind of examination based on plausibility and coherence. By *plausibility,* Johnson and Raye mean that the memory must fit in with other knowledge about the world. A memory of flying by flapping arms is an extreme example of a lack of plausibility. *Coherence* refers to how well the memory fits in with other memories. For example, if supporting memories are available that make the memory of uncertain origin fit in with the grand scheme of things, then the uncertain memory is likely to be of a real event.

Note that these methods are not foolproof. There are likely to be many sorts of memories that fall into the middle category of uncertain. For example, Shepard (1984) points out that, to be useful, intentions and plans need to be specific and detailed. Your memory for the plan, however, is quite likely to have many of the attributes of an external memory, even though it was internally generated.

Many experiments support the general outline proposed by Johnson and Raye (1981). For example, Johnson, Raye, Wang, and Taylor (1979) divided subjects into two groups on the basis of their scores from a test that required them to remember details of pictures. During the experimental session, the subjects were shown pictures of common objects. Every so often, instead of a picture, the subjects saw the name of an object and were asked to create an image of the object. Johnson et al. varied the number of times each object was imaged. At the end of the session, the subjects were given an unexpected test in which they were asked to indicate the number of times they had seen a picture and to ignore the number of times they had imagined seeing it. Subjects who were deemed vivid imagers were less accurate than were subjects classified as less vivid imagers. According to Johnson et al., the rich imagery of the former group made it more difficult to distinguish instances of the imagined object from instances of the presented object.

The more similar the events in terms of their features, the more difficult it becomes to discriminate real from imagined. For example, Foley, Johnson, and Raye (1983) found that subjects were less accurate in determining whether they had spoken a word or imagined speaking the word than they were in deciding whether they had heard a word or imagined hearing the word. Similar results were reported by Anderson (1984).

Another quite systematic bias is known as the "it had to be you" effect (Anderson, 1984; Johnson & Raye, 1981). Here, the subjects appear to have adopted the position that if they had really performed some action, then it would be more memorable than if they only imagined it. This causes them to adopt a conservative criterion when distinguishing between an imagined and a perceived event. The result of this bias is that imagined events are more likely to be judged real than real events are likely to be judged imagined. Thus, memories of uncertain origins are more likely to be judged as originating externally than internally.

Further evidence comes from a study by Johnson, Kounios, and Reeder (1994), in which subjects saw some pictures and imagined others; at test, they received words and were asked to decide whether the object named had been seen, perceived, or neither. Johnson et al. (1994) used a procedure whereby the subjects had to give a response as soon as they heard a tone. The tone could occur 300, 500, 900, or 1500 ms after the test item was displayed. At the short lags, Johnson et al. found that subjects were more accurate in determining "old" or "new" than they were in determining "seen" or "perceived." The researchers interpreted this as consistent with the idea that real and imagined events are made up of differing attributes and that the availability of these attributes can vary over time.

Johnson, Kahan, and Raye (1984) had subjects pair up and tell their partner about dreams they had actually dreamed, dreams they had made up, or dreams they had read about. Subjects were then given a discrimination test in which they had to decide whether a target event was one they had reported or one their partner had told them. Subjects had more difficulty with real dreams than with dreams they had read about or made up. In other words, they had difficulty recalling whether they had dreamed the dream or whether their partner had dreamed the dream. According to the reality monitoring view, this is because dreams lack evidence of cognitive processes that are included in the memory when an event is imagined or read about. Based on this and other work, Johnson (1985) has suggested that memories generated under hypnosis may be more difficult to distinguish from real events (Dywan & Bowers, 1983) because of the extra vividness and degree of detail often present. Furthermore, such memories should lack evidence of cognitive operations because they were generated largely outside of conscious intent. According to this view, memories generated under hypnosis should be very difficult to distinguish from externally produced memories. We shall have more to say about the effects of hypnosis on memory in Chapter 15.

# Eidetic Imagery

*Eidetic imagery* is the technical name given to *photographic memory*. The criteria of true photographic memory are very stringent. For example, a complex picture from *Alice's Adventures in Wonderland* might be shown for about 30 seconds; and then a variety of questions would be asked about specific details. For example, the subject might be asked the number of stripes on the Cheshire Cat's tail or how many whiskers the cat had. To be truly photographic, the memory must preserve all the details that a photograph would.

The evaluation of eidetic imagery has remained constant between articles by Woodworth (1938, p. 45), Gray and Gummerman (1975), and Crowder (1992). Eidetic images are more vivid and contain more detail than normal visual images do, they have a far longer duration than do afterimages or iconic memory, and they are found almost exclusively in preadolescent children.

Haber and Haber (1964) examined 150 preadolescent school children. The children were first shown afterimages (see Chapter 3) to get them used to talking about information not physically present. They were shown pictures for 30 seconds, and then the pictures were removed. The experimenters interviewed the children as they gazed at a blank sheet of cardboard where the picture had been. Although 84 demonstrated some evidence of imagery, only 12 (8% of the original sample) demonstrated eidetic imagery. These subjects were highly accurate and never used the past tense when answering. Furthermore, their eyes moved to the location on the blank where the target information had been displayed. Virtually no other children scanned the blank when answering.

Although the prevalence in preadolescent children is estimated at around 8% (Gray & Gummerman, 1975; Haber, 1979; Paivio & Cohen, 1979), the frequency in adults has been estimated as low as none in a million (Merrit, 1979). The notable exceptions to this are a report by Stromeyer and Psotka (1970) and one by Coltheart and Glick (1974); in the latter study, the subject could take a 10-word sentence and read off the letters backwards. It is possible that the incidence of eidetic imagery is greater in elderly populations (Giray, Altkin, Vaught, & Roodin, 1985), but more data are needed on this point. Some authors assert that the famous Russian mnemonist S. used eidetic imagery. A careful reading of Luria's (1968) report, however, shows that although S. did make extensive use of visual imagery, he did not use eidetic imagery (see Chapter 17).

Many explanations have been offered for the drop in prevalence of eidetic imagery from around 8% in preadolescent children to around 0% in normal adults, but none are universally accepted (Crowder, 1992). One popular explanation is that, as degree of literacy increases, reliance on the earlier pictoral form that gives rise to eidetic imagery decreases. However, Doob (1966) showed that degree of literacy, both within and between groups, is unrelated to prevalence of eidetic imagery.

As Crowder (1992) summarized the literature, "The most important conclusion about eidetic imagery is that it is a genuine phenomenon, capable of objective measurement and study" (pp. 155–156). Its cause and the reason for its disappearance and possible resurgence in older age are still unclear.

## Other Forms of Imagery

So far, we have examined only visual imagery, and to be specific we have not distinguished the two different forms (Farah, Hammond, Levine, & Calvanio, 1988). More is known about both visual perception and visual imagery than about other forms of perception and imagery but, nonetheless, some research has focused on auditory imagery.

Although Perky (1910) included reports of auditory images and Seashore (1938) included a discussion in his text, much of the work on auditory imagery has been even more recent than that on visual imagery (see Reisberg, 1992). The nontemporal properties of a tone include pitch, loudness, and timbre. It is clear that the auditory image can contain information about pitch, although intensity is less reliably imaged (Intons-Peterson, 1992). Crowder (1989) has used an interference demonstration to show that timbre can also be represented. Timbre is a potentially more interesting aspect, because it is more difficult for a subject to reproduce, physically, the unique sound of an oboe or cello than it is to produce a sound of a particular frequency or intensity.

Crowder's (1989) experiment involved two phases, the first demonstrating the perceptual effect and the second showing a similar effect in imagery. He presented two tones,

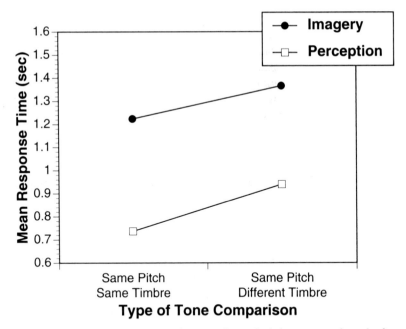

**Figure 13.8**  Mean response time to say the second tone had the same pitch as the first tone when the timbre was the same or different. Subjects either heard (perception) or imaged (imagery) the timbre of the second tone.   Source: Crowder (1989).

and the subjects' task was to decide whether they were the same or a different pitch. The pitches were either F, G, or A and the timbres were of a flute, guitar, or trumpet. Subjects correctly said "same" more quickly when the pitch and timbre were identical than when only the pitches were identical and the timbres differed (see Figure 13.8). In the second phase, the tone was always a sine wave — a tone that essentially has no timbre — at one of the three pitches. After this tone was played, the subjects were asked to imagine a tone of that pitch as produced by either a flute, guitar, or trumpet. The subject indicated when the image had been formed by pressing a button, and then the second note — this time by a flute, guitar, or trumpet — was played. The task was to judge whether the pitch was the same or different, regardless of the timbre. Subjects again more quickly said "same" when the imagined and perceptual timbres matched than when they mismatched.

Voices can also be imaged (e.g., Geiselman & Bjork, 1980; Nairne & Pusen, 1984), although this work has been less psychophysical than has research on auditory imagery for pitch, loudness, and timbre. For example, Geiselman and Glenny (1977) had subjects listen to a tape of either a male or female voice. They then saw words and were asked to imagine these words being pronounced by one of the voices they had just heard. At test, the subjects again heard words spoken in a male or female voice, but their task was simply to indicate whether the word spoken was a studied word. Subjects were more accurate for imagined words if the test word was presented in the same voice as imagined. MacKay (1992) reviewed work on a related area, termed *inner speech*.

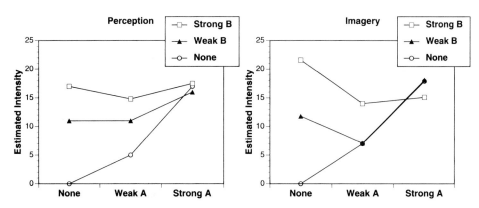

**Figure 13.9**   Estimated intensity when odors are perceived (left panel) or when odors are imaged (right panel).   Source: Algom & Cain (1991).

There are relatively few theories of auditory imagery; indeed, in her review, Intons-Peterson (1992) states that "I have not been able to find a single model of auditory imagery, per se" (p. 65). What models exist are either general models of imagery (Hebb, 1968) or simply adaptations of accounts of visual imagery.

There has been relatively little work on tactile imagery. However, Marchant and Malloy (1984) did find that creating a tactile image facilitated memory for word pairs that were rated high in imagability, just as using visual imagery facilitates memory for word pairs rated high in concreteness.

Imagery for odors has been reviewed by Crowder and Schab (1995). Unlike visual and auditory imagery, imagery for odor appears somewhat different, at least according to the results from memory psychophysics experiments. Algom and Cain (1991) first trained subjects to associate a color with a particular odor. The odors were actually all the same (amyl acetate), but they differed in intensity. To ensure accurate memory, the subject sampled an odor and then gave its name (such as red). Twenty-four hours after learning, the magnitude estimation procedure began. Contrary to findings with visual stimuli, the exponents were almost identical for both perceptual and memory conditions. Thus, imagery for visual stimuli may be quite different from imagery for odors.

The best evidence for imagery for odors comes from a study in which subjects were able to combine and manipulate images of odors. Algom and Cain (1991) found that subjects performed very similarly when giving estimations of a mixture of two odors and when giving estimates of an imagined mixture. In this latter condition, the subjects first learned the individual odors (as described above), and in the psychophysical phase they were asked to judge the intensity of mixing, for example, brown with red. Even though they had no physical experience with this mixture, their estimates were very similar to those given in the perceptual condition (see Figure 13.9).

Since 1960, the study of imagery has gone from a marginal, barely respectable area of research to a central component of memory and cognitive research. Indeed, one of the two main subsystems in Baddeley's (1986) Working Memory is a store devoted to processing visual information in an analog form. The study of auditory imagery has begun to catch up with the study of visual imagery, and imagery for tactile stimuli and imagery for odors is also being reported. Although there is no (as yet) universal theory of imagery, the basic properties and processes involved are becoming quite well understood, and there are several successful models for particular kinds of imagery.

# References

Algom, D., & Cain, W. S. (1991). Remembered odors and mental mixtures: Tapping reservoirs of olfactory knowledge. *Journal of Experimental Psychology: Human Perception and Performance, 17,* 1104–1119.

Algom, D., Wolf, Y., & Bergman, B. (1985). Integration of stimulus dimensions in perception and memory: Composition rules and psychophysical relations. *Journal of Experimental Psychology: General, 114,* 451–471.

Anderson, J. R. (1976). *Language, memory, and thought.* Hillsdale, NJ: Erlbaum.

Anderson, J. R. (1978). Arguments concerning representations for mental imagery. *Psychological Review, 85,* 249–277.

Anderson, R. E. (1984). Did I do it or did I only imagine doing it? *Journal of Experimental Psychology: General, 113,* 594–613.

Baddeley, A. D. (1986). *Working memory.* New York: Oxford University Press.

Baddeley, A. D., & Hitch, G. J. (1974). Working memory. In G. H. Bower (Ed.), *The psychology of learning and motivation, Vol. 8.* New York: Academic Press.

Bisiach, E., & Luzzatti, C. (1978). Unilateral neglect of representational space. *Cortex, 14,* 129–133.

Bisiach, E., Luzzatti, C., & Perani, D. (1979). Unilateral neglect, representational schema and consciousness. *Brain, 102,* 609–618.

Bower, G. H., & Clapper, J. P. (1989). Experimental methods in cognitive science. In M. I. Posner (Ed.), *Foundations of cognitive science.* Cambridge, MA: MIT Press.

Brooks, L. R. (1968). Spatial and verbal components of the act of recall. *Canadian Journal of Psychology, 22,* 349–368.

Coltheart, M., & Glick, M. J. (1974). Visual imagery: A case study. *Quarterly Journal of Experimental Psychology, 26,* 438–453.

Cooper, L. A., & Shepard, R. N. (1973). Chronometric studies of the rotation of mental images. In W. G. Chase (Ed.), *Visual information processing.* New York: Academic Press.

Crowder, R. G. (1976). *Principles of learning and memory.* Hillsdale, NJ: Erlbaum.

Crowder, R. G. (1989). Imagery for musical timbre. *Journal of Experimental Psychology: Human Perception and Performance, 15,* 472–478.

Crowder, R. G. (1992). Eidetic imagery. In L. R. Squire (Ed.), *Encyclopedia of learning and memory.* New York: Macmillan.

Crowder, R. G., & Schab, F. R. (1995). Imagery for odors. In F. R. Schab & R. G. Crowder (Eds.), *Memory for odors.* Mahwah, NJ: Erlbaum.

DeBeni, R., & Cornoldi, C. (1988). Imagery limitations in totally congenitally blind subjects. *Journal of Experimental Psychology: Learning, Memory, and Cognition, 14,* 650–655.

den Heyer, K., & Barrett, B. (1971). Selective loss of visual and verbal information in STM by means of visual and verbal interpolated tasks. *Psychonomic Science, 25,* 100–102.

Doob, L. W. (1966). Eidetic imagery: A cross-cultural will-o'-the-wisp? *Journal of Psychology, 63,* 13–34.

Dywan, J., & Bowers, K. (1983). The use of hypnosis to enhance recall. *Science, 222,* 184–185.

Farah, M. J. (1988). Is visual imagery really visual? Overlooked evidence from neuropsychology. *Psychological Review, 95,* 307–317.

Farah, M. J. (1989). Mechanisms of imagery-perception interaction. *Journal of Experimental Psychology: Human Perception and Performance, 15,* 203–211.

Farah, M. J., Hammond, K. M., Levine, D. N., & Calvanio, R. (1988). Visual and spatial mental imagery: Dissociable systems of representation. *Cognitive Psychology, 20,* 439–462.

Finke, R. A. (1989). *Principles of mental imagery.* Cambridge, MA: MIT Press.

Finke, R. A., & Pinker, S. (1982). Spontaneous imagery scanning in mental extrapolation. *Journal of Experimental Psychology: Learning, Memory, and Cognition, 8,* 142–147.

Foley, M. A., Johnson, M. K., & Raye, C. L. (1983). Age-related changes in confusion between memories for thoughts and memories for speech. *Child Development, 54,* 51–60.

Geiselman, R. E., & Bjork, R. A. (1980). Primary versus secondary rehearsal in imagined voices: Differential effects on recognition. *Cognitive Psychology, 12,* 188–205.

Geiselman, R. E., & Glenny, J. (1977). Effects of imagining speakers' voices on the retention of words presented visually. *Memory & Cognition, 5,* 499–504.

Giray, E. F., Altkin, W. M., Vaught, G. M., & Roodin, P. A. (1985). A life span approach to the study of eidetic imagery. *Journal of Mental Imagery, 9,* 21–32.

Gray, C. R., & Gummerman, K. (1975). The enigmatic eidetic image: A critical examination of methods, data, and theory. *Psychological Bulletin, 82,* 383–407.

Haber, R. N. (1979). Twenty years of haunting eidetic imagery: Where's the ghost? *Behavioral and Brain Sciences, 2,* 583–629.

Haber, R. N., & Haber, R. B. (1964). Eidetic imagery: I. Frequency. *Perceptual & Motor Skills, 19,* 131–138.

Hebb, D. O. (1968). Concerning imagery. *Psychological Review, 75,* 466–467.

Humphreys, G. W., & Bruce, V. (1989). *Visual cognition: Computational, experimental, and neuropsychological perspectives.* Hove, UK: Erlbaum.

Intons-Peterson, M. J. (1983). Imagery paradigms: How vulnerable are they to experimenters' expectations? *Journal of Experimental Psychology: Human Perception and Performance, 9,* 394–412.

Intons-Peterson, M. J. (1992). Components of auditory imagery. In D. Reisberg (Ed.), *Auditory imagery.* Hillsdale, NJ: Erlbaum.

Johnson, M. K. (1985). The origin of memories. In P. C. Kendall (Ed.), *Advances in cognitive behavioral research and therapy, Vol. 4.* New York: Academic Press.

Johnson, M. K. (1988). Reality monitoring: An experimental phenomenological approach. *Journal of Experimental Psychology: General, 117,* 390–394.

Johnson, M. K., Kahan, T. L., & Raye, C. L. (1984). Dreams and reality monitoring. *Journal of Experimental Psychology: General, 113,* 329–344.

Johnson, M. K., Kounios, J., & Reeder, J. A. (1994). Time-course studies of reality monitoring and recognition. *Journal of Experimental Psychology: Learning, Memory, and Cognition, 20,* 1409–1419.

Johnson, M. K., & Raye, C. L. (1981). Reality monitoring. *Psychological Review, 88,* 67–85.

Johnson, M. K., Raye, C. L., Wang, A. Y., & Taylor, T. H. (1979). Fact and fantasy: The roles of accuracy and variability in confusing imaginations with perceptual experiences. *Journal of Experimental Psychology: Learning, Memory, and Cognition, 5,* 229–240.

Jolicoeur, P., & Kosslyn, S. M. (1985). Is time to scan visual images due to demand characteristics? *Memory & Cognition, 13,* 320–332.

Kerr, N. H. (1983). The role of vision in "visual imagery" experiments: Evidence from the congenitally blind. *Journal of Experimental Psychology: General, 112,* 265–277.

Kerst, S. M., & Howard, J. H. (1978). Memory psychophysics for visual area and length. *Memory & Cognition, 6,* 327–335.

Kosslyn, S. M. (1976). Can imagery be distinguished from other forms of internal representation? Evidence from studies of information retrieval times. *Memory & Cognition, 4,* 291–297.

Kosslyn, S. M. (1980). *Image and mind.* Cambridge, MA: Harvard University Press.

Kosslyn, S. M., Ball, T., & Reiser, B. J. (1978). Visual images preserve metric spatial information: Evidence from studies of image scanning. *Journal of Experimental Psychology: Human
Perception and Performance, 4,* 47–60.

Levine, D. N., Warach, J., & Farah, M. J. (1985). Two visual systems in mental imagery: Dissociation of "what" and "where" in imagery disorders due to bilateral posterior cerebral lesions. *Neurology, 35,* 1010–1018.

Luria, A. R. (1968). *The mind of a mnemonist.* New York: Basic Books.

MacKay, D. G. (1992). Constraints on theories of inner speech. In D. Reisberg (Ed.), *Auditory
imagery.* Hillsdale, NJ: Erlbaum.

Madigan, S. (1983). Picture memory. In J. C. Yuille (Ed.), *Imagery, memory, and cognition: Essays
in honour of Allan Paivio.* Hillsdale, NJ: Erlbaum.

Marchant, B., & Malloy, T. E. (1984). Auditory, tactile, and visual imagery in PA learning by
congenitally blind, deaf, and normal adults. *Journal of Mental Imagery, 8,* 19–32.

Marschark, M. (1992). Imagery. In L. R. Squire (Ed.), *Encyclopedia of learning and memory.* New
York: Macmillan.

Merrit, J. O. (1979). None in a million: Results of mass screening for eidetic ability using objective tests published in newspapers and magazines. *Behavioral and Brain Sciences, 2,* 612.

Moyer, R. S., Bradley, D. R., Sorensen, M. H., Whiting, J. D., & Mansfield, D. P. (1978). Psychophysical functions for perceived and remembered size. *Science, 200,* 330–332.

Nairne, J. S., & Pusen, C. (1984). Serial recall of imagined voices. *Journal of Verbal Learning and
Verbal Behavior, 23,* 331–342.

Neath, I. (1997). Modality, concreteness, and set-size effects in a free reconstruction of order
task. *Memory & Cognition, 25,* 256–263.

Paivio, A. (1969). Mental imagery in associative learning and memory. *Psychological Review, 76,*
241–263.

Paivio, A. (1971). *Imagery and verbal processes.* New York: Holt, Rinehart & Winston.

Paivio, A. (1986). *Mental representations: A dual-coding approach.* Oxford: Oxford University
Press.

Paivio, A., & Cohen, M. (1979). Eidetic imagery and cognitive abilities. *Journal of Mental Imagery, 3,* 53–64.

Perky, C. W. (1910). An experimental study of imagination. *American Journal of Psychology, 21,*
422–452.

Posner, M. I., Walker, J. A., Friedrich, F. J., & Rafal, R. D. (1984). Effects of parietal lobe injury
on covert orienting of visual attention. *Journal of Neuroscience, 4,* 1863–1874.

Potter, M. C. (1979). Mundane symbolism: The relations among objects, names, and ideas. In
N. R. Smith & M. B. Franklin (Eds.), *Symbolic functioning in childhood.* Hillsdale, NJ: Erlbaum.

Pylyshyn, Z. W. (1973). What the mind's eye tells the mind's brain: A critique of mental imagery. *Psychological Bulletin, 80,* 1–24.

Pylyshyn, Z. W. (1979). The rate of "mental rotation" of images: A test of a holistic analog hypothesis. *Memory & Cognition, 7,* 19–28.

Pylyshyn, Z. W. (1981). The imagery debate: Analog media versus tacit knowledge. *Psychological Review, 88,* 16–45.

Reisberg, D. (1992). (Ed.). *Auditory imagery.* Hillsdale, NJ: Erlbaum.

Riddoch, M. J., & Humphreys, G. W. (1987). A case of integrative visual agnosia. *Brain, 110,* 1431–1462.

Rosenthal, R. (1966). *Experimenter effects in behavioral research.* New York: Appleton-Century-Crofts.

Schnorr, J. A., & Atkinson, R. C. (1969). Repetition versus imagery instructions in the short- and long-term retention of paired associates. *Psychonomic Science, 15,* 183–184.

Seashore, C. E. (1938). *Psychology of music.* New York: McGraw-Hill.

Segal, S. J., & Fusella, V. (1970). Influence of imagined pictures and sounds on detection of visual and auditory signals. *Journal of Experimental Psychology, 83,* 458–464.

Shepard, R. N. (1984). Ecological constraints in internal representation: Resonant kinematics of perceiving, imagining, thinking, and dreaming. *Psychological Review, 91,* 417–446.

Shepard, R. N., & Cooper, L. A. (1983). *Mental images and their transformations.* Cambridge, MA: MIT Press.

Shepard, R. N., & Metzler, J. (1971). Mental rotation of three-dimensional objects. *Science, 171,* 701–703.

Stromeyer, C. F., & Psotka, J. (1970). The detailed texture of eidetic images. *Nature, 225,* 346–349.

Woodworth, R. S. (1938). *Experimental psychology.* New York: Henry Holt and Company.

# CHAPTER FOURTEEN

# Memory for When

*Interviewer: "How many words did you have to say as King Lear?"*
*Actor: "Ah, well, I don't want you to get the impression that it's just the number of*
*words. I mean, getting them in the right order is just as important."*

—*Monty Python*

Many types of memory questions require a person to recall when something happened. When trying to recall where you parked your car, you are concerned not only with a spatial location (the "where") but also a temporal location (where you parked *today* rather than where you parked yesterday). In this chapter, we will be concerned with how people do this, what kinds of errors they make, and how general the findings are. We begin with an example of typical performance on a dating task and then refine the ideas through laboratory studies of memory for order.

An earthquake occurred on Friday, January 31, 1986 at 11:50 EST in Ohio, where earthquakes are extremely rare. Friedman (1987) had subjects complete a survey during September 1986 to assess memory for when the event occurred. Recall of the day of the week and date were at guessing levels, and the month was inaccurate by an average of 2 months. Memory for the time of occurrence was far better than chance, being accurate to within an hour. This study illustrates several common findings that theories of *memory for when* must take into account. First, time is represented cyclically, not linearly. Thus, subjects can be accurate on certain cycles (hours) and wildly inaccurate on other cycles (weeks). Second, subjects are often significantly more accurate than chance but seldom exactly right. Estimated time is often highly correlated with actual time, but people rarely locate an event in time exactly. Third, people use whatever useful knowledge or fixed points they can to figure out the time of occurrence. One reason that time of day was accurate in the earthquake study was that it occurred around lunch time, a common reference point.

## Data to Be Accounted For

Any theory of memory for time must take into account not only the general characteristics outlined above but also several types of results frequently observed in both laboratory and environmental studies.

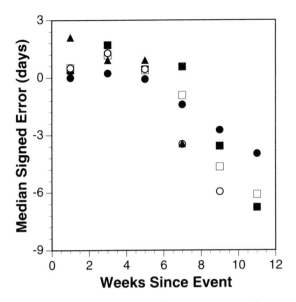

**Figure 14.1**   Accuracy in recalling when a naturally occurring event happened. Negative values indicate telescoping.   Source: Data from four experiments reported by Thompson, Skowronski, & Lee (1988).

*Recency and primacy effects.*   One ubiquitous finding is that temporal accuracy is better for events that happened toward the end of the sequence than for items in the middle of the sequence (Zimmerman & Underwood, 1968). This is true not only for lab studies (Hintzman, Block, & Summers, 1973) but also for autobiographical events (Baddeley, Lewis, & Nimmo-Smith, 1978). A similar finding is that subjects are more accurate in judging when the first item in a series occurred than in judging when later items occurred (Zimmerman & Underwood, 1968). For example, Hintzman, Block, and Summers (1973) presented two lists of 40 words each to subjects. At test, the subjects were asked to indicate which third of each list contained the target word. Judgments were most accurate for items from the beginning of list 1 and the end of list 2; the least accurate were from the middle of list 1 and middle of list 2.

*Telescoping.*   There are two kinds of telescoping: forward and backward (Rubin & Baddeley, 1989). Forward telescoping refers to the finding that people often give estimates of time of occurrence that are too recent. For example, Thompson, Skowronski, and Lee (1988) had students keep diaries of events for 12 weeks. At test, the experimenter would name an event, and the subject was asked to say when the event occurred. The measure of telescoping is the signed error: the actual date is subtracted from the estimated date. A negative number indicates telescoping, where the estimated date occurs closer to the testing date than the actual date. The results are shown in Figure 14.1; in four studies, substantial telescoping occurred.

   One consequence of telescoping is that people often inflate their estimates of the frequency of certain events (Bradburn, Rips, & Shevell, 1987). For example, if asked how

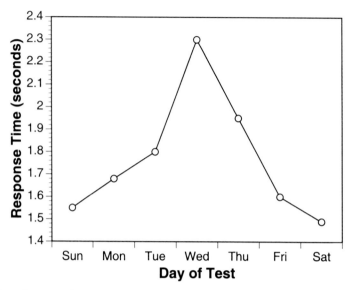

**Figure 14.2**   The time taken by U.S. subjects to respond to the question, "What day is today?" as a function of the actual day of week.   Source: Shannon (1979).

many times you have been to see a physician in the last 6 months, you are likely to include visits that occurred more than 6 months ago.

A related phenomenon is backward telescoping (Hinrichs & Buschke, 1968). Here, events that occurred more recently than a specified time are included, as if they were judged to be older than they really are.

*Better accuracy with longer intervals.*   Many studies find that accuracy in judging when something occurred increases, the longer the duration between the events (Underwood, 1977; Yntema & Trask, 1963). For example, Tzeng and Cotton (1980) presented a list of 50 words at a rate of 2 seconds per word with a 3-second interval between words. At test, the subject saw two words and was asked to indicate which had appeared more recently. Subjects were correct just about 50% of the time when less than 9 items separated the two test items, but they were correct more than 80% of the time when 30 items or more separated the two test items.

*Independent time scales.*   Many times, subjects may report an accurate date on one scale but an inaccurate date on another. For example, Hintzman, Block, and Summers (1973) found that subjects might recall an item on the wrong list but in the correct position; accuracy on one scale (position) can be better than on a more coarse scale (list). Friedman and Wilkins (1985) showed that memory for day of the week, date of the month, month, and year were essentially independent: accurate memory for one was unrelated to accuracy on others.

*Boundaries.*   Within each scale, there are anchor points. For example, Shannon (1979) asked subjects to name the day of week as quickly as they could. As Figure 14.2 shows, they were fastest for Sunday and Saturday, and slowest for Wednesday. Furthermore, the data differed depending on the culture and on whether Saturday or Sunday was the Sabbath.

One final characteristic should be discussed before considering theories of time. Sometimes, people directly encode the particular time, day, and date of an event (e.g., their marriage ceremony, the birth of a child). Direct recall of the time of occurrence can occur, but it is so rare (Friedman, 1993) that it should be viewed as the exception rather than the rule. As Friedman (1990) concluded, "time memory seems more of a makeshift affair, requiring a patchwork of processes and considerable effort — and usually ending in imprecision" (p. 43).

# Models That Don't Work

Friedman (1993) identified eight theories of time and divided them into three major classes (see Table 14.1). Although all of these theories have been proposed at one time or another, some are more well developed than others. In this section, we discuss six of the eight theories identified by Friedman and illustrate why he concluded that they are not viable candidates for a general theory of memory for time.

Distance theories (Hinrichs, 1970) are based on some process correlated with the passage of time. For example, *strength theories* suggest that people make judgments about when an event occurred by assessing the strength of the memory trace or some other measure related to strength, such as the accessibility of the trace or the elaborateness of the information. Strength theories have trouble explaining the primacy effect, where accuracy is not correlated with the passage of time, and the finding that people evaluate time on independent scales.

*Chronological organization theories* (Koffka, 1935) say that temporal information is reflected in the way memories are stored. For example, Koffka assumed that as events are perceived their traces are laid down by a continuously moving process. The result, which he called the *trace column,* is not unlike a tape recording, where time becomes spatialized. The traces in the column are assumed to be subject to the same spatial grouping principles that determine visual phenomena: the most recent items temporally would be the most distinct,

**Table 14.1**   Eight theories of memory for time, the class of theory to which they belong, and the main source of temporal information.

| Theory | Class | Source of Temporal Information |
|---|---|---|
| Strength | Distance | trace strength, accessibility, elaborateness |
| Chronological Organization | Distance | position in memory |
| Contextual Overlap | Distance | amount of context shared with the present |
| Time Tagging | Location | specific temporal tags |
| Perturbation | Location | associations with control elements during encoding |
| Reconstruction | Location | associations with contextual information and general knowledge |
| Associative Chaining | Relative Time | links between events and immediate successors |
| Order Code | Relative Time | pointers link events to specific prior events |

Source: Friedman (1993).

just as in visual perception the closest items spatially would be the most distinct. This view has difficulty explaining primacy effects, telescoping, and independent multiple scales.

The final distance theory is the *contextual overlap view* (Glenberg, Bradley, Kraus, & Renzaglia, 1983). According to this view, temporal judgments are based on the degree to which the contextual information encoded at study overlaps with current context: the larger the change, the older the time judgment. Like the other distance theories, this view has difficulty with both primacy effects and independent time scales.

There are three types of theories based on location rather than distance. The earliest uses *time-tagging* as its basic mechanism (Yntema & Trask, 1963). Essentially, this view maintains that the time of occurrence is stored with the memory for each event as it happens. Judgments of time are made by inspecting the tag, which can become dislodged from the item. The key claim is that time is encoded automatically (Hasher & Zacks, 1979). One major problem with this type of view is that time-tagging theories are generally not sufficiently detailed to make accurate predictions (see Friedman, 1993, for a review). In addition, the evidence suggests that direct retrieval of the date is rare, and although accuracy on judgments is usually better than chance, exact times are rarely given. Finally, studies find only a weak relation between the amount remembered about an event and the date assigned to it. For example, Brown, Rips, and Shevell (1985) had subjects judge which of two news events from a 5-year period was the most recent. Subjects were very accurate in dating the events even though they could often recall very little information about them.

We shall postpone discussion of the two other location-based views—reconstruction and perturbation—because these two account best for the data. The final two theories we address here both rely on relative time and, to be fair, were designed to explain only relative order judgments (e.g., which of two items occurred first). TODAM (Lewandowsky & Murdock, 1989; see Chapter 11), an *associative chaining theory*, was developed primarily as a model of serial order; nonetheless, Lewandowsky and Murdock (1989, p. 25) suggest that similar principles apply when, for example, determining which of two Canadian prime ministers came first. TODAM accomplishes this by the formation of links between successive events. This type of view, though, will have difficulty explaining how the memory system knows the time scale of links to form prior to the retrieval attempt.

*Order code theories* were also designed primarily to explain relative recency judgments. Unlike associative chaining views, though, order code theories (Tzeng & Cotton, 1980) allow for links to be established at any time. For example, hearing about one plane crash reminds you of earlier crashes, and thus an order link is formed. These views were not designed to explain time judgments of unrelated events.

We are left with two theories as viable candidates for a general theory of memory for time. We first examine perturbation theory and then describe the reconstructive view. To anticipate, although both can explain much of the data, perturbation theory makes more precise predictions, whereas the reconstructive view has the edge in intuitive appeal.

# Perturbation Theory

Estes (1972) proposed the initial version of *perturbation theory*. The key idea is that associations are formed between items and control elements; thus, item and order information are separate. For example, if I want to remember my office phone number, I take advan-

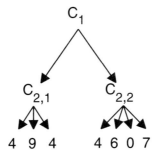

**Figure 14.3** The representation of a phone number using Estes' (1972) perturbation model. Each C represents a control element, the first subscript indicates the level within the hierarchy, and the second subscript indicates the group within a particular level.

tage of the fact that phone numbers in the United States are divided into a group of 3 and a group of 4. One control element, $C_1$, is associated with two lower-level units (see Figure 14.3). The subscript 1 indicates that it is on the first level of the hierarchy. The two control elements that are associated with $C_1$ are called $C_{2,1}$ and $C_{2,2}$. The first subscripts here indicate they are second-level control elements, and the second subscripts indicate their order. The prefix 494 is associated with control element $C_{2,1}$ and the remaining four digits, 4607, are associated with the second control element, $C_{2,2}$. In an immediate test, recall begins with the highest-level control element. From there, the hierarchical structure is decoded, so that $C_{2,1}$ leads to the prefix and "494" is produced. Then, $C_{2,2}$ is accessed, and the rest of the number is reported. With this kind of structure, one might expect a slight pause between recall of the two units.

If recall is required after a delay, rehearsal is necessary to keep the items in order. This is accomplished by a reverberatory loop: the association between a particular item and its corresponding control element is refreshed, with each association being refreshed slightly after the preceding one. Thus, the sequential activation preserves the order. Errors happen when variations occur in the timing of the reverberatory loop. This means that one loop, say between 6 and $C_{2,2}$, might be activated after the 0 and $C_{2,2}$ loop. The order of the digits 6 and 0 has now been swapped, or perturbed (hence the name, *perturbation* theory), and my phone number is now recalled as 494 4067. Because perturbations are due to random variations in timing, there will be more order errors, on average, with longer delays. Items cannot perturb between groups: the '9' will never swap places with the last four items because it is associated with a different control element.

An experiment reported by Healy (1974) illustrates the basic phenomena. She had subjects read aloud a list of four consonants, after which either 3, 8, or 18 digits were also read aloud. The purpose of the digits was to prevent rehearsal and to delay recall. At the end of the sequence, the subject was given 16 seconds to write down the four consonants in four boxes so that the first consonant was in the first box, the second consonant in the second box, and so forth. The results are shown in Figure 14.4. It is clear that the curves are bowed, and that the loss of information about position is gradual.

These results are consistent with what Estes' (1972) perturbation theory would predict. The more digits that need to be shadowed, the longer the delay between presentation and test, and so the more opportunities there are for perturbations to occur. Overall

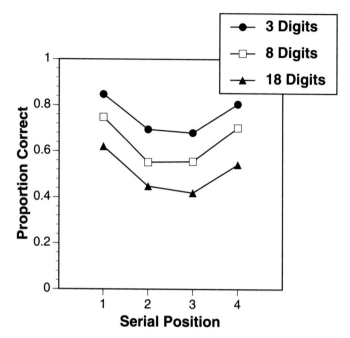

**Figure 14.4**   The proportion of correct responses as a function of input serial position when ordered recall follows shadowing of 3, 8, or 18 digits.   Source: Healy (1974).

performance decreases as the retention interval increases. In perturbation theory, the end items can perturb in only one direction, and so they are more likely to remain in the correct timing sequence. Because interior items can perturb in either direction, performance is better for the end items than for interior items.

This simple model also describes the loss of order information over far longer delays. Nairne (1992) performed an experiment similar to Healy's (1974) but one in which the retention interval varied in duration from 30 seconds to 24 hours. He presented five lists of five words, each of which was a common noun. As each word was presented, the subject was asked to make a pleasantness rating on a scale from 1 (unpleasant) to 3 (pleasant). The words were presented via a tape recorder, and subjects had 2.5 seconds to make their judgment. Each list began with the word *ready,* and lists were separated by a 5-second pause. Subjects in the 2-, 4-, 6-, 8-, and 24-hour retention interval conditions were then excused and asked to return at the appropriate time. Subjects in the 30-second retention interval condition were asked to count backward for 30 seconds.

After the retention interval, subjects were handed a new response sheet that contained five rows of blank lines. Above each blank line was a word from the original list, but they were presented in a new random order. Everyone was told that the words were in the correct list and was asked to indicate the original presentation order. Note that this is a direct test but one that follows incidental learning: subjects were not intentionally trying to learn the items because they were unaware that a test would follow. The results are shown in Figure 14.5 for three of the conditions.

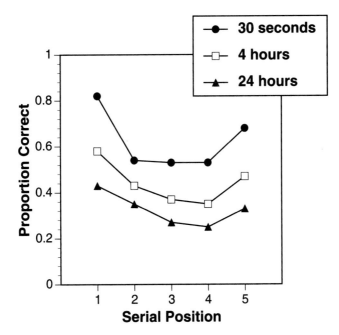

**Figure 14.5**   The proportion of correct responses as a function of input serial position when the surprise reconstruction of order task occurred after delays of 30 seconds, 4 hours, or **24 hours.**   Source: Based on data from Nairne (1992).

Note how similar these data are to those collected by Healy (1974) and shown in Figure 14.4. Nairne (1992) offered an interpretation of perturbation theory that differed from Estes' (1972) original version primarily because Nairne argued that the same principles applied regardless of the time scale. Estes (1972) had originally suggested that additional mechanisms and processes were required to explain memory for order over the long term. These data also suggest that rehearsal is not necessary for perturbations to occur because the subjects had no reason to rehearse during the retention interval.

Let's examine the perturbation model in more detail. The presentation of an event (such as a word in a list) leads to an initial representation of values on a number of different dimensions (Lee & Estes, 1977, 1981), at least one of which is serial order (Fuchs, 1969; Schulz, 1955). For example, in a typical serial recall test, there might be two relevant levels: list number and position within the list. This can be conveniently represented as a two-dimensional array, $S[i][j]$, where the variable $i$ counts the lists and variable $j$ counts the items within a list. If *greyhound* were the fourth word on the third list, then it could be represented as $S[3][4]$.

During forgetting, each of the originally encoded values loses precision. This process, known as *perturbation,* occurs when two encoded values swap positions with neighboring values (see Figure 14.6). For example, if a perturbation occurred for item $S[3][4]$ along the dimension that represented position within a list, it might now be represented by $S[3][3]$ or $S[3][5]$. If a perturbation occurred for item $S[3][4]$ along the dimension that represented the list number, it might now be represented by $S[2][4]$ or $S[4][4]$.

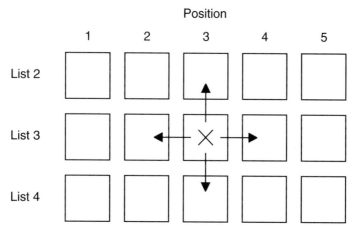

**Figure 14.6**   The four possible directions in which item $x$ (the third item on the third list) can perturb. For example, it can perturb from $S[3][3]$ to $S[3][4]$ by perturbing to the right, or from $S[3][3]$ to $S[2][3]$ by perturbing to the previous list.

---

**Experiment**   Memory for Position

**Purpose:**   To demonstrate the similar results obtained when memory for position is tested after 30 seconds or after 24 hours.

**Subjects:**   Twenty-four subjects are recommended; 12 should be assigned to the Immediate Group, and 12 to the Delayed Group. Subject 1 should be in the Immediate Group, Subject 2 in the Delayed Group, Subject 3 in the Immediate Group, and so on.

**Materials:**   Table E in the Appendix lists 25 common two-syllable nouns. Create five lists of five words each by randomly assigning the words to a list. Each subject should get a different random ordering of items. Also, make two response sheets for each subject. The first answer sheet should have five rows of five boxes for the pleasantness ratings. The second answer sheet should show the words that the subject rated, but in a new random order. Below each list, there should be five boxes in which subjects will indicate the original presentation order.

**Design:**   Because each subject experiences only one condition, delay is a between-subjects factor.

**Procedure:**   Inform the subjects that in this experiment they will be rating lists of words for pleasantness. Read each word clearly, and give equal emphasis to each item. Subjects should have 2 seconds in which to make their rating. At the end of each list, wait 2 seconds and then say, "That's the end of list 1. Here's list 2." After reading all of the lists, dismiss the delayed group, requesting them to return in 24 hours. For the immediate group, tell them the next part will begin as soon as you get all the papers together. Spend 30 seconds shuffling papers, then pass out the second answer sheet. Ask the subjects to indicate the original presentation order. Give the delay group the second answer sheet when they return.

**Instructions for the Immediate Group:**   "This experiment has two phases. In the first phase, you will be asked to rate five lists of words on how pleasant or unpleasant each word is. If you think a word has pleasant connotations, give it a 4 or 5. If you think it has neutral connotations, give it a 3. If you think it has unpleasant connotations, give it a 1 or a 2. You

There are three constraints on the perturbation process. First, the range of permissible values is constrained by the experiment. If the study uses nine-item lists, then the range of values for the dimension that represents position within a list must be between 1 and 9. If list 1 of an experiment contained bird names, list 2 contained dog names, and list 3 contained fish names, there would be very little movement along the list dimension. Second, each dimension can have its own perturbation rate. This rate is typically expressed as a probability that a perturbation will occur during a particular time interval. Third, most versions assume that movement is equally likely in either direction, but this need not always be the case. With this assumption, the end points of a particular dimension will always move more slowly than the middle points because half of the time the direction of movement will be constrained (for example, an item in position 1 cannot have the value of its representation perturb to position 0, only to position 2). It is this factor that will produce primacy and recency effects: memory is better for the first few and last few items because the boundaries prevent them from perturbing as far as middle items.

This theory has the advantage of being described by a simple equation. Assume that we are dealing with perturbations along only one dimension. We can calculate the probability that an item, S, will occupy a particular position, n, during the next time slice,

---

**Experiment    Memory for Position** (*continued*)

will have 2 seconds in which you can make your judgment and write down your answer. Any questions?" (When you have finished reading all the items, spend 30 seconds shuffling papers, then pass out the second answer sheet.) "For the second phase, please indicate the original presentation order for the lists of words you heard yesterday. The answer sheets give you all the items in the correct lists, but in a different order. Below each word, indicate what position in the list it occupied. It is better to guess than to leave a box blank."

**Instructions for the Delayed Group:** "This experiment has two phases; the second phase will take place tomorrow. In the first phase, you will be asked to rate five lists of words on how pleasant or unpleasant each word is. If you think a word has pleasant connotations, give it a 4 or 5. If you think it has neutral connotations, give it a 3. If you think it has unpleasant connotations, give it a 1 or a 2. You will have 2 seconds in which you can make your judgment and write down your answer. Any questions?" (When you have finished reading all the items, collect the answer sheet and dismiss the subjects, reminding them to return tomorrow.) "For the second phase, please indicate the original presentation order for the lists of words you heard yesterday. The answer sheets give you all of the items in the correct lists, but in a different order. Below each word, indicate what position in the list it occupied. It is better to guess than to leave a box blank."

**Scoring and Analysis:** For each subject, count the number of times the first word was correctly placed in the first slot. This number will range from 0 to 5. Do the same for each serial position. Construct two serial position functions, one for the immediate subjects and one for the delay subjects. To do this, add up the individual subject data and divide by the number of subjects. The graph should resemble Figure 14.5.

**Optional Enhancements:** Include more intermediate delay conditions and perhaps even a longer delay. Plot the position error gradients (see Figure 14.7).

Source: Based on an experiment by Nairne (1992).

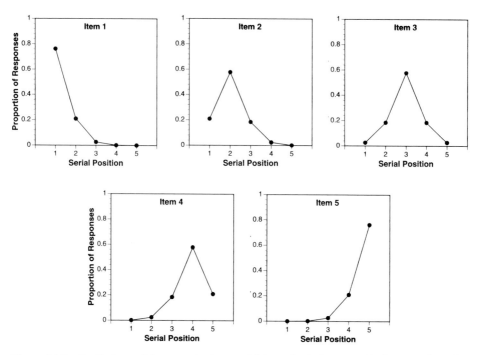

**Figure 14.7**   Predictions of the perturbation model for order judgments of a five-item list. The graph shows the distribution of probabilities that an item presented at the indicated position (e.g., item 1) would be assigned by the subject to each possible serial position at the time of recall. Thus, 76% of the time, the subject is likely to indicate that item 1 was presented at position 1; 21% of the time it will be recalled incorrectly at position 2; 2.6% of the time it will be recalled incorrectly at position 3; 0.2% of the time it will be recalled incorrectly at position 4; and it will almost never be incorrectly recalled at position 5. For this simulation, $\theta = 0.12$, the equations were applied five times, and perturbations in either direction were equally likely.

$t + 1$, by taking into account where the item is at time $t$ and what the probability of a perturbation is. Typically, the probability that an item will undergo a perturbation is represented by the Greek letter theta, $\theta$. The probability that an item will be represented as being in serial position 3 at time $t + 1$ will be equal to (a) the probability that it was at position 3 at time $t$ and no perturbation occurred $(1 - \theta)$, plus (b) the probability that it was at position 2 at time $t$ and a forward perturbation occurred $(\theta/2)$, plus (c) the probability that it was at position 4 at time $t$ and a backward perturbation occurred $(\theta/2)$. Put together, the whole equation is:

$$S_{n,t+1} = (1 - \theta)S_{n,t} + \left(\frac{\theta}{2}\right)S_{n-1,t} + \left(\frac{\theta}{2}\right)S_{n+1,t} \tag{14.1}$$

This equation assumes movement in either direction is equally likely. Because this assumption is not valid for the end points, the equation is changed slightly:

$$S_{1,t+1} = \left(1 - \left(\frac{\theta}{2}\right)\right)S_{1,t} + \left(\frac{\theta}{2}\right)S_{2,t} \tag{14.2}$$

The probability that an item will leave the end point is $\theta/2$ because it can move in only one direction. Similarly, there is only one position in the list, position 2, from which an item can perturb into the first position. These equations allow one to calculate, as a function of elapsed time, the likelihood that an encoded item will occupy a particular value along a particular dimension (Lee & Estes, 1977). Figure 14.7 shows the results of one such calculation. Each panel shows the probability that a particular item (item 1 in the first panel, item 2 in the second panel) will be recalled as having occurred in a particular position. The original serial position is typically most likely, with farther positions becoming increasingly less likely.

It is important to note that the perturbation model is *not* a decay model of memory. The model assumes that as time passes there will be more opportunities for perturbations to take place. This does not, however, mean that memory will always be worse after longer periods. The model allows for an item to perturb out of its original position, but it also allows for the item to perturb back to its original position. Thus, it is possible to recall the position of an item correctly at time $t$, to recall it incorrectly at time $t + 1$, and to recall it correctly again at time $t + 2$.

Although there are more complex versions of perturbation theory (Cunningham, Healy, & Williams, 1984; Lee & Estes, 1981; Healy, Fendrich, Cunningham, & Till, 1987), the simple version seems to account for both Healy's (1974) and Nairne's (1992) data remarkably well. For example, the positional uncertainty gradients can be calculated for each retention interval, and simulations of the perturbation model can then be compared with the data. Nairne (1992) was able to fit his data by setting theta to 0.12 and then applying the equations 5 times to fit the 30-second group, and then applying the equations an additional 5 times for every additional 2 hours in the retention interval. For example, the equations were applied 15 times for the 4-hour retention interval group. The results are shown in Figure 14.8.

In accordance with the model, subjects are more likely to correctly position the end items than the interior items; and when an error is made, it is likely to be close to the original position. As the duration of the retention interval increases, the gradients flatten and errors are more likely to include more distant positions.

The chapter began with a list of data to be explained, and perturbation theory can explain all five types. Recency and primacy effects in temporal judgments arise because the end items have less opportunity to perturb than middle items do. The second result was telescoping—the finding that people think temporally remote events occurred more recently than they actually did. (The name comes from the metaphor of looking at distant objects through a telescope and having them appear closer than they really are.) Telescoping is accounted for by the same principle that explains primacy and recency effects. When an old item perturbs, it moves closer to the end of the list because of the boundary at position 1, and this produces forward telescoping. When a more recent item perturbs, it moves closer to the beginning of the list, and this produces backward telescoping. Nairne (1992) includes a fit of perturbation theory to both forward and backward telescoping phenomena.

The third result was better accuracy with longer intervals between items. This is readily understood within perturbation theory because an item is thought of as being encoded as a point in multidimensional space. Figure 14.6 showed an item represented as a point in two-dimensional space, where the two dimensions were list and position. It would be easy to add a third dimension (e.g., block), and a fourth (experimental session), and so

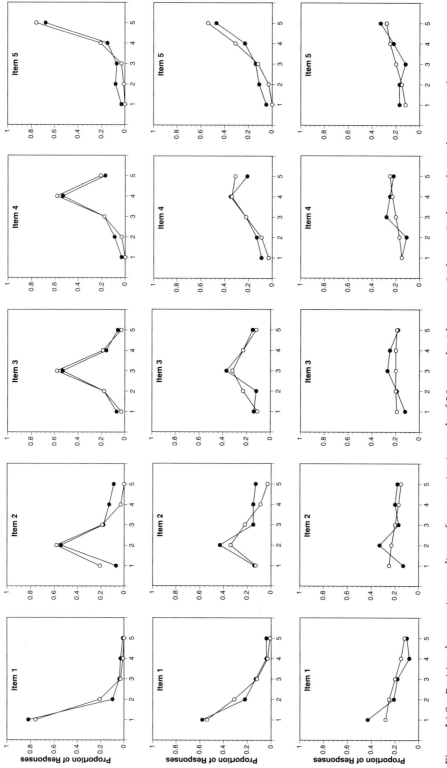

**Figure 14.8** Positional uncertainty gradients after retention intervals of 30 seconds, 4 hours, or 24 hours. Each row shows the positional uncertainty gradient for serial positions 1 through 5; lines with black circles represent the data, and lines with open circles are the predictions of the model. *Source:* Nairne (1992).

on. Multidimensional space, then, simply includes all possible dimensions that represent order information. If perturbation is considered as drifting along one of these dimensions (as opposed to the earlier idea of swapping control elements), then the longer the distance to drift, the more time it will take.

According to perturbation theory, people can be accurate on one time scale and inaccurate on another because the rates of perturbation can be independent. Thus, in the laboratory, position information might be lost more quickly than list information (Nairne, 1991), just as in dating studies, people can remember hour information better than month information. Finally, the boundary effects are a fundamental part of the model.

Although most of the illustrations involving perturbation theory have been used to model data from laboratory studies, these data are also found in studies of naturally occurring events. For example, Huttenlocher, Hedges, and Prohaska (1992) asked subjects to recall the day on which they participated in a telephone survey. The survey took place between 1 and 10 weeks prior to the dating question. The data from weeks 1 through 5 are shown as black circles in Figure 14.9, along with the predictions of the perturbation model (open circles). Theta was set to 0.05, and the number of applications of the equations was 80 for Monday through Friday, and 10 each on Saturday and Sunday. Monday and Friday are considered boundary points of a five-item range, and Saturday and Sunday are boundary points of a two-item range. Because many subjects indicated that they were unsure of their response, a correction-for-guessing procedure was added to the model. The panel labeled "guessing" is the pattern of responses that would be predicted by chance. Most people do not like to respond with end items, and this inflates the number of guesses for Wednesday; these guesses are simply added to the values predicted by perturbation theory. As Figure 14.9 shows, the model captures the important aspects of the data. Perturbation theory fits these everyday data as well as it fit the laboratory data.

The main advantages of perturbation theory are its ability (1) to account for all five main results described above; (2) to describe memory for spatial order as well as temporal and positional order (Nairne & Dutta, 1992); and (3) to make precise, quantitative predictions. The main disadvantage of perturbation theory is that it is rather vague on the psychological processes underlying dimensional drift. Although the early versions (Estes, 1972) offered a very precise and detailed description of the psychological processes, the more recent versions (Nairne, 1992) lack this detail. This weakness is the major advantage of the other main theory of memory for when.

# The Inference Model of Memory for When

According to the *inference* or *reconstructive model* of memory for time (Friedman, 1993; see also Underwood, 1977), people use "general time knowledge and inferential processes at the time of recall" (Friedman, 1993, p. 47) to infer or reconstruct likely temporal sequences. For example, many related memories provide clues to the likely time on one of many scales. Snow on the footpath may indicate winter, heading to lunch may indicate the hour, and wearing new mittens may indicate after Christmas rather than before.

This view predicts recency effects by assuming that there is less information available for judgments for older than for more recent information. Primacy effects are explained in a way similar to perturbation theory. Whenever there is a landmark event (such as the first

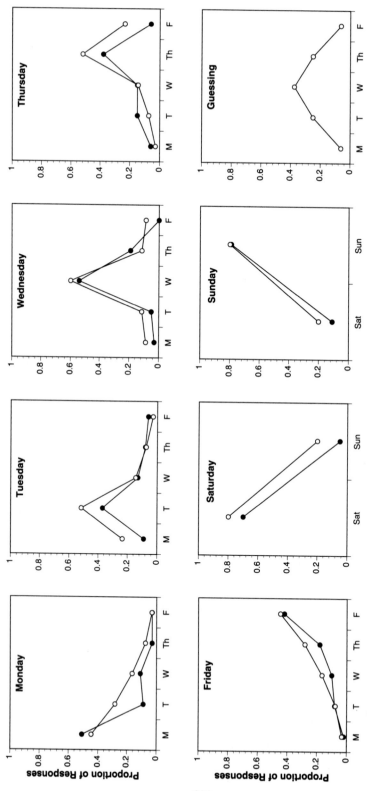

**Figure 14.9** The ability of perturbation theory to account for data from events that occurred between 1 and 5 weeks ago. *Source:* Based on data from Huttenlocher, Hedges, & Prohaska (1992).

time you drove a car), there will be more information available and more chance of accurately inferring the correct time.

The third result was better accuracy when a long rather than a short interval separates two items. This can be seen as an example of a general principle of cognition: the larger the difference between two items, the easier the discrimination. Temporal separation functions just as differences in size, frequency, or any other dimension do.

Telescoping is accounted for in a similar manner as recency effects. Older events have less other information available, so there is more uncertainty about these events. Events that occurred earlier than the cut-off date will be included because of this, and telescoping will be observed. For many events, subjects will have so little information that they may guess; this will produce both forward and backward telescoping. The finding of accuracy on some scales with inaccuracy on other scales is also readily handled. As the examples above show, different sources of information will be available for the different scales.

The major strength of the inference model is that it accords with intuitions of how people date events and with studies showing that subjects make more accurate judgments when told to remember information about the event itself. This process seems more plausible and more sensible than having temporal information drift along multiple dimensions. The major weakness of the inference model is its imprecision. Although it can account for the major results, it does not provide enough detail to say how much primacy will be observed or how much better memory will be with an interval of 60 seconds than with an interval of 10 seconds. It is also harder to test: with its lack of detail, it is easy to accommodate a wide range of results.

It is likely that the inference model and perturbation theory can be combined in some fashion. The perturbation theory does include some knowledge (such as the boundaries), and it seems relatively straightforward to add more top-down information. For example, Huttenlocher, Hedges, and Bradburn (1990) identify two processes commonly used that give rise to telescoping. First, there are bounding processes, much like those described above and already included in the perturbation model. The second is rounding. When there is some indecision about a date, subjects prefer to use a number that corresponds to some meaningful time. Huttenlocher, Hedges, and Bradburn (1990) identify 14, 21, 30, and 60 days as typical values. It is easy to see how these values could be used as boundaries within a revised perturbation model.

Whether this combined approach is successful or not, it is clear that memory for time is not based simply on memory of a linear code and that memory for when is not an automatic process. It is based on inference and reconstruction and includes memory for item information and memory for order. The last part of this chapter examines item and order information in more depth.

## Item versus Order Information

In the typical memory experiment, the subject has to remember when a particular item occurred: was the word *greyhound* presented on list 3 or on list 4? Within the list, was the word *greyhound* the fourth item or the fifth item? When subjects forget a particular item, they do not forget the word itself; they are perfectly capable of producing the word *greyhound* at some time in the future. Indeed, the subject usually 'knows' all of the item information prior to the experiment as well as after the experiment. What they do forget is the precise temporal occurrence of the word. This difference between item and order information is just another way of looking at when and how people date the occurrence of events, but it affords the possibility of separating these two factors.

One long-standing theoretical bone of contention has been the relationship between item and order information. Many researchers have offered theories that are centrally concerned with the relationship between item and order information (Brown, 1958; Crossman, 1960; Wickelgren, 1966). There is good evidence that item and order information are related, but there is also considerable evidence that there are dissociations between item and order information (Bjork & Healy, 1974; Healy, 1974, 1982; Murdock, 1976; Murdock & Vom Saal, 1967). Some models, such as those of Murdock (1976), Shiffrin and Cook (1978), and Drewnowski (1980), include separate and distinct representations of item and order information, but the loss of one type of information can affect the other. The original version of the perturbation model (Estes, 1972; Lee & Estes, 1977) postulates only a single way of losing information — when a perturbation alters order information — and Conrad's (1965) slot model also proposes only a single mechanism for forgetting, but in this model order errors are completely dependent on item errors.

Crowder (1979) argued that there is no fundamental difference between item and order information because each type of information is really a point on a scale. As discussed above, most memory judgments concern whether a particular item occurred at a particular time (for example, was the word *greyhound* on list 2 or list 3, did we have apple pie last Thanksgiving or the one before). According to Crowder, item information is simply order information at a more coarse level. If the subject decides that an item occurred during a particular interval, the subject will report that particular item. If incorrect, the experimenter may interpret this as an item error, whereas Crowder argued it could simply be an order error: the subject mistakenly believed the item occurred in list 6 whereas it actually occurred in list 7.

Even though it seems plausible to think of item and order information as related, there do seem to be important differences: some manipulations seem to enhance one type of information at the expense of the other. The *generation effect* refers to the finding that memory is often better for items that are generated compared to those that are merely read (Heller, 1956; Slamecka & Graf, 1978; see also Chapter 6). Nairne, Riegler, and Serra (1991) suggested that generation effects are not seen when the test emphasizes order information rather than item information. Serra and Nairne (1993) tested the idea that generation disrupts order information but enhances item information by comparing performance on pure lists (a pure list contains only one condition, read or generate) and mixed lists (a mixed list contains both read and generated items). Using a reconstruction of order task, Serra and Nairne found a negative generation effect: better memory for pure read lists than for pure generated lists. Approximately 68% of the read items were ordered correctly, whereas only 58% of the generated items were ordered correctly. There was no difference in performance for read items in a mixed list versus generated items in the mixed list. Serra and Nairne replicated these results in a second experiment in which the subjects were not expecting a memory test.

A third experiment used free recall of pure and mixed lists. This time, there was a generation effect for generated items in mixed lists compared to read items in mixed lists. Free recall of pure read lists was still better than recall of pure generated lists. In this experiment, Serra and Nairne also had subjects perform the reconstruction of order test *after* performing the free recall test. Even though they found a generation effect for generated items in the mixed list with free recall, there was no generation effect for these items on the subsequent reconstruction test.

Serra and Nairne (1993) argued that the act of generating an item disrupts order information but enhances item information. It disrupts order information by inducing item-specific processing; subjects focus more on the individual item than on relating the item to others in the list (Hunt & Einstein, 1981; see Chapter 6). When item but not order information is important at test — as in standard recognition tests — there will be a generation effect because the act of generation enhances memory for individual items. When order but not item information is important at test — as in the reconstruction of order test — there will be a negative generation effect because the act of generation disrupts memory for order. When both sources of information are required at test — as in a free recall test — the magnitude of the generation or negative generation effect will depend on the design. For example, in a pure generated list, the act of generation will enhance item information, but the output strategy, which typically relies heavily on order information, can mask the advantage. In a pure read list, there is no item information enhancement, but there is also no output strategy disadvantage. One prediction of this view is that if a different output strategy is induced, there should be a generation effect for pure generated items in free recall. This prediction has been confirmed: if category cues are used as aids in free recall, a generation effect can be seen with free recall of a pure generated list (McDaniel, Waddill, & Einstein, 1988).

Although the concepts of item and order information appear simple, it is difficult to tease apart the effects due to each. Finding manipulations, such as generation, that differentially affect each kind of information holds the promise of shedding light on the larger issue of how people remember when things happened and how people remember the order in which actions should be performed.

# References

Baddeley, A. D., Lewis, V., & Nimmo-Smith, I. (1978). When did you last . . . ? In M. M. Gruneberg & R. N. Sykes (Eds.), *Practical aspects of memory*. San Diego, CA: Academic Press.

Bjork, E. L., & Healy, A. F. (1974). Short-term order and item retention. *Journal of Verbal Learning and Verbal Behavior, 13*, 80–97.

Bradburn, N. M., Rips, L. J., & Shevell, S. K. (1987). Answering autobiographical questions: The impact of memory and inference on surveys. *Science, 236*, 157–161.

Brown, J. (1958). Some tests of the decay theory of immediate memory. *Quarterly Journal of Experimental Psychology, 10*, 12–21.

Brown, N. R., Rips, L. J., & Shevell, S. K. (1985). The subjective dates of natural events in very-long-term memory. *Cognitive Psychology, 17*, 139–177.

Conrad, R. (1965). Order error in immediate recall of sequences. *Journal of Verbal Learning and Verbal Behavior, 4*, 161–169.

Crossman, W. R. F. W. (1960). Information and serial order in human immediate memory. In C. Cherry (Ed.), *Information theory*. London: Butterworth.

Crowder, R. G. (1979). Similarity and order in memory. In G. H. Bower (Ed.), *The psychology of learning and memory, Vol. 13.* New York: Academic Press.

Cunningham, T. F., Healy, A. F., & Williams, D. M. (1984). Effects of repetition on short-term retention of order information. *Journal of Experimental Psychology: Learning, Memory, and Cognition, 10,* 575–597.

Drewnowski, A. (1980). Attributes and priorities in short-term recall: A new model of memory span. *Journal of Experimental Psychology: General, 109,* 208–250.

Estes, W. K. (1972). An associative basis for coding and organization in memory. In A. W. Melton & E. Martin (Eds.), *Coding processes in human memory.* Washington, DC: Winston.

Friedman, W. J. (1987). A follow-up to "Scale effects in memory for the time of events": The earthquake study. *Memory & Cognition, 15,* 518–520.

Friedman, W. J. (1990). *About time: Inventing the fourth dimension.* Cambridge, MA: MIT Press.

Friedman, W. J. (1993). Memory for the time of past events. *Psychological Bulletin, 113,* 44–66.

Friedman, W. J., & Wilkins, A. J. (1985). Scale effects in memory for the time of events. *Memory & Cognition, 13,* 168–175.

Fuchs, A. H. (1969). Recall for order and content of serial word lists in short-term memory. *Journal of Experimental Psychology, 82,* 14–21.

Glenberg, A. M., Bradley, M. M., Kraus, T. A., & Renzaglia, G. J. (1983). Studies of the long-term recency effect: Support for the contextually guided retrieval hypothesis. *Journal of Experimental Psychology: Learning, Memory, and Cognition, 9,* 231–255.

Hasher, L., & Zacks, R. T. (1979). Automatic and effortful processes in memory. *Journal of Experimental Psychology: General, 108,* 356–388.

Healy, A. F. (1974). Separating item from order information in short-term memory. *Journal of Verbal Learning and Verbal Behavior, 13,* 644–655.

Healy, A. F. (1982). Short-term memory for order information. In G. H. Bower (Ed.), *The psychology of learning and motivation, Vol. 16.* New York: Academic Press.

Healy, A. F., Fendrich, D. W., Cunningham, T. F., & Till, R. E. (1987). Effects of cueing on short-term retention of order information. *Journal of Experimental Psychology: Learning, Memory, and Cognition, 13,* 413–425.

Heller, N. (1956). An application of psychological learning theory. *Journal of Marketing, 20,* 248–254.

Hinrichs, J. V. (1970). A two-process memory-strength theory for judgment of recency. *Psychological Review, 77,* 223–233.

Hinrichs, J. V., & Buschke, H. (1968). Judgment of recency under steady-state conditions. *Journal of Experimental Psychology, 78,* 574–579.

Hintzman, D. L., Block, R. A., & Summers, J. J. (1973). Contextual associations and memory for serial position. *Journal of Experimental Psychology, 97,* 220–229.

Hunt, R. R., & Einstein, G. O. (1981). Relational and item-specific information in memory. *Journal of Verbal Learning and Verbal Behavior, 20,* 497–514.

Huttenlocher, J., Hedges, L. V., & Bradburn, N. M. (1990). Reports of elapsed time: Bounding and rounding processes in estimation. *Journal of Experimental Psychology: Learning, Memory, and Cognition, 16,* 196–213.

Huttenlocher, J., Hedges, L. V., & Prohaska, V. (1992). Memory for day of the week: A 5 + 2 day cycle. *Journal of Experimental Psychology: General, 121,* 313–326.

Koffka, K. (1935). *Principles of gestalt psychology.* London: Routledge & Kegan Paul.

Lee, C. L., & Estes, W. K. (1977). Order and position in primary memory for letter strings. *Journal of Verbal Learning and Verbal Behavior, 16,* 395–418.

Lee, C. L., & Estes, W. K. (1981). Item and order information in short-term memory: Evidence for multilevel perturbation processes. *Journal of Experimental Psychology: Human Learning and Memory, 7,* 149–169.

Lewandowsky, S., & Murdock, B. B., Jr. (1989). Memory for serial order. *Psychological Review, 96,* 25–57.

McDaniel, M. A., Waddill, P. J., & Einstein, G. O. (1988). A contextual account of the generation effect: A three-factor theory. *Journal of Memory and Language, 27,* 521–536.

Murdock, B. B., Jr. (1976). Item and order information in short-term memory. *Journal of Experimental Psychology: General, 105,* 191–216.

Murdock, B. B., Jr. & Vom Saal, W. (1967). Transpositions in short-term memory. *Journal of Experimental Psychology, 74,* 137–143.

Nairne, J. S. (1991). Positional uncertainty in long-term memory. *Memory & Cognition, 19,* 332–340.

Nairne, J. S. (1992). The loss of positional certainty in long-term memory. *Psychological Science, 3,* 199–202.

Nairne, J. S., & Dutta, A. (1992). Spatial and temporal uncertainty in long-term memory. *Journal of Memory and Language, 31,* 396–407.

Nairne, J. S., Riegler, G. L., & Serra, M. (1991). Dissociative effects of generation on item and order retention. *Journal of Experimental Psychology: Learning, Memory, and Cognition, 17,* 702–709.

Rubin, D. C., & Baddeley, A. D. (1989). Telescoping is not time compression: A model of the dating of autobiographical events. *Memory & Cognition, 17,* 653–661.

Schulz, R. (1955). Generalization of serial position in rote serial learning. *Journal of Experimental Psychology, 49,* 267–272.

Serra, M., & Nairne, J. S. (1993). Design controversies and the generation effect: Support for an item-order hypothesis. *Memory & Cognition, 21,* 34–40.

Shannon, B. (1979). Yesterday, today, and tomorrow. *Acta Psychologica, 43,* 469–476.

Shiffrin, R. M., & Cook, J. R. (1978). Short-term forgetting of item and order information. *Journal of Verbal Learning and Verbal Behavior, 17,* 189–218.

Slamecka, N. J., & Graf, P. (1978). The generation effect: Delineation of a phenomenon. *Journal of Experimental Psychology: Human Learning and Memory, 4,* 592–604.

Thompson, C. P., Skowronski, J. J., & Lee, D. J. (1988). Telescoping in dating naturally occurring events. *Memory & Cognition, 16,* 461–468.

Tzeng, O. J. L., & Cotton, B. (1980). A study-phase retrieval model of temporal coding. *Journal of Experimental Psychology: Human Learning and Memory, 6,* 705–716.

Underwood, B. J. (1977). *Temporal codes for memories: Issues and problems.* Hillsdale, NJ: Erlbaum.

Wickelgren, W. A. (1966). Associative intrusions in short-term recall. *Journal of Experimental Psychology, 78,* 853–858.

Yntema, D. B., & Trask, F. P. (1963). Recall as a search process. *Journal of Verbal Learning and Verbal Behavior, 2,* 65–74.

Zimmerman, J., & Underwood, B. J. (1968). Ordinal position knowledge within and across lists as a function of instructions. *Journal of General Psychology, 79,* 301–307.

# CHAPTER FIFTEEN

# Reconstructive Processes in Memory

*"Give us a dozen healthy memories, well-formed, and our own specified world to handle them in. And we'll guarantee to take any one at random and train it to become any type of memory that we might select — hammer, screwdriver, wrench, stop sign, yield sign, Indian chief — regardless of its origin or the brain that holds it."*
— E. F. Loftus and H. G. Hoffman

Although Loftus and Hoffman (1989, p. 103) are parodying a famous quotation by John B. Watson (1939, p. 104), they are making an extremely important point: memories are highly malleable. In this chapter, we review ways in which memories change or are constructed, usually without any awareness of the distortion. Indeed, in all the studies that follow, we can assume that the subjects were being as honest as possible; what is most impressive — or most disturbing — is how pervasive these changes can be.

## Flashbulb Memories

Brown and Kulik (1977) coined the term *flashbulb memory* to refer to a particular kind of memory, such as for where you were when John F. Kennedy was assassinated (or, more recently, when O. J. Simpson was acquitted). They suggested that these memories, which form only for highly surprising and highly consequential events, are "very like a photograph that indiscriminately preserves the scene" (p. 74). The metaphor refers to the scene captured when the flash on a camera goes off: the event is permanently chronicled in a highly detailed manner. Flashbulb memories are "fixed for a very long time, and conceivably permanently" (p. 85) and have their other unique qualities because of a special neurological mechanism. Brown and Kulik's findings were similar to those of Colegrove (1899), who reported that a majority of subjects tested could recall where they were when Abraham Lincoln was assassinated, including details of what they were doing.

There have been numerous studies on flashbulb memories, and even a whole book on the topic (Winograd & Neisser, 1992). For events that are highly surprising and personally relevant, people do report especially vivid memories and do provide lots of details, particularly about where they were when the event happened, who told them, who was with them, and what their emotional reaction was. The main questions of interest have been (1) are these memories really like photographs, and (2) is there any evidence to support the claim for a special process?

Currently, the answer appears to be "no" to both questions. We have already seen that there is virtually no evidence of eidetic imagery (or photographic memory) in adults (see Chapter 13). Even when the criteria of a flashbulb memory is made less stringent, flashbulb memory appears to be no more — or less — accurate than memory for nonflashbulb events. Although much of the research has focused on the explosion of the Space Shuttle *Challenger,* on January 28, 1986, at 11:38 EST, as a flashbulb event, similar results are found for other events.

Neisser and Harsch (1992) had 106 people fill out a questionnaire the day after the space shuttle exploded. The subjects answered questions to indicate what they were doing, who they were with, when they learned of the disaster, and so forth. Just under 3 years later, 44 subjects were asked again to recall this information. Their responses were coded in terms of accuracy of various attributes including location, activity, informant, time, and others present. Even though the event conformed to the criteria for producing a flashbulb memory, the mean score was only 2.95 out of 7 correct. Twenty-five percent of the subjects were wrong about every attribute and received a score of 0; only 3 subjects received perfect scores. Despite the poor overall performance, subjects rated their confidence very highly (4.17 out of 5). Of the 220 attributes tested, 93 were completely wrong, 60 were partially wrong, and 67 were correct. Although the subjects expressed a lot of confidence in the accuracy of their memories, and although they produced detailed and highly vivid recollections, their memories were not necessarily accurate ones (see also Neisser, 1982).

Several methodological problems are inherent in the flashbulb memory literature. One advantage of the Neisser and Harsch (1992) study is that the initial survey of the subjects was undertaken less than 24 hours after the event. After so short a period, it is highly likely that the subjects are reporting what actually happened. On their follow-up test, Neisser and Harsh found that, like regular memories, flashbulb memories can be distorted over time. Some studies that have reported very little distortion may have administered their initial test too late. For example, if the initial questionnaire is not administered until 2 or 4 weeks after the event, the subjects may be reporting already-distorted memories. This delay between the event and the initial assessment has been quite lengthy in many of the reported studies. For example, McCloskey, Wible, and Cohen (1988) administered their initial questionnaire within 1 week of the event; Bohannon (1988) administered his 2 weeks after the shuttle explosion; Conway et al. (1994) administered their questionnaire "within 14 days" after Margaret Thatcher resigned; Pillemer (1984) did not administer his questionnaire until 1 month after the assassination attempt of Ronald Reagan; and Christianson (1989) administered his 6 weeks after the assassination of Swedish prime minister Olof Palme. Only Neisser and Harsch (1992) assessed memory less than 24 hours after the event, and they found substantial inaccuracies and distortions.

A related problem is that because details make for a good story (Bell & Loftus, 1989), many people are tempted to add details to the story. Indeed, these flashbulb memories are the kind of stories that people — including memory researchers (Loftus & Kaufman, 1992) — love to tell and retell. If the "initial" memory is not assessed immediately, then it is likely that these constructed details get incorporated into the memory and are subsequently recalled, giving the illusion of accurate retention. In one sense, this is accurate retention, but it is accurate retention of constructed details.

A final problem is that there is rarely a separation of the effects of emotion and arousal from other effects on memory for a unique event. Most of these problems are due to the nature of the events that cause flashbulb memories: the event is so surprising that the initial memory questionnaire cannot be administered until days, weeks, or even months after the event. Furthermore, there is usually no control group: it is highly unlikely that there will be a cotemporaneous event that is also unique but that is not surprising or does not involve the subject emotionally. Given these problems, the vast majority of researchers have concluded that flashbulb memories are no more accurate and do not have special mechanisms. As McCloskey (1992, p. 234) puts it, "Given that flashbulb memories may not be all that good, and the performance expected from ordinary memory mechanisms may not be all that bad, motivation for postulating a special flashbulb memory mechanism may not be easy to come by." Most researchers agree that there is no special mechanism (see Winograd & Neisser, 1992), and although some researchers make a case for the specialness of flashbulb memories (Conway et al., 1994), most think that the results can be explained with regular principles of memory (Rubin & Kozin, 1984; Neisser & Harsch, 1992).

Weaver (1993) did report a study in which there was a "control" memory. He asked students to complete a typical flashbulb-memory questionnaire after meeting a roommate (or other friend). Coincidentally, later that evening, President Bush ordered the bombing attacks on Iraq, and two days later the same students received a questionnaire about that event. In general, the accuracy of the memories decreased according to Ebbinghaus' forgetting function (see Chapter 2). There was a large drop in accuracy over the first interval and almost no change between three months and one year after the event for both types of events. The most notable difference was that subjects expressed far greater confidence in their memories for the Iraq bombing than for the roommate meeting, even though this elevated confidence did not translate into better accuracy. Weaver (1993) suggests what distinguishes flashbulb memories from other memories are two characteristics: (1) the elevated confidence and (2) the compulsion or intent to remember the event. This latter characteristic appears to arise spontaneously in flashbulb memories and is often missing for more prosaic events. However, as Weaver's study shows, if one tries to remember a prosaic event, then accuracy can be as good as for a flashbulb event.

# Schemas

One frequently reported characteristic of people in flashbulb memory studies is *confabulation*—supplying additional information and details that were not part of the original episode. Rather than thinking of memory as some object that gradually becomes less clear or more distorted, most memory researchers believe that memories change because they are continually constructed and reconstructed. This repeated processing can change the memory in any number of ways, depending on the schema that is active at the time of recollection.

A *schema* is an organized knowledge structure that reflects an individual's knowledge, experience, and expectations about some aspect of the world. Information contained within a schema is usually recruited to help recall various events, and this is especially likely in situations such as those for flashbulb memories. Although not all researchers define schemas in the same way, most agree that a schema has five general characteristics (see Rumelhart & Norman, 1985; Rumelhart & Ortony, 1977).

First, schemas represent knowledge. This means that an individual's experience is reflected in a schema rather than abstract or objective knowledge, and it also means that a particular schema can change with new experiences. Second, schemas can represent knowledge at all levels, from a schema of a penny (Nickerson & Adams, 1979) to a schema of social structure (Schank & Abelson, 1977). Third, schemas can be embedded within each other. A schema about buying ice cream would involve an embedded schema about a commercial transaction (handing over money, receiving change), and that could have an embedded schema about coins (did you get a real coin or a funny foreign one).

The actual information within a schema is general; a restaurant schema applies to most restaurants. Information that is not common to all restaurants is represented by the fourth characteristic: schemas have variables. One variable in a restaurant schema might be whether you seat yourself or you wait and are seated. Variables can also have default values, which are the most common value for a variable for a particular individual. Thus, in schemas involving coffee, the default value is that the coffee is hot, even though it is not uncommon to see restaurants serving ice coffee.

The fifth characteristic is that schemas are active, dynamic, and continually changing. Schemas are used to comprehend sentences, to understand sensations, to organize information, to make predictions, and to foster expectations.

An experiment by Bransford and Johnson (1972) illustrates the usefulness of schemas in understanding. They presented subjects with a passage, such as the following (Bransford & Johnson, 1972):

> The procedure is actually quite simple. First you arrange items into different groups. Of course, one pile may be sufficient depending on how much there is to do. If you have to go somewhere else due to lack of facilities that is the next step, otherwise you are pretty well set. It is important not to overdo things. That is, it is better to do too few things at once than too many. In the short run this may not seem important but complications can easily arise. A mistake can be expensive as well. At first, the whole procedure will seem complicated. Soon, however, it will become just another facet of life. It is difficult to foresee any end to the necessity for this task in the immediate future, but then one never can tell. After the procedure is completed one arranges the materials into different groups again. Then they can be put into their appropriate places. Eventually they will be used once more and the whole cycle will then have to be repeated. However, that is part of life. (p. 722)

Subjects rated the passage on a scale of 1 to 7, where 1 equals very difficult to understand and 7 means very easy to understand. Half of the subjects rated the passage as very difficult, and half rated it as very easy. Furthermore, those who rated the passage as easy recalled almost twice as much as those who rated it as more difficult. The only difference between the groups was whether they had been told that the passage was about washing clothes. By giving the subjects this information, the experimenters ensured that the subjects could use the appropriate schema while reading, and thus integrate the information with knowledge they already had. At recall, the schema was again useful for providing structure: if you know the general procedure of washing clothes, then it is easy to generate the next step in the process.

Schemas can also introduce errors. Bower, Black, and Turner (1979) had subjects read 18 stories, each of which was based on a particular generic schema. These generic schemas were identified through a series of pilot experiments. (Actually, Bower et al. were looking at scripts, which refer to certain situation-action routines. For current purposes, think of a script as one particular type of schema.) In their study, a particular generic schema could be

**Table 15.1**   Average recognition ratings for three kinds of statements as a function of the number of script versions.

| Number of Script Versions | Stated Script Actions | Unstated Script Actions | Other Actions |
|---|---|---|---|
| 1 | 5.46 | 3.91 | 1.71 |
| 2 | 5.40 | 4.62 | 1.76 |
| 3 | 5.59 | 4.81 | 1.86 |

Source: Bower, Black, & Turner (1979).

the basis of 1, 2, or 3 different stories. One generic schema might be "Visiting a health professional" and subjects might read one story about "Going to the doctor" and another about "Going to the dentist." In this case, there would be two versions of the same generic schema.

The subjects were then given a recognition test. Some of the items on the test were stated schema actions that came from the stories, some were actions that had previously been identified as being in the generic schema but that did not appear in the stories, and some were novel actions that were neither in the generic schema nor in the stories. For each item on the test, the subjects gave a rating on a scale of 1 to 7, with 1 indicating "Very sure I did not read this sentence" and 7 indicating "Very sure I did read this sentence." The results are shown in Table 15.1.

Subjects gave higher ratings for sentences that were in the stories than for sentences that were not; however, sentences that were in the generic schema received higher ratings than novel actions did. Furthermore, the more stories a subject read that tapped a particular generic schema, the more likely it was that the subject would incorrectly say that an unstated sentence had been read. In other words, subjects were quite likely to falsely recognize actions as being from the passage if these actions were in their schema. Actions not in the schema (and not in the passage) were rarely falsely recognized or recalled.

The idea is that if you recall the passage was about washing clothes, one action is putting in the detergent. But did this action occur in the event or just in the schema that was activated? Did the passage above mention that sometimes you have to insert coins? Many of the details that subjects in flashbulb memory studies recall fit in this category: the information recalled is attributed to being from the original event but it is also information that is found in a schema of the event. Similar distortions and changes have been found by other researchers (Hasher & Griffin, 1978; Spiro, 1980).

Although schemas can introduce errors, it is important to remember that they can also improve recall. Switching from an inappropriate to an appropriate schema can facilitate memory. Anderson and Pichert (1978) had subjects read a story about two boys skipping school from the perspective of either a burglar or a person interested in buying a home. After recalling the story, the subjects were asked to recall the story a second time but now were asked to change perspective. On their second recall, the subjects produced more details important to the second perspective (that they had not recalled on the first attempt) and fewer details important to the first perspective (that they had recalled on the first attempt).

This basic idea is not new. Plato, in the Theatetus, recognized that the memory of an event is quite likely to be different now than when the event was originally experienced. More recently, Sir Frederic Bartlett (1932) proposed that new information is remembered in terms of already existing structures. In one famous experiment, he had subjects read a Native American folk tale called "The War of the Ghosts." Because the story followed different narrative conventions than those previously experienced by English students, the effect was not unlike reading the laundry passage above without knowing about laundry. Bartlett had his subjects recall the story after varying intervals ranging from immediately to several years. In general, the recalled story became shorter and, from a British perspective, more coherent: most of the supernatural elements disappeared resulting in a more traditional story about fighting and dying. Bartlett identified three particular types of reconstructive errors: (1) omissions, in which unusual or unfamiliar items tended not to be reported; (2) linkages, where made-up reasons — or rationalizations — were added by the subjects to give the story greater coherence; and (3) transformations, where unfamiliar names or terms were changed into more familiar ones (e.g. *canoe* becomes *boat, seal hunting* becomes *fishing*). These characteristics were noted in the reproduction of other stories (see Chapter VII of Bartlett, 1932). Although some of Bartlett's conclusions have proved difficult to replicate (see Chapter 1; Gauld & Stephenson, 1967; Roediger, Wheeler, & Rajaram, 1993; Wheeler & Roediger, 1992), the generally reconstructive nature of recollection has been consistently supported.

## Specific Schemas

The most common criticism of the idea of a schema is that it is too vague to be a useful concept. It is one of those ideas that explains everything but predicts nothing. David Rumelhart and his colleagues (Rumelhart, Smolensky, McClelland, & Hinton, 1986) have attempted to give a more precise definition and to derive and test predictions.

The basic idea is that a schema preserves general information at the expense of particular details. A simple implementation is represented in Figure 15.1 in the form of a regression equation. This example represents a paired-associate task, where the subject is asked to respond with a B item when prompted with an A item. In this case, both A and B items are numbers. The first stimulus is 1 and the correct response is 2.9; the second stimulus is 2 and the correct response is 3.1, and the final pair is 10-24. The black squares show perfect performance. In order to do well, 10 pairs must be learned. The schema for these relationships would reduce the memory load to just 1 item, the schema itself. In this case, the general relationship can be summarized as:

$$\text{response} = (2 \times \text{stimulus}) + 1 \tag{15.1}$$

If a schema is thought of as an equation that relates two (or more) pieces of information, the concept of schema is now precise, unambiguous, and testable. Furthermore, it follows all the properties listed above. For example, subjects using this schema would be quite accurate on most pairs; for example instead of 2.9 for the first response, the subject gives 3.0. One reason for using schemas is that they do work well enough most of the time. However, on some pairs the answer is much less accurate: instead of 11.5 for response 4, the subject responds with 9; instead of 24 for response 10, 21 is given. The increase in efficiency (having to remember only one thing, the schema, rather than 10 pairs) results in a loss of accuracy. There is another advantage of a schema: if a stimulus of 40 is given, the subject can give a plausible response (in this case 81). The person may not know whether this is correct or not, but the schema will allow expectations to be generated. If only the

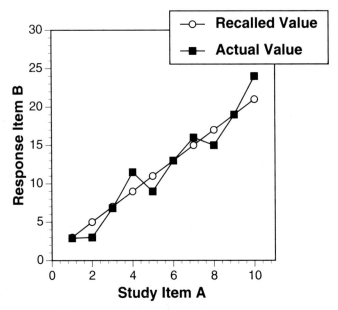

**Figure 15.1**   An illustration of how a schema can be made more precise.

10 pairs were stored, then it would be far more difficult, if not impossible, to extrapolate to novel situations.

Although a very simple example, this illustrates the kind of model Rumelhart et al. (1986) developed. They derived a set of equations that represented room schemas. More precisely, they implemented their descriptions of schemas as particular connections between items that might be found in different sorts of rooms. Thus, bathtub has a strong link with sink (as in a bathroom), and sink has a strong link with stove (as in a kitchen), but bathtub and stove are not linked. The schema, then, is the pattern of activation over all the elements within the network. The model can be questioned in much the same way that a person might be: What kind of room would have a telephone? There are several possibilities (probably more now that portable phones are more common), but one common answer is the kitchen; in most houses in the United States, the kitchen has a phone. In general, the responses given by the model were much the same as those given by people (see Rumelhart et al., 1986, for more details). This is not the only way to refine the concept of a schema so that it becomes more precise and able to make predictions, but it does illustrate one successful way.

## Malleability of Generic Memory

So far we have examined reconstructive processes in autobiographical memory. Generic memory is also quite malleable, even for such well-known information as that George Washington was the first president of the United States or that the Eiffel Tower is in Paris (Gerrig, 1989). The initial motivation behind the experiments that demonstrate this was

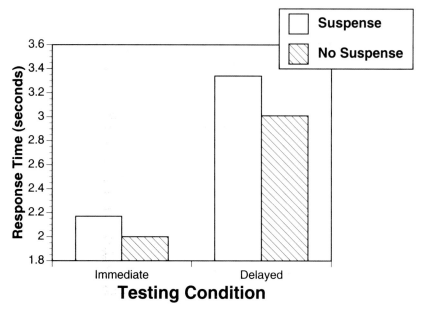

**Figure 15.2** Mean time (in seconds) to verify a target sentence either immediately after reading a passage or approximately 10 minutes after reading the passage. Source: Data from Experiments 1 and 3 of Gerrig (1989).

trying to understand how a person could see a movie or read a book for the second or third time and still have a sense of uncertainty about the outcome. Gerrig (1989) presented subjects with two different versions of a short story, one that contained no suspense and one that created suspense. The no-suspense version of one story went like this:

> George Washington was a famous figure after the Revolutionary War. Washington was a popular choice to lead the new country. Few people had thought that the British could be defeated. The success of the Revolutionary War was attributed largely to Washington. His friends worked to convince him to go on serving his country. Washington agreed that he had abundant experience as a leader.

The suspense version was slightly different:

> George Washington was a famous figure after the Revolutionary War. Washington was a popular choice to lead the new country. Washington, however, wanted to retire after the war. The long years as general had left him tired and frail. Washington wrote that he would be unable to accept the nomination. Attention turned to John Adams as the next most qualified candidate.

In both cases, the key target sentence was identical: George Washington was elected first president of the United States. The results are shown in Figure 15.2; subjects were slower to verify this sentence following a suspenseful passage than after a passage with no suspense. Perhaps more surprising, this difference is quite long-lasting; subjects in the delayed condition showed a similar effect when the target sentence was presented 10 minutes after the key passage.

Gerrig (1989) argued that this experiment reflects the memory processes that occur when watching a movie or reading a book for the second time. You have knowledge about the outcome, but this knowledge interferes with the enjoyment of the movie: Why watch "Terminator" again if you cannot recreate the suspense of seeing it the first time? What happens is that the viewer does not access all the relevant knowledge, or even the key parts of the relevant knowledge, if that information would destroy the suspense. It is as though subjects were able to ignore the information that would interfere with pleasure, and this leads to the surprisingly long-lasting effect shown in Figure 15.2. Access to even well-learned information is not necessarily obligatory.

# Eyewitness Memory

Perhaps the most disturbing area where reconstructive processes occur is in the memory of eyewitnesses. One summary has proved profoundly prophetic: Spiro (1980) suggested that in general, when memory changes to accommodate new information added after the original experience, (1) the chance of such changes increases with time, (2) the confidence the subject has that the memory is accurate will be as high or higher than for "accurate" memories, and (3) there is no way to distinguish inaccurate memories from accurate memories without some objective external evidence.

One line of research supporting these statements was initiated by Elizabeth Loftus and her colleagues. The basic experiment begins with the subjects' seeing a series of slides or a film that depicts some event like a robbery, car accident, or other naturalistic eyewitness event. The experimenters then ask the subjects a series of questions. Typically, Loftus and her colleagues change the way one question is asked to determine its effects on subsequent recall.

In one study, Loftus and Palmer (1974) asked subjects the following question: "How fast were the cars going when they _____ each other?" The researchers varied the intensity of the verb that described the collision, using *smashed, collided, bumped, hit,* and *contacted.* When the verb was *smashed,* the estimates averaged 41 mph; when the verb was *contacted,* the estimates averaged 32 mph (see Figure 15.3). A follow-up question asked whether there was broken glass. Nearly one-third of the subjects who had the verb *smashed* said "yes," but only one-tenth of those who had the verb *contacted* said there was broken glass. There was actually no broken glass. Clearly, the verb used led to the subjects' reconstructing their memory to be consistent with the implied speed of the verb.

Several other studies show that the words used in questions can change the answers, all of which are presumed to be based on memory. For example, subjects will say "yes" more often to a question like "Did you see *the* broken headlight?" than "Did you see *a* broken headlight?" (Loftus & Zanni, 1975). When asked "Do you get headaches frequently, and if so how often?" one sample of subjects gave an estimate of 2.2 headaches per week. When the word *frequently* was replaced by *occasionally,* the estimate dropped to 0.71 headaches per week (Loftus, 1975).

Perhaps the most famous of these studies is the so-called Red Datsun study (Loftus, Miller, & Burns, 1978). Subjects saw a sequence of 30 slides that followed a red Datsun as the car makes a turn and hits a pedestrian. Half of the subjects saw a stop sign at the intersection, and the other half saw a yield sign. Buried among the questions was one that

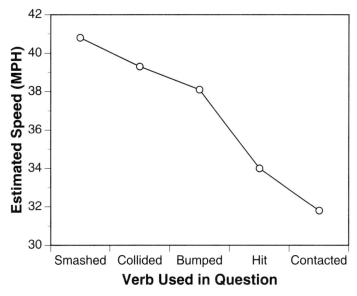

**Figure 15.3** Estimated speed at the time of the crash (in miles per hour) as a function of the verb used in the question. Source: Data from Loftus & Palmer (1974).

contained either consistent or misleading information: "Did another car pass the red Datsun while it was stopped at the ____ sign?" Half of the subjects, then, received consistent information (saw a stop sign and the question mentioned a stop sign, or saw a yield sign and the question mentioned a yield sign), and half received misleading information. Twenty minutes later, the subjects received a recognition test in which they were shown two photographs: one had a stop sign and one had a yield sign, and the subjects were asked which one they had seen.

Subjects who received consistent information were accurate about 75% of the time, but those who received misleading information were accurate only about 40% of the time. When tested after 2 weeks rather than 20 minutes, the effect was larger: subjects who received the misleading information were accurate only about 20% of the time. The subjects in the misleading condition were far more likely to recall the planted information than the original information. Similar findings have been reported when changing other details, for example, the color of the car (Loftus, 1979a). Note that this paradigm is very similar to the paired-associate learning discussed in Chapter 7, and it is an interference paradigm.

Subjects who are misled and who recall the misleading rather than the original information respond just as quickly (Cole & Loftus, 1979) and express just as much confidence (Loftus, Donders, Hoffman, & Schooler, 1989) as do their counterparts who remember accurately. Furthermore, even when told of the experimental design, nearly 90% of the misled subjects believe they received consistent information which they reported accurately (Loftus, Miller, & Burns, 1978). Even offering a financial incentive does not improve accuracy (Loftus, 1979b).

One controversy concerns whether the original information is completely and permanently lost (Loftus & Loftus, 1980) or is retained but has become inaccessible (Capaldi

& Neath, 1995). The biased-guessing account (McCloskey & Zaragoza, 1985; Zaragoza & Koshmider, 1989) emphasizes the fact that the misleading information is more recent than the original information. In its most simple form, a *misleading information experiment* compares performance between a control group, which receives consistent information, and an experimental group, which receives inconsistent (misleading) information. At test, the subjects are forced to make a choice between the original and the misleading information. The typical finding is that the control subjects identify the original information far more accurately than the experimental subjects do.

In this situation, McCloskey and Zaragoza's argument goes like this: Assume that half of the control subjects recall the event perfectly and the other half have forgotten. If this is the case, 50% of the subjects will get the answer correct because they remember it, and 25% will get the answer correct by chance (they guess and there are two possibilities). This gives an average of 75% correct for the control group. Assume further that the experimental subjects will remember as accurately as the control subjects will, so that half of them will recall the original information; thus, 50% will get the answer correct. The key to the biased-guessing explanation concerns the remaining half of the experimental subjects. Unlike the control subjects who cannot remember, some of the experimental subjects will have something else to remember — the misleading information. If 30% of the subjects recall this information, which is more recent than the original, then that leaves only 20% who do not remember either. This remaining portion will be split evenly over the two options. Adding this up, the control group will be 75% accurate and the experimental group will be only 60% accurate (see Table 15.2). These numbers were picked for simplicity; if we assume some retroactive interference from the misleading information (the A-D pair) on the original information (the A-B pair), then the percent of experimental subjects correctly recalling the original would be lower and overall performance lower.

McCloskey and Zaragoza (1985) designed an experiment to distinguish between these accounts. Rather than presenting the subjects with a forced-choice between the original and the misleading item, they used the original and a novel item. According to the impairment account (Loftus & Loftus, 1980), the control subjects should be more accurate than the experimental subjects because their memory for the original item was not over-

**Table 15.2**  An example of how the biased-guessing account explains the misleading information effect. The same number of people remember the original information, and when they remember nothing, half will pick the original and half will pick the misleading. The key is that some of the experimental group will remember only the misleading information, whereas none of the control group can. This reduces the number of subjects who remember nothing and reduces overall performance.

|  | *Percentage of Subjects Who* | | | | |
|  | *Remember and Pick* | | *Forget and Guess* | | *Total Correct* |
|  | *Original* | *Misleading* | *Original* | *Misleading* |  |
|---|---|---|---|---|---|
| Control | 50% | — | 25% | 25% | 75% |
| Experimental | 50% | 30% | 10% | 10% | 60% |

written. According to the biased-guessing account, performance should be nearly equivalent for the two groups: this test change removes the other responding option (remember and pick the misleading item), so all the experimental subjects who do not remember the original item should guess in exactly the same way as the control subjects do. This is what happened: performance by the control and experimental groups did not differ (McCloskey & Zaragoza, 1985; Loftus et al., 1989). The biased-guessing account can explain more data than the overwriting account, but only a few experiments have been done to test it. Regardless of the outcome of the controversy, it is important to emphasize that no one doubts the basic effect: people are very likely to incorporate and report extraneous information into their memories (Weingardt, Loftus, & Lindsay, 1995). In most practical situations, we do not have the luxury of wondering whether the effect is due to overwriting or biased guessing; the inaccuracy will be what is important.

One criticism of some of this research is that the events are not as emotionally intense or arousing as real events. Even if this criticism were correct, research has shown similar results from situations that are undeniably emotionally intense: even very intense, very traumatic, and very long-lasting events do not guarantee an accurate memory. For example, Wagenaar and Groeneweg (1990) studied the memory of concentration camp survivors. The researchers had access to films, photographs, and interviews that took place right after the camp was liberated. Some 40 years later, they questioned some of the survivors about conditions in the camp, guards, fellow prisoners, and other issues. Although some prisoners could recall a lot of information accurately with great detail, they also had many mistakes, including failing to remember whether they were housed in tents or wooden barracks or misremembering a prisoner as a guard. The general conclusion was that "the intensity of the emotion at the encoding of information is no guarantee for accurate eyewitness testimony" (p. 87). For example, memories of more brutal events were no more accurate than were memories of more ordinary events.

So far, we have presented cases in which the errors are mostly content errors — recalling a sign that was not present or being housed in a tent rather than a wooden hut. Many times, the content of the memories of eyewitnesses can be accurate, but there is an attribution error. Baddeley (1990) relates one such case. Donald Thomson, an Australian psychologist who, ironically, has studied eyewitness memory, was picked up by police and identified by a woman as the man who had raped her. His alibi was that he had been on a television talk show at the time and that he had an assistant police commissioner as a witness. The police interrogator reportedly responded with "Yes, and I suppose you've got Jesus Christ and the Queen of England too!" (Baddeley, 1990, p. 27). Later released and exonerated, Thomson found out that the woman had been watching TV when she was raped and had attributed the face she remembered (Thomson's) as the face of her attacker.

Attribution errors can be very common; for example, we have seen them operate in the reality monitoring paradigm, where an item is attributed to either an external or internal source; and they also play a large role in the false fame paradigm (see Chapter 9) discussed later in this chapter. The larger point is that when a memory is recollected, the source of the memory can be attributed either accurately (e.g., I participated in the event or read about the event or I imagined the event) or inaccurately. Even if all the details are correct, an attribution error can result in a fundamentally inaccurate memory.

Researchers in this area have concluded that there is no way to assess whether a memory is accurate or not without objective corroborative evidence (Kihlstrom, 1994; Loftus,

1993). Neither vividness, nor speed of recall, nor intensity of the experience, nor emotionality is correlated with accuracy. The subject may be accurately reporting the contents of memory and is thus not lying or trying to be deceitful. Nonetheless, the contents of memory can include information from other sources. Furthermore, as we saw when discussing reality monitoring, it is often difficult to distinguish between events that were experienced and those that were imagined (Anderson, 1984). If the only evidence is from an eyewitness and there is no other objective or corroborative evidence, then there is no way to assess the accuracy of the memory.

# Hypnosis and Memory

Many people believe that hypnosis can increase the accuracy of eyewitness' memory (Daglish & Wright, 1991; Wagstaff, Vella, & Perfect, 1992). Even therapists trained in hypnosis report widespread belief in the power of hypnosis to unlock previously hidden memories and that memories obtained through hypnosis are more likely to be accurate than are those that are simply recalled (Yapko, 1994). Mingay (1987) recently reviewed two different areas that have explored the effects of hypnosis on memory. Studies from experimental psychology generally show that hypnosis in and of itself does not lead to better recall (see also Orne, 1979; Roediger, 1996; Smith, 1983). If you cannot recall something when not under hypnosis, this research suggests, you will not be able to recall it under hypnosis. This also applies when the material is presented under incidental learning conditions (Mingay, 1986; Murray-Smith, Kinoshita, & McConkey, 1990). On the other hand, studies from the forensic literature cite many case studies where a person recalls additional information when under hypnosis. Which of these claims is more accurate, and why is there a difference?

The problem with most case and forensic studies is that they lack objective evidence that can be compared with the memory produced under hypnosis. Although a person might produce new information and might express great confidence, the validity of this information cannot usually be assessed. There is no way of assessing the accuracy of the information without objective corroborative evidence.

Hypnotically obtained testimony was first used in a U.S. court of law in an 1846 murder trial (Gravitz, 1995). One controversial issue is whether it should be allowed today. The consensus, at least of researchers, is that the possibility of producing an inaccurate memory is too high to warrant the risk (Orne, 1979). Hypnotized subjects are also more easy to mislead than are nonhypnotized subjects (Sanders & Simmons, 1983), and they have great difficulty distinguishing between events that happened prior to the hypnotic session and those that happened during the session (Dywan & Bowers, 1983; Whitehouse, Orne, Orne, & Dinges, 1991). The question of concern is whether hypnosis per se facilitates retrieval from memory. This is a separate issue from whether hypnosis is a useful therapeutic process, where the distorting effects on memory can sometimes be beneficial (Gravitz, 1994).

Yet another problem with hypnotically enhanced memories is the potential increase in confidence the subject reports. For example, Sheehan and Tilden (1983) presented subjects with a 24-slide sequence that depicted a wallet-snatching incident, after which questions were administered to determine how accurate the subjects' memories were. Half of

**Table 15.3** Accuracy (percent correct) and confidence levels
(percent of answers given the highest confidence rating) for
hypnoitized and control subjects.

|          | Suggestibility | % Correct | % "Certain" |
|----------|----------------|-----------|-------------|
| Hypnotic | High           | 79.5      | 64.5        |
|          | Low            | 79.5      | 57.2        |
| Control  | High           | 86.1      | 46.7        |
|          | Low            | 84.5      | 51.7        |

Source: Sheehan & Tilden (1983).

the subjects were hypnotized and half were not, and within each of these groups, half of the subjects were characterized as being highly suggestible and half were low suggestible. The data of interest are shown in Table 15.3. First, there was very little effect of suggestibility on overall accuracy; second, the nonhypnotized subjects were slightly more accurate. Sheehan and Tilden also had each subject rate his or her confidence in having answered the questions correctly. The final column in Table 15.3 shows the percentage of questions that the subject gave the highest confidence rating. Not only were the hypnotized subjects more confident but, of the hypnotized subjects, the more suggestible were even more confident. Thus, relative to a nonhypnotized control group, hypnotized subjects can express more confidence in their memories even though those memories are less accurate.

Of the few studies that do suggest an increase in accuracy with hypnosis, a large proportion can be attributed to processes other than hypnosis itself. Hypermnesia (the opposite of amnesia) is the finding that memory can improve with repeated tests. Erdelyi (1994) suggests that the repeated retrieval efforts made during the typical hypnotic session are what produces the enhanced memory, and that this is no different from hypermnesia studies that do not use hypnosis (Payne, 1987).

The majority of studies do not find that hypnosis allows recollection of information that could not otherwise be recalled. When hypnosis does lead to enhanced recollection, it is almost always the case that some other principle, such as hypermnesia, is producing the benefit. There is a far better alternative to hypnosis (and, also, to regular questioning) that does enhance recollection but that does not have the undesirable side effects of increasing errors and elevating confidence ratings that hypnosis does. Developed by Geiselman and his colleagues (Fisher, Geiselman, Raymond, & Jurkeich, 1987; Geiselman, Fisher, MacKinnon, & Holland, 1985), the method is called the *cognitive interview*, and it draws on findings from current memory research. Witnesses are asked to mentally reinstate the physical and psychological environment of the original events. According to transfer appropriate processing (Chapter 6), this should help in recreating the appropriate cues. The types of questions asked and the form of the questions are customized for each witness so that they take account of and conform to the witness' knowledge. This ensures that both the interviewer and the witness share common ground. A typical study showed that the cognitive interview yielded 45% more correct information than did the stan-dard police interview, without any measurable increase in errors. Geiselman and his colleagues suggest this as a replacement for hypnosis and also suggest that, on those occasions when hypnosis does help, it is likely that the hypnotist has stumbled on to the techniques proposed for the cognitive interview.

# Implanting Memories

There is a growing literature showing that memories can be easily created (Loftus, 1993; Roediger & McDermott, 1995); that is, after a particular experimental manipulation, a person "remembers" something that did not happen. One note on terminology is important here: these kinds of memories unfortunately have been termed *false memories*. This leads to an implied dichotomy between those memories that are true and those that are false. This is unfortunate for several reasons. First, as the evidence reviewed above shows, almost all memories are a combination of episodic details supplemented by information from generic memory or from other sources. Thus, at least parts of your memory for everything you have experienced is a false memory. To divide memory up as either true or false masks the fact that all memories are constructed and that the construction process draws on a lot of different types of information. Second, the term *false memory* suggests that the memory system *stored* false information. This obscures the important point that the memory system is dynamic and continuously changing. A particular inaccurate memory might be accurate in all respects except one (as in the case with Donald Thomson, described above). What is important are the processes that lead to this result, not the simple-minded assertion that a memory is true or false.

Memory for items that were not presented has recently been demonstrated by Roediger and McDermott (1995). They describe a paradigm first used by Deese (1959a, 1959b) in which he used lists of 12 words, such as *thread, pin, eye, sewing, sharp, point, pricked, thimble, haystack, pain, hurt,* and *injection.* All these words are related to *needle*, which does not appear in the list. Deese found that many subjects would recall *needle* as one of the list items, and Roediger and McDermott (1995) replicated this result: the critical omitted word was recalled approximately 40% of the time. Following recall, the subjects were given a recognition test and were asked to indicate on a scale of 1 to 4 whether each item was from one of the lists or not. A 4 meant Sure Old, a 3 meant Probably Old, and 2 meant Probably New, and 1 meant Sure New. Along with the studied items, there were three types of lures. Some were unrelated, some were weakly related, and some were the strongly related critical lure. The results are shown in Table 15.4.

Subjects treated the critical lures (mean rating 3.3) more as a studied item (mean rating 3.6) than as a nonstudied item (mean ratings: 1.2 and 1.8). Similar results were reported by Read (1996) and Payne, Elie, Blackwell, and Neuschatz (1996). Note that both spreading activation and compound cue models (see Chapter 12) can explain this finding. In a second experiment, Roediger and McDermott (1995) had subjects make a remember-know judgment (see Chapter 10). Surprisingly, the proportion of studied items that received a remember judgment (0.79) was almost identical to the proportion of critical lures that received a remember judgment (0.73). This underscores one of the main findings from the misleading information paradigm (Weingardt, Loftus, & Lindsay, 1995): people can be very confident that information they recall is accurate despite the fact that the information is completely wrong.

Once again, it may be objected that these memories are different from ones in which real-life events happened, but a recent study illustrates that this objection is not well

**Table 15.4**   The proportion of items rated as Sure Old (4), Probably Old (3), Probably New (2) and Sure New (1) and the overall mean rating for studied items and three types of lures in a recognition test.

|  | Old | | New | | Mean Rating |
|---|---|---|---|---|---|
|  | 4 | 3 | 2 | 1 | |
| Studied | .75 | .11 | .09 | .05 | 3.6 |
| Unrelated Lure | .00 | .02 | .18 | .80 | 1.2 |
| Weakly Related | .04 | .17 | .35 | .44 | 1.8 |
| Critical Lure | .58 | .26 | .08 | .08 | 3.3 |

Source: Roediger & McDermott (1995).

founded. Loftus and Coan (cited by Loftus, 1993) developed a way of implanting a specific memory — getting lost when age 5. Using a trusted family member, the procedure involves the subject in a game of "Remember when...?" where all but one of the events described is genuine. The subject of the study was a 14-year-old boy named Chris whose older brother convinced him that Chris had been lost in a shopping mall when age 5. The brother told

---

**Experiment   Memory for Words Not Presented**

**Purpose:** To demonstrate recall of words that were not present on the list.

**Subjects:** Thirty subjects are recommended.

**Materials:** Table J in the Appendix contains 6 lists of 15 words each. You will also need an answer sheet.

**Procedure:** Inform the subjects that in this experiment they will be hearing a list of words. Read the words at a rate of 1 word every 2 seconds. Before beginning each list, say "List 1," etc. Allow 2 minutes for free recall, and then ask the subjects to rate their confidence for each word on a scale from 1 to 4.

**Instructions:** "In this experiment, you will hear a list of words and will then be asked to re-call as many words as you can. You may write down the words in any order you like. Then, I will ask you to judge your confidence in your responses using a scale of 1 to 4. A 1 means you are not very sure and a 4 means you are absolutely sure that the word was on the list. Then the next list will start. Any questions?"

**Scoring and Analysis:** For each subject, calculate the mean proportion of items recalled. Count up the number of words recalled and divide by the total number of words. Then, count up the number of times each critical item was recalled and also divide by 6. Also calculate the average confidence for the studied words and compare with the average confidence on the critical lure. The results should be similar to those shown in Table 15.4.

**Optional Enhancements:** Add a recognition test after presenting all 6 lists. Prepare some distractor words by including some unrelated words as well as the critical lures. Have the subjects respond using the same scale described in Table 15.4.

Source: Based on an experiment by Roediger & McDermott (1995).

the story, including details of the parents' panic and of finding Chris being led through the mall by an old man. Within 2 days of hearing the story, Chris began supplying details on how he felt. After about 2 weeks, Chris produced the following report (Loftus, 1993):

> I was with you guys for a second and I think I went over to look at the toy store, the Kay-bee toy and uh, we got lost and I was looking around and I thought, "Uh-oh. I'm in trouble now." You know. And then I . . . I thought I was never going to see my family again. I was really scared you know. And then this old man, I think he was wearing a blue flannel, came up to me . . . he was kind of old. He was kind of bald on top . . . he had like a ring of gray hair . . . and he had glasses. (p. 532)

According to both the older brother and Chris' mother, this event never happened. Chris, on the other hand, described the memory as being reasonably clear and vivid. Being lost at the mall was the implanted memory, and all the other memories were of genuine episodes that Chris had experienced. When debriefed and asked to pick out the planted memory, Chris picked a genuine one. It is likely that even this elaborate a procedure is unnecessary for planting memories. For example, Garry, Manning, Loftus, and Sherman (1996) have shown that simply imagining that some childhood event occurred can elevate confidence ratings that the event actually did occur (see also Hyman & Pentland, 1996).

One well-known example of a memory of an entire sequence that never happened concerns the famous Swiss psychologist Jean Piaget (see Loftus & Ketchum, 1991, p. 19). He had a memory of being kidnapped when he was an infant and found out later that his nanny had made up the story. It is likely that you have memories of events that did not happen. A student in one of my memory classes had a memory of a favorite pet golden retriever. After hearing my lecture on this topic, she checked with her parents: the dog had died 2 years before she was born. Apparently, she had heard stories and seen slides, and was attributing memory for these as memory for real events. Along similar lines, I received a nasty e-mail from a journal editor asking where was my review of an article that he had sent some months previously. It was all too easy to imagine receiving the manuscript, placing it somewhere in my office, and then having it disappear under a mountain of papers. A couple of days later, I received an apologetic e-mail from the editor saying that an overzealous automated warning system had fired off the missive and that he had not actually sent the manuscript. For those two days, however, I was so convinced that I had lost the paper that I conducted a frantic search of home and office.

# Memory Illusions

As Roediger (1996) points out, although there are hundreds if not thousands of studies on perceptual illusions, there are relatively few that deal specifically with memory illusions. One reason may be that with a perceptual illusion, such as those shown in Figures 15.4 and 15.5, both the objective and subjective version can be continually experienced. With a memory illusion, only the subjective version remains. An additional reason may be that memory illusions are often referred to by other names and are not specifically identified as illusions. A recent issue of the *Journal of Memory and Language* is devoted to the topic of memory illusions (Murphy, 1996) and illustrates many effects. Here, we follow Roediger's terminology and describe some of these illusions.

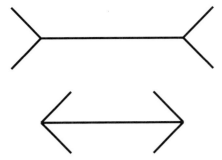

**Figure 15.4**   The Müller-Lyer illusion: most people report that the top horizontal line looks longer than the bottom horizontal line even though they are the same length.

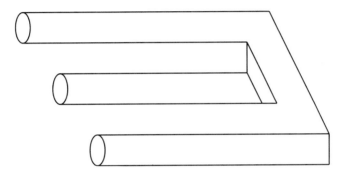

**Figure 15.5**   An impossible object.

*Verbal overshadowing.*   Carmichael, Hogan, and Walter (1932; see also Moore, 1910) demonstrated that memory for simple line drawings is affected by the verbal label (see Chapter 6). Two circles connected by a line can be remembered as either a pair of glasses or as a set of dumbbells, depending on the label. Melcher and Schooler (1996) showed that novice wine drinkers could not recognize wines when they engaged in verbal description because their descriptions were not accurate. Experienced wine drinkers, on the other hand, showed no impairment because their verbal labels were accurate. As Roediger (1996) put it, "people remember the events as they described them to themselves, not as they actually happened" (p. 87).

*Reality monitoring.*   As reviewed in Chapter 13, the reality monitoring paradigm (Johnson & Raye, 1981) is fundamentally concerned with distinguishing memories of perceived events from memories of imagined events. Like research begun almost a century ago (Perky, 1910), this line of research has shown that it is often difficult for people to recall the source of a memory. Memories for events are often attributed to an incorrect source rather than to the actual one.

**Target Figures**

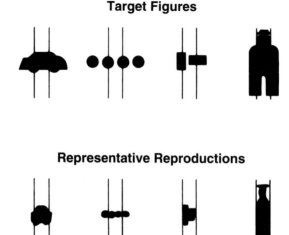

**Representative Reproductions**

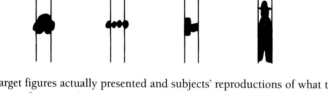

**Figure 15.6**   Target figures actually presented and subjects' reproductions of what they saw. The size of the target figures is shown relative to the size of the slit behind which they moved. In the experiment subjects could see only what was revealed in the space between the two lines.   Source: McCloskey & Watkins (1978).

*Misattributions of memory.*   Many memory illusions are due to a misattribution. Jacoby, Woloshyn, and Kelley (1989) presented subjects with a list of nonfamous names and told the subjects that all the names are nonfamous. Subjects then were shown a list of mixed famous and nonfamous names and were asked to indicate which are famous. Some of the nonfamous names were new (they have not been seen before by the subject) and some were from the previous phase. The typical finding was that many of the nonfamous old names were judged as famous. The idea is that if a subject can recall seeing a name from the first phase, they know the name is nonfamous. If, on the other hand, they cannot recall this but instead are relying on overall familiarity, they should be more likely to say the old nonfamous name is famous. Ease of processing is often taken, in many situations, as an indication that the information is well known (Begg, Duft, Lalonde, Melnick, & Sanvito, 1989; Kelley & Jacoby, 1996).

*Remembering more than is seen.*   When people see a moving picture through a small aperture, they remember more of the object than was actually seen (McCloskey & Watkins, 1978; see Figure 15.6). Motion is not necessary for this effect: when people see a still photograph, their memories include additional information that was not seen, relating to both the object and the background scene (Intraub & Richardson, 1989). The explanation is the use of schemas: if the picture is of two-thirds of a car, the remaining one-third can be filled in by knowledge contained in a schema.

This is by no means an exhaustive list of memory illusions; indeed, many others are described throughout this text. For example, we will see in the next chapter that self-reports of memory problems are usually unrelated to the actual number and severity of memory problems. The important point to remember is that most illusions will go unnoticed because, unlike perceptual illusions, there is nothing objective to compare with your internal representation.

# References

Anderson, R. C., & Pichert, J. W. (1978). Recall of previously unrecallable information following a shift in perspective. *Journal of Verbal Learning and Verbal Behavior, 17,* 1–12.

Anderson, R. E. (1984). Did I do it or did I only imagine doing it? *Journal of Experimental Psychology: General, 113,* 594–613.

Baddeley, A. D. (1990). *Human memory.* Boston: Allyn & Bacon.

Bartlett, F. C. (1932). *Remembering: A study in experimental and social psychology.* Cambridge: Cambridge University Press. (Reprinted 1977.)

Begg, I., Duft, S., Lalonde, P., Melnick, R., & Sanvito, J. (1989). Memory predictions are based on ease of processing. *Journal of Memory and Language, 28,* 610–632.

Bell, B. E., & Loftus, E. F. (1989). Trivial persuasion in the courtroom: The power of (a few) minor details. *Journal of Personality and Social Psychology, 56,* 669–679.

Bohannon, J. N. (1988). Flashbulb memories of the space shuttle disaster: A tale of two theories. *Cognition, 29,* 179–196.

Bower, G. H., Black, J. B., & Turner, T. J. (1979). Scripts in memory for text. *Cognitive Psychology, 11,* 177–220.

Bransford, J. D., & Johnson, M. K. (1972). Contextual prerequisites for understanding: Some investigations of comprehension and recall. *Journal of Verbal Learning and Verbal Behavior, 11,* 717–726.

Brown, R., & Kulik, J. (1977). Flashbulb memories. *Cognition, 5,* 73–99.

Capaldi, E. J., & Neath, I. (1995). Remembering and forgetting as context discrimination. *Learning & Memory, 2,* 107–132.

Carmichael, L., Hogan, H. P., & Walter, A. A. (1932). An experimental study of the effect of language on the reproductions of visually perceived forms. *Journal of Experimental Psychology, 15,* 73–86.

Christianson, S.-A. (1989). Flashbulb memories: Special, but not so special. *Memory & Cognition, 17,* 435–443.

Cole, W. G., & Loftus, E. F. (1979). Incorporating new information into memory. *American Journal of Psychology, 92,* 413–425.

Colegrove, F. W. (1899). Individual memories. *American Journal of Psychology, 10,* 228–255.

Conway, M. A., Anderson, S. J., Larsen, S. F., Donnelly, C. M., McDaniel, M. A., McClelland, A. G. R., Rawles, R. E., & Logie, R. H. (1994). The formation of flashbulb memories. *Memory & Cognition, 22,* 326–343.

Daglish, M. R., & Wright, P. (1991). Opinions about hypnosis among medical and psychology students. *Contemporary Hypnosis, 8,* 51–55.

Deese, J. (1959a). Influence of inter-item associative strength upon immediate free recall. *Psychological Reports, 5,* 305–312.

Deese, J. (1959b). On the prediction of occurrence of particular verbal intrusions in immediate recall. *Journal of Experimental Psychology, 58,* 17–22.

Dywan, J., & Bowers, K. (1983). The use of hypnosis to enhance recall. *Science, 222,* 184–185.

Erdelyi, M. H. (1994). Hypnotic hypermnesia: The empty set of hypermnesia. *International Journal of Clinical and Experimental Hypnosis, 42,* 379–390.

Fisher, R. P., Geiselman, R. E., Raymond, D. S., & Jurkeich, L. M. (1987). Enhancing enhanced eyewitness memory: Refining the cognitive interview. *Journal of Police Science and Administration, 15,* 291–297.

Garry, M., Manning, C. G., Loftus, E. F., & Sherman, S. J. (1996). Imagination inflation: Imagining a childhood event inflates confidence that it occurred. *Psychonomic Bulletin & Review, 3,* 208–214.

Gauld, A., & Stephenson, G. M. (1967). Some experiments related to Bartlett's theory of remembering. *British Journal of Psychology, 58,* 39–49.

Geiselman, R. E., Fisher, R. P., MacKinnon, D. P., & Holland, H. L. (1985). Eyewitness memory enhancement in the police interview: Cognitive retrieval mnemonics versus hypnosis. *Journal of Applied Psychology, 70,* 401–412.

Gerrig, R. J. (1989). Suspense in the absence of uncertainty. *Journal of Memory and Language, 28,* 633–648.

Gravitz, M. A. (1994). Memory reconstruction by hypnosis as a therapeutic technique. *Psychotherapy, 31,* 687–691.

Gravitz, M. A. (1995). First admission (1846) of hypnotic testimony in court. *American Journal of Clinical Hypnosis, 37,* 326–330.

Hasher, L., & Griffin, M. (1978). Reconstructive and reproductive processes in memory. *Journal of Experimental Psychology: Human Learning and Memory, 4,* 318–330.

Hyman, I. E., Jr., & Pentland, J. (1996). The role of mental imagery in the creation of false childhood memories. *Journal of Memory and Language, 35,* 101–117.

Intraub, H., & Richardson, M. (1989). Wide-angle memories of close-up scenes. *Journal of Experimental Psychology: Learning, Memory, and Cognition, 15,* 179–187.

Jacoby, L. L., Woloshyn, V., & Kelley, C. (1989). Becoming famous without being recognized: Unconscious influences of memory produced by dividing attention. *Journal of Experimental Psychology: General, 118,* 115–125.

Johnson, M. K., & Raye, C. L. (1981). Reality monitoring. *Psychological Review, 88,* 67–85.

Kelley, C. M., & Jacoby, L. L. (1996). Adult egocentrism: Subjective experience versus analytic bases for judgment. *Journal of Memory and Language, 35,* 157–175.

Kihlstrom, J. F. (1994). Hypnosis, delayed recall, and the principles of memory. *International Journal of Clinical and Experimental Hypnosis, 42,* 337–345.

Loftus, E. F. (1975). Leading questions and the eyewitness report. *Cognitive Psychology, 7,* 560–572.

Loftus, E. F. (1979a). Shifting human color memory. *Memory & Cognition, 5,* 696–699.

Loftus, E. F. (1979b). *Eyewitness testimony.* Cambridge, MA: Harvard University Press.

Loftus, E. F. (1993). The reality of repressed memories. *American Psychologist, 48,* 518–537.

Loftus, E. F., Donders, K., Hoffman, H. G., & Schooler, J. W. (1989). Creating new memories that are quickly accessed and confidently held. *Memory & Cognition, 17,* 607–616.

Loftus, E. F., & Hoffman, H. G. (1989). Misinformation and memory: The creation of new memories. *Journal of Experimental Psychology: General, 118,* 100–104.

Loftus, E. F., & Kaufman, L. (1992). Why do traumatic experiences sometimes produce good memory (flashbulbs) and sometimes no memory (repression)? In E. Winograd & U. Neisser (Eds.), *Affect and accuracy in recall: Studies of "flashbulb" memories.* New York : Cambridge University Press.

Loftus, E. F., & Ketchum, K. (1991). *Witness for the defense.* New York: St. Martin's Press.

Loftus, E. F., & Loftus, G. R. (1980). On the permanence of stored information in the human brain. *American Psychologist, 35,* 409–420.

Loftus, E. F., Miller, D. G., & Burns, H. J. (1978). Semantic integration of verbal information into a visual memory. *Journal of Experimental Psychology: Human Learning and Memory, 4,* 19–31.

Loftus, E. F., & Palmer, J. C. (1974). Reconstruction of automobile destruction: An example of the interaction between language and memory. *Journal of Verbal Learning and Verbal Behavior, 13,* 585–589.

Loftus, E. F., & Zanni, G. (1975). Eyewitness testimony: The influence of the wording of a question. *Bulletin of the Psychonomic Society, 5,* 86–88.

McCloskey, M. (1992). Special versus ordinary memory mechanisms in the genesis of flashbulb memories. In E. Winograd & U. Neisser (Eds.), *Affect and accuracy in recall: Studies of "flashbulb" memories.* New York : Cambridge University Press.

McCloskey, M., & Watkins, M. J. (1978). The seeing-more-than-is-there phenomenon: Implications for the locus of iconic storage. *Journal of Experimental Psychology: Human Perception and Performance, 4,* 553–564.

McCloskey, M., Wible, C. G., & Cohen, N. J. (1988). Is there a special flashbulb memory mechanism? *Journal of Experimental Psychology: General, 117,* 171–181.

McCloskey, M., & Zaragoza, M. S. (1985). Misleading postevent information and memory for events: Arguments and evidence against memory impairment hypotheses. *Journal of Experimental Psychology: General, 114,* 1–16.

Melcher, J. M., & Schooler, J. W. (1996). The misremembrance of wines past: Verbal and perceptual expertise differentially mediate verbal overshadowing of wine. *Journal of Memory and Language, 35,* 231–245.

Mingay, D. J. (1986). Hypnosis and memory for incidentally learned scenes. *British Journal of Experimental and Clinical Hypnosis, 3,* 173–183.

Mingay, D. J. (1987). The effect of hypnosis on eyewitness memory: Reconciling forensic claims and research findings. *Applied Psychology: An International Review, 36,* 163–183.

Moore, T. V. (1910). The process of abstraction: An experimental study. *California University Publications in Psychology, 1,* 73–197.

Murphy, G. L. (1996). Illusions of memory. *Journal of Memory and Language, 35,* 75.

Murray-Smith, D., Kinoshita, S., & McConkey, K. M. (1990). Hypnotic memory and retrieval cues. *British Journal of Experimental and Clinical Hypnosis, 7,* 1–8.

Neisser, U. (1982). *Memory observed.* San Francisco: Freeman.

Neisser, U., & Harsch, N. (1992). In E. Winograd & U. Neisser (Eds.), *Affect and accuracy in recall: Studies of "flashbulb" memories.* New York: Cambridge University Press.

Nickerson, R. S., & Adams, M. J. (1979). Long-term memory for a common object. *Cognitive Psychology, 11,* 287–307.

Orne, M. T. (1979). The use and misuse of hypnosis in court. *International Journal of Clinical and Experimental Hypnosis, 27,* 311–341.

Payne, D. G. (1987). Hypermnesia and reminiscence in recall: A historical and empirical review. *Psychological Bulletin, 101,* 5–27.

Payne, D. G., Elie, C. J., Blackwell, J. M., & Neuschatz, J. S. (1996). Memory illusions: Recalling, recognizing, and recollecting events that never occurred. *Journal of Memory and Language, 35,* 261–285.

Perky, C. W. (1910). An experimental study of imagination. *American Journal of Psychology, 21,* 422–452.

Pillemer, D. B. (1984). Flashbulb memories of the assassination attempt on President Reagan. *Cognition, 16,* 63–80.

Read, J. D. (1996). From a passing thought to a false memory in 2 minutes: Confusing real and illusory events. *Psychonomic Bulletin & Review, 3,* 105–111.

Roediger, H. L., III. (1996). Memory illusions. *Journal of Memory and Language, 35,* 76–100.

Roediger, H. L., III, & McDermott, K. B. (1995). Creating false memories: Remembering words not presented in lists. *Journal of Experimental Psychology: Learning, Memory, and Cognition, 21,* 803–814.

Roediger, H. L., III, Wheeler, M. A., & Rajaram, S. (1993). Remembering, knowing, and reconstructing the past. In D. L. Medin (Ed.), *The psychology of learning and motivation: Advances in research and theory.* San Diego, CA: Academic Press.

Rubin, D. C., & Kozin, M. (1984). Vivid memories. *Cognition, 16,* 81–95.

Rumelhart, D. E., & Norman, D. A. (1985). Representation of knowledge. In A. M. Aitkenhead & J. M. Slack (Eds.), *Issues in cognitive modelling.* London: Erlbaum.

Rumelhart, D. E., & Ortony, A. (1977). The representation of knowledge in memory. In R. C. Anderson, R. J. Spiro, & W. E. Montague (Eds.), *Schooling and the acquisition of knowledge.* Hillsdale, NJ: Erlbaum.

Rumelhart, D. E., Smolensky, P., McClelland, J. L., & Hinton, G. E. (1986). Schemata and sequential thought processes in PDP models. In J. L. McClelland & D. E. Rumelhart (Eds.), *Parallel distributed processing: Explorations in the microstructure of cognition (Vol. 2).* Cambridge, MA: MIT Press.

Sanders, G. S., & Simmons, W. L. (1983). Use of hypnosis to enhance eyewitness accuracy: Does it work? *Journal of Applied Psychology, 68,* 70–77.

Schank, R. C., & Abelson, R. (1977). *Scripts, plans, goals and understanding.* Hillsdale, NJ: Erlbaum.

Sheehan, P. W., & Tilden, J. (1983). Effects of suggestibility and hypnosis on accurate and distorted retrieval from memory. *Journal of Experimental Psychology: Learning, Memory, and Cognition, 9,* 283–293.

Smith, M. C. (1983). Hypnotic memory enhancement of witnesses: Does it work? *Psychological Bulletin, 94,* 387–407.

Spiro, R. J. (1980). Accommodative reconstruction in prose recall. *Journal of Verbal Learning and Verbal Behavior, 19,* 84–95.

Wagenaar, W. A., & Groeneweg, J. (1990). The memory of concentration camp survivors. *Applied Cognitive Psychology, 4,* 77–87.

Wagstaff, G. F., Vella, M., & Perfect, T. (1992). The effect of hypnotically elicited testimony on jurors' judgments of guilt and innocence. *Journal of Social Psychology, 132,* 591–595.

Watson, J. B. (1939). *Behaviorism* (2nd ed.). Chicago: University of Chicago Press.

Weaver, C. A., III. (1993). Do you need a "flash" to form a flashbulb memory? *Journal of Experimental Psychology: General, 122,* 39–46.

Weingardt, K. R., Loftus, E. F., & Lindsay, D. S. (1995). Misinformation revisited: New evidence on the suggestibility of memory. *Memory & Cognition, 23,* 72–82.

Wheeler, M. A., & Roediger, H. L., III (1992). Disparate effects of repeated testing: Reconciling Ballard's (1913) and Bartlett's (1932) results. *Psychological Science, 3,* 240–245.

Whitehouse, W. G., Orne, E. C., Orne, M. T., & Dinges, D. F. (1991). Distinguishing the source of memories reported during prior waking and hypnotic recall attempts. *Applied Cognitive Psychology, 5,* 51–59.

Winograd, E., & Neisser, U. (Eds.). (1992). *Affect and accuracy in recall: Studies of "flashbulb" memories.* New York : Cambridge University Press.

Yapko, M. D. (1994). Suggestibility and repressed memories of abuse: A survey of psychotherapists' beliefs. *American Journal of Clinical Hypnosis, 36,* 163–171.

Zaragoza, M. S., & Koshmider, J. W., III. (1989). Misled subjects may know more than their performance implies. *Journal of Experimental Psychology: Learning, Memory, and Cognition, 15,* 246–255.

# CHAPTER SIXTEEN

# Developmental Changes in Memory

*"The phenomenon of Self and that of memory, are two sides of the same fact, or two different modes of viewing the same fact. We may, as psychologists, set out from either of them, and refer the other to it. We may in treating of memory, say it is the idea of a past sensation associated with the idea of myself as having it. Or we may say, in treating of Identity, that the meaning of Self is the memory of certain past sensations."*
—*John Stuart Mill*

Throughout this book so far, most of the studies have focused on memory in people between the ages of 18 and 25. An important area of study is how these people developed their memory and what is likely to happen to their memory as they age. Both cognitive and developmental psychologists study memory as it changes.

## Memory in Infancy

Although the memories of infants are quite different from those of the average 20-year-old, some of the basic processes and phenomena can still be observed. One big difference is the way the studies are conducted. Because infants do not yet have language, do not understand instructions, and do not have the capability of writing or saying their answer, memory studies of infants are more like those of rats and pigeons than of older humans. Thus, memory in infants is often assessed by using learning techniques such as *habituation*.

Friedman (1972) used an habituation procedure to see whether newborn infants (around 1 day old) could remember which objects they had seen. This procedure is based on the assumption that infants will look longer at a novel stimulus than at a previously seen stimulus. Friedman used checkerboard patterns, because these have enough discriminability that even a 1-day-old child with 20/400 vision can see the difference. The more times a particular pattern was displayed, the less time the infant spent looking at it. However, when a novel pattern was shown, the infants spent more time looking at it. This suggests that infants can remember quite accurately which items they have seen before.

Another technique is to place a mobile over an infant's crib and tie a ribbon from the infant's leg to the mobile. When the infant kicks, the mobile moves, providing novel stimulation. This procedure has been used to investigate a variety of different aspects of infants' memory. For example, Rovee-Collier and her colleagues have shown that 2-month-olds retain the response for up to 3 days (Greco, Rovee-Collier, Hayne, Griesler, & Earley, 1986), whereas by age 6 months retention has increased to 2 weeks (Hill, Borovsky, & Rovee-Collier, 1988).

Even when 3-month-olds no longer show memory for the relationship between the ribbon and the mobile — the memory is not accessible — it is likely that they still do remember something, that the memory is potentially available (Tulving & Pearlstone, 1966). Sullivan (1982) used a procedure known as *reinstatement,* where a cue is given to the infant prior to the memory test. It is important that the cue does not allow new learning, because then nothing could be claimed about the old memory. A number of 3-month-olds were trained on a ribbon-mobile apparatus. One group was tested after two weeks, and showed little memory. Another group received a reminder the day before the test, which consisted of having the infants watch the experimenter pull the ribbon. The next day, the infants' memory for the relationship was shown by immediately kicking. Rovee-Collier and Fagen (1981) have shown reinstatement after a delay of 28 days.

Kicking a leg is one type of memory, but do infants have memory for specific episodes? Bauer and her colleagues (see Bauer, 1996, for a review) have developed a procedure for assessing memory for specific episodes. She first shows the infants a series of events using props. At recall, the props are again available, but the subject has to put them together in the correct temporal sequence to recreate the activity. For example, one event is to use a goalpost-shaped base, a bar, a hooked metal plate, and a mallet to make a gong. The child would be told the following (Bauer, 1996): "Let's make a gong. Put on the bar [placing the bar across the base to form a cross piece]. Hang up the bell [hanging the metal plate from the cross piece]. Ring the bell [hitting the metal plate with the mallet]" (p. 32).

The important claim is that performance on these tasks engages the same cognitive processes as verbal recall does. Results consistent with this claim come from studies with amnesics, who cannot perform verbal recall and also cannot perform this event sequence task (McDonough, Mandler, McKee, & Squire, 1995). Children as young as 11 months can recall novel event sequences when tested immediately, and the number of steps recalled in order systematically increases as they get older (see Figure 16.1).

Bauer, Hertsgaard, and Dow (1994) tested 21-month-olds, 24-month-olds, and 29-month-olds for sequences they had learned 8 months previously. All three age groups performed better than a control group, indicating retention of the specific sequences after an 8-month interval. As with memory in adults, memory in infants benefits from repetition and from the presence of appropriate retrieval cues at test (Bauer, 1996).

Even infants as young as 3 months encode and retain contextual information (see Rovee-Collier & Shyi, 1992, for a review). For example, Butler and Rovee-Collier (1989) tested infants in a crib in the mobile-kicking paradigm. The crib liner could be either the same or different at test as it had been during acquisition, and the mobile could be the same or different. A group of 3-month-olds were tested 5 days after acquisition, but only those subjects in the same liner and same mobile showed evidence of retention. That is, the same mobile was not itself a sufficiently useful retrieval cue unless accompanied by the same context. Infants as young as 3 months also show a misinformation effect (Rovee-Collier, Borza, Adler, & Boller, 1993).

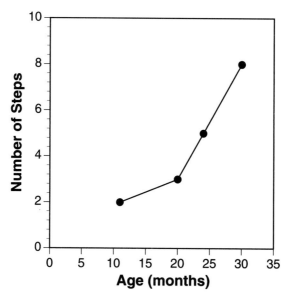

**Figure 16.1**    The number of steps in novel event sequences that children can immediately reproduce in order as a function of the child's age.    Source: From data summarized in Bauer (1996).

## Infantile Amnesia

One topic of much speculation is infantile amnesia — the finding that most people cannot recall events that involved them prior to the age of about 3 or 4 years (Waldfogel, 1948). For example, Sheingold and Tenney (1982) asked college students to recall events surrounding the birth of a sibling. Subjects who were younger than 3 at the time of their sibling's birth recalled almost no information, whereas those older than 3 had quite good recollection. Winograd and Killinger (1983) found that few people who were younger than 3 years old at the time could recall where they were when John F. Kennedy was assassinated.

One problem with this type of research is the extent to which the memories are of the actual event rather than of some external source. Just over 90% of the subjects in the study by Usher and Neisser (1993) indicated that external sources of information (such as photographs, family stories) had been available to them. A second potential problem is in determining the accuracy of these memories. When people recall events from this early part of their lives, it is difficult to distinguish between recollection of specific episodes versus reconstruction from generic memory (Loftus, 1993; see Chapter 15).

A report by Pillemer, Picariello, and Pruett (1994) is noteworthy because they had objective information about the event recollected. They tested children aged either 3 years, 8 months or 4 years, 7 months for their memory of an emergency evacuation of their school after a fire alarm. Although all the children could answer some questions after 2 weeks, only those in the older age range demonstrated memory for the event 7 years later. This result supports the general conclusion that infantile amnesia can last until age

3 or so; once a child is older than about 3, there is relatively little information about earlier experiences that can be remembered (Kihlstrom & Harackiewicz, 1982).

It is important to note that prior to the age of 3 or 4, children can recall information about events that had occurred much earlier in their lives. For example, Fivush and Hamond (1990) found that 2½-year-old children could readily recall events that took place 6 months earlier, and Myers, Clifton, and Clarkson (1987) found that almost all 3-year-olds could remember a visit to the psychology laboratory 2 years previously. Perris, Myers, and Clifton (1990) found that 2½-year-olds could remember a laboratory task learned at age 6½ months. Given successful recollection prior to age 3, why is recollection so poor or even nonexistent after age 3?

The general consensus is that no theory of infantile amnesia accounts for all the data, although this is not because of a shortage of theories (Howe & Courage, 1993; Perner & Ruffman, 1995). Some theories emphasize the development of language, consciousness, and sense of self. As these become more available to the child, information begins to be processed differently than previously. To use a computer analogy, this change in operating system renders earlier memories incompatible and inaccessible. One weakness with this view is that it is unable to account for infantile amnesia observed in nonhuman animals. For example, rats demonstrate infantile amnesia, but guinea pigs do not (Campbell, Misanin, White, & Lytle, 1974). One important difference between rats and guinea pigs is that, compared to rats, guinea pigs undergo very little brain growth after birth. Guinea pigs that learn an avoidance response in infancy retain it when tested as adults, whereas rats do not.

Another explanation emphasizes biological factors. To the extent that an animal is relatively well developed (as are guinea pigs), there will be little or no infantile amnesia. Whenever there is substantial biological development between infancy and adulthood, there will be infantile amnesia. One weakness with this approach is that infantile amnesia, in both humans and other animals, is not an all-or-none phenomenon. For example, recollection need not necessarily be completely absent. Newcombe and Fox (1994) found poor but above chance performance when 9- and 10-year-old children were asked to recognize the faces of preschool classmates. In addition, both rats and infants show evidence of memory when additional retrieval cues are used (Richardson, Riccio, & Axiotis, 1986; Rovee-Collier, 1993). The problem for the biological view is how to explain that the apparent loss can be reinstated.

One other suggestion, although speculative, is that infantile amnesia is due to telescoping (see Chapter 14), which is observed when people think that an event occurred more recently than it really did. Rubin and Baddeley (1989) suggest that people may think memories of events from earlier than age 4 are "telescoped" and report them as occurring later than they did. This explanation might also be applied to animals, because they show similar patterns of temporal compression (Spetch & Rusak, 1992).

# Memory in Older Children

One of the major differences between memory in infants and memory in older children is the development of strategies, including rehearsal. Although not well developed until later, some precursors of these strategies can be seen in children as young as 2 years.

DeLoache, Cassidy, and Brown (1985) observed children between the ages of 18 and 24 months use a variety of strategies to help keep alive information that has to be remembered. For example, the experimenter might hide a doll under a pillow and then distract the children with tempting toys before giving permission to retrieve the doll. During this time, the children frequently looked where the doll was hidden, would point at it, or would repeat its name. To demonstrate that this was a memory effect rather than, for example, a simple desire to get the toy, DeLoache et al. repeated the study, but this time putting the doll on top of the pillow. In this case, very few orienting behaviors occurred.

With more complex tasks, the frequency of using self-generated strategies is delayed. For example, Ritter (1978) hid some candy under 6 cups on a turntable. There were gold stars and paper clips that could potentially be used to mark the cup that covered the candy, and the children were aware that they would have to close their eyes while the turntable was being spun. The third-graders placed the retrieval cues spontaneously, but all the preschoolers required prompting. Even with prompting, nearly one-third of the youngest preschoolers (ages 3 to 4½ years) failed to use the retrieval cues. It is clear, though, that preschoolers do consciously try to memorize information in certain situations (Baker-Ward, Ornstein, & Holden, 1984; Hudson & Fivush, 1983).

Researchers have taken advantage of the relative lack of sophisticated strategies in 3-year-olds to test hypotheses about adult memory. For example, the *spacing effect* refers to the finding that although repeated presentations of an item in a list can aid memory, the repetitions must be spaced. This finding is robust, occurring for both recall and recognition tests (Hintzman, 1974) and with large variations in presentation rate (Melton, 1970). One explanation is that the effect in free recall is due to automatic rather than strategic processes (Greene, 1989). Toppino (1991) reasoned that, if this view is correct, then even children as young as 3 and 4 should show a spacing effect. To test this hypothesis, children were shown a 22-item list; some items were presented only once, some were repeated adjacent to the first occurrence, and some were repeated 3 items after the first occurrence. As Figure 16.2 shows, both age groups performed better with distributed than with massed repetitions, and massed repetitions were no better than no repetition. Children as young as 3 show a spacing effect, suggesting that it is not due to complex strategies.

There has been an enormous amount of research on the development of rehearsal. Flavell, Beach, and Chinsky (1966) examined list learning in children aged 5, 7, and 10 years. The experimenter watched the child's mouth to see whether the child was rehearsing. Using this as the measure, the researchers found that only a few of the 5-year-olds displayed multiple-item rehearsal, compared to almost all of the older children. Most of the early work asked subjects to rehearse out loud, and the typical instructions were to tell the children that if they thought about a word, they should say it out loud. Ornstein, Naus, and Liberty (1975) compared overt rehearsal in third-, sixth-, and eighth-graders. The overall amount of rehearsal was equal for all three age groups, and total rehearsal correlated weakly with amount recalled, which did increase with age. The differences turned out to be in the size of the rehearsal set, which is simply the number of items rehearsed together. The youngest subjects rehearsed only one item at a time; as the age of the subjects increased, so did the number of items in the rehearsal set. Kunzinger (1985) has demonstrated an average increase from 1.7 items in 7-year-olds, to 2.6 items in the same subjects 2 years later.

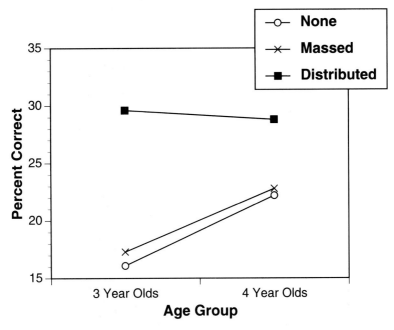

**Figure 16.2** Recall as a function of the type of repetitions (no repetitions, massed or distributed repetitions) as a function of age. Both 3- and 4-year-olds show benefits of distributed repetitions.    Source: Data from Toppino (1991).

Children can have very good memory for events that happened earlier in their lives if the retrieval cues are appropriate. For example, Fivush, Hudson, and Nelson (1984) interviewed 15 first-graders about a museum trip. When given a general prompt such as "What happened when you went to the museum?" only 7% of the children recalled it. When given a more specific prompt such as "Do you remember, you learned about archaeology?" nearly 60% recalled the event. In a follow-up study 6 years later, Hudson and Fivush (1991) asked similar questions. With a general prompt, only 1 child reported remembering the information; when more specific prompts were used, including pictures, 13 children provided accurate information.

Lehman, Mikesell, and Doherty (1985) compared memory for various contextual features in children (third- and fourth-graders) and adults (college students). A list of 200 words was presented for continuous recognition judgments; that is, the subject sees or hears a word and is asked to decide whether the word is old or new. In this particular experiment, the subjects then also indicated, for words judged old, whether the presentation modality was the same or different. On the immediate test, there were no differences in accuracy of modality identification, and even on the delayed test, the young children forgot modality information no more quickly than adults did. Given these results that show good retention of contextual information, it should not be surprising that children show the same context- and state-dependent memory effects as adults do (Bartlett & Santrock, 1979).

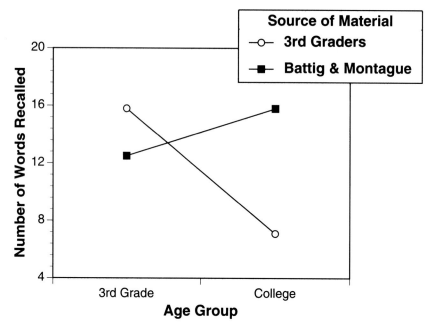

**Figure 16.3**   The number of words recalled by third-graders and college students as a function of the source of material, either third-graders' or Battig and Montague's (1969) norms. Source: Lindberg (1980).

As children age, they acquire more knowledge. There is a large literature showing that the amount recalled is positively related to the amount known about the subject matter. (In many of these studies, it is impossible to separate the effects of knowledge from the effects of interest; see Schneider & Pressley, 1989, for a discussion.) One particularly interesting study was reported by Lindberg (1980). He compared recall of 30-item lists by 9-year-old third-graders and 20-year-old college students. One list was constructed using items the third-graders supplied during interviews, including names of cartoon characters, games they played, and the names of characters from *Charlie's Angels*. The second list was constructed from category norms obtained from college students (Battig & Montague, 1969) that were similar to the third-graders', such as natural earth formations, types of reading material, and female first names. The lists were presented to both groups of subjects at a rate of 1 item every 3 seconds, and the results are shown in Figure 16.3. Each group recalled more information from the list that they knew more about. It was not the case that the college students outperformed the third-graders on every task: the third-graders recalled more information from the list that they knew more about.

Much of the recent work on memory development in children has been organized around the ideas of Baddeley's (1986) Working Memory (see Chapter 5). For example, increases in memory span have been linked to the speed at which subjects can articulate. Hulme, Thomson, Muir, and Lawrence (1984) found that as children mature their speech rate increases. Figure 16.4 shows the relationship they observed between increasing

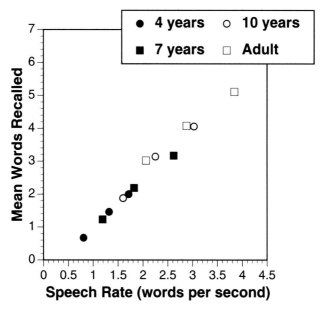

**Figure 16.4** Mean number of words recalled as a function of speech rate (in words per second) and the age of subject—either 4, 7, or 10 years old or adult. Source: Hulme, Thomson, Muir, & Lawrence (1984).

speech rate with age and increasing memory. Note that it is not age per se that is driving this effect: some adults fall in the 7-year-old range. The word-length effect, better recall of short compared to long items, is present from about age 4 if the to-be-remembered items are spoken (Hulme & Tordoff, 1989). If the items are either read silently or are the names of objects presented as pictures, the word-length effect is not observed until later (Hitch, Halliday, Dodd, & Littler, 1989).

In 5-year-olds, recall of the names of pictures does not show a word-length effect; but by age 11, there is a clear word-length effect and, furthermore, this effect is eliminated by articulatory suppression (Halliday, Hitch, Lennon, & Pettipher, 1990). The phonological similarity effect—worse recall for lists of items that sound similar—is evident with pictoral stimuli by about age 7 (Conrad, 1972), and with auditory stimuli it is evident by age 5 (Hulme & Tordoff, 1989).

An increase in speech rate is not the only factor contributing to increased memory performance. Samuel (1978) tested first- (mean age 6.4 years), third- (8.3 years), and sixth- (11.4 years) grade children and compared their performance on a modified digit span task to that of college students (19.1 years). Of most interest is an analysis of output order. Here, the experimenter calculates the percent correct responses of the first response, the second response, and so on. Usually, researchers report only input serial position curves, which shows the percent correct as a function of input position; the output serial position curve shows the percent correct as a function of output position. To achieve optimal performance, a subject should recall the item most likely to be correct first, then the second most likely item second, and so on. This would result in a correlation of 1.0 between accuracy and output position. The idea is that it is not useful to delay recall of an item that is likely to be correct because it may be forgotten or interfered with before it can be recalled. Samuel found that the correlation between output position and accuracy was 0.481 for the first-graders, 0.698 for the third-graders, 0.715 for the sixth-graders, and 0.884 for the college students. Samuel interpreted this result as showing that as children get older they are more likely to use more effective or appropriate retrieval strategies.

# Implicit Memory in Children

Although Lewicki (1986) did find implicit learning in children, there are almost no studies that examine developmental changes in implicit learning from early to late childhood. Maybery, Taylor, and O'Brien-Malone (1995) have reported one of the few. They compared performance on an implicit learning task by young children (mean age 6 years, 6 months) and older children (mean age 11 years, 1 month). The task was adapted from Lewicki (1986, Experiment 5.2) and consisted of three phases: learning, indirect test, and direct test. The children were told: "In this game I will bring over a board that has lots of pictures on it. When I take the cover off, all that I want you to do is look closely at all of the pictures and point to the one of the house" (Maybery, Taylor, & O'Brien-Malone, 1995, p. 11). There were 16 pictures in a $4 \times 4$ matrix; when the apparatus was blue, the house was in the left half, and when the apparatus was red, the house was in the right half. Furthermore, when the experimenter approached from the right, the house was in the upper half, and when the experimenter approached from the left, the house was in the lower half. These two cues indicated the correct quadrant, but the subject still needed to search for the exact location.

During the test phase, the pictures were covered and the child responded by lifting a cover, and if unsuccessful, by lifting a second. They were awarded 1 point for the correct quadrant, with the maximum possible score of 16 (2 attempts on 8 trials). Chance accuracy is 4 points. The young group did not perform better than chance (mean score 3.63) whereas the older group was significantly better than chance (mean score 5.37). The researchers also tested both groups on an explicit learning task and found typical age-related differences. Contrary to the predictions of Lewicki (1986), there were age-related changes in implicit learning tasks in young children.

The literature on indirect tests of implicit memory in children is both small and mixed. Several studies report no age-related differences (Carrol, Byrne, & Kirsner, 1985; Ellis, Ellis, & Hosie, 1993; Greenbaum & Graf, 1989; Russo, Nichelli, Gibertoni, & Cornia, 1995), whereas others do report age-related differences (Drummey & Newcombe, 1995; Naito, 1990); yet other studies show no clear pattern (Parkin & Streete, 1988, and the reanalysis by Parkin, 1993). One explanation may be that, by around age 7, there are no more developmental differences but there are differences between younger children and older children (Naito, 1990). One clear result, though, is that children as young as 3 show clear evidence of implicit memory.

# Memory and Aging

The typical view is that, the older we get, the worse our memories will become. For example, Delbecq-Derouesné and Beauvois (1989) measured immediate free recall of 15 words in several different age groups. The results, shown in Table 16.1, were that performance dropped by 20% over 40 years. However, this is not always the case. Indeed, numerous studies find no age-related decrement, and some even find an advantage for the more elderly subjects. For the remainder of this chapter, we examine memory in healthy older people, focusing on where memory deficits occur and where they do not.

There are two basic ways of conducting research on developmental changes in older adults, and both are fraught with difficulties. One way is to use a *cross-sectional design*, in which the researcher compares memory performance in people of different ages. For example, a researcher might give the Brown-Peterson task to four groups: groups of 20-year-olds, 40-year-olds, 60-year-olds, and 80-year-olds. Performance typically declines with age. There are three main problems with this kind of research. First, there is usually a larger proportion of nonhealthy individuals in the older age groups, and these health problems and the medications taken for them can adversely affect memory. Second, there are likely to be differences in educational levels. Today's average college graduate is likely to be very different from a college graduate of 60 years ago, especially in socioeconomic status. Third, current college students are likely to be more practiced at taking timed tests with apparently arbitrary instructions, after having taken the PSAT, the SAT, the GRE, and other such tests. Finally, there are likely to be cohort effects. A *cohort* is the name given to a group of subjects of similar ages and experiences. Today's 80-year-olds experienced the great depression, World War II, the Korean War, and the Vietnam war; today's 20-year-olds did not. These differences could affect responding as, for example, could increasingly better nutrition and prenatal care with the younger samples.

The alternative to cross-sectional research is to use *longitudinal designs*. Here, a group of subjects is followed for a long time, so changes in performance of particular individuals can be tracked. Although this controls for many of the weaknesses inherent in cross-sectional designs, it has its own set of problems. First, over the course of the study, many subjects will drop out, either because of health problems, relocation, or lack of interest. Subjects who drop out for lack of interest are typically those who score lower on the test. Second, there are practice effects: repeatedly taking the same test can increase scores, which can mask any possible decrements in performance. Third, these studies are very expensive and therefore tend to have a very small sample size. Finally, because they take

**Table 16.1**  Percent correct as a function of the age group of the subjects.

| Age Group | 20–25 | 26–40 | 41–55 | 56–55 | 65–86 |
|---|---|---|---|---|---|
| % Correct | 54.7% | 47.9% | 48.1% | 41.6% | 34.8% |

Source: Data from Delbecq-Derouesné & Beauvois (1989).

so long to conduct, the researcher can leave (or die), and studies started 40 or 50 years earlier may continue to use methods that are no longer appropriate. Salthouse (1991) provides an excellent discussion of both types of methodologies and a review of the longitudinal studies.

Fortunately, researchers have been able to overcome or work around these difficulties. For example, many studies use a cross-sectional design but use several different kinds of older subject groups. Other studies use a design in which a critical variable has two possible values: at one level, there is predicted no age-related difference, but at another level there is predicted a large age-related difference. When these patterns occur, it is difficult to argue that they are due to the problems with cross-sectional design noted above.

## What Gets Worse?

Immediate memory tests generally show smaller decrements than delayed memory tests; furthermore, the more complex the task, the more likely age decrements will be found. For example, measures of memory span decline only slightly with age, from 6.4 to 5.8 (Parkinson, 1982). Span was less affected by age when the stimuli were digits than when they were words (Salthouse & Babcock, 1991).

In a span task, recall is assessed immediately, whereas in a Brown-Peterson task, recall is assessed after varying delays. Parkinson, Inman, and Dannenbaum (1985) found that young adults (mean age 19.2 years) performed more accurately on a Brown-Peterson task than did older adults (mean age 74.2 years), and that the difference in performance between young and old was larger with longer delays between study and test. In their second experiment, however, the researchers equated performance on the immediate test. Each subject was pretested to determine the number of repetitions of each to-be-remembered item such that the subject was approximately 89% correct on the immediate serial recall test. The young group needed an average of 2.25 repetitions, compared to 2.8 for the old group. With performance equated on the immediate test, performance on the delayed test was also equivalent. Because forgetting in Brown-Peterson is attributable to the role of proactive interference (see Chapter 7), these studies show that when performance is equated, older subjects are not differentially affected by proactive interference (although the authors interpreted the data in terms of equivalent forgetting rates).

One question of enduring interest has been whether older subjects differ from younger subjects in terms of encoding ability. As Craik and Jennings (1992) summarized the situation: "What are we to make of the situation in which there are good data to support the conclusions that (a) older people benefit more than do their younger counterparts from more supportive encoding conditions, (b) older and younger subjects profit to the same extent, and (c) younger subjects profit to a greater extent" (p. 75). The problem is that many studies examine only one variable at a time, rather than examining several levels of several tasks.

However, there is some evidence that older subjects tend to remember fewer specific features than younger subjects do. For example, Kausler and Puckett (1980, 1981) found that older subjects had more difficulty remembering whether visually presented words were shown in upper- or lowercase or which voice spoke the words. Although older subjects perform worse on tests that require knowledge of contextual information, their performance can improve if specifically asked to study this information. Naveh-Benjamin and Craik (1995) had two groups of older (mean age 72 and 73 years) and younger (mean age 21 and 20 years) subjects listen to a list of words, which were spoken by two different male speakers. The test of interest was the voice memory test, in which subjects judged whether the word was spoken by Voice A or by Voice B. In one experiment, the subjects were asked to rate the voice in terms of pitch, whereas in the second they were asked to rate the word in terms of pleasantness. The proportion of hits (correctly identifying Voice A and Voice B words) was the same for both old (.55) and young (.56) subjects when subjects rated the words for pitch. When subjects rated the words for pleasantness, younger subjects were reliably better (.55) than older subjects (.51). Although this latter result looks small, it is reliable and replicable: a second study found that younger subjects again outperformed older subjects, this time .61 to .53.

Given this result, the reality monitoring framework (Johnson & Raye, 1981; see Chapter 13) predicts that older subjects should have more difficulty determining whether a word was perceived or imagined or whether an action was intended or performed. Results tend to confirm this. For example, Hashtroudi, Johnson, and Chrosniak (1989) found that although older subjects were almost as good as younger at distinguishing between whether they had generated an item or whether it was spoken by an experimenter, the older subjects were worse at discriminating between items they had spoken and items they had imagined speaking. Older subjects are also typically worse at discriminating which of two speakers spoke a word (Johnson, De Leonardis, Hashtroudi, & Ferguson, 1995). Hashtroudi, Johnson, and Chrosniak (1990) found that older subjects had more difficulty determining whether complex events (such as packing a picnic basket) had been seen or imagined 3 weeks previously.

Cohen and Faulkner (1989) found that older subjects (mean age 70.4) were more likely to be influenced by misleading information than younger subjects were and, furthermore, were more confident on these errors than the younger subjects were. The older subjects gave a rating of "very sure" to over one-third of their responses that were incorrect, compared to under 10% of the responses for the young group.

Micco and Masson (1992) compared younger (mean age 21.1) and older (mean age 70.2) subjects in their ability to generate and use cues. In Phase I, both groups were asked to provide cues that would help another person generate a given target word. In Phase II, a second group of old and young subjects were given the cues and asked to generate the target word. Cues generated by the first group of old subjects were less effective for both the old and young subjects in Phase II. Furthermore, even when using the cues provided by the young subjects, the older subjects still performed worse.

Consistent with the results of Micco and Masson (1992) is the finding that whenever the task offers reduced retrieval cues, performance will be impaired for elderly compared to younger subjects (Craik, 1983, 1994). Thus, the typical recall test offers fewer retrieval cues than does the typical recognition test. Craik and McDowd (1987) compared performance between young and old subjects on both a recall test and a recognition test. As shown in Figure 16.5, the older subjects were impaired on the free recall task but not on the recognition task. This demonstration is important because Craik and McDowd's study obviates objections to previous work. Typically, recognition scores are very high—so high, in fact, that a difference between old and young subjects might be hidden by a

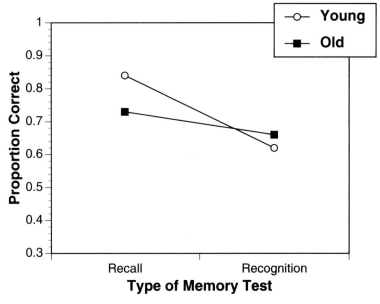

**Figure 16.5** Proportion correct on recall and recognition tests for younger and older subjects.
Source: Data from Craik & McDowd (1987).

ceiling effect. For example, if old and young subjects were presented with a two-item list for immediate free recall, there would probably be no difference in performance; both groups are recalling perfectly and the measure is not sensitive enough to detect a difference. In the Craik and McDowd study, recognition performance is nowhere near ceiling, and so we can be far more confident of the result.

Craik, Byrd, and Swanson (1987) showed that performance on a cued-recall test falls in between performance on free recall and recognition tests; more important, however, they included three different groups of old subjects. All old subjects were around 74 years old, but they differed in various other ways (see Table 16.2). Old 1 had relatively low socioeconomic status, had a relatively low vocabulary score on the Wechsler Adult Intelli-

**Table 16.2**  Characteristics of the four groups of subjects in Craik, Byrd, and Swanson (1987).

|  | *Group* | | | |
|---|---|---|---|---|
|  | *Old 1* | *Old 2* | *Old 3* | *Young* |
| Mean Age | 76.2 | 73.5 | 73.3 | 19.7 |
| Socioeconomic Status | Low | Low | High | Moderate |
| Vocabulary Score | 31.2 | 35.0 | 52.2 | 48.1 |
| Activity Level | Low | High | High | High |

Source: Table from Craik (1994).

**Table 16.3**   Recall scores for the four groups of subjects in Craik, Byrd, and Swanson (1987). Scores within the same shaded area can be considered equivalent.

|  | Group | | | |
| --- | --- | --- | --- | --- |
|  | Old 1 | Old 2 | Old 3 | Young |
| Cued Learning/Cued Recall | 5.5 | 7.3 | 8.1 | 7.8 |
| Cued Learning/Free Recall | 2.2 | 5.4 | 5.8 | 5.6 |
| Free Learning/Cued Recall | 2.2 | 4.5 | 5.3 | 5.8 |
| Free Learning/Free Recall | 2.4 | 4.6 | 4.7 | 6.0 |

Source: Table from Craik (1994).

gence Scale-Revised (WAIS-R), and were not very active. Old 2 were quite similar except that they were active in the community, volunteering for a local Foster Grandparents program, for example. Old 3 were affluent, had high verbal scores, and were socially active. The young group were college undergraduates, to whom Craik, Byrd, and Swanson assigned a socioeconomic status of moderate. This design enables the researchers to explore differences between different elderly populations.

Craik, Byrd and Swanson manipulated both study and test conditions. In the free learning/free recall test, a list of ten words was presented and the subjects attempted to recall the words without cues. In the cued learning/cued recall test, a list of ten words was again presented, but this time each word was accompanied by a cue. At learning the cue might be "a type of bird—LARK," and at test the cue might be "what was the type of bird?" Two other conditions had either the cue at learning or the cue at test. The results are shown in Table 16.3.

All groups did better with cued learning/cued recall, but the Old 2, Old 3, and young groups did better than Old 1 did. In fact, Old 1 did worse on all tests than Old 2, which differed only in terms of activity level. Old 3 and the young group were comparable on all tests except free learning and free recall, in which the young group performed better. Less active older subjects were significantly worse on all the tests, but even the more active older subjects were impaired relative to the college students when the task relied on internally generated cues.

Einstein and McDaniel (1990) compared prospective memory between young and older subjects. *Prospective memory* refers to remembering to perform some action at some point in the future. Older (60- to 78-year-olds) and younger (17- to 24-year-olds) subjects were given the vocabulary test of the WAIS-R, a free recall test, and a recognition test. The subjects were also asked to press a particular key whenever a specified target word was shown. These target words could be familiar (rake, method) or unfamiliar (sone, monad). The data were then scored in terms of the proportion of times the subject responded when the target word was shown; the results are shown in Table 16.4.

There were no age differences on the WAIS-R vocabulary score, although the elderly did do worse on the free recall tests. On the prospective measure, however, there were no differences; if anything, the elderly subjects performed slightly better. Both groups performed better when the target word was unfamiliar than when it was familiar.

**Table 16.4**  Performance on a retrospective memory task (free recall) and a prospective memory task (remembering to press a key when a target word was shown) for two different age groups with the same WAIS-R score. The older subjects show impairment on the retrospective memory task but no impairment on the prospective memory task.

|  | Young | | Older | |
| --- | --- | --- | --- | --- |
| Measure | Familiar | Unfamiliar | Familiar | Unfamiliar |
| WAIS-R | 53.33 | 50.50 | 57.42 | 56.42 |
| Free Recall | .58 | .51 | .41 | .47 |
| Prospective Memory | .28 | .83 | .36 | .94 |

Source: Data from Einstein & McDaniel (1990).

This lack of an age-related difference was explored further in a second study (Einstein, McDaniel, Richardson, Guynn, & Cunfer, 1995). There are two different ways in which prospective memory tasks can be signaled. In a time-based task, the subject must perform some activity at a certain time; in an event-based task, the subject must perform the activity when a certain event occurs. Examples are remembering to take a pill every 8 hours versus remembering to give Bob a message when you see him. Using a similar pool of subjects as in the previous study, Einstein et al. (1995) again found no age-related differences on an event-based prospective memory task, but they did find age-related differences with a time-based task. One difference between event-based and time-based prospective memory is whether the retrieval cue is present in the environment or is internally generated. When it is internally generated (time-based), there are age-related differences.

One final finding relevant to evaluating memory deficits in the elderly is the accuracy of self-reports. Rabbitt and Abson (1991) found that older subjects' estimates of their performance were uncorrelated with their actual performance on recognition, memory span, recall, and cumulative learning tasks. Nonetheless, there were significant correlations between estimated memory ability and reports of depression. Thus, although the elderly may report many more memory problems than younger adults do, and although this perceived loss may contribute to depression, self-reported memory problems may not be related to actual memory problems. Memory tasks that require self-generated cues are likely to suffer, but as we shall see in the next section, there are many tasks on which the elderly are not impaired.

## What Doesn't Get Worse?

Performance on tasks that offer sufficient retrieval cues and performance on indirect tasks frequently show no age-related impairment. That is, to the extent that self-initiated retrieval processes are important, there will probably be age-related differences; to the extent that the task provides sufficient retrieval cues, there will probably be few or no age-related differences.

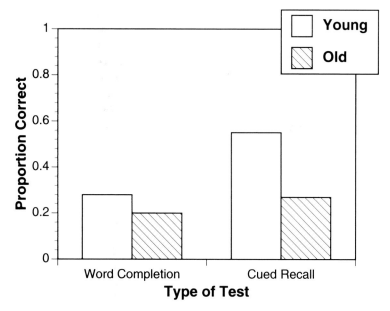

**Figure 16.6** Mean proportion of word stems completed with words from the studied list. The sole difference between the word completion and cued recall tests was the instructions. Source: Data from Light & Singh (1987).

Light and Singh (1987) compared memory performance on both direct and indirect tests of memory. A group of young subjects (mean age 23.1) and a group of old subjects (mean age 68.3) saw a list of words and were asked to rate each word's pleasantness. After the list had been presented, half of the subjects received a word completion test and half received a cued-recall test. The only difference between the tests were the instructions. In the word stem completion test, the subjects were asked to write the first word that came to mind for each word stem. In the cued-recall test, the subjects were told that some of the stems came from the list they had just rated, and they were asked to treat the stems as clues for recall. Note that this test used incidental learning and then had either an indirect test or a direct test. The results are shown in Figure 16.6. There was a large difference when the test asked the subjects to refer back to the learning episode (cued recall), but there was no reliable difference when the task did not refer back (word completion).

Many other studies have found reduced or absent age-related differences on indirect tests (Chiarello & Hoyer, 1988; Craik & Jennings, 1992; Graf, 1990; Light & Burke, 1988). For example, Java and Gardiner (1991) found that older subjects (age 62–87 years) showed a reliable decrement in free recall, but found almost no influence of age on a word-stem completion task.

Parkin and Walter (1992) examined performance on a recognition test using the re-member-know procedure (see Chapter 10) with subjects in three age groups—old (mean age 81.6 years), middle-old (mean age 67.7), and young (mean age 21.5)—all of whom performed equivalently on three different assessments of cognitive functioning. Subjects

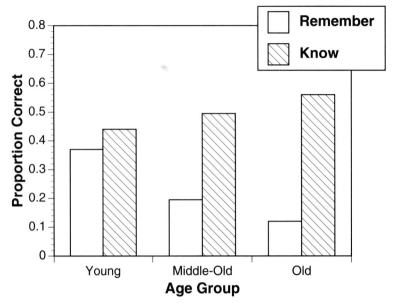

**Figure 16.7**   The proportion of "remember" and "know" responses given by young, middle-old, and old subjects. Older subjects were more likely to give fewer "remember" responses and more "know" responses than younger subjects, even though overall accuracy did not differ.
Source: Parkin & Walter (1992).

saw a list of 36 words printed on index cards for 2 seconds each and were asked to remember the words. At the end of the list, the subjects were engaged in "genial conversation" for about 10 minutes. Then the subjects saw 72 words and were asked to indicate which words were from the list and to mark whether they remembered the item or simply knew the item was on the list. The results are shown in Figure 16.7.

Although overall accuracy did not differ substantially between the groups, with increasing age, subjects were more likely to give a "know" response and less likely to give a "remember" response. This result has also been found in other studies (Mäntylä, 1993; Maylor, 1995). A second study showed equivalent confidence ratings between older and younger subjects, indicating that they were not basing their remember-know decisions on their level of confidence (see also Rajaram, 1993).

One interesting parallel is that older subjects' performance is often like that of subjects with human amnesic syndrome (see Chapter 9), although with far less impairment. Both groups of subjects show relatively unimpaired performance on indirect tests and impairment on direct tests. When recognition performance is broken down into conscious recollection versus just knowing, then differences emerge. Consistent with this idea is an experiment by Dywan and Jacoby (1990), who compared performance of younger (mean age 19.5 years) and older (mean age 71.2 years) subjects in the false fame paradigm. Subjects see a list of nonfamous names and are told they are nonfamous; they then see a list of mixed famous and nonfamous names and are asked to indicate which are famous. Some of the nonfamous names have not been seen before by the subject, and some are from the previous phase. If subjects recall seeing a name from the previous phase, they know the name is nonfamous. If, on the other hand, they cannot recall that the name was from the old nonfamous list but instead rely on overall familiarity, they should be more likely to say the old nonfamous name is famous. Dywan and Jacoby found that the probability of saying an old nonfamous name was famous was higher (.20) for the older subjects than for younger subjects (.14). They argued that although both old and young subjects have similar feelings of familiarity, younger subjects are better able to recall the source of the familiarity and attribute it to seeing the name in the earlier phase of the experiment. Older subjects, on the other hand, are more likely to attribute the familiarity to the name's being famous.

Incidental learning also seems relatively unimpaired, at least when assessed by indirect tests. Howard and Howard (1992) compared performance by a young group (mean age 19.4 years) and an old group (mean age 73.4 years) who were similar in their WAIS-R vocabulary scores and WAIS Digits Backward scores. The task was implicit serial pattern learning, in which subjects were asked to press one of four keys as quickly as they could when an asterisk appeared in one of four locations (see Chapter 8). With A indicating the left-most location, there were two patterns: DBCACBDCBA and BCACDCD-BADADACAD, but we will focus on only the short pattern. The first two blocks had trials that followed the pattern, the third block had a random pattern, and the fourth block again had the repeating pattern.

The older subjects' response times were consistently slower than those of the younger group, a standard finding (Salthouse, 1991). The older subjects were slightly more accurate than the young, with accuracy of .97, .97, .95, and .96 for blocks 1 through 4 for the young subjects, compared to .98, .98, .97, and .97 for the old subjects. The indirect test of pattern learning was to see if the median response times on block 3 were reliably greater than on block 2. Both groups were slower on the random patterns — the young group by 108 ms and the old group by 85 ms, which is not a reliable difference. Thus, on an indirect test of incidental learning, there was no age-related impairment. The direct test occurred in the fifth block. Here, subjects were asked to predict the next location prior to the appearance of the asterisk, and the measure was simply proportion correct. The young subjects were more accurate (.76) than the old subjects (.53). Thus, on indirect tests of incidental learning, there are no age-related differences; on direct tests of incidental learning, there are age-related differences. One qualification could be that this lack of impairment for indirect tests of incidental learning applies only for high-functioning elderly adults (Cherry & Stadler, 1995).

# Theoretical Explanations of Aging and Memory

Of the many explanations for the effects of normal aging on memory, three main accounts are easily distinguishable: the disuse view, the multiple systems view, and the processing view. The latter view contains several differing approaches, including a transfer appropriate processing account and one based on reduced resources.

*The disuse view.*   One explanation for age-related declines has been termed the "use it or lose it" view. The analogy is to muscles, where exercise increases performance and lack of exercise induces atrophy, and can be traced back to at least Vives in 1523. Some support for this view comes from numerous studies showing that rats raised in enriched environments show significantly better performance and more complex brain organization and functioning than do rats raised in sterile environments (Greenough, Black, & Wallace, 1987; Rosenzweig, 1984). Thus, given that use promotes brain functioning, the idea is that disuse depresses brain functioning. Many memory tasks require processing that may be unfamiliar to elderly subjects: because of their long-standing removal from academic environments, they may not have performed similar tasks for several decades, or even at all. According to this view, then, tasks that tap processes still used by elderly subjects will reveal no deficits, whereas tasks that require less frequently used processes will show deficits.

Some support for this idea comes from a study of aging university professors (Shimamura, Berry, Mangels, Rusting, & Jurica, 1995). The reason for using this group of subjects is that all (both young and elderly) are cognitively active; have similar levels of academic training; and have similar cultural, economic, and social environments. The young professors had a mean age of 38.4 years, the middle-aged professors had a mean age of 52.2 years, and the senior professors had a mean age of 64.7 years. Although the older professors were impaired relative to the younger on tests of response time and paired-associate learning, there was no difference in measures of proactive interference and prose recall. These latter two results are different from most aging studies. Shimamura et al. (1995) suggested that one possibility for their findings was that "mental activity reduces the changes that typically occur as a result of aging" (p. 276). An alternative, however, could be that the "professors' preserved performance on behavioral measures is the result of an enhanced ability to compensate for decrements" (p. 276).

Although an intriguing idea, there are three main problems with this view. First, Salthouse (1991, pp. 134–136) lists about 40 tasks on which researchers have found an age-related impairment. All of these tasks are described as meaningful or ecologically valid and are ones that the elderly subjects are likely to be still performing. Examples include memory for bridge hands by bridge players, memory for conversations, memory for faces, memory for songs, and memory for what one previously said or wrote. These results are a problem for the disuse view because all the tasks in this list are ones that the group is still performing. Even though they are still using these processes, the elderly subjects show an age-related decrement.

A second problem is that the disuse view is potentially circular. Although older people with good memories may have good memories because they used them more, it could be the case that only those people with good memories are able to still use them. This is related to the third problem: the disuse view is rarely spelled out in enough detail to make predictions or to overcome the circularity problem. To quote Salthouse (1991), "Despite the attractiveness of this simple idea, it seems to have little convincing empirical support at the present time" (p. 351).

***Multiple memory systems.***   Craik (Craik & Jennings, 1992; Craik, 1994) argues that the multiple memory systems view has not fared well in explaining age-related memory changes. For example, one key distinction according to multiple systems theorists is the difference between episodic and semantic memory (see Chapter 8). In the elderly, it is argued, age differences will be small or nonexistent for tasks that tap semantic memory, compared to substantial age differences for tasks that tap episodic memory. Although age differences are indeed relatively small on some tasks thought to tap semantic memory, there can be substantial age differences on other tasks that are also thought to tap semantic memory. For example, age differences are apparent when subjects are asked to retrieve words in response to definitions (Bowles & Poon, 1985) and in the time that inhibition of priming remains (Bowles, 1994). This type of result, Craik argues, suggests that it is a process that is affected, rather than a system. Similar problems arise when considering impairments on episodic tasks: although the systems view says that these tasks should show substantial impairment, the actual impairment can be either minimal (as with cued-recall or recognition) or large (as with free recall).

*Speed of processing view.* One of the main reduced resources views is that declines in performance that accompany normal aging are due to a general slowing down of processing speed (Birren, 1956; Salthouse, 1985). For example, Chapter 12 discussed associative priming, where seeing the word *doctor* facilitates processing the word *nurse*. Howard, Shaw, and Heisey (1986) found that whereas younger subjects showed priming when the prime and target were separated by as little as 150 ms, the older subjects required about 500 ms between prime and target before priming was seen. According to a spreading activation view of priming, this can be interpreted as a reduction in the speed at which activation spreads. According to a compound-cue view of priming, the search of memory takes longer to perform. More generally, this view holds that age-related decrements are due to a reduced capacity caused by a reduction in speed of processing. Although there is much evidence that at least some age differences are due to differences in speed of processing, this view is incomplete by itself and requires other factors to give a more general explanation (Salthouse, 1991).

*Impaired inhibition view.* The impaired inhibition view (Hasher & Zacks, 1988) is in some ways similar to the reduced speed of processing view. Both focus on processing differences between younger and older subjects, and both posit a general reduction in one particular area. According to the inhibitory view, deficits seen in memory performance by elderly subjects are due to an impairment in inhibiting irrelevant information (see also Rabbitt, 1965), one consequence of which is increased interference. In this sense, the inhibitory view is much like the interference view of amnesia discussed in Chapter 9. However, the inhibitory view predicts not only worse performance on a variety of memory tasks but also an improvement under certain circumstances. For example, one major prediction is that older adults will have more difficulty eliminating information from working memory when it is activated but becomes irrelevant. The key is that "irrelevance" is in the eye of the beholder: what is irrelevant from the experimenter's point of view may not be irrelevant for the subject. The additional information can lead to richer or more elaborate processing. Thus, older subjects may have a more integrative interpretation of metaphors (Boswell, 1979) and be judged better storytellers (Mergler, Faust, & Goldstein, 1985) because of the additional information that remains activated. A summary of this approach is offered by Stoltzfus, Hasher, and Zacks (1996).

*Transfer appropriate processing.* The transfer appropriate processing framework differs from the other processing views in that it offers an explanation of memory performance in both the young and the elderly. Under this view, "Encoding is simply the set of processes involved in the perception and interpretation of the original event . . . and retrieval is the attempted recapitulation of the original pattern of encoding activity" (Craik, 1994, p. 156). Recollection will be successful when the cues available at test, either internally or externally, allow recapitulation of the results of processing at study. Age-related declines are typically less when good external cues are available, and differences increase to the extent that internally generated cues must be relied on. Performance on most indirect tasks is well preserved because the task itself affords good cues. Although by no means a complete theory of age-related declines, it accounts better for the known data (Craik, 1994).

# References

Baddeley, A. D. (1986). *Working memory.* New York: Oxford University Press.

Baker-Ward, L., Ornstein, P. A., & Holden, D. J. (1984). The expression of memorization in early childhood. *Journal of Experimental Child Psychology, 37,* 555–575.

Bartlett, J. C., & Santrock, J. W. (1979). Affect-dependent episodic memory in young children. *Child Development, 50,* 513–518.

Battig, W. F., & Montague, W. E. (1969). Category norms for verbal items in 56 categories: A replication and extension of the Connecticut category norms. *Journal of Experimental Psychology: Monograph, 80,* 1–46.

Bauer, P. J. (1996). What do infants recall of their lives? *American Psychologist, 51,* 29–41.

Bauer, P. J., Hertsgaard, L. A., & Dow, G. A. (1994). After 8 months have passed: Long-term recall of events by 1- to 2-year-old children. *Memory, 2,* 353–382.

Birren, J. E. (1956). The significance of age changes in speed of perception and psychomotor response. In J. E. Anderson (Ed.), *Psychological aspects of aging.* Washington, DC: American Psychological Association.

Boswell, D. A. (1979). Metaphoric processing in the mature years. *Human Development, 22,* 373–384.

Bowles, N. L. (1994). Age and rate of activation in semantic memory. *Psychology and Aging, 9,* 414–429.

Bowles, N. L., & Poon, L. W. (1985). Aging and retrieval of words in semantic memory. *Journal of Gerontology, 40,* 71–77.

Butler, J., & Rovee-Collier, C. (1989). Contextual gating of memory retrieval. *Developmental Psychobiology, 22,* 533–552.

Campbell, B. A., Misanin, J. R., White, B. C., & Lytle, L. D. (1974). Species difference in ontogeny of memory: Indirect support for neural maturation as a determinant of forgetting. *Journal of Comparative and Physiological Psychology, 87,* 193–202.

Carrol, M., Byrne, B., & Kirsner, K. (1985). Autobiographical memory and perceptual learning: A developmental study using picture recognition, naming latency, and perceptual identification. *Memory & Cognition, 13,* 273–279.

Cherry, K. E., & Stadler, M. A. (1995). Implicit learning of a nonverbal sequence in younger and older adults. *Psychology and Aging, 10,* 379–394.

Chiarello, C., & Hoyer, W. J. (1988). Adult age differences in implicit and explicit memory: Time course and encoding effects. *Psychology and Aging, 3,* 358–366.

Cohen, G., & Faulkner, D. (1989). Age differences in source forgetting: Effects on reality monitoring and on eyewitness testimony. *Psychology and Aging, 4,* 10–17.

Conrad, R. (1972). Speech and reading. In J. F. Kavanagh & I. G. Mattingley (Eds.), *Language by ear and by eye.* Cambridge, MA: MIT Press.

Craik, F. I. M. (1983). On the transfer of information from temporary to permanent memory. *Philosophical Transactions of the Royal Society of London B, 302,* 341–359.

Craik, F. I. M. (1994). Memory changes in normal aging. *Current Directions in Psychological Science, 3,* 155–158.

Craik, F. I. M., Byrd, M., & Swanson, J. M. (1987). Patterns of memory loss in three elderly samples. *Psychology and Aging, 2,* 79–86.

Craik, F. I. M., & Jennings, J. M. (1992). Human memory. In F. I. M. Craik & T. A. Salthouse (Eds.), *The handbook of aging and cognition.* Hillsdale, NJ: Erlbaum.

Craik, F. I. M., & McDowd, J. M. (1987). Age differences in recall and recognition. *Journal of Experimental Psychology: Learning, Memory, and Cognition, 13,* 474–479.

Delbecq-Derouesné, J., & Beauvois, M. F. (1989). Memory processes and aging: A defect of automatic rather than controlled processes? *Archives of Gerontology and Geriatrics, Supplement, 1,* 121–150.

DeLoache, J. S., Cassidy, D. J., & Brown, A. L. (1985). Precursors of mnemonic strategies in very young children's memory. *Child Development, 56,* 125–137.

Drummey, A. B., & Newcombe, N. (1995). Remembering versus knowing the past: Children's explicit and implicit memories for pictures. *Journal of Experimental Child Psychology, 59,* 549–565.

Dywan, J., & Jacoby, L. L. (1990). Effects of aging on source monitoring: Differences in susceptibility to false fame. *Psychology and Aging, 5,* 379–387.

Einstein, G. O., & McDaniel, M. A. (1990). Normal aging and prospective memory. *Journal of Experimental Psychology: Learning, Memory, and Cognition, 16,* 717–726.

Einstein, G. O., McDaniel, M. A., Richardson, S. L., Guynn, M. J., & Cunfer, A. R. (1995). Aging and prospective memory: Examining the influences of self-initiated retrieval processes. *Journal of Experimental Psychology: Learning, Memory, and Cognition, 21,* 996–1007.

Ellis, H. D., Ellis, D. M., & Hosie, J. A. (1993). Priming effects in children's face recognition. *British Journal of Psychology, 84,* 101–110.

Fivush, R., & Hamond, N. (1990). Autobiographical memory across the preschool years: Towards reconceptualizing childhood amnesia. In R. Fivush and J. A. Hudson (Eds.), *Knowing and remembering in young children.* Cambridge: Cambridge University Press.

Fivush, R., Hudson, J. A., & Nelson, K. (1984). Children's long-term memory for a novel event: An exploratory study. *Merrill-Palmer Quarterly, 30,* 303–316.

Flavell, J. H., Beach, D. H., & Chinsky, J. M. (1966). Spontaneous verbal rehearsal in a memory task as a function of age. *Child Development, 37,* 283–299.

Friedman, S. (1972). Newborn visual attention to repeated exposure of redundant vs. "novel" targets. *Perception & Psychophysics, 12,* 291–294.

Graf, P. (1990). Life-span changes in implicit and explicit memory. *Bulletin of the Psychonomic Society, 28,* 353–358.

Greco, C., Rovee-Collier, C., Hayne, H., Griesler, P., & Earley, L. (1986). Ontogeny of early event memory: I. Forgetting and retrieval by 2- and 3-month-olds. *Infant Behavior and Development, 9,* 441–460.

Greenbaum, J. L., & Graf, P. (1989). Preschool period development of implicit and explicit remembering. *Bulletin of the Psychonomic Society, 27,* 417–420.

Greene, R. L. (1989). Spacing effects in memory: Evidence for a two-process account. *Journal of Experimental Psychology: Learning, Memory, and Cognition, 15,* 371–377.

Greenough, W. T., Black, J. E., & Wallace, C. S. (1987). Experience and brain development. *Child Development, 58,* 539–559.

Halliday, M. S., Hitch, G. J., Lennon, B., & Pettipher, C. (1990). Verbal short-term memory in children: The role of the articulatory loop. *European Journal of Cognitive Psychology, 2,* 23–38.

Hasher, L., & Zacks, R. T. (1988). Working memory, comprehension, and aging: A review and a new view. In G. H. Bower (Ed.), *The psychology of learning and motivation, Vol. 22.* San Diego, CA: Academic Press.

Hashtroudi, S., Johnson, M. K., & Chrosniak, L. D. (1989). Aging and source monitoring. *Psychology and Aging, 4,* 106–112.

Hashtroudi, S., Johnson, M. K., & Chrosniak, L. D. (1990). Aging and qualitative characteristics of memories for perceived and imagined complex events. *Psychology and Aging, 5,* 119–126.

Hill, W. L., Borovsky, D., & Rovee-Collier, C. (1988). Continuities in infant memory development. *Developmental Psychobiology, 21,* 43–62.

Hintzman, D. L. (1974). Theoretical implications of the spacing effect. In R. L. Solso (Ed.), *Theories of cognitive psychology: The Loyola symposium.* Hillsdale, NJ: Erlbaum.

Hitch, G. J., Halliday, M. S., Dodd, A., & Littler, J. E. (1989). Development of rehearsal in short-term memory: Differences between pictorial and spoken stimuli. *British Journal of Developmental Psychology, 7,* 347–362.

Howard, D. V., & Howard, J. H. (1992). Adult age differences in the rate of learning serial patterns: Evidence from direct and indirect tests. *Psychology and Aging, 7,* 232–241.

Howard, D. V., Shaw, R. J., & Heisey, J. G. (1986). Aging and the time course of semantic activation. *Journal of Gerontology, 41,* 195–203.

Howe, M. L., & Courage, M. L. (1993). On resolving the enigma of infantile amnesia. *Psychological Bulletin, 113,* 305–326.

Hudson, J. A., & Fivush, R. (1991). As time goes by: Sixth graders remember a kindergarten experience. *Applied Cognitive Psychology, 5,* 346–360.

Hudson, J., & Fivush, R. (1983). Categorical and schematic organization and the development of retrieval strategies. *Journal of Experimental Child Psychology, 36,* 32–42.

Hulme, C., Thomson, N., Muir, C., & Lawrence, A. (1984). Speech rate and the development of short-term memory span. *Journal of Experimental Child Psychology, 38,* 241–253.

Hulme, C., & Tordoff, V. (1989). Working memory development: The effects of speech rate, word length, and acoustic similarity on serial recall. *Journal of Experimental Child Psychology, 47,* 72–87.

Java, R. I., & Gardiner, J. M. (1991). Priming and aging: Further evidence of preserved memory function. *American Journal of Psychology, 104,* 89–100.

Johnson, M. K., De Leonardis, D. M., Hashtroudi, S., & Ferguson, S. A. (1995). Aging and single versus multiple cues in source monitoring. *Psychology and Aging, 10,* 507–517.

Johnson, M. K., & Raye, C. L. (1981). Reality monitoring. *Psychological Review, 88,* 67–85.

Kausler, D. H., & Puckett, J. M. (1980). Adult age differences in recognition memory for a nonsemantic attribute. *Experimental Aging Research, 6,* 349–355.

Kausler, D. H., & Puckett, J. M. (1981). Adult age differences in memory for modality attributes. *Experimental Aging Research, 7,* 117–125.

Kihlstrom, J. F., & Harackiewicz, J. M. (1982). The earliest recollection: A new survey. *Journal of Personality, 50,* 134–138.

Kunzinger, E. L. (1985). A short-term longitudinal study of memorial development during early grade school. *Developmental Psychology, 21,* 642–646.

Lehman, E. B., Mikesell, J. W., & Doherty, S. C. (1985). Long term retention of information about presentation modality by children and adults. *Memory & Cognition, 13,* 21–28.

Lewicki, P. (1986). *Nonconscious social information processing.* Orlando, FL: Academic Press.

Light, L. L., & Burke, D. M. (1988). Patterns of language and memory in old age. In L. L. Light & D. M. Burke (Eds.), *Language, memory, and aging.* New York: Cambridge University Press.

Light, L. L., & Singh, A. (1987). Implicit and explicit memory in young and older adults. *Journal of Experimental Psychology: Learning, Memory, and Cognition, 13,* 531–541.

Lindberg, M. A. (1980). Is knowledge base development a necessary and sufficient condition for memory development? *Journal of Experimental Child Psychology, 30,* 401–410.

Loftus, E. F. (1993). Desperately seeking memories of the first few years of childhood: The reality of early memories. *Journal of Experimental Psychology: General, 122,* 274–277.

Mäntylä, T. (1993). Knowing but not remembering: Adult age differences in recollective experience. *Memory & Cognition, 21,* 379–388.

Maybery, M., Taylor, M., & O'Brien-Malone, A. (1995). Implicit learning: Sensitive to age but not IQ. Special Issue: Cognitive development. *Australian Journal of Psychology, 47,* 8–17.

Maylor, E. A. (1995). Remembering versus knowing television theme tunes in middle-aged and elderly adults. *British Journal of Psychology, 86,* 21–25.

McDonough, L., Mandler, J. M., McKee, R. D., & Squire, L. R. (1995). The deferred imitation task as a nonverbal measure of declarative memory. *Proceedings of the National Academy of Sciences, 92,* 7580–7584.

Melton, A. W. (1970). The situation with respect to the spacing of repetitions and memory. *Journal of Verbal Learning and Verbal Behavior, 9,* 596–606.

Mergler, N., Faust, M., & Goldstein, M. (1985). Storytelling as an age-dependent skill. *International Journal of Aging and Human Development, 20,* 205–228.

Micco, A., & Masson, M. E. J. (1992). Age-related differences in the specificity of verbal encoding. *Memory & Cognition, 20,* 244–253.

Myers, N. A., Clifton, R. K., & Clarkson, M. G. (1987). When they were very young: Almost-threes remember two years ago. *Infant Behavior and Development, 10,* 123–132.

Naito, M. (1990). Repetition priming in children and adults: Age-related dissociation between implicit and explicit memory. *Journal of Experimental Child Psychology, 50,* 462–484.

Naveh-Benjamin, M., & Craik, F. I. M. (1995). Memory for context and its use in item memory: Comparisons of younger and older persons. *Psychology and Aging, 10,* 284–293.

Newcombe, N., & Fox, N. A. (1994). Infantile amnesia: Through a glass darkly. *Child Development, 65,* 31–40.

Ornstein, P. A., Naus, M. J., & Liberty, C. (1975). Rehearsal and organizational processes in children's memory. *Child Development, 46,* 818–830.

Parkin, A. J. (1993). Implicit memory across the lifespan. In P. Graf & M. E. Masson (Eds.), *Implicit memory: New directions in cognition, development, and neuropsychology.* Hillsdale, NJ: Erlbaum.

Parkin, A. J., & Streete, S. (1988). Implicit and explicit memory in young children and adults. *British Journal of Psychology, 79,* 361–369.

Parkin, A. J., & Walter, B. M. (1991). Aging, short-term memory and frontal dysfunction. *Psychobiology, 19,* 175–179.

Parkin, A. J., & Walter, B. M. (1992). Recollective experience, normal aging, and frontal dysfunction. *Psychology and Aging, 7,* 290–298.

Parkinson, S. R. (1982). Performance deficits in short-term memory tasks: A comparison of amnesic Korsakoff patients and the aged. In L. S. Cermak (Ed.), *Human memory and amnesia.* Hillsdale, NJ: Erlbaum.

Parkinson, S. R., Inman, V. W., & Dannenbaum, S. E. (1985). Adult age differences in short-term forgetting. *Acta Psychologica, 60,* 83–101.

Perner, J., & Ruffman, T. (1995). Episodic memory and autonoetic consciousness: Developmental evidence and a theory of childhood amnesia. *Journal of Experimental Child Psychology, 59,* 516–548.

Perris, E. E., Myers, N. A., & Clifton, R. K. (1990). Long-term memory for a single infancy experience. *Child Development, 61,* 1796–1807.

Pillemer, D. B., Picariello, M. L., & Pruett, J. C. (1994). Very long-term memories of a salient preschool event. *Applied Cognitive Psychology, 8,* 95–106.

Rabbitt, P. M. A. (1965). An age decrement in the ability to ignore irrelevant information. *Journal of Gerontology, 20,* 233–238.

Rabbitt, P. M. A., & Abson, V. (1991). Do older people know how good they are? *British Journal of Psychology, 82,* 137–151.

Rajaram, S. (1993). Remembering and knowing: Two means of access to the personal past. *Memory & Cognition, 21,* 89–102.

Richardson, R., Riccio, D. C., & Axiotis, R. (1986). Alleviation of infantile amnesia in rats by internal and external contextual cues. *Developmental Psychobiology, 19,* 453–462.

Ritter, K. (1978). The development of knowledge of an external retrieval cue strategy. *Child Development, 49,* 1227–1230.

Rosenzweig, M. R. (1984). Experience, memory, and the brain. *American Psychologist, 39,* 365–376.

Rovee-Collier, C. (1989). The joy of kicking: Memories, motives, and mobiles. In P. R. Solomon, G. R. Goethals, C. M. Kelley, & B. R. Stephens (Eds.), *Memory: Interdisciplinary approaches.* New York: Springer-Verlag.

Rovee-Collier, C. (1993). The capacity for long-term memory in infancy. *Current Directions in Psychological Science, 2,* 130–135.

Rovee-Collier, C., Borza, M. A., Adler, S. A., & Boller, K. (1993). Infants' eyewitness testimony: Effects of postevent information on a prior memory representation. *Memory & Cognition, 21,* 267–279.

Rovee-Collier, C., & Fagen, J. W. (1981). The retrieval of memory in early infancy. In L. P. Lipsitt (Ed.), *Advances in infancy research, Vol. 1.* Norwood, NJ: Ablex.

Rovee-Collier, C., & Shyi, C.-W. G. (1992). A functional and cognitive analysis of infant long-term retention. In M. L. Howe, C. J. Brainerd, & V. F. Reyna (Eds.), *Development of long-term retention.* New York: Springer-Verlag.

Rubin, D. C., & Baddeley, A. D. (1989). Telescoping is not time compression: A model of the dating of autobiographical events. *Memory & Cognition, 17,* 653–661.

Russo, R., Nichelli, P., Gibertoni, M., & Cornia, C. (1995). Developmental trends in implicit and explicit memory: A picture completion study. *Journal of Experimental Child Psychology, 59,* 566–578.

Salthouse, T. A. (1985). *A theory of cognitive aging.* Amsterdam: North-Holland.

Salthouse, T. A. (1991). *Theoretical perspectives on cognitive aging.* Hillsdale, NJ: Erlbaum.

Salthouse, T. A., & Babcock, R. L. (1991). Decomposing adult age differences in working memory. *Developmental Psychology, 27,* 763–776.

Samuel, A. G. (1978). Organizational vs. retrieval factors in the development of digit span. *Journal of Experimental Child Psychology, 26,* 308–319.

Schneider, W., & Pressley, M. (1989). *Memory development between 2 and 20.* New York: Springer-Verlag.

Sheingold, K., & Tenney, Y. J. (1982). Memory for a salient childhood event. In U. Neisser (Ed.), *Memory observed.* San Francisco: Freeman.

Shimamura, A. P., Berry, J. M., Mangels, J. A., Rusting, C. L., & Jurica, P. J. (1995). Memory and cognitive abilities in university professors: Evidence for successful aging. *Psychological Science, 6,* 271–277.

Spetch, M. L., & Rusak, B. (1992). Time present and time past. In W. K. Honig & J. G. Fetterman (Eds.), *Cognitive aspects of stimulus control.* Hillsdale, NJ: Erlbaum.

Stoltzfus, E. R., Hasher, L., & Zacks, R. T. (1996). Working memory and aging: Current status of the inhibitory view. In J. T. E. Richardson (Ed.), *Working memory and human cognition.* New York: Oxford University Press.

Sullivan, M. W. (1982). Reactivation: Priming forgotten memories in human infants. *Child Development, 57,* 100–104.

Toppino, T. C. (1991). The spacing effect in young children's free recall: Support for automatic process explanations. *Memory & Cognition, 19,* 159–167.

Tulving, E., & Pearlstone, Z. (1966). Availability versus accessibility of information in memory for words. *Journal of Verbal Learning and Verbal Behavior, 5,* 381–391.

Usher, J. A., & Neisser, U. (1993). Childhood amnesia and the beginnings of memory for four early life events. *Journal of Experimental Psychology: General, 122,* 155–165.

Waldfogel, S. (1948). The frequency and affective character of childhood memories. *Psychological Monographs, 62* (Whole No. 291).

Winograd, E., & Killinger, W. A., Jr. (1983). Relating age at encoding in early childhood to adult recall: Development of flashbulb memories. *Journal of Experimental Psychology: General, 112,* 413–422.

# CHAPTER SEVENTEEN

# Mnemonics

*"The 'secret of a good memory' is thus the secret of forming diverse and multiple associations with every fact we care to retain."*

—*William James (1890, p. 623)*

## Can I Improve My Memory?

When people find out that I am a cognitive psychologist who studies memory, they invariably tell me that their memory is terrible and ask how they can improve it. The answer usually does not satisfy them because it is rather prosaic and the methods often involve a moderate amount of effort. They also do not appreciate it when I point out that they appear to have an excellent memory because they can remember every time their memory failed them. Indeed, the correlation between actual memory ability and perceived memory ability is typically very low (Hertzog, 1992).

Memory improvement books can be divided into two kinds: popular and scholarly. Typically, the popular books are written by people with no formal training in memory; they are either professional entertainers who have discovered techniques for memorizing a large amount of novel information for a brief period of time, or they are promoters of seminars and training sessions that, among other things, are designed to improve memory. Indeed, on the covers of many of these books are phrases such as "More Money! Higher Grades! More Friends!" Most of the popular books report the same techniques, and almost none offer much by way of explanation of how or why these methods work. The good news is that most of the methods do lead to substantial improvements in memory performance. The bad news, however, is that because many of these authors are removed from the scientific literature, these books often contain many errors, omissions, or statements that are simply meaningless. Furthermore, there is no easy or magical way to develop a perfect memory overnight. To anticipate the end of this chapter, the easiest way to improve your memory is simply to practice.

# The Bad News

One common theme in popular memory improvement books is that "one only uses 10 percent of the potential of the brain" (Lapp, 1992, pp. 19–20) or "we use only a small percentage of our brain power" (Lorayne, 1957, p. 10). Other books quote figures as low as 1% (Herold, 1982), but in no case are references cited nor is there any indication of what this means or how it was determined. In fact, this type of statement, although widely believed, is entirely meaningless. Consider the brain from an evolutionary perspective: Why would humans develop such large brains but use only 10% of it? An analogous situation would be that we evolved with 20 legs but use only 2 of them. Although it would be nice to believe that we all have an enormous untapped potential (90% of our brains are in permanent idle), we can still believe in potential without resorting to meaningless statements. Given the frequency of this belief, where might it have come from?

One possible source is Lashley's (1950) report concerning rats trained to run in a maze. After the rats had learned where to go to reach food, Lashley destroyed parts of the rat's visual cortex. The animals were still able to find their way through the maze when 90% of their visual cortex had been destroyed, although their performance was diminished. Lashley's conclusion was not that rats use only 10% of their brain but rather that brain function is not localized: many different parts of the brain are involved in any given activity (see Chapter 9).

Calvin and Ojemann (1994, p. 15) speculate that this myth of untapped potential originally came from the observation that a slow-growing tumor has to destroy approximately 80% of the cells in a particular area within the motor strip of the brain before movement and control is lost. They also point out, however, that in skilled situations such as finger movements by a pianist, a loss of some control would be easily detectable far earlier. Moreover, if a sudden loss of as few as 30% of the neurons in the motor strip occurred (through a stroke, for example), complete paralysis could occur.

A third possible source comes from a misunderstanding about the results of a famous series of studies by Wilder Penfield (Penfield, 1969). Prior to performing brain surgery, surgeons must map out areas of the brain to ensure that areas responsible for things like speech and language are not damaged during the operation. This process of mapping out areas involves using a mild electrical current to stimulate a particular area. Because the patient is usually awake, the neurosurgeon can observe the patient's response and can find motor areas, speech areas, and so forth. Penfield (1969) reported that he triggered long-forgotten memories when stimulating various regions in the cortex and argued that "it is clear that the neuronal action that accompanies each succeeding state of consciousness leaves its permanent imprint on the brain. The imprint, or record, is a trail of facilitation of neuronal connections that can be followed again by an electric current many years later with no loss of detail, as though a tape recorder had been receiving it all" (p. 165). Many memory improvement books (Buzan, 1984) follow this interpretation. They assume that the brain automatically records everything but that very little is actually recallable. The unused potential lies in trying to gain access to these memories, as Penfield's patients did. The problem is that less than 3% of all patients Penfield tested produced any response — that is, 97% of the patients produced *no* responses — and of these, each recovered memory is highly generic and appears to be more an inference or likely happening, rather than a particular memory (Loftus & Loftus, 1980; Neisser, 1967; Squire, 1987).

Many books (Buzan, 1984; Herold, 1982) say that one reason many people have poor memories is that they do not use the right brain and they depend too much on the left brain. The left side of the brain is the seat of language in almost all right-handed people and in approximately 70% of left-handed people (Corballis, 1980). The left hemisphere is concerned with logic and reason, whereas the right hemisphere is the artistic, intuitive, holistic side. Although there have been many popular books aimed at right-brain educa-tion, there is little scientific evidence to support the claims (Hellige, 1990; Springer & Deutsch, 1989).

Other statements in the popular memory improvement books do not reflect the facts about memory accurately. For example, Lapp (1992, p. 9) reasserts the common idea that elderly people have trouble remembering the most recent events and are particularly good at recalling older events. Research has consistently failed to find support that healthy older adults remember the past more clearly than they remember the present (Squire, 1974; Warrington & Sanders, 1971). Most studies do show a memory loss for the older subjects relative to younger subjects, but the loss is uniform rather than concentrated on recent events. Lapp (1992) also claims that "recognition memory is easy, whereas free recall is not" (p. 110). If this really were the case, then there should not be the phenomenon of recognition failure of recallable words. People can recall words they cannot recognize when the cues presented to them as part of the recall test are better than the cues pre-sented to them as part of the recognition test (Watkins & Tulving, 1975; see Chapter 10). Lorayne (1957, p. 42) says that creating bizarre (or to use his word, ridiculous) images leads to better memory. As discussed later, it is the interacting nature of the image that affords mnemonic staying power, not its bizarreness or ridiculousness (Wollen, Weber, & Lowry, 1972). The reason that many people believe bizarre images do increase retention is that bizarre images are typically interactive images. As a final example, Lorayne (1957) states that "Things that we see register upon our brains with much more emphasis than what we hear" (p. 121). This depends upon the type of material and the type of test. The modality effect (Chapter 3) contradicts this statement when serial recall is the test, and Roediger, Weldon, and Challis (1989; see Chapter 8) document other situations where au-ditory presentation leads to better performance.

Another method of improving memory that is often invoked is playing tapes while asleep. Greenwald, Spangenberg, Pratkanis, and Eskenazi (1991) tested whether sublimi-nal audiotapes could improve memory. When played, these tapes appear to contain only relaxing sounds, such as music or waterfalls, but also recorded on them — according to manufacturers — is material that will improve memory. Greenwald et al. (1991) had four important features in their experimental design. First, a double-blind method was used so that neither the subject nor the experimenter knew the actual content of the tape. Second, the tape was used according to the instructions provided by the manufacturer. Third, the study (actually, three separate replications) used subjects who were highly motivated and who expressed a desire to improve memory. Fourth, the research used both pretest and posttest measures to determine whether any change had occurred as a result of using the tapes. Two types of tapes were tested: self-esteem and memory. One of the manipulations was whether the tape was labeled correctly; thus, half the subjects listened to a tape that was labeled correctly (the tape was designed by the manufacturers to improve memory

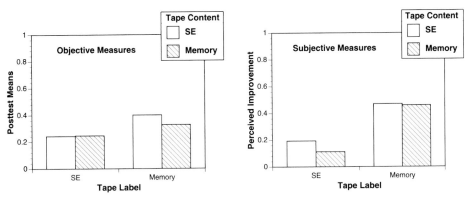

**Figure 17.1** The left panel shows the average posttest score on the memory scale (in the form of a standardized score) as a function of audiotape subliminal content and tape label. The mean of the pretest scores was zero. The right panel shows the percentage of subjects perceiving improvement in memory as a function of audiotape subliminal content and tape label. Source: Greenwald, Spangenberg, Pratkanis, & Eskenazi (1991).

and was labeled as a memory improvement tape), and half listened to a tape that was labeled incorrectly (the memory tape was labeled as a self-esteem tape). The results are shown in Figure 17.1.

Although approximately 50% of the subjects reported an improvement in the domain listed on the tape label, a comparison of pre- and posttest scores on objective measures of memory performance led the researchers to conclude that "there was no trace of a subliminal content effect" (Greenwald et al., 1991, p. 121). Basically, if the tape said it improved memory, then the content was irrelevant: subjects perceived an improvement in memory even though there was no increase in memory performance on objective tests. Greenwald et al. termed this an *illusory placebo effect*.

## The Good News

The good news is that many of the suggestions for improving memory offered in the popular books do work, although these methods are neither new nor particularly surprising. The good news is also somewhat qualified by the fact that most popular books fail to mention some of the easiest but nonetheless most potent strategies. One such overlooked contribution is the difference in acquisition and retention due to distributed rather than massed rehearsal. This omission is surprising because this is an easy way to greatly increase retention of material, and studies demonstrating the advantage were reported by Ebbinghaus (1885, Section 34) and have been systematically explored ever since (see Underwood, 1961, for a review).

When trying to learn a motor skill, such as typing, playing a computer game, or any other such activity, people become better faster when they take a short break between each trial (distributed practice) than when no such break occurs (massed practice). An early study by Lorge (1930) examined performance on a mirror drawing task in which a

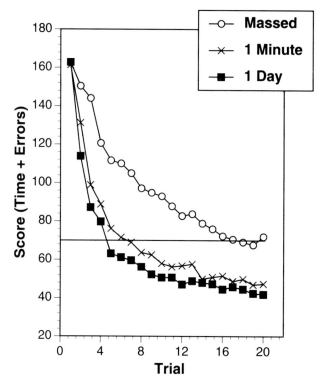

**Figure 17.2** Performance learning in a mirror maze task as a function of interpolated activity. The massed group had no interval. The horizontal line shows that by the end of 20 sessions, the massed group was performing at the level achieved by the two distributed groups after 5 (1 day) and 6 (1 minute) trials.   Source: Data from Table V of Lorge (1930).

channel in the shape of a 6-pointed star was cut out of brass. The subject's task was to move a stylus around the channel without touching the sides, but the subject did not see the channel directly, only through a mirror. The score is simply the time taken to complete a circuit plus the number of times the stylus touched either edge of the channel. Subjects either had a 1-day interval between trials, a 1-minute interval between trials, or no interval between trials (massed). Performance after 20 trials with massed practice was the same as performance after only 5–6 trials with distributed practice (see Figure 17.2).

There does not seem to be any difference in the rate of acquisition when verbal material is learned using massed compared to distributed rehearsal (Underwood, 1961). The difference for verbal material shows up in measures of retention (Cain & Willey, 1939), particularly when the interval between practice is longer than 24 hours (Underwood & Schulz, 1961). For example, Keppel (1964, 1967) conducted two experiments that examined retention after 1 day or 8 days when practice was massed (4-second interval) versus distributed (24-hour interval). The difference between the two experiments was the degree of proactive interference: subjects in the single list experiment learned only one list, and subjects in the multiple list experiment learned a total of four lists but were tested for

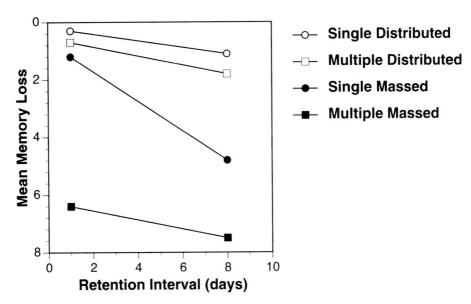

**Figure 17.3** The effects of massed and distributed practice on the retention of verbal information. Distributed practice has only a small effect after a short delay but has a substantial effect after longer delays.   Source: Keppel (1967).

just the final list. The results are shown in Figure 17.3. There was little difference after a 1-day retention interval except for the multiple list groups. However, by 8 days after studying, both of the massed groups had lost a substantial portion of the information, whereas there was relatively little loss for the distributed groups. These results generalize to a whole host of tasks including multiplication tables, spelling, lecture material, foreign language vocabulary, and information from textbooks (Rea & Modigliani, 1988).

It should be emphasized that distributed rehearsal takes no more time than massed rehearsal does; the only difference is that 2 hours of massed study might be broken up into four 30-minute sessions distributed over 4 days. The advantage of distributed over massed is so great and the results so reliable that it is one of the most often mentioned techniques for improving memory in the more scholarly memory improvement books (Herrmann, Weingartner, Searleman, & McEvoy, 1992). It is also a technique most people do not believe works (Zechmeister & Shaughnessy, 1980). One reason students may not believe there is a difference is because massed practice does work, but only for the short run. Cramming the night before an exam is fine for performance on that exam because the retention interval is less than one day. However, if you have a cumulative final at the end of the semester and you used massed practice, you will recall very little. If you want to retain the information so that you will remember it for the final, then distributed practice is the way to go.

If you take breaks to distribute your study, what should you do during the interval? One easy thing is to sleep. As described in Chapter 7, Jenkins and Dallenbach (1924) showed that subjects were able to recall more of the items following a period of sleep than

**Table 17.1**   The two main sources of interference when learning Spanish vocabulary. Studying Italian vocabulary after the Spanish can result in retroactive interference, but studying Italian before studying the Spanish can result in proactive interference. Interference occurs because Spanish is similar to Italian.

|  | *Study First* | *Study Second* | *Tested On* |
|---|---|---|---|
| *RI* | | | |
| Experimental | Spanish | Italian | Spanish |
| Control | Spanish | Math | Spanish |
| *PI* | | | |
| Experimental | Italian | Spanish | Spanish |
| Control | Math | Spanish | Spanish |

following a period of wakefulness. Of course, it is not sleep in and of itself that helps memory retention; rather, it is the absence of (or reduction in) potentially interfering material. During the intervals created by using distributed processing, you should avoid performing tasks that can interfere. This can be quite difficult, because there are two important kinds of interference.

When two kinds of activities are similar, they can interfere. If you are learning Spanish and Italian concurrently, you can easily become confused about which word means what in which language. Let's say you have a test on Spanish vocabulary on Wednesday, and you study on Monday night. If you study Spanish vocabulary first and then Italian vocabulary, you will suffer from retroactive interference when you take the test: studying the Italian interferes with the material you learned earlier. What happens if you reverse the order of studying to avoid retroactive interference? Your memory for the Spanish will be interfered with by the material you learned earlier, the Italian. This is proactive interference (see Table 17.1). To avoid retroactive interference, you should study something quite different (such as math). Or you can take a nap.

Most scholarly books suggest that, when studying, we should use processing that elaborates on the to-be-remembered information. One of the most influential papers on memory in the past 30 years formally introduced the idea of levels of processing (Craik & Lockhart, 1972; see Chapter 6). Depending on the type of material and the type of test, different elaborative processes can help in retaining the information.

For factual information, such as that conveyed by many textbooks, one of the best ways of performing elaborative processing is to ask yourself, why? Several studies (Woloshyn, Willoughby, Wood, & Pressley, 1990; Wood, Pressley, & Winne, 1990) have investigated the effects of using this elaborative interrogation. The technique involves asking people to think beyond the facts as stated and to construct reasons that explain why the factual relationships hold. The advantage, presumably, is in getting people to make use of prior knowledge when they process new information. This research has shown beneficial effects for college students, adults, and even for young children (grades 4 through 8).

For certain types of tests, a shallow level of processing can lead to better performance than a deep level does. As described in Chapter 6, Morris, Bransford, and Franks (1977) found that when the test required semantic processing, a deep level produced better performance; however, when the test required more shallow processing, a shallow level produced better performance. This *transfer appropriate processing approach* retains much of the levels of processing view but includes the processing done at test. The key is to ensure that the cues available at retrieval are effective for identifying the to-be-remembered material.

Many of the techniques that the less scholarly memory improvement books offer do work. The most common first suggestion is to pay attention during encoding. For example, a common problem many people report is that they are not able to remember people's names. A technique that works well begins with repeating the name out loud when introduced to a person for the first time to ensure that you have the correct basic information. Many failures to remember a person's name can be attributed to a failure to encode the material in the first place. If the name is unusual, do not hesitate to ask for spelling.

# Technical Mnemonics

Most books agree with William James (1890) on the basic method for improving memory: forming meaningful associations. For example, to remember the names of the Great Lakes, simply remember the acronym HOMES: Huron, Ontario, Michigan, Erie, Superior. Many biology and physiology students know the phrase, "On old Olympus' towering top, a Fin and German viewed some hops." The first letters here give you the first letters of the 12 cranial nerves (olfactory, optic, oculomotor, trochlear, trigeminal, abducens, facial, auditory, glossopharyngeal, vagus, spinal accessory, and hypoglossal). ROY G. BIV is the formal name of the spectrum of colors: red, orange, yellow, green, blue, indigo, and violet. These techniques are useful for providing cues: all you need do is search for a word that begins with a particular letter, and the mnemonic provides you with the letter and the number of targets.

Other mnemonic techniques require a preliminary learning stage before they can be applied. Almost all books mention what is variously referred to as the Phonetic Alphabet, the Phonetic Numeral Code, or the Major System. Attributed originally to Stanislaus Mink von Wennsshein around 1650 and subsequently modified by Richard Grey in 1730, this system has been mentioned by most writers on memory, including William James (1890, p. 629). Its main goal is to help with memory for numbers. One problem with trying to remember numbers is that they are relatively abstract and have very little that can be readily associated with them. So the phonetic alphabet links a particular sound with a particular digit. To recall the number, just remember the sounds that are associated with that number.

First, each of the digits from 0 to 9 are associated with the sound of a particular consonant (see Table 17.2). Because it is the sound that is important, sometimes more than one letter is associated with a particular number. There is even a mnemonic to help remember the basic ten associations needed. The letter is typically chosen based on visual

**Table 17.2**   The phonetic alphabet, in which each number is associated with the sound of a particular consonant. Two or more consonant sounds are sometimes listed when the sounds are very similar.

| Number | Phonetic Counterpart |
|--------|----------------------|
| 0 | z or s, because these letters can sound like the first letter of zero |
| 1 | t or d, because t looks like a 1 and d has one downstroke, like the number 1 |
| 2 | n, because n has two downstrokes |
| 3 | m, because m has three downstrokes |
| 4 | r, because r is the last letter in four |
| 5 | L, because L is the Roman numeral for 50 |
| 6 | j, soft g, ch, sh, because 6 looks like an uppercase G |
| 7 | k, hard c, hard g, because you can see two rotated 7s in the uppercase letter K |
| 8 | f or v, because a cursive f can look like an 8 |
| 9 | p or b, because p is a mirror image of 9 |

similarity with a hand-written form of the letter, on the acoustic similarity, or some other relatively simple facet. The key, though, will be using the sound that is represented by the letters. The vowels (a, e, i, o, and u) and the letters w, h, and y (why?) are not used; these letters are ignored for mnemonic purposes and are used in the second stage to form words using the consonant sounds.

The second step is to associate the sounds (and thus, the numbers) to particular words. Note that only the key sound is important; the remaining letters fill out the word but do not provide any extra information. The most popular suggestions include:

0 = zoo
1 = tie
2 = new
3 = ma
4 = rye
5 = law
6 = shoe
7 = cow
8 = foe
9 = bee

Other numbers use combinations of these basic sounds. For example, the number 10 might be associated with the word *toes*. Notice how the first consonant sound (*t*) is used for first digit (1) and the second consonant sound (*z*) is used for the second digit (0). The number 100 might be associated with the word *disease*. Buzan (1984) lists words for the first 1000 numbers (0–999) using the phonetic alphabet. Edward Pick (1888) provides an illustration of how to use this method:

To briefly show its use, suppose it is desired to fix 1142 feet in a second as the velocity of sound: t, t, r, n, are the letters and order required. Fill up with vowels forming a phrase, like "tight run," and connect it by some such flight of the imagination as that if a man tried to keep up with the velocity of sound, he would have a tight run. When you recall this a few days later great care must be taken not to get confused with the velocity of light, nor to think he had a hard run, which would be 3000 feet too fast. (p. 7)

The phonetic alphabet depends on imagery for the final stage, as illustrated in the quotation above. As with all techniques, the key is having a cue at test that will trigger the appropriate response. When trying to recall the speed of sound, a natural image is of running, and that easily translates into a man running. The hardest part is then moving on to a man racing sound and having a "tight run."

It is perfectly fine to use idiosyncratic associations. Some may be straightforward, as noting that 1066 is when the Battle of Hastings occurred, whereas others may simply be odd, as when people recall that the number 42 is crucially important in metaphysics (see Adams, 1981, p. 180). This technique can work quite dramatically as long as the cue is easy to generate. Dramatic empirical support for this was provided by Mäntylä (1986, Experiment 2). He presented subjects with 504 words, and each subject generated three properties of the word. At test, the experimenter presented the properties, and the subject had to respond with the original word. When tested immediately, subjects recalled approximately 91% of the words. Compare this figure with the 88% obtained by Shepard (1967) for recognition of 540 words. Recall without such cues was terrible.

One might object that getting any three properties would let a person guess the target word. Mäntylä included an important control condition. If subjects were simply generating the target item based on the properties, performance should not get worse over time. If, on the other hand, the properties were serving only as a cue to memory proper, then one might well expect performance to decrease. When the retention interval was 1 week, recall had dropped to about 65% correct. This is still an impressive feat, however: after 1 week, these subjects could recall nearly 330 words correctly!

The method of loci is a similar but far older method. Yates (1966) provides a superb history of this particular technique. According to Cicero (as translated by Sutton, 1942), it was invented by Simonides:

> There is a story that Simonides was dining at the house of a wealthy nobleman named Scopas at Crannon in Thessaly, and chanted a lyric poem which he had composed in honour of his host, in which he followed the custom of the poets by including for decorative purposes a long passage referring to Castor and Pollux; whereupon Scopas with excessive meanness told him he would pay him half the fee agreed on for the poem, and if he liked he might apply for the balance to his sons of Tyndareus, as they had gone halves in the panegyric. The story runs that a little later a message was brought to Simonides to go outside, as two young men were standing at the door who earnestly requested him to come out; so he rose from his seat and went out, and could not see anybody; but in the interval of his absence the roof of the hall where Scopas was giving the banquet fell in, crushing Scopas himself and his relations underneath the ruins and killing them; and when their friends wanted to bury them but were altogether unable to know them apart as they had been completely crushed, the story goes that Simonides was enabled by his recollection of the place in which each of them had been reclining at table to identify them for separate internment; and that this circumstance suggested to him the discovery of the truth that the best aid to clearness of memory consists in orderly arrangement. He inferred that persons desiring to train this faculty must select localities and form mental images of the facts they wish to remember and store those images in the localities, with the result

that the arrangement of the localities will preserve the order of the facts, and the images of the facts will designate the facts themselves. (Sutton, 1942, pp. 465–467)

There are three steps to this system. First, a well-known series of locations is chosen: for example, your route from your dorm room or apartment to class is well known to you and there are many different locations along the route. You can even use imaginary locations; the importance of the locations is to provide a structure to retain the order information. The second step involves creating a mental image of the item you want to remember interacting with a particular location along your route. The most common use of this technique in the Roman world was as an aid for remembering speeches. Each point to be made would be represented by an image in a particular location. For example, if you were delivering a speech on the imminent demise of civilization and your third point concerns the fact that the amount of graffiti is rising, you could imagine seeing a person spray-painting the word *graffiti* on the side of the fountain, the third notable location you walk by on the way to class. The final step is simply to "walk" from one location to the next, recalling the images and reconstructing the desired memory.

Although it may seem that a lot of effort is required, the method of loci does in fact work and is particularly useful to remembering order information. For example, Ross and Lawrence (1968) reported that with no more than two practice trials, subjects could recall a list of 40 or 50 items in order close to perfectly. One subject, after only 2 trials, could recall 52 items in backward order. Another study by De Beni and Cornoldi (1985) showed that the method of loci had benefits observable in both free recall and recognition tests that were delayed by 1 week after study. The key to the method of loci lies in two components: interactive imagery affords better memory than noninteractive imagery, and the known locations provide an organizational structure.

Is it important, as many popular books suggest, that the images be bizarre? Wollen, Weber and Lowry (1972) compared memory when subjects used bizarre interactive images, bizarre images that were not interactive, common interactive images, and common images that were not interactive. Bizarreness neither helped nor hurt; memory was better with interactive images than with noninteractive images. Neisser and Kerr (1973) found similar results, and Einstein and McDaniel (1987) reviewed 44 studies of normal versus bizarre imagery. For tests after very short delays, an advantage for bizarre items occurs only (1) when both bizarre and normal images are used, (2) when used with free recall, and (3) when imagery instructions are emphasized. For tests after longer delays, they conclude that "the conflicting results within the four categories make these experiments difficult to summarize" (p. 86). Given these, at best weak, results and the fact that no bizarre imagery effects are seen when only bizarre imagery is used, bizarreness should not be the prime criterion in creating an image.

When learning complex material, the mnemonics most often mentioned in popular books are not very good. Technical mnemonics are best for remembering a particular series of items, but writing down a shopping list can be far easier than using the method of loci. Indeed, such external means of remembering are used far more often, even by people familiar with and trained using the mnemonic techniques (Bellezza, 1983; Park, Smith, & Cavanaugh, 1990). One reason is that if you do not keep changing the locations or the key words, an enormous amount of proactive interference can build up. For example, most books mention the peg-word method: each digit is associated with a word that sounds like the number, so 1 is a bun, 2 is a shoe, 3 is a tree, and so on. For each item you want to remember, associate the word with the appropriate item. When going to the grocery store, you may need milk, pretzels, cheese, and so on; you would imagine a bun being dunked in the milk, a shoe stomping on the pretzels, a tree oozing cheese, and so

---

**Experiment    Imagery and Mnemonics**

**Purpose:** To demonstrate the use of visual imagery as a mnemonic device.

**Subjects:** Thirty-two subjects are recommended; 16 should be assigned to the control group, and 16 to the imagery group.

**Materials:** Table 1 in the Appendix lists 80 concrete nouns. Create 20 random pairings of the nouns. The test list consists of the first item in a pair, and the target list consists of the second item in a pair. Write each word in large, clear form on a notecard. Each subject should get a different random ordering and pairing of items. Each subject should also get an answer sheet.

**Design:** Because each subject experiences only one condition, rehearsal instruction is a between-subjects factor.

**Procedure:** Inform the subjects that in this experiment they will be asked to learn an association between two words so that when they are given the first word, they will be able to produce the second word. The control group is given no special instructions on how to do this. The imagery group is asked to form an interacting visual image. Each word pair should be shown for 5 seconds. At test, present the first word of each pair for 5 seconds, during which time the subject should try to write down the second word.

**Instructions Control Group:** "In this experiment, I would like you to try to learn a list of word pairs. You will see each pair for 5 seconds. Please study the pair so that when you see the first word again, you will be able to produce the second word. For example, if you see the pair DOG-BICYCLE, at test you will see just DOG and you will be asked to produce BICYCLE. Any questions?"

**Instructions Imagery Group:** "In this experiment, I would like you to try to learn a list of word pairs. You will see each pair for 5 seconds. Please study the pair so that when you see the first word again, you will be able to produce the second word. Try to visualize the two members interacting in some way. For example, if you see the pair DOG-BICYCLE, you might visualize a dog riding a bicycle. At test you will see just DOG and you will be asked to produce BICYCLE. Any questions?"

**Test Instructions for Both Groups:** "I will show you the first word from each pair that you just studied. Please write down the second word from the pair on your answer sheet. Any questions?"

**Scoring and Analysis:** The dependent variable is the number of words correctly recalled. Calculate this for each group, and then use a $t$ test for independent groups to see whether the mean number of words recalled differs. You should find that the imagery group recalled significantly more words than the control group did.

**Optional Enhancements:** Change the experiment to test three groups: control, interactive imagery, and noninteractive imagery. The group that receives instructions to create interacting images should recall more than the group that creates noninteracting images.

Source: Based on an experiment by Bower (1972).

on. The limit occurs the next time you go to the store: Does bun still go with milk, or does it now go with lettuce?

For the type of material a typical college student must master, the technical mnemonics offer very little. The suggestions from the scientific literature, however, are exactly what you need. The goal of the preceding sections was to help you improve your memory performance. There have been many reports of mnemonists, people who appear to have exceptional memory abilities. We now turn to examine this subject, and in particular we will be interested in whether their memories are simply better or are actually different.

# Exceptional Memories

Perhaps the most famous case of an exceptional memory was reported by Luria (1968). The English version is called *The Mind of a Mnemonist* and documents the remarkable memory of a Russian man named S., who appeared to have a limitless memory. All the following information and quotations come from that source.

S. was a reporter who took no notes during meetings, even though his assignments would involve complex instructions on where to go to meet people or what information to seek out. His editor, thinking that S. was not paying attention, told him to repeat the assignment just given. S. did so perfectly. It was this editor who directed S. to Luria's laboratory. It is of interest that S. apparently did not think himself unusual; he believed everybody else's memory worked this way also.

Luria gave S. a standard battery of tests and quickly concluded that "there was no limit either to the capacity of S.'s memory or to the durability of the traces he retained" (p. 11). As long as there was a pause of approximately 3–4 seconds between each piece of information, S. could retain the information indefinitely. For example, when Luria presented S. with a table of 50 numbers, S. needed 3 minutes to learn the table and 40 seconds to recall it. However, he could recall the table by rows (as if reading across), by columns (as if reading down), or by diagonals or zig-zag patterns, and his performance did not decrease even after an interval of several months.

On June 11, 1936, S. learned a lengthy table composed only of the syllables ma, na, sa, and va. For example, the first two rows could have been: ma, va, na, sa, na, va and na, sa, na, ma, va. On April 6, 1944, S. recalled the table perfectly.

S. appeared to owe his exceptional memory to a process called *synesthesia,* which is perceiving one sensory modality with a different sensory modality. In S.'s case, when he heard a sound, he would also see lights and colors: "There was no distinct line, as there is for others of us, separating vision from hearing, or hearing from a sense of touch or taste" (p. 27). He reportedly told Vygotsky, the influential Russian developmental psychologist, "what a crumbly yellow voice you have" (p. 24). He said of a fence, "it has such a salty taste and feels so rough; furthermore, it has such a sharp, piercing sound" (p. 38).

The few errors of memory that S. did make tended to be errors of omission (failing to report an item) rather than errors in recalling a different item. In one case, S. forgot to recall the word *pencil.* He explains why: "I put the image of *pencil* near a fence . . . the one down the street, you know. But what happened was that the image fused with that of the fence and I walked right on past without noticing it" (p. 36).

S. quit his job at the newspaper and became a professional mnemonist. Because he would often perform several shows a night, he became more economical in using his synesthesia and a variation of the method of loci, but the processes were essentially the same. His major problem was forgetting: he would sometimes recall a lengthy series of unrelated items perfectly, only to realize that it was the list from last week rather than the list for the current performance. He tried several ways of forgetting. He would imagine writing down the items he wished to forget on paper and then imagine setting the paper on fire. The problem was that he could see, in the charred remains, the writing on the paper. It is unclear exactly how he solved his problem. He told Luria only that one day, when trying desperately to forget a chart of numbers he had previously memorized, he looked to see if the chart was still there: "The chart of numbers isn't turning up now and it's clear why — it's because I don't want it to! Aha! That means if I don't want the chart to show up it won't. And all it took was for me to realize this" (p. 71).

Having a perfect memory, particularly one that depended upon synesthesia, caused S. severe emotional and mental problems; in fact, he ended up in a Soviet asylum for the mentally ill. The primary reason was his inability to distinguish between reality and fantasy. An examination of various accounts of mnemonists, however, shows that S. was the exception rather than the rule. Most mnemonists seem to be otherwise normal people who have extensive practice with a limited range of material.

Susukita (1933, 1934) described a 26-year-old mnemonist named Sigeyuki Ishihara whose memory abilities appear to be as remarkable as those of S. Unlike S., however, Ishihara seemed to use more conventional mnemonic techniques and, according to the reports, did not suffer any of the emotional problems that made S.'s life so tragic.

Ishihara became interested in memory while at school, and he became a professional mnemonist. Because of his genuine interest, however, he participated in experiments in Susukita's laboratory and freely gave away his performance secrets. Typically, he was tested on random orders of digits, on male and female names, on Roman consonants, and on Japanese nonsense syllables. His memory for color names, for example, was no better than average. One difference between Ishihara and other noted mnemonists was that Ishihara could learn a list of digits much more quickly. For example, he could learn a series of 204 digits in approximately 5 minutes, 23 seconds and recall them in order in 3 minutes, 20 seconds. He learned the names of all 124 emperors of Japan in order in only 22 minutes, 38 seconds. For many of the lists of items learned, Ishihara organized the information such that there were markers every fifth item. Once learned, he could instantly give the name of the appropriate emperor when cued using the number — for example, to name the 22nd emperor, he would first find the 20th and from there retrieve the 22nd.

Perhaps most surprisingly, Ishihara required the same amount of time to learn any given item in a list regardless of the length of the list to be learned. Figure 17.4 shows the average amount of time needed to learn lists of names (left panel) and digits (right panel) of various lengths. Susukita determined that the mathematical relationship between the amount of material to be learned, $x$, and the learning rate, $y$, was approximately linear,

$$y = kx \tag{17.1}$$

where $k$ is a proportionality constant. The main difference between the data for Ishihara compared to other mnemonists was that $k$ was smaller.

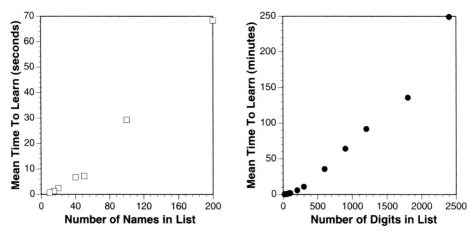

**Figure 17.4** Average time needed by Ishihara to learn lists of 10, 15, 20, 40, 50, 100, and 200 names (in seconds) and lists of 20, 42, 60, 90, 102, 204, 300, 600, 900, 1200, 1800, and 2400 digits (in minutes). Source: From data reported in Susukita (1934).

The technique used was superficially similar to the method of loci but had important differences. Each digit automatically conjured up in Ishihara's mind a particular visual image, such as the field behind his house, a rice paddy, or an elbow. These images could be combined, so that in the field behind his house there might also be a pear tree and a pile of wheat in front of the barn. In this way, he made random strings of numbers more meaningful, and from the image he could determine what the numbers were. Using eight basic images, he could combine them in different ways to learn a list of up to 2500 digits in about 3½ hours. The more frequently a basic image was used, however, the greater chance of an error.

Some images, such as a room for the number 163, led to errors: at recall, it was not clear what was important because the code word used meant "breadth" or "width." Similarly, sometimes the image did not convey the order. For example, the basic image for 47 is China, and that for 32 is spoon; the association for 4732 was therefore a Chinese man selling spoons. At retrieval, this combined image was interpreted as a "'spoon-selling Chinese man" and the number recalled was 3247.

Ishihara learned a list of 600 digits and, 31 days later, he could report 357; his forgetting curve resembled that of Ebbinghaus. Susukita emphasized that when Ishihara "forgot" something, this was not a permanent loss but rather an inability to find the appropriate image. This image could be reported later on, sometimes with repeated testing, or *hypermnesia*. For example, at the first attempt to recall a list of 900 numbers, Ishihara failed to recall 12. A second retrieval attempt, immediately after the first, yielded four of the missing 12. A test 10 minutes later resulted in an additional two. An hour later, two more were retrieved, and the next day, two of the remaining four items were produced. A more extreme example came from a test conducted 27 weeks after learning a list of 600 items. Although Ishihara could recall only 88, nine of these were items he had failed to recall on the original test. If distributed rehearsal took place, such as 1, 3, 7, 14, 21, and 31 days after learning, then he could recall about 75% of the items 27 weeks later.

Ishihara was not easily distracted except by visual stimuli. For example, when he requested moving to a darker lab to reduce the interference, the loud noises that came from an adjacent room did not bother him and did not affect his performance. However, one factor that was referred to as "disadvantageous" for memory was earthquakes. The laboratory was on the second floor, and during the middle of one testing session where Ishihara was learning a list of 200 female names, an earthquake hit, shaking the building quite violently. Recall of the items learned post-earthquake was worse than those learned prior to the earthquake. Consistent with the idea that forgetting was not permanent loss, however, Ishihara was subsequently able to reproduce the missing items. The reason for the initial poor performance could be interpreted as mood-dependent memory: what is learned during a period of calm cannot easily be recalled in a state of shock.

Unlike S.'s, then, Ishihara's memory was not qualitatively different from normal memories but rather was the result of practice with a particular process for a limited range of stimuli. Other mnemonists are very much like Ishihara. For example, Hunter (1962) described a professor of mathematics, A. C. Aitken, who could recall 25 unrelated words in order 27 years after learning them; Rajan (Thompson, Cowan, & Frieman, 1991) has memorized pi to 31,811 places. Like Ishihara, both of these mnemonists were limited in the type of material that could be remembered. Rajan, for example, has exceptional memory only for digits.

V. P., a mnemonist studied by Hunt and Love (1972), also had an exceptional memory but claimed not to use the method of loci or synesthetic processes. Rather, he used idiosyncratic verbal associations to provide a far richer encoding format than most people used. His ability to do this was fostered by his knowledge of foreign languages (he could speak English, French, German, and Spanish as well as Russian, Latvian, and Estonian) and the fact that his early schooling stressed rote memorization, so he received lots of practice (see below). His most noted memory feat was retaining the text of Bartlett's "War of the Ghosts" for over a year with very little distortion.

One question that has concerned researchers on exceptional memory is the degree to which it can be acquired versus the degree to which you are (or are not) born with an exceptional memory. K. Anders Ericsson takes perhaps the most extreme position — that exceptional memory abilities are learned rather than innate — but he also offers a remarkable array of data to support the idea that exceptional memory abilities can be learned. He and his colleagues (Chase & Ericsson, 1981, 1982; Ericsson, 1985; Ericsson, Chase, & Faloon, 1980) have produced two exceptional mnemonists, both of whom began as average college students.

Most people's memory span for a random series of digits is approximately 7, and S. F.'s span was this prior to practice. After 2 years of practice, it had increased to 84 and had shown no signs of reaching asymptote (see Figure 17.5). S. F. did this using his already extensive knowledge about long-distance running. For various distances, there are certain times that have important meanings to a distance runner. For example, 2942 can be seen as 29 minutes and 42 seconds, a time associated with a 10K race. This strategy posed a couple of problems. First, although all 3-digit numbers from 100–959 can be made into times, any number with a 6, 7, 8, or 9 in the middle digits creates an invalid time. At one

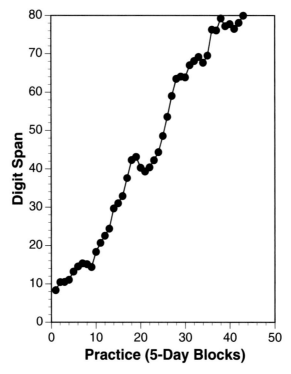

**Figure 17.5**   Average digit span as a function of practice for subject S. F. Each training session lasted approximately 1 hour, and each point is based on five training sessions.   Source: Adapted from Ericsson & Faivre (1988).

point in training, S. F. was given a list entirely of numbers like this, and his digit span was severely reduced. A second problem is that this strategy works only for numbers. His ability to remember a random list of letters was no better than that of any other average college student: 6. D. D., another distance runner, was trained using S. F.'s techniques, and his digit span has reached 106 (Ericsson & Staszewski, 1989).

Ericsson and Faivre (1988) suggest that exceptional abilities are not necessarily beyond the reach of nonexceptional people: "There is no reason to believe that exceptional memory performance is possible only for a small number of special individuals" (p. 450). Although practice in and of itself is not sufficient to develop an exceptional memory, it is certainly necessary. Practice in a variety of different areas can result in processes that are quite different from processes used when there is little or no practice (Ericsson, Krampe, & Tesch-Römer, 1993). There appears to be relatively little difference in performance between subjects who claim exceptional abilities and subjects who have acquired exceptional abilities through practice. For example, Ericsson and Staszewski (1989) found that their two trained experts (S. F. and D. D.) learned and recalled a matrix of 25 digits as fast or even faster than did others with exceptional memories (for example, Luria's S.). This was also true when recall was backward or by diagonals. Furthermore, with the exception of S., most acclaimed mnemonists use similar techniques and show similar patterns of responding as do laboratory-trained subjects. As Ericsson and Faivre (1988) state, "The pattern of memory performance is so similar between subjects alleging exceptional abilities and subjects with acquired memory skill that the same basic mechanisms in both cases can be inferred" (p. 449).

Skilled memory theory, developed by Ericsson and his colleagues, summarizes what has been said above about memory improvement in general. First, the to-be-remembered material must be encoded in a meaningful manner. Most mnemonists use associations that are meaningful to them (Ericsson & Faivre, 1988; Hunt & Love, 1972; Hunter, 1962; Susukita, 1933): S. F. and D. D. used running times, and V. P. used his extensive knowledge of languages. The second key is to have useful retrieval cues available at test that will identify the target material. It seems likely, when trying to recall the speed of sound, that running against sound would produce a "tight run." Finally, the processes must be practiced. Although spending 500 hours practicing some task may seem unduly long and burdensome, it is little more than an hour a day for a little more than one year. For example, it might seem impossible for someone to learn to take dictation while simultaneously reading a novel. Even if it were possible, there must surely be some loss of speed or accuracy on the dictation task and a loss of speed or comprehension on the reading task. Spelke, Hirst, and Neisser (1976) showed that people can in fact learn to do this after sufficient practice: their two subjects could read a novel and take dictation at the same time. Compared to their original performance on these tasks separately, after extended practice there was no loss of comprehension of the novel and no increase in errors or decrease in speed when both tasks were performed simultaneously.

Wenger and Payne (1995) conducted a series of experiments to test some of the ideas of skilled memory theory. What makes their study unique is both the number of subjects and the highly controlled design. Subject S. F. was able to recall approximately 80 digits in order after 2 years of sessions (see Figure 17.5). Wenger and Payne had subjects use similar conditions of practice (with no explicit instruction on mnemonic techniques) but substituted words for the digits, and the results were even more remarkable. In less than 15 weeks, three subjects were able to recall, in order, over 80 items, and an additional five subjects reached performance levels that were 4 to 5 times higher than their baseline performance. *All* subjects showed the type of organization in encoding and recall that S. F. showed: just as S. F. made use of his running knowledge to guide encoding and retrieval, the subjects in Wenger and Payne's study used their verbal knowledge, particularly the ability to generate associations as the lists were being presented. The results were all well described by skilled memory theory.

Ericsson is aware that this explanation of exceptional memory performance may remove something mysterious or some magical quality and turn it into something more prosaic. But this is entirely in accord with two of the main goals of memory research: to explain how and why memory works and to offer guidance for improving memory. If all we could say was that some people are mysteriously better than others, we would fail to achieve both of these goals.

With the exception of S., the vast majority of people exhibiting exceptional memories are otherwise normal, and the type of material that they can retain is limited. The keys to developing an exceptional memory are neither mysterious nor difficult to master, and they echo the advice presented in this chapter and throughout the book for improving your own. First, associate the to-be-remembered material with something that you already know so that you can take advantage of already-existing structures and organizations. Second, process the material in a way that is appropriate for the test. Third, distribute your rehearsals over time. The old joke is almost right: How do you get to Carnegie Hall? Practice, wait a while, practice, wait a while, practice.

# References

Adams, D. (1981). *The hitchhiker's guide to the galaxy.* New York: Pocket Books.

Bellezza, F. S. (1983). Mnemonic-device instruction with adults. In M. Pressley & J. R. Levin (Eds.), *Cognitive strategy research: Psychological foundations.* New York: Springer-Verlag.

Bower, G. H. (1972). Mental imagery and associative learning. In L. W. Gregg (Ed.), *Cognition in learning and memory.* New York: Wiley.

Buzan, T. (1984). *Use your perfect memory: A complete program of new techniques for remembering.* New York: Dutton.

Cain, L. F., & Willey, R. de V. (1939). The effect of spaced learning on the curve of retention. *Journal of Experimental Psychology, 25,* 209–214.

Calvin, W. H., & Ojemann, G. A. (1994). *Conversations with Neil's brain: The neural nature of thought and language.* Reading, MA: Addison-Wesley.

Chase, W. G., & Ericsson, K. A. (1981). Skilled memory. In J. R. Anderson (Ed.), *Cognitive skills and their acquisition.* Hillsdale, NJ: Erlbaum.

Chase, W. G., & Ericsson, K. A. (1982). Skill and working memory. In G. H. Bower (Ed.), *The psychology of learning and motivation, Vol. 16.* New York: Academic Press.

Cicero. (1942). *De oratore.* (E. W. Sutton, Trans.). Loeb Classical Library. London: William Heinemann.

Corballis, M. C. (1980). Laterality and myth. *American Psychologist, 35,* 284–295.

Craik, F. I. M., & Lockhart, R. S. (1972). Levels of processing: A framework for memory research. *Journal of Verbal Learning and Verbal Behavior, 11,* 671–684.

De Beni, R., & Cornoldi, C. (1985). Effects of the mnemotechnique of loci in the memorization of concrete words. *Acta Psychologica, 60,* 11–24.

Ebbinghaus, H. (1885). *Über das Gedächtnis: Untersuchungen zur experimentellen Psychologie.* Leipzig: Duncker and Humboldt. [Reprinted as H. E. Ebbinghaus (1964). Memory: A contribution to experimental psychology (H. A. Ruger, Trans.). New York: Dover.]

Einstein, G. O., & McDaniel, M. A. (1987). Distinctiveness and the mnemonic benefits of bizarre imagery. In M. A. McDaniel & M. Pressley (Eds.), *Imagery and related mnemonic processes: Theories, individual differences, and applications.* New York: Springer-Verlag.

Ericsson, K. A. (1985). Memory skill. *Canadian Journal of Psychology, 39,* 188–231.

Ericsson, K. A., Chase, W. G., & Faloon, S. F. (1980). Acquisition of a memory skill. *Science, 208,* 1181–1182.

Ericsson, K. A., & Faivre, I. A. (1988). What's exceptional about exceptional abilities? In L. K. Obler & D. Fein (Eds.), *The exceptional brain: Neuropsychology of talent and special abilities.* New York: Guilford.

Ericsson, K. A., & Krampe, R. Th., & Tesch-Römer, C. (1993). The role of deliberate practice in the acquisition of expert. *Psychological Review, 100,* 363–406.

Ericsson, K. A., & Staszewski, J. (1989). Skilled memory and expertise: Mechanisms of exceptional performance. In D. Klahr & K. Kotovsky (Eds.), *Complex information processing: The impact of Herbert A. Simon.* Hillsdale, NJ: Erlbaum.

Greenwald, A. G., Spangenberg, E. R., Pratkanis, A. R., & Eskenazi, J. (1991). Double-blind tests of subliminal self-help audiotapes. *Psychological Science, 2,* 119–122.

Hellige, J. B. (1990). Hemispheric asymmetry. *Annual Review of Psychology, 41,* 55–80.

Herold, M. (1982). *You can have a near-perfect memory.* Chicago: Contemporary Books.

Herrmann, D. J., Weingartner, H., Searleman, A., & McEvoy, C. (Eds.). (1992). *Memory improvement: Implications for memory theory.* New York: Springer-Verlag.

Hertzog, C. (1992). Improving memory: The possible roles of metamemory. In D. J. Herrmann, H. Weingartner, A. Searleman, & C. McEvoy (Eds.), *Memory improvement: Implications for memory theory.* New York: Springer-Verlag.

Hunt, E., & Love, T. (1972). How good can memory be? In A. W. Melton & E. Martin (Eds.), *Coding processes in human memory.* Washington, DC: Winston.

Hunter, I. M. L. (1962). An exceptional talent for calculative thinking. *British Journal of Psychology, 53,* 243–258.

James, W. (1890). *The principles of psychology.* New York: Holt and Company. [Reprinted as W. James. (1983). *The principles of psychology.* Cambridge, MA: Harvard University Press.]

Jenkins, J. G., & Dallenbach, K. M. (1924). Obliviscence during sleep and waking. *American Journal of Psychology, 35,* 605–612.

Keppel, G. (1964). Facilitation in short- and long-term retention of paired-associates following distributed practice in learning. *Journal of Verbal Learning and Verbal Behavior, 3,* 91–111.

Keppel, G. (1967). A reconsideration of the extinction-recovery theory. *Journal of Verbal Learning and Verbal Behavior, 6,* 476–486.

Lapp, D. C. (1992). *(Nearly) total recall: A guide to better memory at any age.* Stanford, CA: Stanford Alumni Association.

Lashley, K. S. (1950). In search of the engram. In *Symposium of the society for experimental biology, Vol. 4.* New York: Cambridge University Press.

Loftus, E. F., & Loftus, G. R. (1980). On the permanence of stored information in the human brain. *American Psychologist, 35,* 409–420.

Lorayne, H. (1957). *How to develop a super power memory.* Hollywood, FL: Fell.

Lorge, I. (1930). Influence of regularly interpolated time intervals upon subsequent learning. *Contributions to Education* (Whole No. 438).

Luria, A. R. (1968). *The mind of a mnemonist.* New York: Basic Books.

Mäntylä, T. (1986). Optimizing cue effectiveness: Recall of 500 and 600 incidentally learned words. *Journal of Experimental Psychology: Learning, Memory, and Cognition, 12,* 66–71.

Melton, A. W. (1970). The situation with respect to the spacing of repetitions and memory. *Journal of Verbal Learning and Verbal Behavior, 9,* 596–606.

Morris, C. D., Bransford, J. D., & Franks, J. J. (1977). Levels of processing versus transfer appropriate processing. *Journal of Verbal Learning and Verbal Behavior, 16,* 519–533.

Neisser, U. (1967). *Cognitive psychology.* New York: Appleton-Century-Crofts.

Neisser, U., & Kerr, N. (1973). Spatial and mnemonic properties of visual images. *Cognitive Psychology, 5,* 138–150.

Park, D. C., Smith, A. D., & Cavanaugh, J. C. (1990). Metamemories of memory researchers. *Memory & Cognition, 18,* 321–327.

Penfield, W. (1969). Consciousness, memory, and man's conditioned reflexes. In K. Pribram (Ed.), *On the biology of learning.* New York: Harcourt, Brace, and World.

Pick, E. (1888). *Memory and its doctors.* London: Trubner.

Rea, C. P., & Modigliani, V. (1988). Educational implications of the spacing effect. In M. M. Gruneberg, P. E. Morris, & R. N. Sykes (Eds.), *Practical aspects of memory: Current research and issues, Vol. 1: Memory in everyday life.* Chichester, UK: Wiley.

Roediger, H. L., III, Weldon, M. S., & Challis, B. H. (1989). Explaining dissociations between implicit and explicit measures of retention: A processing account. In H. L. Roediger, III & F. I. M. Craik (Eds.), *Varieties of memory and consciousness: Essays in honour of Endel Tulving.* Hillsdale, NJ: Erlbaum.

Ross, J., & Lawrence, K. A. (1968). Some observations on memory artifice. *Psychonomic Science, 13,* 107–108.

Shepard, R. N. (1967). Recognition memory for words, sentences, and pictures. *Journal of Verbal Learning and Verbal Behavior, 6,* 156–163.

Spelke, E., Hirst, W., & Neisser, U. (1976). Skills of divided attention. *Cognition, 4,* 215–230.

Springer, S. P., & Deutsch, G. (1989). *Left brain, right brain* (3rd ed.). New York: W. H. Freeman.

Squire, L. R. (1974). Remote memory as affected by aging. *Neuropsychologia, 12,* 429–435.

Squire, L. R. (1987). *Memory and brain.* New York: Oxford University Press.

Susukita, T. (1933). Untersuchung eines ausserordentlichen Gedächtnisses in Japan (I). *Tohoku Psychologica Folia, 1,* 111–134.

Susukita, T. (1934). Untersuchung eines außerordentlichen Gedächtnisses in Japan (II). *Tohoku Psychologica Folia, 2,* 15–42.

Thompson, C. P., Cowan, T., & Frieman, J. (1991). Rajan: A study of a memorist. *Journal of Memory and Language, 30,* 702–724.

Underwood, B. J. (1961). Ten years of massed practice on distributed practice. *Psychological Review, 68,* 229–247.

Underwood, B. J., & Schulz, R. W. (1961). Studies of distributed practice: XX. Sources of interference associated with differences in learning and retention. *Journal of Experimental Psychology, 61,* 228–235.

Warrington, E. K., & Sanders, H. J. (1971). The fate of old memories. *Quarterly Journal of Experimental Psychology, 23,* 432–442.

Watkins, M. J., & Tulving, E. (1975). Episodic memory: When recognition fails. *Journal of Experimental Psychology: General, 104,* 5–29.

Wenger, M. J., & Payne, D. G. (1995). On the acquisition of mnemonic skill: Application of skilled memory theory. *Journal of Experimental Psychology: Applied, 1,* 194–215.

Wollen, K. A., Weber, A., & Lowry, D. H. (1972). Bizarreness versus interaction of mental images as determinants of learning. *Cognitive Psychology, 3,* 518–523.

Woloshyn, V. E., Willoughby, T., Wood, E., & Pressley, M. (1990). Elaborative interrogation facilitates adult learning of factual paragraphs. *Journal of Educational Psychology, 82,* 513–524.

Wood, E., Pressley, M., & Winne, P. H. (1990). Elaborative interrogation effects on children's learning of factual information. *Journal of Educational Psychology, 82,* 741–748.

Yates, F. A. (1966). *The art of memory.* Chicago: University of Chicago Press.

Zechmeister, E. B., & Shaughnessy, J. J. (1980). When you know that you know and when you think that you know but you don't. *Bulletin of the Psychonomic Society, 15,* 41–44.

# Appendix

**Table A**   Twenty-four nonsense syllables (CVCs)

| BAF | NUM | SAQ |
|-----|-----|-----|
| BAP | PEC | SIM |
| BEF | PIM | SUC |
| GIF | QAW | TAY |
| HAB | QIR | VAM |
| JUV | QOG | VEN |
| KES | ROL | VEZ |
| NEM | SAH | VOT |

Source:  Glaze (1928).

**Table B** Random arrangements of the digits 1–9

| | | |
|---|---|---|
| 5 1 3 9 7 2 4 6 8 | 5 7 2 3 6 8 9 1 4 | 9 4 2 6 7 5 3 1 8 |
| 8 4 9 1 2 7 3 5 6 | 1 9 3 2 5 7 6 4 8 | 1 7 3 9 8 4 5 2 6 |
| 1 6 3 9 5 4 7 8 2 | 2 1 3 5 7 8 4 9 6 | 9 1 8 6 4 7 3 5 2 |
| 4 7 2 3 8 6 9 1 5 | 8 4 5 1 6 7 2 9 3 | 2 5 4 7 9 3 1 6 8 |
| 5 3 1 7 4 9 6 2 8 | 6 2 5 1 3 9 4 8 7 | 8 4 1 7 2 6 9 3 5 |
| 8 5 1 6 2 4 3 7 9 | 9 6 2 7 3 5 1 4 8 | 3 9 2 1 4 8 6 7 5 |
| 3 2 1 7 5 8 6 9 4 | 4 3 8 6 9 1 5 7 2 | 8 7 2 9 6 1 3 5 4 |
| 6 1 4 2 8 5 9 7 3 | 5 1 3 2 9 7 6 8 4 | 5 2 4 7 1 6 8 9 3 |
| 9 6 3 1 8 7 4 5 2 | 2 4 9 6 3 8 5 1 7 | 5 1 3 8 9 6 7 2 4 |
| 7 1 9 2 4 8 3 6 5 | 3 6 4 5 9 7 2 8 1 | 6 9 2 7 4 1 5 8 3 |
| 6 3 7 8 9 4 2 5 1 | 6 3 1 7 8 4 9 5 2 | 3 1 2 4 7 5 8 6 9 |
| 7 9 6 4 2 3 8 1 5 | 7 2 3 9 1 4 8 6 5 | 1 5 4 2 6 9 8 7 3 |
| 2 9 3 4 1 6 7 5 8 | 6 4 8 1 5 9 7 2 3 | 5 2 9 7 6 3 8 4 1 |
| 5 2 6 7 1 9 4 8 3 | 9 3 6 2 5 8 7 4 1 | 4 6 7 3 1 5 9 8 2 |
| 3 6 1 9 5 2 7 8 4 | 4 6 5 1 3 9 8 2 7 | 7 8 1 5 9 4 3 2 6 |
| 4 5 9 3 7 2 1 6 8 | 7 1 8 3 6 2 4 9 5 | 2 4 8 5 7 1 6 3 9 |
| 9 2 7 3 1 6 4 8 5 | 2 8 7 3 6 5 9 1 4 | 7 1 5 6 8 3 9 4 2 |
| 3 1 7 6 2 9 8 5 4 | 8 2 9 4 5 7 3 6 1 | 4 1 2 7 6 5 9 8 3 |
| 3 4 6 2 7 5 1 9 8 | 6 4 2 1 7 5 8 3 9 | 5 3 7 9 6 1 4 8 2 |
| 5 7 9 4 8 2 1 3 6 | 3 1 9 8 7 5 2 6 4 | 4 5 9 7 2 3 8 1 6 |
| 8 3 9 1 7 5 2 6 4 | 2 6 5 1 3 9 4 8 7 | 5 4 5 8 1 9 7 7 5 |
| 2 6 3 8 1 7 4 5 9 | 6 4 1 9 2 5 8 7 3 | 8 7 6 1 2 8 6 4 1 |
| 1 4 2 3 5 9 6 7 8 | 1 8 3 7 4 9 6 2 5 | 2 9 4 4 7 6 8 5 4 |
| 9 2 8 5 7 4 3 6 1 | 8 2 5 4 7 6 3 1 9 | 6 5 8 6 8 5 2 8 7 |
| 8 7 9 3 1 4 2 6 5 | 2 3 8 1 7 5 6 4 9 | 3 8 3 2 9 7 1 3 9 |
| 7 6 8 9 1 4 5 2 3 | 7 4 1 9 6 8 3 5 2 | 4 2 7 9 4 3 4 1 8 |
| 6 3 4 2 7 9 1 5 8 | 8 4 2 3 7 5 9 1 6 | 9 1 9 5 3 2 3 6 2 |
| 7 3 2 4 9 6 8 5 1 | 3 5 8 2 4 6 9 7 1 | 1 3 1 7 5 1 9 9 3 |
| 9 3 5 6 4 8 1 2 7 | 2 1 8 9 5 6 3 4 7 | 7 6 2 3 6 4 5 2 6 |
| 8 6 4 2 5 3 7 1 9 | 4 1 6 2 9 5 3 8 7 | 8 5 1 5 4 3 6 2 7 |
| 5 9 1 2 7 3 8 6 4 | 6 2 4 8 5 9 1 7 3 | 9 3 9 4 5 1 2 4 6 |
| 3 6 2 4 9 8 1 7 5 | 2 1 6 5 4 8 7 9 3 | 5 7 3 3 8 8 9 6 1 |
| 7 9 3 8 6 4 5 1 2 | 3 9 5 2 1 6 8 4 7 | 7 6 4 6 2 2 4 1 2 |
| 6 2 9 3 7 4 1 5 8 | 5 1 8 4 3 2 6 7 9 | 3 4 5 7 6 4 5 9 4 |
| 1 8 3 2 5 6 9 4 7 | 4 9 8 1 7 6 3 2 5 | 6 1 6 8 7 9 8 7 3 |
| 2 4 9 6 7 1 3 8 5 | 2 6 1 7 5 3 8 9 4 | 2 9 7 1 1 7 3 3 9 |
| 4 5 8 2 1 9 6 3 7 | 9 3 7 4 2 5 6 8 1 | 1 8 2 9 9 5 1 8 5 |
| 3 5 7 9 8 4 2 1 6 | 9 5 1 7 3 6 8 4 2 | 4 2 8 2 3 6 7 5 8 |
| 2 6 3 9 1 7 4 8 5 | 6 7 4 1 8 3 9 5 2 | 9 3 1 7 4 6 2 8 5 |
| 2 6 8 1 3 4 9 7 5 | 4 7 1 6 2 9 5 8 3 | 9 4 8 3 5 2 7 1 6 |

**Table C**    Ninety-six two-syllable words

| | | | |
|---|---|---|---|
| able | depart | herself | proclaim |
| achieve | describe | honest | proper |
| although | destroy | humble | protect |
| amuse | dispose | impulse | publish |
| anger | dispute | include | punish |
| approve | dissolve | lightly | really |
| attain | elect | linger | relief |
| away | enough | lively | resign |
| awhile | enter | locate | service |
| backward | every | loyal | shallow |
| began | explain | lucky | shortly |
| betray | faithful | meaning | sincere |
| beyond | farewell | method | slowly |
| chosen | firmly | mighty | slumber |
| climate | forward | modern | softly |
| command | friendly | obtain | suggest |
| confirm | frighten | open | suppose |
| confuse | function | oppose | survive |
| control | funny | pointed | thinking |
| correct | future | possess | travel |
| costly | gallant | prefer | trifle |
| deadly | going | present | trouble |
| decay | gravely | prevent | within |
| degree | happy | proceed | writing |

Source: Ninety-six words randomly selected from Friendly, Franklin, Hoffman, & Rubin (1982).

**Table D**    Eight short and eight long words

| | |
|---|---|
| beast | alcohol |
| bronze | amplifier |
| dirt | gallery |
| golf | mosquito |
| inn | musician |
| lump | officer |
| star | orchestra |
| wife | property |

Source:  LaPointe & Engle (1990).

# Appendix

**Table E**  Twenty-five common two-syllable nouns

| Noun | Imageability | Concreteness | Frequency |
|------|--------------|--------------|-----------|
| ankle | 6.77 | 7.00 | 21 |
| apple | 6.73 | 7.00 | 9 |
| arrow | 6.57 | 7.00 | 37 |
| barrel | 6.57 | 6.94 | 32 |
| butter | 6.57 | 6.96 | 27 |
| cabin | 6.47 | 6.96 | 23 |
| candy | 6.63 | 6.56 | 32 |
| cellar | 6.27 | 6.83 | 32 |
| coffee | 6.73 | 6.89 | 78 |
| cottage | 6.50 | 6.90 | 46 |
| elbow | 6.30 | 6.94 | 26 |
| engine | 6.33 | 6.76 | 50 |
| fireplace | 6.83 | 6.96 | 19 |
| flower | 6.57 | 6.96 | 21 |
| hammer | 6.73 | 6.96 | 34 |
| hotel | 6.40 | 6.83 | 126 |
| infant | 6.33 | 6.76 | 22 |
| lemon | 6.83 | 6.96 | 27 |
| meadow | 6.43 | 6.69 | 47 |
| mountain | 6.77 | 7.00 | 33 |
| oven | 6.40 | 6.96 | 29 |
| palace | 6.50 | 6.73 | 38 |
| salad | 6.53 | 6.83 | 28 |
| slipper | 6.47 | 6.94 | 20 |
| sugar | 6.57 | 6.96 | 34 |

Source: Paivio, Yuille, & Madigan (1968).

**Table F** Thirty-two consonant trigrams

| | | |
|---|---|---|
| BMZ | HZP | QKB |
| BPF | JBW | RJP |
| CGW | JMC | RJX |
| CJX | KFH | SGC |
| DJF | LRB | SJF |
| DLH | MQH | TJQ |
| FQD | NWB | TZJ |
| FZH | NZK | XNZ |
| GKW | PNB | ZFK |
| GJX | PXZ | ZSB |
| HFP | QCF | |

Source: Witmer (1935).

**Table G** Fifty-six category names

| | | |
|---|---|---|
| Precious Stone | Country | Area of Science |
| Unit of Time | Crime | Toy |
| Relative | Carpenter's Tool | Type of Dance |
| Unit of Distance | Member of the Clergy | Vegetable |
| Metal | Substance for Flavoring Food | Type of Footgear |
| Type of Reading Material | Type of Fuel | Insect |
| Military Title | Occupation | Girl's First Name |
| Four-Footed Animal | Natural Earth Formation | Boy's First Name |
| Kind of Cloth | Sport | Flower |
| Kitchen Utensil | Weather Phenomenon | Disease |
| Religious Building | Article of Clothing | Tree |
| Part of Speech | Part of a Building | Type of Ship |
| Article of Furniture | Chemical Element | Fish |
| Human Body Part | Musical Instrument | Snake |
| Fruit | Kind of Money | City |
| Weapon | Type of Music | State |
| Elective Office | Bird | College or University |
| Type of Dwelling | Nonalcoholic Beverage | |
| Alcoholic Beverage | Type of Vehicle | |

Source: Battig & Montague (1969).

**Table H**   Sixty word fragments

| | | |
|---|---|---|
| AARDVARK | ESPRESSO | PHARAOH |
| ABATTOIR | FLANNEL | PIGMENT |
| AGNOSTIC | GAZETTE | PLANKTON |
| ALMANAC | GRANARY | QUARTET |
| ANATOMY | HEXAGON | RAINBOW |
| ANYBODY | HORIZON | RHUBARB |
| APPROVAL | HYDRANT | ROTUNDA |
| BACHELOR | IDEOLOGY | RUFFIAN |
| BANDANNA | ISTHMUS | SAPPHIRE |
| BASSOON | KEROSENE | SHERIFF |
| BEHAVIOR | LAGGARD | SILICON |
| BOROUGH | LETTUCE | SPATULA |
| BROCCOLI | LITHIUM | THEOREM |
| CABARET | MIGRAINE | TOBOGGAN |
| CHIMNEY | MONOGRAM | TRICYCLE |
| CLARINET | MYSTERY | UNIVERSE |
| COCONUT | NOCTURNE | VERANDAH |
| CUPCAKE | ORATION | WARRANTY |
| DINOSAUR | OUTSIDER | YOGHURT |
| ELLIPSE | PENDULUM | ZEPPELIN |

Note: The letters that should be missing from the fragment are underlined. For example, the target word AARDVARK should be tested with _AR_VA__.

Source: Tulving, Schacter, & Stark (1982).

**Table I** Eighty concrete and eighty abstract words

*Concrete Words:*

| | | | | | |
|---|---|---|---|---|---|
| accordion | cellar | gold | missile | rattle | tablespoon |
| acrobat | chair | grandmother | mother | refrigerator | thorn |
| alligator | child | hammer | newspaper | restaurant | tree |
| ambulance | coffee | hospital | ocean | river | truck |
| arrow | diamond | hotel | paper | salad | trumpet |
| automobile | doctor | hurricane | peach | seat | umbrella |
| avalanche | dollar | lake | pepper | slipper | valley |
| bagpipe | dress | lemonade | photograph | spinach | village |
| barrel | elbow | letter | physician | stagecoach | window |
| book | factory | library | piano | storm | woods |
| bottle | forehead | magazine | potato | strawberry | |
| butcher | forest | meadow | prairie | student | |
| cabin | garden | meat | pudding | sugar | |
| caterpillar | girl | microscope | railroad | swamp | |

*Abstract Words:*

| | | | | | |
|---|---|---|---|---|---|
| adversity | distinction | gender | law | ownership | theory |
| amount | duty | greed | length | pact | thought |
| animosity | economy | hearing | magnitude | pledge | tribute |
| aptitude | effort | hint | malady | position | trouble |
| atrocity | encore | hope | malice | prestige | truth |
| attitude | episode | hour | method | quality | upkeep |
| boredom | equity | idea | mind | quantity | vanity |
| capacity | event | idiom | moment | rating | vigilance |
| chance | exclusion | illusion | mood | reaction | violation |
| cost | facility | impulse | moral | reminder | vocation |
| crisis | fantasy | incident | namesake | sensation | |
| custom | fault | irony | nonsense | session | |
| deduction | folly | jeopardy | obedience | style | |
| democracy | franchise | justice | occasion | tendency | |

| | Concreteness | Imageability | Frequency | Length |
|---|---|---|---|---|
| Concrete | 6.51 | 6.82 | 50.26 | 6.73 |
| Abstract | 3.18 | 2.58 | 50.66 | 6.74 |

Source: Paivio, Yuille, & Madigan (1968).

**Table J** Six lists of words related to a critical item

| CHAIR | MOUNTAIN | SLEEP |
|---|---|---|
| table | hill | bed |
| sit | valley | rest |
| legs | climb | awake |
| seat | summit | tired |
| couch | top | dream |
| desk | molehill | wake |
| recliner | peak | snooze |
| sofa | plain | blanket |
| wood | glacier | doze |
| cushion | goat | slumber |
| swivel | bike | snore |
| stool | climber | nap |
| sitting | range | peace |
| rocking | steep | yawn |
| bench | ski | drowsy |
| NEEDLE | ROUGH | SWEET |
| thread | smooth | sour |
| pin | bumpy | candy |
| eye | road | sugar |
| sewing | tough | bitter |
| sharp | sandpaper | good |
| point | jagged | taste |
| prick | ready | tooth |
| thimble | coarse | nice |
| haystack | uneven | honey |
| thorn | riders | soda |
| hurt | rugged | chocolate |
| injection | sand | heart |
| syringe | boards | cake |
| cloth | ground | tart |
| knitting | gravel | pie |

Note: The words in uppercase are the predicted intrusion errors for each list.

Source: Roediger & McDermott (1995).

# Name Index

# Subject Index

TO THE OWNER OF THIS BOOK:

I hope that you have found *Human Memory* useful. So that this book can be improved in a future edition, would you take the time to complete this sheet and return it? Thank you.

School and address: —————————————————————————————————

Department: ————————————————————————————————————

Instructor's name: ————————————————————————————————

1. What I like most about this book is: —————————————————————

————————————————————————————————————————

————————————————————————————————————————

2. What I like least about this book is: —————————————————————

————————————————————————————————————————

————————————————————————————————————————

3. My general reaction to this book is: —————————————————————

————————————————————————————————————————

4. The name of the course in which I used this book is: ——————————————

————————————————————————————————————————

5. Were all of the chapters of the book assigned for you to read? ———————————

If not, which ones weren't? ———————————————————————————

6. In the space below, or on a separate sheet of paper, please write specific suggestions for improving this book and anything else you'd care to share about your experience in using the book.

————————————————————————————————————————

————————————————————————————————————————

————————————————————————————————————————

————————————————————————————————————————

————————————————————————————————————————

Optional:

Your name: _____ Date: _____

May Brooks/Cole quote you, either in promotion for *Human Memory* or in future publishing ventures?

Yes: _____ No: _____

Sincerely,

*Ian Neath*